Microsoft® Office

Word 2007

Comprehensive Concepts and Techniques

Gary B. Shelly
Thomas J. Cashman
Misty E. Vermaat

THOMSON COURSE TECHNOLOGY   25 THOMSON PLACE   BOSTON MA 02210

Australia • Canada • Denmark • Japan • Mexico • New Zealand • Philippines • Puerto Rico • Singapore • South Africa • Spain • United Kingdom • United States

THOMSON
COURSE TECHNOLOGY

Microsoft Office Word 2007
Comprehensive Concepts and Techniques

Gary B. Shelly

Thomas J. Cashman

Misty E. Vermaat

Executive Editor
Alexandra Arnold

Senior Product Manager
Reed Curry

Associate Product Manager
Klenda Martinez

Editorial Assistant
Jon Farnham

Senior Marketing Manager
Joy Stark-Vancs

Marketing Coordinator
Julie Schuster

Print Buyer
Julio Esperas

Director of Production
Patty Stephan

Production Editor
Jill Klaffky

Developmental Editor
Jill Batistick

Proofreader
Kim Kosmatka

Indexer
Rich Carlson

QA Manuscript Reviewers
John Freitas, Serge Palladino,
Chris Scriver, Danielle Shaw,
Marianne Snow, Teresa Storch

Art Director
Bruce Bond

Cover and Text Design
Joel Sadagursky

Cover Photo
Jon Chomitz

Compositor
GEX Publishing Services

Printer
Banta Menasha

Contents

Appendices

APPENDIX A

Project Planning Guidelines

APPENDIX B

Introduction to Microsoft Office 2007

APPENDIX C

Microsoft Office Word 2007 Help

APPENDIX D

Publishing Office 2007 Web Pages to a Web Server

APPENDIX E

Customizing Microsoft Office Word 2007

APPENDIX F

Steps for the Windows XP User

APPENDIX G

Microsoft Business Certification Program

Preface

The Shelly Cashman Series® offers the finest textbooks in computer education. We are proud of the fact that our series of Microsoft Office 4.3, Microsoft Office 95, Microsoft Office 97, Microsoft Office 2000, Microsoft Office XP, and Microsoft Office 2003 textbooks have been the most widely used books in education. With each new edition of our Office books, we have made significant improvements based on the software and comments made by instructors and students.

Microsoft Office 2007 contains more changes in the user interface and feature set than all other previous versions combined. Recognizing that the new features and functionality of Microsoft Office 2007 would impact the way that students are taught skills, the Shelly Cashman Series development team carefully reviewed our pedagogy and analyzed its effectiveness in teaching today's Office student. An extensive customer survey produced results confirming what the series is best known for: its step-by-step, screen-by-screen instructions, its project-oriented approach, and the quality of its content.

We learned, though, that students entering computer courses today are different than students taking these classes just a few years ago. Students today read less, but need to retain more. They need not only to be able to perform skills, but to retain those skills and know how to apply them to different settings. Today's students need to be continually engaged and challenged to retain what they're learning.

As a result, we've renewed our commitment to focusing on the user and how they learn best. This commitment is reflected in every change we've made to our Office 2007 books.

Objectives of This Textbook

Microsoft Office Word 2007: Comprehensive Concepts and Techniques is intended for a ten- to fifteen-week period in a course that teaches Word 2007 as the primary component. No experience with a computer is assumed, and no mathematics beyond the high school freshman level is required. The objectives of this book are:

- To offer a comprehensive presentation of Microsoft Office Word 2007
- To expose students to practical examples of the computer as a useful tool
- To acquaint students with the proper procedures to create documents suitable for coursework, professional purposes, and personal use
- To help students discover the underlying functionality of Word 2007 so they can become more productive
- To develop an exercise-oriented approach that allows learning by doing

The Shelly Cashman Approach

Features of the Shelly Cashman Series Microsoft Office Word 2007 books include:

- **Project Orientation** Each chapter in the book presents a project with a practical problem and complete solution in an easy-to-understand approach.
- **Plan Ahead Boxes** The project orientation is enhanced by the inclusion of Plan Ahead boxes. These new features prepare students to create successful projects by encouraging them to think strategically about what they are trying to accomplish before they begin working.
- **Step-by-Step, Screen-by-Screen Instructions** Each of the tasks required to complete a project is clearly identified throughout the chapter. Now, the step-by-step instructions provide a context beyond point-and-click. Each step explains why students are performing a task, or the result of performing a certain action. Found on the screens accompanying each step, call-outs give students the information they need to know when they need to know it. Now, we've used color to distinguish the content in the call-outs. The Explanatory call-outs (in black) summarize

Q&A

What is a maximized window?

A maximized window fills the entire screen. When you maximize a window, the Maximize button changes to a Restore Down button.

Other Ways

1. Click Italic button on Mini toolbar
2. Right-click selected text, click Font on shortcut menu, click Font tab, click Italic in Font style list, click OK button
3. Click Font Dialog Box Launcher, click Font tab, click Italic in Font style list, click OK button
4. Press CTRL+I

BTW

Minimizing the Ribbon
If you want to minimize the Ribbon, right-click the Ribbon and then click Minimize the Ribbon on the shortcut menu, double-click the active tab, or press CTRL+F1. To restore a minimized Ribbon, right-click the Ribbon and then click Minimize the Ribbon on the shortcut menu, double-click any top-level tab, or press CTRL+F1. To use commands on a minimized Ribbon, click the top-level tab.

what is happening on the screen and the Navigational call-outs (in red) show students where to click.

- **Q&A**   Found within many of the step-by-step sequences, Q&As raise the kinds of questions students may ask when working through a step sequence and provide answers about what they are doing, why they are doing it, and how that task might be approached differently.

- **Experimental Steps**   These new steps, within our step-by-step instructions, encourage students to explore, experiment, and take advantage of the features of the Office 2007 new user interface. These steps are not necessary to complete the projects, but are designed to increase the confidence with the software and build problem-solving skills.

- **Thoroughly Tested Projects**   Unparalleled quality is ensured because every screen in the book is produced by the author only after performing a step, and then each project must pass Thomson Course Technology's Quality Assurance program.

- **Other Ways Boxes and Quick Reference Summary**   The Other Ways boxes displayed at the end of most of the step-by-step sequences specify the other ways to do the task completed in the steps. Thus, the steps and the Other Ways box make a comprehensive reference unit. A Quick Reference Summary at the end of the book contains all of the tasks presented in the chapters, and all ways identified of accomplishing the tasks.

- **BTW**   These marginal annotations provide background information, tips, and answers to common questions that complement the topics covered, adding depth and perspective to the learning process.

- **Integration of the World Wide Web**   The World Wide Web is integrated into the Word 2007 learning experience by (1) BTW annotations that send students to Web sites for up-to-date information and alternative approaches to tasks; (2) a Microsoft Business Certification Program Web page so students can prepare for the certification examinations; (3) a Quick Reference Summary Web page that summarizes the ways to complete tasks (mouse, Ribbon, shortcut menu, and keyboard); and (4) the Learn It Online section at the end of each chapter, which has chapter reinforcement exercises, learning games, and other types of student activities.

- **End-of-Chapter Student Activities**   Extensive student activities at the end of each chapter provide the student with plenty of opportunities to reinforce the materials learned in the chapter through hands-on assignments. Several new types of activities have been added that challenge the student in new ways to expand their knowledge, and to apply their new skills to a project with personal relevance.

Organization of This Textbook

Microsoft Office Word 2007: Comprehensive Concepts and Techniques consists of nine chapters on Microsoft Office Word 2007, three special features, seven appendices, and a Quick Reference Summary.

End-of-Chapter Student Activities

A notable strength of the Shelly Cashman Series Microsoft Office Word 2007 books is the extensive student activities at the end of each chapter. Well-structured student activities can make the difference between students merely participating in a class and students retaining the information they learn. The activities in the Shelly Cashman Series Office books include the following.

CHAPTER SUMMARY A concluding paragraph, followed by a listing of the tasks completed within a chapter together with the pages on which the step-by-step, screen-by-screen explanations appear.

LEARN IT ONLINE Every chapter features a Learn It Online section that is comprised of six exercises. These exercises include True/False, Multiple Choice, Short Answer, Flash Cards, Practice Test, and Learning Games.

APPLY YOUR KNOWLEDGE This exercise usually requires students to open and manipulate a file from the Data Files that parallels the activities learned in the chapter. To obtain a copy of the Data Files for Students, follow the instructions on the inside back cover of this text.

EXTEND YOUR KNOWLEDGE This exercise allows students to extend and expand on the skills learned within the chapter.

MAKE IT RIGHT This exercise requires students to analyze a document, identify errors and issues, and correct those errors and issues using skills learned in the chapter.

IN THE LAB Three all new in-depth assignments per chapter require students to utilize the chapter concepts and techniques to solve problems on a computer.

CASES AND PLACES Five unique real-world case-study situations, including Make It Personal, an open-ended project that relates to student's personal lives, and one small-group activity.

Instructor Resources CD-ROM

The Shelly Cashman Series is dedicated to providing you with all of the tools you need to make your class a success. Information about all supplementary materials is available through your Thomson Course Technology representative or by calling one of the following telephone numbers: Colleges, Universities, and Continuing Ed departments, 1-800-648-7450; High Schools, 1-800-824-5179; and Career Colleges, Business, Government, Library and Resellers, 1-800-477-3692.

The Instructor Resources CD-ROM for this textbook includes both teaching and testing aids. The contents of each item on the Instructor Resources CD-ROM (ISBN 1-4239-1226-8) are described on the following pages.

INSTRUCTOR'S MANUAL The Instructor's Manual consists of Microsoft Word files, which include chapter objectives, lecture notes, teaching tips, classroom activities, lab activities, quick quizzes, figures and boxed elements summarized in the chapters, and a glossary page. The new format of the Instructor's Manual will allow you to map through every chapter easily.

LECTURE SUCCESS SYSTEM The Lecture Success System consists of intermediate files that correspond to certain figures in the book, allowing you to step through the creation of a project in a chapter during a lecture without entering large amounts of data.

SYLLABUS Sample syllabi, which can be customized easily to a course, are included. The syllabi cover policies, class and lab assignments and exams, and procedural information.

FIGURE FILES Illustrations for every figure in the textbook are available in electronic form. Use this ancillary to present a slide show in lecture or to print transparencies for use in lecture with an overhead projector. If you have a personal computer and LCD device, this ancillary can be an effective tool for presenting lectures.

POWERPOINT PRESENTATIONS PowerPoint Presentations is a multimedia lecture presentation system that provides slides for each chapter. Presentations are based on chapter objectives. Use this presentation system to present well-organized lectures that are both interesting and knowledge based. PowerPoint Presentations provides consistent coverage at schools that use multiple lecturers.

SOLUTIONS TO EXERCISES Solutions are included for the end-of-chapter exercises, as well as the Chapter Reinforcement exercises. Rubrics and annotated solution files, as described below, also are included.

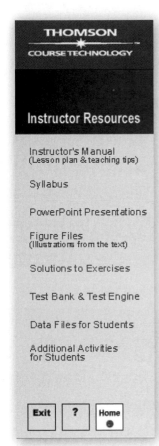

RUBRICS AND ANNOTATED SOLUTION FILES The grading rubrics provide a customizable framework for assigning point values to the laboratory exercises. Annotated solution files that correspond to the grading rubrics make it easy for you to compare students' results with the correct solutions whether you receive their homework as hard copy or via e-mail.

TEST BANK & TEST ENGINE In the ExamView test bank, you will find our standard question types (40 multiple-choice, 25 true/false, 20 completion) and new objective-based question types (5 modified multiple-choice, 5 modified true/false and 10 matching). Critical Thinking questions also are included (3 essays and 2 cases with 2 questions each) totaling the test bank to 112 questions for every chapter with page number references, and when appropriate, figure references. A version of the test bank you can print also is included. The test bank comes with a copy of the test engine, ExamView, the ultimate tool for your objective-based testing needs. ExamView is a state-of-the-art test builder that is easy to use. ExamView enables you to create paper-, LAN-, or Web-based tests from test banks designed specifically for your Thomson Course Technology textbook. Utilize the ultra-efficient QuickTest Wizard to create tests in less than five minutes by taking advantage of Thomson Course Technology's question banks, or customize your own exams from scratch.

LAB TESTS/TEST OUT The Lab Tests/Test Out exercises parallel the In the Lab assignments and are supplied for the purpose of testing students in the laboratory on the material covered in the chapter or testing students out of the course.

DATA FILES FOR STUDENTS All the files that are required by students to complete the exercises are included. You can distribute the files on the Instructor Resources CD-ROM to your students over a network, or you can have them follow the instructions on the inside back cover of this book to obtain a copy of the Data Files for Students.

ADDITIONAL ACTIVITIES FOR STUDENTS These additional activities consist of Chapter Reinforcement Exercises, which are true/false, multiple-choice, and short answer questions that help students gain confidence in the material learned.

Assessment & Training Solutions
SAM 2007
SAM 2007 helps bridge the gap between the classroom and the real world by allowing students to train and test on important computer skills in an active, hands-on environment.

SAM 2007's easy-to-use system includes powerful interactive exams, training or projects on critical applications such as Word, Excel, Access, PowerPoint, Outlook, Windows, the Internet, and much more. SAM simulates the application environment, allowing students to demonstrate their knowledge and think through the skills by performing real-world tasks.

Designed to be used with the Shelly Cashman series, SAM 2007 includes built-in page references so students can print helpful study guides that match the Shelly Cashman series textbooks used in class. Powerful administrative options allow instructors to schedule exams and assignments, secure tests, and run reports with almost limitless flexibility.

Student Edition Labs
Our Web-based interactive labs help students master hundreds of computer concepts, including input and output devices, file management and desktop applications, computer ethics, virus protection, and much more. Featuring up-to-the-minute content, eye-popping graphics, and rich animation, the highly interactive Student Edition Labs offer students an alternative way to learn through dynamic observation, step-by-step practice, and challenging review questions.

Online Content

Blackboard is the leading distance learning solution provider and class-management platform today. Thomson Course Technology has partnered with Blackboard to bring you premium online content. Instructors: Content for use with *Microsoft Office Word 2007: Comprehensive Concepts and Techniques* is available in a Blackboard Course Cartridge and may include topic reviews, case projects, review questions, test banks, practice tests, custom syllabi, and more.

Thomson Course Technology also has solutions for several other learning management systems. Please visit http://www.course.com today to see what's available for this title.

Blackboard

CourseCasts Learning on the Go. Always Available...Always Relevant.

Want to keep up with the latest technology trends relevant to you? Visit our site to find a library of podcasts, CourseCasts, featuring a "CourseCast of the Week," and download them to your portable media player at http://coursecasts.course.com.

Our fast-paced world is driven by technology. You know because you are an active participant — always on the go, always keeping up with technological trends, and always learning new ways to embrace technology to power your life.

Ken Baldauf, a faculty member of the Florida State University (FSU) Computer Science Department, is responsible for teaching technology classes to thousands of FSU students each year. He knows what you know; he knows what you want to learn. He is also an expert in the latest technology and will sort through and aggregate the most pertinent news and information so you can spend your time enjoying technology, rather than trying to figure it out.

Visit us at http://coursecasts.course.com to learn on the go!

CourseNotes

Course Technology's CourseNotes are six-panel quick reference cards that reinforce the most important and widely used features of a software application in a visual and user-friendly format. CourseNotes will serve as a great reference tool during and after the student completes the course. CourseNotes for Microsoft Office 2007, Word 2007, Excel 2007, Access 2007, PowerPoint 2007, Windows Vista, and more are available now!

About Our New Cover Look

Learning styles of students have changed, but the Shelly Cashman Series' dedication to their success has remained steadfast for over 30 years. We are committed to continually updating our approach and content to reflect the way today's students learn and experi-

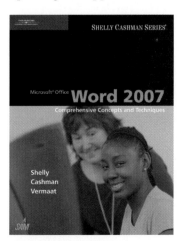

ence new technology. This focus on the user is reflected in our bold new cover design, which features photographs of real students using the Shelly Cashman Series in their courses. Each book features a different user, reflecting the many ages, experiences, and backgrounds of all of the students learning with our books. When you use the Shelly Cashman Series, you can be assured that you are learning computer skills using the most effective courseware available. We would like to thank the administration and faculty at the participating schools for their help in making our vision a reality. Most of all, we'd like to thank the wonderful students from all over the world who learn from our texts and now appear on our covers.

To the Student . . . Getting the Most Out of Your Book

Welcome to *Microsoft Office Word 2007: Comprehensive Concepts and Techniques*. You can save yourself a lot of time and gain a better understanding of the Office 2007 programs if you spend a few minutes reviewing the figures and callouts in this section.

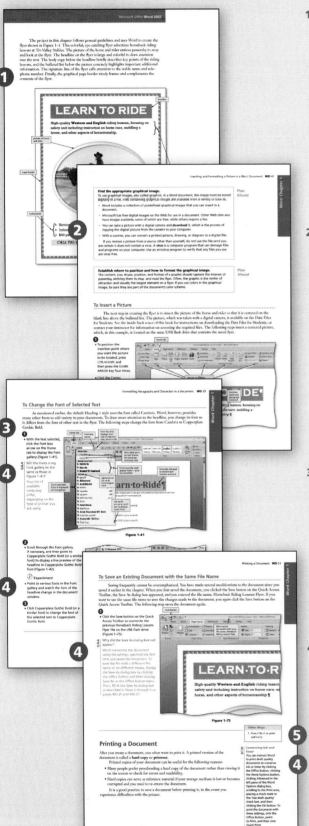

1 PROJECT ORIENTATION

Each chapter's project presents a practical problem and shows the solution in the first figure of the chapter. The project orientation lets you see firsthand how problems are solved from start to finish using application software and computers.

2 PROJECT PLANNING GUIDELINES AND PLAN AHEAD BOXES

Overall planning guidelines at the beginning of a chapter and Plan Ahead boxes throughout encourage you to think critically about how to accomplish the next goal before you actually begin working.

3 CONSISTENT STEP-BY-STEP, SCREEN-BY-SCREEN PRESENTATION

Chapter solutions are built using a step-by-step, screen-by-screen approach. This pedagogy allows you to build the solution on a computer as you read through the chapter. Generally, each step includes an explanation that indicates the result of the step.

4 MORE THAN JUST STEP-BY-STEP

BTW annotations in the margins of the book, Q&As in the steps, and substantive text in the paragraphs provide background information, tips, and answers to common questions that complement the topics covered, adding depth and perspective. When you finish with this book, you will be ready to use the Office programs to solve problems on your own. Experimental steps provide you with opportunities to step out on your own to try features of the programs, and pick up right where you left off in the chapter.

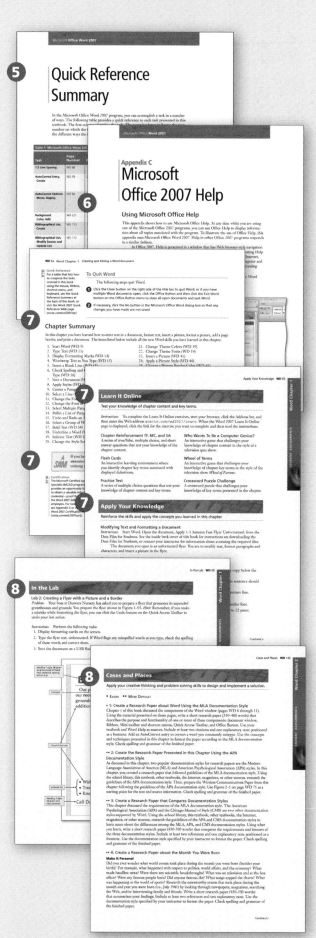

5 OTHER WAYS BOXES AND QUICK REFERENCE SUMMARY
Other Ways boxes that follow many of the step sequences and a Quick Reference Summary at the back of the book explain the other ways to complete the task presented, such as using the mouse, Ribbon, shortcut menu, and keyboard.

6 EMPHASIS ON GETTING HELP WHEN YOU NEED IT
The first project of each application and Appendix C show you how to use all the elements of Office Help. Being able to answer your own questions will increase your productivity and reduce your frustrations by minimizing the time it takes to learn how to complete a task.

7 REVIEW, REINFORCEMENT, AND EXTENSION
After you successfully step through a project in a chapter, a section titled Chapter Summary identifies the tasks with which you should be familiar. Terms you should know for test purposes are bold in the text. The SAM Training feature provides the opportunity for addional reinforcement on important skills covered in each chapter. The Learn It Online section at the end of each chapter offers reinforcement in the form of review questions, learning games, and practice tests. Also included are exercises that require you to extend your learning beyond the book.

8 LABORATORY EXERCISES
If you really want to learn how to use the programs, then you must design and implement solutions to problems on your own. Every chapter concludes with several carefully developed laboratory assignments that increase in complexity.

1 | Creating and Editing a Word Document

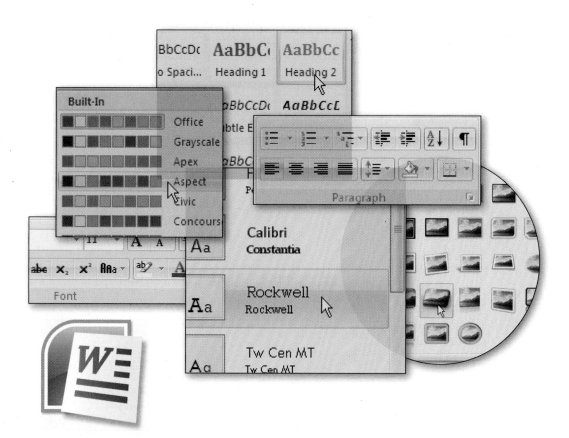

Objectives

You will have mastered the material in this chapter when you can:

- Start and quit Word
- Describe the Word window
- Enter text in a document
- Check spelling as you type
- Save a document
- Format text, paragraphs, and document elements
- Undo and redo commands or actions

- Insert a picture and format it
- Print a document
- Change document properties
- Open a document
- Correct errors in a document
- Use Word's Help

1 | Creating and Editing a Word Document

What Is Microsoft Office Word 2007?

Microsoft Office Word 2007 is a full-featured word processing program that allows you to create professional-looking documents and revise them easily. A document is a printed or electronic medium people use to communicate with others. With Word, you can develop many types of documents, including flyers, letters, memos, resumes, reports, fax cover sheets, mailing labels, and newsletters. Word also provides tools that enable you to create Web pages. From within Word, you can place these Web pages directly on a Web server.

Word has many features designed to simplify the production of documents and make documents look visually appealing. Using Word, you easily can change the shape, size, and color of text. You can include borders, shading, tables, images, pictures, charts, and Web addresses in documents.

While you are typing, Word performs many tasks automatically. For example, Word detects and corrects spelling and grammar errors in several languages. Word's thesaurus allows you to add variety and precision to your writing. Word also can format text, such as headings, lists, fractions, borders, and Web addresses, as you type.

This latest version of Word has many new features to make you more productive. For example, Word has many predefined text and graphical elements designed to assist you with preparing documents. Word also includes new charting and diagramming tools; uses themes so that you can coordinate colors, fonts, and graphics; and has a tool that enables you to convert a document to a PDF format.

To illustrate the features of Word, this book presents a series of projects that use Word to create documents similar to those you will encounter in academic and business environments.

Project Planning Guidelines

The process of developing a document that communicates specific information requires careful analysis and planning. As a starting point, establish why the document is needed. Once the purpose is determined, analyze the intended readers of the document and their unique needs. Then, gather information about the topic and decide what to include in the document. Finally, determine the document design and style that will be most successful at delivering the message. Details of these guidelines are provided in Appendix A. In addition, each project in this book provides practical applications of these planning considerations.

Project — Document with a Picture

To advertise a sale, promote a business, publicize an event, or convey a message to the community, you may want to create a flyer and post it in a public location. Libraries, schools, churches, grocery stores, and other places often provide bulletin boards or windows for flyers. These flyers announce personal items for sale or rent (car, boat, apartment); garage or block sales; services being offered (animal care, housecleaning, lessons); membership, sponsorship, or donation requests (club, church, charity); and other messages. Flyers are an inexpensive means of reaching the community, yet many go unnoticed because they are designed poorly.

The project in this chapter follows general guidelines and uses Word to create the flyer shown in Figure 1–1. This colorful, eye-catching flyer advertises horseback riding lessons at Tri-Valley Stables. The picture of the horse and rider entices passersby to stop and look at the flyer. The headline on the flyer is large and colorful to draw attention into the text. The body copy below the headline briefly describes key points of the riding lessons, and the bulleted list below the picture concisely highlights important additional information. The signature line of the flyer calls attention to the stable name and telephone number. Finally, the graphical page border nicely frames and complements the contents of the flyer.

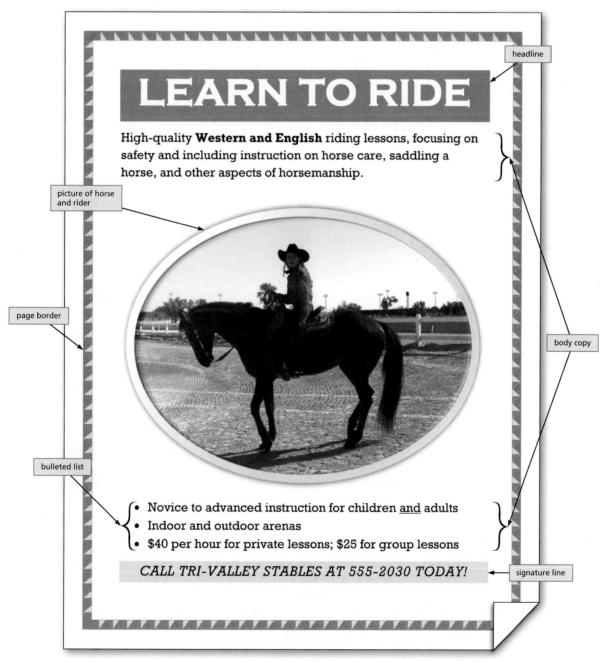

Figure 1–1

Overview

As you read this chapter, you will learn how to create the flyer shown in Figure 1–1 on the previous page by performing these general tasks:

- Enter text in the document.
- Save the document.
- Format the text in the document.
- Insert a picture in the document.
- Format the picture.
- Add a border to the page.
- Print the document.

Plan Ahead

> **General Project Guidelines**
>
> When creating a Word document, the actions you perform and decisions you make will affect the appearance and characteristics of the finished document. As you create a flyer, such as the project shown in Figure 1–1, you should follow these general guidelines:
>
> 1. **Choose the words for the text.** Follow the *less is more* principle. The less text, the more likely the flyer will be read. Use as few words as possible to make a point.
>
> 2. **Determine where to save the flyer.** You can store a document permanently, or **save** it, on a variety of storage media including a hard disk, USB flash drive, or CD. You also can indicate a specific location on the storage media for saving the document.
>
> 3. **Identify how to format various elements of the text.** The overall appearance of a document significantly affects its ability to communicate clearly. Examples of how you can modify the appearance, or **format**, of text include changing its shape, size, color, and position on the page.
>
> 4. **Find the appropriate graphical image.** An eye-catching graphical image should convey the flyer's overall message. It could show a product, service, result, or benefit, or visually convey a message that is not expressed easily with words.
>
> 5. **Establish where to position and how to format the graphical image.** The position and format of the graphical image should grab the attention of passersby and draw them into reading the flyer.
>
> 6. **Determine whether the flyer needs a page border, and if so, its style and format.** A graphical, color-coordinated page border can further draw attention to a flyer and nicely frame its contents. Be careful, however, that a page border does not make the flyer look too cluttered.
>
> When necessary, more specific details concerning the above guidelines are presented at appropriate points in the chapter. The chapter also will identify the actions performed and decisions made regarding these guidelines during the creation of the flyer shown in Figure 1–1.

Starting Word

If you are using a computer to step through the project in this chapter and you want your screen to match the figures in this book, you should change your screen's resolution to 1024 × 768. For information about how to change a computer's resolution, read Appendix E.

Note: If you are using Windows XP, see Appendix F for alternate steps.

To Start Word

The following steps, which assume Windows Vista is running, start Word based on a typical installation. You may need to ask your instructor how to start Word for your computer.

- Click the Start button on the Windows Vista taskbar to display the Start menu.

- Click All Programs at the bottom of the left pane on the Start menu to display the All Programs list.

- Click Microsoft Office in the All Programs list to display the Microsoft Office list (Figure 1–2).

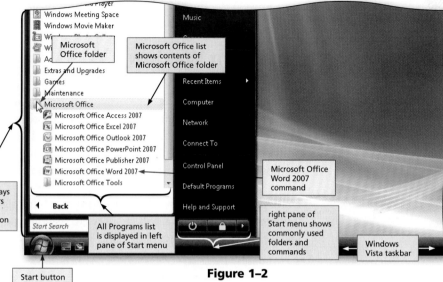

Figure 1–2

- Click Microsoft Office Word 2007 to start Word and display a new blank document in the Word window (Figure 1–3).

- If the Word window is not maximized, click the Maximize button next to the Close button on its title bar to maximize the window.

Q&A

What is a maximized window?

A maximized window fills the entire screen. When you maximize a window, the Maximize button changes to a Restore Down button.

- If the Print Layout button is not selected, click it so that your screen layout matches Figure 1–3.

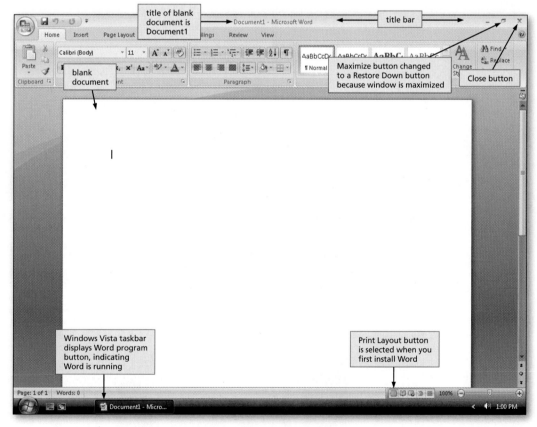

Figure 1–3

Other Ways
1. Double-click Word icon on desktop, if one is present   2. Click Microsoft Office Word 2007 on Start menu

The Word Window

The Word window consists of a variety of components to make your work more efficient and documents more professional. These include the document window, Ribbon, Mini toolbar and shortcut menus, Quick Access Toolbar, and Office Button. Some of these components are common to other Microsoft Office 2007 programs; others are unique to Word.

Document Window

You view a portion of a document on the screen through a **document window** (Figure 1–4). The default (preset) view is **Print Layout view**, which shows the document on a mock sheet of paper in the document window.

The Word document window in Figure 1–4 contains an insertion point, mouse pointer, scroll bar, and status bar. Other elements that may appear in the document window are discussed later in this and subsequent chapters.

Insertion Point The **insertion point** is a blinking vertical bar that indicates where text, graphics, and other items will be inserted. As you type, the insertion point moves to the right, and when you reach the end of a line, it moves downward to the beginning of the next line.

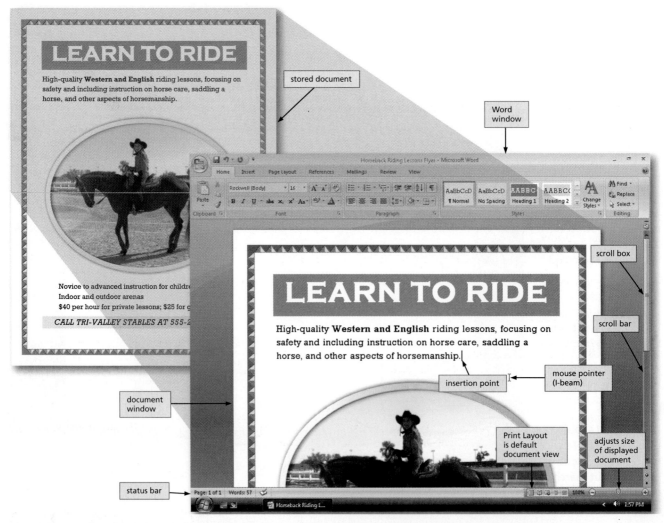

Figure 1–4

Mouse Pointer The **mouse pointer** becomes different shapes depending on the task you are performing in Word and the pointer's location on the screen. The mouse pointer in Figure 1–4 is the shape of an I-beam.

Scroll Bar You use a **scroll bar** to display different portions of a document in the document window. At the right edge of the document window is a vertical scroll bar. If a document is too wide to fit in the document window, a horizontal scroll bar also appears at the bottom of the document window. On a scroll bar, the position of the **scroll box** reflects the location of the portion of the document that is displayed in the document window. A **scroll arrow** is located at each end of a scroll bar. To scroll through, or display different portions of the document in the document window, you can click a scroll arrow or drag the scroll box.

Status Bar The **status bar**, located at the bottom of the document window above the Windows Vista taskbar, presents information about the document, the progress of current tasks, and the status of certain commands and keys; it also provides controls for viewing the document. As you type text or perform certain commands, various indicators and buttons may appear on the status bar.

The left edge of the status bar in Figure 1–4 shows the current page followed by the total number of pages in the document, the number of words in the document, and a button to check spelling and grammar. Toward the right edge are buttons and controls you can use to change the view of a document and adjust the size of the displayed document.

Ribbon

The **Ribbon**, located near the top of the Word window, is the control center in Word (Figure 1–5a). The Ribbon provides easy, central access to the tasks you perform while creating a document. The Ribbon consists of tabs, groups, and commands. Each **tab** surrounds a collection of groups, and each group contains related commands.

When you start Word, the Ribbon displays seven top-level tabs: Home, Insert, Page Layout, References, Mailings, Review, and View. The **Home tab**, called the primary tab, contains the more frequently used commands. To display a different tab on the Ribbon, click the top-level tab. That is, to display the Insert tab, click Insert on the Ribbon. To return to the Home tab, click Home on the Ribbon. The tab currently displayed is called the **active tab**.

To display more of the document in the document window, some users prefer to minimize the Ribbon, which hides the groups on the Ribbon and displays only the top-level tabs (Figure 1–5b). To use commands on a minimized Ribbon, click the top-level tab.

BTW

Minimizing the Ribbon
If you want to minimize the Ribbon, right-click the Ribbon and then click Minimize the Ribbon on the shortcut menu, double-click the active tab, or press CTRL+F1. To restore a minimized Ribbon, right-click the Ribbon and then click Minimize the Ribbon on the shortcut menu, double-click any top-level tab, or press CTRL+F1. To use commands on a minimized Ribbon, click the top-level tab.

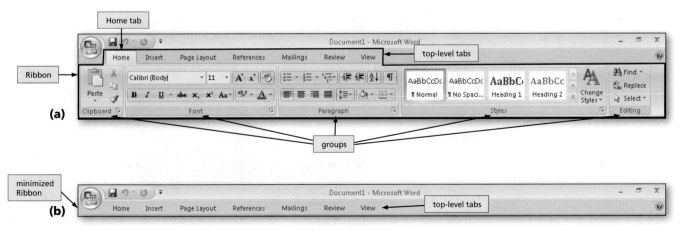

Figure 1–5

Each time you start Word, the Ribbon appears the same way it did the last time you used Word. The chapters in this book, however, begin with the Ribbon appearing as it did at the initial installation of the software. If you are stepping through this chapter on a computer and you want your Ribbon to match the figures in this book, read Appendix E.

In addition to the top-level tabs, Word displays other tabs, called **contextual tabs**, when you perform certain tasks or work with objects such as pictures or tables. If you insert a picture in the document, for example, the Picture Tools tab and its related subordinate Format tab appear (Figure 1–6). When you are finished working with the picture, the Picture Tools and Format tabs disappear from the Ribbon. Word determines when contextual tabs should appear and disappear based on tasks you perform. Some contextual tabs, such as the Table Tools tab, have more than one related subordinate tab.

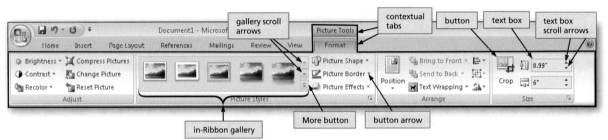

Figure 1–6

Commands on the Ribbon include buttons, boxes (text boxes, check boxes, etc.), and galleries (Figure 1–6). A **gallery** is a set of choices, often graphical, arranged in a grid or in a list. You can scroll through choices on an in-Ribbon gallery by clicking the gallery's scroll arrows. Or, you can click a gallery's More button to view more gallery options on the screen at a time. Some buttons and boxes have arrows that, when clicked, also display a gallery; others always cause a gallery to be displayed when clicked. Most galleries support **live preview**, which is a feature that allows you to point to a gallery choice and see its effect in the document — without actually selecting the choice (Figure 1–7).

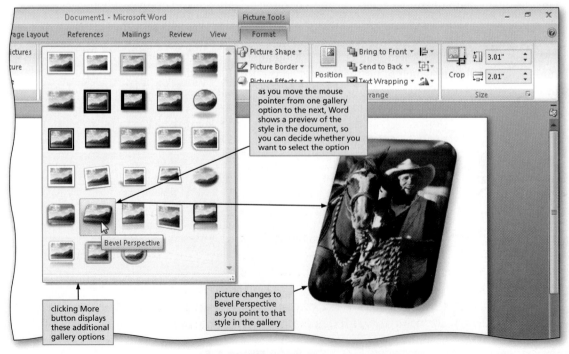

Figure 1–7

Some commands on the Ribbon display an image to help you remember their function. When you point to a command on the Ribbon, all or part of the command glows in shades of yellow and orange, and an Enhanced ScreenTip appears on the screen. An **Enhanced ScreenTip** is an on-screen note that provides the name of the command, available keyboard shortcut(s), a description of the command, and sometimes instructions for how to obtain help about the command (Figure 1–8). Enhanced ScreenTips are more detailed than a typical ScreenTip, which usually only displays the name of the command.

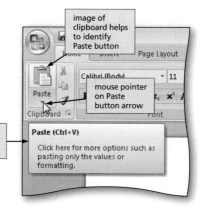

Figure 1–8

The lower-right corner of some groups on the Ribbon has a small arrow, called a **Dialog Box Launcher**, that when clicked, displays a dialog box or a task pane with additional options for the group (Figure 1–9). When presented with a dialog box, you make selections and must close the dialog box before returning to the document. A **task pane**, by contrast, is a window that can remain open and visible while you work in the document.

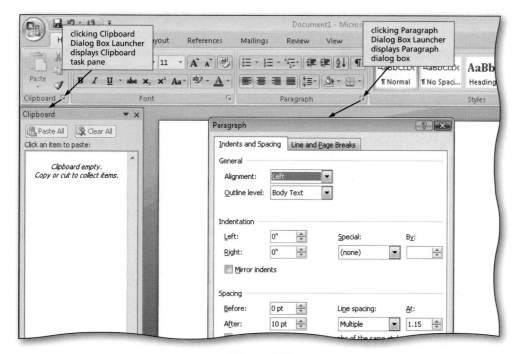

Figure 1–9

Mini Toolbar and Shortcut Menus

The **Mini toolbar**, which appears automatically based on tasks you perform, contains commands related to changing the appearance of text in a document. All commands on the Mini toolbar also exist on the Ribbon. The purpose of the Mini toolbar is to minimize mouse movement. For example, if you want to use a command that currently is not displayed on the active tab, you can use the command on the Mini toolbar — instead of switching to a different tab to use the command.

When the Mini toolbar appears, it initially is transparent (Figure 1–10a). If you do not use the transparent Mini toolbar, it disappears from the screen. To use the Mini toolbar, move the mouse pointer into the toolbar, which causes the Mini toolbar to change from a transparent to bright appearance (Figure 1–10b).

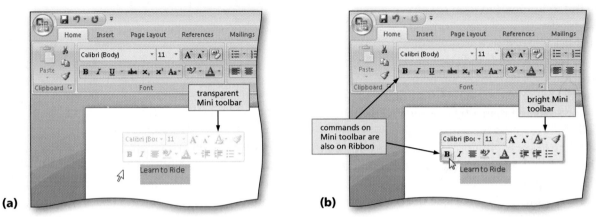

(a)   **(b)**

Figure 1–10

A **shortcut menu**, which appears when you right-click an object, is a list of frequently used commands that relate to the right-clicked object. When you right-click a scroll bar, for example, a shortcut menu appears with commands related to the scroll bar. If you right-click an item in the document window, Word displays both the Mini toolbar and a shortcut menu (Figure 1–11).

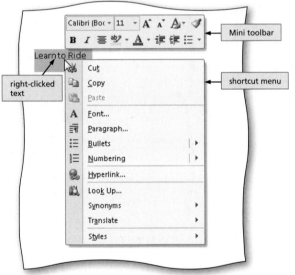

Figure 1–11

Quick Access Toolbar

The **Quick Access Toolbar**, located by default above the Ribbon, provides easy access to frequently used commands (Figure 1–12a). The commands on the Quick Access Toolbar always are available, regardless of the task you are performing. Initially, the Quick Access Toolbar contains the Save, Undo, and Redo commands. If you click the Customize Quick Access Toolbar button, Word provides a list of commands you quickly can add to and remove from the Quick Access Toolbar (Figure 1–12b).

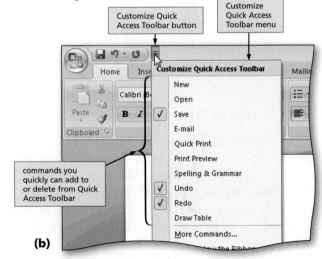

(a)   **(b)**

Figure 1–12

You also can add other commands to or delete commands from the Quick Access Toolbar so that it contains the commands you use most often. As you add commands to the Quick Access Toolbar, its commands may interfere with the document title on the title bar. For this reason, Word provides an option of displaying the Quick Access Toolbar below the Ribbon (Figure 1–13).

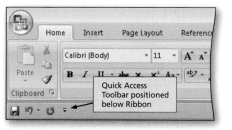

Figure 1–13

BTW

Quick Access Toolbar Commands
To add a Ribbon command to the Quick Access Toolbar, right-click the command on the Ribbon and then click Add to Quick Access Toolbar on the shortcut menu. To delete a command from the Quick Access Toolbar, right-click the command on the Quick Access Toolbar and then click Remove from Quick Access Toolbar on the shortcut menu. To display the Quick Access Toolbar below the Ribbon, right-click the Quick Access Toolbar and then click Show Quick Access Toolbar Below the Ribbon on the shortcut menu.

Each time you start Word, the Quick Access Toolbar appears the same way it did the last time you used Word. The chapters in this book, however, begin with the Quick Access Toolbar appearing as it did at the initial installation of the software. If you are stepping through this chapter on a computer and you want your Quick Access Toolbar to match the figures in this book, you should reset your Quick Access Toolbar. For more information about how to reset the Quick Access Toolbar, read Appendix E.

Office Button

While the Ribbon is a control center for creating documents, the **Office Button** is a central location for managing and sharing documents. When you click the Office Button, located in the upper-left corner of the window, Word displays the Office Button menu (Figure 1–14a). A **menu** contains a list of commands.

When you click the New, Open, Save As, and Print commands on the Office Button menu, Word displays a dialog box with additional options. The Save As, Print, Prepare, Send, and Publish commands have an arrow to their right. If you point to this arrow, Word displays a **submenu**, which is a list of additional commands associated with the selected command (Figure 1–14b). For the Prepare, Send, and Publish commands that do not display a dialog box when clicked, you can point either to the command or the arrow to display the submenu.

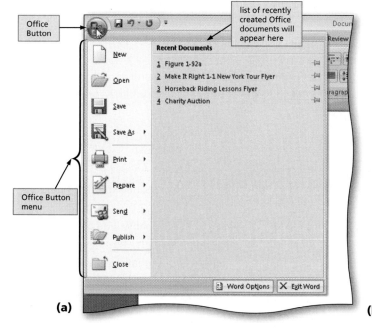
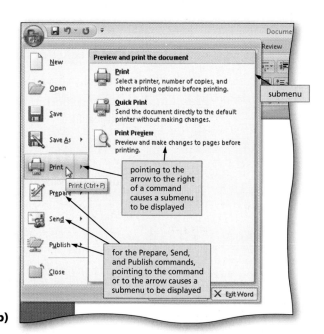

(a) **(b)**

Figure 1–14

Key Tips

If you prefer using the keyboard instead of the mouse, you can press the ALT key on the keyboard to display a **Key Tip badge**, or keyboard code icon, for certain commands (Figure 1–15). To select a command using the keyboard, press its displayed code letter, or **Key Tip**. When you press a Key Tip, additional Key Tips related to the selected command may appear. For example, to select the New command on the Office Button menu, press the ALT key, then press the F key, and then press the N key.

To remove the Key Tip badges from the screen, press the ALT key or the ESC key until all Key Tip badges disappear, or click the mouse anywhere in the Word window.

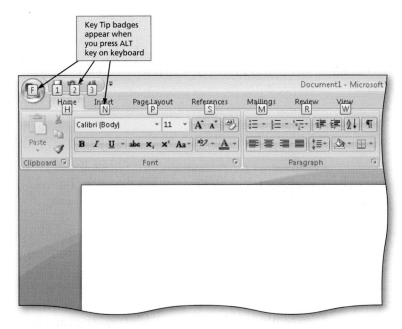

Key Tip badges appear when you press ALT key on keyboard

Figure 1–15

Entering Text

The first step in creating a document is to enter its text by typing on the keyboard. By default, Word positions text you type at the left margin. In a later section of this chapter, you will learn how to format, or change the appearance of, the entered text.

Plan Ahead

Choose the words for the text.
The text in a flyer is organized into three areas: headline, body copy, and signature line.

- The headline is the first line of text on the flyer. It conveys the product or service being offered, such as a car for sale or personal lessons, or the benefit that will be gained, such as a convenience, better performance, greater security, higher earnings, or more comfort.

- The body text consists of all text between the headline and the signature line. This text highlights the key points of the message in as few words as possible. It should be easy to read and follow. While emphasizing the positive, the body text must be realistic, truthful, and believable.

- The signature line, which is the last line of text on the flyer, contains contact information or identifies a call to action.

To Type Text

To begin creating the flyer in this chapter, you type the headline in the document window. The following steps type this first line of text in the document.

1

- **Type** Learn to Ride **as the headline (Figure 1–16).**

 What if I make an error while typing?

You can press the **BACKSPACE** key until you have deleted the text in error and then retype the text correctly.

 Why did the Spelling and Grammar Check icon appear on the status bar?

When you begin typing text, the **Spelling and Grammar Check icon** appears on the status bar with an animated pencil writing on paper that indicates Word is checking for spelling and grammar errors. When you stop typing, the pencil changes to a blue check mark (no errors) or a red X (potential errors found). Word flags potential errors in the document with a red or green wavy underline. Later, this chapter shows how to fix flagged errors.

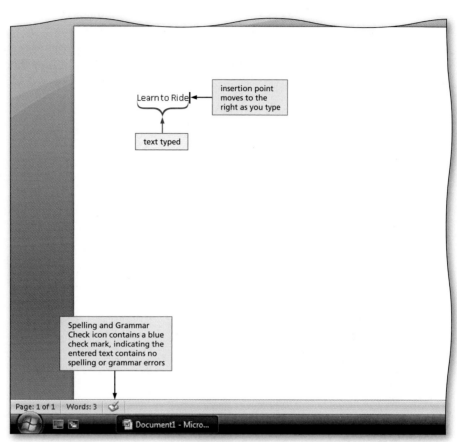

Figure 1–16

2

- **Press the ENTER key to move the insertion point to the beginning of the next line (Figure 1–17).**

 Why did blank space appear between the headline and the insertion point?

Each time you press the ENTER key, Word creates a new paragraph and inserts blank space between the two paragraphs. Later in this chapter, you will learn how to adjust the spacing between paragraphs.

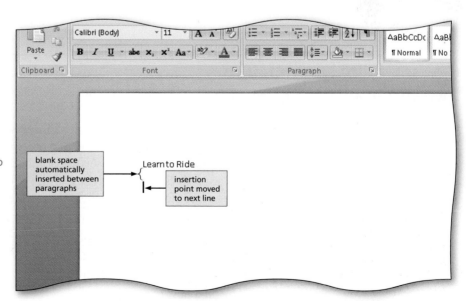

Figure 1–17

To Display Formatting Marks

To indicate where in a document you press the ENTER key or SPACEBAR, you may find it helpful to display formatting marks. A **formatting mark**, sometimes called a **nonprinting character**, is a character that Word displays on the screen but is not visible on a printed document. For example, the paragraph mark (¶) is a formatting mark that indicates where you pressed the ENTER key. A raised dot (·) shows where you pressed the SPACEBAR. Other formatting marks are discussed as they appear on the screen.

Depending on settings made during previous Word sessions, your Word screen already may display formatting marks (Figure 1–18). The following step displays formatting marks, if they do not show already on the screen.

1

- If necessary, click Home on the Ribbon to display the Home tab.

- If it is not selected already, click the Show/Hide ¶ button on the Home tab to display formatting marks on the screen (Figure 1–18).

Q&A

What if I do not want formatting marks to show on the screen?

If you feel the formatting marks clutter the screen, you can hide them by clicking the Show/Hide ¶ button again. It is recommended that you display formatting marks so that you visually can identify when you press the ENTER key, SPACEBAR, and other keys associated with nonprinting characters; therefore, the document windows presented in this book show the formatting marks.

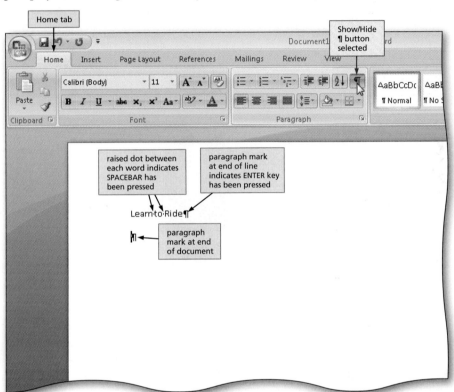

Figure 1–18

Other Ways
1. Press CTRL+SHIFT+*

Wordwrap

Wordwrap allows you to type words in a paragraph continually without pressing the ENTER key at the end of each line. When the insertion point reaches the right margin, Word automatically positions the insertion point at the beginning of the next line. As you type, if a word extends beyond the right margin, Word also automatically positions that word on the next line along with the insertion point.

Word creates a new paragraph each time you press the ENTER key. Thus, as you type text in the document window, do not press the ENTER key when the insertion point reaches the right margin. Instead, press the ENTER key only in these circumstances:

1. To insert blank lines in a document
2. To begin a new paragraph
3. To terminate a short line of text and advance to the next line
4. To respond to questions or prompts in Word dialog boxes, task panes, and other on-screen objects

To Wordwrap Text as You Type

The next step in creating the flyer is to type the body copy. The following step wordwraps the text in the body copy.

- **Type** High-quality Western and English riding lessons, focusing on safety and including instruction on horse care, saddling a horse, and other aspects of horsemanship.

 Why does my document wrap on different words?

Differences in wordwrap relate to the printer used by your computer. That is, the printer controls where wordwrap occurs for each line in your document. Thus, it is possible that the same document could wordwrap differently if printed on different printers.

- Press the ENTER key to position the insertion point on the next line in the document (Figure 1–19).

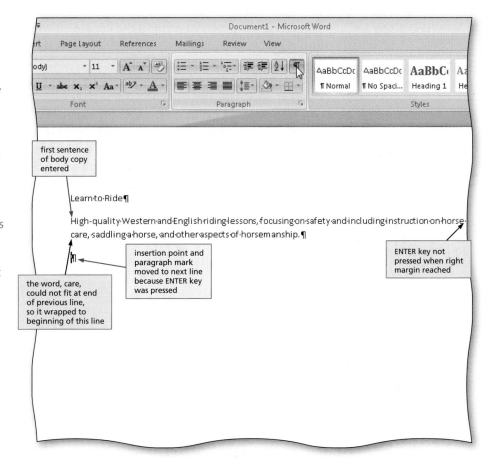

Figure 1–19

To Insert a Blank Line

In the flyer, the picture of the horse and rider should be positioned below the paragraph just entered. The picture will be inserted after all text is entered and formatted. Thus, you will leave a blank line in the document for the picture. To enter a blank line in a document, press the ENTER key without typing any text on the line. The following step inserts one blank line below the first paragraph of body copy.

- Press the ENTER key to insert a blank line in the document (Figure 1–20).

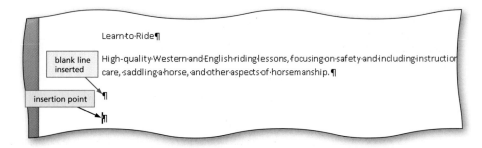

Figure 1–20

BTW

Automatic Spelling Correction

As you type, Word automatically corrects some misspelled words. For example, if you type recieve, Word automatically fixes the misspelling and displays the word, receive, when you press the SPACEBAR or type a punctuation mark. To see a complete list of automatically corrected words, click Office Button, click the Word Options button, click Proofing in the left pane of the Word Options dialog box, click the AutoCorrect Options button, and then scroll through the list of words near the bottom of the dialog box.

Spelling and Grammar Check

As you type text in a document, Word checks your typing for possible spelling and grammar errors. If all of the words you have typed are in Word's dictionary and your grammar is correct, as mentioned earlier, the Spelling and Grammar Check icon on the status bar displays a blue check mark. Otherwise, the icon shows a red X. In this case, Word flags the potential error in the document window with a red or green wavy underline. A red wavy underline means the flagged text is not in Word's dictionary (because it is a proper name or misspelled). A green wavy underline indicates the text may be incorrect grammatically. Although you can check the entire document for spelling and grammar errors at once, you also can check these flagged errors as they appear on the screen.

To display a list of corrections for flagged text, right-click the flagged text. When you right-click a flagged word, for example, a list of suggested spelling corrections appears on the screen. A flagged word, however, is not necessarily misspelled. For example, many names, abbreviations, and specialized terms are not in Word's main dictionary. In these cases, you tell Word to ignore the flagged word. As you type, Word also detects duplicate words while checking for spelling errors. For example, if your document contains the phrase, to the the store, Word places a red wavy underline below the second occurrence of the word, the.

To Check Spelling and Grammar as You Type

In the following steps, the word, instruction, has been misspelled intentionally as intrution to illustrate Word's check spelling as you type feature. If you are doing this project on a computer, your flyer may contain other misspelled words, depending on the accuracy of your typing.

• **Type** Novice to advanced intrution **and then press the** SPACEBAR (Figure 1–21).

Q&A

What if Word does not flag my spelling and grammar errors with wavy underlines?

To verify that the check spelling and grammar as you type features are enabled, click the Office Button and then click the Word Options button. When the Word Options dialog box is displayed, click Proofing, and then ensure the 'Check spelling as you type' and 'Mark grammar errors as you type' check boxes have check marks. Also ensure the 'Hide spelling errors in this document only' and 'Hide grammar errors in this document only' check boxes do not have check marks. Click the OK button.

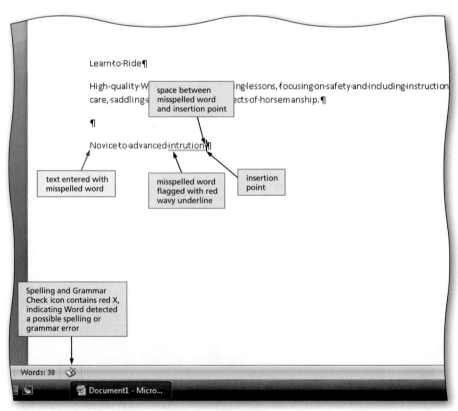

Figure 1–21

2

- Right-click the flagged word (intrution, in this case) to display a shortcut menu that includes a list of suggested spelling corrections for the flagged word (Figure 1–22).

Q&A What if, when I right-click the misspelled word, my desired correction is not in the list on the shortcut menu?

You can click outside the shortcut menu to close the menu and then retype the correct word, or you can click Spelling on the shortcut menu to display the Spelling dialog box. Chapter 2 discusses the Spelling dialog box.

Q&A What if a flagged word actually is, for example, a proper name and spelled correctly?

Right-click it and then click Ignore All on the shortcut menu to instruct Word not to flag future occurrences of the same word.

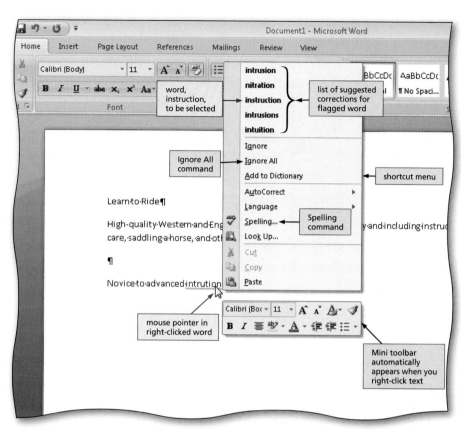

Figure 1–22

3

- Click instruction on the shortcut menu to replace the misspelled word in the document (intrution) with the word, instruction (Figure 1–23).

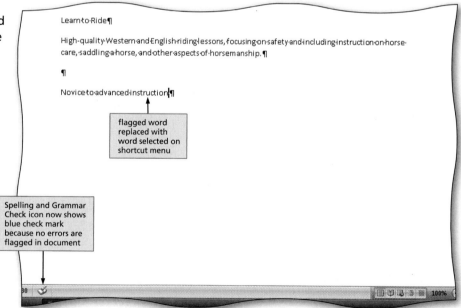

Figure 1–23

Other Ways

1. Click Spelling and Grammar Check icon on status bar, click correct word on shortcut menu

To Enter More Text

In the flyer, the text yet to be entered includes the remainder of the body copy, which will be formatted as a bulleted list, and the signature line. The following steps enter the remainder of text in the flyer.

1 Press the END key to move the insertion point to the end of the current line.

2 Type `for children and adults` and then press the ENTER key.

3 Type `Indoor and outdoor arenas` and then press the ENTER key.

4 Type `$40 per hour for private lessons; $25 for group lessons` and then press the ENTER key.

5 To complete the text in the flyer, type `Call Tri-Valley Stables at 555-2030 today!` (Figure 1–24).

BTW

Character Widths
Many word processing documents use variable character fonts, where some characters are wider than others; for example, the letter w takes up more space than the letter i.

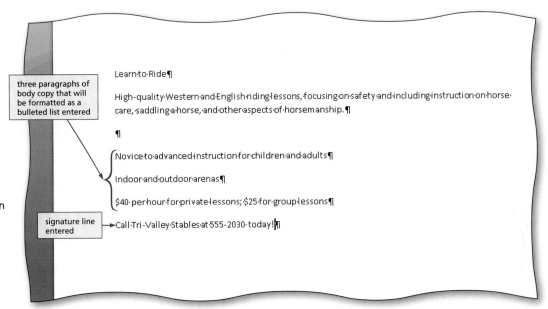

three paragraphs of body copy that will be formatted as a bulleted list entered

signature line entered

Learn·to·Ride¶

High-quality·Western·and·English·riding·lessons,·focusing·on·safety·and·including·instruction·on·horse·care,·saddling·a·horse,·and·other·aspects·of·horsemanship.¶

¶

Novice·to·advanced·instruction·for·children·and·adults¶

Indoor·and·outdoor·arenas¶

$40·per·hour·for·private·lessons;·$25·for·group·lessons¶

Call·Tri-Valley·Stables·at·555-2030·today!¶

Figure 1–24

Saving the Project

BTW

File Type
Depending on your Windows Vista settings, the file type .docx may be displayed immediately to the right of the file name after you save the file. The file type .docx is a Word 2007 document. Previous versions of Word had a file type of .doc.

While you are creating a document, the computer stores it in memory. When you save a document, the computer places it on a storage medium such as a USB flash drive, CD, or hard disk. A saved document is referred to as a **file**. A **file name** is the name assigned to a file when it is saved.

It is important to save a document frequently for the following reasons:

• The document in memory will be lost if the computer is turned off or you lose electrical power while Word is open.

• If you run out of time before completing your project, you may finish your document at a future time without starting over.

Determine where to save the document.
When saving a document, you must decide which storage medium to use.

- If you always work on the same computer and have no need to transport your projects to a different location, then your computer's hard disk will suffice as a storage location. It is a good idea, however, to save a backup copy of your projects on a separate medium in case the file becomes corrupted or the computer's hard disk fails.

- If you plan to work on your projects in various locations or on multiple computers, then you should save your projects on a portable medium, such as a USB flash drive or CD. The projects in this book use a USB flash drive, which saves files quickly and reliably and can be reused. CDs are easily portable and serve as good backups for the final versions of projects because they generally can save files only one time.

To Save a Document

You have performed many tasks while creating this project and do not want to risk losing the work completed thus far. Accordingly, you should save the document. The following steps save a document on a USB flash drive using the file name, Horseback Riding Lessons Flyer.

Note: If you are using Windows XP, see Appendix F for alternate steps.

1

- With a USB flash drive connected to one of the computer's USB ports, click the Save button on the Quick Access Toolbar to display the Save As dialog box (Figure 1–25).

- If the Navigation pane is not displayed in the Save As dialog box, click the Browse Folders button to expand the dialog box.

- If a Folders list is displayed below the Folders button, click the Folders button to remove the Folders list.

Q&A

Do I have to save to a USB flash drive?

No. You can save to any device or folder. A **folder** is a specific location on a storage medium. You can save to the default folder or a different folder. You also can create your own folders, which is explained later in this book.

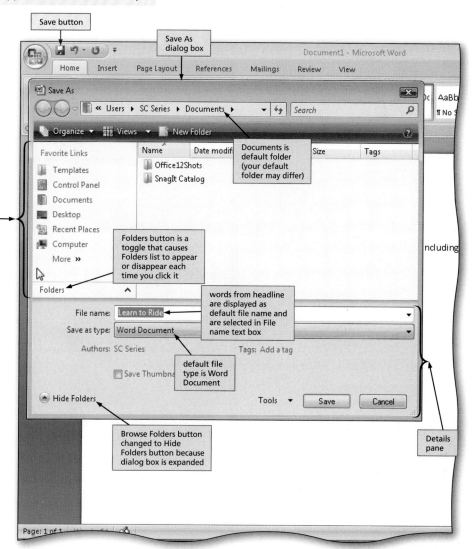

Figure 1–25

2

- **Type** Horseback Riding Lessons Flyer in the File name text box to change the file name. Do not press the ENTER key after typing the file name (Figure 1–26).

Q&A

What characters can I use in a file name?

A file name can have a maximum of 260 characters, including spaces. The only invalid characters are the backslash (\), slash (/), colon (:), asterisk (*), question mark (?), quotation mark ("), less than symbol (<), greater than symbol (>), and vertical bar (|).

Q&A

What are file properties and tags?

File properties contain information about a file such as the file name, author name, date the file was modified, and tags. A tag is a file property that contains a word or phrase about a file. You can organize and locate files based on their file properties.

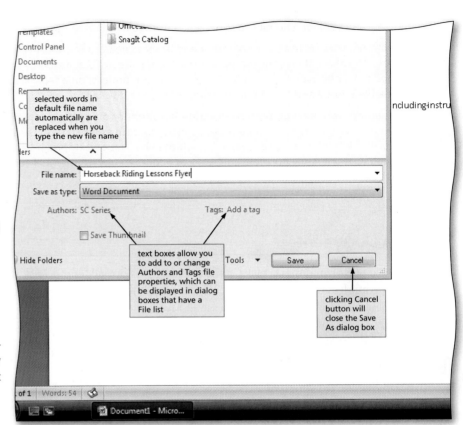

Figure 1–26

3

- If Computer is not displayed in the Favorite Links section, drag the top or bottom edge of the Save As dialog box until Computer is displayed.

- Click Computer in the Favorite Links section to display a list of available drives (Figure 1–27).

- If necessary, scroll until UDISK 2.0 (E:) appears in the list of available drives.

Q&A

Why is my list of drives arranged and named differently?

The size of the Save As dialog box and your computer's configuration determine how the list is displayed and how the drives are named.

Q&A

How do I save the file if I am not using a USB flash drive?

Use the same process, but select your desired save location in the Favorite Links section.

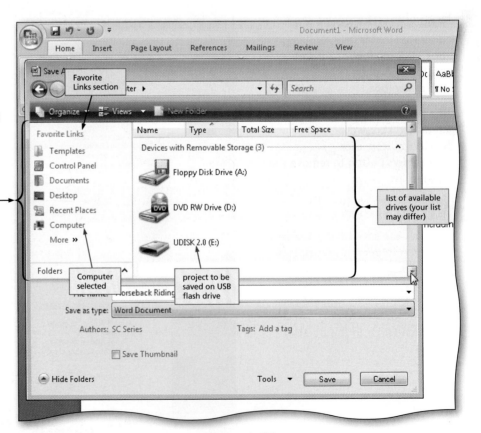

Figure 1–27

4

- Double-click UDISK 2.0 (E:) in the Computer list to select the USB flash drive, Drive E in this case, as the new save location (Figure 1–28).

What if my USB flash drive has a different name or letter?

It is very likely that your USB flash drive will have a different name and drive letter and be connected to a different port. Verify the device in your Computer list is correct.

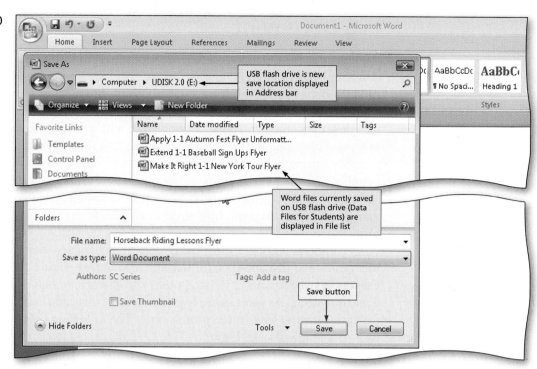

Figure 1–28

5

- Click the Save button in the Save As dialog box to save the document on the USB flash drive with the file name, Horseback Riding Lessons Flyer (Figure 1–29).

How do I know that the project is saved?

While Word is saving your file, it briefly displays a message on the status bar indicating the amount of the file saved. In addition, your USB drive may have a light that flashes during the save process.

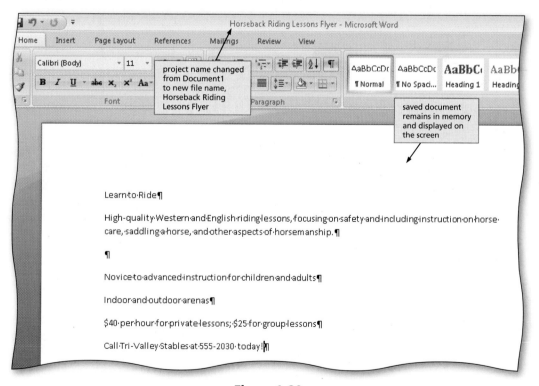

Figure 1–29

Other Ways
1. Click Office Button, click Save, type file name, click Computer, select drive or folder, click Save button   2. Press CTRL+S or press SHIFT+F12, type file name, click Computer, select drive or folder, click Save button

Formatting Paragraphs and Characters in a Document

With the text for the flyer entered, the next step is to format its paragraphs and characters. Paragraphs encompass the text from the first character in a paragraph up to and including a paragraph mark (¶). **Paragraph formatting** is the process of changing the appearance of a paragraph. For example, you can center or indent a paragraph. Characters include letters, numbers, punctuation marks, and symbols. **Character formatting** is the process of changing the way characters appear on the screen and in print. You use character formatting to emphasize certain words and improve readability of a document. For example, you can italicize or underline characters. Often, you apply both paragraph and character formatting to the same text. For example, you may center a paragraph (paragraph formatting) and bold some of the characters in a paragraph (character formatting).

Although you can format paragraphs and characters before you type, many Word users enter text first and then format the existing text. Figure 1–30a shows the flyer in this chapter before formatting its paragraphs and characters. Figure 1–30b shows the flyer after formatting. As you can see from the two figures, a document that is formatted is easier to read and looks more professional. The following pages discuss how to format the flyer so that it looks like Figure 1–30b.

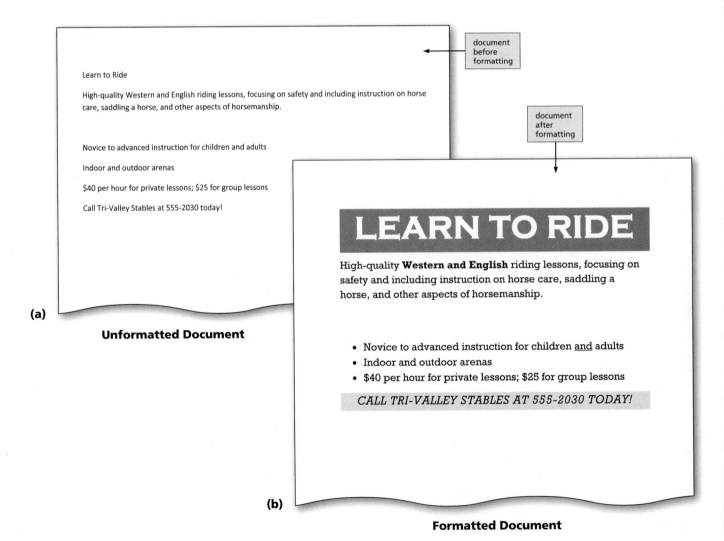

(a)

Unformatted Document

(b)

Formatted Document

Figure 1–30

Fonts, Font Sizes, Styles, and Themes

Characters that appear on the screen are a specific shape and size. The **font**, or typeface, defines the appearance and shape of the letters, numbers, and special characters. In Word, the default font usually is Calibri (Figure 1–31 on the next page). You can leave characters in the default font or change them to a different font. **Font size** specifies the size of the characters and is determined by a measurement system called points. A single **point** is about 1/72 of one inch in height. The default font size in Word typically is 11 (Figure 1–31). A character with a font size of 11 is about 11/72 or a little less than 1/6 of one inch in height. You can increase or decrease the font size of characters in a document.

When you create a document, Word formats the text using a particular style. A **style** is a named group of formatting characteristics, including font and font size. The default style in Word is called the **Normal style**, which most likely uses 11-point Calibri font. If you do not specify a style for text you type, Word applies the Normal style to the text. In addition to the Normal style, Word has many other built-in, or predefined, styles that you can use to format text. You also can create your own styles. Styles make it easy to apply many formats at once to text. After you apply a style to text, you easily can modify the text to include additional formats. You also can modify the style.

To assist you with coordinating colors and fonts and other formats, Word uses document themes. A document **theme** is a set of unified formats for fonts, colors, and graphics. The default theme fonts are Cambria for headings and Calibri for body text (Figure 1–31). Word includes a variety of document themes. By changing the document theme, you quickly give your document a new look. You also can define your own document themes.

Plan Ahead

Identify how to format various elements of the text.
By formatting the characters and paragraphs in a document, you can improve its overall appearance. In a flyer, consider the following formatting suggestions.

- **Increase the font size of characters.** Flyers usually are posted on a bulletin board or in a window. Thus, the font size should be as large as possible so that passersby easily can read the flyer. To give the headline more impact, its font size should be larger than the font size of the text in the body copy. If possible, make the font size of the signature line larger than the body copy but smaller than the headline.

- **Change the font of characters.** Use fonts that are easy to read. Try to use only two different fonts in a flyer, for example, one for the headline and the other for all other text. Too many fonts can make the flyer visually confusing.

- **Change paragraph alignment.** The default alignment for paragraphs in a document is **left-aligned**, that is, flush at the left margin of the document with uneven right edges. Consider changing the alignment of some of the paragraphs to add interest and variety to the flyer.

- **Highlight key paragraphs with bullets.** A **bullet** is a dot or other symbol positioned at the beginning of a paragraph. Use bullets to highlight important paragraphs in a flyer.

- **Emphasize important words.** To call attention to certain words or lines, you can underline them, italicize them, or bold them. Use these formats sparingly, however, because overuse will minimize their effect and make the flyer look too busy.

- **Use color.** Use colors that complement each other and convey the meaning of the flyer. Vary colors in terms of hue and brightness. Headline colors, for example, can be bold and bright. Signature lines should stand out more than body copy but less than headlines. Keep in mind that too many colors can detract from the flyer and make it difficult to read.

To Apply Styles

In the flyer, you want the headline and the signature line to be emphasized more than the other text. Word provides heading styles designed to emphasize this type of text. The first step in formatting the flyer is to apply the Heading 1 style to the headline and the Heading 2 style to the signature line. The default Heading 1 style is a 14-point Cambria bold font. The default Heading 2 style is a 13-point Cambria bold font. The default theme color scheme uses shades of blue for headings.

To apply a style to a paragraph, you first position the insertion point in the paragraph and then apply the style. The following steps apply heading styles to paragraphs.

1

- Press CTRL+HOME (that is, press and hold down the CTRL key, press the HOME key, and then release both keys) to position the insertion point at the top of the document (Figure 1–31).

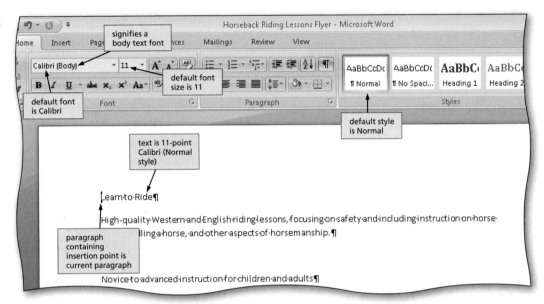

Figure 1–31

2

- Point to Heading 1 in the Styles gallery to display a live preview in the document of the Heading 1 style (Figure 1–32).

Q&A

What happens if I move the mouse pointer?

If you move the mouse pointer away from the gallery, the text containing the insertion point returns to the Normal style.

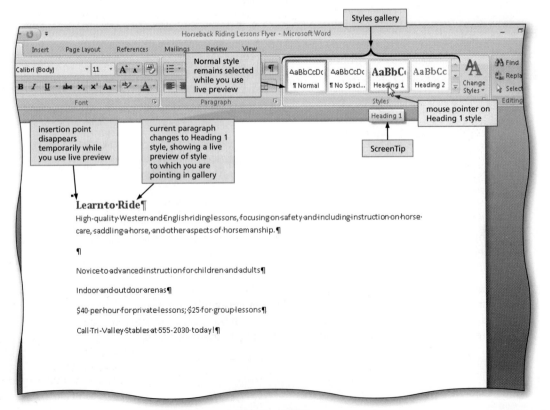

Figure 1–32

3

- Click Heading 1 in the Styles gallery to apply the Heading 1 style to the headline (Figure 1–33).

Q&A

Why did a square appear on the screen near the left edge of the headline?

The square is a nonprinting character, like the paragraph mark, that indicates text to its right has a special paragraph format applied to it.

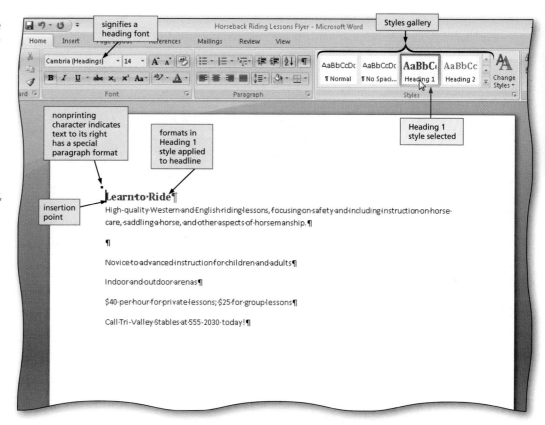

Figure 1–33

4

- Press CTRL+END (that is, press and hold down the CTRL key, press the END key, and then release both keys) to position the insertion point at the end of the document.

- Click Heading 2 in the Styles gallery to apply the Heading 2 style to the signature line (Figure 1–34).

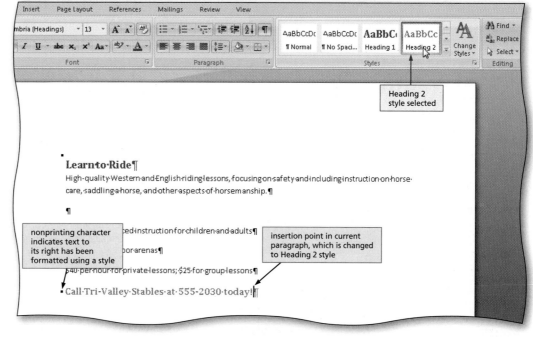

Figure 1–34

Other Ways
1. Click Styles Dialog Box Launcher, click desired style in Styles task pane   2. Press CTRL+SHIFT+S, click Style Name box arrow in Apply Styles task pane, click desired style in list

To Center a Paragraph

The headline in the flyer currently is left-aligned (Figure 1–35). You want the headline to be **centered**, that is, positioned horizontally between the left and right margins on the page. Thus, you will center the paragraph containing the headline. Recall that Word considers a single short line of text, such as the three-word headline, a paragraph. The following steps center a paragraph.

- Click somewhere in the paragraph to be centered (in this case, the headline) to position the insertion point in the paragraph to be formatted (Figure 1–35).

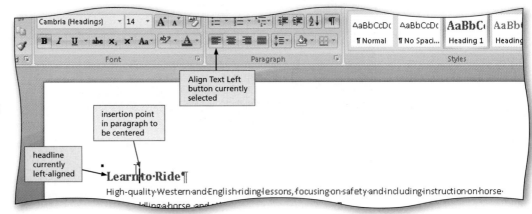

Figure 1–35

- Click the Center button on the Home tab to center the headline (Figure 1–36).

Q&A

What if I want to return the paragraph to left-aligned?

Click the Align Text Left button on the Home tab.

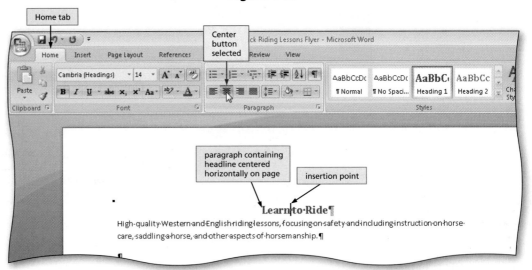

Figure 1–36

Other Ways

1. Right-click paragraph, click Center button on Mini toolbar

2. Right-click paragraph, click Paragraph on shortcut menu, click Indents and Spacing tab, click Alignment box arrow, click Centered, click OK button

3. Click Paragraph Dialog Box Launcher, click Indents and Spacing tab, click Alignment box arrow, click Centered, click OK button

4. Press CTRL+E

Formatting Single Versus Multiple Paragraphs and Characters

As shown in the previous pages, to format a single paragraph, simply move the insertion point in the paragraph and then format the paragraph. Likewise, to format a single word, position the insertion point in the word and then format the word.

To format *multiple* paragraphs or words, however, you first must select the paragraphs or words you want to format and then format the selection. If your screen normally displays dark letters on a light background, which is the default setting in Word, then selected text displays light letters on a dark background.

To Select a Line

The font size of characters in the Heading 1 style, 14 point, is too small for passersby to read in the headline of the flyer. To increase the font size of the characters in the headline, you must first select the line of text containing the headline. The following steps select a line.

1

• Move the mouse pointer to the left of the line to be selected (in this case, the headline) until the mouse pointer changes to a right-pointing block arrow (Figure 1–37).

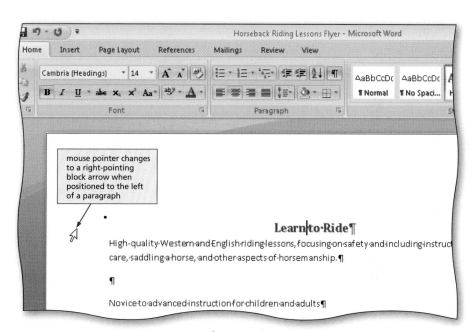

Figure 1–37

2

• While the mouse pointer is a right-pointing block arrow, click the mouse to select the entire line to the right of the mouse pointer (Figure 1–38).

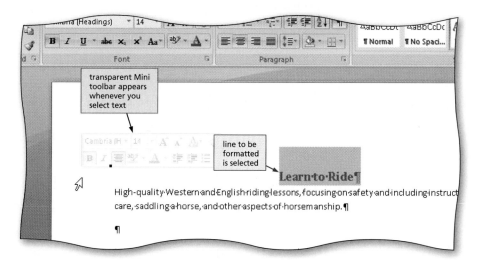

Figure 1–38

Other Ways	
1. Drag mouse through line	2. With insertion point at beginning of desired line, press SHIFT+DOWN ARROW

To Change the Font Size of Selected Text

The next step is to increase the font size of the characters in the selected headline. You would like the headline to be as large as possible and still fit on a single line, which in this case is 48 point. The following steps increase the font size of the headline from 14 to 48 point.

- With the text selected, click the Font Size box arrow on the Home tab to display the Font Size gallery (Figure 1–39).

Q&A Why are the font sizes in my Font Size gallery different from those in Figure 1–39?

Font sizes may vary depending on the current font and your printer driver.

Q&A What happened to the Mini toolbar?

The Mini toolbar disappears if you do not use it. These steps use the Font Size box arrow on the Home tab instead of the Font Size box arrow on the Mini toolbar. If a command exists both on the currently displayed tab and the Mini toolbar, this book uses the command on the tab. When the command is not on the currently displayed tab, the Mini toolbar is used.

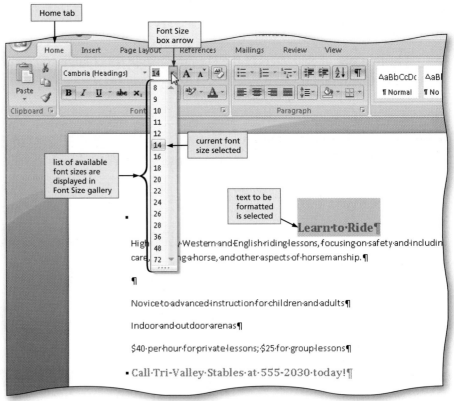

Figure 1–39

- Point to 48 in the Font Size gallery to display a live preview of the headline at 48 point (Figure 1–40).

 **Experiment**

- Point to various font sizes in the Font Size gallery and watch the font size of the headline change in the document window.

- Click 48 in the Font Size gallery to increase the font size of the selected text to 48.

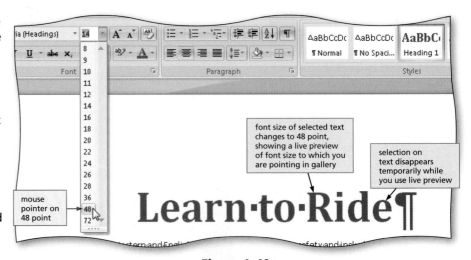

Figure 1–40

Other Ways

1. Click Font Size box arrow on Mini toolbar, click desired font size in Font Size gallery
2. Right-click selected text, click Font on shortcut menu, click Font tab, select desired font size in Size list, click OK button
3. Click Font Dialog Box Launcher, click Font tab, select desired font size in Size list, click OK button
4. Press CTRL+SHIFT+P, click Font tab, select desired font size in Size list, click OK button

To Change the Font of Selected Text

As mentioned earlier, the default Heading 1 style uses the font called Cambria. Word, however, provides many other fonts to add variety to your documents. To draw more attention to the headline, you change its font so it differs from the font of other text in the flyer. The following steps change the font from Cambria to Copperplate Gothic Bold.

1

- With the text selected, click the Font box arrow on the Home tab to display the Font gallery (Figure 1–41).

Q&A

Will the fonts in my Font gallery be the same as those in Figure 1–41?

Your list of available fonts may differ, depending on the type of printer you are using.

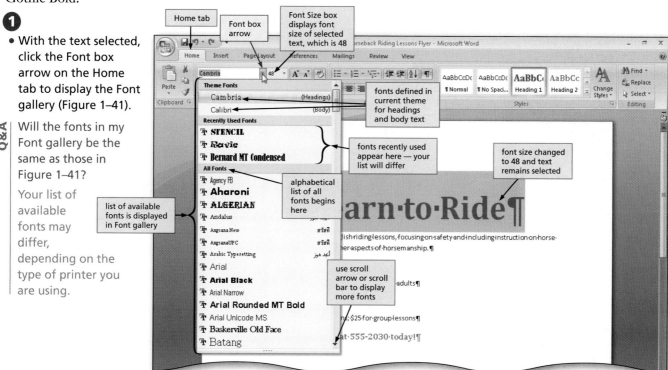

Figure 1–41

2

- Scroll through the Font gallery, if necessary, and then point to Copperplate Gothic Bold (or a similar font) to display a live preview of the headline in Copperplate Gothic Bold font (Figure 1–42).

Experiment

- Point to various fonts in the Font gallery and watch the font of the headline change in the document window.

3

- Click Copperplate Gothic Bold (or a similar font) to change the font of the selected text to Copperplate Gothic Bold.

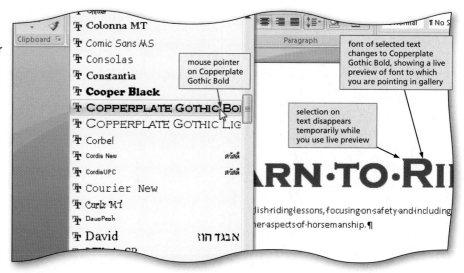

Figure 1–42

Other Ways
1. Click Font box arrow on Mini toolbar, click desired font in Font gallery
2. Right-click selected text, click Font on shortcut menu, click Font tab, select desired font in Font list, click OK button
3. Click Font Dialog Box Launcher, click Font tab, select desired font in Font list, click OK button
4. Press CTRL+SHIFT+F, click Font tab, select desired font in the Font list, click OK button

To Select Multiple Paragraphs

The next formatting step in creating the flyer is to increase the font size of the characters between the headline and the signature line so that they are easier to read from a distance. To change the font size of the characters in multiple lines, you first must select all the lines to be formatted. The following steps select multiple lines.

1

- Move the mouse pointer to the left of the first paragraph to be selected until the mouse pointer changes to a right-pointing block arrow (Figure 1–43).

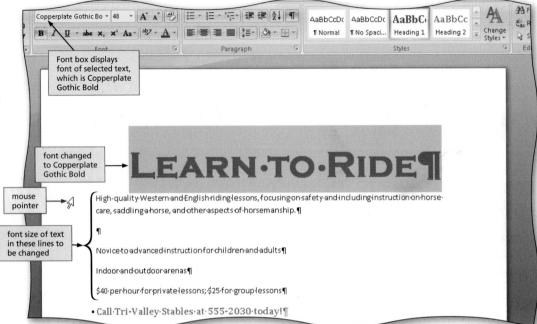

Figure 1–43

2

- Drag downward to select all lines that will be formatted (Figure 1–44).

Q&A

How do I *drag* the mouse?

Dragging is the process of holding down the mouse button while moving the mouse and then releasing the mouse button.

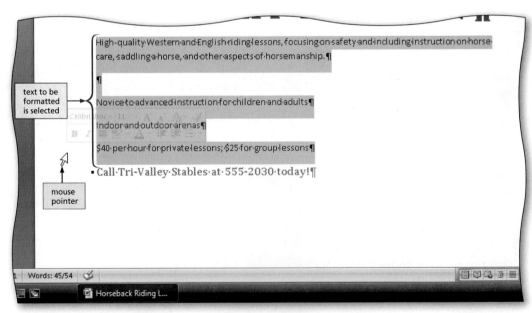

Figure 1–44

Other Ways

1. With insertion point at beginning of desired line, press SHIFT+DOWN ARROW repeatedly until all lines are selected

To Change the Font Size of Selected Text

The characters between the headline and the signature line in the flyer currently are 11 point. To make them easier to read from a distance, this flyer uses 16 point for these characters. The following steps change the font size of the selected text.

1 With the text selected, click the Font Size box arrow on the Home tab to display the Font Size gallery.

2 Click 16 in the Font Size gallery to increase the font size of the selected text to 16.

To Format a Line

In the flyer, the signature line is to be centered to match the paragraph alignment of the headline. Also, its text should have a font size larger than the rest of the body copy. The following steps center the line and increase its font size to 18.

1 Click somewhere in the paragraph to be centered (in this case, the signature line) to position the insertion point in the paragraph to be formatted.

2 Click the Center button on the Home tab to center the signature line.

3 Move the mouse pointer to the left of the line to be selected (in this case, the signature line) until the mouse pointer changes to a right-pointing block arrow and then click to select the line.

4 With the signature line selected, click the Font Size box arrow on the Home tab and then click 18 in the Font Size gallery to increase the font size of the selected text to 18 (Figure 1–45).

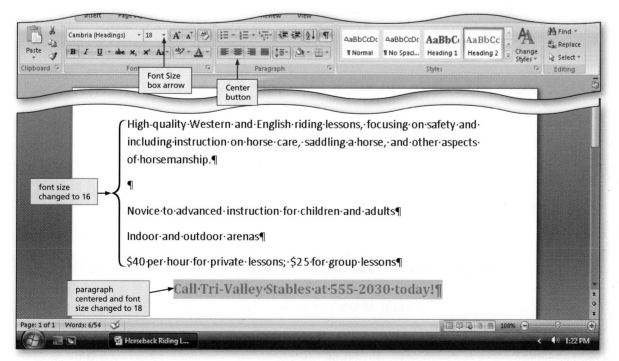

Figure 1–45

To Bullet a List of Paragraphs

The next step is to format the three important points above the signature line in the flyer as a bulleted list. A **bulleted list** is a series of paragraphs, each beginning with a bullet character. The three lines each end with a paragraph mark because you pressed the ENTER key at the end of each line. Thus, these three lines actually are three separate paragraphs.

To format a list of paragraphs with bullets, you first must select all the lines in the paragraphs. The following steps bullet a list of paragraphs.

- Move the mouse pointer to the left of the first paragraph to be selected until the mouse pointer changes to a right-pointing block arrow.

- Drag downward until all paragraphs (lines) that will be formatted with a bullet character are selected.

- Click the Bullets button on the Home tab to place a bullet character at the beginning of each selected paragraph (Figure 1–46).

Q&A

How do I remove bullets from a list or paragraph?

Select the list or paragraph and click the Bullets button again.

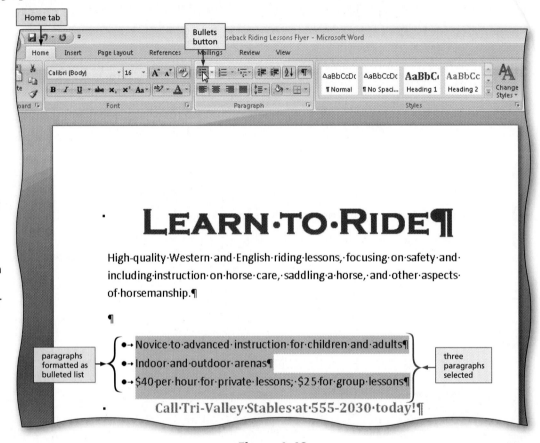

Figure 1–46

Other Ways

1. Right-click selected paragraphs, click Bullets button on Mini toolbar

2. Right-click selected paragraphs, point to Bullets on shortcut menu, click desired bullet style

To Undo and Redo an Action

Word provides a means of canceling your recent command(s) or action(s). For example, if you format text incorrectly, you can undo the format and try it again. When you point to the Undo button, Word displays the action you can undo as part of the ScreenTip.

If, after you undo an action, you decide you did not want to perform the undo, you can redo the undone action. Word does not allow you to undo or redo some actions, such as saving or printing a document. The next steps undo the bullet format just applied and then redo the bullet format.

1

- Click the Undo button on the Quick Access Toolbar to remove the bullets from the selected paragraphs (Figure 1–47).

2

- Click the Redo button on the Quick Access Toolbar to place a bullet character at the beginning of each selected paragraph again (shown in Figure 1–46).

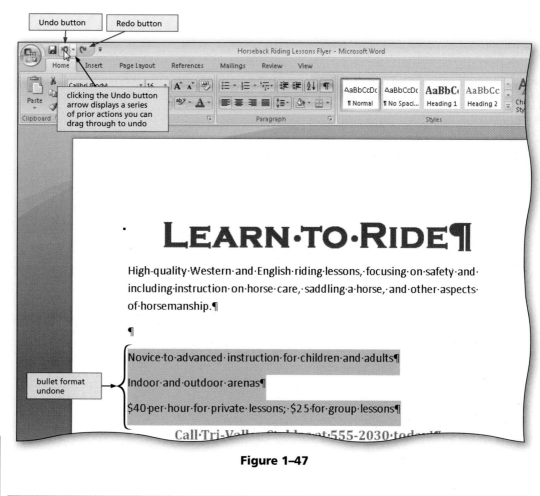

Figure 1–47

Other Ways
1. Press CTRL+Z; press CTRL+Y

To Select a Group of Words

To emphasize the types of riding lessons, Western and English, these words are bold in the flyer. To format a group of words, you first must select them. The following steps select a group of words.

1

- Position the mouse pointer immediately to the left of the first character of the text to be selected, in this case, the W in Western (Figure 1–48).

Q&A

Why did the shape of the mouse pointer change?

The mouse pointer's shape is an I-beam when positioned in unselected text in the document window.

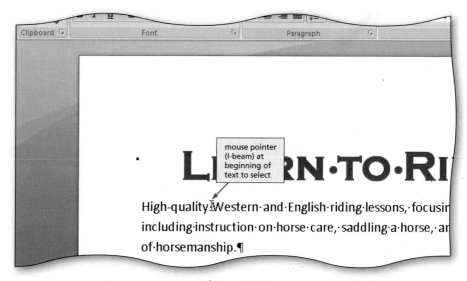

Figure 1–48

2

- Drag the mouse pointer through the last character of the text to be selected, in this case, the h in English (Figure 1–49).

Q&A

Why did the mouse pointer shape change again?

When the mouse pointer is positioned in selected text, its shape is a left-pointing block arrow.

Other Ways

1. With insertion point at beginning of first word in group, press CTRL+SHIFT+RIGHT ARROW repeatedly until all words are selected

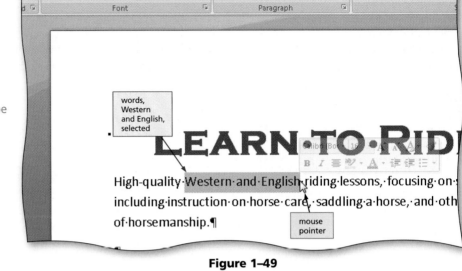

Figure 1–49

To Bold Text

Bold characters display somewhat thicker and darker than those that are not bold. The following step formats the selected words, Western and English, as bold.

1

- With the text selected, click the Bold button on the Home tab to format the selected text in bold (Figure 1–50).

Q&A

How would I remove a bold format?

You would click the Bold button a second time, or you immediately could click the Undo button on the Quick Access Toolbar.

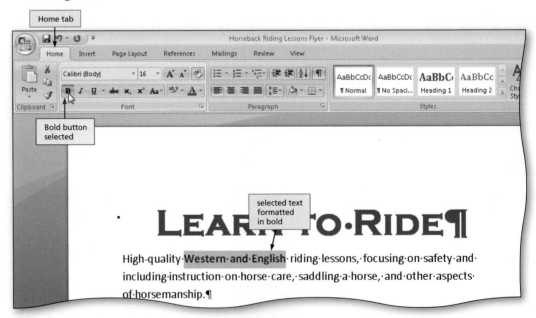

Figure 1–50

Other Ways

1. Click Bold button on Mini toolbar

2. Right-click selected text, click Font on shortcut menu, click Font tab, click Bold in Font style list, click OK button

3. Click Font Dialog Box Launcher, click Font tab, click Bold in Font style list, click OK button

4. Press CTRL+B

To Underline a Word

As with bold text, underlines are used to emphasize or draw attention to specific text. **Underlined** text prints with an underscore (_) below each character. In the flyer, the word, and, in the first bulleted paragraph is emphasized with an underline.

As with a single paragraph, if you want to format a single word, you do not need to select the word. Simply position the insertion point somewhere in the word and apply the desired format. The following step formats a word with an underline.

1

- Click somewhere in the word to be underlined (and, in this case).

- Click the Underline button on the Home tab to underline the word containing the insertion point (Figure 1–51).

Q&A How would I remove an underline?

You would click the Underline button a second time, or you immediately could click the Undo button on the Quick Access Toolbar.

Q&A Are other types of underlines available?

In addition to the basic solid underline shown in Figure 1–51, Word has many decorative underlines, such as double underlines, dotted underlines, and wavy underlines. You can access the decorative underlines and also change the color of an underline through the Underline gallery.

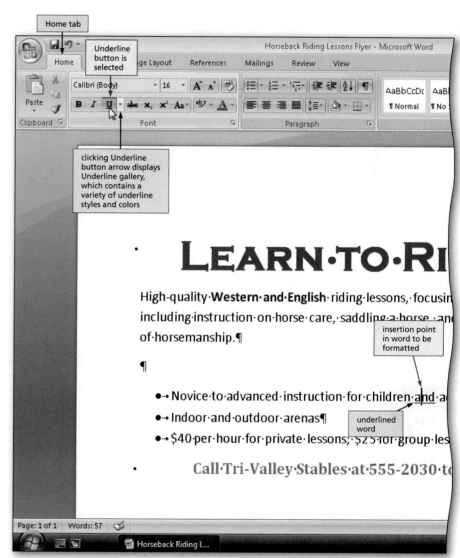

Figure 1–51

Other Ways

1. Right-click text, click Font on shortcut menu, click Font tab, click Underline style box arrow, click desired underline style, click OK button

2. Click Font Dialog Box Launcher, click Font tab, click Underline style box arrow, click desired underline style, click OK button

3. Press CTRL+U

To Italicize Text

To further emphasize the signature line, this line is italicized in the flyer. **Italicized** text has a slanted appearance. The following steps select the text and then italicize it.

- Point to the left of the line to be selected (in this case, the signature line) and click when the mouse pointer is a right-pointing block arrow.

- Click the Italic button on the Home tab to italicize the selected text.

- Click inside the selected text to remove the selection (Figure 1–52).

Q&A How would I remove an italic format?

You would click the Italic button a second time, or you immediately could click the Undo button on the Quick Access Toolbar.

Q&A How can I tell what formatting has been applied to text?

The selected buttons and boxes on the Home tab show formatting characteristics of the location of the insertion point. With the insertion point in the signature line, the Home tab shows these formats: 18-point Cambria bold italic font, centered paragraph, and Heading 2 style.

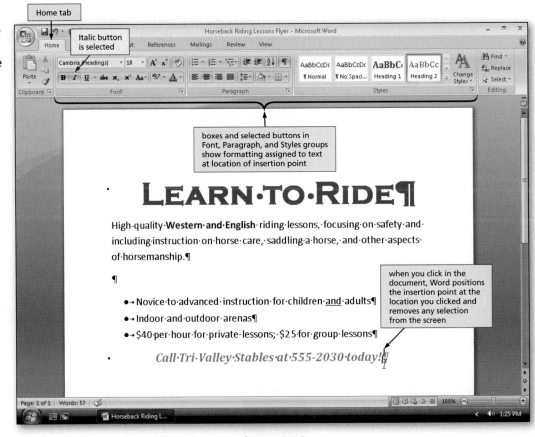

Figure 1–52

Other Ways

1. Click Italic button on Mini toolbar
2. Right-click selected text, click Font on shortcut menu, click Font tab, click Italic in Font style list, click OK button
3. Click Font Dialog Box Launcher, click Font tab, click Italic in Font style list, click OK button
4. Press CTRL+I

Document Formats

One advantage of using styles to format text is that you easily can change the formats of styles and themes in your document to give it a different or new look. Recall that a style is a named group of formatting characteristics and a theme is a set of unified formats for fonts, colors, and graphics. In Word, you can change the style set, theme colors, and theme fonts.

- The predefined styles in the Styles gallery, such as Heading 1 and Heading 2, each known as a **Quick Style**, are part of a style set. A **style set** consists of a group of frequently used styles formatted so they look pleasing when used together. When you change the style set, formats assigned to each Quick Style also change.

- Each **color scheme** in a theme identifies 12 complementary colors for text, background, accents, and links in a document. With more than 20 predefined color schemes, Word provides a simple way to select colors that work well together.

- Each theme has a **font set** that defines formats for two fonts: one for headings and another for body text. In Word, you can select from more than 20 predefined coordinated font sets to give the document's text a new look.

Use color.

Plan Ahead

When choosing color, associate the meaning of color to your message:

- Red expresses danger, power, or energy, and often is associated with sports or physical exertion.

- Brown represents simplicity, honesty, and dependability.

- Orange denotes success, victory, creativity, and enthusiasm.

- Yellow suggests sunshine, happiness, hope, liveliness, and intelligence.

- Green symbolizes growth, healthiness, harmony, blooming, and healing, and often is associated with safety or money.

- Blue indicates integrity, trust, importance, confidence, and stability.

- Purple represents wealth, power, comfort, extravagance, magic, mystery, and spirituality.

- White stands for purity, goodness, cleanliness, precision, and perfection.

- Black suggests authority, strength, elegance, power, and prestige.

- Gray conveys neutrality and thus often is found in backgrounds and other effects.

To Change the Style Set

To symbolize perfection and precision in the flyer, the characters in the headline are white. The style set, called Modern, formats Heading 1 characters in white. It also formats the Heading 1 and Heading 2 styles in all capital letters and places a background color around the paragraphs, which further emphasize the headline and signature line in the flyer. Thus, you will change the style set from Default to Modern. The following steps change a style set.

- Click the Change Styles button on the Home tab to display the Change Styles menu (Figure 1–53).

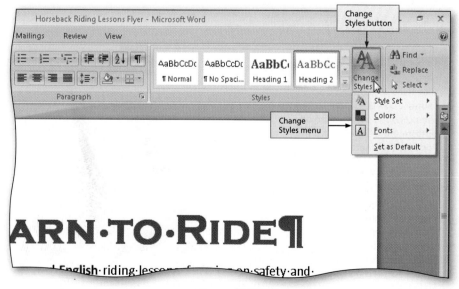

Figure 1–53

- Point to Style Set on the Change Styles menu to display the Style Set gallery.

- Point to Modern in the Style Set gallery to display a live pre-view of the formats associated with the Modern style set (Figure 1–54).

 **Experiment**

- Point to various style sets in the Style Set gallery and watch the formats of the styled text change in the document window.

- Click Modern in the Style Set gallery to change the docu-ment style set to Modern.

Q&A What if I want to return to the original style set?

You would click the Change Styles button, click Style Set on the Change Styles menu, and then click Default in the Style Set gallery, or you could click the Undo button on the Quick Access Toolbar.

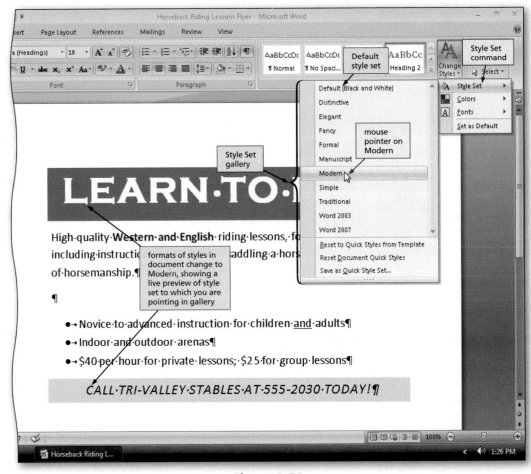

Figure 1–54

BTW

Style Formats
To see the formats assigned to a particular style in a document, click the Styles Dialog Box Launcher on the Home tab and then click the Style Inspector button in the Styles task pane. Position the insertion point in the style and then point to the Paragraph formatting or Text level formatting areas in the Style Inspector task pane to display an Enhanced ScreenTip describing formats assigned to the location of the insertion point. You also can click the Reveal Formatting button in the Style Inspector to display the Reveal Formatting task pane.

To Change Theme Colors

To suggest enthusiasm, success, and honesty, the background colors around the headline and signature line paragraphs in the flyer use shades of orange and brown. In Word, the color scheme called Aspect uses these colors. Thus, you will change the color scheme to Aspect. The following steps change theme colors.

- Click the Change Styles button on the Home tab to display the Change Styles menu.

- Point to Colors on the Change Styles menu to display the Colors gallery.

- Point to Aspect in the Colors gallery to display a live preview of the Aspect color scheme (Figure 1–55).

Experiment

- Point to various color schemes in the Colors gallery and watch the paragraph background colors change in the document window.

- Click Aspect in the Colors gallery to change the document theme colors to Aspect.

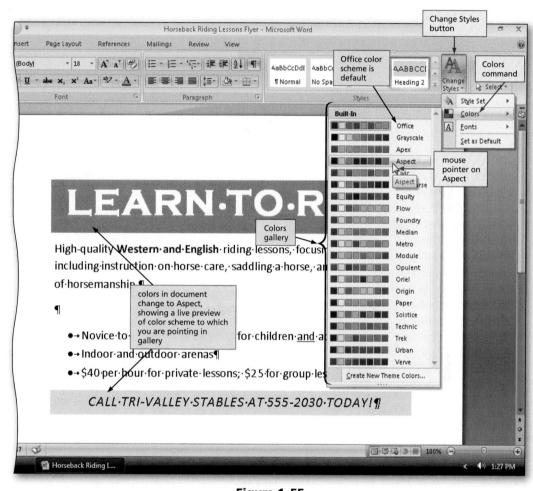

Figure 1–55

Q&A | What if I want to return to the original color scheme?

You would click the Change Styles button, click Colors on the Change Styles menu, and then click Office in the Colors gallery.

Other Ways

1. Click Theme Colors button arrow on Page Layout tab, select desired color scheme

---

To Change Theme Fonts

Earlier in this chapter, you changed the font of the headline to Copperplate Gothic Bold. In this flyer, all text below the headline should be the Rockwell font, instead of the Calibri font, because it better matches the western tone of the flyer. Thus, the next step is to change the current font set, which is called Office, to a font set called Foundry, which uses the Rockwell font for headings and body text.

If you previously changed a font using buttons on the Ribbon or Mini toolbar, Word will not alter those when you change the font set because changes to the font set are not applied to fonts changed individually. This means the font headline in the flyer will stay as Copperplate Gothic Bold when you change the font set. The following steps change the font set to Foundry.

- Click the Change Styles button on the Home tab.

- Point to Fonts on the Change Styles menu to display the Fonts gallery.

- Scroll through the Fonts gallery until Foundry is displayed and then point to Foundry to display a live preview of the Foundry font set (Figure 1–56).

Experiment

- Point to various font sets in the Fonts gallery and watch the fonts below the headline change in the document window.

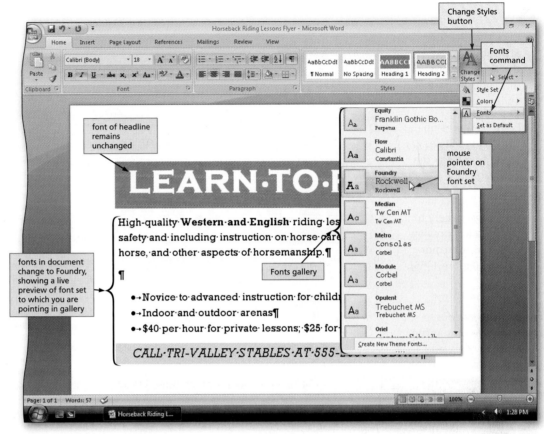

Figure 1–56

- Click Foundry in the Fonts gallery to change the document theme fonts to Foundry.

Q&A

What if I want to return to the original font set?

You would click the Change Styles button, click Fonts on the Change Styles menu, and then click Office in the Fonts gallery.

Other Ways
1. Click Theme Fonts button arrow on Page Layout tab, select desired font set

Inserting and Formatting a Picture in a Word Document

With the text formatted in the flyer, the next step is to insert a picture in the flyer and format the picture. Flyers usually contain graphical images, such as a picture, to attract the attention of passersby.

Note: If you are using Windows XP, see Appendix F for alternate steps.

Plan
Ahead

Find the appropriate graphical image.

To use graphical images, also called graphics, in a Word document, the image must be stored digitally in a file. Files containing graphical images are available from a variety of sources:

- Word includes a collection of predefined graphical images that you can insert in a document.

- Microsoft has free digital images on the Web for use in a document. Other Web sites also have images available, some of which are free, while others require a fee.

- You can take a picture with a digital camera and **download** it, which is the process of copying the digital picture from the camera to your computer.

- With a scanner, you can convert a printed picture, drawing, or diagram to a digital file.

  If you receive a picture from a source other than yourself, do not use the file until you are certain it does not contain a virus. A **virus** is a computer program that can damage files and programs on your computer. Use an antivirus program to verify that any files you use are virus free.

Plan
Ahead

Establish where to position and how to format the graphical image.

The content, size, shape, position, and format of a graphic should capture the interest of passersby, enticing them to stop and read the flyer. Often, the graphic is the center of attraction and visually the largest element on a flyer. If you use colors in the graphical image, be sure they are part of the document's color scheme.

To Insert a Picture

The next step in creating the flyer is to insert the picture of the horse and rider so that it is centered on the blank line above the bulleted list. The picture, which was taken with a digital camera, is available on the Data Files for Students. See the inside back cover of this book for instructions on downloading the Data Files for Students, or contact your instructor for information about accessing the required files. The following steps insert a centered picture, which, in this example, is located on the same USB flash drive that contains the saved flyer.

- To position the insertion point where you want the picture to be located, press CTRL+HOME and then press the DOWN ARROW key four times.

- Click the Center button on the Home tab to center the paragraph that will contain the picture.

- Click Insert on the Ribbon to display the Insert tab (Figure 1–57).

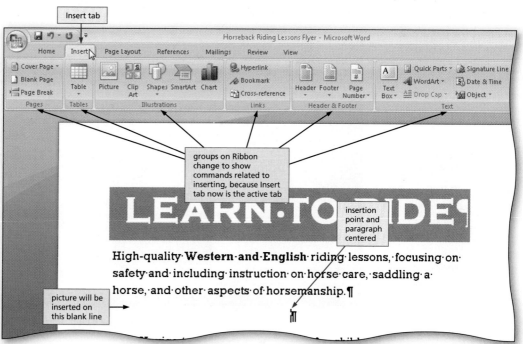

Figure 1–57

• With your USB flash drive connected to one of the computer's USB ports, click the Insert Picture from File button on the Insert tab to display the Insert Picture dialog box.

• If the Folders list is displayed below the Folders button, click the Folders button to remove the Folders list.

• If necessary, click Computer in the Favorite Links section and then scroll until UDISK 2.0 (E:) appears in the list of available drives.

• Double-click UDISK 2.0 (E:) to select the USB flash drive, Drive E in this case, as the device that contains the picture.

• Click Horse and Rider to select the file name (Figure 1–58).

Q&A What if the picture is not on a USB flash drive?

Use the same process, but select the device containing the picture in the Favorite Links section.

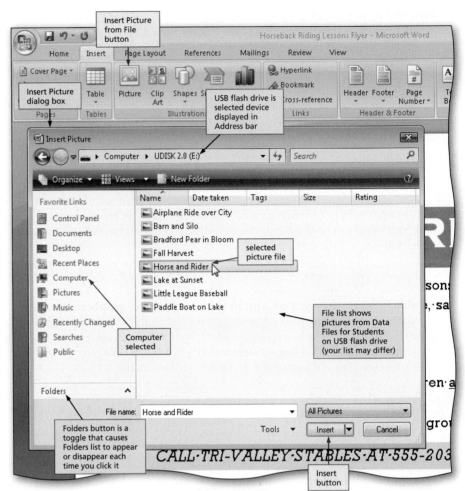

Figure 1–58

• Click the Insert button in the dialog box to insert the picture at the location of the insertion point in the document (Figure 1–59).

Q&A What are the symbols around the picture?

A selected graphic appears surrounded by a **selection rectangle**, which has small squares and circles, called **sizing handles**, at each corner and middle location.

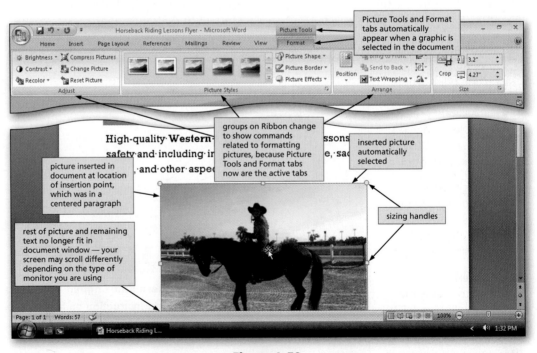

Figure 1–59

Scrolling

As mentioned at the beginning of this chapter, you view only a portion of a document on the screen through the document window. At some point when you type text or insert graphics, Word will **scroll** the top or bottom portion of the document off the screen. Although you cannot see the text and graphics once they scroll off the screen, they remain in the document.

As shown in Figure 1–59, when you insert the picture in the flyer, the text and graphics are too long to fit in the document window. Thus, to see the bottom of the flyer, you will need to scroll downward.

You may use either the mouse or the keyboard to scroll to a different location in a document. With the mouse, you can use the scroll arrows or the scroll box on the scroll bar to display a different portion of the document in the document window, and then click the mouse to move the insertion point to that location. Table 1–1 explains various techniques for using the scroll bar to scroll vertically with the mouse.

BTW

Minimize Wrist Injury
Computer users frequently switch between the keyboard and the mouse during a word processing session; such switching strains the wrist. To help prevent wrist injury, minimize switching. For instance, if your fingers already are on the keyboard, use keyboard keys to scroll. If your hand already is on the mouse, use the mouse to scroll.

Table 1–1 Using the Scroll Bar to Scroll with the Mouse	
SCROLL DIRECTION	**MOUSE ACTION**
Up	Drag the scroll box upward.
Down	Drag the scroll box downward.
Up one screen	Click anywhere above the scroll box on the vertical scroll bar.
Down one screen	Click anywhere below the scroll box on the vertical scroll bar.
Up one line	Click the scroll arrow at the top of the vertical scroll bar.
Down one line	Click the scroll arrow at the bottom of the vertical scroll bar.

When you use the keyboard to scroll, the insertion point automatically moves when you press the appropriate keys. Table 1–2 outlines various techniques to scroll through a document using the keyboard, some of which you have seen used in this chapter.

Table 1–2 Scrolling with the Keyboard	
SCROLL DIRECTION	**KEY(S) TO PRESS**
Left one character	LEFT ARROW
Right one character	RIGHT ARROW
Left one word	CTRL+LEFT ARROW
Right one word	CTRL+RIGHT ARROW
Up one line	UP ARROW
Down one line	DOWN ARROW
To end of line	END
To beginning of line	HOME
Up one paragraph	CTRL+UP ARROW
Down one paragraph	CTRL+DOWN ARROW
Up one screen	PAGE UP
Down one screen	PAGE DOWN
To top of document window	ALT+CTRL+PAGE UP
To bottom of document window	ALT+CTRL+PAGE DOWN
To beginning of document	CTRL+HOME
To end of document	CTRL+END

To Apply a Picture Style

Earlier in this chapter, you applied the heading styles to the headline and signature line in the flyer. Word also provides styles for pictures, allowing you easily to change the basic rectangle format to a more visually appealing style. Word provides a gallery of more than 25 picture styles, which include a variety of shapes, angles, borders, and reflections. The flyer in this chapter uses an oval picture style that has a border around its edges. The following steps apply a picture style to the picture in the flyer.

1
- Click the down scroll arrow on the vertical scroll bar as many times as necessary until the entire picture is displayed in the document window (Figure 1–60).

Q&A What if the Picture Tools and Format tabs no longer are displayed on my Ribbon?

Double-click the picture to display the Picture Tools and Format tabs.

Figure 1–60

2
- Click the More button in the Picture Styles gallery, which shows more gallery options.

- Point to Metal Oval in the Picture Styles gallery to display a live preview of that style applied to the picture in the document (Figure 1–61).

Experiment
- Point to various picture styles in the Picture Styles gallery and watch the format of the picture change in the document window.

3
- Click Metal Oval in the Picture Styles gallery to apply the selected style to the picture.

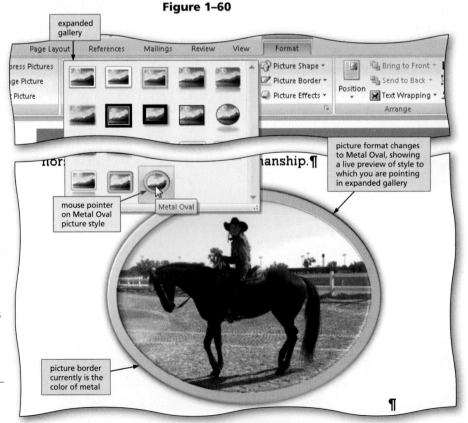

Figure 1–61

To Change a Picture Border Color

The flyer in this chapter has a tan border around the picture. Earlier in this chapter, you changed the color scheme to Aspect. To coordinate the border color with the other colors in the document, you will use a shade of tan in Aspect color scheme for the picture border. Any color galleries you display show colors defined in this current color scheme. The following steps change the picture border color.

1

- Click the Picture Border button arrow on the Format tab to display the Picture Border gallery.

What if the Picture Tools and Format tabs no longer are displayed on my Ribbon?

Double-click the picture to display the Picture Tools and Format tabs.

- Point to Tan, Background 2 (third theme color from left in the first row) in the Picture Border gallery to display a live preview of that border color on the picture (Figure 1–62).

Experiment

- Point to various colors in the Picture Border gallery and watch the border color on the picture change in the document window.

2

- Click Tan, Background 2 in the Picture Styles gallery to change the picture border color.

Figure 1–62

To Zoom the Document

The next step in formatting the picture is to resize it. Specifically, you will increase the size of the picture. You do not want it so large, however, that it causes the flyer text to flow to a second page. You can change the zoom so that you can see the entire document on the screen at once. Seeing the entire document at once helps you determine the appropriate size of the picture. The steps on the next page zoom the document.

1

  Experiment

- Repeatedly click the Zoom Out and Zoom In buttons on the status bar and watch the size of the document change in the document window.

2

- Click the Zoom Out or Zoom In button as many times as necessary until the Zoom level button displays 50% on its face (Figure 1–63).

Q&A If I change the zoom percentage, will the document print differently?

Changing the zoom has no effect on the printed document.

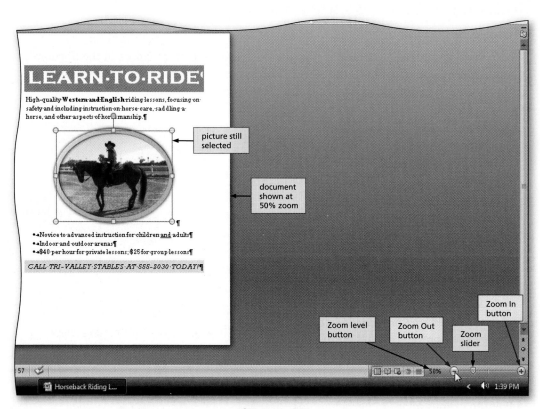

Figure 1–63

Other Ways		
1. Drag Zoom slider on status bar	2. Click Zoom level button on status bar, select desired zoom percent or type, click OK button	3. Click Zoom button on View tab, select desired zoom percent or type, click OK button

To Resize a Graphic

The next step is to resize the picture. **Resizing** includes both enlarging and reducing the size of a graphic. The picture in the flyer should be as large as possible, without causing any flyer text to flow to a second page.

With the entire document displaying in the document window, you will be able to see how the resized graphic will look on the entire page. The following steps resize a selected graphic.

1

- With the graphic still selected, point to the upper-right corner sizing handle on the picture so that the mouse pointer shape changes to a two-headed arrow (Figure 1–64).

Q&A What if my graphic (picture) is not selected?

To select a graphic, click it.

Figure 1–64

2

- Drag the sizing handle diagonally outward until the crosshair mouse pointer is positioned approximately as shown in Figure 1–65.

3

- Release the mouse button to resize the graphic.

Q&A What if the graphic is the wrong size?

Repeat Steps 1, 2, and 3.

as you drag a corner sizing handle, Word changes mouse pointer to a crosshair shape

transparent image of how the graphic will look at that proposed size appears in document window

Figure 1–65

4

- Click outside the graphic to deselect it (Figure 1–66).

Q&A What happened to the Picture Tools and Format tabs?

When you click outside of a graphic or press a key to scroll through a document, Word deselects the graphic and removes the Picture Tools and Format tabs from the screen.

Q&A What if I want to return a graphic to its original size and start again?

With the graphic selected, click the Size Dialog Box Launcher on the Format tab to display the Size dialog box, click the Size tab, click the Reset button, and then click the Close button.

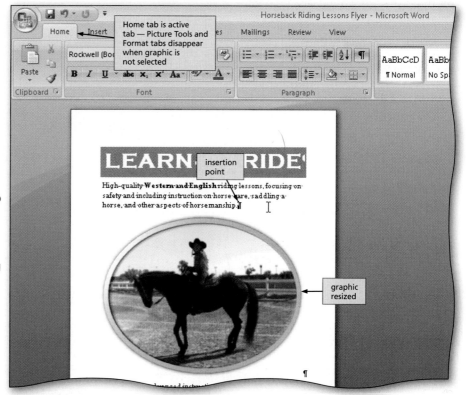

Home tab is active tab — Picture Tools and Format tabs disappear when graphic is not selected

insertion point

graphic resized

Figure 1–66

Other Ways

1. Enter graphic height and width in Shape Height and Shape Width text boxes in Size group on Format tab in Picture Tools tab

2. Click Size Dialog Box Launcher on Format tab in Picture Tools tab, click Size tab, enter desired height and width values in text boxes, click Close button

Enhancing the Page

With the text and graphics entered and formatted, the next step is to look at the page as a whole and determine if it looks finished in its current state. As you review the page, answer these questions:

- Does it need a page border to frame its contents, or would a page border make it look too busy?
- Is the spacing between paragraphs and graphics on the page adequate? Do any sections of text or graphics look as if they are positioned too closely to the items above or below them?

You determine that a graphical, color-coordinated border would enhance the flyer. You also notice that the flyer would look more proportionate if it had a little more space below the headline and above the graphic. The following pages make these enhancements to the flyer.

To Add a Page Border

In Word, you can add a border around the perimeter of an entire page. In this flyer, you add a graphical border that uses a shade of brown from the Aspect color scheme. The following steps add a graphical page border.

- Click Page Layout on the Ribbon to display the Page Layout tab.

- Click the Page Borders button on the Page Layout tab to display the Borders and Shading dialog box (Figure 1–67).

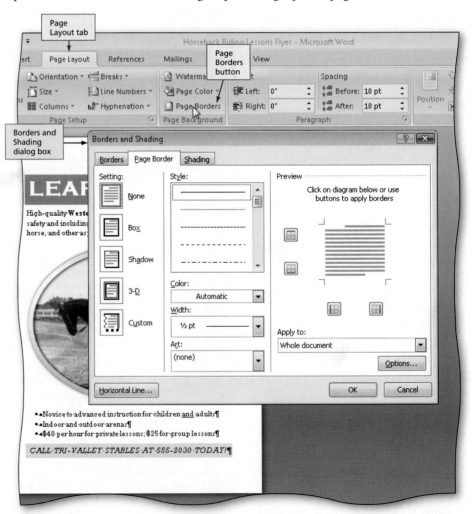

Figure 1–67

2

- Click the Art box arrow to display the Art gallery.

- Click the down scroll arrow in the Art gallery until the art border shown in Figure 1–68 appears.

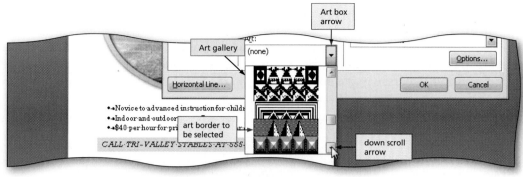

Figure 1–68

3

- Click the art border shown in Figure 1–68 to display a preview of the selection in the Preview area of the dialog box.

- Click the Color box arrow to display a Color gallery (Figure 1–69).

Q&A Do I have to use an art border?

No. You can select a solid or decorative line in the Style list.

Q&A Can I add color to every border type?

You can color all of the line styles and many of the art borders.

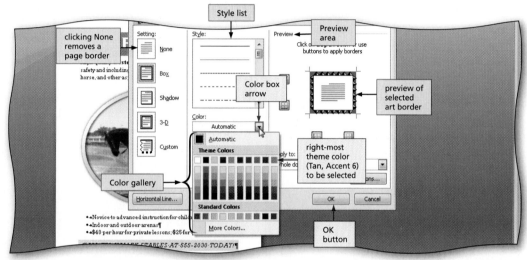

Figure 1–69

4

- Click the right-most theme color (Tan, Accent 6) in the Color gallery to display a preview of the selection in the Preview area.

- Click the OK button to add the border to the page (Figure 1–70).

Q&A What if I wanted to remove the border?

Click None in the Setting list in the Borders and Shading dialog box.

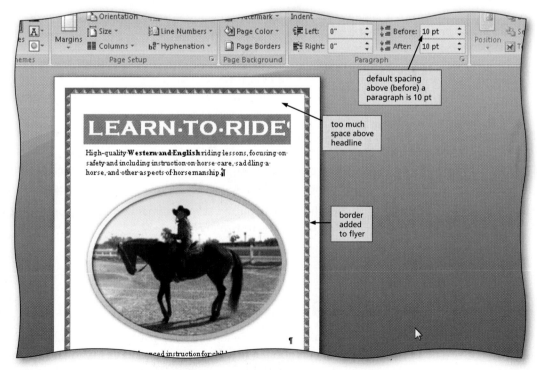

Figure 1–70

To Change Spacing Above and Below Paragraphs

The default spacing above a heading paragraph in Word is 10 points. In the flyer, you want to remove this spacing so the headline is closer to the page border. The default spacing below (after) a body text paragraph is 0 points. Below the first paragraph of body copy in the flyer, you want to increase this space. The following steps change the spacing above and below paragraphs.

1

- Position the insertion point in the paragraph to be adjusted, in this case, the headline.

- Click the Spacing Before box down arrow on the Page Layout tab as many times as necessary until 0 pt is displayed in the Spacing Before text box (Figure 1–71).

Q&A

Why is a blank space still between the border and the headline?

The space is a result of Word's preset left, right, top, and bottom margins and other settings.

2

- Position the insertion point in the paragraph below the headline.

- Click the Spacing After box up arrow on the Page Layout tab as many times as necessary until 24 pt is displayed in the Spacing After text box, shown in Figure 1–72. (If the text flows to two pages, resize the picture so that it is smaller.)

Figure 1–71

Centering Page Contents Vertically
You can center page contents vertically between the top and bottom margins. To do this, click the Page Setup Dialog Box Launcher on the Page Layout tab, click the Layout tab in the dialog box, click the Vertical alignment box arrow, click Center in the list, and then click the OK button.

To Zoom the Document

You are finished enhancing the page and no longer need to view the entire page in the document window. Thus, the following step changes the zoom back to 100 percent.

1 Click the Zoom In button as many times as necessary until the Zoom level button displays 100% on its face, shown in Figure 1–72.

Changing Document Properties and Saving Again

Word helps you organize and identify your files by using **document properties**, which are the details about a file. Document properties, also known as **metadata**, can include such information as the project author, title, or subject. **Keywords** are words or phrases that further describe the document. For example, a class name or document topic can describe the file's purpose or content.

Document properties are valuable for a variety of reasons:

- Users can save time locating a particular file because they can view a document's properties without opening the document.
- By creating consistent properties for files having similar content, users can better organize their documents.
- Some organizations require Word users to add document properties so that other employees can view details about these files.

Five different types of document properties exist, but the more common ones used in this book are standard and automatically updated properties. **Standard properties** are associated with all Microsoft Office documents and include author, title, and subject. **Automatically updated properties** include file system properties, such as the date you create or change a file, and statistics, such as the file size.

BTW

Printing Document Properties
To print document properties, click the Office Button to display the Office Button menu, point to Print on the Office Button menu to display the Print submenu, click Print on the Print submenu to display the Print dialog box, click the Print what box arrow, click Document properties to instruct Word to print the document properties instead of the document, and then click the OK button.

To Change Document Properties

The **Document Information Panel** contains areas where you can view and enter document properties. You can view and change information in this panel at any time while you are creating a document. Before saving the flyer again, you want to add your name and course information as document properties. The following steps use the Document Information Panel to change document properties.

1

- Click the Office Button to display the Office Button menu.

- Point to Prepare on the Office Button menu to display the Prepare submenu (Figure 1–72).

Q&A

What other types of actions besides changing properties can you take to prepare a document for distribution?

The Prepare submenu provides commands related to sharing a document with others, such as allowing or restricting people to view and modify your document, checking to see if your document will open in earlier versions of Word, and searching for hidden personal information.

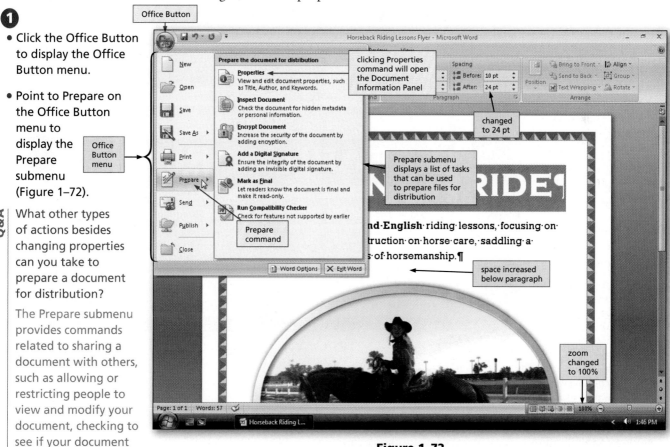

Figure 1–72

2

- Click Properties on the Prepare submenu to display the Document Information Panel (Figure 1–73).

Why are some of the document properties in my Document Information Panel already filled in?

The person who installed Microsoft Office 2007 on your computer or network may have set or customized the properties.

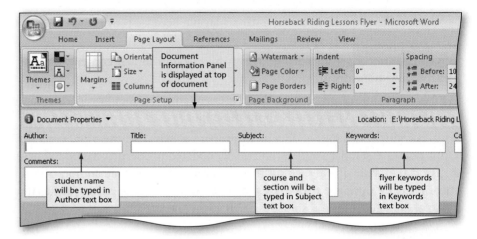

Figure 1–73

3

- Click the Author text box, if necessary, and then type your name as the Author property. If a name already is displayed in the Author text box, delete it before typing your name.

- Click the Subject text box, if necessary delete any existing text, and then type your course and section as the Subject property.

- If an AutoComplete dialog box appears, click its Yes button.

- Click the Keywords text box, if necessary delete any existing text, and then type `Tri-Valley Stables` as the Keywords property (Figure 1–74).

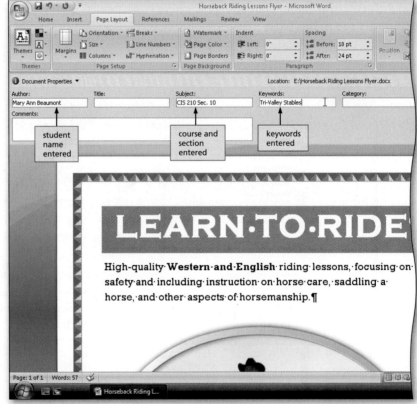
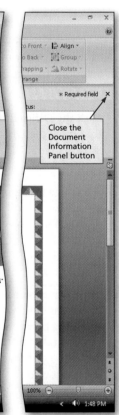

Figure 1–74

What types of document properties does Word collect automatically?

Word records such details as how long you worked at creating your project, how many times you revised the document, and what fonts and themes are used.

4

- Click the Close the Document Information Panel button so that the Document Information Panel no longer is displayed.

To Save an Existing Document with the Same File Name

Saving frequently cannot be overemphasized. You have made several modifications to the document since you saved it earlier in the chapter. When you first saved the document, you clicked the Save button on the Quick Access Toolbar, the Save As dialog box appeared, and you entered the file name, Horseback Riding Lessons Flyer. If you want to use the same file name to save the changes made to the document, you again click the Save button on the Quick Access Toolbar. The following step saves the document again.

- Click the Save button on the Quick Access Toolbar to overwrite the previous Horseback Riding Lessons Flyer file on the USB flash drive (Figure 1–75).

Q&A

Why did the Save As dialog box not appear?

Word overwrites the document using the settings specified the first time you saved the document. To save the file with a different file name or on different media, display the Save As dialog box by clicking the Office Button and then clicking Save As on the Office Button menu. Then, fill in the Save As dialog box as described in Steps 2 through 5 on pages WD 20 and WD 21.

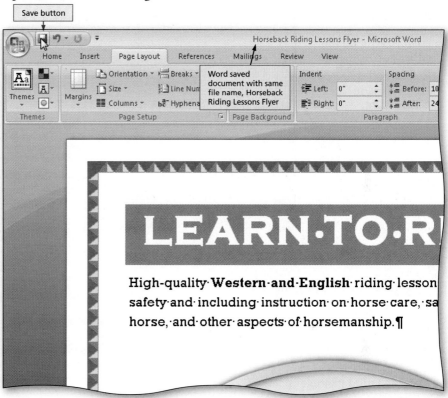

Figure 1–75

Other Ways

1. Press CTRL+S or press SHIFT+F12

Printing a Document

After you create a document, you often want to print it. A printed version of the document is called a **hard copy** or **printout**.

Printed copies of your document can be useful for the following reasons:

- Many people prefer proofreading a hard copy of the document rather than viewing it on the screen to check for errors and readability.

- Hard copies can serve as reference material if your storage medium is lost or becomes corrupted and you need to re-create the document.

It is a good practice to save a document before printing it, in the event you experience difficulties with the printer.

BTW

Conserving Ink and Toner
You can instruct Word to print draft quality documents to conserve ink or toner by clicking the Office Button, clicking the Word Options button, clicking Advanced in the left pane of the Word Options dialog box, scrolling to the Print area, placing a check mark in the 'Use draft quality' check box, and then clicking the OK button. To print the document with these settings, click the Office Button, point to Print, and then click Quick Print.

To Print a Document

With the completed document saved, you may want to print it. The following steps print the contents of the saved Horseback Riding Lessons Flyer project.

1

• Click the Office Button to display the Office Button menu.

• Point to Print on the Office Button menu to display the Print submenu (Figure 1–76).

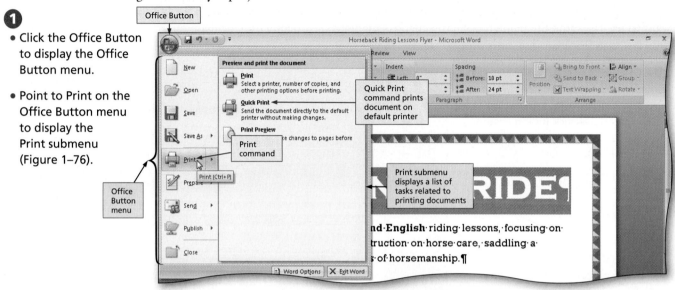

Figure 1–76

2

• Click Quick Print on the Print submenu to print the document.

• When the printer stops, retrieve the hard copy of the Horseback Riding Lessons Flyer (Figures 1–77).

Q&A How can I print multiple copies of my document other than issuing the Quick Print command twice?

Click the Office Button, point to Print on the Office Button menu, click Print on the Print submenu, increase the number in the Number of copies box, and then click the OK button.

Q&A Do I have to wait until my document is complete to print it?

No, you can follow these steps to print a document at any time while you are creating it.

BTW **Printed Borders**
If one or more of your borders do not print, click the Page Borders button on the Page Layout tab, click the Options button in the dialog box, click the Measure from box arrow and click Text, change the four text boxes to 15 pt, and then click the OK button in each dialog box. Try printing the document again. If the borders still do not print, adjust the text boxes in the dialog box to a number smaller than 15 point.

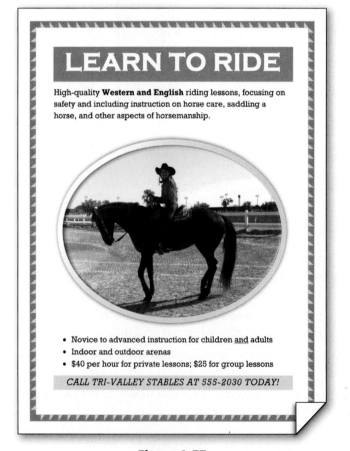

Figure 1–77

Other Ways

1. Press CTRL+P, press ENTER

Quitting Word

When you quit Word, if you have made changes to a document since the last time the file was saved, Word displays a dialog box asking if you want to save the changes you made to the file before it closes that window. The dialog box contains three buttons with these resulting actions: the Yes button saves the changes and then quits Word; the No button quits Word without saving changes; and the Cancel button closes the dialog box and redisplays the document without saving the changes.

If no changes have been made to an open document since the last time the file was saved, Word will close the window without displaying a dialog box.

To Quit Word with One Document Open

You saved the document prior to printing and did not make any changes to the project. The Horseback Riding Lessons Flyer project now is complete, and you are ready to quit Word. When one Word document is open, the following steps quit Word.

- Point to the Close button on the right side of the Word title bar (Figure 1–78).

- Click the Close button to quit Word.

Q&A

What if I have more than one Word document open?

You would click the Close button for each open document. When you click the last open document's Close button, Word also quits. As an alternative, you could click the Office Button and then click the Exit Word button on the Office Button menu, which closes all open Word documents and then quits Word.

Figure 1–78

Starting Word and Opening a Document

Once you have created and saved a document, you may need to retrieve it from your storage medium. For example, you might want to revise the document or reprint it. Opening a document requires that Word is running on your computer.

To Start Word

The following steps, which assume Windows Vista is running, start Word.

1. Click the Start button on the Windows Vista taskbar to display the Start menu.

2. Click All Programs at the bottom of the left pane on the Start menu to display the All Programs list and then click Microsoft Office in the All Programs list to display the Microsoft Office list.

3. Click Microsoft Office Word 2007 in the Microsoft Office list to start Word and display a new blank document in the Word window.

4. If the Word window is not maximized, click the Maximize button on its title bar to maximize the window.

Note: If you are using Windows XP, see Appendix F for alternate steps.

To Open a Document from Word

Earlier in this chapter you saved your project on a USB flash drive using the file name, Horseback Riding Lessons Flyer. The following steps open the Horseback Riding Lessons Flyer file from the USB flash drive.

1

• With your USB flash drive connected to one of the computer's USB ports, click the Office Button to display the Office Button menu (Figure 1–79).

Q&A

What files are shown in the Recent Documents list?

Word displays the most recently opened document file names in this list. If the name of the file you want to open appears in the Recent Documents list, you could click it to open the file.

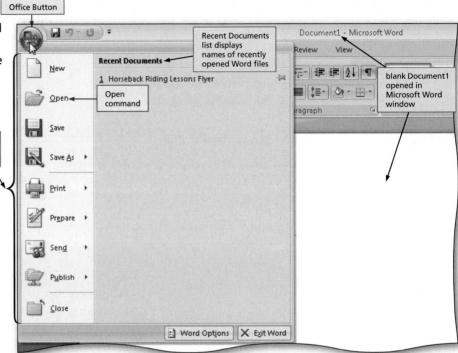

Figure 1–79

2

• Click Open on the Office Button menu to display the Open dialog box.

• If the Folders list is displayed below the Folders button, click the Folders button to remove the Folders list.

• If necessary, click Computer in the Favorite Links section and then scroll until UDISK 2.0 (E:) appears in the list of available drives.

• Double-click UDISK 2.0 (E:) to select the USB flash drive, Drive E in this case, as the new open location.

• Click Horseback Riding Lessons Flyer to select the file name (Figure 1–80).

Q&A

How do I open the file if I am not using a USB flash drive?

Use the same process, but be certain to select your device in the Computer list.

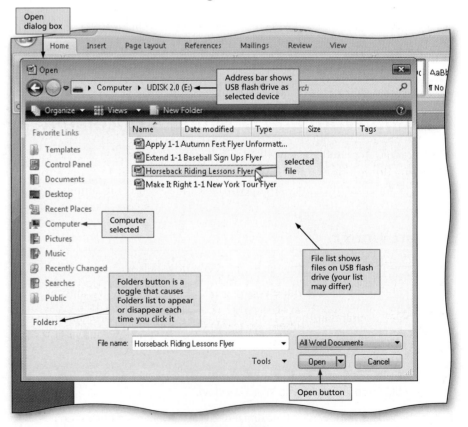

Figure 1–80

3

- Click the Open button to open the selected file and display the Horseback Riding Lessons Flyer document in the Word window (Figure 1–81).

Q&A

Why is the Word icon and document name on the Windows Vista taskbar?

When you open a Word file, a Word program button is displayed on the taskbar. The button in Figure 1–81 contains an ellipsis because some of its contents do not fit in the allotted button space. If you point to a program button, its entire contents appear in a ScreenTip, which in this case would be the file name followed by the program name.

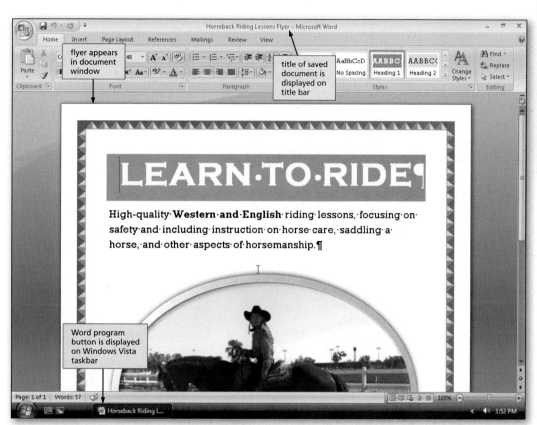

Figure 1–81

Other Ways

1. Click Office Button, click file name in Recent Documents list
2. Press CTRL+O, select file name, press ENTER

Correcting Errors

After creating a document, you often will find you must make changes to it. For example, the document may contain an error, or new circumstances may require you to add text to the document.

Types of Changes Made to Documents

The types of changes made to documents normally fall into one of the three following categories: additions, deletions, or modifications.

Additions   Additional words, sentences, or paragraphs may be required in a document. Additions occur when you omit text from a document and want to insert it later. For example, additional types of riding lessons may be offered.

BTW

Print Preview
You can preview a document before printing it by clicking the Office Button, pointing to Print, and then clicking Print Preview. When finished previewing the document, click the Close Print Preview button.

Deletions   Sometimes, text in a document is incorrect or is no longer needed. For example, group lessons might not be offered. In this case, you would delete the words, $25 for group lessons, from the flyer.

Modifications   If an error is made in a document or changes take place that affect the document, you might have to revise a word(s) in the text. For example, the fee per hour may change from $40 to $50 for private lessons.

To Insert Text in an Existing Document

Word inserts text to the left of the insertion point. The text to the right of the insertion point moves to the right and downward to fit the new text. The following steps insert the word, various, to the left of the word, aspects, in the flyer.

- Scroll through the document and then click to the left of the location of text to be inserted (in this case, the a in aspects) to position the insertion point where text should be inserted (Figure 1–82).

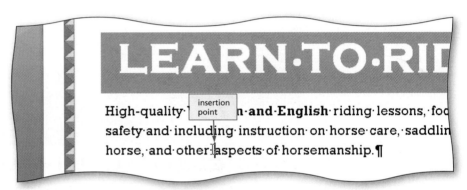

Figure 1–82

- Type various and then press the SPACEBAR to insert the word, various, to the left of the insertion point (Figure 1–83).

Why did the text move to the right as I typed?

In Word, the default typing mode is **insert mode**, which means as you type a character, Word moves all the characters to the right of the typed character one position to the right.

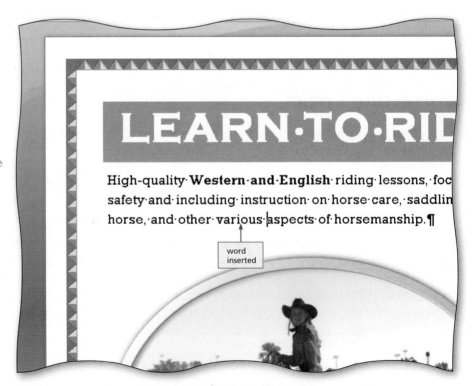

Figure 1–83

Deleting Text from an Existing Document

It is not unusual to type incorrect characters or words in a document. As discussed earlier in this chapter, you can click the Undo button on the Quick Access Toolbar to immediately undo a command or action — this includes typing. Word also provides other methods of correcting typing errors.

To delete an incorrect character in a document, simply click next to the incorrect character and then press the BACKSPACE key to erase to the left of the insertion point, or press the DELETE key to erase to the right of the insertion point.

To Select a Word and Delete It

To delete a word or phrase, you first must select the word or phrase. The following steps select the word, various, that was just added in the previous steps and then delete the selection.

- Position the mouse pointer somewhere in the word to be selected (in this case, various), as shown in Figure 1–84.

Figure 1–84

2

- Double-click the word to select it (Figure 1–85).

3

- With the text selected, press the DELETE key to delete the selected text (shown in Figure 1–82).

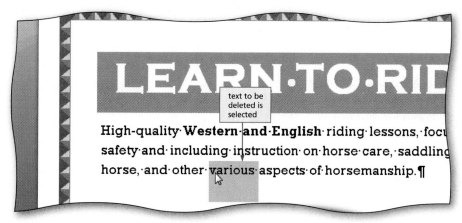

Figure 1–85

Closing the Entire Document

Sometimes, everything goes wrong. If this happens, you may want to close the document entirely and start over with a new document. You also may want to close a document when you are finished with it so you can begin your next document. If you wanted to close a document, you would use the steps on the next page.

TO CLOSE THE ENTIRE DOCUMENT AND START OVER

1. Click the Office Button and then click Close.
2. If Word displays a dialog box, click the No button to ignore the changes since the last time you saved the document.
3. Click the Office Button and then click New on the Office Button menu. When Word displays the New Document dialog box, click Blank document and then click the Create button.

BTW

Word Help
The best way to become familiar with Word Help is to use it. Appendix C includes detailed information about Word Help and exercises that will help you gain confidence in using it.

Word Help

At any time while using Word, you can find answers to questions and display information about various topics through **Word Help**. Used properly, this form of assistance can increase your productivity and reduce your frustrations by minimizing the time you spend learning how to use Word.

This section introduces you to Word Help. Additional information about using Word Help is available in Appendix C.

To Search for Word Help

Using Word Help, you can search for information based on phrases such as save a document or format text, or key terms such as copy, save, or format. Word Help responds with a list of search results displayed as links to a variety of resources. The following steps, which use Word Help to search for information about selecting text, assume you are connected to the Internet.

1

- Click the Microsoft Office Word Help button near the upper-right corner of the Word window to open the Word Help window.

- Type `select text` in the 'Type words to search for' text box at the top of the Word Help window (Figure 1–86).

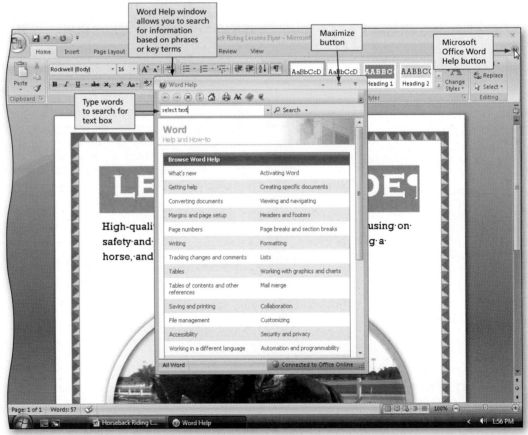

Figure 1–86

2

- Press the ENTER key to display the search results.

- Click the Maximize button on the Word Help window title bar to maximize the Help window (Figure 1–87).

Where is the Word window with the Horseback Riding Lessons Flyer document?

Word is open in the background, but the Word Help window is overlaid on top of the Word window. When the Word Help window is closed, the document will reappear.

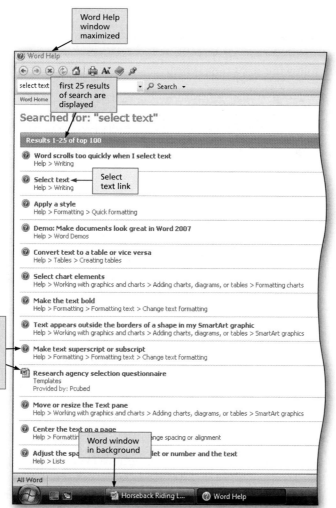

Figure 1–87

3

- Click the Select text link to display information about selecting text (Figure 1–88).

What is the purpose of the buttons at the top of the Word Help window?

Use the buttons in the upper-left corner of the Word Help window to navigate through Help, change the display, show the Word Help table of contents, and print the contents of the window.

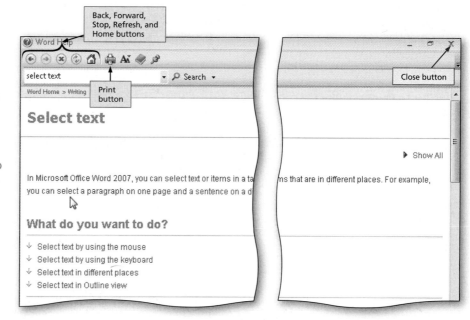

4

- Click the Close button on the Word Help window title bar to close the Word Help window and redisplay the Word window.

Figure 1–88

Other Ways
1. Press F1

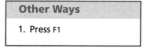

BTW

Quick Reference
For a table that lists how to complete the tasks covered in this book using the mouse, Ribbon, shortcut menu, and keyboard, see the Quick Reference Summary at the back of this book, or visit the Word 2007 Quick Reference Web page (scsite.com/wd2007/qr).

To Quit Word

The following steps quit Word.

1 Click the Close button on the right side of the title bar to quit Word; or if you have multiple Word documents open, click the Office Button and then click the Exit Word button on the Office Button menu to close all open documents and quit Word.

2 If necessary, click the No button in the Microsoft Office Word dialog box so that any changes you have made are not saved.

Chapter Summary

In this chapter you have learned how to enter text in a document, format text, insert a picture, format a picture, add a page border, and print a document. The items listed below include all the new Word skills you have learned in this chapter.

1. Start Word (WD 5)
2. Type Text (WD 13)
3. Display Formatting Marks (WD 14)
4. Wordwrap Text as You Type (WD 15)
5. Insert a Blank Line (WD 15)
6. Check Spelling and Grammar as You Type (WD 16)
7. Save a Document (WD 19)
8. Apply Styles (WD 24)
9. Center a Paragraph (WD 26)
10. Select a Line (WD 27)
11. Change the Font Size of Selected Text (WD 28)
12. Change the Font of Selected Text (WD 29)
13. Select Multiple Paragraphs (WD 30)
14. Bullet a List of Paragraphs (WD 32)
15. Undo and Redo an Action (WD 32)
16. Select a Group of Words (WD 33)
17. Bold Text (WD 34)
18. Underline a Word (WD 35)
19. Italicize Text (WD 36)
20. Change the Style Set (WD 37)
21. Change Theme Colors (WD 39)
22. Change Theme Fonts (WD 39)
23. Insert a Picture (WD 41)
24. Apply a Picture Style (WD 44)
25. Change a Picture Border Color (WD 45)
26. Zoom the Document (WD 45)
27. Resize a Graphic (WD 46)
28. Add a Page Border (WD 48)
29. Change Spacing Above and Below Paragraphs (WD 50)
30. Change Document Properties (WD 51)
31. Save an Existing Document with the Same File Name (WD 53)
32. Print a Document (WD 54)
33. Quit Word with One Document Open (WD 55)
34. Open a Document from Word (WD 56)
35. Insert Text in an Existing Document (WD 58)
36. Select a Word and Delete It (WD 59)
37. Close the Entire Document and Start Over (WD 60)
38. Search for Word Help (WD 60)

 If you have a SAM user profile, you may have access to hands-on instruction, practice, and assessment. Log in to your SAM account (http://sam2007.course.com) to launch any assigned training activities or exams that relate to the skills covered in this chapter.

BTW

Certification
The Microsoft Certified Application Specialist (MCAS) program provides an opportunity for you to obtain a valuable industry credential – proof that you have the Word 2007 skills required by employers. For more information, see Appendix G or visit the Word 2007 Certification Web page (scsite.com/wd2007/cert).

Learn It Online

Test your knowledge of chapter content and key terms.

Instructions: To complete the Learn It Online exercises, start your browser, click the Address bar, and then enter the Web address scsite.com/wd2007/learn. When the Word 2007 Learn It Online page is displayed, click the link for the exercise you want to complete and then read the instructions.

Chapter Reinforcement TF, MC, and SA
A series of true/false, multiple choice, and short answer questions that test your knowledge of the chapter content.

Flash Cards
An interactive learning environment where you identify chapter key terms associated with displayed definitions.

Practice Test
A series of multiple choice questions that test your knowledge of chapter content and key terms.

Who Wants To Be a Computer Genius?
An interactive game that challenges your knowledge of chapter content in the style of a television quiz show.

Wheel of Terms
An interactive game that challenges your knowledge of chapter key terms in the style of the television show *Wheel of Fortune*.

Crossword Puzzle Challenge
A crossword puzzle that challenges your knowledge of key terms presented in the chapter.

Apply Your Knowledge

Reinforce the skills and apply the concepts you learned in this chapter.

Modifying Text and Formatting a Document
Instructions: Start Word. Open the document, Apply 1-1 Autumn Fest Flyer Unformatted, from the Data Files for Students. See the inside back cover of this book for instructions on downloading the Data Files for Students, or contact your instructor for information about accessing the required files.

The document you open is an unformatted flyer. You are to modify text, format paragraphs and characters, and insert a picture in the flyer.

Perform the following tasks:
1. Delete the word, entire, in the sentence of body copy below the headline.
2. Insert the word, Creek, between the text, Honey Farm, in the sentence of body copy below the headline. The sentence should end: ...Honey Creek Farm.
3. At the end of the signature line, change the period to an exclamation point. The sentence should end: ...This Year's Fest!
4. Apply the Heading 1 style to the headline. Apply the Heading 2 style to the signature line.
5. Center the headline and the signature line.
6. Change the font and font size of the headline to 48-point Cooper Black, or a similar font.
7. Change the font size of body copy between the headline and the signature line to 22 point.
8. Change the font size of the signature line to 28 point.
9. Bullet the three lines (paragraphs) of text above the signature line.
10. Bold the text, October 4 and 5.

Continued >

Apply Your Knowledge *continued*

11. Underline the word, and, in the first bulleted paragraph.

12. Italicize the text in the signature line.

13. Change the theme colors to the Civic color scheme.

14. Change the theme fonts to the Opulent font set.

15. Change the zoom to 50 percent so the entire page is visible in the document window.

16. Change the spacing before the headline paragraph to 0 point. Change the spacing after the headline paragraph to 12 point.

17. Insert the picture of the combine centered on the blank line above the bulleted list. The picture is called Fall Harvest and is available on the Data Files for Students. Apply the Snip Diagonal Corner, White picture style to the inserted picture. Change the color of the picture border to Orange, Accent 6.

18. The entire flyer now should fit on a single page. If it flows to two pages, resize the picture or decrease spacing before and after paragraphs until the entire flyer text fits on a single page.

19. Enter the text, Honey Creek, as the keywords. Change the other document properties, as specified by your instructor.

20. Click the Office Button and then click Save As. Save the document using the file name, Apply 1-1 Autumn Fest Flyer Formatted.

21. Position the Quick Access Toolbar below the Ribbon. Save the document again by clicking the Save button. Reposition the Quick Access Toolbar above the Ribbon.

22. Submit the revised document, shown in Figure 1–89, in the format specified by your instructor.

Heading 1 style; 48-point Cooper Black font; centered; spacing before 0 pt; spacing after 12 pt

Civic theme colors; Opulent theme fonts

bold

Snip Diagonal Corner, White picture style; Orange, Accent 6 picture border

22-point font size

underlined

bulleted list

Heading 2 style; 28-point font size; centered; italicized

Figure 1–89

Extend Your Knowledge

Extend the skills you learned in this chapter and experiment with new skills. You may need to use Help to complete the assignment.

Modifying Text and Graphics Formats

Instructions:　Start Word. Open the document, Extend 1-1 Baseball Sign Ups Flyer, from the Data Files for Students. See the inside back cover of this book for instructions on downloading the Data Files for Students, or contact your instructor for information about accessing the required files.

　　You will enhance the look of the flyer shown in Figure 1–90.

Perform the following tasks:

1. Use Help to learn about the following formats: grow font, shrink font, change text color, decorative underline, and change bullet.

2. Select the headline and use the Grow Font button to increase its font size just enough so that the headline still fits on a single line. If it wraps to two lines, use the Shrink Font button.

3. Change the font color of all body copy between the headline and the signature line to a color other than Automatic, or Black.

4. Change the picture style of the picture so that it is not the Drop Shadow Rectangle picture style. Add a Glow picture effect to the picture of the baseball player.

5. Change the solid underline below the words, Indoor facility, to a decorative underline.

6. Change the color and width of the border.

7. Change the style of the bullets to a character other than the dot.

8. Change the document properties, including keywords, as specified by your instructor. Save the revised document with a new file name and then submit it in the format specified by your instructor.

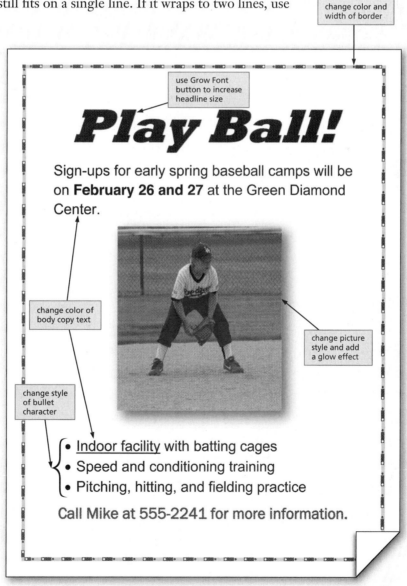

Figure 1–90

Make It Right

Analyze a document and correct all errors and/or improve the design.

Correcting Spelling and Grammar Errors

Instructions: Start Word. Open the document, Make It Right 1-1 New York Tour Flyer, from the Data Files for Students. See the inside back cover of this book for instructions on downloading the Data Files for Students, or contact your instructor for information on accessing the required files.

The document is a flyer that contains spelling and grammar errors, as shown in Figure 1–91. You are to correct each spelling (red wavy underline) and grammar error (green wavy underline) by right-clicking the flagged text and then clicking the appropriate correction on the shortcut menu. If your screen does not display the wavy underlines, click the Office Button and then click the Word Options button. When the Word Options dialog box is displayed, click Proofing, be sure the 'Hide spelling errors in this document only' and 'Hide grammar errors in this document only' check boxes do not have check marks, and then click the OK button. If your screen still does not display the wavy underlines, redisplay the Word Options dialog box, click Proofing, and then click the Recheck Document button.

Change the document properties, including keywords, as specified by your instructor. Save the revised document with a new file name and then submit it in the format specified by your instructor.

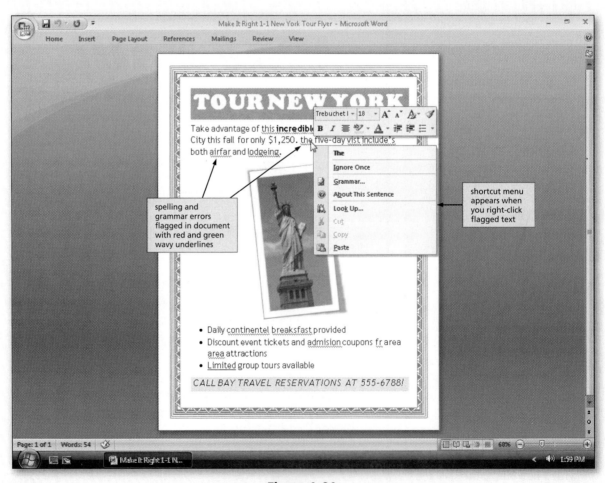

Figure 1–91

In the Lab

Design and/or create a document using the guidelines, concepts, and skills presented in this chapter. Labs are listed in order of increasing difficulty.

Lab 1: Creating a Flyer with a Picture

Problem: You work part-time at Scenic Air. Your boss has asked you to prepare a flyer that advertises aerial tours over the city of Campton. First, you prepare the unformatted flyer shown in Figure 1–92a, and then you format it so that it looks like Figure 1–92b on the next page. *Hint:* Remember, if you make a mistake while formatting the flyer, you can click the Undo button on the Quick Access Toolbar to undo your last action.

Instructions: Perform the following tasks:

1. Display formatting marks on the screen.
2. Type the flyer text, unformatted, as shown in Figure 1–92a. If Word flags any misspelled words as you type, check the spelling of these words and correct them.
3. Save the document on a USB flash drive using the file name, Lab 1-1 Airplane Rides Flyer.
4. Apply the Heading 1 style to the headline. Apply the Heading 2 style to the signature line.
5. Center the headline and the signature line.
6. Change the font and font size of the headline to 48-point Arial Rounded MT Bold, or a similar font.
7. Change the font size of body copy between the headline and the signature line to 22 point.
8. Change the font size of the signature line to 28 point.
9. Bullet the three lines (paragraphs) of text above the signature line.
10. Bold the text, change your view.
11. Italicize the word, aerial.

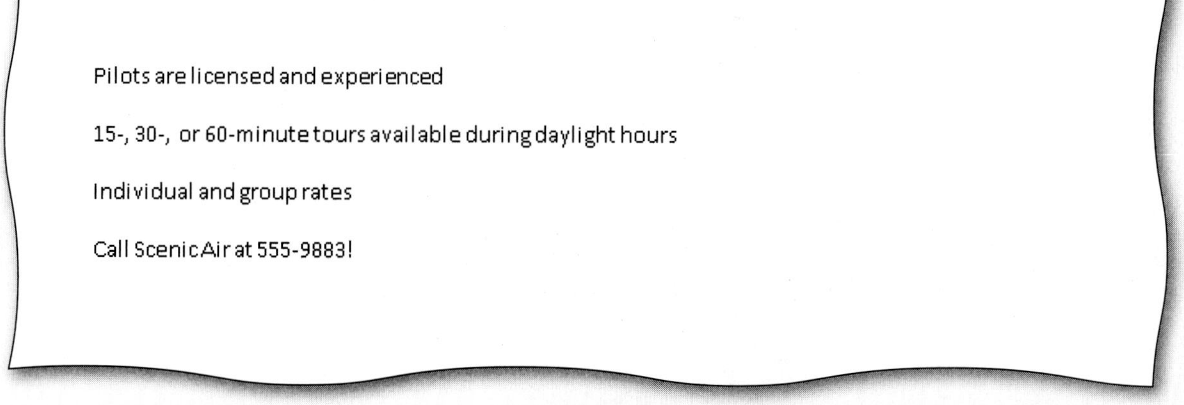

Airplane Rides

Gain an entirely new vision of Campton by taking an aerial tour. Visitor or local, business or pleasure, the trip will change your view of the city.

Pilots are licensed and experienced

15-, 30-, or 60-minute tours available during daylight hours

Individual and group rates

Call Scenic Air at 555-9883!

Figure 1–92a

Continued >

In the Lab *continued*

12. Underline the word, and, in the first bulleted paragraph.

13. Change the style set to Formal.

14. Change the theme fonts to the Metro font set.

15. Change the zoom to 50 percent so the entire page is visible in the document window.

16. Change the spacing before the headline to 0 point. Change the spacing after the first paragraph of body copy to 0 point. Change the spacing before the first bulleted paragraph to 12 point.

17. Insert the picture on the blank line above the bulleted list. The picture is called Airplane Ride over City and is available on the Data Files for Students. Apply the Relaxed Perspective, White picture style to the inserted picture.

18. The entire flyer should fit on a single page. If it flows to two pages, resize the picture or decrease spacing before and after paragraphs until the entire flyer text fits on a single page.

19. Change the document properties, including keywords, as specified by your instructor.

20. Save the flyer again with the same file name.

21. Submit the document, shown in Figure 1–92b, in the format specified by your instructor.

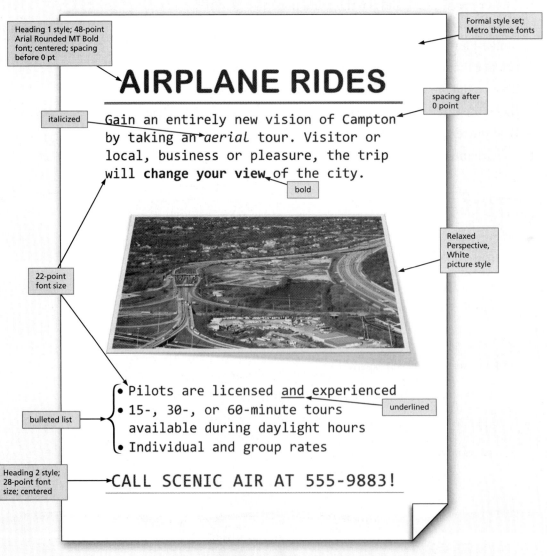

Figure 1–92b

In the Lab

Lab 2: Creating a Flyer with a Picture and a Border

Problem: Your boss at Danvers Nursery has asked you to prepare a flyer that promotes its expanded greenhouses and grounds. You prepare the flyer shown in Figure 1–93. *Hint:* Remember, if you make a mistake while formatting the flyer, you can click the Undo button on the Quick Access Toolbar to undo your last action.

Instructions: Perform the following tasks:

1. Display formatting marks on the screen.

2. Type the flyer text, unformatted. If Word flags any misspelled words as you type, check the spelling of these words and correct them.

3. Save the document on a USB flash drive using the file name, Lab 1-2 Nursery Expansion Flyer.

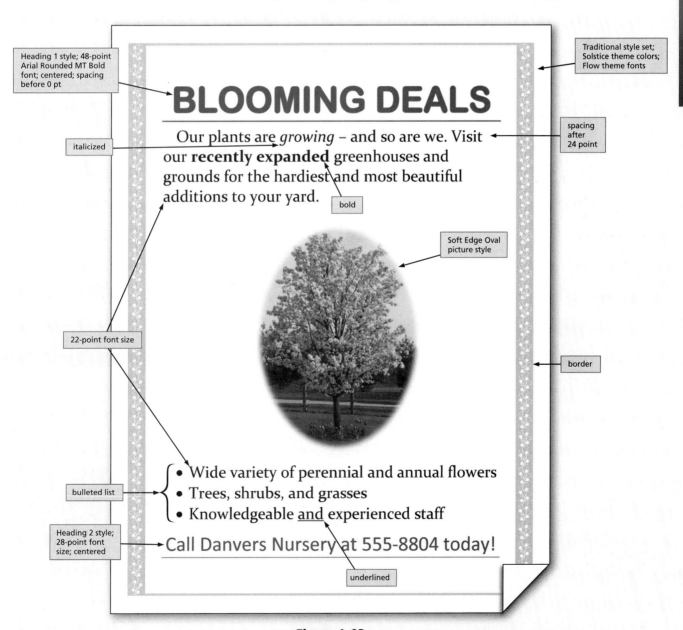

Figure 1–93

Continued >

In the Lab *continued*

4. Apply the Heading 1 style to the headline. Apply the Heading 2 style to the signature line.

5. Center the headline and the signature line.

6. Change the font and font size of the headline to 48-point Arial Rounded MT Bold, or a similar font.

7. Change the font size of body copy between the headline and the signature line to 22 point.

8. Change the font size of the signature line to 28 point.

9. Bullet the three lines (paragraphs) of text above the signature line.

10. Italicize the word, growing.

11. Bold the text, recently expanded.

12. Underline the word, and, in the third bulleted paragraph.

13. Change the style set to Traditional.

14. Change the theme colors to the Solstice color scheme.

15. Change the theme fonts to the Flow font set.

16. Change the zoom to 50 percent so the entire page is visible in the document window.

17. Change the spacing before the headline to 0 point. Change the spacing after the first paragraph of body copy to 24 point. Change the spacing before the first bulleted paragraph to 12 point.

18. Insert the picture on the blank line above the bulleted list. The picture is called Bradford Pear in Bloom and is available on the Data Files for Students. Apply the Soft Edge Oval picture style to the inserted picture.

19. The entire flyer should fit on a single page. If it flows to two pages, resize the picture or decrease spacing before and after paragraphs until the entire flyer text fits on a single page.

20. Add the graphic border, shown in Figure 1–93 on the previous page (about one-third down in the Art gallery). Change the color of the border to Tan, Background 2.

21. Change the document properties, including keywords, as specified by your instructor.

22. Save the flyer again with the same file name.

23. Submit the document, shown in Figure 1–93, in the format specified by your instructor.

In the Lab

Lab 3: Creating a Flyer with a Picture and Resized Border Art

Problem: Your neighbor has asked you to prepare a flyer that promotes her cabin rental business. You prepare the flyer shown in Figure 1–94.

Instructions: Enter the text in the flyer, checking spelling as you type, and then format it as shown in Figure 1–94. The picture to be inserted is called Paddle Boat on Lake and is available on the Data Files for Students. After adding the page border, reduce the point size of its width so that the border is not so predominant on the page. Change the document properties, including keywords, as specified by your instructor. Save the document on a USB flash drive using the file name, Lab 1-3 Cabin Rentals Flyer. Submit the document, shown in Figure 1–94, in the format specified by your instructor.

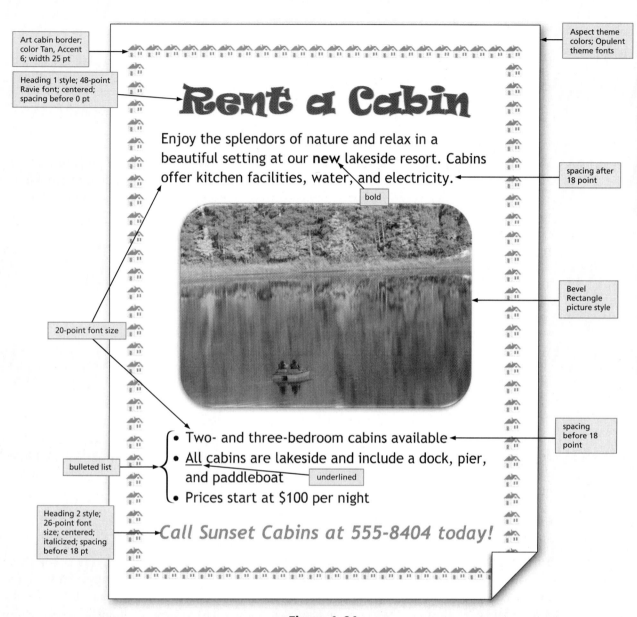

Figure 1–94

Cases and Places

Apply your creative thinking and problem solving skills to design and implement a solution.

● Easier ●● More Difficult

● 1: Design and Create a Grand Reopening Flyer

Your friend owns the Craft Barn, a large, year-round craft fair. She recently has renovated and remodeled the facility and is planning a grand reopening. She has asked you to create a flyer advertising this fact. The flyer should contain the following headline: Craft Barn. The first paragraph of text below the headline should read: Pick up a jar of homemade jam or a handcrafted gift at the completely remodeled and renovated Craft Barn, located at 8701 County Road 300 West. Insert the photograph named, Barn and Silo, which is available on the Data Files for Students. The bullet items

Continued >

Cases and Places *continued*

under the photograph should read as follows: first bullet – Expanded and paved parking; second bullet – More than 150 booths; and third bullet – Open Monday through Saturday, 10:00 a.m. to 7:00 p.m. The last line should read: Call 555-5709 for more information! Use the concepts and techniques presented in this chapter to create and format this flyer. Be sure to check spelling and grammar.

• 2: Design and Create a Property Advertisement Flyer

As a part-time employee of Markum Realty, you have been assigned the task of preparing a flyer advertising lakefront property. The headline should read: Lakefront Lot. The first paragraph of text should read as follows: Build the house of your dreams or a weekend getaway on this beautiful lakeside property located on the north side of Lake Pleasant. Insert the photograph named, Lake at Sunset, which is available on the Data Files for Students. Below the photograph, insert the following bullet items: first bullet — City sewer and water available; second bullet – Lot size 110 × 300; third bullet – List price $65,000. The last line should read: Call Markum Realty at 555-0995 for a tour! Use the concepts and techniques presented in this chapter to create and format this flyer. Be sure to check spelling and grammar.

• • 3: Design and Create a Flyer for the Sale of a Business

After 25 years, your Uncle Mitch has decided to sell his ice cream shop and wants you to help him create a sales flyer. The shop is in a choice location at the corner of 135th and Main Street and has an established customer base. The building has an adjacent, paved parking lot, as well as an outdoor seating area. He wants to sell the store and all its contents, including the equipment, tables, booths, and chairs. The 1200-square-foot shop recently was appraised at $200,000, and your uncle is willing to sell for cash or on contract. Use the concepts and techniques presented in this chapter to create and format a sales flyer. Include a headline, descriptive body copy, a signature line, an appropriate photograph or clip art image, a bulleted list, a decorative underline, and if appropriate, a page border. Be sure to check spelling and grammar in the flyer.

• • 4: Design and Create a Flyer that Advertises You

Make It Personal

Everyone has at least one skill, talent, or special capability, which if shared with others, can lead to opportunity for growth, experience, and personal reward. Perhaps you play a musical instrument. If so, you could offer lessons. Maybe you are a skilled carpenter or other tradesman who could advertise your services. If you speak a second language, you could offer tutoring. Budding athletes might harbor a desire to pass on their knowledge by coaching a youth sports team. You may have a special knack for singing, sewing, knitting, photography, typing, housecleaning, or pet care. Carefully consider your own personal capabilities, skills, and talents and then use the concepts and techniques presented in this chapter to create a flyer advertising a service you can provide. Include a headline, descriptive body copy, a signature line, an appropriate photograph or clip art image, a bulleted list, a decorative underline, and if appropriate, a page border. Be sure to check spelling and grammar in the flyer.

• • 5: Redesign and Enhance a Poorly Designed Flyer

Working Together

Public locations, such as stores, schools, and libraries, have bulletin boards or windows for people to post flyers. Often, these bulletin boards or windows have so many flyers that some go unnoticed. Locate a posted flyer on a bulletin board or window that you think might be overlooked. Copy the text from the flyer and distribute it to each team member. Each member then independently should use this text, together with the techniques presented in this chapter, to create a flyer that would be more likely to catch the attention of passersby. Be sure to check spelling and grammar. As a group, critique each flyer and have team members redesign their flyer based on the group's recommendations. Hand in each team member's original and final flyers.

2 | Creating a Research Paper

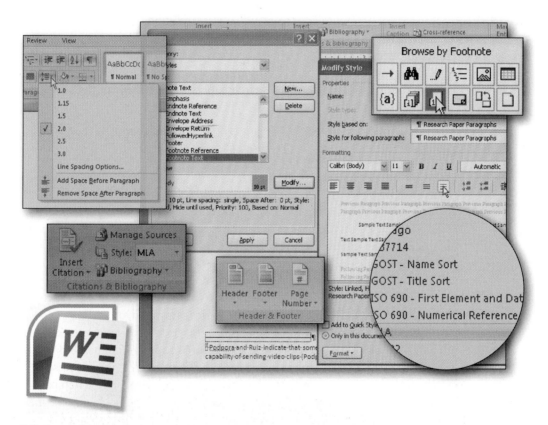

Objectives

You will have mastered the material in this chapter when you can:

- Describe the MLA documentation style for research papers

- Change line and paragraph spacing in a document

- Use a header to number pages of a document

- Apply formatting using shortcut keys

- Modify paragraph indentation

- Create and modify styles

- Insert and edit citations and their sources

- Add a footnote to a document

- Insert a manual page break

- Create a bibliographical list of sources

- Move text

- Find and replace text

- Use the Research task pane to look up information

2 | Creating a Research Paper

Introduction

In both academic and business environments, you will be asked to write reports. Business reports range from proposals to cost justifications to five-year plans to research findings. Academic reports focus mostly on research findings. A **research paper** is a document you can use to communicate the results of research findings. To write a research paper, you learn about a particular topic from a variety of sources (research), organize your ideas from the research results, and then present relevant facts and/or opinions that support the topic. Your final research paper combines properly credited outside information along with personal insights. Thus, no two research papers — even if about the same topic — will or should be the same.

Project — Research Paper

When preparing a research paper, you should follow a standard documentation style that defines the rules for creating the paper and crediting sources. A variety of documentation styles exists, depending on the nature of the research paper. Each style requires the same basic information; the differences in styles relate to requirements for presenting the information. For example, one documentation style uses the term bibliography for the list of sources, whereas another uses references, and yet a third prefers the title works cited. Two popular documentation styles for research papers are the **Modern Language Association of America (MLA)** and **American Psychological Association (APA)** styles. This chapter uses the MLA documentation style because it is used in a wide range of disciplines.

The project in this chapter follows research paper guidelines and uses Word to create the short research paper shown in Figure 2–1. This paper, which discusses three types of wireless communications, follows the MLA documentation style. Each page contains a page number. The first two pages present the heading (name, course, and date information), paper title, an introduction with a thesis statement, details that support the thesis, and a conclusion. This section of the paper also includes references to research sources. The third page contains a detailed, alphabetical list of the sources used in the research paper.

Overview

As you read through this chapter, you will learn how to create the research paper shown in Figure 2–1 by performing these general tasks:

- Change the document settings.
- Type the research paper.
- Save the research paper.
- Create an alphabetical list of sources.
- Proof and revise the research paper.
- Print the research paper.

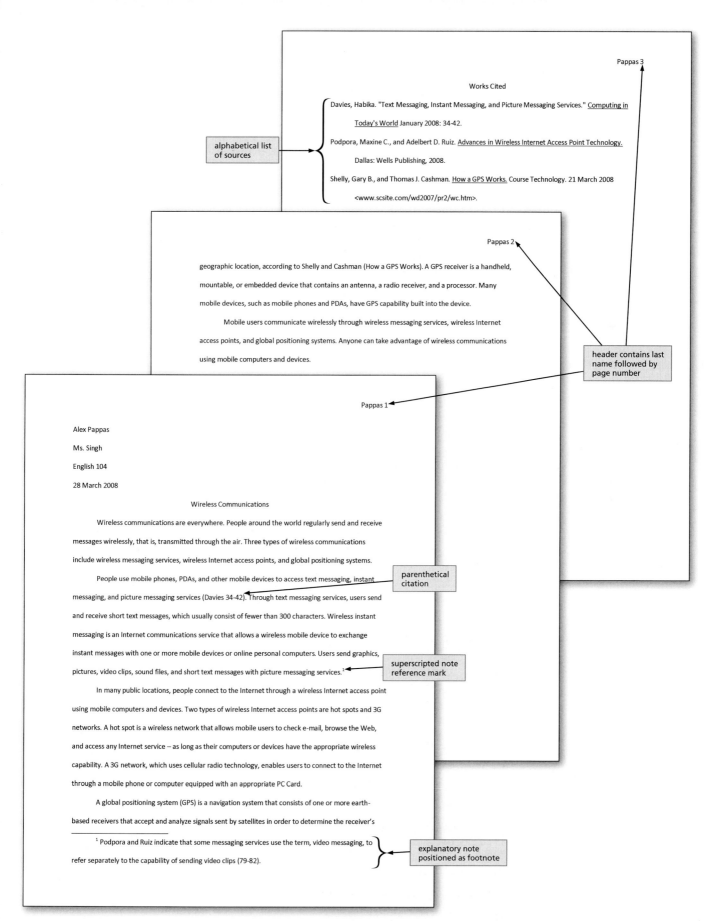

Pappas 3

Works Cited

Davies, Habika. "Text Messaging, Instant Messaging, and Picture Messaging Services." Computing in

Today's World January 2008: 34-42.

Podpora, Maxine C., and Adelbert D. Ruiz. Advances in Wireless Internet Access Point Technology.

Dallas: Wells Publishing, 2008.

Shelly, Gary B., and Thomas J. Cashman. How a GPS Works. Course Technology. 21 March 2008

<www.scsite.com/wd2007/pr2/wc.htm>.

alphabetical list of sources

Pappas 2

geographic location, according to Shelly and Cashman (How a GPS Works). A GPS receiver is a handheld,

mountable, or embedded device that contains an antenna, a radio receiver, and a processor. Many

mobile devices, such as mobile phones and PDAs, have GPS capability built into the device.

Mobile users communicate wirelessly through wireless messaging services, wireless Internet

access points, and global positioning systems. Anyone can take advantage of wireless communications

using mobile computers and devices.

header contains last name followed by page number

Pappas 1

Alex Pappas

Ms. Singh

English 104

28 March 2008

Wireless Communications

Wireless communications are everywhere. People around the world regularly send and receive

messages wirelessly, that is, transmitted through the air. Three types of wireless communications

include wireless messaging services, wireless Internet access points, and global positioning systems.

People use mobile phones, PDAs, and other mobile devices to access text messaging, instant

messaging, and picture messaging services (Davies 34-42). Through text messaging services, users send

and receive short text messages, which usually consist of fewer than 300 characters. Wireless instant

messaging is an Internet communications service that allows a wireless mobile device to exchange

instant messages with one or more mobile devices or online personal computers. Users send graphics,

pictures, video clips, sound files, and short text messages with picture messaging services.[1]

In many public locations, people connect to the Internet through a wireless Internet access point

using mobile computers and devices. Two types of wireless Internet access points are hot spots and 3G

networks. A hot spot is a wireless network that allows mobile users to check e-mail, browse the Web,

and access any Internet service — as long as their computers or devices have the appropriate wireless

capability. A 3G network, which uses cellular radio technology, enables users to connect to the Internet

through a mobile phone or computer equipped with an appropriate PC Card.

A global positioning system (GPS) is a navigation system that consists of one or more earth-

based receivers that accept and analyze signals sent by satellites in order to determine the receiver's

parenthetical citation

superscripted note reference mark

[1] Podpora and Ruiz indicate that some messaging services use the term, video messaging, to

refer separately to the capability of sending video clips (79-82).

explanatory note positioned as footnote

Figure 2–1

General Project Guidelines

When creating a Word document, the actions you perform and decisions you make will affect the appearance and characteristics of the finished document. As you create a research paper, such as the project shown in Figure 2–1 on the previous page, you should follow these general guidelines:

1. **Select a topic.** Spend time brainstorming ideas for a topic. Choose one you find interesting. For shorter papers, narrow down the scope of the topic; for longer papers, broaden the scope. Identify a tentative thesis statement, which is a sentence describing the paper's subject matter.

2. **Research the topic and take notes.** Gather credible, relevant information about the topic that supports the thesis statement. Sources of research include books, magazines, newspapers, and the Internet. As you record facts and ideas, list details about the source: title, author, place of publication, publisher, date of publication, etc. When taking notes, be careful not to **plagiarize**. That is, do not use someone else's work and claim it to be your own. If you copy information directly, place it in quotation marks and identify its source.

3. **Organize your ideas.** Classify your notes into related concepts. Make an outline from the categories of notes. In the outline, identify all main ideas and supporting details.

4. **Write the first draft, referencing sources.** From the outline, compose the paper. Every research paper should include an introduction containing the thesis statement, supporting details, and a conclusion. Follow the guidelines identified in the required documentation style. Reference all sources of information.

5. **Create the list of sources.** Using the formats specified in the required documentation style, completely list all sources referenced in the body of the research paper in alphabetical order.

6. **Proofread and revise the paper.** If possible, proofread the paper with a fresh set of eyes, that is, at least one to two days after completing the first draft. Proofreading involves reading the paper with the intent of identifying errors (spelling, grammar, etc.) and looking for ways to improve the paper (wording, transitions, flow, etc.). Try reading the paper out loud, which helps to identify unclear or awkward wording. Ask someone else to proofread the paper and give you suggestions for improvements.

When necessary, more specific details concerning the above guidelines are presented at appropriate points in the chapter. The chapter also will identify the actions performed and decisions made regarding these guidelines during the creation of the research paper shown in Figure 2–1.

BTW

APA Documentation Style
In the APA style, a separate title page is required instead of placing name and course information on the paper's first page. Double-space all pages of the paper with 1.5" top, bottom, left, and right margins. Indent the first word of each paragraph .5" from the left margin. In the upper-right margin of each page, including the title page, place a running head that consists of the page number double-spaced below a brief summary of the paper title.

MLA Documentation Style

The research paper in this project follows the guidelines presented by the MLA. To follow the MLA style, double-space text on all pages of the paper using one-inch top, bottom, left, and right margins. Indent the first word of each paragraph one-half inch from the left margin. At the right margin of each page, place a page number one-half inch from the top margin. On each page, precede the page number by your last name.

The MLA style does not require a title page. Instead, place your name and course information in a block at the left margin beginning one inch from the top of the page. Center the title one double-space below your name and course information.

In the text of the paper, place author references in parentheses with the page number(s) of the referenced information. The MLA style uses in-text **parenthetical citations** instead of noting each source at the bottom of the page or at the end of the paper. In the MLA style, notes are used only for optional explanatory notes.

If used, explanatory notes elaborate on points discussed in the paper. Use a superscript (raised number) to signal that an explanatory note exists, and also to sequence the notes. Position explanatory notes either at the bottom of the page as footnotes or at the end of the paper as endnotes. Indent the first line of each explanatory note one-half inch from the left margin. Place one space following the superscripted number before beginning the note text. Double-space the note text. At the end of the note text, you may list bibliographic information for further reference.

The MLA style uses the term **works cited** to refer to the bibliographic list of sources at the end of the paper. The works cited page alphabetically lists sources that are referenced directly in the paper. Place the list of sources on a separate numbered page. Center the title, Works Cited, one inch from the top margin. Double-space all lines. Begin the first line of each source at the left margin, indenting subsequent lines of the same source one-half inch from the left margin. List each source by the author's last name, or, if the author's name is not available, by the title of the source. Underline or italicize the title of each source.

Changing Document Settings

The MLA documentation style defines some global formats that apply to the entire research paper. Some of these formats are the default in Word. For example, the default left, right, top, and bottom margin settings in Word are one inch, which meets the MLA style. You will modify, however, the paragraph and line spacing and header formats as required by the MLA style.

After starting Word, the following pages adjust line and paragraph spacing and define a header for the current document.

To Start Word

If you are using a computer to step through the project in this chapter and you want your screens to match the figures in this book, you should change your computer's resolution to 1024×768. For information about how to change a computer's resolution, read Appendix E.

The following steps, which assume Windows Vista is running, start Word based on a typical installation. You may need to ask your instructor how to start Word for your computer.

Note: If you are using Windows XP, see Appendix F for alternate steps.

1 Click the Start button on the Windows Vista taskbar to display the Start menu and then click All Programs at the bottom of the left pane on the Start menu to display the All Programs list.

2 Click Microsoft Office in the All Programs list to display the Microsoft Office list and then click Microsoft Office Word 2007 to start Word and display a new blank document in the Word window.

3 If the Word window is not maximized, click the Maximize button next to the Close button on its title bar to maximize the window.

4 If the Print Layout button is not selected, click it so that your screen layout matches Figure 2–2 on the next page.

5 If your zoom percent is not 100, click the Zoom Out or Zoom In button as many times as necessary until the Zoom level button displays 100% on its face.

To Display Formatting Marks

As discussed in Chapter 1, it is helpful to display formatting marks that indicate where in the document you pressed the ENTER key, SPACEBAR, and other keys. The following step displays formatting marks.

1 If necessary, click Home on the Ribbon to display the Home tab. If the Show/Hide ¶ button on the Home tab is not selected already, click it to display formatting marks on the screen.

BTW

Line Spacing
If the top of a set of characters or a graphical image is chopped off, then line spacing may be set to Exactly. To remedy the problem, change line spacing to 1.0, 1.15, 1.5, 2.0, 2.5, 3.0, or At least (in the Paragraph dialog box), all of which accommodate the largest font or image.

Adjusting Line and Paragraph Spacing

Line spacing is the amount of vertical space between lines of text in a paragraph. **Paragraph spacing** is the amount of space above and below a paragraph. By default, the Normal style places 10 points of blank space after each paragraph and inserts a vertical space equal to 1.15 lines between each line of text. It also automatically adjusts line height to accommodate various font sizes and graphics.

The MLA documentation style requires that you **double-space** the entire research paper. That is, the amount of vertical space between each line of text and above and below paragraphs should be equal to one blank line. The next sets of steps adjust line spacing and paragraph spacing according to the MLA documentation style.

To Double-Space Text

To double-space the lines in the research paper, change the line spacing to 2.0. The following steps change line spacing to double.

1

- Click the Line spacing button on the Home tab to display the Line spacing gallery (Figure 2–2).

Q&A

What do the numbers in the Line spacing gallery represent?

The default line spacing is 1.15 lines. The options 1.0, 2.0, and 3.0 set line spacing to single, double, and triple, respectively. Similarly, the 1.5 and 2.5 options set line spacing to 1.5 and 2.5 lines. All these options adjust line spacing automatically to accommodate the largest font or graphic on a line.

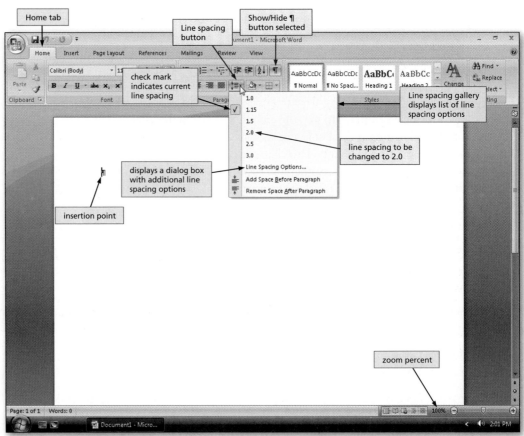

Figure 2–2

2

- Click 2.0 in the Line spacing gallery to change the line spacing to double at the location of the insertion point.

Q&A

Can I change the line spacing of existing text?

Yes. Select the text first and then change the line spacing as described in these steps.

Other Ways

1. Right-click paragraph, click Paragraph on shortcut menu, click Indents and Spacing tab, click Line

   spacing box arrow, click Double, click OK button

2. Click Paragraph Dialog Box Launcher, click Indents

   and Spacing tab, click Line spacing box arrow, click Double, click OK button

3. Press CTRL+2

To Remove Space after a Paragraph

The research paper should not have additional blank space after each paragraph. The following steps remove space after a paragraph.

- Click the Line spacing button on the Home tab to display the Line spacing gallery (Figure 2–3).

- Click Remove Space After Paragraph in the Line spacing gallery so that no blank space appears after a paragraph.

Q&A Can I remove space after existing paragraphs?

Yes. Select the paragraphs first and then remove the space as described in these steps.

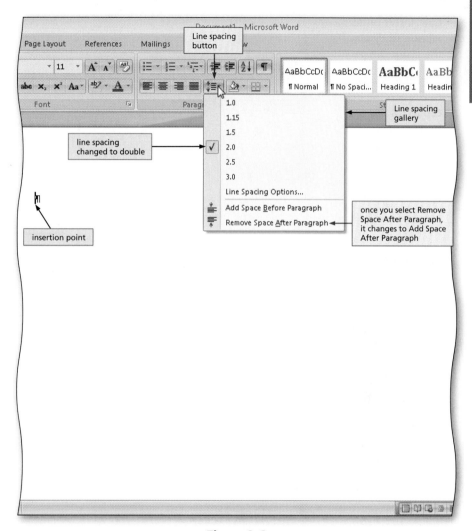

Figure 2–3

Other Ways

1. Click Spacing After box arrow on Page Layout tab until 0 pt is displayed

2. Right-click paragraph, click Paragraph on shortcut menu, click Indents and Spacing tab, click Spacing After box arrow until 0 pt is displayed, click OK button

3. Click Paragraph Dialog Box Launcher, click Indents and Spacing tab, click Spacing After box arrow until 0 pt is displayed, click OK button

Headers and Footers

A **header** is text and graphics that print at the top of each page in a document. Similarly, a **footer** is text and graphics that print at the bottom of every page. In Word, headers print in the top margin one-half inch from the top of every page, and footers print in the bottom margin one-half inch from the bottom of each page, which meets the MLA style. In addition to text and graphics, headers and footers can include document information such as the page number, current date, current time, and author's name.

In this research paper, you are to precede the page number with your last name placed one-half inch from the upper-right edge of each page. The procedures on the following pages enter your name and the page number in the header, as specified by the MLA style.

To Switch to the Header

To enter text in the header, you instruct Word to edit the header. The following steps switch from editing the document text to editing the header.

- Click Insert on the Ribbon to display the Insert tab.

- Click the Header button on the Insert tab to display the Header gallery (Figure 2–4).

Q&A
Can I use a built-in header for this research paper?

None of the built-in headers adhere to the MLA style. Thus, you enter your own header contents, instead of using a built-in header, for this research paper.

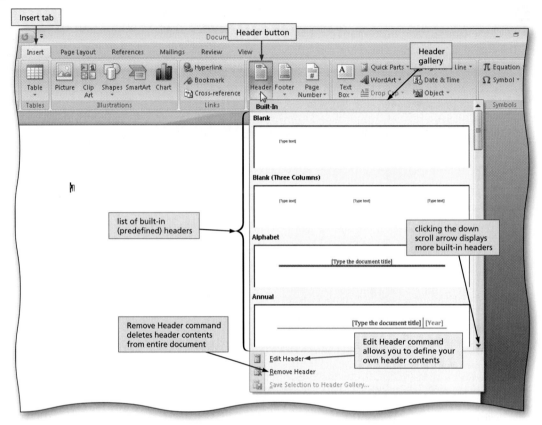

Figure 2–4

Experiment

- Click the down scroll arrow in the Header gallery to see the available built-in headers.

- Click Edit Header in the Header gallery to switch from the document text to the header, which allows you to edit the contents of the header (Figure 2–5).

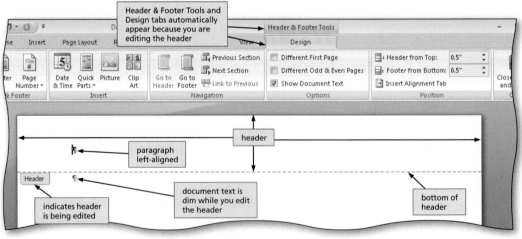

Figure 2–5

Q&A
How do I remove the Header & Footer Tools and Design tabs from the Ribbon?

When you are finished editing the header, you will close it, which removes the Header & Footer Tools tabs.

Other Ways

1. Double-click dimmed header

To Right-Align a Paragraph

The paragraph in the header currently is left-aligned (Figure 2–5). Your last name and the page number should print **right-aligned**, that is, at the right margin. The following step right-aligns a paragraph.

1

- Click Home on the Ribbon to display the Home tab.

- Click the Align Text Right button on the Home tab to right-align the paragraph in the header (Figure 2–6).

Q&A

What if I wanted to return the paragraph to left-aligned?

Click the Align Text Right button again, or click the Align Text Left button.

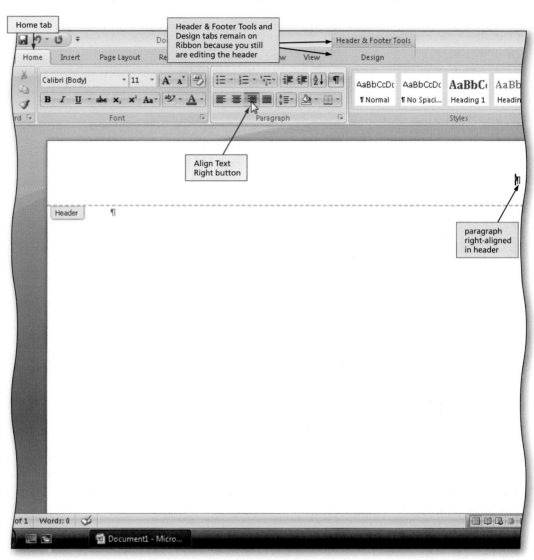

Figure 2–6

To Enter Text

The following steps enter your last name right-aligned in the header area.

1 Click Design on the Ribbon to display the Design tab.

2 Type Pappas and then press the SPACEBAR to enter the last name in the header.

BTW

Footers
If you wanted to create a footer, you would click the Footer button on the Insert tab and then select the desired built-in footer or click Edit Footer to create a customized footer.

To Insert a Page Number

The next task is to insert the current page number in the header. The following steps insert a page number at the location of the insertion point.

- Click the Insert Page Number button on the Design tab to display the Insert Page Number menu.

- Point to Current Position on the Insert Page Number menu to display the Current Position gallery (Figure 2–7).

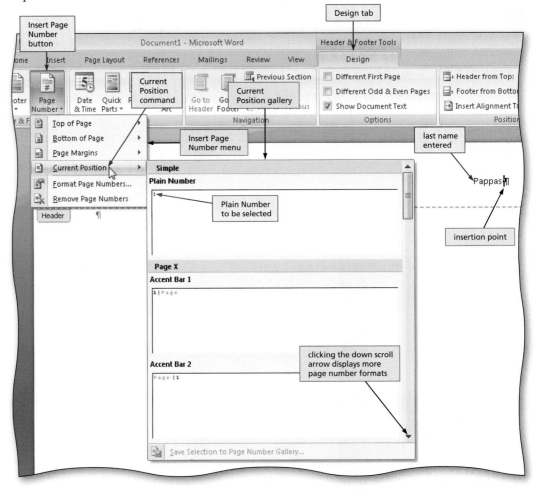

Figure 2–7

- Click the down scroll arrow in the Current Position gallery to see the available page number formats.

② Experiment

③

- If necessary, scroll to the top of the Current Position gallery. Click Plain Number in the Current Position gallery to insert an unformatted page number at the location of the insertion point (Figure 2–8).

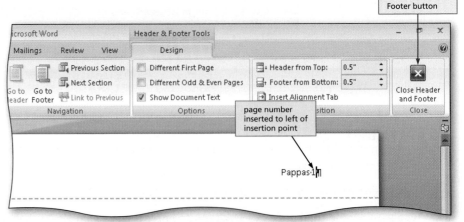

Figure 2–8

Other Ways

1. Click Insert Page Number button on Insert tab	2. Click Quick Parts button on Insert tab or on Design tab on Header & Footer Tools tab,	click Field on Quick Parts menu, select Page in Field names list, click OK button

To Close the Header

You are finished entering text in the header. Thus, the next task is to switch back to the document text. The following step closes the header.

- Click the Close Header and Footer button on the Design tab (shown in Figure 2–8) to close the header and switch back to the document text (Figure 2–9).

Q&A

How do I make changes to existing header text?

Switch to the header using the steps described on page WD 80, edit the header as you would edit text in the document window, and then switch back to the document text.

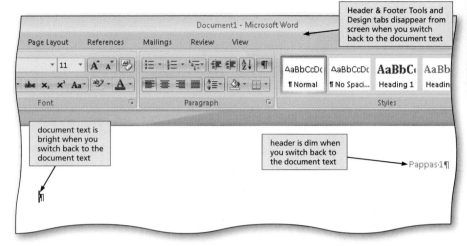

Figure 2–9

Other Ways
1. Double-click dimmed document text

Typing the Research Paper Text

The text of the research paper in this chapter encompasses the first two pages of the paper. You will type the text of the research paper and then modify it later in the chapter, so that it matches Figure 2–1 on page WD 75.

Plan Ahead

Write the first draft, referencing sources.
As you write the first draft of your research paper, be sure it includes the proper components, uses credible sources, and does not contain any plagiarism.

- **Include an introduction, body, and conclusion.** The first paragraph of the paper introduces the topic and captures the reader's attention. The body, which follows the introduction, consists of several paragraphs that support the topic. The conclusion summarizes the main points in the body and restates the topic.

- **Evaluate sources for authority, currency, and accuracy.** Be especially wary of information obtained from the Web. Any person, company, or organization can publish a Web page on the Internet. Ask yourself these questions about the source:

  - Authority: Does a reputable institution or group support the source? Is the information presented without bias? Are the author's credentials listed and verifiable?

  - Currency: Is the information up to date? Are dates of sources listed? What is the last date revised or updated?

  - Accuracy: Is the information free of errors? Is it verifiable? Are the sources clearly identified?

- **Acknowledge all sources of information; do not plagiarize.** Not only is plagiarism unethical, but it is considered an academic crime that can have severe punishments such as failing a course or being expelled from school.

  When you summarize, paraphrase (rewrite information in your own words), present facts, give statistics, quote exact words, or show a map, chart, or other graphical image, you

(continued)

Plan
Ahead

(continued)

must acknowledge the source. Information that commonly is known or accessible to the audience constitutes common knowledge and does not need to be acknowledged. If, however, you question whether certain information is common knowledge, you should document it — just to be safe.

To Enter Name and Course Information

As discussed earlier in this chapter, the MLA style does not require a separate title page for research papers. Instead, place your name and course information in a block at the top of the page, below the header, at the left margin. The following steps enter the name and course information in the research paper.

BTW

Date Formats
The MLA style prefers the day-month-year (28 March 2008) or month-day-year (March 28, 2008) format. Whichever format you select, use it consistently throughout the paper.

1 Type Alex Pappas as the student name and then press the ENTER key.

2 Type Ms. Singh as the instructor name and then press the ENTER key.

3 Type English 104 as the course name and then press the ENTER key.

4 Type 28 March 2008 as the paper due date and then press the ENTER key (Figure 2–10).

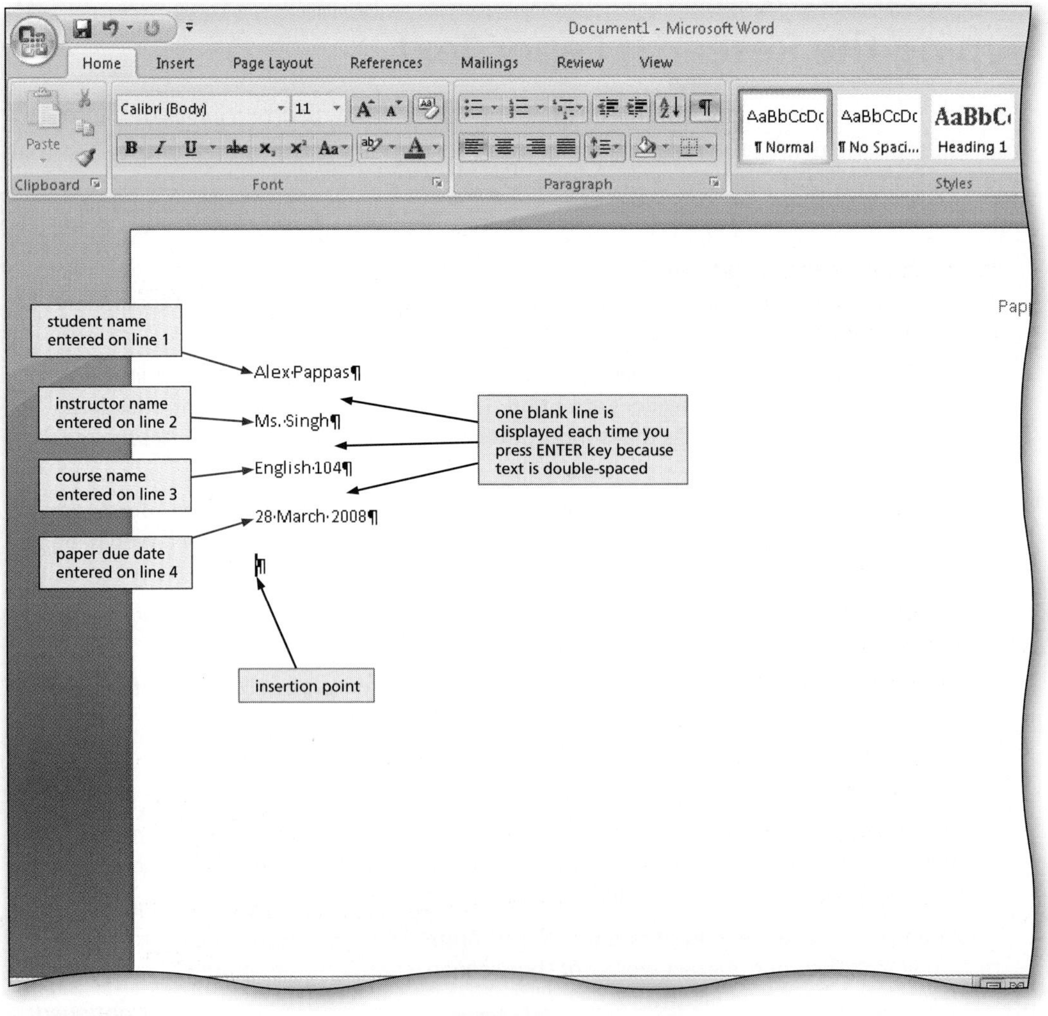

Figure 2–10

To Click and Type

The next step is to enter the title of the research paper centered between the page margins. In Chapter 1, you used the Center button on the Home tab to center text and graphics. As an alternative, you can use **Click and Type** to format and enter text, graphics, and other items. To use Click and Type, you double-click a blank area of the document window. Word automatically formats the item you enter according to the location where you just double-clicked. The following steps use Click and Type to center and then type the title of the research paper.

 1

 Experiment

- Move the mouse pointer around the document below the entered name and course information and observe the various icons that appear with the I-beam.

2

- Position the mouse pointer in the center of the document at the approximate location for the research paper title until a center icon appears below the I-beam (Figure 2–11).

Q&A What are the other icons that appear in the Click and Type pointer?

A left-align icon appears to the right of the I-beam when the Click and Type pointer is in certain locations on the left side of the document window. A right-align icon appears to the left of the icon when the Click and Type pointer is in certain locations on the right side of the document window.

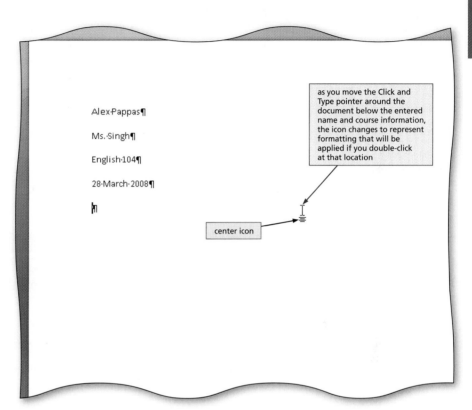

Alex·Pappas¶

Ms.·Singh¶

English·104¶

28·March·2008¶

as you move the Click and Type pointer around the document below the entered name and course information, the icon changes to represent formatting that will be applied if you double-click at that location

center icon

Figure 2–11

 3

- Double-click to center the paragraph mark and insertion point between the left and right margins.

- **Type** Wireless Communications as the paper title and then press the ENTER key (Figure 2–12).

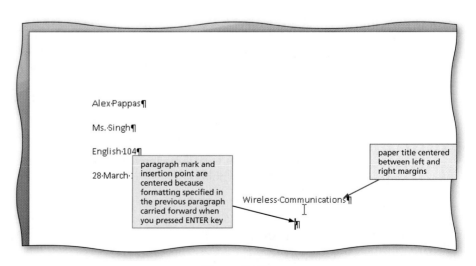

Alex·Pappas¶

Ms.·Singh¶

English·104¶

28·March·

paragraph mark and insertion point are centered because formatting specified in the previous paragraph carried forward when you pressed ENTER key

Wireless·Communications¶

paper title centered between left and right margins

Figure 2–12

Shortcut Keys

Word has many shortcut keys for your convenience while typing. Table 2–1 lists the common shortcut keys for formatting characters. Table 2–2 lists common shortcut keys for formatting paragraphs.

Table 2–1 Shortcut Keys for Formatting Characters

Character Formatting Task	Shortcut Keys	Character Formatting Task	Shortcut Keys
All capital letters	CTRL+SHIFT+A	Italic	CTRL+I
Bold	CTRL+B	Remove character formatting (plain text)	CTRL+SPACEBAR
Case of letters	SHIFT+F3	Small uppercase letters	CTRL+SHIFT+K
Decrease font size	CTRL+SHIFT+<	Subscript	CTRL+EQUAL SIGN
Decrease font size 1 point	CTRL+[	Superscript	CTRL+SHIFT+PLUS SIGN
Double-underline	CTRL+SHIFT+D	Underline	CTRL+U
Increase font size	CTRL+SHIFT+>	Underline words, not spaces	CTRL+SHIFT+W
Increase font size 1 point	CTRL+]		

Table 2–2 Shortcut Keys for Formatting Paragraphs

Paragraph Formatting	Shortcut Keys	Paragraph Formatting	Shortcut Keys
1.5 line spacing	CTRL+5	Justify paragraph	CTRL+J
Add/remove one line above paragraph	CTRL+0 (ZERO)	Left-align paragraph	CTRL+L
Center paragraph	CTRL+E	Remove hanging indent	CTRL+SHIFT+T
Decrease paragraph indent	CTRL+SHIFT+M	Remove paragraph formatting	CTRL+Q
Double-space lines	CTRL+2	Right-align paragraph	CTRL+R
Hanging indent	CTRL+T	Single-space lines	CTRL+1
Increase paragraph indent	CTRL+M		

BTW

Shortcut Keys
To print a complete list of shortcut keys in Word, click the Microsoft Office Word Help button near the upper-right corner of the Word window, type shortcut keys in the 'Type words to search for' text box at the top of the Word Help window, press the ENTER key, click the Keyboard shortcuts for Microsoft Office Word link, click the Show All link in the upper-right corner of the Help window, click the Print button in the Help window, and then click the Print button in the Print dialog box.

To Format Text Using Shortcut Keys

The paragraphs below the paper title should be left-aligned, instead of centered. Thus, the next step is to left-align the paragraph below the paper title. When your fingers are already on the keyboard, you may prefer using **shortcut keys**, or keyboard key combinations, to format text as you type it. The following step left-aligns a paragraph using the shortcut keys CTRL+L. (Recall from Chapter 1 that a notation such as CTRL+L means to press the letter l on the keyboard while holding down the CTRL key.)

 Press CTRL+L to left-align the current paragraph, that is, the paragraph containing the insertion point.

Q&A Why would I use a keyboard shortcut, instead of the Ribbon, to format text?

Switching between the mouse and the keyboard takes time. If your hands are already on the keyboard, use a keyboard shortcut. If your hand is on the mouse, use the Ribbon.

To Save a Document

You have performed many tasks while creating the research paper and do not want to risk losing the work completed thus far. Accordingly, you should save the document. For a detailed example of the procedure summarized below, refer to pages WD 19 through WD 21 in Chapter 1.

Note: If you are using Windows XP, see Appendix F for alternate steps.

1 With a USB flash drive connected to one of the computer's USB ports, click the Save button on the Quick Access Toolbar to display the Save As dialog box.

2 Type `Wireless Communications Paper` in the File name text box to change the file name.

3 If Computer is not displayed in the Favorite Links section, drag the top or bottom edge of the Save As dialog box until Computer is displayed. Click Computer in the Favorite Links section and then double-click your USB flash drive in the list of available drives.

4 Click the Save button in the Save As dialog box to save the document on the USB flash drive with the file name, Wireless Communications Paper.

To Display the Rulers

According to the MLA style, the first line of each paragraph in the research paper is to be indented one-half inch from the left margin. Although you can use a dialog box to indent paragraphs, Word provides a quicker way through the **horizontal ruler**. This ruler displays at the top edge of the document window just below the Ribbon. Word also provides a **vertical ruler** that displays along the left edge of the Word window. The following steps display the rulers.

1

Experiment

• Repeatedly click the View Ruler button on the vertical scroll bar to see the how this button is used to both show and hide the rulers.

2

• If the rulers are not displayed, click the View Ruler button on the vertical scroll bar because you want to use the ruler to indent paragraphs (Figure 2–13).

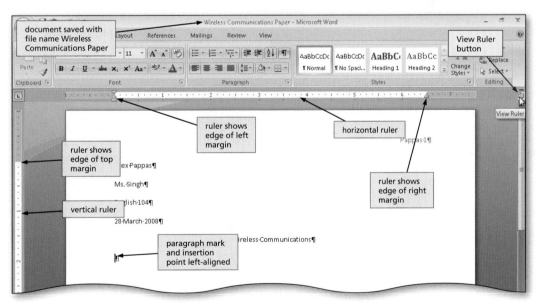

Figure 2–13

Q&A

Can I use the rulers for other tasks?

In addition to indenting paragraphs, you can use the rulers to set tab stops, change page margins, and adjust column widths.

Other Ways

1. Click View Ruler check box on View tab

To First-Line Indent Paragraphs

The first line of each paragraph in the research paper is to be indented one-half inch from the left margin. You can use the horizontal ruler, usually simply called the **ruler**, to indent just the first line of a paragraph, called **first-line indent**.

The left margin on the ruler contains two triangles above a square. The **First Line Indent marker** is the top triangle at the 0" mark on the ruler (Figure 2–14). The bottom triangle is discussed later in this chapter. The small square at the 0" mark is the Left Indent marker. The **Left Indent marker** allows you to change the entire left margin, whereas the First Line Indent marker indents only the first line of the paragraph. The following steps first-line indent paragraphs in the research paper.

- With the insertion point on the paragraph mark below the research paper title, point to the First Line Indent marker on the ruler (Figure 2–14).

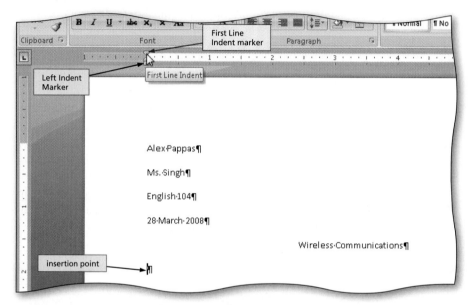

Figure 2–14

- Drag the First Line Indent marker to the .5" mark on the ruler to display a vertical dotted line in the document window, which indicates the proposed location of the first line of the paragraph (Figure 2–15).

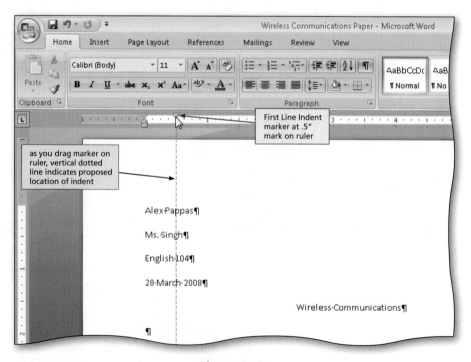

Figure 2–15

3

- Release the mouse button to place the First Line Indent marker at the .5" mark on the ruler, or one-half inch from the left margin (Figure 2–16).

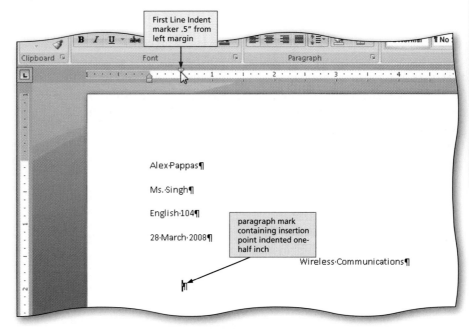

Figure 2–16

4

- Type Wireless communications are everywhere. People around the world regularly send and receive messages wirelessly, that is, transmitted through the air. and notice that Word automatically indented the first line of the paragraph by one-half inch (Figure 2–17).

Will I have to set first-line indent for each paragraph in the paper?

No. Each time you press the ENTER key, paragraph formatting in the previous paragraph carries forward to the next paragraph. Thus, once you set the first-line indent, its format carries forward automatically to each subsequent paragraph you type.

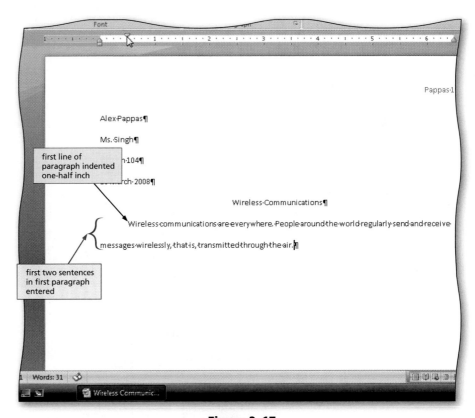

Figure 2–17

Other Ways
1. Right-click paragraph, click Paragraph on shortcut menu, click Indents and Spacing tab, click Special box arrow, click First line, click OK button   2. Click Paragraph Dialog Box Launcher, click Indents and Spacing tab, click Special box arrow, click First line, click OK button   3. Press TAB key at beginning of paragraph

To Create a Quick Style

Recall from Chapter 1 that a Quick Style is a predefined style that appears in the Styles gallery on the Ribbon. You use styles in the Styles gallery to apply defined formats to text. Later in this chapter, you will apply the formats of the research paper paragraph to the paragraphs in the footnote. To accomplish this task, you can create a Quick Style based on the formats in the current paragraph. That is, text is double-spaced with the first line of the paragraph indented and no space after the paragraph. The following steps first select the paragraph and then create a Quick Style based on the formats in the selected paragraph.

- Position the mouse pointer in the paragraph below the title and then triple-click; that is, press the mouse button three times in rapid succession, to select the paragraph.

- Right-click the selected paragraph to display a shortcut menu.

- Point to Styles on the shortcut menu to display the Styles submenu (Figure 2–18).

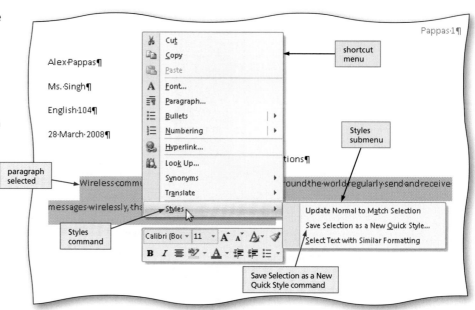

Figure 2–18

- Click Save Selection as a New Quick Style on the Styles sub-menu to display the Create New Style from Formatting dialog box.

- Type `Research Paper Paragraphs` in the Name text box (Figure 2–19).

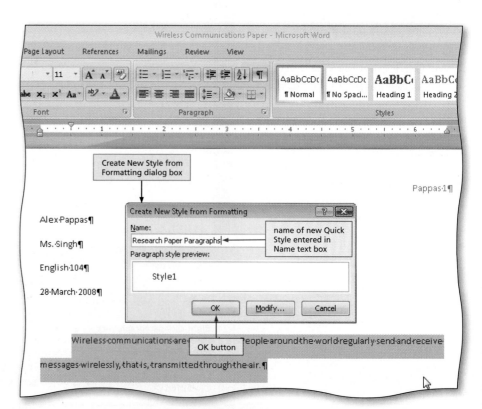

Figure 2–19

3

- Click the OK button to create the new Quick Style and add it to the Styles gallery (Figure 2–20).

Q&A

How can I see the formats assigned to a Quick Style?

Click the Styles Dialog Box Launcher. When the Styles task pane appears, position the mouse pointer on any style to display its formats in a ScreenTip. When finished, click the Close button in the task pane.

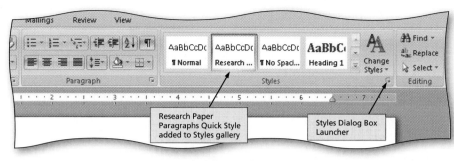

Figure 2–20

Other Ways

1. Click More button in Styles gallery on Home tab, click Save Selection as a New Quick Style, enter name of new Quick Style, click OK button

To AutoCorrect as You Type

As you type, you may make typing, spelling, capitalization, or grammar errors. For this reason, Word provides an **AutoCorrect** feature that automatically corrects these kinds of errors as you type them in the document. For example, if you type the text ahve, Word automatically changes it to the correct spelling, have, when you press the SPACEBAR or a punctuation mark key such as a period or comma.

Word has predefined many commonly misspelled words, which it automatically corrects for you. In the following steps, the word wireless is misspelled intentionally as wreless to illustrate the AutoCorrect as you type feature.

1

- Press CTRL+END to move the insertion point to the end of the document.

- Press the SPACEBAR.

- Type the beginning of the next sentence, misspelling the word, wireless, as follows: Three types of wireless communications include wireless messaging services, wreless (Figure 2–21).

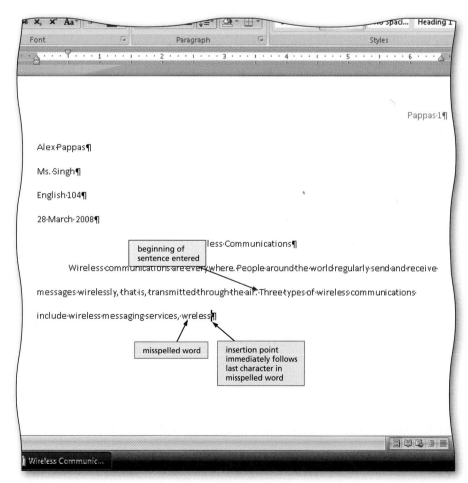

Figure 2–21

● **2**

- Press the SPACEBAR and watch Word automatically correct the misspelled word.

- Type the rest of the sentence (Figure 2–22): Internet access points, and global positioning systems.

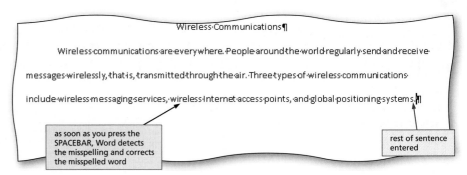

as soon as you press the SPACEBAR, Word detects the misspelling and corrects the misspelled word

rest of sentence entered

Figure 2–22

To Use the AutoCorrect Options Button

When you position the mouse pointer on text that Word automatically corrected, a small blue box appears below the text. If you point to the small blue box, Word displays the AutoCorrect Options button. When you click the **AutoCorrect Options button**, Word displays a menu that allows you to undo a correction or change how Word handles future automatic corrections of this type. The following steps illustrate the AutoCorrect Options button and menu.

● **1**

- Position the mouse pointer in the text automatically corrected by Word (in this case, the word wireless) to display a small blue box below the automatically corrected word (Figure 2–23).

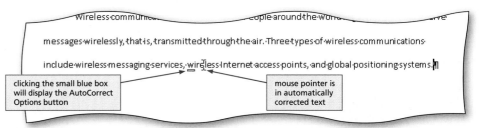

clicking the small blue box will display the AutoCorrect Options button

mouse pointer is in automatically corrected text

Figure 2–23

● **2**

- Point to the small blue box to display the AutoCorrect Options button.

- Click the AutoCorrect Options button to display the AutoCorrect Options menu (Figure 2–24).

- Press the ESCAPE key to remove the AutoCorrect Options menu from the screen.

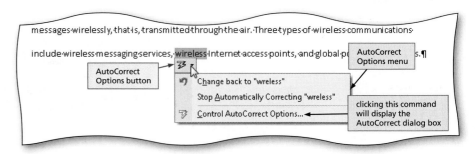

AutoCorrect Options button

AutoCorrect Options menu

Change back to "wreless"

Stop Automatically Correcting "wreless"

Control AutoCorrect Options...

clicking this command will display the AutoCorrect dialog box

Figure 2–24

Q&A

Do I need to remove the AutoCorrect Options button from the screen?

No. When you move the mouse pointer, the AutoCorrect Options button will disappear from the screen. If, for some reason, you wanted to remove the AutoCorrect Options button from the screen, you could press the ESCAPE key a second time.

To Create an AutoCorrect Entry

In addition to the predefined list of AutoCorrect spelling, capitalization, and grammar errors, you can create your own AutoCorrect entries to add to the list. For example, if you tend to type the word mobile as moble, you should create an AutoCorrect entry for it. The following steps create an AutoCorrect entry.

1
- Click the Office Button to display the Office Button menu (Figure 2–25).

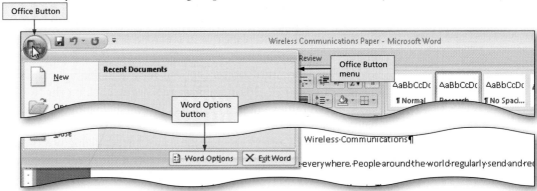

Figure 2–25

2
- Click the Word Options button on the Office Button menu to display the Word Options dialog box.

- Click Proofing in the left pane to display proofing options in the right pane.

- Click the AutoCorrect Options button in the right pane to display the AutoCorrect dialog box.

- When Word displays the AutoCorrect dialog box, type moble in the Replace text box.

- Press the TAB key and then type mobile in the With text box (Figure 2–26).

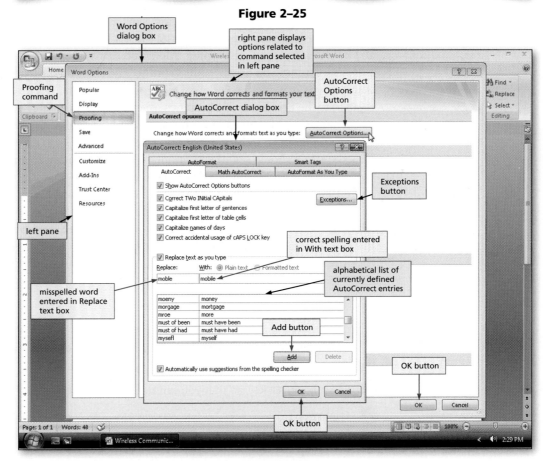

Figure 2–26

3
- Click the Add button in the AutoCorrect dialog box. (If your dialog box displays a Replace button instead, click it and then click the Yes button in the Microsoft Office Word dialog box.)

- Click the OK button to add the entry alphabetically to the list of words to correct automatically as you type.

- Click the OK button in the Word Options dialog box.

The AutoCorrect Dialog Box

In addition to creating AutoCorrect entries for words you commonly misspell or mistype, you can create entries for abbreviations, codes, and so on. For example, you could create an AutoCorrect entry for asap, indicating that Word should replace this text with the phrase, as soon as possible.

If, for some reason, you do not want Word to correct automatically as you type, you can turn off the Replace text as you type feature by clicking the Word Options button on the Office Button menu, clicking Proofing in the left pane of the Word Options dialog box, clicking the AutoCorrect Options button in the right pane of the Word Options dialog box (Figure 2–26 on the previous page), clicking the 'Replace text as you type' check box to remove the check mark, and then clicking the OK button in each open dialog box.

The AutoCorrect sheet in the AutoCorrect dialog box (Figure 2–26) contains other check boxes that correct capitalization errors if the check boxes are selected. If you type two capital letters in a row, such as TH, Word makes the second letter lowercase, Th. If you begin a sentence with a lowercase letter, Word capitalizes the first letter of the sentence. If you type the name of a day in lowercase, such as tuesday, Word capitalizes the first letter of the day, Tuesday. If you leave the CAPS LOCK key on and begin a new sentence, such as aFTER, Word corrects the typing, After, and turns off the CAPS LOCK key.

Sometimes you do not want Word to AutoCorrect a particular word or phrase. For example, you may use the code WD. in your documents. Because Word automatically capitalizes the first letter of a sentence, the character you enter following the period will be capitalized (in the previous sentence, it would capitalize the letter i in the word, in). To allow the code WD. to be entered into a document and still leave the AutoCorrect feature turned on, you should set an exception. To set an exception to an AutoCorrect rule, click the Word Options button on the Office Button menu, click Proofing in the left pane of the Word Options dialog box, click the AutoCorrect Options button in the right pane of the Word Options dialog box, click the Exceptions button (Figure 2–26), click the appropriate tab in the AutoCorrect Exceptions dialog box, type the exception entry in the text box, click the Add button, click the Close button in the AutoCorrect Exceptions dialog box, and then click the OK button in each of the remaining dialog boxes.

To Enter More Text

The next step is to continue typing text in the research paper up to the location of the citation.

1 Press the ENTER key, so that you can begin typing the text in the second paragraph.

2 Type People use mobile phones, PDAs, and other mobile devices to access text messaging, instant messaging, and picture messaging services and then press the SPACEBAR.

Citations

Both the MLA and APA guidelines suggest the use of in-text parenthetical citations (placed at the end of a sentence), instead of footnoting each source of material in a paper. These parenthetical acknowledgments guide the reader to the end of the paper for complete information about the source.

Reference all sources.
During your research, be sure to record essential publication information about each of your sources. Following is a sample list of types of required information.

• Book: full name of author(s), complete title of book, edition (if available), volume (if available), publication city, publication year

• Magazine: full name of author(s), complete title of article, magazine title, date of magazine, page numbers of article

• Web site: full name of author(s), title of Web site, date viewed, Web address

Word provides tools to assist you with inserting citations in a paper and later generating a list of sources from the citations. With a documentation style selected, Word automatically formats the citations and list of sources. The process for adding citations in Word is as follows:

1. Modify the documentation style, if necessary.
2. Insert a citation placeholder.
3. Enter the source information for the citation.

You can combine Steps 2 and 3, where you insert the citation placeholder and enter the source information at once. Or, you can insert the citation placeholder as you write and then enter the source information for the citation at a later time. While entering the research paper in this chapter, you will use both methods.

To Change the Bibliography Style

The first step in inserting a citation is to be sure the citations and sources will be formatted using the correct documentation style, called the bibliography style in Word. The following steps change the specified documentation style.

1

• Click References on the Ribbon to display the References tab.

• Click the Bibliography Style box arrow on the References tab to display a gallery of predefined documentation styles (Figure 2–27).

2

• Click MLA in the Bibliography Style gallery to change the documentation style to MLA.

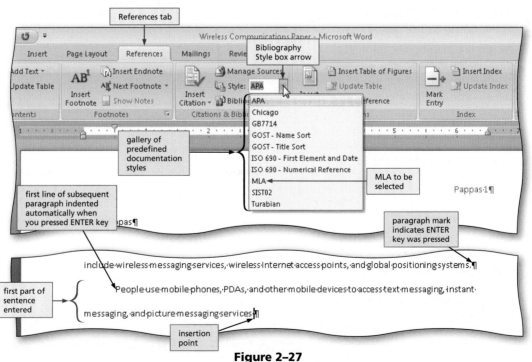

Figure 2–27

To Insert a Citation and Create Its Source

With the documentation style selected, the next task is to insert a citation placeholder and enter the source information. You can accomplish these steps at once by instructing Word to add a new source. The following steps add a new source for a magazine (periodical) article.

• Click the Insert Citation button on the References tab to display the Insert Citation menu (Figure 2–28).

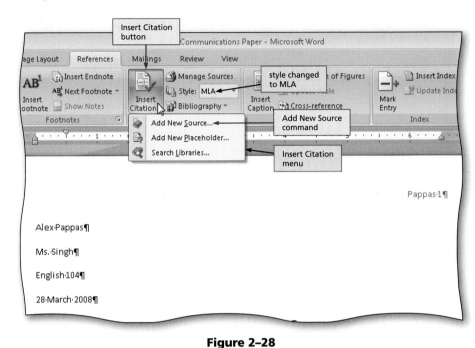

Figure 2–28

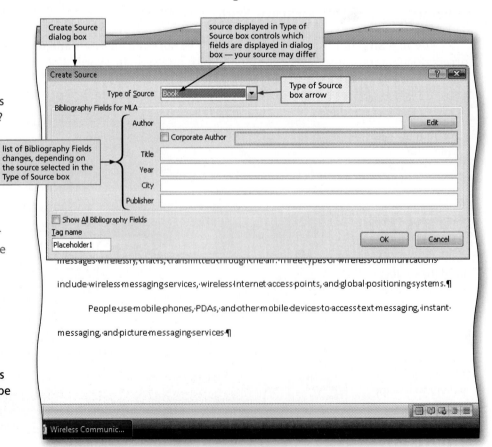

• Click Add New Source on the Insert Citation menu to display the Create Source dialog box (Figure 2–29).

Q&A What are the Bibliography Fields in the Create Source dialog box?

A **field** is a placeholder for data whose contents can change. You enter data in some fields; Word supplies data for others. In this case, you enter the contents of the fields for a particular source, for example, the author name in the Author field.

Experiment

• Click the Type of Source box arrow and then click one of the source types in the list, so that you can see how the list of fields changes to reflect the source type you selected.

Figure 2–29

3

- If necessary, click the Type of Source box arrow and then click Article in a Periodical, so that the list shows fields required for a magazine (periodical).

- Click the Author text box. Type Davies, Habika as the author.

- Click the Title text box. Type Text Messaging, Instant Messaging, and Picture Messaging as the article title.

- Press the TAB key and then type Computing in Today's World as the periodical title.

- Press the TAB key and then type 2008 as the year.

- Press the TAB key and then type January as the month.

- Press the TAB key twice and then type 34–42 as the pages (Figure 2–30).

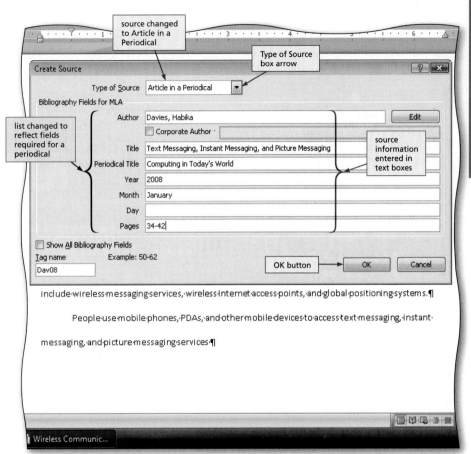

Figure 2–30

4

- Click the OK button to close the dialog box, create the source, and insert the citation in the document at the location of the insertion point (Figure 2–31).

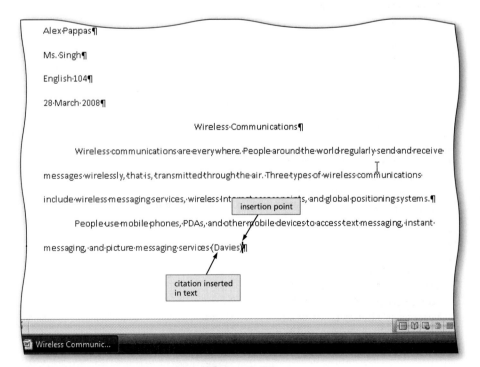

Figure 2–31

To Edit a Citation

In the MLA style, if a source has page numbers, you should include them in the citation. Thus, Word provides a means to enter the page numbers to be displayed in the citation. The following steps edit a citation, so that the page numbers appear in it.

- Click somewhere in the citation to be edited, in this case somewhere in (Davies), which selects the citation and displays the Citation Options box arrow.

- Click the Citation Options box arrow to display the Citation Options menu (Figure 2–32).

Q&A

What is the purpose of the tab to the left of the selected citation?

If, for some reason, you wanted to move a citation to a different location in the document, you would select it and then drag the citation tab to the desired location.

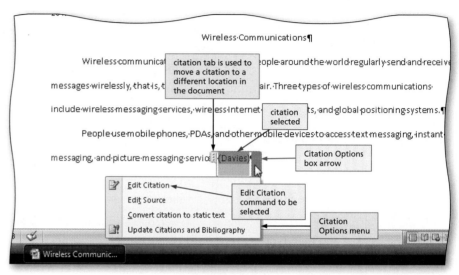

Figure 2–32

- Click Edit Citation on the Citation Options menu to display the Edit Citation dialog box.

- Type 34–42 in the Pages text box (Figure 2–33).

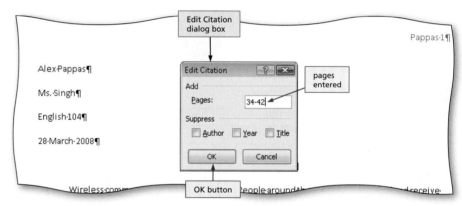

Figure 2–33

- Click the OK button to close the dialog box and add the page numbers to the citation in the document (Figure 2–34).

❹

- Press the END key to move the insertion point to the end of the line, which also deselects the citation.

- Press the PERIOD key to end the sentence.

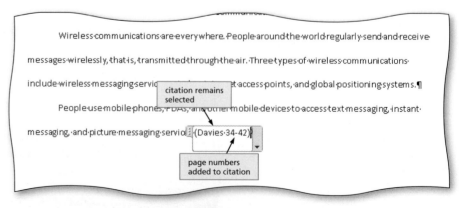

Figure 2–34

To Enter More Text

The next step is to continue typing text in the research paper up to the location of the footnote.

1 Press the SPACEBAR.

2 Type these three sentences (Figure 2–35): Through text messaging services, users send and receive short text messages, which usually consist of fewer than 300 characters. Wireless instant messaging is an Internet communications service that allows a wireless mobile device to exchange instant messages with one or more mobile devices or online personal computers. Users send graphics, pictures, video clips, sound files, and short text messages with picture messaging services.

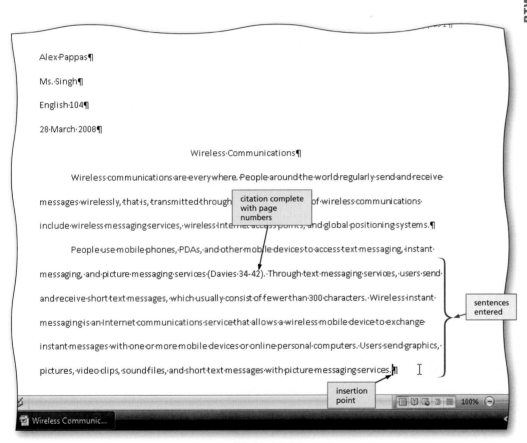

BTW

Edit a Source
To edit a source, click somewhere in the citation, click the Citation Options box arrow, and then click Edit Source on the Citation Options menu to display the Edit Source dialog box (which resembles the Create Source dialog box). Make necessary changes and then click the OK button.

Figure 2–35

Footnotes

As discussed earlier in this chapter, explanatory notes are optional in the MLA documentation style. They are used primarily to elaborate on points discussed in the body of a research paper. The MLA style specifies that a superscript (raised number) be used for a **note reference mark** to signal that an explanatory note exists either at the bottom of the page as a **footnote** or at the end of the document as an **endnote**.

In Word, **note text** can be any length and format. Word automatically numbers notes sequentially by placing a note reference mark in the body of the document and also to the left of the note text. If you insert, rearrange, or remove notes, Word renumbers any subsequent note reference marks according to their new sequence in the document.

To Insert a Footnote Reference Mark

The following step inserts a footnote reference mark in the document at the location of the insertion point and also at the location where the footnote text will be typed.

- With the insertion point positioned as shown in Figure 2–35 on the previous page, click the Insert Footnote button on the References tab to display a note reference mark (a superscripted 1) in two places: (1) in the document window at the location of the insertion point and (2) at the bottom of the page where the footnote will be positioned, just below a separator line (Figure 2–36).

Q&A What if I wanted explanatory notes to be positioned as endnotes instead of as footnotes?

You would click the Insert Endnote button on the References tab, which places the separator line and the endnote text at the end of the document, instead of the bottom of the page containing the reference.

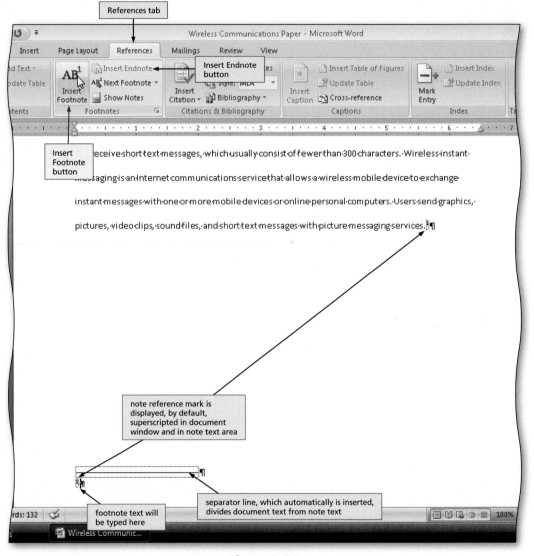

Figure 2–36

Other Ways

1. Press CTRL+ALT+F

To Enter Footnote Text

The next step is to type the footnote text to the right of the note reference mark below the separator line.

 Type the footnote text up to the citation: Podpora and Ruiz indicate that some messaging services use the term, video messaging, to refer separately to the capability of sending video clips **and then press the SPACEBAR.**

To Insert a Citation Placeholder

Earlier in this chapter, you inserted a citation and its source at once. Sometimes, you may not have the source information readily available and would prefer entering it at a later time.

In the footnote, you will insert a placeholder for the citation and enter the source information later. The following steps insert a citation placeholder.

- With the insertion point positioned as shown in Figure 2–37, click the Insert Citation button on the References tab to display the Insert Citation menu (Figure 2–37).

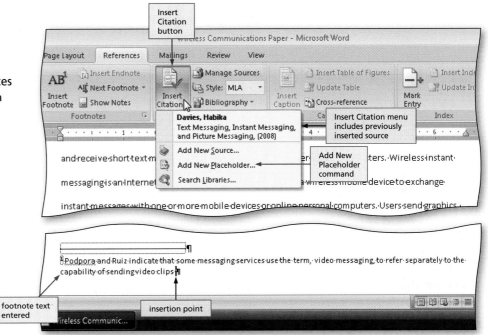

Figure 2–37

- Click Add New Placeholder on the Insert Citation menu to display the Placeholder Name dialog box.

- Type Podpora as the tag name for the source (Figure 2–38).

Q&A

What is a tag name?

A tag name is an identifier that links a citation to a source. Word automatically creates a tag name when you enter a source. When you create a citation placeholder, enter a meaningful tag name, which will appear in the citation placeholder until you edit the source.

- Click the OK button to close the dialog box and insert the tag name in the citation placeholder.

- Press the PERIOD key to end the sentence.

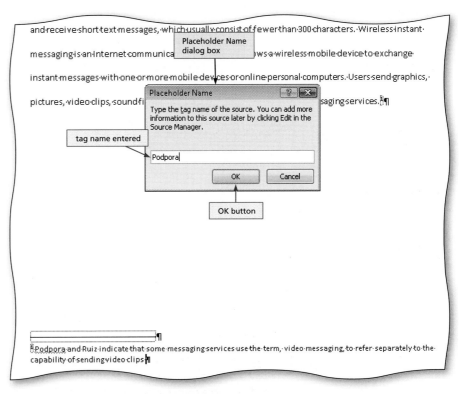

Figure 2–38

Footnote Text Style

When you insert a footnote, Word formats it using the Footnote Text style, which does not adhere to the MLA documentation style. For example, notice in Figure 2–38 on the previous page that the footnote text is single-spaced, left-aligned, and a smaller font size than the text in the research paper. According to the MLA style, notes should be formatted like all other paragraphs in the paper.

You could change the paragraph formatting of the footnote text to first-line indent and double-spacing and then change the font size from 10 to 11 point. If you use this technique, however, you will need to change the format of the footnote text for each footnote you enter into the document.

A more efficient technique is to modify the format of the Footnote Text style so that every footnote you enter in the document will use the formats defined in this style.

To Modify a Style Using a Shortcut Menu

The Footnote Text style should be based on the Research Paper Paragraphs style defined earlier in this chapter. Because the Footnote Text style specifically set paragraphs to single-spaced and the font size to 10 point, you will need to modify those formats to double-spaced paragraphs and 11-point font. The following steps modify the Footnote Text style.

- Right-click the note text in the footnote to display a shortcut menu related to footnotes (Figure 2–39).

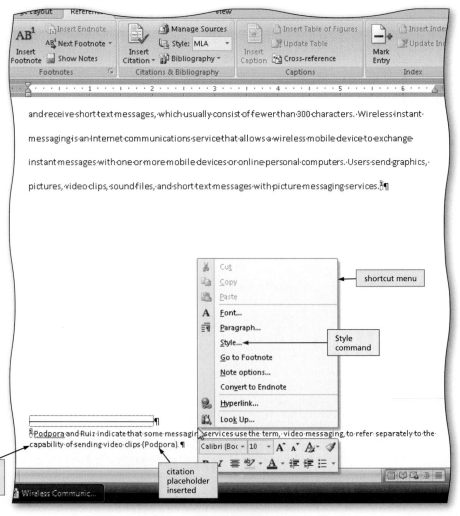

footnote paragraphs should be formatted the same as other paragraphs in the research paper

citation placeholder inserted

Figure 2–39

2

- Click Style on the shortcut menu to display the Style dialog box. If necessary, click Footnote Text in the Styles list.

- Click the Modify button in the Style dialog box to display the Modify Style dialog box.

- Click the 'Style based on' box arrow and then click Research Paper Paragraphs so that the Footnote Text style is based on the Research Paper Paragraphs style.

- Click the 'Style for following paragraph' box arrow and then scroll to and click Research Paper Paragraphs so that the additional footnote paragraphs are based on the Research Paper Paragraphs style.

- Click the Font Size box arrow and then click 11 in the Font Size list to change the font size to 11.

- Click the Double Space button to set the line spacing to double (Figure 2–40).

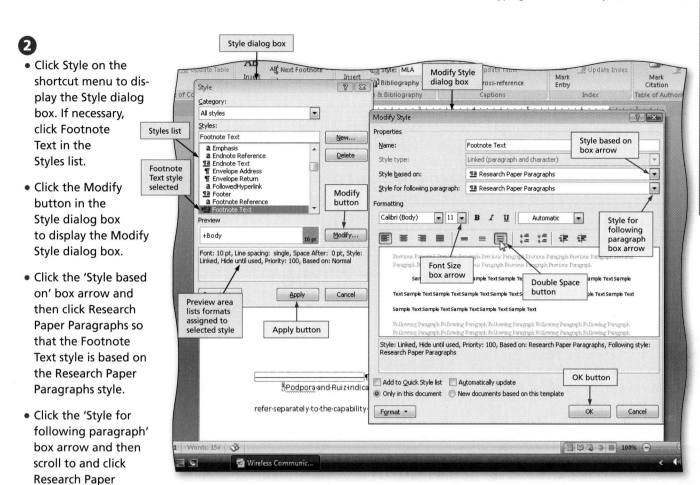

Figure 2–40

3

- Click the OK button in the Modify Style dialog box to close the dialog box.

- Click the Apply button in the Style dialog box to apply the style changes to the footnote text (Figure 2–41).

Q&A

Will all footnotes use this modified style?

Yes. Any future footnotes entered in the document will use an 11-point font with the paragraphs first-line indented and double-spaced.

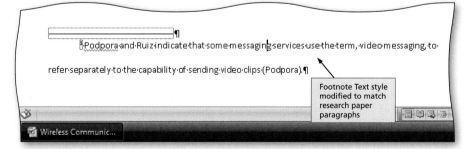

Figure 2–41

Other Ways

1. Click Styles Dialog Box Launcher, click Footnote Text in list, click Footnote Text box arrow, click Modify, change settings, click OK button

2. Click Styles Dialog Box Launcher, click Manage Styles button, scroll to Footnote Text and then select it, click Modify button, change settings, click OK button in each dialog box

To Edit a Source

When you typed the footnote text for this research paper, you inserted a citation placeholder for the source. You now have the source information and are ready to enter it. The following steps edit the source.

- Click somewhere in the citation placeholder to be edited, in this case (Podpora), to select the citation placeholder.

- Click the Citation Options box arrow to display the Citation Options menu (Figure 2–42).

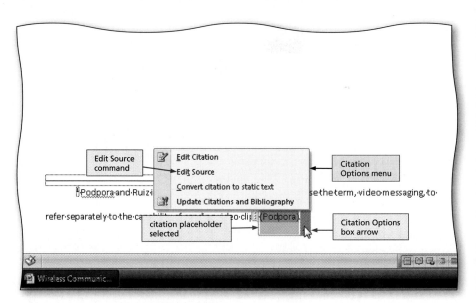

Figure 2–42

- Click Edit Source on the Citation Options menu to display the Edit Source dialog box.

- If necessary, click the Type of Source box arrow and then click Book, so that the list shows fields required for a book.

- Click the Author text box. Type `Podpora, Maxine C., and Adelbert D. Ruiz` as the author.

- Click the Title text box. Type `Advances in Wireless Internet Access Point Technology` as the book title.

- Press the TAB key and then type `2008` as the year.

- Press the TAB key and then type `Dallas` as the city.

- Press the TAB key and then type `Wells Publishing` as the publisher (Figure 2–43).

- Click the OK button to close the dialog box and create the source.

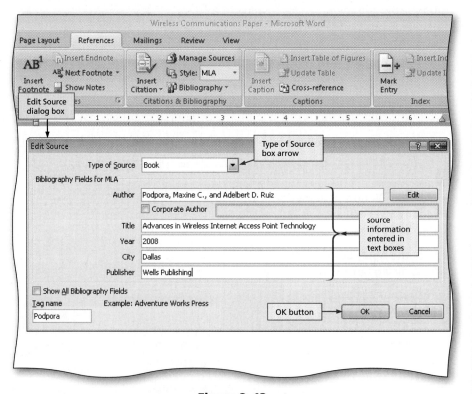

Figure 2–43

Other Ways

1. Click Manage Sources button on References tab, click placeholder source in Current List, click Edit button

To Edit a Citation

In the MLA style, if you reference the author's name in the text, you should not list it again in the parenthetical citation. Instead, just list the page number in the citation. The following steps edit the citation, suppressing the author but displaying the page numbers.

1 If necessary, click somewhere in the citation to be edited, in this case (Podpora), to select the citation and display the Citation Options box arrow.

2 Click the Citation Options box arrow to display the Citation Options menu.

3 Click Edit Citation on the Citation Options menu to display the Edit Citation dialog box.

4 Type 79-82 in the Pages text box.

5 Click the Author check box to place a check mark in it (Figure 2–44).

6 Click the OK button to close the dialog box, remove the author name from the citation in the footnote, and add page numbers to the citation.

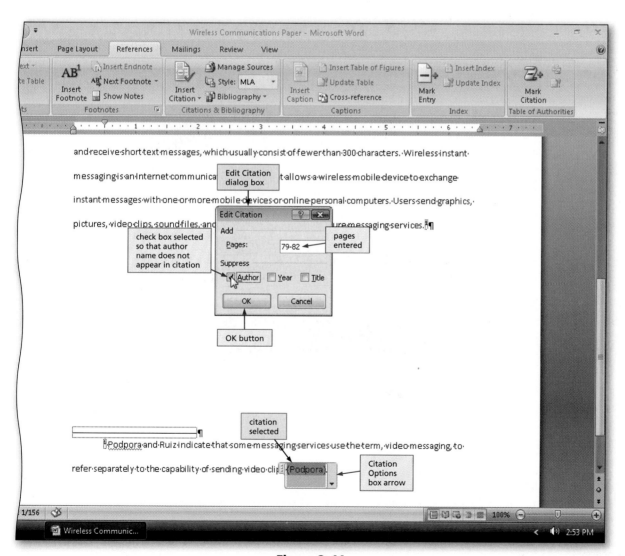

Figure 2–44

Working with Footnotes and Endnotes

You edit footnote text just as you edit any other text in the document. To delete or move a note reference mark, however, you must be in the document text (not in the footnote text).

To delete a note, select the note reference mark in the document text (not in the footnote text) by dragging through the note reference mark and then click the Cut button on the Home tab. Another way to delete a note is to click immediately to the right of the note reference mark in the document text and then press the BACKSPACE key twice, or click immediately to the left of the note reference mark in the document text and then press the DELETE key twice.

To move a note to a different location in a document, select the note reference mark in the document text (not in the footnote text), click the Cut button on the Home tab, click the location where you want to move the note, and then click the Paste button on the Home tab. When you move or delete notes, Word automatically renumbers any remaining notes in the correct sequence.

If you position the mouse pointer on the note reference mark, the note text displays above the note reference mark as a ScreenTip. To remove the ScreenTip, move the mouse pointer.

If, for some reason, you wanted to change the format of note reference marks in footnotes or endnotes (i.e., from 1, 2, 3, to A, B, C), you would click the Footnotes Dialog Box Launcher to display the Footnote and Endnote dialog box, click the Number format box arrow, click the desired number format in the list, and then click the OK button.

If, for some reason, you wanted to convert footnotes to endnotes, you would click the Footnotes Dialog Box Launcher to display the Footnote and Endnote dialog box, click the Convert button, make sure the 'Convert all footnotes to endnotes' option button is selected, click the OK button, and then click the Close button in the Footnote and Endnote dialog box.

To Enter More Text

The next step is to continue typing text in the body of the research paper.

1 Position the insertion point after the note reference mark in the document, and then press the ENTER key.

2 Type the third paragraph of the research paper (Figure 2–45): `In many public locations, people connect to the Internet through a wireless Internet access point using mobile computers and devices. Two types of wireless Internet access points are hot spots and 3-G networks. A 3-G network, which uses cellular radio technology, enables users to connect to the Internet through a mobile phone or computer equipped with an appropriate PC Card. A hot spot is a wireless network that allows mobile users to check e-mail, browse the Web, and access any Internet service - as long as their computers or devices have the proper wireless capability.`

BTW

Spacing after Punctuation
Because word processing documents use variable character fonts, it often is difficult to determine in a printed document how many times someone has pressed the SPACEBAR between sentences. The rule is to press the SPACEBAR only once after periods, colons, and other punctuation marks.

To Count Words

Often when you write papers, you are required to compose the papers with a minimum number of words. The minimum requirement for the research paper in this chapter is 325 words. You can look on the status bar and see the total number of words thus far in a document. For example, Figure 2–45 shows the research paper has 250 words, but you are not sure if that count includes the words in your footnote. The following steps display the Word Count dialog box, so that you can verify whether the footnote text is included in the count.

1

- Click the Word Count indicator on the status bar to display the Word Count dialog box.

- If necessary, place a check mark in the 'Include textboxes, footnotes and endnotes' check box (Figure 2-45).

Q&A Why do the statistics in my Word Count dialog box differ from Figure 2–45?

Depending on the accuracy of your typing, your statistics may differ.

2

- Click the Close button to close the dialog box.

Q&A Can I display statistics for just a section of the document?

Yes. Select the section and then click the Word Count indicator on the status bar to display statistics about the selected text.

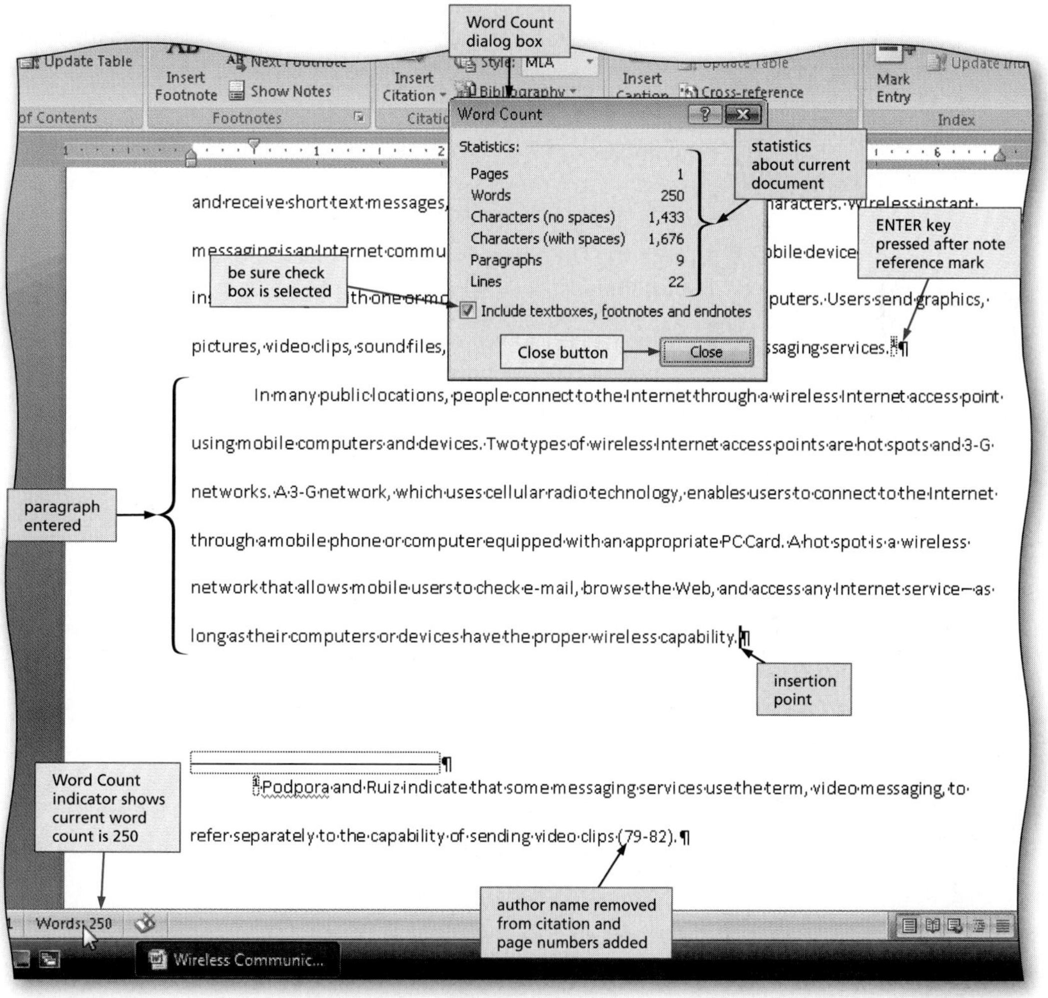

Figure 2–45

Other Ways

1. Click Word Count button on Review tab
2. Press CTRL+SHIFT+G

Automatic Page Breaks

As you type documents that exceed one page, Word automatically inserts page breaks, called **automatic page breaks** or **soft page breaks**, when it determines the text has filled one page according to paper size, margin settings, line spacing, and other settings. If you add text, delete text, or modify text on a page, Word recomputes the location of automatic page breaks and adjusts them accordingly.

Word performs page recomputation between the keystrokes, that is, in between the pauses in your typing. Thus, Word refers to the automatic page break task as **background repagination**. The steps on the next page illustrate Word's automatic page break feature.

To Enter More Text and Insert a Citation Placeholder

The next task is to type the fourth paragraph in the body of the research paper.

1 With the insertion point positioned at the end of the third paragraph as shown in Figure 2–45 on the previous page, press the ENTER key. Type the fourth paragraph of the research paper (Figure 2–46): `A global positioning system (GPS) is a navigation system that consists of one or more earth-based receivers that accept and analyze signals sent by satellites in order to determine the receiver's geographic location, according to Shelly and Cashman` and then press the SPACEBAR.

2 Click the Insert Citation button on the References tab to display the Insert Citation menu. Click Add New Placeholder on the Insert Citation menu to display the Placeholder Name dialog box.

3 Type `Shelly` as the tag name for the source.

4 Click the OK button to close the dialog box and insert the tag name in the citation placeholder.

5 Press the PERIOD key to end the sentence. Press the SPACEBAR. Type `A GPS receiver is a handheld, mountable, or embedded device that contains an antenna, a radio receiver, and a processor. Many mobile devices, such as mobile phones and PDAs, have GPS capability built into the device.`

6 Press the ENTER key.

Page Break Locations
As you type, your page break may occur at different locations depending on Word settings and the type of printer connected to the computer.

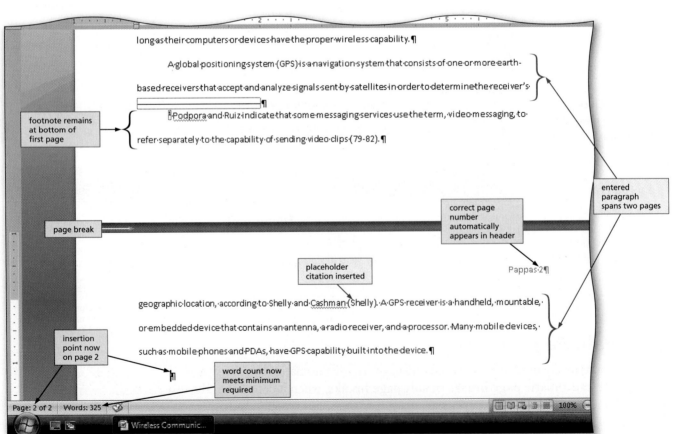

Figure 2–46

To Edit a Source

When you typed the fourth paragraph of the research paper, you inserted a citation placeholder, Shelly, for the source. You now have the source information, which is for a Web site, and are ready to enter it. The following steps edit the source for the Shelly citation placeholder.

1 Click somewhere in the citation placeholder to be edited, in this case (Shelly), to select the citation placeholder.

2 Click the Citation Options box arrow to display the Citation Options menu.

3 Click Edit Source on the Citation Options menu to display the Edit Source dialog box.

4 If necessary, click the Type of Source box arrow; scroll to and then click Web site, so that the list shows fields required for a Web site.

5 Place a check mark in the Show All Bibliography Fields check box to display more fields related to Web sites.

6 Click the Author text box. Type `Shelly, Gary B., and Thomas J. Cashman` as the author.

7 Click the Name of Web Page text box. Type `How a GPS Works` as the Web page title.

8 Click the Production Company text box. Type `Course Technology` as the production company.

9 Click the Year Accessed text box. Type `2008` as the year.

10 Press the TAB key and then type `March` as the month accessed.

Q&A

What if some of the text boxes disappear as I enter the Web site fields?

With the Show All Bibliography Fields check box selected, all Web site fields may not be able to be displayed in the dialog box at the same time. In this case, some may scroll up.

11 Press the TAB key and then type `21` as the day accessed.

12 Press the TAB key and then type `www.scsite.com/wd2007/pr2/wc.htm` as the URL (Figure 2–47).

13 Click the OK button to close the dialog box and create the source.

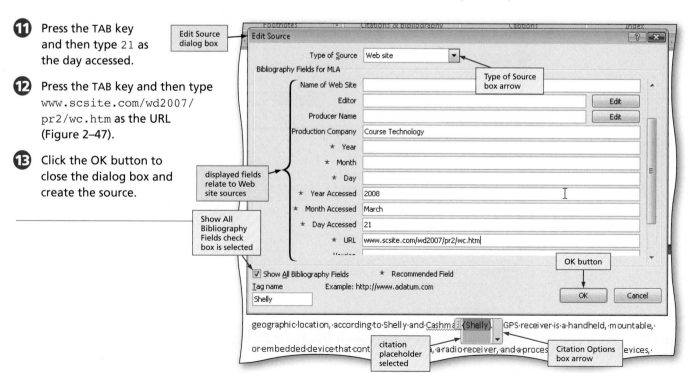

Figure 2–47

To Edit a Citation

As mentioned earlier, if you reference the author's name in the text, you should not list it again in the parenthetical citation. For Web site citations, when you suppress the author's name, the citation shows the Web site name because page numbers do not apply. The following steps edit the citation, suppressing the author and displaying the name of the Web site instead.

1 If necessary, click somewhere in the citation to be edited, in this case (Shelly), to select the citation and display the Citation Options box arrow.

2 Click the Citation Options box arrow and then click Edit Citation on the Citation Options menu to display the Edit Citation dialog box.

3 Click the Author check box to place a check mark in it (Figure 2–48).

4 Click the OK button to close the dialog box, remove the author name from the citation, and show the name of the Web site in the citation.

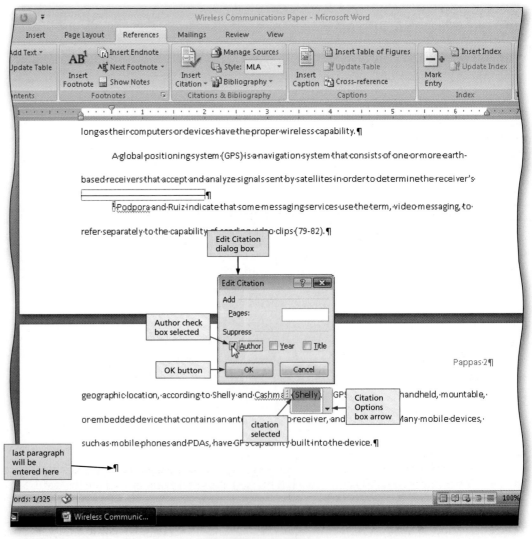

Figure 2–48

To Enter More Text

The next step is to type the last paragraph of text in the research paper.

1 Position the insertion point on the paragraph mark below the fourth paragraph in the research paper (Figure 2–48).

2 Type the last paragraph of the research paper (Figure 2–49):
Mobile users communicate wirelessly through wireless messaging services, wireless Internet access points, and global positioning systems. Anyone can take advantage of wireless communications using mobile computers and devices.

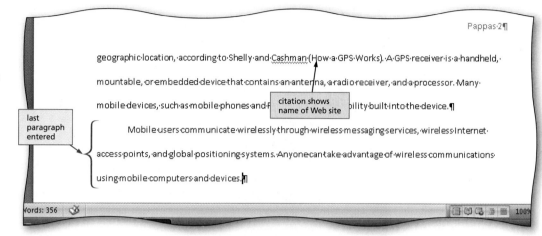

Pappas·2¶

geographic·location,·according·to·Shelly·and·Cashman·(How·a·GPS·Works).·A·GPS·receiver·is·a·handheld,·
mountable,·or·embedded·device·that·contains·an·antenna,·a·radio·receiver,·and·a·processor.·Many·
mobile·devices,·such·as·mobile·phones·and·P_____·bility·built·into·the·device.¶

citation shows name of Web site

Mobile·users·communicate·wirelessly·through·wireless·messaging·services,·wireless·Internet·
access·points,·and·global·positioning·systems.·Anyone·can·take·advantage·of·wireless·communications·
using·mobile·computers·and·devices.¶

last paragraph entered

Words: 356   100%

Figure 2–49

To Save an Existing Document with the Same File Name

You have made several edits to the research paper since you last saved it. Thus, you should save it again. The following step saves the document again.

1 Click the Save button on the Quick Access Toolbar to overwrite the previous Wireless Communications Paper file on the USB flash drive.

Creating an Alphabetical Works Cited Page

According to the MLA style, the **works cited page** is a list of sources that are referenced directly in a research paper. You place the list on a separate numbered page with the title, Works Cited, centered one inch from the top margin. The works are to be alphabetized by the author's last name or, if the work has no author, by the work's title. The first line of each entry begins at the left margin. Indent subsequent lines of the same entry one-half inch from the left margin.

Create the list of sources.
A **bibliography** is an alphabetical list of sources referenced in a paper. Whereas the text of the research paper contains brief references to the source (the citations), the bibliography lists all publication information about the source. Documentation styles differ significantly in their guidelines for preparing a bibliography. Each style identifies formats for various sources including books, magazines, pamphlets, newspapers, Web sites, television programs, paintings, maps, advertisements, letters, memos, and much more. You can find information about various styles and their guidelines in printed style guides and on the Web.

Plan Ahead

To Page Break Manually

The works cited are to be displayed on a separate numbered page. Thus, you must insert a manual page break following the body of the research paper so that the list of sources is displayed on a separate page. A **manual page break**, or **hard page break**, is one that you force into the document at a specific location.

Word never moves or adjusts manual page breaks; however, Word adjusts any automatic page breaks that follow a manual page break. Word inserts manual page breaks immediately above the location of the insertion point. The following step inserts a manual page break after the text of the research paper.

- With the insertion point at the end of the text of the research paper (Figure 2-49 on the previous page), press the ENTER key.

- Then, press CTRL+ENTER to insert a manual page break immediately above the insertion point and position the insertion point immediately below the manual page break (Figure 2–50).

- Scroll to position the top of the third page closer to the ruler.

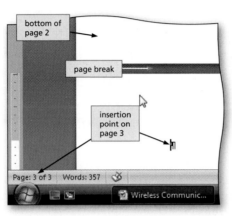
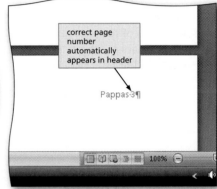

Figure 2–50

Other Ways

1. Click Page Break button on Insert tab

To Center the Title of the Works Cited Page

The works cited title is to be centered between the margins of the paper. If you simply issue the Center command, the title will not be centered properly. Instead, it will be one-half inch to the right of the center point because earlier you set first-line indent at one-half inch. Recall that Word is indenting the first line of every paragraph one-half inch.

To properly center the title of the works cited page, you must move the First Line Indent marker back to the left margin before centering the paragraph.

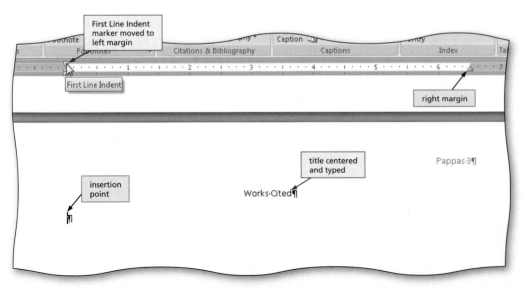
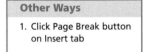

Figure 2–51

1️⃣ Drag the First Line Indent marker to the 0" mark on the ruler, which is at the left margin, to remove the first-line indent setting.

2️⃣ Press CTRL+E to center the paragraph mark.

3️⃣ Type Works Cited as the title.

4️⃣ Press the ENTER key.

5️⃣ Press CTRL+L to left-align the paragraph mark (Figure 2–51).

To Create the Bibliographical List

While typing the research paper, you created several citations and their sources. Word can format the list of sources and alphabetize them in a **bibliographical list**, saving you time looking up style guidelines. That is, Word will create a bibliographical list with each element of the source placed in its correct position with proper formatting and punctuation, according to the specified style. For example, in this research paper, the book source will list, in this order, the author name(s), book title, publisher city, publishing company name, and publication year with the book title underlined and the correct punctuation between each element according to the MLA style. The following steps create a MLA formatted bibliographical list from the sources previously entered.

1

- With the insertion point positioned as shown in Figure 2–52, click the Bibliography button on the References tab to display the Bibliography gallery (Figure 2–52).

Will I select Works Cited from the Bibliography gallery?

No. The title it inserts is not formatted according to the MLA style. Thus, you will use the Insert Bibliography command instead.

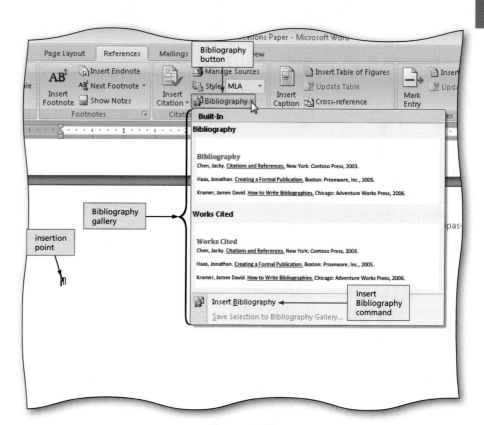

Figure 2–52

2

- Click Insert Bibliography in the Bibliography gallery to insert a list of sources at the location of the insertion point.

- If necessary, scroll to display the entire list of sources in the document window (Figure 2–53).

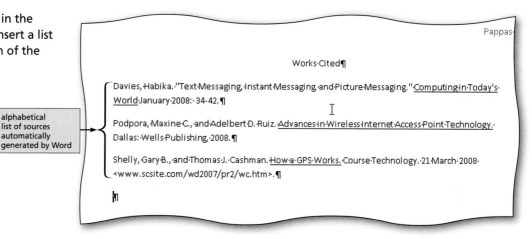

Figure 2–53

To Modify a Style Using the Styles Task Pane

Although the format within each entry in the bibliographical list meets the MLA style, the paragraph formatting does not. Currently, entries are based on the Normal style, which does not have the correct line or paragraph spacing. Thus, you will modify the style so that it is based on the No Spacing style (no blank space before or after a paragraph) and change its line spacing to double. The following steps modify the Bibliography style.

1

- Click somewhere in the list of sources to position the insertion point in a paragraph formatted with the Bibliography style.

Q&A

Why did the list of sources turn gray?

The entire list of sources is a field that Word automatically updates each time you make a change to one of the sources. Word, by default, shades fields gray on the screen to help you identify them. The gray shading, however, will not appear in the printed document.

- Click Home on the Ribbon to display the Home tab.

- Click the Styles Dialog Box Launcher to display the Styles task pane.

- If necessary, scroll to Bibliography in the Styles task pane. Click Bibliography to select it, if necessary, and then click its box arrow to display the Bibliography menu (Figure 2–54).

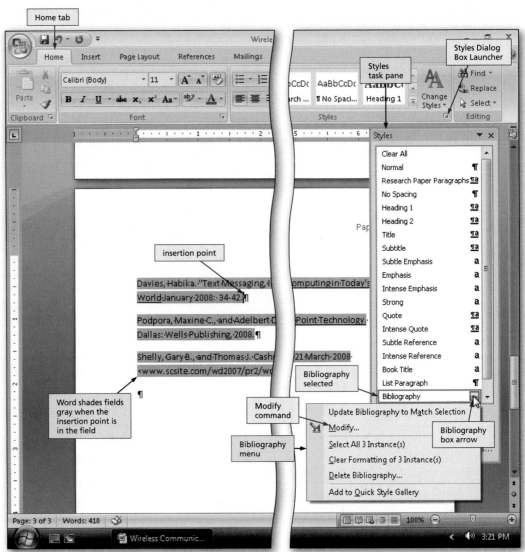

Figure 2–54

2

- Click Modify on the Bibliography menu to display the Modify Style dialog box.

- Click the 'Style based on' box arrow and then click No Spacing to base the Bibliography style on the No Spacing style.

- Click the 'Style for following paragraph' box arrow and then click No Spacing to base additional bibliographical paragraphs on the No Spacing style.

- Click the Double Space button to set the line spacing to double.

- Place a check mark in the Automatically update check box so that any future changes you make to the bibliographical paragraphs will update the Bibliography style automatically (Figure 2–55).

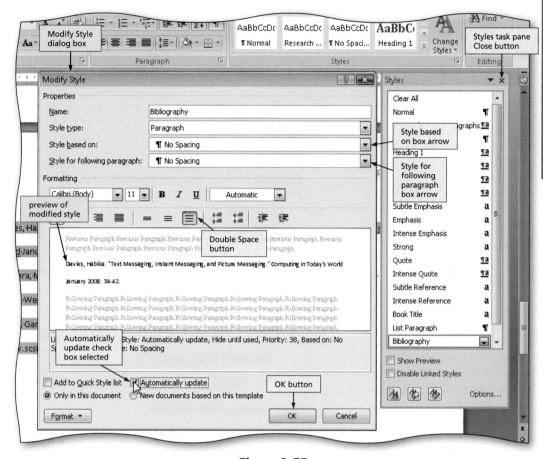

Figure 2–55

3

- Click the OK button in the Modify Style dialog box to close the dialog box and apply the style changes to the paragraphs in the document.

- Click the Close button on the Styles task pane title bar to close the task pane (Figure 2–56).

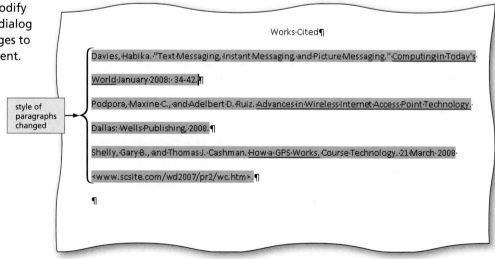

Figure 2–56

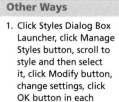

Other Ways

1. Click Styles Dialog Box Launcher, click Manage Styles button, scroll to style and then select it, click Modify button, change settings, click OK button in each dialog box

To Create a Hanging Indent

Currently, the first line of each source entry begins at the left margin. Subsequent lines in the same paragraph are to be indented one-half inch from the left margin. In essence, the first line hangs to the left of the rest of the paragraph; thus, this type of paragraph formatting is called a **hanging indent**.

One method of creating a hanging indent is to use the horizontal ruler. The **Hanging Indent marker** is the bottom triangle at the 0" mark on the ruler (Figure 2–57). The following steps create a hanging indent using the horizontal ruler.

- With the insertion point in the paragraph to format, point to the Hanging Indent marker on the ruler (Figure 2–57).

- Drag the Hanging Indent marker to the .5" mark on the ruler to set the hanging indent to one-half inch from the left margin (Figure 2–58).

Q&A

Why were all three bibliographical paragraphs formatted with a hanging indent?

When you make a change to a paragraph based on the Bibliography style, the style is updated and all paragraphs based on that style also change because you selected the Automatically update check box in the Modify Style dialog box (shown in Figure 2–55 on the previous page).

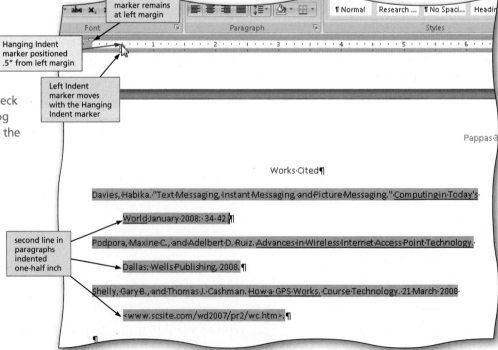

Figure 2–57

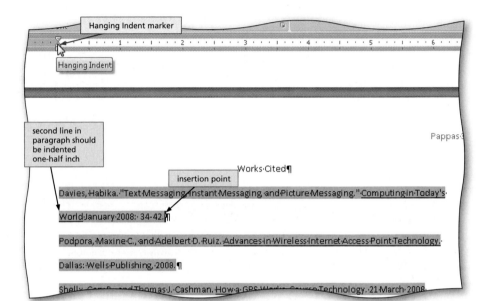

Figure 2–58

Other Ways

1. Right-click paragraph, click Paragraph on shortcut menu, click Indents and Spacing tab, click Special box arrow, click Hanging, click OK button
2. Click Paragraph Dialog Box Launcher, click Indents and Spacing tab, click Special box arrow, click Hanging, click OK button
3. Press CTRL+T

To Modify a Source and Update the Bibliographical List

If you modify the contents of any source, the list of sources automatically updates because the list is a field. The following steps modify the title of the magazine article.

1

- Click References on the Ribbon to display the References tab.

- Click the Manage Sources button on the References tab to display the Source Manager dialog box.

- Click the source you wish to edit in the Current List.

- Click the Edit button to display the Edit Source dialog box.

- In the Title text box, add the word, Services, to the end of the title (Figure 2–59).

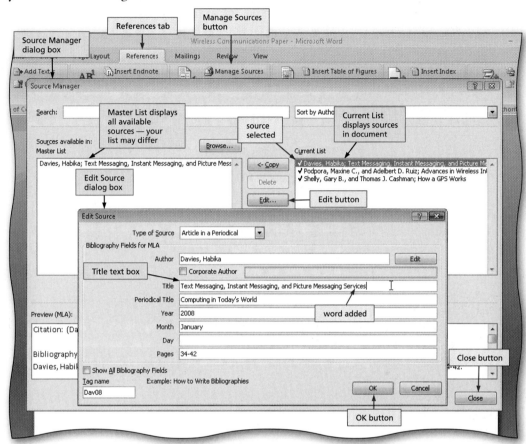

Figure 2–59

2

- Click the OK button to close the Edit Source dialog box.

- If a Microsoft Office Word dialog box appears, click its Yes button to update all occurrences of the source.

- Click the Close button in the Source Manager dialog box to update the list of sources in the document (Figure 2–60).

What if the list of sources in the document does not update automatically?

Click in the list of sources and then press the F9 key, which is the shortcut key to update a field.

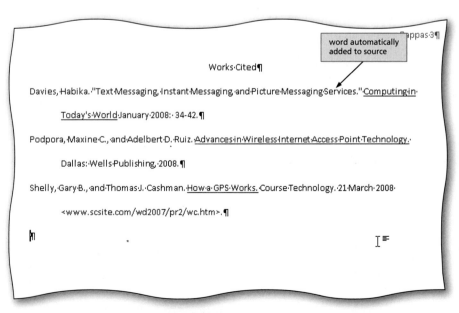

Works Cited¶

Davies, Habika. "Text Messaging, Instant Messaging, and Picture Messaging Services." Computing in

Today's World January 2008: 34-42. ¶

Podpora, Maxine C., and Adelbert D. Ruiz. Advances in Wireless Internet Access Point Technology.

Dallas: Wells Publishing, 2008. ¶

Shelly, Gary B., and Thomas J. Cashman. How a GPS Works. Course Technology. 21 March 2008

<www.scsite.com/wd2007/pr2/wc.htm>. ¶

Figure 2–60

Proofing and Revising the Research Paper

As discussed in Chapter 1, once you complete a document, you might find it necessary to make changes to it. Before submitting a paper to be graded, you should proofread it. While **proofreading**, you look for grammatical errors and spelling errors. You want to be sure the transitions between sentences flow smoothly and the sentences themselves make sense.

<table>
<tr><td>Plan
Ahead</td><td>

Proofread and revise the paper.

As you proofread the paper, look for ways to improve it. Check all grammar, spelling, and punctuation. Be sure the text is logical and transitions are smooth. Where necessary, add text, delete text, reword text, and move text to different locations. Ask yourself these questions:

- Does the title suggest the topic?
- Is the thesis clear?
- Is the purpose of the paper clear?
- Does the paper have an introduction, body, and conclusion?
- Does each paragraph in the body relate to the thesis?
- Is the conclusion effective?
- Are all sources acknowledged?

</td></tr>
</table>

To assist you with the proofreading effort, Word provides several tools. You can go to a specific location in a document, move text, find and replace text, insert a synonym, check spelling and grammar, and look up information. The following pages discuss these tools.

To Use the Select Browse Object Menu

Often, you would like to bring a certain page, footnote, or other object into view in the document window. To accomplish this, you could scroll through the document to find a desired page, footnote, or item. Instead of scrolling through the document, however, you can use Word to go to a specific location via the Select Browse Object menu. The following steps display the footnote in the research paper using the Select Browse Object menu.

- Click the Select Browse Object button on the vertical scroll bar to display the Select Browse Object menu and then position the mouse pointer on the Browse by Footnote icon (Figure 2–61).

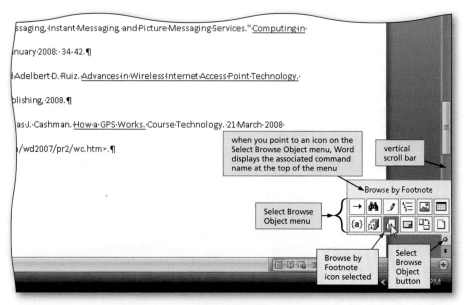

Figure 2–61

2

- Click the Browse by Footnote icon to set the browse object to footnotes.

- Position the mouse pointer on the Previous Footnote button on the vertical scroll bar (Figure 2–62).

Q&A

Did the function of the button change?

Yes. By default, it is the Previous Page button. Depending on the icon you click on the Select Browse Object menu, the function of the buttons above and below the Select Browse Object button on the vertical scroll bar changes.

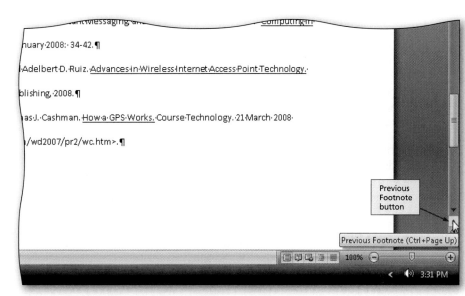

Figure 2–62

3

- Click the Previous Footnote button to display the footnote reference mark in the document window (Figure 2–63).

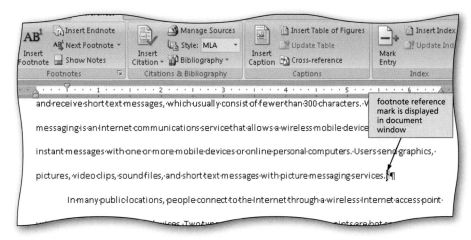

Figure 2–63

Other Ways

1. Click Page Number indicator on status bar, click desired object in Go to what list, type desired object number in Enter object number text box, click Go To button

2. Press ALT+CTRL+HOME

Moving Text

While proofreading the research paper, you realize that text in the third paragraph would flow better if the third sentence were moved to the end of the paragraph.

To move text, such as words, characters, sentences, or paragraphs, you first select the text to be moved and then use drag-and-drop editing or the cut-and-paste technique to move the selected text. With **drag-and-drop editing**, you drag the selected item to the new location and then insert, or *drop*, it there. **Cutting** involves removing the selected item from the document and then placing it on the Clipboard. The **Clipboard** is a temporary Windows storage area. **Pasting** is the process of copying an item from the Clipboard into the document at the location of the insertion point.

When moving text a long distance or between application programs, use the Clipboard task pane to cut and paste. When moving text a short distance, the drag-and-drop technique is more efficient. Thus, the steps on the following pages demonstrate drag-and-drop editing.

To Select a Sentence

To drag-and-drop a sentence in the research paper, you first must select the sentence. The following step selects a sentence.

- Position the mouse pointer in the sentence to be moved (shown in Figure 2–64).

- Press and hold down the CTRL key. While holding down the CTRL key, click the sentence to select the entire sentence.

- Release the CTRL key.

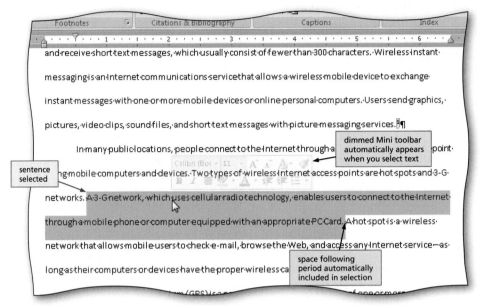

Figure 2–64

Other Ways

1. Drag through the sentence

2. With insertion point at beginning of sentence, press CTRL+SHIFT+RIGHT ARROW until sentence is selected

Selecting Text

In the previous steps and throughout Chapters 1 and 2, you have selected text. Table 2–3 summarizes the techniques used to select various items with the mouse.

BTW

Selecting Nonadjacent Items
In Word, you can select nonadjacent items, that is, items not next to each other. This is helpful when you are formatting multiple items the same way. To select nonadjacent items (text or graphics), do the following: select the first item, such as a word or paragraph, as usual. Press and hold down the CTRL key. While holding down the CTRL key, select any additional items.

Table 2–3 Techniques for Selecting Items with the Mouse	
Item To Select	**Mouse Action**
Block of text	Click at beginning of selection, scroll to end of selection, position mouse pointer at end of selection, hold down SHIFT key and then click; or drag through the text
Character(s)	Drag through character(s)
Document	Move mouse to left of text until mouse pointer changes to a right-pointing block arrow and then triple-click
Graphic	Click the graphic
Line	Move mouse to left of line until mouse pointer changes to a right-pointing block arrow and then click
Lines	Move mouse to left of first line until mouse pointer changes to a right-pointing block arrow and then drag up or down
Paragraph	Triple-click paragraph; or move mouse to left of paragraph until mouse pointer changes to a right-pointing block arrow and then double-click
Paragraphs	Move mouse to left of paragraph until mouse pointer changes to a right-pointing block arrow, double-click, and then drag up or down
Sentence	Press and hold down CTRL key and then click sentence
Word	Double-click the word
Words	Drag through words

To Move Selected Text

With the sentence to be moved selected, you can use drag-and-drop editing to move it. You should be sure that drag-and-drop editing is enabled by clicking the Word Options button on the Office Button menu, clicking Advanced in the left pane of the Word Options dialog box, verifying the 'Allow text to be dragged and dropped' check box is selected, and then clicking the OK button.

The following steps move the selected sentence so that it becomes the last sentence in the paragraph.

- With the mouse pointer in the selected text, press and hold down the mouse button (Figure 2–65).

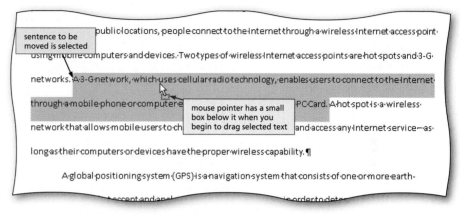

Figure 2–65

- Drag the mouse pointer to the location where the selected text is to be moved, as shown in Figure 2–66.

- Release the mouse button to move the selected text to the location of the mouse pointer.

- Click outside the selected text to remove the selection (Figure 2–67).

Q&A What if I accidentally drag text to the wrong location?

Click the Undo button on the Quick Access Toolbar and try again.

Q&A Can I use drag-and-drop editing to move any selected item?

Yes, you can select words, sentences, phrases, and graphics and then use drag-and-drop editing to move them.

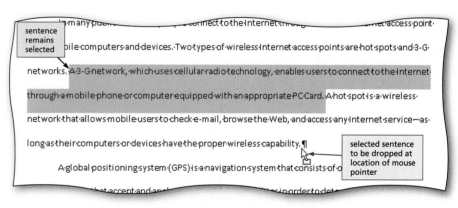

Figure 2–66

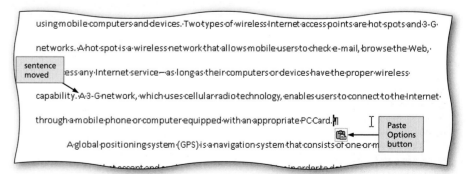

Figure 2–67

Other Ways		
1. Click Cut button on Home tab, click where text is to be pasted, click Paste button on Home tab	2. Right-click selected text, click Cut on shortcut menu, right-click where text is to be pasted, click Paste on shortcut menu	3. Press CTRL+X, position insertion point where text is to be pasted, press CTRL+V

To Display the Paste Options Menu

When you drag-and-drop text, Word automatically displays a Paste Options button near the location of the drag-and-dropped text (Figure 2–67 on the previous page). If you click the **Paste Options button**, a menu appears that allows you to change the format of the item that was moved. The following steps display the Paste Options menu.

- Click the Paste Options button to display the Paste Options menu (Figure 2–68).

Q&A

What is the purpose of the commands on the Paste Options menu?

In general, the first command indicates the pasted text should look the same as it did in its original location. The second command formats the pasted text to match the rest of the text where it was pasted. The third command removes all formatting from the pasted text. The last command displays the Word Options dialog box.

- Press the ESCAPE key to remove the Paste Options menu from the window.

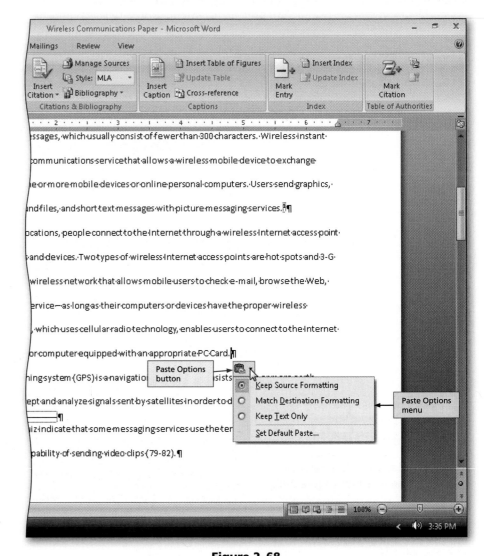

Figure 2–68

BTW

Dragging-and-Dropping
If you hold down the CTRL key while dragging a selected item, Word copies the item instead of moving it.

To Find and Replace Text

While proofreading the paper, you notice that you typed 3-G in the third paragraph (Figure 2–69). You prefer to use 3G, instead. Therefore, you need to change all occurrences of 3-G to 3G. To do this, you can use Word's find and replace feature, which automatically locates each occurrence of a word or phrase and then replaces it with specified text. The following steps use Find and Replace to replace all occurrences of 3-G with 3G.

- Click Home on the Ribbon to display the Home tab.

- Click the Replace button on the Home tab to display the Find and Replace dialog box.

- Type 3-G in the Find what text box.

- Press the TAB key. Type 3G in the Replace with text box (Figure 2–69).

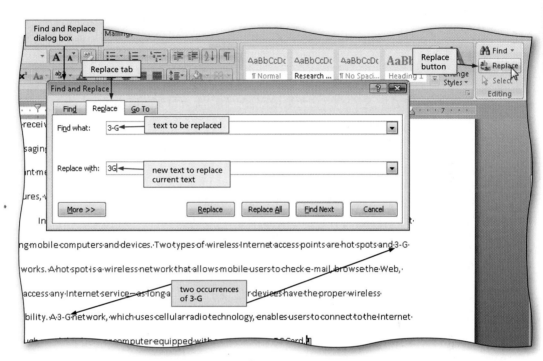

Figure 2–69

- Click the Replace All button in the Find and Replace dialog box to instruct Word to replace all occurrences of the Find what text with the Replace with text (Figure 2–70).

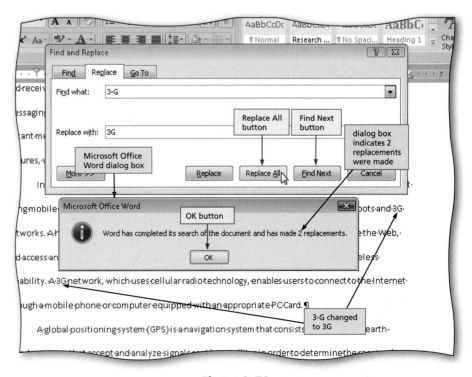

- Click the OK button in the Microsoft Office Word dialog box.

- Click the Close button in the Find and Replace dialog box.

Other Ways

1. Click Select Browse Object button on vertical scroll bar, click Find icon, click Replace tab
2. Click Page Number indicator on status bar, click Replace tab in dialog box
3. Press CTRL+H

Figure 2–70

Find and Replace Dialog Box

The Replace All button in the Find and Replace dialog box replaces all occurrences of the Find what text with the Replace with text. In some cases, you may want to replace only certain occurrences of a word or phrase, not all of them. To instruct Word to confirm each change, click the Find Next button in the Find and Replace dialog box (Figure 2–70 on the previous page), instead of the Replace All button. When Word locates an occurrence of the text, it pauses and waits for you to click either the Replace button or the Find Next button. Clicking the Replace button changes the text; clicking the Find Next button instructs Word to disregard the replacement and look for the next occurrence of the Find what text.

If you accidentally replace the wrong text, you can undo a replacement by clicking the Undo button on the Standard toolbar. If you used the Replace All button, Word undoes all replacements. If you used the Replace button, Word undoes only the most recent replacement.

TO FIND TEXT

Finding Formatting
To search for formatting or a special character, click the More button in the Find dialog box. To find formatting, use the Format button in the Find dialog box. To find a special character, use the Special button.

Sometimes, you may want only to find text, instead of finding and replacing text. To search for just a single occurrence of text, you would follow these steps.

1. Click the Find button on the Home tab; or click the Select Browse Object button on the vertical scroll bar and then click the Find icon on the Select Browse Object menu; or click the page indicator on the status bar and then click the Find tab; or press CTRL+F.

2. Type the text to locate in the Find what text box and then click the Find Next button. To edit the text, click the Cancel button in the Find and Replace dialog box; to find the next occurrence of the text, click the Find Next button.

To Find and Insert a Synonym

When writing, you may discover that you used the same word in multiple locations or that a word you used was not quite appropriate. In these instances, you will want to look up a **synonym**, or a word similar in meaning, to the duplicate or inappropriate word. A **thesaurus** is a book of synonyms. Word provides synonyms and a thesaurus for your convenience.

In this project, you would like a synonym for the word, proper, in the third paragraph of the research paper. The following steps show how to find a suitable synonym.

1

- Locate and then right-click the word for which you want to find a synonym (in this case, proper) to display a shortcut menu related to the word you right-clicked.

- Point to Synonyms on the shortcut menu to display a list of synonyms for the word you right-clicked (Figure 2–71).

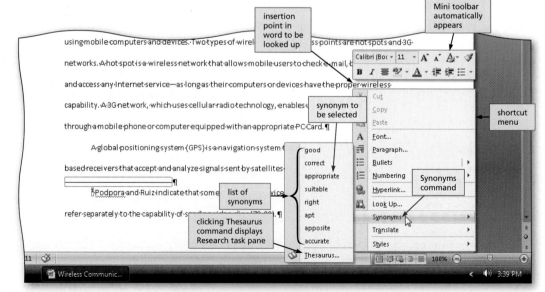

Figure 2–71

2

- Click the synonym you want (appropriate) on the Synonyms submenu to replace the word, proper, in the document with the word, appropriate (Figure 2–72).

What if the synonyms list on the shortcut menu does not display a suitable word?

You can display the thesaurus in the Research task pane by clicking Thesaurus on the Synonyms submenu. The Research task pane displays a complete thesaurus, in which you can look up synonyms for various meanings of a word. You also can look up an **antonym**, or word with an opposite meaning. The Research task pane is discussed later in this chapter.

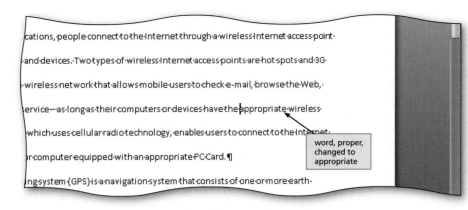

Figure 2–72

Other Ways	
1. Click Thesaurus on Review tab	2. Press SHIFT+F7

To Check Spelling and Grammar at Once

As discussed in Chapter 1, Word checks spelling and grammar as you type and places a wavy underline below possible spelling or grammar errors. Chapter 1 illustrated how to check these flagged words immediately. As an alternative, you can wait and check the entire document for spelling and grammar errors at once.

Note: In the following example the word, world, has been misspelled intentionally as wrld to illustrate the use of Word's check spelling and grammar at once feature. If you are completing this project on a personal computer, your research paper may contain different misspelled words, depending on the accuracy of your typing.

1

- Press CTRL+HOME because you want the spelling and grammar check to begin from the top of the document.

- Click Review on the Ribbon to display the Review tab.

- Click the Spelling & Grammar button on the Review tab to begin the spelling and grammar check at the location of the insertion point, which in this case, is at the beginning of the document (Figure 2–73).

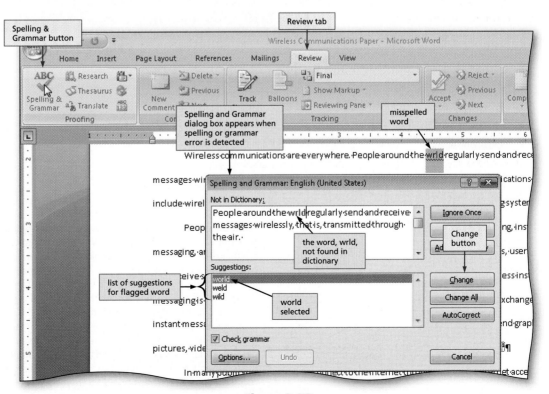

Figure 2–73

2

- With the word, world, selected in the Suggestions list, click the Change button in the Spelling and Grammar dialog box to change the flagged word, wrld, to the selected suggestion, world, and then continue the spelling and grammar check until the next error is identified or the end of the document is reached (Figure 2–74).

3

- Click the Ignore All button in the Spelling and Grammar dialog box to ignore this and future occurrences of the flagged proper noun and then continue the spelling and grammar check until the next error is identified or the end of the document is reached.

4

- When Word flags the proper noun, Podpora, click the Ignore All button.

- When the spelling and grammar check is finished and Word displays a dialog box, click its OK button.

Q&A

Can I check spelling of just a section of a document?

Yes, select the text before starting the spelling and grammar check.

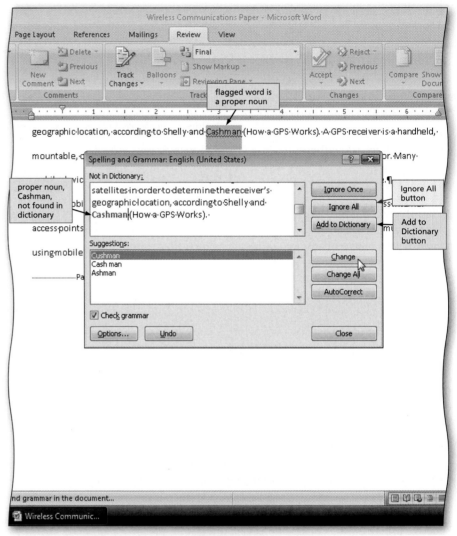

Figure 2–74

Other Ways

1. Click Spelling and Grammar Check icon on status bar, click Spelling on shortcut menu
2. Right-click flagged word, click Spelling on shortcut menu
3. Press F7

BTW

Contextual Spelling Errors

You can instruct Word to check for misuse of homophones and other types of contextual spelling errors. (Homophones are two or more words that are pronounced the same but that have different spellings or meanings, such as one and won.) With this feature, Word flags a contextual spelling error with a blue wavy underline. For example, Word would place a blue wavy underline below the words, one and knight, in this sentence: The team one the game last knight. (The correct sentence would be written as follows: The team won the game last night.) To view Word's suggested replacements for the flagged words, you could right-click each of the flagged words or start the spelling and grammar check by clicking the Spelling & Grammar button on the Review tab. On many installations of Word, the contextual spelling check is not activated by default. To activate it, click the Office Button, click Word Options on the Office Button menu, click Proofing in the left pane, place a check mark in the 'Use contextual spelling' check box, and then click the OK button.

The Main and Custom Dictionaries

As shown in the previous steps, Word may flag a proper noun as an error because the proper noun is not in its main dictionary. To prevent Word from flagging proper nouns as errors, you can add the proper nouns to the custom dictionary. To add a correctly spelled word to the custom dictionary, click the Add to Dictionary button in the Spelling and Grammar dialog box (Figure 2–74) or right-click the flagged word and then click Add to Dictionary on the shortcut menu. Once you have added a word to the custom dictionary, Word no longer will flag it as an error.

To View or Modify Entries in a Custom Dictionary

To view or modify the list of words in a custom dictionary, you would follow these steps.

1. Click the Office Button and then click the Word Options button.
2. Click Proofing in the left pane of the Word Options dialog box.
3. Click the Custom Dictionaries button.
4. When Word displays the Custom Dictionaries dialog box, place a check mark next to the dictionary name to view or modify. Click the Edit Word List button. (In this dialog box, you can add or delete entries to and from the selected custom dictionary.)
5. When finished viewing and/or modifying the list, click the OK button in the dialog box.
6. Click the OK button in the Custom Dictionaries dialog box.
7. If the 'Suggest from main dictionary only' check box is selected in the Word Options dialog box, remove the check mark. Click the OK button in the Word Options dialog box.

To Set the Default Custom Dictionary

If you have multiple custom dictionaries, you can specify which one Word should use when checking spelling. To set the default custom dictionary, you would follow these steps.

1. Click the Office Button and then click the Word Options button.
2. Click Proofing in the left pane of the Word Options dialog box.
3. Click the Custom Dictionaries button.
4. When the Custom Dictionaries dialog box is displayed, place a check mark next to the desired dictionary name. Click the Change Default button.
5. Click the OK button in the Custom Dictionaries dialog box.
6. If the 'Suggest from main dictionary only' check box is selected in the Word Options dialog box, remove the check mark. Click the OK button in the Word Options dialog box.

To Use the Research Task Pane to Look Up Information

From within Word, you can search through various forms of reference information. Earlier, this chapter discussed the Research task pane with respect to looking up a synonym in a thesaurus. Other services available in the Research task pane include a dictionary and if you are connected to the Web, an encyclopedia, a search engine, and other Web sites that provide information such as stock quotes, news articles, and company profiles.

Assume you want to know more about the acronym, PDA. The following steps use the Research task pane to look up information about a word.

- Locate the word you want to look up.

- While holding down the ALT key, click the word you want to look up (in this case, PDAs) to open the Research task pane and display a dictionary entry for the ALT+CLICKED word. Release the ALT key (Figure 2–75).

- If the Research task pane does not display a dictionary entry for the ALT+CLICKED word, click the Search for box arrow and then click All Reference Books.

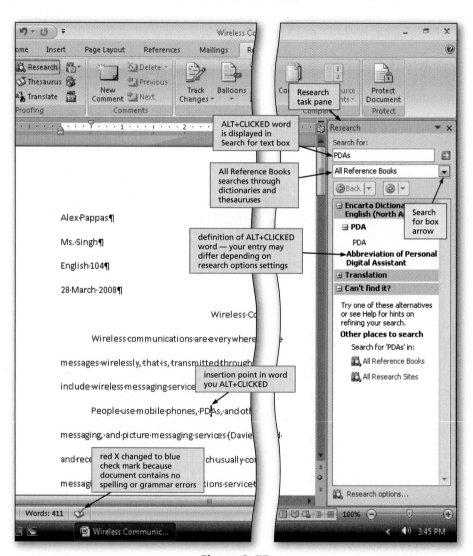

Figure 2–75

- Click the Search for box arrow and then click All Research Sites in the list to display Web sites with information about the ALT+CLICKED word (Figure 2–76).

Q&A

Can I copy information from the Research task pane into my document?

Yes, you can use the Copy and Paste commands. When using Word to insert material from the Research task pane or any other online reference, however, be very careful not to plagiarize.

- Click the Close button in the Research task pane.

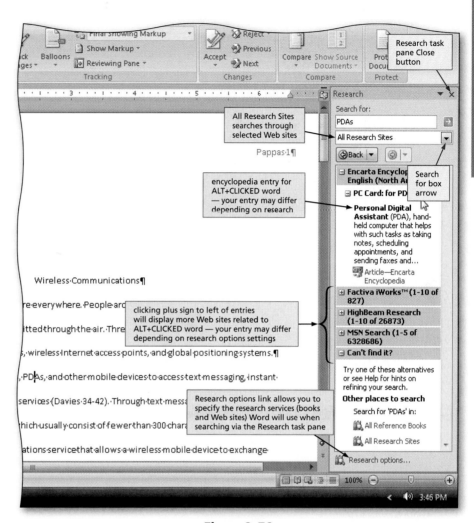

Figure 2–76

Other Ways

1. Click Research button on Review tab
2. Click Insert Citation button on References tab, click Search Libraries

Research Task Pane Options

When you install Word, it selects a series of services (reference books and Web sites) through which it searches when you use the Research task pane. You can view, modify, and update the list of services at any time.

Clicking the Research options link at the bottom of the Research task pane displays the Research Options dialog box, where you can view or modify the list of installed services. You can view information about any installed service by clicking the service in the list and then clicking the Properties button. To activate an installed service, click the check box to its left; likewise, to deactivate a service, remove the check mark. To add a particular Web site to the list, click the Add Services button, enter the Web address in the Address text box, and then click the Add button in the Add Services dialog box. To update or remove services, click the Update/Remove button, select the service in the list, click the Update (or Remove) button in the Update or Remove Services dialog box, and then click the Close button. You also can install parental controls through the Parental Control button in the Research Options dialog box, for example, if you want to restrict Web access from minor children who use Word.

To Change Document Properties

Before saving the research paper again, you want to add your name, course information, and some keywords as document properties. The following steps use the Document Information Panel to change document properties.

1 Click the Office Button to display the Office Button menu, point to Prepare on the Office Button menu, and then click Properties on the Prepare submenu to display the Document Information Panel.

2 Click the Author text box, if necessary, and then type your name as the Author property. If a name already is displayed in the Author text box, delete it before typing your name.

3 Click the Subject text box, if necessary delete any existing text, and then type your course and section as the Subject property.

4 Click the Keywords text box, if necessary delete any existing text, and then type `instant messaging, Internet access points, global positioning systems` as the Keywords property.

5 Click the Close the Document Information Panel button so that the Document Information Panel no longer is displayed.

To Save an Existing Document with the Same File Name

The document now is complete. You should save the research paper again. The following step saves the document again.

1 Click the Save button on the Quick Access Toolbar to overwrite the previous Wireless Communications Paper file on the USB flash drive.

To Print Document Properties and then the Document

With the document properties entered and the completed document saved, you may want to print the document properties along with the document. The following steps print the document properties, followed by the contents of the saved Wireless Communications Paper project.

1

- Click the Office Button to display the Office Button menu and then point to Print on the Office Button menu to display the Print submenu (Figure 2–77).

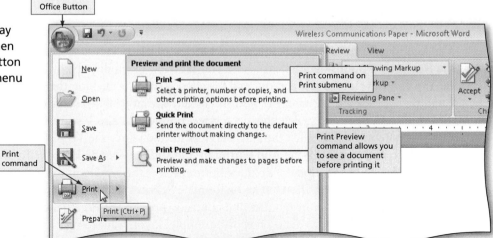

Figure 2–77

- Click Print on the Print submenu to display the Print dialog box.

- Click the Print what box arrow and then click Document properties to instruct Word to print the document properties instead of the document (Figure 2–78).

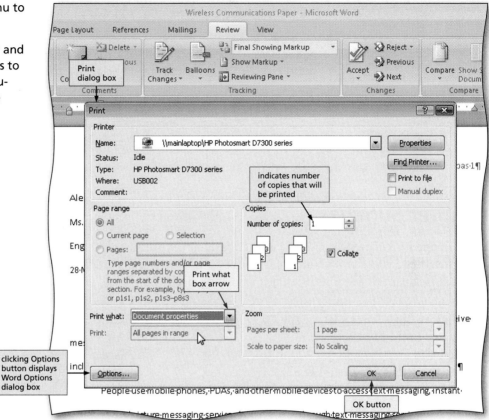

Figure 2–78

- Click the OK button to print the document properties (Figure 2–79).

- Click the Office Button again to display the Office Button menu, point to Print on the Office Button menu, and then click Quick Print on the Print submenu to print the research paper (shown in Figure 2–1 on page WD 75).

printed document properties — your properties may differ, depending on settings

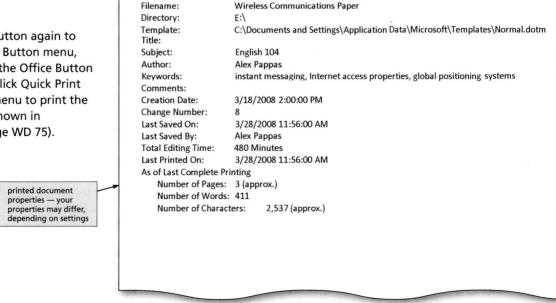

Filename:	Wireless Communications Paper
Directory:	E:\
Template:	C:\Documents and Settings\Application Data\Microsoft\Templates\Normal.dotm
Title:	
Subject:	English 104
Author:	Alex Pappas
Keywords:	instant messaging, Internet access properties, global positioning systems
Comments:	
Creation Date:	3/18/2008 2:00:00 PM
Change Number:	8
Last Saved On:	3/28/2008 11:56:00 AM
Last Saved By:	Alex Pappas
Total Editing Time:	480 Minutes
Last Printed On:	3/28/2008 11:56:00 AM

As of Last Complete Printing
   Number of Pages: 3 (approx.)
   Number of Words: 411
   Number of Characters: 2,537 (approx.)

Figure 2–79

BTW

Certification
The Microsoft Certified Application Specialist (MCAS) program provides an opportunity for you to obtain a valuable industry credential — proof that you have the Word 2007 skills required by employers. For more information, see Appendix G or visit the Word 2007 Certification Web page (scsite.com/wd2007/cert).

To Quit Word

This project is complete. The following steps quit Word.

1 Click the Close button on the right side of the title bar to quit Word; or if you have multiple Word documents open, click the Office Button and then click the Exit Word button on the Office Button menu to close all open documents and quit Word.

2 If necessary, click the Yes button in the Microsoft Office Word dialog box so that any changes you have made are saved.

Chapter Summary

In this chapter you have learned how to change document settings, use headers to number pages, create and modify styles, insert and edit citations and their sources, add footnotes, create a bibliographical list of sources, and use the Research task pane. The items listed below include all the new Word skills you have learned in this chapter.

1. Double-Space Text (WD 78)
2. Remove Space after a Paragraph (WD 79)
3. Switch to the Header (WD 80)
4. Right-Align a Paragraph (WD 81)
5. Insert a Page Number (WD 82)
6. Close the Header (WD 83)
7. Click and Type (WD 85)
8. Display the Rulers (WD 87)
9. First-Line Indent Paragraphs (WD 88)
10. Create a Quick Style (WD 90)
11. AutoCorrect as You Type (WD 91)
12. Use the AutoCorrect Options Button (WD 92)
13. Create an AutoCorrect Entry (WD 93)
14. Change the Bibliography Style (WD 95)
15. Insert a Citation and Create Its Source (WD 96)
16. Edit a Citation (WD 98)
17. Insert a Footnote Reference Mark (WD 100)
18. Insert a Citation Placeholder (WD 101)
19. Modify a Style Using a Shortcut Menu (WD 102)
20. Edit a Source (WD 104)
21. Count Words (WD 107)
22. Page Break Manually (WD 112)
23. Create the Bibliographical List (WD 113)
24. Modify a Style Using the Styles Task Pane (WD 114)
25. Create a Hanging Indent (WD 116)
26. Modify a Source and Update the Bibliographical List (WD 117)
27. Use the Select Browse Object Menu (WD 118)
28. Select a Sentence (WD 120)
29. Move Selected Text (WD 121)
30. Display the Paste Options Menu (WD 122)
31. Find and Replace Text (WD 123)
32. Find Text (WD 124)
33. Find and Insert a Synonym (WD 124)
34. Check Spelling and Grammar at Once (WD 125)
35. View or Modify Entries in a Custom Dictionary (WD 127)
36. Set the Default Custom Dictionary (WD 127)
37. Use the Research Task Pane to Look Up Information (WD 128)
38. Print Document Properties and then the Document (WD 130)

 If you have a SAM user profile, you may have access to hands-on instruction, practice, and assessment. Log in to your SAM account (http://sam2007.course.com) to launch any assigned training activities or exams that relate to the skills covered in this chapter.

BTW

Quick Reference
For a table that lists how to complete the tasks covered in this book using the mouse, Ribbon, shortcut menu, and keyboard, see the Quick Reference Summary at the back of this book, or visit the Word 2007 Quick Reference Web page (scsite.com/wd2007/qr).

Learn It Online

Test your knowledge of chapter content and key terms.

Instructions: To complete the Learn It Online exercises, start your browser, click the Address bar, and then enter the Web address scsite.com/wd2007/learn. When the Word 2007 Learn It Online page is displayed, click the link for the exercise you want to complete and then read the instructions.

Chapter Reinforcement TF, MC, and SA
A series of true/false, multiple choice, and short answer questions that test your knowledge of the chapter content.

Flash Cards
An interactive learning environment where you identify chapter key terms associated with displayed definitions.

Practice Test
A series of multiple choice questions that test your knowledge of chapter content and key terms.

Who Wants To Be a Computer Genius?
An interactive game that challenges your knowledge of chapter content in the style of a television quiz show.

Wheel of Terms
An interactive game that challenges your knowledge of chapter key terms in the style of the television show *Wheel of Fortune*.

Crossword Puzzle Challenge
A crossword puzzle that challenges your knowledge of key terms presented in the chapter.

Apply Your Knowledge

Reinforce the skills and apply the concepts you learned in this chapter.

Revising Text and Paragraphs in a Document
Instructions: Start Word. Open the document, Apply 2-1 Software Paragraphs Draft, from the Data Files for Students. See the inside back cover of this book for instructions on downloading the Data Files for Students, or contact your instructor for information about accessing the required files.

The document you open has a header and three paragraphs of text. You are to revise the document as follows: move a paragraph, move a word and change the format of the moved word, change paragraph indentation, change line spacing and paragraph spacing, replace all occurrences of a word with another word, and edit the header.

Perform the following tasks:
1. Select the last (third) paragraph. Use drag-and-drop editing to move this paragraph, so that it is the second paragraph in the document.
2. Select the underlined word, effectively, in the second sentence of the first paragraph. Use drag-and-drop editing to move the selected word, effectively, so that it follows the word, software, in the same sentence. Click the Paste Options button that displays to the right of the moved word, effectively. Remove the underline format from the moved sentence by clicking Keep Text Only on the shortcut menu.
3. Select the three paragraphs of text in the document.
4. Display the ruler, if necessary. With the paragraphs selected, use the ruler to indent the first line of the selected paragraphs one-half inch.
5. With the paragraphs still selected, change the line spacing of the selected paragraphs from single to double.

Continued >

Apply Your Knowledge *continued*

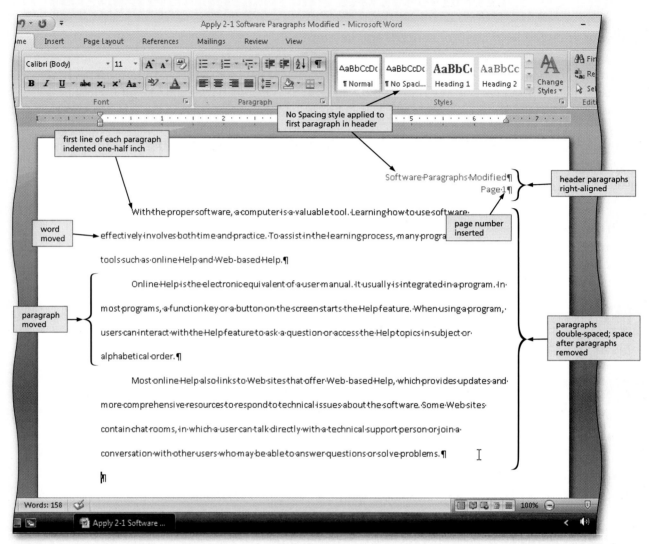

Figure 2–80

6. With the paragraphs still selected, use Line spacing box arrow to remove extra space below (after) the paragraphs. Click anywhere to remove the selection.

7. Use the Find and Replace dialog box to replace all occurrences of the word, Internet, with the word, Web. How many replacements were made?

8. Use the Find dialog box to locate the word, incorporated. Use Word's thesaurus to change the word, incorporated, to the word, integrated, in the first sentence of the second paragraph.

9. Switch to the header so that you can edit it. In the first line of the header, change the word, Draft, to the word, Modified, so that it reads: Software Paragraphs Modified. Change the first line of the header from the Normal style to the No Spacing style.

10. In the second line of the header, insert the page number (with no formatting) one space after the word, Page.

11. Change the alignment of both lines of text in the header from left-aligned to right-aligned. Switch back to the document text.

12. Change the document properties, as specified by your instructor.

13. Click the Office Button and then click Save As. Save the document using the file name, Apply 2-1 Software Paragraphs Modified.

14. Print the document properties and then print the revised document, shown in Figure 2–80.

15. Use the Research task pane to look up the definition of the word, online, in the first sentence of the second paragraph. Handwrite the COMPUTING definition of the word, online, on your printout.

16. Display the Research Options dialog box and on your printout, handwrite the currently active Reference Books, Research Sites, and Business and Financial Sites. If your instructor approves, activate one of the services.

Extend Your Knowledge

Extend the skills you learned in this chapter and experiment with new skills. You may need to use Help to complete the assignment.

Working with References and Proofing Tools

Instructions: Start Word. Open the document, Extend 2-1 Computing Options Paper Draft, from the Data Files for Students. See the inside back cover of this book for instructions on downloading the Data Files for Students, or contact your instructor for information on accessing the required files.

You will add another footnote to the paper, use the thesaurus, convert the document from MLA to APA style, convert the footnotes to endnotes, modify the Endnote Text style, change the format of the note reference marks, and translate the document to another language.

Perform the following tasks:

1. Insert a second footnote at an appropriate place in the research paper. Use the following footnote text: The Americans with Disabilities Act (ADA) requires any company with 15 or more employees to make reasonable attempts to accommodate the needs of physically challenged workers.

2. Use the Replace dialog box to find the word, imagine, in the document and then replace it with a word of your choice.

3. Save the document with a new file name and then print it. Select the entire document and then change the style of the citations and bibliography from MLA to APA. Save the APA version of the document with a new file name and then print it. Compare the two versions. Circle the differences between the two documents.

4. Convert the footnotes to endnotes.

5. Modify the Endnote Text style to 11-point Calibri font, double-spaced text with a first-line indent.

6. Change the format of the note reference marks to capital letters (A, B, etc.).

7. Save the revised document with endnotes with a new file name and then print it. On the printout with the endnotes, write the number of words, characters without spaces, characters with spaces, paragraphs, and lines in the document. Be sure to include endnote text in the statistics.

8. Translate the research paper into a language of your choice (Figure 2–81 on the next page) using the Translate button on the Review tab. Print the translated document.

Continued >

Extend Your Knowledge *continued*

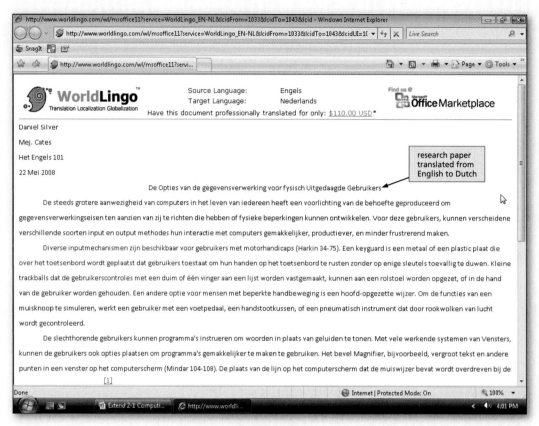

research paper translated from English to Dutch

Figure 2–81

Make It Right

Analyze a document and correct all errors and/or improve the design.

Inserting Missing Elements in an MLA Style Research Paper

Instructions: Start Word. Open the document, Make It Right 2-1 Certification Paper Draft, from the Data Files for Students. See the inside back cover of this book for instructions on downloading the Data Files for Students, or contact your instructor for information on accessing the required files.

The document is a research paper that is missing several elements. You are to insert these missing elements, all formatted according to the MLA documentation style: header with a page number, heading (name, course, and date information), paper title, footnote, and source information for the first citation and the citation in the footnote.

Perform the following tasks:

1. Insert a header with a page number, heading (use your own information: name, course information, and date), and an appropriate paper title, all formatted according to the MLA style.

2. Use the Select Browse Object button to go to page 2. How many bibliographical entries currently are on the Works Cited page? You will create additional source entries in Steps 3 and 4.

3. The Otoole placeholder (tag name) is missing its source information (Figure 2–82). Use the following source information to edit the source: magazine article titled "Career Builders and Boosts," written by Sarah W. O'Toole, magazine name is *IT World and Certifications*, publication date is March 2008, article is on pages 88-93. Edit the citation so that it displays the author name and the page numbers.

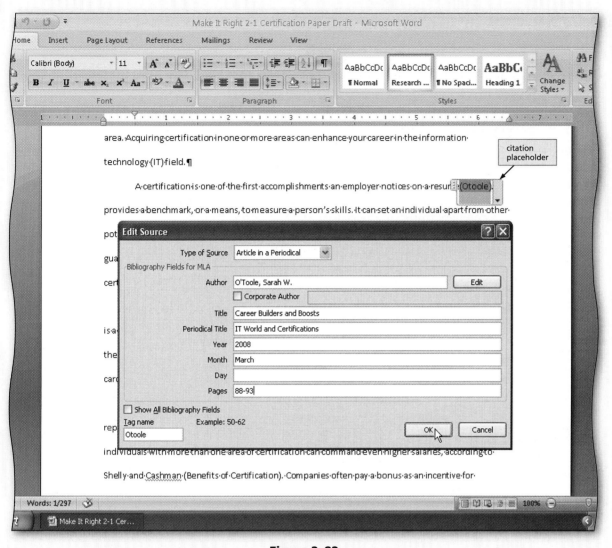

Figure 2–82

4. Insert the following footnote with the note reference at an appropriate place in the paper, formatted according to the MLA style: Debbins points out that, as an additional bonus, some certification training can be used for college credit. The citation for this footnote should be at the end of the footnote. The source information is as follows: book named *Preparing for the Future: IT Strategies*, authored by Floyd I. Debbins, published in 2008 at IT World Press in Chicago, pages 99-104. Edit the citation so that it displays only page numbers.

5. Use the Select Browse Object button to go to page 3. Be sure the bibliographical list on the Works Cited page contains all three entries. If necessary, use the F9 key to update the bibliographical list. Format the bibliographical paragraphs with a one-half inch hanging indent.

6. Modify the source of the book authored by Floyd I. Debbins, so that the publisher city is Boston instead of Chicago.

7. Use the Select Browse Object button to go to the footnote. Be sure the footnote is formatted properly.

8. Change the document properties, as specified by your instructor. Save the revised document with a new file name and then submit it in the format specified by your instructor.

In the Lab

Design and/or create a document using the guidelines, concepts, and skills presented in this chapter. Labs are listed in order of increasing difficulty.

Lab 1: Preparing a Short Research Paper

Problem: You are a college student currently enrolled in an introductory business class. Your assignment is to prepare a short research paper (300-350 words) about a computer-related job. The requirements are that the paper be presented according to the MLA documentation style and have three references. One of the three references must be from the Web. You prepare the paper shown in Figure 2–83, which discusses the computer forensics specialist.

Hankins 1

Mary Hankins

Mr. Habib

Business 102

14 March 2008

Computer Forensics Specialist

Computer forensics, also called digital forensics, network forensics, or cyberforensics, is a rapidly growing field that involves gathering and analyzing evidence from computers and networks. Because computers and the Internet are the fastest growing technology used for criminal activity, the need for computer forensics specialists will increase in years to come.

A computer forensics specialist examines computer media, programs, data, and log files on computers, servers, and networks. According to Shelly and Cashman (Computer Careers), many areas employ computer forensics specialists, including law enforcement, criminal prosecutors, military intelligence, insurance agencies, and information security departments in the private sector. A computer forensics specialist must have knowledge of the law, technical experience with many types of hardware and software products, superior communication skills, a willingness to learn and update skills, and a knack for problem solving.

When a problem occurs, it is the responsibility of the computer forensics specialist to carefully take several steps to identify and retrieve possible evidence that may exist on a suspect's computer. These steps include protecting the suspect's computer, discovering all files, recovering deleted files, revealing hidden files, accessing protected or encrypted files, analyzing all the data, and providing expert consultation and/or testimony as required (Reinman 52-58).

A computer forensics specialist must have knowledge of all aspects of the computer, from the operating system to computer architecture and hardware design. In the past, many computer forensics specialists were self-taught computer users. Today, extensive training, usually from several different

(a)

Figure 2–83

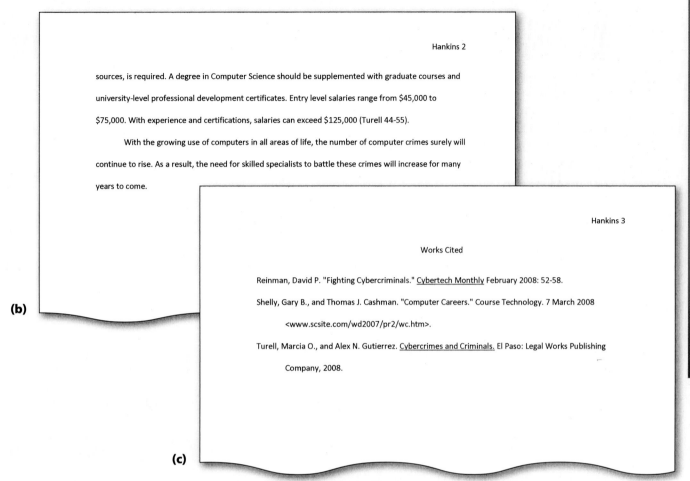

(b)

(c)

Figure 2–83 (continued)

Instructions: Perform the following tasks:

1. If necessary, display formatting marks on the screen.

2. Adjust line spacing to double.

3. Remove space below (after) paragraphs.

4. Create a header to number pages.

5. Type the name and course information at the left margin. Center and type the title.

6. Set first-line indent for paragraphs in the body of the research paper.

7. Create a Quick Style for the research paper paragraphs.

8. Type the research paper as shown in Figures 2–83a and 2–83b. Change the bibliography style to MLA. As you insert citations, enter their source information (shown in Figure 2–83c). Edit the citations so that they display according to Figures 2–83a and 2–83b.

9. At the end of the research paper text, press the ENTER key and then insert a manual page break so that the Works Cited page begins on a new page. Enter and format the works cited title (Figure 2–83c). Use Word to insert the bibliographical list (bibliography). Format the paragraphs in the list with a hanging indent.

10. Check the spelling and grammar of the paper at once.

11. Save the document on a USB flash drive using Lab 2-1 Computer Forensics Paper as the file name.

12. Print the research paper. Handwrite the number of words, paragraphs, and characters in the research paper above the title of your printed research paper.

In the Lab

Lab 2: Preparing a Research Report with a Footnote

Problem: You are a college student enrolled in an introductory English class. Your assignment is to prepare a short research paper in any area of interest to you. The requirements are that the paper be presented according to the MLA documentation style, contain at least one explanatory note positioned as a footnote, and have three references. One of the three references must be from the Internet. You prepare a paper about antivirus programs (Figure 2–84).

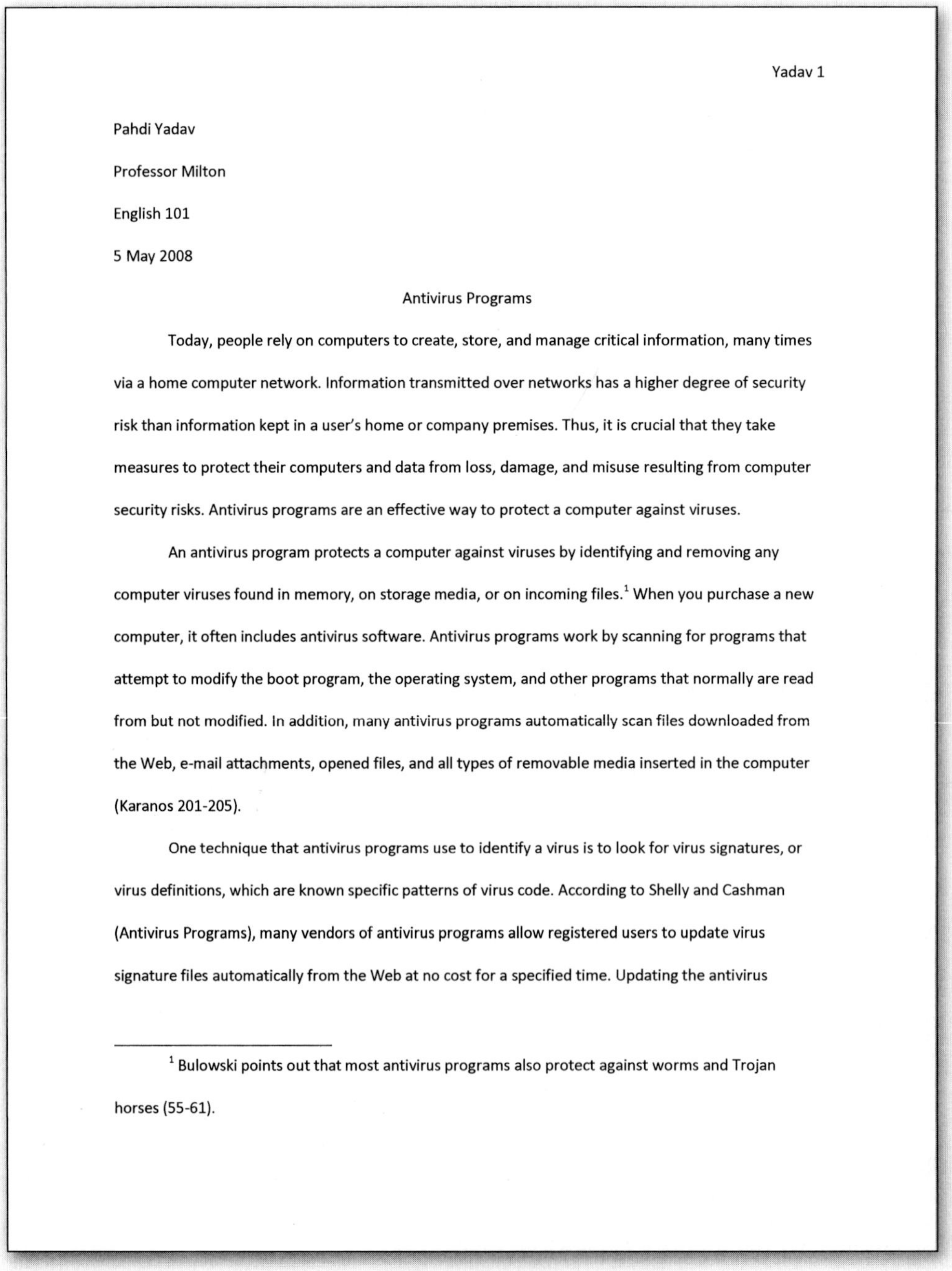

Yadav 1

Pahdi Yadav

Professor Milton

English 101

5 May 2008

Antivirus Programs

Today, people rely on computers to create, store, and manage critical information, many times via a home computer network. Information transmitted over networks has a higher degree of security risk than information kept in a user's home or company premises. Thus, it is crucial that they take measures to protect their computers and data from loss, damage, and misuse resulting from computer security risks. Antivirus programs are an effective way to protect a computer against viruses.

An antivirus program protects a computer against viruses by identifying and removing any computer viruses found in memory, on storage media, or on incoming files.[1] When you purchase a new computer, it often includes antivirus software. Antivirus programs work by scanning for programs that attempt to modify the boot program, the operating system, and other programs that normally are read from but not modified. In addition, many antivirus programs automatically scan files downloaded from the Web, e-mail attachments, opened files, and all types of removable media inserted in the computer (Karanos 201-205).

One technique that antivirus programs use to identify a virus is to look for virus signatures, or virus definitions, which are known specific patterns of virus code. According to Shelly and Cashman (Antivirus Programs), many vendors of antivirus programs allow registered users to update virus signature files automatically from the Web at no cost for a specified time. Updating the antivirus

---
[1] Bulowski points out that most antivirus programs also protect against worms and Trojan horses (55-61).

(a)

Figure 2–84

Yadav 2

program's signature files regularly is important, because it will download any new virus definitions that

have been added since the last update.

    Methods that guarantee a computer or network is safe from computer viruses simply do not

exist. Installing, updating, and using an antivirus program, though, is an effective technique to safeguard

your computer from loss.

(b)

Figure 2–84 (continued)

Instructions: Perform the following tasks:

1. Adjust line spacing to double and remove space below (after) paragraphs. Create a header to number pages. Type the name and course information at the left margin. Center and type the title. Set first-line indent for paragraphs in the body of the research paper. Create a Quick Style for the research paper paragraphs.

2. Type the research paper as shown in Figures 2–84a and 2–84b. Add the footnote as shown in Figure 2–84a. Change the Footnote Text style to the format specified in the MLA style. Change the bibliography style to MLA. As you insert citations, use the following source information:

   a. Type of Source: Periodical
      Author: Bulowski, Dana
      Title: Protection and Precaution: Keeping Your Computer Healthy
      Periodical Title: Computing Today
      Year: 2008
      Month: February
      Pages 55-61
   b. Type of Source: Book
      Author: Karanos, Hector
      Title: Internet Security
      Year: 2008
      City: Indianapolis
      Publisher: Citywide Cyber Press
   c. Type of Source: Web site
      Author: Shelly, Gary B., and Thomas J. Cashman
      Name of Web page: Antivirus Programs
      Production Company: Course Technology
      Year Accessed: 2008
      Month Accessed: February
      Day Accessed: 7
      URL: www.scsite.com/wd2007/pr2/wc.htm

3. At the end of the research paper text, press the ENTER key once and insert a manual page break so that the Works Cited page begins on a new page. Enter and format the works cited title. Use Word to insert the bibliographical list. Format the paragraphs in the list with a hanging indent.

4. Check the spelling and grammar of the paper.

5. Save the document on a USB flash drive using Lab 2-2 Antivirus Programs Paper as the file name.

6. Print the research paper. Handwrite the number of words, including the footnotes, in the research paper above the title of your printed research paper.

In the Lab

Lab 3: Composing a Research Paper from Notes

Problem: You have drafted the notes shown in Figure 2–85. Your assignment is to prepare a short research paper from these notes.

Home networks:
- Home users connect multiple computers and devices together in a home network.
- Home networking saves money and provides conveniences.
- Approximately 39 million homes have more than one computer.
- Many vendors offer home networking packages that include all the necessary hardware and software to network a home using wired or wireless techniques.

Three types of wired home networks: Ethernet, powerline cable, and phoneline (source: "Wired vs. Wireless Networks," an article on pages 24-29 in March 2008 issue of Modern Networking by Mark A. Travis).
- Traditional Ethernet networks require that each computer have built-in network capabilities or contain a network card, which connects to a central network hub or similar device with a physical cable. This may involve running cable through walls, ceilings, and floors in the house.
- The hardware and software of an Ethernet network can be difficult to configure for the average home user (source: a book called Home Networking by Frank A. Deakins, published at Current Press in New York in 2008).
- A phoneline network is an easy-to-install and inexpensive network that uses existing telephone lines in the home.
- A home powerline cable network is a network that uses the same lines that bring electricity into the house. This network requires no additional wiring.

Two types of wireless home networks: HomeRF and Wi-Fi (source: a Web site titled "Wired and Wireless Networks" by Gary B. Shelly and Thomas J. Cashman of Course Technology, viewed on April 23, 2008. Web address is www.scsite.com/wd2007/pr2/wc.htm).
- Wireless networks have the disadvantage of interference, because walls, ceilings, and other electrical devices such as cordless telephones and microwave ovens can disrupt wireless communications.
- A HomeRF (radio frequency) network uses radio waves, instead of cables, to transmit data.
- A Wi-Fi network sends signals over a wider distance than the Home RF network, which can be up to 1,500 feet in some configurations.

Figure 2–85

Instructions: Perform the following tasks:
1. Review the notes in Figure 2–85 and then rearrange and reword them. Embellish the paper as you deem necessary. Present the paper according to the MLA documentation style. Create an AutoCorrect entry that automatically corrects the spelling of the misspelled word, wird, to the correct spelling, wired. Add a footnote that refers the reader to the Web for more information. Enter citations and their sources as shown. Create the works cited page (bibliography) from the listed sources.

2. Check the spelling and grammar of the paper. Save the document on a USB flash drive using Lab 2-3 Home Networks Paper as the file name.

3. Use the Research task pane to look up a definition of a word in the paper. Copy and insert the definition into the document as a footnote. Be sure to quote the definition and cite the source.

4. Print the research paper. Handwrite the number of words, including the footnotes, in the research paper above the title of the printed research paper.

Cases and Places

Apply your creative thinking and problem solving skills to design and implement a solution.

• EASIER   •• MORE DIFFICULT

• 1: Create a Research Paper about Word Using the MLA Documentation Style

Chapter 1 of this book discussed the components of the Word window (pages WD 6 through 11). Using the material presented on those pages, write a short research paper (350–400 words) that describes the purpose and functionality of one or more of these components: document window, Ribbon, Mini toolbar and shortcut menus, Quick Access Toolbar, and Office Button. Use your textbook and Word Help as sources. Include at least two citations and one explanatory note positioned as a footnote. Add an AutoCorrect entry to correct a word you commonly mistype. Use the concepts and techniques presented in this chapter to format the paper according to the MLA documentation style. Check spelling and grammar of the finished paper.

•• 2: Create the Research Paper Presented in this Chapter Using the APA Documentation Style

As discussed in this chapter, two popular documentation styles for research papers are the Modern Language Association of America (MLA) and American Psychological Association (APA) styles. In this chapter, you created a research paper that followed guidelines of the MLA documentation style. Using the school library, this textbook, other textbooks, the Internet, magazines, or other sources, research the guidelines of the APA documentation style. Then, prepare the Wireless Communications Paper from this chapter following the guidelines of the APA documentation style. Use Figure 2–1 on page WD 75 as a starting point for the text and source information. Check spelling and grammar of the finished paper.

•• 3: Create a Research Paper that Compares Documentation Styles

This chapter discussed the requirements of the MLA documentation style. The American Psychological Association (APA) and the Chicago Manual of Style (CMS) are two other documentation styles supported by Word. Using the school library, this textbook, other textbooks, the Internet, magazines, or other sources, research the guidelines of the APA and CMS documentation styles to learn more about the differences among the MLA, APA, and CMS documentation styles. Using what you learn, write a short research paper (450-500 words) that compares the requirements and formats of the three documentation styles. Include at least two references and one explanatory note positioned as a footnote. Use the documentation style specified by your instructor to format the paper. Check spelling and grammar of the finished paper.

•• 4: Create a Research Paper about the Month You Were Born

Make It Personal

Did you ever wonder what world events took place during the month you were born (besides your birth)? For example, what happened with respect to politics, world affairs, and the economy? What made headline news? Were there any scientific breakthroughs? What was on television and at the box office? Were any famous people born? Did anyone famous die? What songs topped the charts? What was happening in the world of sports? Research the newsworthy events that took place during the month and year you were born (i.e., July 1981) by looking through newspapers, magazines, searching the Web, and/or interviewing family and friends. Write a short research paper (450-500 words) that summarizes your findings. Include at least two references and one explanatory note. Use the documentation style specified by your instructor to format the paper. Check spelling and grammar of the finished paper.

Continued >

STUDENT ASSIGNMENTS

Cases and Places *continued*

•• 5: Create a Research Paper about Spring Break Vacation Destinations

Working Together

With spring break just two months away, you and your fellow classmates are thinking about various spring break vacation destinations. Many options are available. Should you vacation close to home or travel across the country? Stay at a hotel, rent a condominium, or camp outdoors? Travel by car, train, or airplane? Book through a travel agent or the Web? Each team member is to research the attractions, accommodations, required transportation, and total cost of one spring break destination by looking through newspapers, magazines, searching the Web, and/or visiting a travel agency. Each team member is to write a minimum of 200 words summarizing his or her findings. Each team member also is to write at least one explanatory note and supply his or her source information for the citation and bibliography. Then, the team should meet as a group to compose a research paper that includes all team members' write-ups. Start by copying and pasting the text into a single document and then write an introduction and conclusion as a group. Use the documentation style specified by your instructor to format the paper. Check spelling and grammar of the finished paper. Set the default dictionary. If Word flags any of your last names as an error, add the name(s) to the custom dictionary. Hand in printouts of each team member's original write-up, as well as the final research paper.

3 | Creating a Cover Letter and a Resume

Objectives

You will have mastered the material in this chapter when you can:

- Format characters and paragraphs
- Insert and format clip art
- Set and use tab stops
- Identify the components of a business letter
- Insert the current date
- Create and insert a building block
- Insert a Word table, enter data in the table, and format the table
- Use a template to create a document

- Fill in a document template
- Copy and paste using the Office Clipboard
- Indent paragraphs
- Insert a Quick Part
- Sort a list
- Use print preview to view and print a document
- Address and print an envelope

3 | Creating a Cover Letter and a Resume

Introduction

In a business environment, people use documents to communicate with others. Business documents can include letters, memos, newsletters, proposals, and resumes. An effective business document clearly and concisely conveys its message and has a professional, organized appearance.

Some people prefer to use their own creative skills to design and compose business documents. Using Word, for example, you can develop the content and decide on the location of each item in a document. On occasion, however, you may have difficulty composing a particular type of document. To assist with the task of creating certain types of documents, such as resumes and fax cover letters, Word provides templates. A **template** is similar to a form with prewritten text; that is, Word prepares the requested document with text and/or formatting common to all documents of this nature. After Word creates a document from a template, you fill in the blanks or replace prewritten words in the document.

Project — Cover Letter and Resume

At some time in your professional life, you will prepare a cover letter along with a resume to send to prospective employers. In addition to some personal information, a **resume** usually contains the applicant's educational background and job experience. Employers review many resumes for each vacant position. Thus, you should design your resume carefully so that it presents you as the best candidate for the job. You also should attach a personalized cover letter to each resume you send. A **cover letter** enables you to elaborate on positive points in your resume; it also provides you with an opportunity to show a potential employer your writing skills.

The project in this chapter follows generally accepted guidelines for writing letters and resumes and uses Word to create the cover letter shown in Figure 3–1 and the resume shown in Figure 3–2 on page WD 148. The personalized cover letter to the prospective employer (Juniper Culinary Academy) includes a custom-made letterhead, as well as all essential business letter components. The resume for Lana Halima Canaan, a recent graduate of the culinary arts program, uses a Word template to present relevant information to a potential employer.

Overview

As you read through this chapter, you will learn how to create the cover letter and resume shown in Figures 3–1 and 3–2 by performing these general tasks:

- Design and compose a letterhead.
- Compose a cover letter.
- Print the cover letter.
- Use a template to create a resume.
- Print the resume.
- Address and print an envelope.

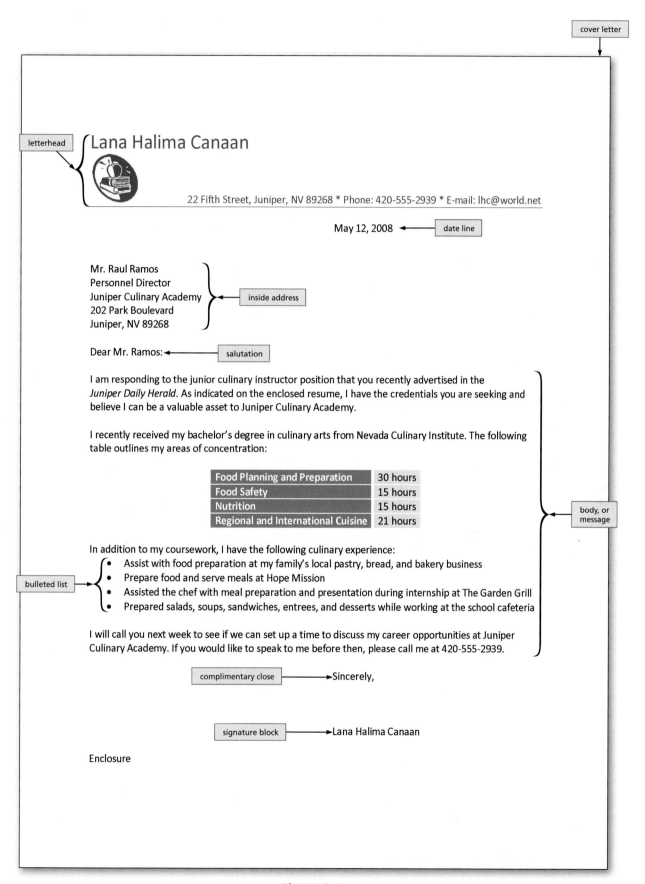

Figure 3–1

resume

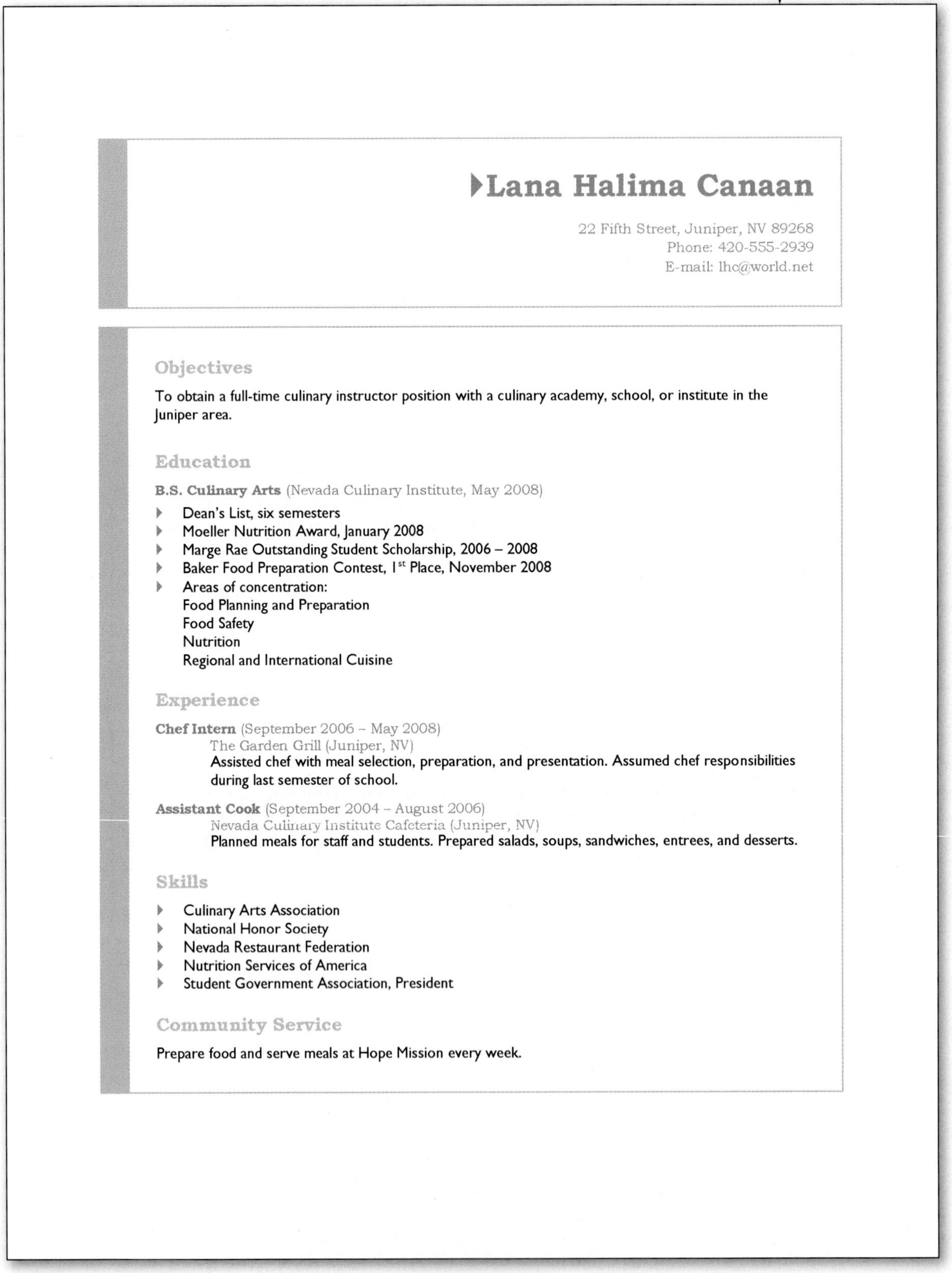

▶Lana Halima Canaan

22 Fifth Street, Juniper, NV 89268
Phone: 420-555-2939
E-mail: lhc@world.net

Objectives

To obtain a full-time culinary instructor position with a culinary academy, school, or institute in the Juniper area.

Education

B.S. Culinary Arts (Nevada Culinary Institute, May 2008)

▸ Dean's List, six semesters
▸ Moeller Nutrition Award, January 2008
▸ Marge Rae Outstanding Student Scholarship, 2006 – 2008
▸ Baker Food Preparation Contest, 1st Place, November 2008
▸ Areas of concentration:
  Food Planning and Preparation
  Food Safety
  Nutrition
  Regional and International Cuisine

Experience

Chef Intern (September 2006 – May 2008)
    The Garden Grill (Juniper, NV)
    Assisted chef with meal selection, preparation, and presentation. Assumed chef responsibilities during last semester of school.

Assistant Cook (September 2004 – August 2006)
    Nevada Culinary Institute Cafeteria (Juniper, NV)
    Planned meals for staff and students. Prepared salads, soups, sandwiches, entrees, and desserts.

Skills

▸ Culinary Arts Association
▸ National Honor Society
▸ Nevada Restaurant Federation
▸ Nutrition Services of America
▸ Student Government Association, President

Community Service

Prepare food and serve meals at Hope Mission every week.

Figure 3–2

General Project Guidelines

When creating a Word document, the actions you perform and decisions you make will affect the appearance and characteristics of the finished document. As you create a cover letter and resume, such as the project shown in Figure 3–1 on page WD 147 and Figure 3–2, you should follow these general guidelines:

1. **Design a creative letterhead.** Use text, graphics, formats, and colors that reflect your personality or employment goals. Include your name, postal mailing address, and telephone number. If you have an e-mail address and Web address, include those as well.

2. **Compose an effective cover letter.** A finished business letter (i.e., cover letter) should look like a symmetrically framed picture with evenly spaced margins, all balanced below an attractive letterhead. A well-written, properly formatted cover letter presents solid evidence of your writing skills and provides insight into your personality. The content of a letter should contain proper grammar, correct spelling, logically constructed sentences, flowing paragraphs, and sound ideas. Be sure to proofread it carefully.

3. **Craft a successful resume.** Your resume should present, at a minimum, your contact information, objective, educational background, and work experience to a potential employer. It should honestly present all your positive points. As with the cover letter, the resume should be error free. Ask someone else to proofread your resume and give you suggestions for improvements.

When necessary, more specific details concerning the above guidelines are presented at appropriate points in the chapter. The chapter also will identify the actions performed and decisions made regarding these guidelines during the creation of the cover letter shown in Figure 3–1 and the resume shown in Figure 3–2.

Plan Ahead

Creating a Letterhead

In many businesses, letterhead is preprinted on stationery that everyone in the company uses for correspondence. For personal letters, the cost of preprinted letterhead can be high. An alternative is to create your own letterhead and save it in a file. At a later time, when you want to create a letter using the letterhead, simply open the letterhead file and then save the file with a new name to preserve the original letterhead file. The letterhead in this project (Figure 3–1), follows this process; that is, you design and create a letterhead and then save it in a file.

Design a creative letterhead.

A letterhead often is the first section a reader notices on a letter. Thus, it is important your letterhead appropriately reflect the essence of the individual or business (i.e., formal, youthful, technical, etc.). The letterhead should leave ample room for the contents of the letter. When designing a letterhead, consider its contents, placement, and appearance.

- **Contents of letterhead.** A letterhead should contain these elements:
  - Complete legal name of the individual, group, or company
  - Complete mailing address: street address including building, room, suite number, or post office box, along with city, state, and postal code
  - Telephone number(s) and fax number, if one exists

  Many letterheads also include a Web address, e-mail address, and a logo or other image. If you use an image, select one that expresses your personality or goals.

  (continued)

Plan Ahead

Plan
Ahead

(continued)

- **Placement of elements in the letterhead.** Some letterheads center their elements across the top of the page. Others align some or all of the elements with the left or right margins. Sometimes, the elements are split between the top and bottom of the page. For example, a name and logo may be at the top of the page with the address at the bottom of the page.

- **Appearance of letterhead elements.** Use fonts that are easy to read. Give your name impact by making its font size larger than the rest of the text in the letterhead. For additional emphasis, consider formatting the name in bold or italic. Choose colors that complement each other and convey your goals or personality.

When finished designing the letterhead, determine if a divider line would help to visually separate the letterhead from the text of the letter.

The following pages start Word, enter and format the text and graphics in the letterhead, shown in Figure 3–1 on page WD 147, and then save the personal letterhead file.

To Start Word and Display Formatting Marks

If you are using a computer to step through the project in this chapter and you want your screens to match the figures in this book, you should change your computer's resolution to 1024×768. For information about how to change a computer's resolution, read Appendix D.

The following steps start Word and display formatting marks.

❶ Start Word. If necessary, maximize the Word window.

❷ If the Print Layout button is not selected, click it so that your screen layout matches Figure 3–3.

❸ If your zoom level is not 100%, change it to 100%.

❹ If the Show/Hide ¶ button on the Home tab is not selected already, click it to display formatting marks on the screen.

Normal Style
If your screen settings differ from Figure 3–3, it is possible the default settings in your Normal style have been changed. Normal style settings are saved in the normal.dotm file. To restore the original Normal style settings, quit Word and use Windows Explorer to locate the normal.dotm file (be sure that hidden files and folders are displayed, and include system and hidden files in your search). Rename the normal.dotm file to oldnormal.dotm file. After renaming the normal.dotm file, it no longer will exist as normal.dotm. The next time you start Word, it will recreate a normal .dotm file using the original default settings.

To Apply a Quick Style

When you press the ENTER key in the letterhead, you want the insertion point to advance to the next line, with no blank space between the lines. Recall that, by default, the Normal style in Word places 10 points of blank space after each paragraph and inserts a blank space equal to 1.15 lines between each line of text. The No Spacing style, however, does not put any extra blank space between lines when you press the ENTER key. The following step applies the No Spacing style to the current paragraph.

❶ Click No Spacing in the Styles gallery to apply the No Spacing style to the current paragraph.

To Change Theme Colors

Recall that Word provides document themes that contain a variety of color schemes to assist you in selecting complementary colors in a document. In your own letterhead, you would select a color scheme that reflects your personality or goals. This letterhead uses the Urban color scheme. The following steps change theme colors.

❶ Click the Change Styles button on the Home tab to display the Change Styles menu, and then point to Colors on the Change Styles menu to display the Colors gallery.

❷ Click Urban in the Colors gallery to change the document theme colors to Urban.

To Type Text

To begin creating the personal letterhead file in this chapter, type your name in the document window. The following step types this first line of text in the document.

1 Type `Lana Halima Canaan` and then press the ENTER key.

Q&A Why not type the name in all capital letters?

Studies show that all capital letters can be more difficult to read.

Mini Toolbar

Recall from Chapter 1 that the Mini toolbar, which automatically appears based on certain tasks you perform, contains commands related to changing the appearance of text in a document. All commands on the Mini toolbar also exist on the Ribbon.

When the Mini toolbar appears, it initially is transparent. If you do not use the transparent Mini toolbar, it disappears from the screen. To use the Mini toolbar, move the mouse pointer into the toolbar, which causes the Mini toolbar to change from a transparent to a bright appearance. The following steps illustrate the use of the Mini toolbar.

To Use the Grow Font Button to Increase Font Size

You want the font size of the name to be larger than the rest of the text in the letterhead. In previous chapters, you used the Font Size box arrow on the Home tab to change the font size of text. Word also provides a Grow Font button, which increases the font size of selected text each time you click the button. The following steps use the Grow Font button on the Mini toolbar to increase the font size of the name.

1

• Move the mouse pointer to the left of the line to be selected (in this case, the line containing your name) until the mouse pointer changes to a right-pointing block arrow, and then click the mouse to select the line (Figure 3–3).

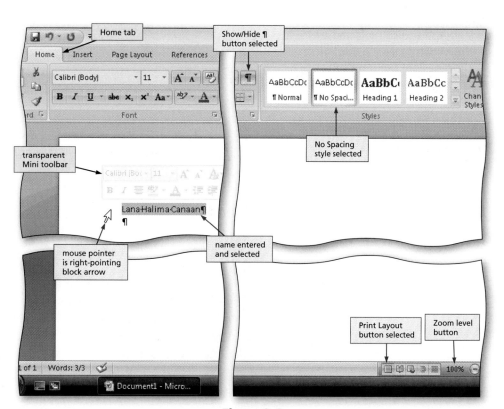

Figure 3–3

2

- Move the mouse pointer into the transparent Mini toolbar, so that it changes to a bright toolbar.

- Repeatedly click the Grow Font button on the Mini toolbar until the Font Size box displays 20, for 20 point (Figure 3–4).

Q&A

What if I click the Grow Font button too many times and make the font size too big?

Click the Shrink Font button until the desired font size is displayed.

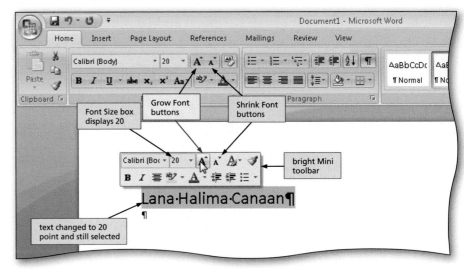

Figure 3–4

3

🔍 **Experiment**

- Repeatedly click the Grow Font and Shrink Font buttons on the Mini toolbar and watch the font size of the selected name change in the document window. When you have finished experimenting, set the font size to 20 point.

Other Ways

1. Click Grow Font button on Home tab
2. Press CTRL+>

To Color Text

The text in the letterhead is to be a shade of teal. The following steps change the color of the entered text.

1

- With the text still selected and the Mini toolbar still displaying, click the Font Color button arrow on the Mini toolbar to display the Font Color gallery (Figure 3–5).

Q&A

What if my Mini toolbar no longer is displayed?

Use the Font Color button arrow on the Home tab.

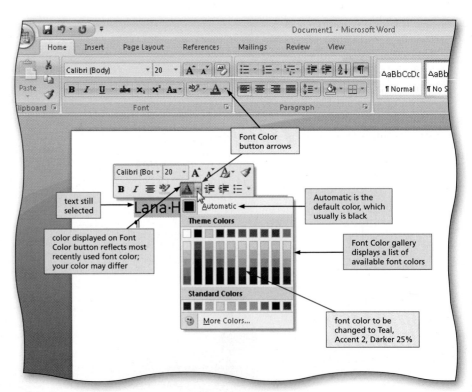

Figure 3–5

2

- Click Teal, Accent 2, Darker 25%, which is the sixth color in the fifth row in the Theme Colors area, to change the color of the selected text to a shade of teal.

- Click the paragraph mark below the name to deselect the text and position the insertion point on line 2 of the document (Figure 3–6).

Q&A

How would I change the text color back to black?

If, for some reason, you wanted to change the text color back to black at this point, you would select the text, click the Font Color button arrow again, and then click Automatic in the Font Color gallery.

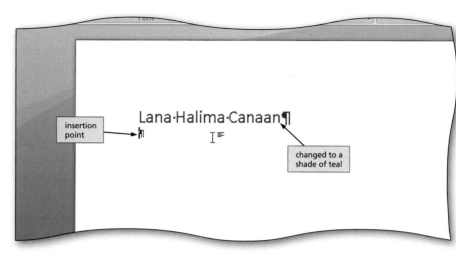

insertion point

changed to a shade of teal

Lana·Halima·Canaan¶

Figure 3–6

Other Ways

1. Click the Font Color button arrow on Home tab, click desired color

2. Click Font Dialog Box Launcher, click Font tab, click Font color box arrow, click desired color, click OK button

To Insert Clip Art

Files containing graphical images, or **graphics**, are available from a variety of sources. In Chapter 1, you inserted a digital picture taken with a digital camera in a document. In this project, you insert **clip art**, which is a predefined graphic. In the Microsoft Office programs, clip art is located in the **Clip Organizer**, which contains a collection of clip art, photographs, sounds, and videos.

The letterhead in this project contains clip art of an apple on a stack of books (Figure 3–1 on page WD 147), which represents Lana's desire to be an instructor. Thus, the next steps insert clip art on line 2 of the letterhead below the job seeker's name.

1

- With the insertion point on line 2 below the name, click Insert on the Ribbon to display the Insert tab.

- Click the Clip Art button on the Insert tab to display the Clip Art task pane.

Q&A

What is a task pane?

A **task pane** is a separate window that enables you to carry out some Word tasks more efficiently.

- If the Search for text box displays text, drag through the text to select it.

- Type teacher in the Search for text box (Figure 3–7).

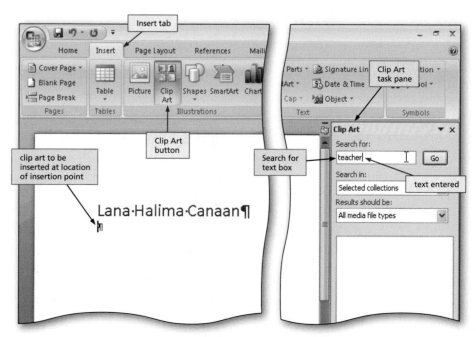

Insert tab

Clip Art task pane

Clip Art button

clip art to be inserted at location of insertion point

Search for text box

text entered

Lana·Halima·Canaan¶

Figure 3–7

2

- Click the Go button to display a list of clips that match the description, teacher (Figure 3–8).

Why is my list of clips different from Figure 3–8?

If you are connected to the Internet, the Clip Art task pane displays clips from the Web as well as those installed on your hard disk.

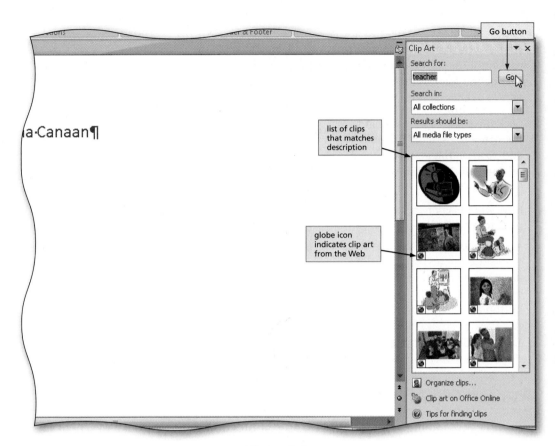

Figure 3–8

3

- Click the clip art of the apple on the stack of books to insert it in the document at the location of the insertion point (Figure 3–9).

4

- Click the Close button on the Clip Art task pane title bar to close the task pane.

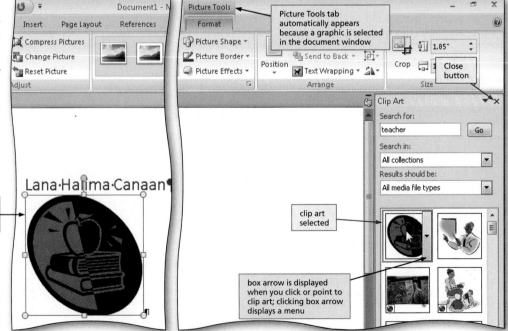

Figure 3–9

To Resize a Graphic Using the Size Dialog Box

In this project, the graphic is 35 percent of its original size. Instead of dragging the sizing handle to change the graphic's size, as you learned how to do in Chapter 1, you can use the Size dialog box to set exact size percentages. The following steps resize a graphic using the Size dialog box.

- With the graphic still selected, click the Size Dialog Box Launcher on the Format tab to display the Size dialog box (Figure 3–10).

Q&A

What if the Format tab is not the active tab on my Ribbon?

Double-click the graphic or click Format on the Ribbon to display the Format tab.

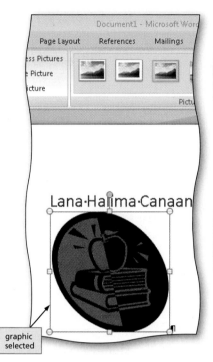
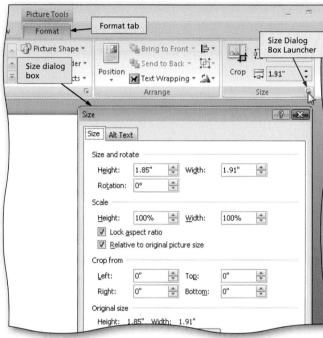

Figure 3–10

- In the Scale area, triple-click the Height text box to select it.

- Type 35 and then press the TAB key to display 35% in the Height and Width text boxes and resize the selected graphic to 35 percent of its original size (Figure 3–11).

Q&A

How do I know to use 35 percent for the resized graphic?

The larger graphic consumed too much room on the page. Try various percentages to determine the size that works best in the letterhead design.

- Click the Close button in the Size dialog box to close the dialog box.

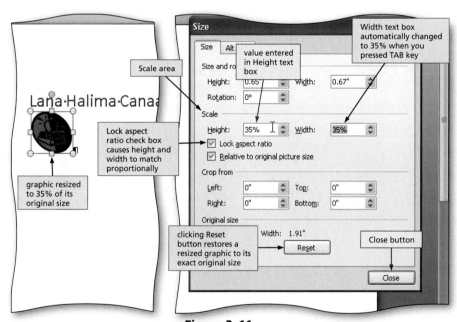

Figure 3–11

Other Ways
1. Right-click graphic, click Size on shortcut menu, click Size tab, enter Height and Width values, click Close button

To Recolor a Graphic

The clip art currently is bright red and black, which does not blend well with the current color scheme. In Word, you can change the color of a graphic. The following steps change the color of the graphic to a shade in the current color scheme.

- With the graphic still selected, click the Recolor button on the Format tab to display the Recolor gallery (Figure 3–12).

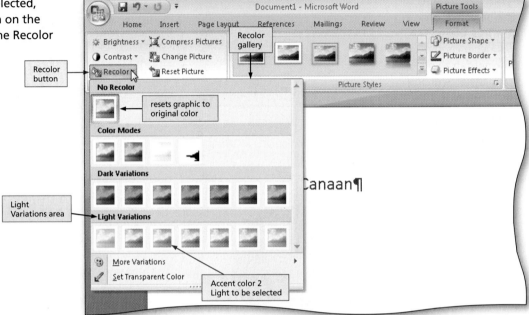

Figure 3–12

- Click Accent color 2 Light in the Recolor gallery (third color in Light Variations area) to change the color of the selected graphic in the document window (Figure 3–13).

Q&A

How would I change a graphic back to its original colors?

With the graphic selected, you would click the Reset Picture button on the Format tab or click No Recolor in the Recolor gallery.

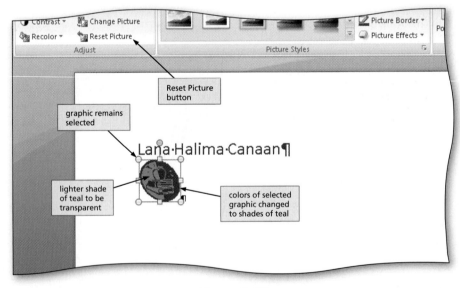

Figure 3–13

Other Ways

1. Right-click graphic, click Format Picture on shortcut menu, click Picture in left pane, click Recolor button, select color, click Close button

To Set a Transparent Color in a Graphic

Although the graphic now is the right color scheme, it is difficult to distinguish the objects in the graphic because they use shades of the same color. In Word, you can make one color in a graphic transparent, that is, remove the color. In this project, you make the lighter shades of teal in the graphic transparent, which results in a graphic that is teal and white — making the image easier to identify. The following steps set a transparent color in a graphic.

- With the graphic still selected, click the Recolor button on the Format tab to display the Recolor gallery (Figure 3–14).

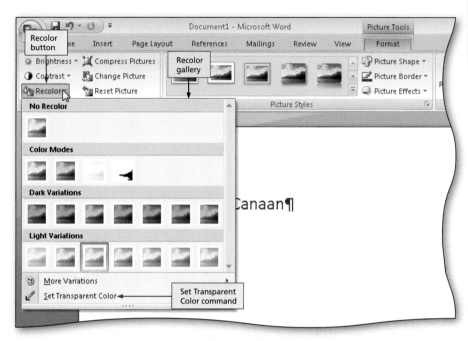

Figure 3–14

- Click Set Transparent Color in the Recolor gallery to display a pen mouse pointer in the document window.

- Position the pen mouse pointer in the graphic where you want to make the color transparent (Figure 3–15).

Figure 3–15

- Click the location in the graphic where you want the color to be transparent (Figure 3–16).

- Press the END key to deselect the graphic and move the insertion point to the end of the line, which is between the graphic and the paragraph mark.

Figure 3–16

Using Tab Stops to Align Text

In the letterhead, the graphic of the apple and the stack of books is left-aligned. The address, phone, and e-mail information in the letterhead is to be positioned at the right margin on the same line. In Word, a paragraph cannot be both left-aligned and right-aligned. If you click the Align Text Right button on the Ribbon, for example, the graphic will be right-aligned. To place text at the right margin of a left-aligned paragraph, you set a tab stop at the right margin. A **tab stop** is a location on the horizontal ruler that tells Word where to position the insertion point when you press the TAB key on the keyboard.

To Display the Ruler

You want to see the location of tab stops on the horizontal ruler. The following step displays the ruler in the document window.

 If the rulers are not displayed already, click the View Ruler button on the vertical scroll bar.

To Set Custom Tab Stops Using the Tabs Dialog Box

Word, by default, places a tab stop at every .5" mark on the ruler (shown in Figure 3–17). These default tab stops are indicated at the bottom of the horizontal ruler by small vertical tick marks. You also can set your own custom tab stops.

The next step in creating the letterhead for this project is to set a custom tab stop at the right margin, that is, at the 6.5" mark on the ruler, because you want the address, phone, and e-mail information at the right margin. One method of setting custom tab stops is to click the ruler at the desired location of the tab stop. You cannot click, however, at the right margin location. Thus, the following steps use the Tabs dialog box to set a custom tab stop.

- With the insertion point positioned between the paragraph mark and the graphic, click the Paragraph Dialog Box Launcher to display the Paragraph dialog box (Figure 3–17).

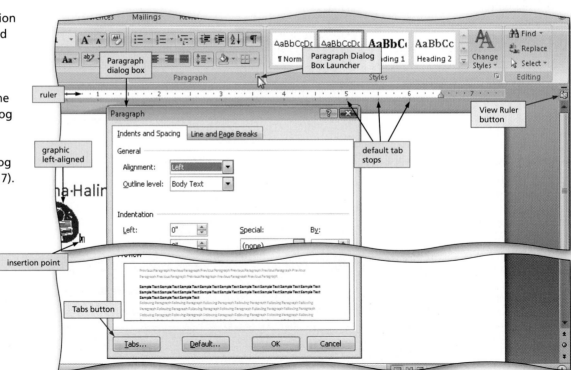

Figure 3–17

2

- Click the Tabs button in the Paragraph dialog box to display the Tabs dialog box.

- Type 6.5 in the Tab stop position text box.

- Click Right in the Alignment area to specify alignment for text at the tab stop (Figure 3–18).

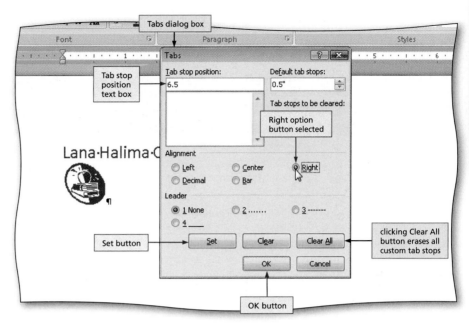

Figure 3–18

3

- Click the Set button in the Tabs dialog box to set a right-aligned custom tab stop.

- Click the OK button to place a right tab marker at the 6.5" mark on the ruler (Figure 3–19).

 What happened to all the default tab stops on the ruler?

When you set a custom tab stop, Word clears all default tab stops to the left of the newly set custom tab stop on the ruler.

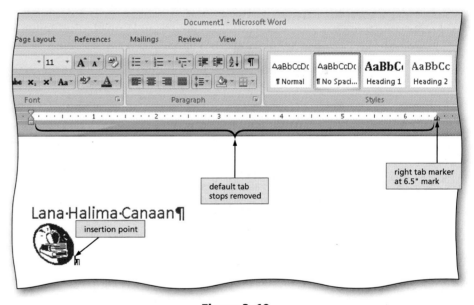

Figure 3–19

Tab Stops

Tab settings are a paragraph format. Thus, each time you press the ENTER key, any custom tab stops are carried forward to the next paragraph.

To move the insertion point from one tab stop to another, press the TAB key on the keyboard. When you press the TAB key, a **tab character** formatting mark appears in the empty space between the tab stops.

When you set a custom tab stop, you specify how the text will align at a tab stop. The tab marker on the ruler reflects the alignment of the characters at the location of the tab stop. Table 3–1 shows types of tab stop alignments in Word and their corresponding tab markers. To change an existing tab stop's alignment, double-click the tab marker on the ruler to display the Tabs dialog box (or display the Tabs dialog box as described in the steps on the previous page), click the tab stop position you wish to change, click the new alignment, and then click the OK button. You can remove an existing tab stop by clicking the tab stop position in the Tabs dialog box and then clicking the Clear button in the dialog box. To remove all tab stops, click the Clear All button in the Tabs dialog box.

Table 3–1 Types of Tab Stop Alignments

Tab Stop	Tab Marker	Result of Pressing TAB Key	Example
Left Tab	L	Left-aligns text at the location of the tab stop	toolbar ruler
Center Tab	⊥	Centers text at location of the tab stop	toolbar ruler
Right Tab	⌐	Right-aligns text at location of the tab stop	toolbar ruler
Decimal Tab	⊥·	Aligns text on decimal point at location of the tab stop	45.72 223.75
Bar Tab	I	Aligns text at a bar character at the location of the tab stop	toolbar ruler

To Specify Font Color before Typing

The address, phone, and e-mail information should be the same color as the name. The following steps enter text using the most recently defined color.

1 Click the Font Color button on the Home tab so that the text you type will be the color displayed on the face of the button.

Q&A What if the color I want is not displayed on the face of the Font Color button?

Click the Font Color button arrow and then click the desired color in the Font Color gallery.

2 With the insertion point positioned between the graphic and the paragraph mark (as shown in Figure 3–19 on the previous page), press the TAB key to move the insertion point to the 6.5" mark on the ruler.

3 Type 22 Fifth Street, Juniper, NV 89268 * Phone: 420-555-2939 * E-mail: lhc@world.net in the letterhead (Figure 3–20).

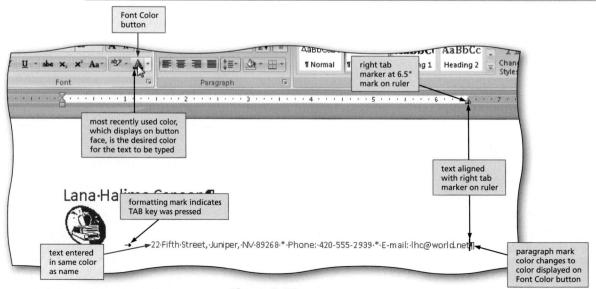

Font Color button

right tab marker at 6.5" mark on ruler

most recently used color, which displays on button face, is the desired color for the text to be typed

text aligned with right tab marker on ruler

Lana·Ha~~lima Cansan~~

formatting mark indicates TAB key was pressed

22·Fifth·Street,·Juniper,·NV·89268·*·Phone:·420-555-2939·*·E-mail:·lhc@world.net¶

text entered in same color as name

paragraph mark color changes to color displayed on Font Color button

Figure 3–20

To Bottom Border a Paragraph

The letterhead in this project has a horizontal line that extends from the left margin to the right margin immediately below the address, phone, and e-mail information. In Word, you can draw a solid line, called a **border**, at any edge of a paragraph. That is, borders may be added above or below a paragraph, to the left or right of a paragraph, or in any combination of these sides. The following steps add a bottom border to the paragraph containing address, phone, and e-mail information.

1
- With the insertion point in the paragraph to border, click the Border button arrow on the Home tab to display the Border gallery (Figure 3–21).

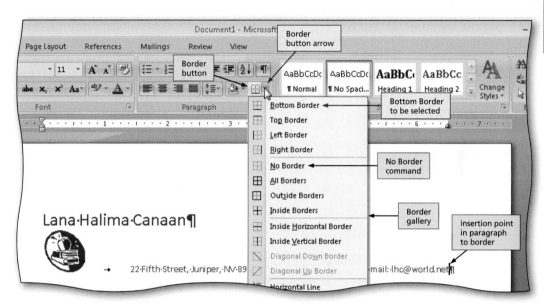

Figure 3–21

2
- Click Bottom Border in the Border gallery to place a border below the paragraph containing the insertion point (Figure 3–22).

Q&A If the face of the Border button displays the border icon I want to use, can I click the Border button instead of using the Border button arrow?

Yes.

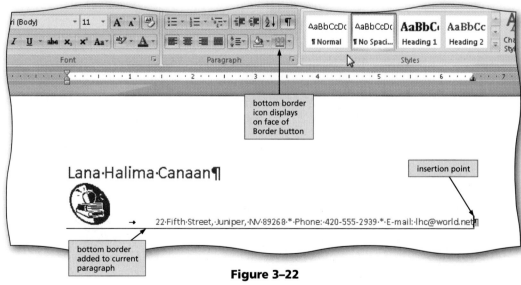

Figure 3–22

Q&A How would I remove an existing border from a paragraph?

If, for some reason, you wanted to remove a border from a paragraph, you would position the insertion point in the paragraph, click the Border button arrow on the Home tab, and then click No Border (Figure 3–21) in the Border gallery.

Other Ways
1. Click Page Borders on Page Layout tab, click Borders tab in Borders and Shading	dialog box, select desired border, click OK button

To Clear Formatting

The next step is to position the insertion point below the letterhead, so that you can type the content of the letter. When you press the ENTER key at the end of a paragraph containing a border, Word moves the border forward to the next paragraph. It also retains all current settings. That is, the paragraph text will be teal and will have a bottom border. Instead, you want the paragraph and characters on the new line to use the Normal style: black font with no border. In Word, the term, **clear formatting**, refers to returning the formatting to the Normal style. The following steps clear formatting at the location of the insertion point.

- With the insertion point between the e-mail address and paragraph mark (as shown in Figure 3–22 on the previous page), press the ENTER key (Figure 3–23).

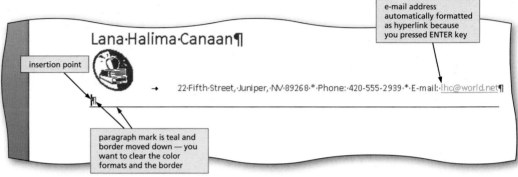

Figure 3–23

- Click the Clear Formatting button on the Home tab to apply the Normal style to the location of the insertion point (Figure 3–24).

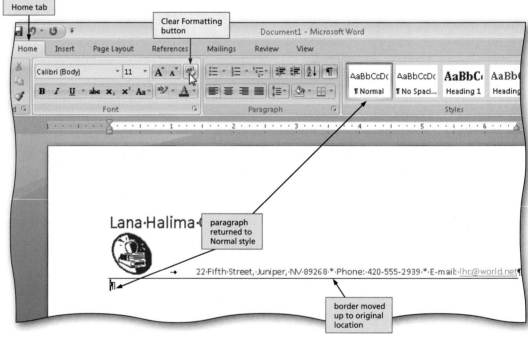

Figure 3–24

Other Ways

1. Click More button in Styles gallery on Home tab, click Clear Formatting
2. Click Styles Dialog Box Launcher, click Clear All in Styles task pane
3. Press CTRL+SPACEBAR, press CTRL+Q

AutoFormat As You Type

As you type text in a document, Word automatically formats it for you. For example, when you press the ENTER key or SPACEBAR after typing an e-mail address or Web address, Word automatically formats the address as a hyperlink, that is, colored blue and underlined. In Figure 3–23, Word formatted the e-mail address as a hyperlink because you pressed the ENTER key at the end of the line. Table 3–2 outlines commonly used AutoFormat As You Type options and their results.

Table 3–2 Commonly Used AutoFormat As You Type Options

Typed Text	AutoFormat Feature	Example
Quotation marks or apostrophes	Changes straight quotation marks or apostrophes to curly ones	"the" becomes "the"
Text, a space, one hyphen, one or no spaces, text, space	Changes the hyphen to an en dash	ages 20 - 45 becomes ages 20 – 45
Text, two hyphens, text, space	Changes the two hyphens to an em dash	Two types--yellow and red becomes Two types—yellow and red
Web or e-mail address followed by SPACEBAR or ENTER key	Formats Web or e-mail address as a hyperlink	www.scsite.com becomes www.scsite.com
Three hyphens, underscores, equal signs, asterisks, tildes, or number signs and then ENTER key	Places a border above a paragraph	--- This line becomes _____ This line
Number followed by a period, hyphen, right parenthesis, or greater than sign and then a space or tab followed by text	Creates a numbered list when you press the SPACEBAR or TAB key	1. Word 2. Excel becomes 1. Word 2. Excel
Asterisk, hyphen, or greater than sign and then a space or tab followed by text	Creates a bulleted list when you press the SPACEBAR or TAB key	* Home tab * Insert tab becomes • Home tab • Insert tab
Fraction and then a space or hyphen	Condenses the fraction entry so that it consumes one space instead of three	1/2 becomes ½
Ordinal and then a space or hyphen	Makes part of the ordinal a superscript	3rd becomes 3rd

To Convert a Hyperlink to Regular Text

The e-mail address in the letterhead should be formatted as regular text; that is, it should not be blue or underlined. Thus, the next step is to remove the hyperlink format from the e-mail address in the letterhead.

- Right-click the hyperlink (in this case, the e-mail address) to display the Mini toolbar and a shortcut menu (Figure 3–25).

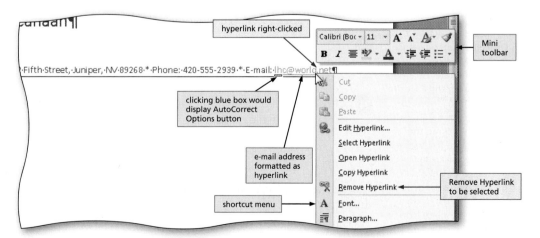

Figure 3–25

2

- Click Remove Hyperlink on the shortcut menu to remove the hyperlink format from the e-mail address.

- Position the insertion point on the paragraph mark below the border (Figure 3–26).

Q&A

Could I have used the AutoCorrect Options button instead of the Remove Hyperlink command?

Yes. Alternatively, you could have pointed to the small blue box at the beginning of the hyperlink, clicked the AutoCorrect Options button, and then clicked Undo Hyperlink on the AutoCorrect Options menu.

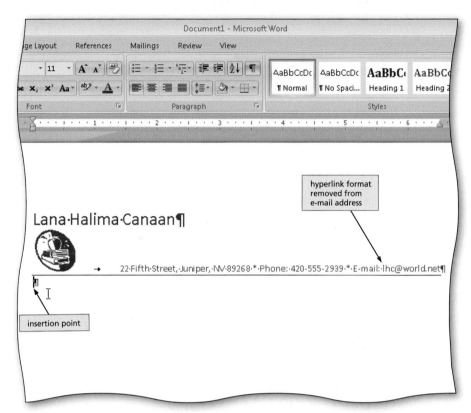

Figure 3–26

Other Ways

1. With insertion point in hyperlink, click Hyperlink button on Insert tab, click Remove Link button

To Save the Letterhead

The letterhead now is complete. Thus, you should save it in a file. For a detailed example of the procedure summarized below, refer to pages WD 19 through WD 21 in Chapter 1.

Note: If you are using Windows XP, see Appendix F for alternate steps.

1 With a USB flash drive connected to one of the computer's USB ports, click the Save button on the Quick Access Toolbar to display the Save As dialog box.

2 Type `Canaan Letterhead` in the File name text box to change the file name.

3 If Computer is not displayed in the Favorite Links section, drag the top or bottom edge of the Save As dialog box until Computer is displayed. Click Computer in the Favorite Links section and then select the USB flash drive.

4 Click the Save button in the Save As dialog box to save the document on the USB flash drive with the file name, Canaan Letterhead.

Q&A

How can I keep reusing this same letterhead file for every letter I create?

If the letterhead file is not yet opened, you can instruct Word to create a new document window that contains the contents of an existing document. If the letterhead file is already opened, you can save the file with a new file name.

BTW

Saving a Template
As an alternative to saving the letterhead as a Word document, you could save it as a template by clicking the Office Button, pointing to Save As, clicking Word Template, clicking Templates in the Favorite Links section, entering the template name, and then clicking the Save button. To use the template, click the Office Button, click New, click My templates in the left pane, and then double-click the template icon or name.

TO CREATE A NEW FILE FROM AN EXISTING FILE

If you wish to open a new document window that contains the contents of an existing file, you would follow these steps.

1. Click the Office Button and then click New to display the New Document dialog box.
2. Click 'New from existing' in the Templates area to display the New from Existing Document dialog box.
3. Locate and select the file from which you wish to create a new file.
4. Click the Create New button in the dialog box.

Creating a Cover Letter

You have created a letterhead for the cover letter. The next step is to compose the cover letter. The following pages use Word to compose a cover letter that contains a table and a bulleted list.

Plan Ahead

> **Compose an effective cover letter.**
> You always should send a personalized cover letter with a resume. The cover letter should highlight aspects of your background relevant to the position. To help you recall past achievements and activities, keep a personal file containing documents that outline your accomplishments.
>
> A cover letter is a type of business letter. When composing a business letter, you need to be sure to include all essential elements and to decide which letter style to use.
>
> - **Include all essential letter elements.** All business letters, including cover letters, contain the same basic elements. Essential business letter elements include the date line, inside address, message, and signature block (shown in Figure 3–1 on page WD 147).
>
> - **Determine which letter style to use.** You can follow many different styles when creating business letters. A letter style specifies guidelines for the alignment and spacing of elements in the business letter.

To Save the Document with a New File Name

The current open file has the name Canaan Letterhead, which is the name of the personal letterhead. You want the letterhead to remain intact. Thus, the following steps save the document with a new file name.

1 With a USB flash drive connected to one of the computer's USB ports, click the Office Button to display the Office Button menu and then click Save As on the Office Button menu to display the Save As dialog box.

2 Type `Canaan Cover Letter` in the File name text box to change the file name.

3 If necessary, select the USB flash drive as the save location.

4 Click the Save button in the Save As dialog box to save the document on the USB flash drive with the file name, Canaan Cover Letter.

To Apply a Quick Style

When you press the ENTER key in the letter, you want the insertion point to advance to the next line, with no blank space between the lines. Recall that, by default, the Normal style in Word places 10 points of blank space after each paragraph and inserts a blank space equal to 1.15 lines between each line of text. The No Spacing style, however, does not put any blank space between lines when you press the ENTER key. Thus, the following step applies the No Spacing style to the current paragraph.

 With the insertion point on the paragraph mark below the border, click No Spacing in the Styles gallery to apply the No Spacing style to the current paragraph.

Plan Ahead

> **Include all essential letter elements.**
> Be sure to include all essential business letter elements, properly spaced, in your cover letter.
>
> - The **date line**, which consists of the month, day, and year, is positioned two to six lines below the letterhead.
>
> - The **inside address**, placed three to eight lines below the date line, usually contains the addressee's courtesy title plus full name, job title, business affiliation, and full geographical address.
>
> - The **salutation**, if present, begins two lines below the last line of the inside address. If you do not know the recipient's name, avoid using the salutation "To whom it may concern" — it is impersonal. Instead, use the recipient's title in the salutation, e.g., Dear Personnel Director.
>
> - The body of the letter, the **message**, begins two lines below the salutation. Within the message, paragraphs are single-spaced with one blank line between paragraphs.
>
> - Two lines below the last line of the message, the **complimentary close** is displayed. Capitalize only the first word in a complimentary close.
>
> - Type the **signature block** at least four blank lines below the complimentary close, allowing room for the author to sign his or her name.

Plan Ahead

> **Determine which letter style to use.**
> Three common business letter styles are the block, the modified block, and the modified semi-block. Each style specifies different alignments and indentations.
>
> - In the block letter style, all components of the letter begin flush with the left margin.
>
> - In the modified block letter style, the date, complimentary close, and signature block are positioned approximately one-half inch to the right of center or at the right margin. All other components of the letter begin flush with the left margin.
>
> - In the modified semi-block letter style, the date, complimentary close, and signature block are centered, positioned approximately one-half inch to the right of center or at the right margin. The first line of each paragraph in the body of the letter is indented one-half to one inch from the left margin. All other components of the letter begin flush with the left margin.
>
> The cover letter in this project follows the modified block style.

To Set Custom Tab Stops Using the Ruler

The first required element of the cover letter is the date line, which in this letter is to be positioned two lines below the letterhead. The date line contains the month, day, and year, and begins 3.5 inches from the left margin, which is approximately one-half inch to the right of center. Thus, you should set a custom tab stop at the 3.5" mark on the ruler. Earlier you used the Tabs dialog box to set a tab stop because you could not use the ruler to set a tab stop at the right margin. The following steps set a left-aligned tab stop using the ruler.

- With the insertion point on the paragraph mark below the border, press the ENTER key so that a blank line appears between the letterhead and the date line.

- If necessary, click the tab selector at the left edge of the horizontal ruler until it displays the Left Tab icon.

- Position the mouse pointer on the 3.5" mark on the ruler (Figure 3–27).

Q&A What is the purpose of the tab selector?

Before using the ruler to set a tab stop, you must ensure the correct tab stop icon appears in the tab selector. Each time you click the tab selector, its icon changes. For a list of the types of tab stops, see Table 3–1 on page WD 160.

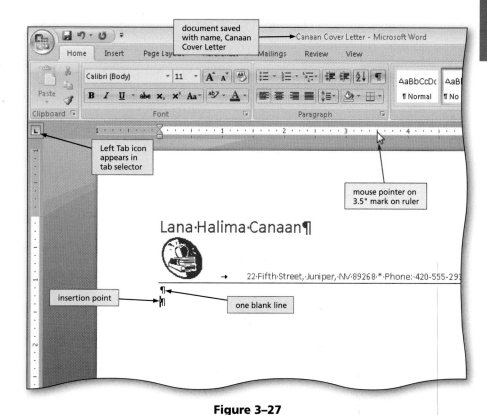

Figure 3–27

- Click the 3.5" mark on the ruler to place a left tab marker at that location on the ruler (Figure 3–28).

Q&A What if I click the wrong location on the ruler?

You can move a custom tab stop by dragging the tab marker to the desired location on the ruler. Or, you can remove a custom tab stop by pointing to the tab marker on the ruler and then dragging the tab marker down and out of the ruler.

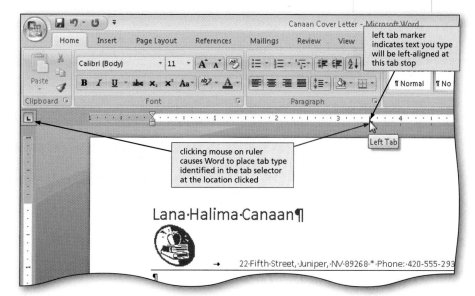

Figure 3–28

To Insert the Current Date in a Document

The next step is to enter the current date at the 3.5" tab stop in the document, as specified in the guidelines for a modified block style letter. Word provides a method of inserting a computer's system date in a document. The following steps insert the current date in the cover letter.

1

- Press the TAB key.

- Click Insert on the Ribbon to display the Insert tab.

- Click the Insert Date and Time button on the Insert tab to display the Date and Time dialog box.

- Click the desired format (in this case, May 12, 2008) in the dialog box.

- If the Update automatically check box is selected, click the check box to remove the check mark (Figure 3–29).

Q&A

Why should the Update automatically check box not be selected?

In this project, the date at the top of the letter should always show today's date. If, however, you wanted the date always to change to reflect the current computer date, for example showing the date you open or print the letter, then you would put a check mark in this check box.

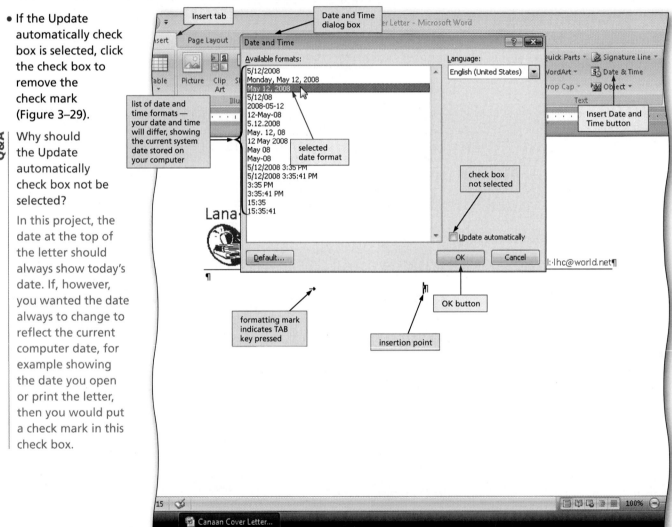

Figure 3–29

2

- Click the OK button to insert the current date at the location of the insertion point (Figure 3–30).

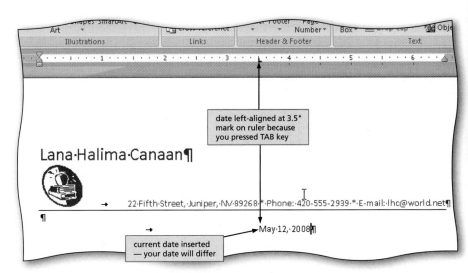

date left-aligned at 3.5" mark on ruler because you pressed TAB key

Lana·Halima·Canaan¶

→ 22·Fifth·Street,·Juniper,·NV·89268·*·Phone:·420-555-2939·*·E-mail:·lhc@world.net¶
¶
→ May·12,·2008¶

current date inserted — your date will differ

Figure 3–30

To Enter the Inside Address and Salutation

The next step in composing the cover letter is to type the inside address and salutation.

1 With the insertion point at the end of the date, press the ENTER key three times.

2 Type `Mr. Raul Ramos` and then press the ENTER key.

3 Type `Personnel Director` and then press the ENTER key.

4 Type `Juniper Culinary Academy` and then press the ENTER key.

5 Type `202 Park Boulevard` and then press the ENTER key.

6 Type `Juniper, NV 89268` and then press the ENTER key twice.

7 Type `Dear Mr. Ramos` and then press the COLON key (:) to complete the entries of the inside address and salutation (Figure 3–31).

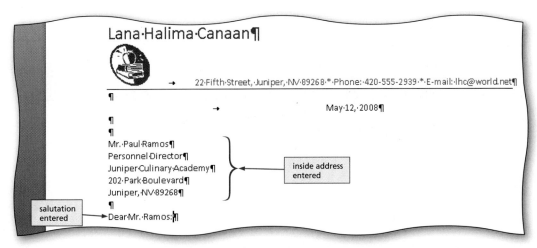

Lana·Halima·Canaan¶

→ 22·Fifth·Street,·Juniper,·NV·89268·*·Phone:·420-555-2939·*·E-mail:·lhc@world.net¶
¶
→ May·12,·2008¶
¶
¶
Mr.·Paul·Ramos¶
Personnel·Director¶
Juniper·Culinary·Academy¶
202·Park·Boulevard¶
Juniper,·NV·89268¶
¶
Dear·Mr.·Ramos:¶

inside address entered

salutation entered

Figure 3–31

To Create a Building Block

If you use the same text or graphic frequently, you can store the text or graphic in a **building block** and then use the stored building block entry in the open document, as well as in future documents. That is, you can create the entry once as a building block, and for all future occurrences of the text or graphic, you can insert the building block as you need it. In this way, you avoid entering the text or graphics inconsistently or incorrectly in different locations throughout the same document.

The next steps create a building block for the prospective employer's name, Juniper Culinary Academy. Later in the chapter, you will insert the building block in the document instead of typing the employer's name.

- Select the text to be a building block, in this case, Juniper Culinary Academy. Do not select the paragraph mark at the end of the text.

Q&A

Why is the paragraph mark not part of the building block?

Only select the paragraph mark if you want to store paragraph formatting, such as indentation and line spacing, as part of the building block.

- Click the Quick Parts button on the Insert tab to display the Quick Parts menu (Figure 3–32).

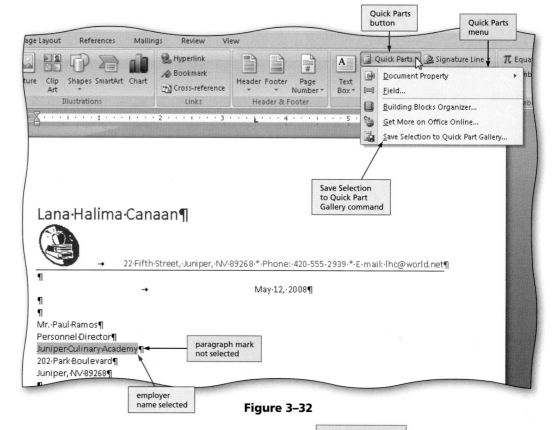

Figure 3–32

- Click Save Selection to Quick Part Gallery on the Quick Parts menu to display the Create New Building Block dialog box.

- Type jca in the Name text box to replace the proposed building block name (Juniper Culinary) with a shorter building block name (Figure 3–33).

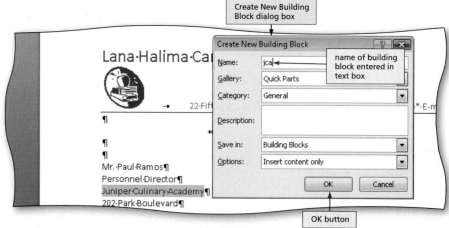

Figure 3–33

- Click the OK button to store the building block entry and close the dialog box.

- If Word displays another dialog box, click the Yes button.

Other Ways

1. Select text, press ALT+F3

To Insert a Nonbreaking Space

Some compound words, such as proper nouns, dates, units of time and measure, abbreviations, and geographic destinations, should not be divided at the end of a line. These words either should fit as a unit at the end of a line or be wrapped together to the next line.

Word provides two special characters to assist with this task: nonbreaking space and nonbreaking hyphen. A **nonbreaking space** is a special space character that prevents two words from splitting if the first word falls at the end of a line. Similarly, a **nonbreaking hyphen** is a special type of hyphen that prevents two words separated by a hyphen from splitting at the end of a line.

The following steps insert a nonbreaking space between the words in the newspaper name.

- Click to the right of the colon in the salutation and then press the ENTER key twice to position the insertion point one blank line below the salutation.

- Type I am responding to the junior culinary instructor position that you recently advertised in the and then press the SPACEBAR.

- Press CTRL+I to turn on italics. Type Juniper as the first word in the newspaper name and then press CTRL+SHIFT+SPACEBAR to insert a nonbreaking space after the word, Juniper (Figure 3–34).

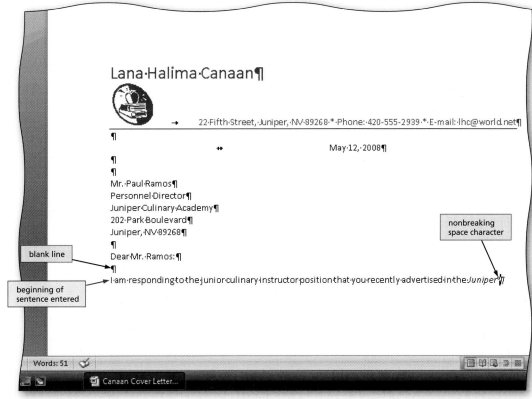

Figure 3–34

2

- Type Daily and then press CTRL+SHIFT+SPACEBAR to insert another nonbreaking space after the word, Daily.

- Type Herald and then press CTRL+I to turn off italics. Press the PERIOD key (Figure 3–35).

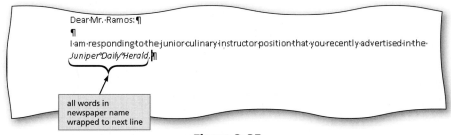

Figure 3–35

Other Ways
1. Click Symbol button on Insert tab, click More Symbols, click Special Characters tab, click   Nonbreaking Space in Character list, click Insert button, click Close button

To Insert a Building Block

At the end of the next sentence in the body of the cover letter, you want the prospective employer name, Juniper Culinary Academy, to be displayed. Recall that earlier in this chapter, you created a building block name of jca for Juniper Culinary Academy. Thus, you will type the building block name and then instruct Word to replace the building block name with the stored building block entry of Juniper Culinary Academy. The following steps insert a building block.

• Press the SPACEBAR. Type As indicated on the enclosed resume, I have the credentials you are seeking and believe I can be a valuable asset to jca as shown in Figure 3–36.

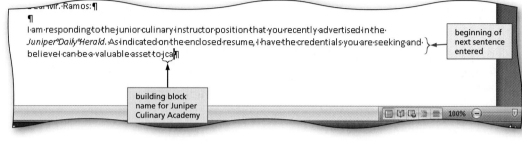

Figure 3–36

• Press the F3 key to instruct word to replace the building block name (jca) with the stored building block entry (Juniper Culinary Academy).

• Press the PERIOD key (Figure 3–37).

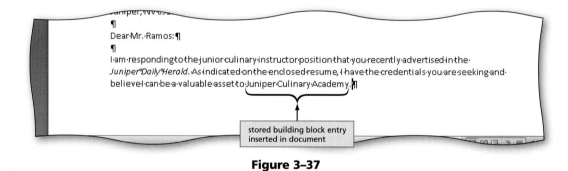

Figure 3–37

Other Ways
1. Click Quick Parts button on Insert tab, click desired building block

Building Blocks vs. AutoCorrect

In Project 2, you learned how to use the AutoCorrect feature, which enables you to insert and create AutoCorrect entries, similarly to how you created and inserted building blocks in this chapter. The difference between an AutoCorrect entry and a building block entry is that the AutoCorrect feature makes corrections for you automatically as soon as you press the SPACEBAR or type a punctuation mark, whereas you must instruct Word to insert a building block. That is, you enter the building block name and then press the F3 key, or click the Quick Parts button and select the building block from the list.

To Enter a Paragraph

The next step in creating the cover letter is to enter a paragraph of text.

Press the ENTER key twice to place a blank line between paragraphs, according to the guidelines of the modified block letter style.

2 Type I recently received my bachelor's degree in culinary arts from Nevada Culinary Institute. The following table outlines my areas of concentration:

3 Press the ENTER key twice.

Tables

The next step in composing the cover letter is to place a table listing the number of credit hours for areas of concentration (shown in Figure 3–1 on page WD 147). A Word **table** is a collection of rows and columns. The intersection of a row and a column is called a **cell**, and cells are filled with text.

The first step in creating a table is to insert an empty table into the document. When inserting a table, you must specify the total number of rows and columns required, which is called the **dimension** of the table. The table in this project has two columns. You often do not know the total number of rows in a table. Thus, many Word users create one row initially and then add more rows as needed. In Word, the first number in a dimension is the number of columns, and the second is the number of rows. For example, in Word, a 2 × 1 (pronounced "two by one") table consists of two columns and one row.

To Insert an Empty Table

The next step is to insert an empty table in the cover letter. The following steps insert a table with two columns and one row at the location of the insertion point.

1
- Click the Table button on the Insert tab to display the Table gallery.

🔍 **Experiment**
- Point to various cells on the grid to see a preview of the table in the document window.

2
- Position the mouse pointer on the cell in the first row and second column of the grid to preview the desired table dimension (Figure 3–38).

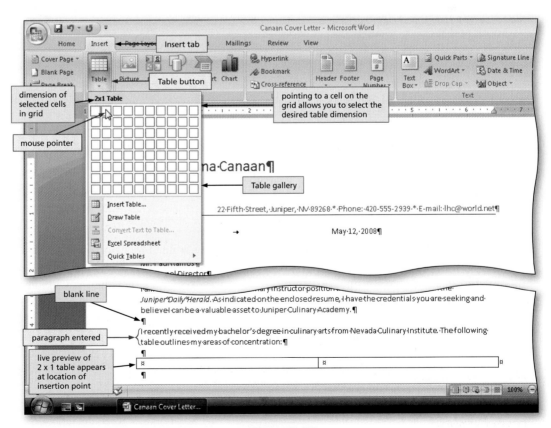

Figure 3–38

3

- Click the cell in the first row and second column of the grid to insert an empty table with one row and two columns in the document (Figure 3–39).

Q&A

What are the small circles in the table cells?

Each table cell has an **end-of-cell mark**, which is a formatting mark that assists you with selecting and formatting cells. Similarly, each row has an **end-of-row mark**, which you can use to add columns to the right of a table. Recall that formatting marks do not print on a hard copy. The end-of-cell marks currently are left-aligned, that is, positioned at the left edge of each cell.

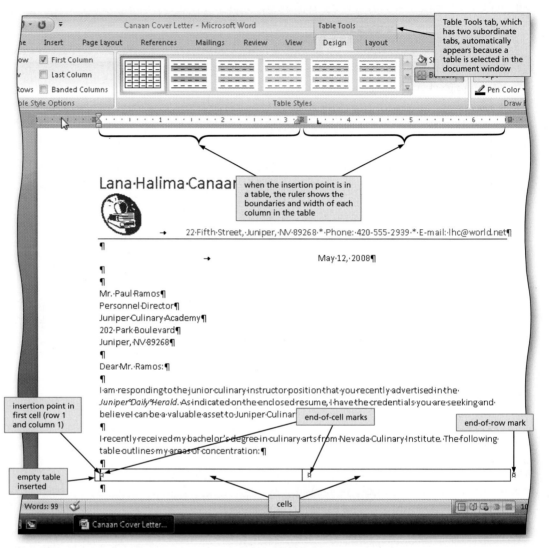

Figure 3–39

Other Ways
1. Click Table on Insert tab, click Insert Table on Table gallery, enter number of columns and rows, click OK button

To Enter Data in a Table

The next step is to enter data in the cells of the empty table. The data you enter in a cell wordwraps just as text wordwraps between the margins of a document. To place data in a cell, you click the cell and then type.

To advance rightward from one cell to the next, press the TAB key. When you are at the rightmost cell in a row, press the TAB key to move to the first cell in the next row; do not press the ENTER key. The ENTER key is used to begin a new paragraph within a cell. One way to add new rows to a table is to press the TAB key when the insertion point is positioned in the bottom-right corner cell of the table. The next steps enter data in the table, adding rows as necessary.

1

- If necessary, scroll the table up in the document window.

- With the insertion point in the left cell of the table, type `Food Planning and Preparation` and then press the TAB key to advance the insertion point to the next cell.

- Type `30 hours` and then press the TAB key to add a second row to the table and position the insertion point in the first column of the new row (Figure 3–40).

Q&A How do I edit cell contents if I make a mistake?

Click in the cell and then correct the entry.

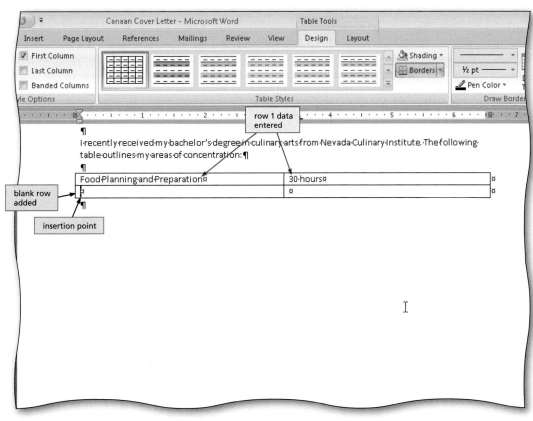

Figure 3–40

2

- Type `Food Safety` and then press the TAB key. Type `15 hours` and then press the TAB key.

- Type `Nutrition` and then press the TAB key. Type `15 hours` and then press the TAB key.

- Type `Regional and International Cuisine` and then press the TAB key. Type `21 hours` to complete the entries in the table (Figure 3–41).

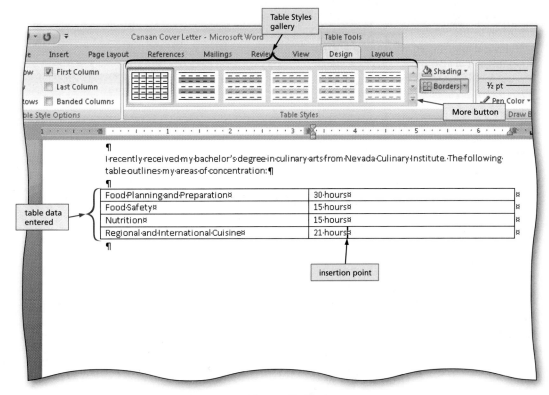

Figure 3–41

To Apply a Table Style

The next step is to apply a table style to the table. Word provides a Table Styles gallery, allowing you to change the basic table format to a more visually appealing style. Word provides a gallery of more than 90 table styles, which include a variety of colors and shading. In this project, you do not want the heading rows or alternating rows to use a different format; that is, you want the formatting applied to the rows in the table to be the same. The following steps apply a table style to the table in the cover letter.

- With the insertion point in the table, remove the check marks from the Header Row and Banded Rows check boxes on the Design tab so that all rows in the table will be formatted the same.

Q&A

What if the Design tab in the Table Tools tab no longer is the active tab?

Click in the table and then click Design on the Ribbon.

- Click the More button in the Table Styles gallery (shown in Figure 3–41 on the previous page) to expand the Table Styles gallery.

- Scroll and then point to Medium Grid 3 - Accent 2 in the Table Styles gallery to display a live preview of that style applied to the table in the document (Figure 3–42).

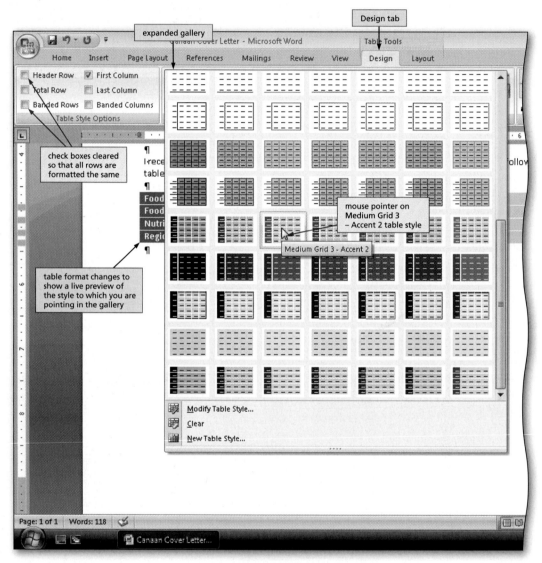

Figure 3–42

Experiment

- Point to various table styles in the Table Styles gallery and watch the format of the table change in the document window.

- Click Medium Grid 3 - Accent 2 in the Table Styles gallery to apply the selected style to the table (Figure 3–43).

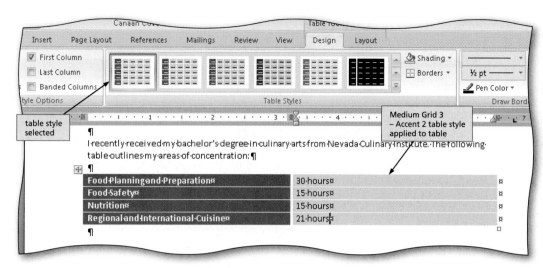

Figure 3–43

To Resize Table Columns to Fit Table Contents

The table in this project currently extends from the left margin to the right margin of the document. You want each column only to be as wide as the longest entry in the table. That is, the first column must be wide enough to accommodate the words, Regional and International Cuisine, and the second column should be only as wide as the hours entered. The following steps instruct Word to fit the width of the columns to the contents of the table automatically.

1

- With the insertion point in the table, click Layout on the Ribbon to display the Layout tab.

- Click the AutoFit button on the Layout tab to display the AutoFit menu (Figure 3–44).

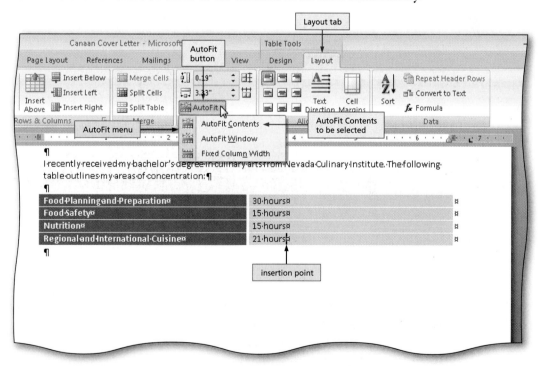

Figure 3–44

2

• Click AutoFit Contents on the AutoFit menu, so that Word automatically adjusts the widths of the columns based on the text in the table (Figure 3–45).

Q&A

Can I resize columns manually?

Yes, you can drag a **column boundary**, the border to the right of a column, until the column is the desired width. Similarly, you can resize a row by dragging the **row boundary**, the border at the bottom of a row, until the row is the desired height. You also can resize the entire table by dragging the **table resize handle**, which is a small square that appears when you point to a corner of the table (shown in Figure 3–46).

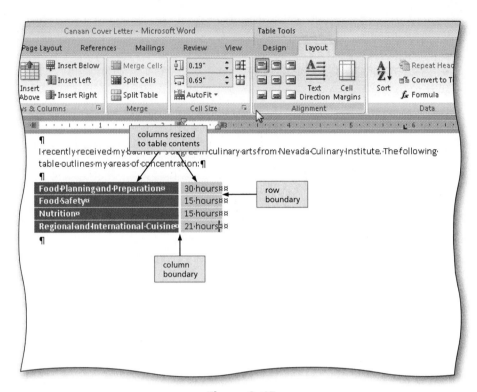

Figure 3–45

Other Ways	
1. Right-click table, point to AutoFit on shortcut menu, click AutoFit to Contents	2. Double-click column boundary

Selecting Table Contents

When working with tables, you may need to select the contents of cells, rows, columns, or the entire table. Table 3–3 identifies ways to select various items in a table.

Table 3–3 Selecting Items in a Table	
Item to Select	**Action**
Cell	Click left edge of cell
Column	Click border at top of column
Multiple cells, rows, or columns adjacent to one another	Drag through cells, rows, or columns
Multiple cells, rows, or columns not adjacent to one another	Select first cell, row, or column and then hold down CTRL key while selecting next cell, row, or column
Next cell	Press TAB key
Previous cell	Press SHIFT+TAB
Row	Click to left of row
Table	Click table move handle

BTW

Tab Character
In a table, the TAB key advances the insertion point from one cell to the next in a table. To insert a tab character in a cell, you must press CTRL+TAB.

To Select a Table

When you first create a table, it is left-aligned, that is, flush with the left margin. In this cover letter, the table should be centered. To center a table, you first select the entire table.

- Position the mouse pointer in the table so that the table move handle appears.

- Click the table move handle to select the entire table (Figure 3–46).

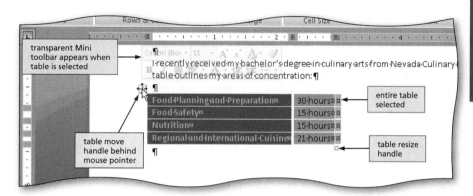

Figure 3–46

Other Ways

1. Click Select button on Layout tab, click Select Table on Select menu

To Center a Selected Table

The following steps center the selected table between the margins.

1 Move the mouse pointer into the Mini toolbar, so that the toolbar changes to a bright toolbar.

2 Click the Center button on the Mini toolbar to center the selected table between the left and right margins (Figure 3–47).

Q&A When should I use the Mini toolbar versus the Ribbon?

If the command you want to use is not on the currently displayed tab on the Ribbon and it is available on the Mini toolbar, use the Mini toolbar instead of switching to a different tab. This technique minimizes mouse movement.

Q&A How would I center the contents of the table cells instead of the entire table?

If you wanted to center the contents of the cells, you would select the cells by dragging through them and then click the Center button.

BTW

Tables
For simple tables, such as the one just created, Word users often select the table dimension in the grid to create the table. For more complex tables, such as one with a varying number of columns per row, Word has a Draw Table feature that allows users to draw a table in the document using a pencil pointer. To use this feature, click Table on the Insert tab and then click Draw Table.

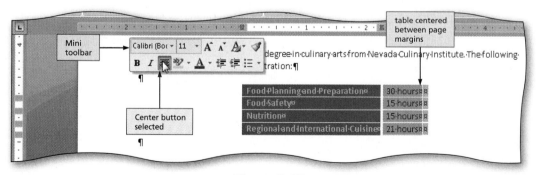

Figure 3–47

Adding and Deleting Table Rows

As discussed in the previous steps, you can add a row to the end of a table by positioning the insertion point in the bottom-right corner cell and then pressing the TAB key. You also can add rows to a table by clicking the Insert Rows Above button or Insert Rows Below button on the Layout tab to insert a row above or below the location of the insertion point in the table. Similarly, you can right-click the table, point to Insert on the shortcut menu, and then click Insert Rows Above or Insert Rows Below.

To add columns to a table, click the Insert Columns to the Left button or Insert Columns to the Right button on the Layout tab to insert a column to the left or right of the location of the insertion point in the table. Similarly, you can right-click the table, point to Insert on the shortcut menu, and then click Insert Columns to the Left or Insert Columns to the Right.

If you want to delete row(s) or delete column(s) from a table, position the insertion point in the row(s) or column(s) to delete, click the Delete button on the Layout tab, and then click Delete Rows or Delete Columns. Or, select the row or column to delete, right-click the selection, and then click Delete Rows or Delete Columns on the shortcut menu.

To delete the contents of a cell, select the cell contents by pointing to the left edge of a cell and clicking when the mouse pointer changes direction, and then press the DELETE key. You also can drag and drop or cut and paste the contents of cells.

To Add More Text

The next step is to add more text below the table.

1 Position the insertion point on the paragraph mark below the table and then press the ENTER key.

2 Type In addition to my coursework, I have the following culinary experience: and then press the ENTER key.

To Bullet a List as You Type

In Chapter 1, you learned how to apply bullets to existing paragraphs. If you know before you type that a list should be bulleted, you can use Word's AutoFormat As You Type feature to bullet the paragraphs as you type them (Table 3–2 on page WD 163). The following steps add bullets to a list as you type.

1
- Press the ASTERISK key (*) as the first character on the line (Figure 3–48).

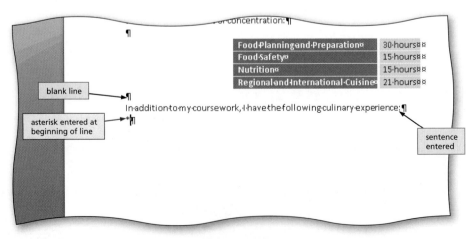

Figure 3–48

2

- Press the SPACEBAR to convert the asterisk to a bullet character.

What if I did not want the asterisk converted to a bullet character?

You would undo the AutoFormat by clicking the Undo button, or by clicking the AutoCorrect Options button and then clicking Undo Automatic Bullets on the AutoCorrect Options menu, or by clicking the Bullets button on the Home tab.

- Type Assist with food preparation at my family's local pastry, bread, and bakery business as the first bulleted item.

- Press the ENTER key to place another bullet character at the beginning of the next line (Figure 3–49).

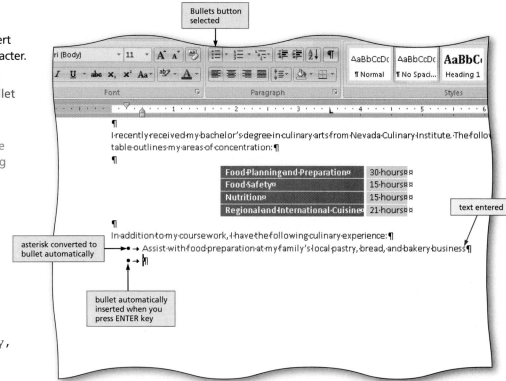

Figure 3–49

3

- Type Prepare food and serve meals at Hope Mission and then press the ENTER key.

- Type Assisted the chef with meal preparation and presentation during internship at The Garden Grill and then press the ENTER key.

- Type Prepared salads, soups, sandwiches, entrees, and desserts while working at the school cafeteria and then press the ENTER key.

- Press the ENTER key to turn off automatic bullets as you type (Figure 3–50).

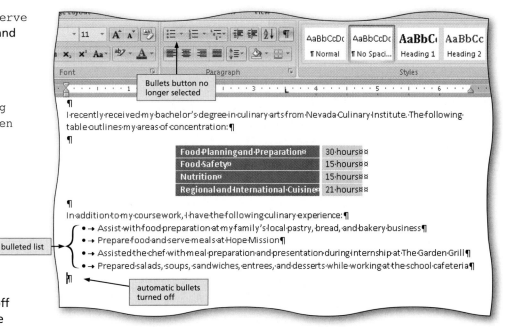

Figure 3–50

Why did automatic bullets stop?

When you press the ENTER key without entering any text after the automatic bullet character, Word turns off the automatic bullets feature.

Other Ways

1. Click Bullets button on Home tab

2. Right-click paragraph to be bulleted, click bullets button on Mini toolbar

3. Right-click paragraph to be bulleted, point to Bullets on shortcut menu, click desired bullet style

To Enter the Remainder of the Cover Letter

The next step is to enter the remainder of the cover letter.

1 Press the ENTER key and then type the paragraph shown in Figure 3–51, making certain you use the building block name, jca, to insert the employer name.

2 Press the ENTER key twice. Press the TAB key. Type Sincerely and then press the COMMA key.

3 Press the ENTER key four times. Press the TAB key. Type Lana Halima Canaan and then press the ENTER key twice. Type Enclosure as the final text in the cover letter (Figure 3–51).

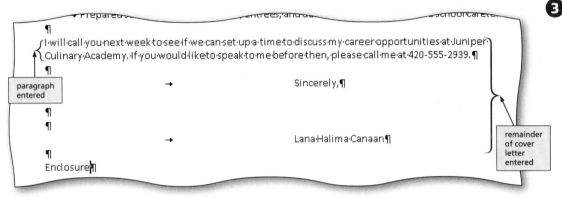

Figure 3–51

To Change Document Properties

Before saving the research paper again, you want to add your name, course and section, and some keywords as document properties. The following steps use the Document Information Panel to change document properties.

1 Display the Office Button menu, point to Prepare on the Office Button menu, and then click Properties on the Prepare submenu to display the Document Information Panel.

2 Click the Author text box, if necessary, and then type your name as the Author property. If a name already is displayed in the Author text box, delete it before typing your name. Click the Subject text box, if necessary delete any existing text, and then type your course and section as the Subject property. Click the Keywords text box, if necessary delete any existing text, and then type Cover Letter as the Keywords property.

3 Close the Document Information Panel.

To Save an Existing Document and Print It

The document now is complete. You should save the cover letter again. The following steps save the document again and then print it. Do not close the Canaan Cover Letter file. You will use it again later in this chapter to copy the address, phone, and e-mail information to the resume.

1 Click the Save button on the Quick Access Toolbar to overwrite the previous Canaan Cover Letter file on the USB flash drive.

2 Display the Office Button menu, point to Print, and then click Quick Print to print the cover letter (shown in Figure 3–1 on page WD 147).

Using a Template to Create a Resume

The next step in this project is to create the resume (Figure 3–2 on page WD 148). Although you could compose a resume in a blank document window, this chapter shows instead how to use a template, where Word formats the resume with appropriate headings and spacing. You customize the resume created by the template by filling in blanks and by selecting and replacing text.

Craft a successful resume.

Two types of resumes are the chronological resume and the functional resume. A chronological resume sequences information by time, with the most recent listed first. This type of resume highlights a job seeker's job continuity and growth. A functional resume groups information by skills and accomplishments. This resume emphasizes a job seeker's experience and qualifications in specialized areas. Some resumes use a combination of the two formats. For an entry-level job search, experts recommend a chronological resume or a combination of the two types of resumes.

When creating your resume, be sure to include necessary information and present it appropriately. Keep descriptions short and concise, using action words and bulleted lists.

- **Include necessary information.** Your resume should include contact information, a clearly written objective, educational background, and experience. Use your complete legal name and mailing address, along with phone number and e-mail address, if one exists. Other sections you might consider including are organizations, recognitions and awards, and skills. Do not include your social security number, marital status, age, height, weight, gender, physical appearance, health, citizenship, previous pay rates, reasons for leaving a prior job, current date, high-school information (if you are a college graduate), and references. Employers assume you will give references, if asked, and this information simply clutters a resume.

- **Present your resume appropriately.** For printed resumes, use a high-quality ink-jet or laser printer to print your resume (and cover letter) on standard letter-size white or ivory paper. Consider using paper that contains cotton fibers for a professional look. Select envelopes that are the same quality and grade as the paper. If you e-mail the resume, consider that the potential employer may not have the same software you used to create the resume and thus may not be able to open it up. As an alternative, you could save the file in a format, such as a PDF, that can be viewed with a reader program. Many job seekers also post their resume on the Web.

To Use a Template

Word installs a variety of templates for letters, fax cover sheets, reports, and resumes on your hard disk. The templates are grouped in five styles: Equity, Median, Oriel, Origin, and Urban. The templates in each style use similar formatting, themes, etc., enabling users to create a set of documents that complement one another. In this chapter, you will create a resume from the template in the Origin style. The following steps create a new document based on a template.

1
- Display the Office Button menu (Figure 3–52).

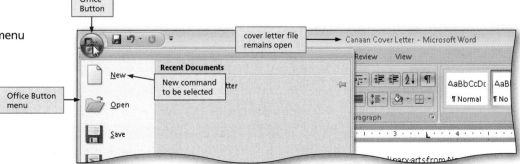

Figure 3–52

2

- Click New on the Office Button menu to display the New Document dialog box.

- Click Installed Templates in the Templates area to display the list of templates on the hard disk.

🔍 **Experiment**

- Click various installed templates in the Installed Templates list and watch the preview of the template display at the right edge of the dialog box.

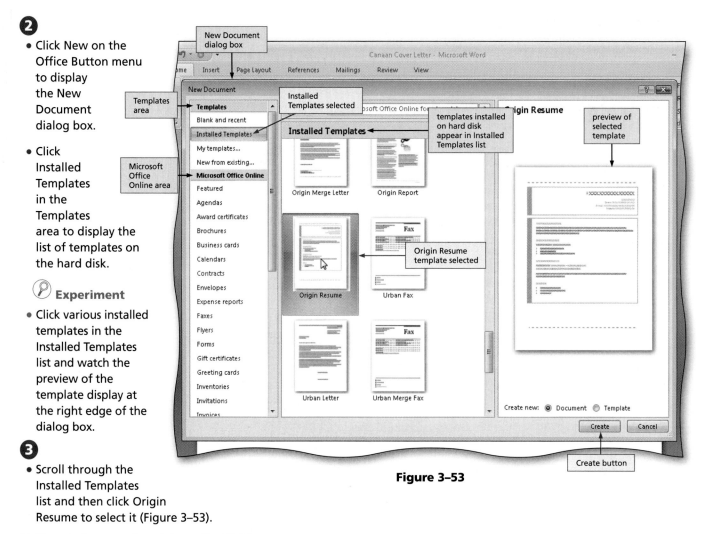

Figure 3–53

3

- Scroll through the Installed Templates list and then click Origin Resume to select it (Figure 3–53).

Q&A How do I access a template on the Web?

If you are connected to the Internet when you click the desired template in the Microsoft Office Online area of the New Document dialog box, Word automatically displays templates from the Microsoft Office Online Web page that you can download.

4

- Click the Create button to create a new document based on the selected template (Figure 3–54).

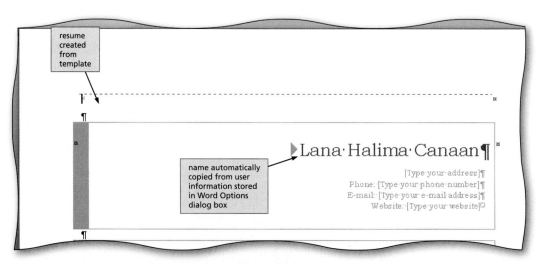

Figure 3–54

To Print the Resume

To see the entire resume created by the resume template, print the document shown in the Word window.

1 Ready the printer. Display the Office Button menu, point to Print, and then click Quick Print to print the resume created from the template (Figure 3–55).

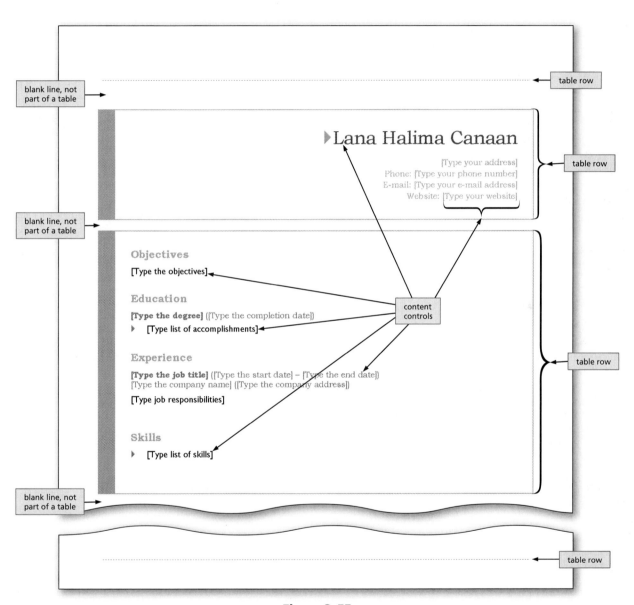

Figure 3–55

Resume Template

The resume created from the template, shown in Figure 3–55, consists of four individual tables, each with one row and one column. The first and last tables contain a decorative blue line; the second table contains the labels and content controls for the job seeker's contact information; and the third table contains labels and content controls for the Objectives, Education, Experience, and Skills sections of the resume. A **content control** contains instructions for filling areas of the template. To select a content control, you click it. As soon as you begin typing in the selected content control, your typing replaces the instruction in the control. Thus, you do not need to delete the selection before you begin typing.

The next step is to personalize the resume. The following pages personalize the resume created by the resume template.

To Delete Rows

The first and last rows of the resume created from the template contain a decorative line. The resume in this project deletes those rows to provide more space for the contents of the resume. The following steps delete the first and last rows on the resume.

- With the insertion point at the top of the document, click Layout on the Ribbon to display the Layout tab.
- Click the Delete button on the Layout tab to display the Delete menu (Figure 3–56).

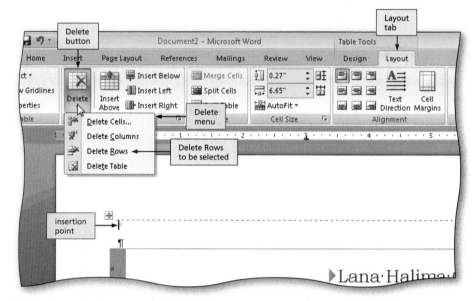

Figure 3–56

- Click Delete Rows on the Delete menu to delete the row containing the insertion point (Figure 3–57).

What happened to the Table Tools tab on the Ribbon?

It is a contextual tab that appears only when the insertion point is in a table. With the row deleted, the insertion point is above the table row containing contact information.

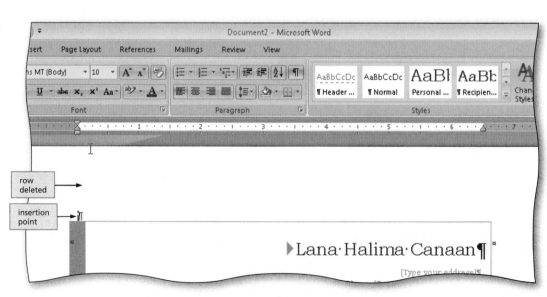

Figure 3–57

- Press CTRL+END and then press the DOWN ARROW key to position the insertion point at the bottom of the document in the last row.

- Click Layout on the Ribbon to display the Layout tab.

- Click the Delete button on the Layout tab to display the Delete menu (Figure 3–58).

- Click Delete Rows on the Delete menu to delete the row containing the insertion point.

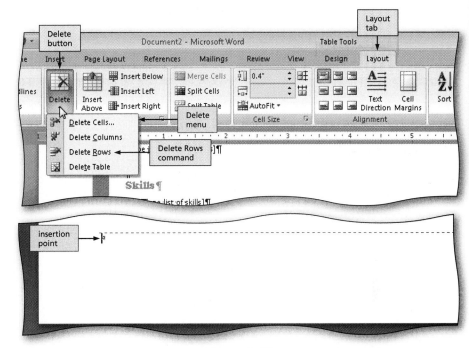

Figure 3–58

Other Ways
1. Right-click selected rows, click Delete Rows on shortcut menu

To Modify Text in a Content Control

The next step is to select text that the template inserted in the resume and replace it with personal information. The name area on your resume may contain a name, which Word copied from the Word Options dialog box, or it may contain the instruction, Type your name. This content control should contain your name. In this project, the name is bold to give it more emphasis on the resume. It also uses the same color as the name on the cover letter.

The following steps modify the text in the content control that contains the job seeker's name.

- Press CTRL+HOME to position the insertion point at the top of the document.

- Click the name content control to select it (if it already contains a name, instead of the instruction, Type name here, drag through the name to select it). Then, type Lana Halima Canaan as the name.

- Triple-click the name content control to select its contents, so that you can format the name (Figure 3–59).

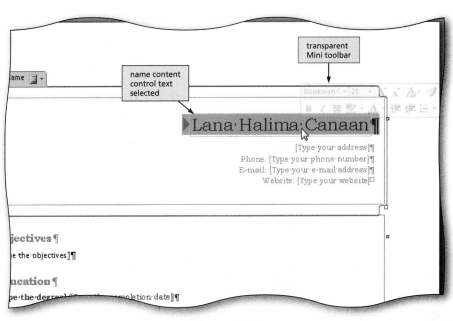

Figure 3–59

2

- Move the mouse pointer into the transparent Mini toolbar, so that it changes to a bright toolbar.

- Click the Bold button on the Mini toolbar to bold the selected name.

- Click the Font Color button on the Mini toolbar to change the font color of the selected name to the most recently used font color, which was the color of the name in the cover letter (Figure 3–60).

Q&A

Instead of using buttons on the Mini toolbar, can I use the Bold and Font Color buttons on the Home tab?

Yes.

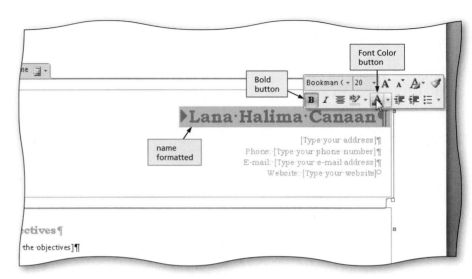

Figure 3–60

To Save the Resume

You have completed several tasks on the resume. Thus, you should save it in a file.

1 Click the Save button on the Quick Access Toolbar.

2 Save the file on your USB flash drive using `Canaan Resume` as the file name.

Copying and Pasting

The next step in personalizing the resume is to enter the address, phone, and e-mail information in the content controls. One way to enter this information in the resume is to type it. Recall, however, that you already typed this information in the cover letter. Thus, a timesaving alternative would be to use the Office Clipboard to copy it from the cover letter to the resume. The **Office Clipboard** is a temporary storage area that holds up to 24 items (text or graphics) copied from any Office program.

Through the Office Clipboard, you can copy multiple items from any Office document and then paste them into the same or another Office document by following these general guidelines:

1. Items are copied *from* a **source document**. If the source document is not the active document, display it in the document window.

2. Display the Office Clipboard task pane and then copy items from the source document to the Office Clipboard.

3. Items are copied *to* a **destination document**. If the destination document is not the active document, display the destination document in the document window.

4. Paste items from the Office Clipboard to the destination document.

The following pages use these guidelines to copy the address, phone, and e-mail information from the letterhead to the resume.

To Switch from One Open Document to Another

The step below switches from the open resume document to the open cover letter document, which is the source document in this case.

1

- Click the Canaan Cover Letter - Microsoft Word program button on the Windows Vista taskbar to switch from the resume document to the cover letter document (Figure 3–61).

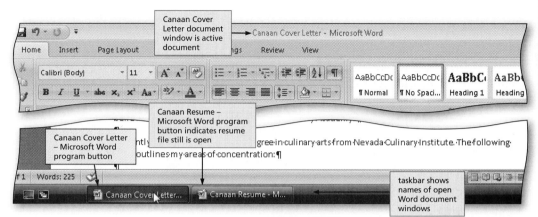

Figure 3–61

Other Ways

1. Click Switch Windows button on View tab, click document name

2. Press ALT+TAB

To Copy Items to the Office Clipboard

You can copy multiple items to the Office Clipboard through the Clipboard task pane and then paste them later. The following steps copy three items from the source document, the Canaan Cover Letter document, to the Office Clipboard.

1

- If necessary, scroll to the top of the cover letter, so that the items to be copied are visible in the document window.

- Click the Clipboard Dialog Box Launcher on the Home tab to display the Clipboard task pane.

- If the Office Clipboard in the Clipboard task pane is not empty, click the Clear All button in the Clipboard task pane (Figure 3–62).

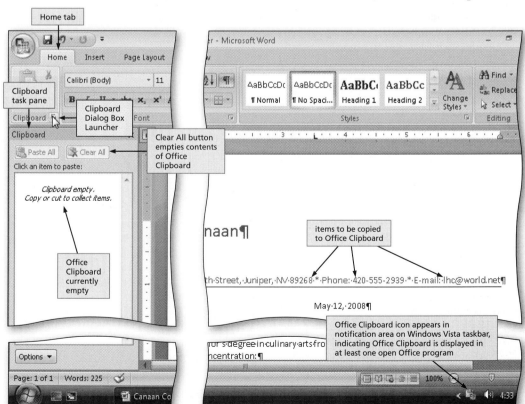

Figure 3–62

2

- In the cover letter, select the address, 22 Fifth Street, Juniper, NV 89268, which is the first item to be copied. Do not include the spaces to the right and left of the address.

- Click the Copy button on the Home tab to copy the selection to the Office Clipboard (Figure 3–63).

Q&A Does the copied item always display in its entirety in the Office Clipboard?

No. If the entry is too long, only the first portion is displayed.

Q&A What appears in the Office Clipboard if I copy a graphic instead of text?

A thumbnail of the copied graphic is displayed.

Figure 3–63

3

- Select the phone number (just the number, not the word Phone: and no spaces before or after the number) and then click the Copy button on the Home tab to copy the selection to the Office Clipboard.

- Select the e-mail address (just the e-mail address, not the word E-mail: and no spaces before or after the address) and then click the Copy button on the Home tab to copy the selection to the Office Clipboard (Figure 3–64).

Q&A What if I copy more than the maximum 24 items allowed in the Office Clipboard?

When you copy a 25th item, Word deletes the first item to make room for the new item.

Q&A Can I delete an item from the Office Clipboard?

Yes. Point to the item in the gallery, click the box arrow to the right of the item, and then click Delete.

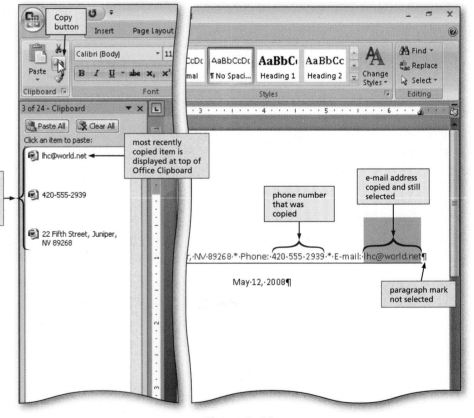

Figure 3–64

Other Ways
1. With Clipboard task pane displayed, right-click selected item, click Copy on shortcut menu   2. With Clipboard task pane displayed and item to copy selected, press CTRL+C

To Paste from the Office Clipboard

The next step is to paste the copied items (the address, phone, and e-mail information) into the destination document, in this case, the resume document. Recall that the address, phone, and e-mail address are part of content controls in the resume.

The following steps paste the address, phone, and e-mail information from the Office Clipboard into the resume.

1

- Click the Canaan Resume - Microsoft Word program button on the Windows Vista taskbar to display the resume document.

Q&A Does the destination document have to be a different document?

No. The source and destination documents can be the same document.

- If the Clipboard task pane is not displayed on the screen, click the Clipboard Dialog Box Launcher on the Home tab to display the Clipboard task pane.

- Click the content control in the resume with the instruction, Type your address, to select it (Figure 3–65).

Q&A What is the function of the Paste All button?

It pastes all items in a row, without any characters between them, at the location of the insertion point or selection.

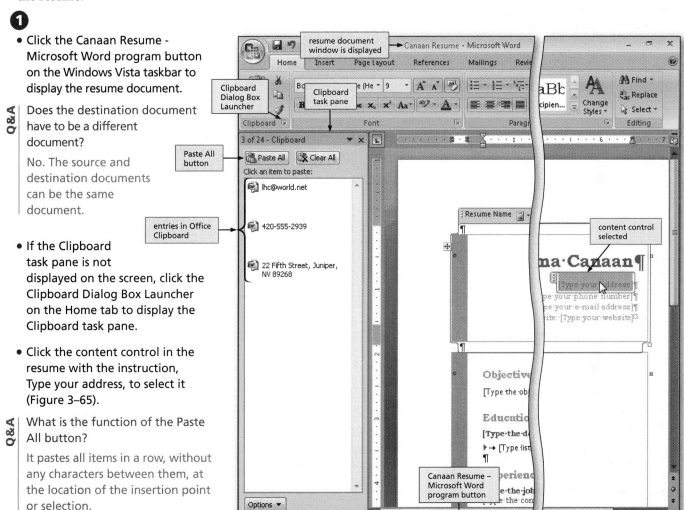

Figure 3–65

BTW

Clipboard Task Pane
The Clipboard task pane may appear on the screen if you click the Copy button or the Cut button twice in succession, or if you copy and paste an item and then copy another item. You can display the Clipboard task pane by clicking the Office Clipboard icon, if it appears in the notification area on the Windows Vista taskbar. If the Office Clipboard icon does not appear, click the Options button at the bottom of the Clipboard task pane and then click Show Office Clipboard Icon on Taskbar.

- Click the address entry in the Office Clipboard to paste it in the document at the location of the selected content control (Figure 3–66).

Q&A

Are the contents of the Office Clipboard erased when you paste?

No.

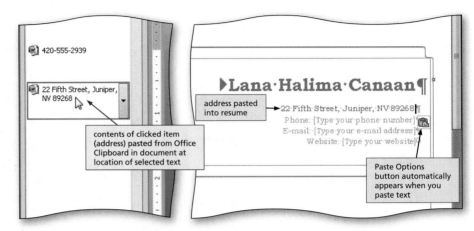

Figure 3–66

- Click the content control in the resume with the instruction, Type your phone number, to select it.

- Click the phone entry in the Office Clipboard to paste it in the document at the location of the selected content control.

- Click the content control in the resume with the instruction, Type your e-mail address, to select it.

- Click the e-mail entry in the Office Clipboard to paste it in the document at the location of the selected content control (Figure 3–67).

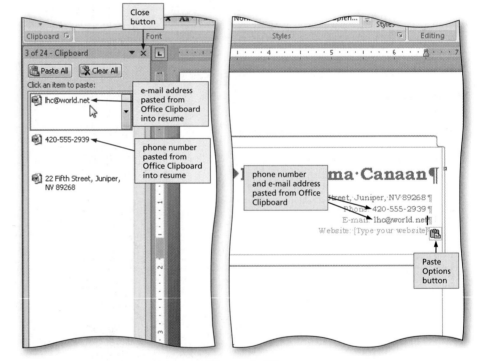

- Click the Close button on the Clipboard task pane title bar.

Figure 3–67

Other Ways

1. With Clipboard task pane displayed, right-click selected item, click Paste on shortcut menu
2. With Clipboard task pane displayed, press CTRL+V

Paste Options Button

When you paste items into a document, Word automatically displays the Paste Options button on the screen. The Paste Options button allows you to change the format of pasted items. For example, you can instruct Word to format the pasted text the same as the text from where it was copied or format it the same as the text to where it was pasted. You also can have Word remove all extra non-text characters that were pasted. For example, if you included a paragraph mark when copying at the end of a line in the address of the resume, the Paste Options button allows you to remove the paragraph mark from the pasted text.

To Change Font Color

The phone and e-mail labels should be the same color as the other contact information. Currently, they are a shade different from each other. The following steps change text color to the most recently used color.

1 Drag through the text, Phone:, to select it. Move the mouse pointer into the transparent Mini toolbar, so that it changes to a bright toolbar. Click the Font Color button on the Mini toolbar to change the color of the Phone: label to the color displayed on the button.

2 Drag through the text, E-mail:, to select it. Move the mouse pointer into the transparent Mini toolbar, so that it changes to a bright toolbar. Click the Font Color button on the Mini toolbar to change the color of the E-mail: label.

To Delete Text and Lines

You do not have a Web address. Thus, the Website content control, its corresponding label, and the line should be deleted. The following steps delete text.

1
- Drag through the text to be deleted, as shown in Figure 3–68.

2
- Press the DELETE key to delete the label and content control.

- Press the UP ARROW key to position the insertion point at the end of the e-mail address.

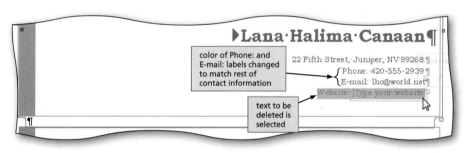

Figure 3–68

- Press the DELETE key to delete the extra paragraph mark and line below the e-mail address.

Other Ways		
1. With text selected, click Cut button on Home tab	2. Right-click selected text, click Cut on shortcut menu	3. With text selected, press CTRL+X

To Zoom the Document

The text in the resume is a little small for you to read. The following step changes the zoom to 110 percent.

1 Use the Zoom slider to change the zoom to 110% (Figure 3–69).

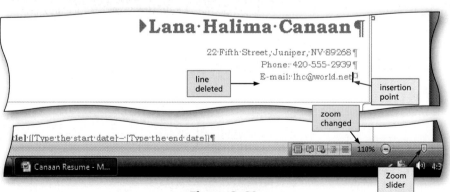

Figure 3–69

To Enter More Text in Content Controls

The next step is to select content controls in the resume and replace their instructions with personal information. The following steps enter text in the Objectives and some of the Education sections of the resume.

1 Scroll to position the Objectives section near the top of the document window. In the Objectives section of the resume, click the content control with the instruction, Type the objectives. Type `To obtain a full-time culinary instructor position with a culinary academy, school, or institute in the Juniper area.`

2 In the Education section of the resume, click the content control with the instruction, Type the degree. Type `B.S. Culinary Arts` and then click the content control with the instruction, Type the completion date.

3 Type `Nevada Culinary Institute, May 2008` and then click the content control with the instruction, Type list of accomplishments. Type `Dean's List, six semesters` and then press the ENTER key. Type `Moeller Nutrition Award, January 2008` and then press the ENTER key. Type `Marge Rae Outstanding Student Scholarship, 2006 - 2008` and then press the ENTER key. Type `Baker Food Preparation Contest, 1st Place, November 2008` (Figure 3–70).

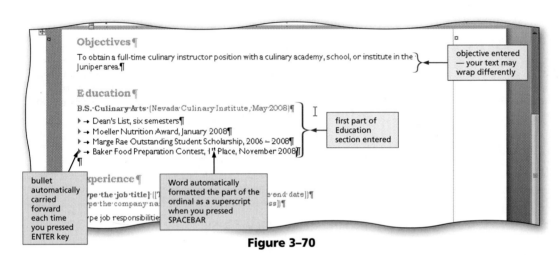

Figure 3–70

To Enter a Line Break

The next step in personalizing the resume is to enter the areas of concentration in the education section. You want only the first line that says, Areas of concentration:, to begin with a bullet. If you press the ENTER key on subsequent lines, Word automatically will carry forward the paragraph formatting, which includes the bullet. Thus, you will not press the ENTER key between each line. Instead, you will create a **line break**, which advances the insertion point to the beginning of the next physical line, ignoring any paragraph formatting. The following steps enter the areas of concentration using a line break, instead of a paragraph break, between each line.

1

- Press the ENTER key.

- Type `Areas of concentration:` and then press SHIFT+ENTER to insert a line break character and move the insertion point to the beginning of the next physical line (Figure 3–71).

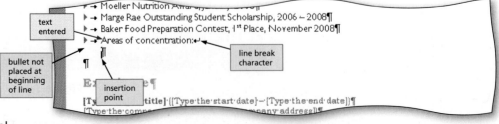

Figure 3–71

- Type Food Planning and Preparation and then press SHIFT+ENTER.

- Type Food Safety and then press SHIFT+ENTER.

- Type Nutrition and then press SHIFT+ENTER.

- Type Regional and International Cuisine as the last entry. Do not press SHIFT+ENTER at the end of this line (Figure 3–72).

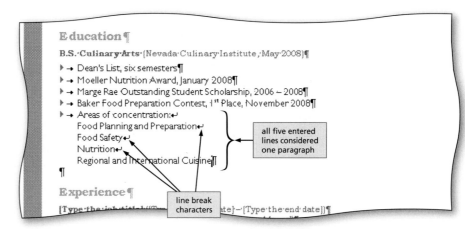

Figure 3–72

To Change Spacing Below Paragraphs

The blank paragraph below the Education section has spacing after (below) of 6 point. You do not want space below this paragraph because you want enough room for all the resume text. The following steps change the spacing after to 0 point.

① Position the insertion point in the paragraph to be adjusted, in this case, the paragraph mark below the Education section on the resume.

② Display the Page Layout tab.

③ Click the Spacing After box down arrow on the Page Layout tab as many times as necessary until 0 pt is displayed in the Spacing After text box (Figure 3–73).

BTW

Line Break Character
Line break characters do not print. A line break character is a formatting mark that indicates a line break at the end of the line.

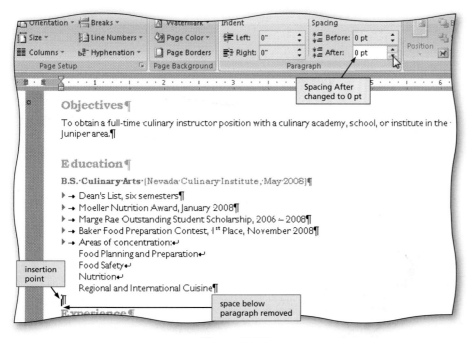

Figure 3–73

To Enter More Text in Content Controls

The next step is to select content controls in the Experience section of the resume and replace their instructions with personalized information.

1 In the Experience section of the resume, click the content control with the instruction, Type the job title.

2 Type `Chef Intern` and then bold the text, Chef Intern.

3 Click the content control with the instruction, Type the start date.

4 Type `September 2006` and then click the content control with the instruction, Type the end date.

5 Type `May 2008` and then click the content control with the instruction, Type the company name.

6 Type `The Garden Grill` and then click the content control with the instruction, Type the company address.

7 Type `Juniper, NV` as the company address.

To Indent a Paragraph

In the resume, the lines below the job title that contain the company name and job responsibilities are to be indented, so that the job titles are easier to see. The following step indents the left edge of a paragraph.

1

- Display the Home tab.

- With the insertion point in the paragraph to indent, click the Increase Indent button on the Home tab to indent the paragraph one-half inch (Figure 3–74).

Q&A

Why did the paragraph indent one-half inch?

Each time you click the Increase Indent button, the current paragraph indents one-half inch. Similarly, when you click the Decrease Indent button, the paragraph decreases the indent by one-half inch.

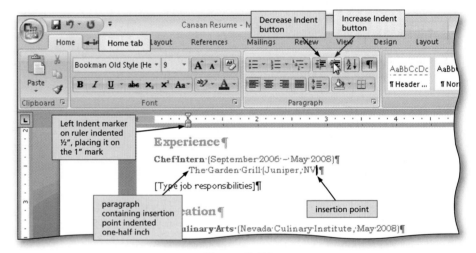

Figure 3–74

Experiment

- Repeatedly click the Increase Indent and Decrease Indent buttons on the Home tab and watch the left indent of the current paragraph change. When you have finished experimenting, use the Increase Indent and Decrease Indent buttons to set the left margin to the one-inch mark on the ruler.

Other Ways

1. Drag Left Indent marker on ruler
2. Enter value in Indent Left text box on Page Layout tab
3. Click Paragraph Dialog Box Launcher on Home tab, click

Indents and Spacing sheet, set indentation in Left text box, click OK button

4. Right-click text, click Paragraph on shortcut menu, click Indents

and Spacing sheet, set indentation in Left text box, click OK button

5. Press CTRL+M

To Change Spacing Below Paragraphs

The next step is to remove the blank space below the company name paragraph, so that the company name and job description paragraphs are closer together. The following steps change the spacing after to 0 point.

1 Display the Page Layout tab.

2 With the insertion point in the paragraph to be adjusted, as shown in Figure 3–74, click the Spacing After box down arrow on the Page Layout tab as many times as necessary until 0 pt is displayed in the Spacing After text box.

To Enter and Format More Text in Content Controls

The next step is to select the job responsibilities content control in the Experience section of the resume and replace its instructions with personal information.

1 In the Experience section of the resume, click the content control with the instruction, Type job responsibilities.

2 Type `Assisted chef with meal selection, preparation, and presentation. Assumed chef responsibilities during last semester of school.`

3 With the insertion point in the paragraph to be adjusted, in this case, the job responsibilities paragraph, click the Spacing After box down arrow on the Page Layout tab as many times as necessary until 6 pt is displayed in the Spacing After text box.

4 Display the Home tab.

5 Click the Increase Indent button on the Home tab to indent the paragraph one-half inch (Figure 3–75).

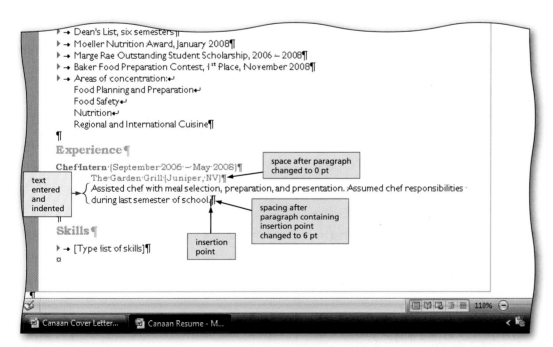

Figure 3–75

To Insert a Building Block Using the Quick Parts Gallery

In this resume, the Experience section contains two jobs. The template, however, inserted content controls for only one job. Word has defined the sections and subsections of the resume in the building blocks, which you can insert in the document. In this case, you want to insert the Experience Subsection building block. The following steps insert a building block.

- Scroll to display the Experience section at the top of the document window.

- Position the insertion point on the paragraph mark below the first job entry.

- Display the Insert tab.

- Click the Quick Parts button on the Insert tab and then scroll through the Quick Parts gallery until Experience Subsection is displayed (Figure 3–76).

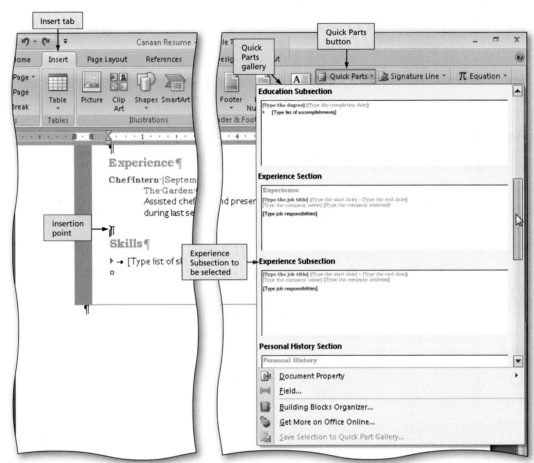

Figure 3–76

- Click Experience Subsection in the Quick Parts gallery to insert the building block in the document at the location of the insertion point.

- Press the DELETE key to remove the extra paragraph mark inserted with the building block (Figure 3–77).

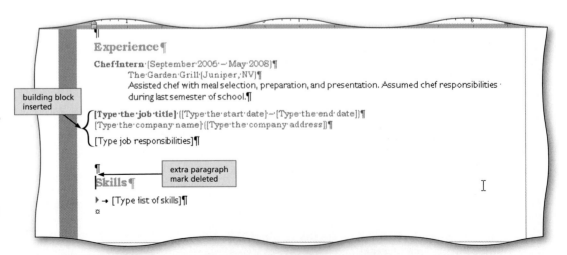

Figure 3–77

To Enter and Format the Experience Subsection and the Skills Section

The next step is to select content controls in the Experience Subsection building block just inserted and the Skills section in the resume and replace the instructions with personal information.

1 Enter `Assistant Cook` as the job title and then bold the job title. Enter `September 2004` as the start date. Enter `August 2006` as the end date. Enter `Nevada Culinary Institute Cafeteria` as the company name. Enter `Juniper, NV` as the company address.

2 Display the Home tab. With the insertion point in the paragraph to indent (company address line), click the Increase Indent button on the Home tab to indent the paragraph one-half inch.

3 Display the Page Layout tab. With the insertion point in the paragraph to be adjusted (company address line), change the Spacing After to 0 point.

4 Enter this text for the job responsibilities: `Planned meals for staff and students. Prepared salads, soups, sandwiches, entrees, and desserts.`

5 With the insertion point in the paragraph to be adjusted, in this case, the job responsibilities paragraph, change Spacing After to 0 point.

6 Display the Home tab. Click the Increase Indent button on the Home tab to indent the paragraph one-half inch.

7 In the Skills section, click the content control with the instruction, Type list of skills, to select it. Type `National Honor Society` and then press the ENTER key. Type `Culinary Arts Association` and then press the ENTER key. Type `Nutrition Services of America` and then press the ENTER key. Type `Student Government Association, President` and then press the ENTER key. Enter `Nevada Restaurant Federation` as the last skill (Figure 3–78).

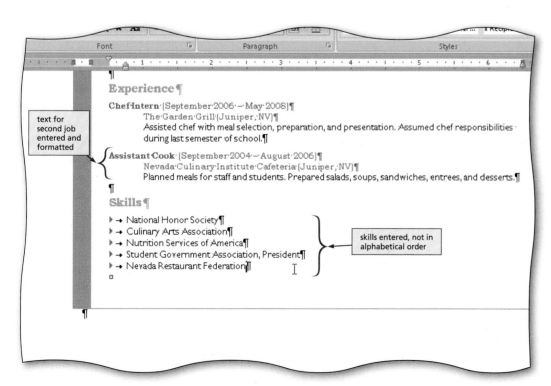

Figure 3–78

To Sort Paragraphs

The next step is to alphabetize the paragraphs in the Skills section of the resume. In Word, you can arrange paragraphs in alphabetic, numeric, or date order based on the first character in each paragraph. Ordering characters in this manner is called **sorting**. The following steps sort paragraphs.

1

- Drag through the paragraphs to be sorted, in this case, the list of skills.

- Click the Sort button on the Home tab to display the Sort Text dialog box (Figure 3–79).

Q&A

What does ascending mean?

Ascending means to sort in alphabetic, numeric or earliest-to-latest date order.

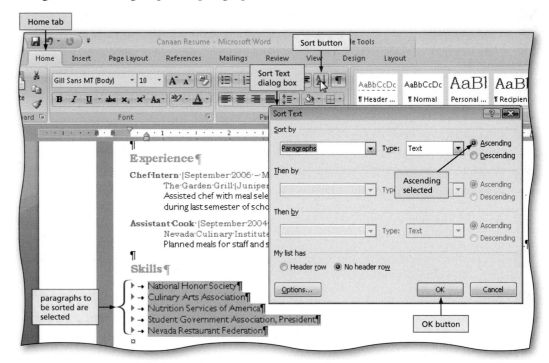

Figure 3–79

2

- Click the OK button to close the dialog box and instruct Word to alphabetize the selected paragraphs.

To Insert Another Building Block

The last section of the resume is the Community Service section. No building block exists for this section; however, the format of the Reference Section building block is the same format you would like for the Community Service section. Thus, you will insert the Reference Section building block and modify its text. The following steps insert a building block.

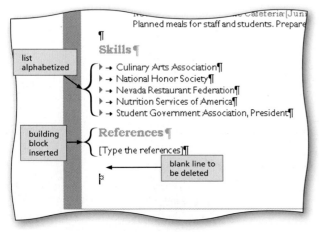

Figure 3–80

1 Position the insertion point on the line below the Skills section on the resume. Display the Insert tab. Click the Quick Parts button on the Insert tab and then scroll through the Quick Parts gallery until Reference Section is displayed. Click Reference Section to insert the building block in the document at the location of the insertion point (Figure 3–80).

2 Press the BACKSPACE key to remove the extra blank line inserted with the building block.

To Enter and Format the Community Service Section

The next step is to select content controls in the section just inserted in the resume and replace its instructions with community service information.

1 Change the title, References, to Community Service.

2 Display the Page Layout tab. With the insertion point in the paragraph to be adjusted (Community Service heading), change the Spacing Before to 12 point.

3 In the last content control, type Prepare food and serve meals at Hope Mission every week.

4 With the insertion point in the paragraph to be adjusted, in this case, the community services paragraph, change Spacing After to 0 point (Figure 3–81).

5 If the document flows to a second page, reduce the space after internal paragraphs so that it fits on a single page.

Figure 3–81

To Change Theme Colors

The cover letter created earlier in this chapter used the Urban color scheme. Because you will be mailing the resume along with the cover letter, you decide also to use the Urban color scheme for the resume. The following step changes theme colors.

1 Display the Home tab. Click the Change Styles button on the Home tab, point to Colors on the Change Styles menu, and then click Urban in the Colors gallery to change the document theme colors to Urban.

To Print Preview a Document

To see exactly how a document will look when you print it, you could display it in print preview. **Print preview** displays the entire document in reduced size on the Word screen. In print preview, you can edit and format text, adjust margins, view multiple pages, reduce the document to fit on a single page, and print the document. The following steps view and print the resume in print preview.

• Click the Office Button and then point to Print on the Office Button menu (Figure 3–82).

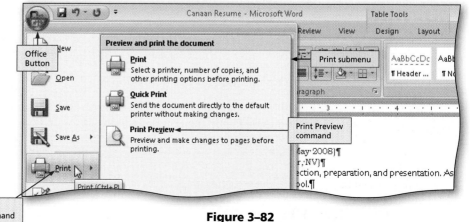

Figure 3–82

2

- Click Print Preview on the Print submenu to display the document in print preview (Figure 3–83).

- If necessary, click the One Page button on the Print Preview tab to display the document as one readable page in the window.

- Click the Print button on the Print Preview tab and then click the OK button in the Print dialog box to print the resume, as shown in Figure 3–2 on page WD 148.

- Click the Close Print Preview button on the Print Preview tab to redisplay the resume in the document window.

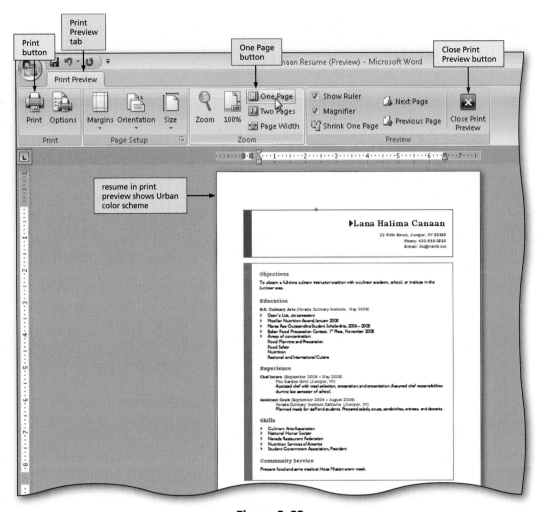

Figure 3–83

BTW

Print Preview
If you want to display two pages in print preview, click the Two Pages button on the Print Preview tab. With the Magnifier check box on the Print Preview tab selected, you can click in the document to zoom in or out. Magnifying a page does not affect the printed document. To edit a document, remove the check mark from the Magnifier check box and then edit the text. If a document spills onto a second page by a line or two, click the Shrink One Page button and Word will try to fit all content on a single page.

To Change Document Properties and Save Again

Before saving the resume a final time, you want to add your name, course and section, and some keywords as document properties. The following steps use the Document Information Panel to change document properties and then save the document again.

1 Display the Office Button menu, point to Prepare on the Office Button menu, and then click Properties on the Prepare submenu to display the Document Information Panel.

2 Enter your name in the Author text box. Enter your course and section in the Subject text box. Enter the text, Resume, in the Keywords text box.

3 Close the Document Information Panel.

4 Click the Save button on the Quick Access Toolbar to overwrite the previous Canaan Resume file on the USB flash drive.

Addressing and Printing Envelopes and Mailing Labels

With Word, you can print address information on an envelope or on a mailing label. Computer-printed addresses look more professional than handwritten ones. Thus, the following steps address and print an envelope.

BTW

Quick Reference
For a table that lists how to complete the tasks covered in this book using the mouse, Ribbon, shortcut menu, and keyboard, see the Quick Reference Summary at the back of this book, or visit the Word 2007 Quick Reference Web page (scsite.com/wd2007/qr).

To Address and Print an Envelope

 1

- Switch to the cover letter by clicking its program button on the Windows Vista taskbar.

- Close the Clipboard task pane.

- Scroll through the cover letter to display the inside address in the document window.

- Drag through the inside address to select it (Figure 3–84).

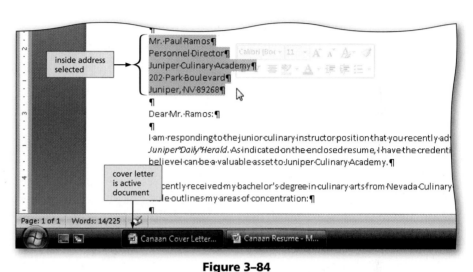

Figure 3–84

2

- Click Mailings on the Ribbon to display the Mailings tab.

- Click the Create Envelopes button on the Mailings tab to display the Envelopes and Labels dialog box.

- If necessary, click the Envelopes tab in the dialog box.

- Click the Return address text box.

- Type Lana Halima Canaan and then press the ENTER key.

- Type 22 Fifth Street and then press the ENTER key.

- Type Juniper, NV 89268 (Figure 3–85).

- Insert an envelope in your printer, as shown in the Feed area of the dialog box (your Feed area may be different depending on your printer).

- Click the Print button in the Envelopes and Labels dialog box to print the envelope.

- If a dialog box is displayed, click the No button.

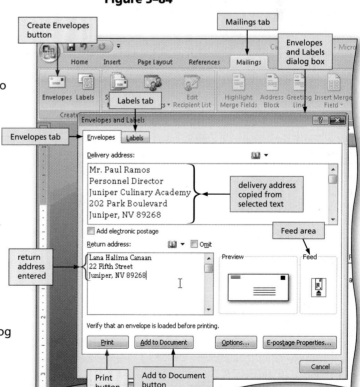

Figure 3–85

Envelopes and Labels

Instead of printing the envelope immediately, you can add it to the document by clicking the Add to Document button in the Envelopes and Labels dialog box. To specify a different envelope or label type (identified by a number on the box of envelopes or labels), click the Options button in the Envelopes and Labels dialog box.

Instead of printing an envelope, you can print a mailing label. To do this, click the Labels tab in the Envelopes and Labels dialog box (Figure 3–85 on the previous page). Type the delivery address in the Address box. To print the same address on all labels on the page, click Full page of the same label. Click the Print button in the dialog box.

To Quit Word

This project is complete. The following step quits Word.

 Click the Office Button and then click the Exit Word button on the Office Button menu to close all open documents and quit Word.

Chapter Summary

In this chapter, you have learned how to use Word to insert and format clip art, set and use tab stops, create and insert building blocks, insert the current date, insert and format tables, use print preview, copy and paste, and use templates. The items listed below include all the new Word skills you have learned in this chapter.

1. Use the Grow Font Button to Increase Font Size (WD 151)
2. Color Text (WD 152)
3. Insert Clip Art (WD 153)
4. Resize a Graphic Using the Size Dialog Box (WD 155)
5. Recolor a Graphic (WD 156)
6. Set a Transparent Color in a Graphic (WD 157)
7. Set Custom Tab Stops Using the Tabs Dialog Box (WD 158)
8. Bottom Border a Paragraph (WD 161)
9. Clear Formatting (WD 162)
10. Convert a Hyperlink to Regular Text (WD 163)
11. Create a New File from an Existing File (WD 165)
12. Set Custom Tab Stops Using the Ruler (WD 167)
13. Insert the Current Date in a Document (WD 168)
14. Create a Building Block (WD 170)
15. Insert a Nonbreaking Space (WD 171)
16. Insert a Building Block (WD 172)
17. Insert an Empty Table (WD 173)
18. Enter Data in a Table (WD 175)
19. Apply a Table Style (WD 176)
20. Resize Table Columns to Fit Table Contents (WD 177)
21. Bullet a List as You Type (WD 180)
22. Use a Template (WD 183)
23. Delete Rows (WD 186)
24. Modify Text in a Content Control (WD 187)
25. Switch from One Open Document to Another (WD 189)
26. Copy Items to the Office Clipboard (WD 189)
27. Paste from the Office Clipboard (WD 191)
28. Delete Text and Lines (WD 193)
29. Enter a Line Break (WD 194)
30. Indent a Paragraph (WD 196)
31. Insert a Building Block Using the Quick Parts Gallery (WD 198)
32. Sort Paragraphs (WD 200)
33. Print Preview a Document (WD 201)
34. Address and Print an Envelope (WD 203)

Learn It Online

Test your knowledge of chapter content and key terms.

Instructions: To complete the Learn It Online exercises, start your browser, click the Address bar, and then enter the Web address scsite.com/wd2007/learn. When the Word 2007 Learn It Online page is displayed, click the link for the exercise you want to complete and then read the instructions.

Chapter Reinforcement TF, MC, and SA
A series of true/false, multiple choice, and short answer questions that test your knowledge of the chapter content.

Flash Cards
An interactive learning environment where you identify chapter key terms associated with displayed definitions.

Practice Test
A series of multiple choice questions that test your knowledge of chapter content and key terms.

Who Wants To Be a Computer Genius?
An interactive game that challenges your knowledge of chapter content in the style of a television quiz show.

Wheel of Terms
An interactive game that challenges your knowledge of chapter key terms in the style of the television show *Wheel of Fortune*.

Crossword Puzzle Challenge
A crossword puzzle that challenges your knowledge of key terms presented in the chapter.

Apply Your Knowledge

Reinforce the skills and apply the concepts you learned in this chapter.

Working with Tabs and a Table
Instructions: Start Word. Open the document, Apply 3-1 Expenses Table Draft, from the Data Files for Students. See the inside back cover of this book for instructions on downloading the Data Files for Students, or contact your instructor for information about accessing the required files.

The document is a Word table that you are to edit and format. The revised table is shown in Figure 3–86.

Monthly Club Expenses

	January	February	March	April
Decorations	170.88	129.72	74.43	167.85
Postage	65.90	62.90	40.19	69.91
Computer Supplies	17.29	18.50	72.50	19.12
Paper Supplies	46.57	41.67	38.82	48.70
Food/Beverages	122.04	99.88	55.43	100.00
Hall Rental	120.00	120.00	120.00	120.00
Total	542.68	472.67	401.37	525.58

Figure 3–86

Continued >

Apply Your Knowledge *continued*

Perform the following tasks:

1. In the line containing the table title, Monthly Club Expenses, remove the tab stop at the 1" mark on the ruler.

2. Set a centered tab at the 3.25" mark on the ruler.

3. Bold the characters in the title. Increase their font size to 14. Change their color to Red, Accent 2, Darker 25%.

4. Add a new row to the bottom of the table. In the first cell of the new row, type Total as the entry. Enter these values in the next three cells: January – 542.68; February – 472.67; April – 525.58.

5. Delete the row containing the Duplicating Fees expenses.

6. Insert a column between the February and April columns. Fill in the column as follows: Column Title – March; Decorations – 74.43; Postage – 40.19; Computer Supplies – 72.50; Paper Supplies – 38.82; Food/Beverages – 55.43; Hall Rental – 120.00; Total – 401.37.

7. In the Design tab, remove the check mark from the Banded Rows check box. Place a check mark in the Total Row check box. The three check boxes that should have check marks are Header Row, Total Row, and First Column. Apply the Medium Grid 3 - Accent 1 style to the table.

8. Make all columns as wide as their contents (AutoFit Contents).

9. Center the table between the left and right margins of the page.

10. Change the document properties, as specified by your instructor.

11. Click the Office Button and then click Save As. Save the document using the file name, Apply 3-1 Expenses Table Modified.

12. Print the document properties.

13. Print the revised table, shown in Figure 3–86.

Extend Your Knowledge

Extend the skills you learned in this chapter and experiment with new skills. You may need to use Help to complete the assignment.

Working with Pictures, Symbols, Borders, and Tables

Instructions: Start Word. Open the document, Extend 3-1 Club Letter Draft, from the Data Files for Students. See the inside back cover of this book for instructions on downloading the Data Files for Students, or contact your instructor for information about accessing the required files.

You will flip the clip art, insert symbols, add a decorative border, add totals to the table, modify the table style, and print mailing labels.

Perform the following tasks:

1. Use Help to learn about rotating objects, inserting symbols, working with borders, entering formulas, and printing mailing labels.

2. Flip the image in the letterhead horizontally so that the fruit faces toward the middle of the letter instead of toward the margin.

3. In the letterhead, replace the asterisk characters that separate the address, phone, and e-mail information with a symbol in one of the Wingdings fonts (Figure 3–87).

4. Remove the bottom border in the letterhead. Add a new bottom border that has a color and style different from the default Word border.

5. Add a row to the bottom of the table with a label indicating it contains totals. For each of the columns, use the Formula button on the Layout tab to sum the contents of the column. Write down the formula that Word uses to sum the contents of a column. Add a column to the right of the table with a label indicating it contains totals. For each of the rows, use a formula to sum the row. Write down the formula that Word uses to sum the contents of a row.

6. Change the table style. One at a time, select and deselect each check box in the Table Style Options group. Write down the function of each check box: Header Row, Total Row, Banded Rows, First Column, Last Column, and Banded Columns. Select the check boxes you prefer for the table.

7. Change the document properties, as specified by your instructor. Save the revised document using a new file name and then submit it in the format specified by your instructor.

8. Print a single mailing label for the letter.

9. Print a full page of mailing labels, each containing the address shown in Figure 3-87.

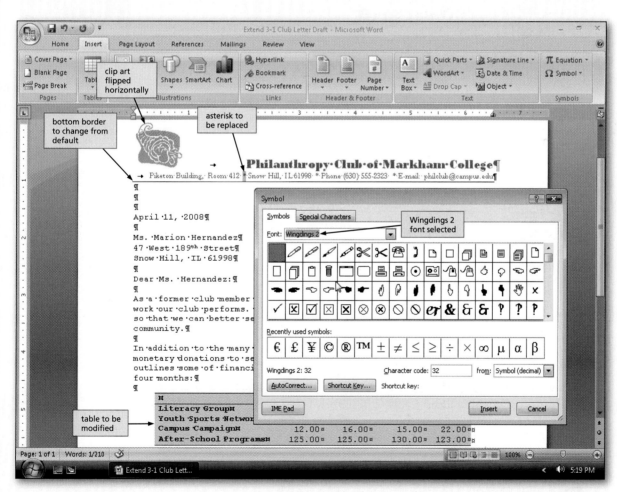

Figure 3–87

Make It Right

Analyze a document and correct all errors and/or improve the design.

Formatting a Business Letter

Instructions: Start Word. Open the document, Make It Right 3-1 Cover Letter Draft, from the Data Files for Students. See the inside back cover of this book for instructions about downloading the Data Files for Students, or contact your instructor for information on accessing the required files.

The document is a cover letter that is missing elements and formatted incorrectly (Figure 3–88). You are to insert and format clip art in the letterhead, change the color of the text and graphic, change the letter style from block to modified block, sort a list, and format the table.

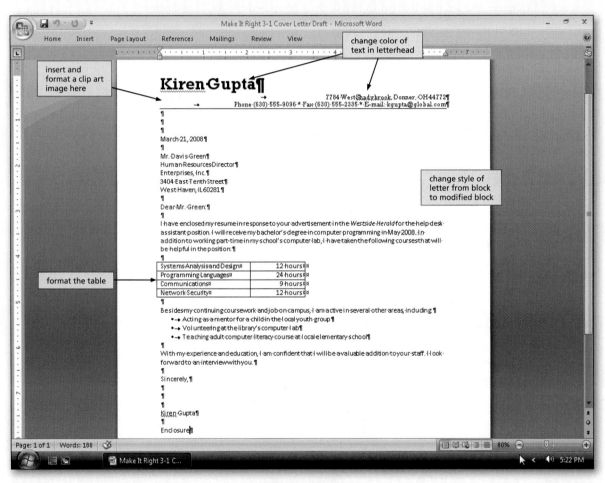

Figure 3–88

Perform the following tasks:

1. Locate and insert an appropriate clip art image. If you have access to the Internet, use one from the Web. Resize the graphic, if necessary.

2. Change the color of the text in the letterhead. Recolor the graphic to match the color of the text. Format one color in the graphic as transparent.

3. The letter currently is the block letter style. It should be the modified block letter style. Format the appropriate paragraphs by setting custom tab stops and then positioning those paragraphs at the tab stops. Be sure to position the insertion point in the paragraph before setting the tab stop.

4. Sort the paragraphs in the bulleted list.

5. Center the table. Apply a table style of your choice. Resize the table columns to fit the contents of the cells.

6. Change the document properties, as specified by your instructor. Save the revised document using a new file name and then submit it in the format specified by your instructor.

In the Lab

Design and/or create a document using the guidelines, concepts, and skills presented in this chapter. Labs are listed in order of increasing difficulty.

Lab 1: Creating a Cover Letter with a Table

Problem: You are a student at Norson Central College. Graduation is approaching quickly and you would like a part-time job while furthering your studies. Thus, you prepare the cover letter shown in Figure 3–89.

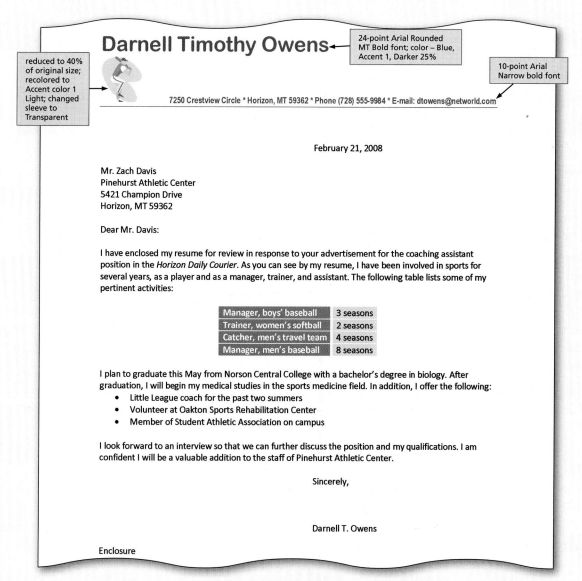

Figure 3–89

Continued >

In the Lab *continued*

Perform the following tasks:

1. Create the letterhead shown at the top of Figure 3–89 on the previous page. Insert the clip art image and then resize and format it as indicated in the figure. Remove the hyperlink format from the e-mail address. If necessary, clear formatting after entering the bottom border. Save the letterhead with the file name, Lab 3-1 Owens Letterhead.

2. Create the letter shown in Figure 3–89. Set a tab stop at the 3.5" mark on the ruler for the date line, complimentary close, and signature block. Insert the current date. After entering the inside address, create a building block for Pinehurst Athletic Center and insert the building block whenever you have to enter the company name. Insert nonbreaking space characters in the newspaper name. Insert and center the table. Format the table using the Medium Grid 3 - Accent 1 table style. Select only the First Column check box in the Table Style Options group. Adjust the column widths so that they are as wide as the contents of the cells. Bullet the list as you type it.

3. Check the spelling of the letter. Change the document properties, as specified by your instructor. Save the letter with Lab 3-1 Owens Cover Letter as the file name.

4. View and print the cover letter from within print preview.

5. Address and print an envelope and a mailing label using the inside and return addresses in the cover letter.

In the Lab

Lab 2: Creating a Resume from a Template

Problem: You are a nursing student at Ferrell College. As graduation is approaching quickly, you prepare the resume shown in Figure 3–90 using one of Word's resume templates.

Perform the following tasks:

1. Use the Equity Resume template to create a resume.

2. Personalize the resume as shown in Figure 3–90. Use your own name and address information when you personalize the resume. If necessary, drag the blue-dotted column border to the right of the name to the right, to make room for a name with a larger font size. Insert the Experience Subsection building block, so that you can enter the second job. Indent the text in the Experience section as shown. Enter line break characters between the job responsibility lines. Adjust line spacing in the Experience section, so that it matches Figure 3–90. Change the title, Skills, to the word, Activities.

3. Change the theme fonts to Aspect.

4. Check the spelling of the resume. Change the document properties, as specified by your instructor. Save the resume with Lab 3-2 Marsh Resume as the file name.

5. View and print the resume from within print preview.

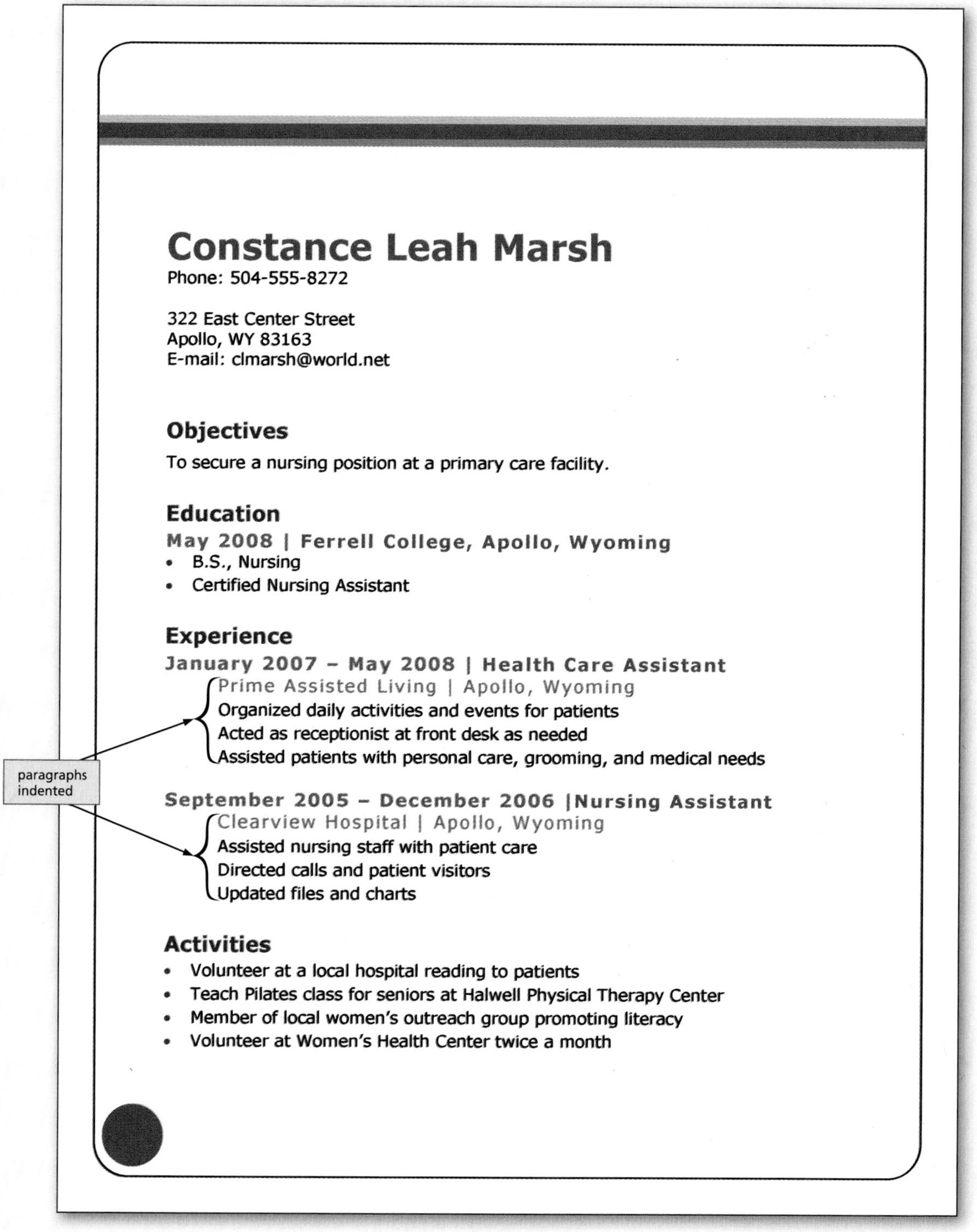

Constance Leah Marsh
Phone: 504-555-8272

322 East Center Street
Apollo, WY 83163
E-mail: clmarsh@world.net

Objectives
To secure a nursing position at a primary care facility.

Education
May 2008 | Ferrell College, Apollo, Wyoming
- B.S., Nursing
- Certified Nursing Assistant

Experience
January 2007 – May 2008 | Health Care Assistant
Prime Assisted Living | Apollo, Wyoming
Organized daily activities and events for patients
Acted as receptionist at front desk as needed
Assisted patients with personal care, grooming, and medical needs

September 2005 – December 2006 |Nursing Assistant
Clearview Hospital | Apollo, Wyoming
Assisted nursing staff with patient care
Directed calls and patient visitors
Updated files and charts

Activities
- Volunteer at a local hospital reading to patients
- Teach Pilates class for seniors at Halwell Physical Therapy Center
- Member of local women's outreach group promoting literacy
- Volunteer at Women's Health Center twice a month

paragraphs
indented

Figure 3–90

In the Lab

Lab 3: Creating a Letter

Problem: You are a president of the Parents Educational Organization for the local high school. The organization currently is taking nominations for outstanding teacher award and you write thank-you letters to nominators, also asking them for donations.

Instructions: Prepare the letter shown in Figure 3–91. Follow the guidelines in the modified semi-block letter style. Use proper spacing between elements of the letter. Check the spelling of the letter. Change the document properties, as specified by your instructor. Save the letter with Lab 3-3 Ling Letter as the file name.

Kim S. Ling
Parents Educational Organization
99 Ohio Avenue, Harrust, NH 03891
(317) 555-1865 * E-mail: ksling@net.com

February 14, 2008

Ms. Laura Ennis
74 MacEnroe Court
Fairview, IN 46142

Dear Ms. Ennis:

Thank you for your recent nomination of Mr. Serensi from Bakersville North High School for our outstanding teacher award. He will be pleased that you believe he was a great influence in your decision to become a teacher.

In addition to the honor of being selected outstanding teacher, we present our candidates with a monetary gift. They use the funds for future classroom needs, including:

- Reading materials to be kept in the classroom
- Emergency funds to assist students in need of supplies
- Supplies for additional projects to be determined by teacher
- Guest author and speaker visits

If you are interested in donating to this worthy cause, please contact me via e-mail or telephone. All donors' names are engraved on a plaque on display in the school auditorium. Listed in the table below are the donation levels.

Donation Level	Donation Amount
Gold	$500
Silver	$250
Bronze	$100

Again, we thank you for your interest in our project.

Yours truly,

Kim Ling
President

Figure 3–91

Cases and Places

Apply your creative thinking and problem solving skills to design and implement a solution.

• Easier   •• More Difficult

• 1: Create a Fax Cover Sheet from a Template

Your boss has asked you to send a fax that includes a fax cover sheet. In the New Document dialog box, click Installed Templates in the Templates pane and then click Equity Fax in the Installed Templates list. Click in each area to enter the following information in the fax cover sheet: the fax is from your boss, Max Henreich; the fax should go to Shirelle Bradley; her fax number is (317) 555-0922; the fax contains three pages; and the phone is (317) 555-1350. Use today's date for the date. The Re: area should contain the following text: Site visit materials. Leave the CC: field blank. The For Review check box should be checked, and your boss wants the following comment on the cover sheet: Here are the notes for tomorrow's site visit.

• 2: Create this Chapter's Resume Using a Different Template

Information can look and be perceived completely differently simply by virtue of the way it is presented. Take the resume created in this chapter and create it using a different template. For example, try the Equity, Median, Oreil, or Urban Resume template in the Installed Templates list. Make sure each section of the resume in this chapter is presented in the new document. You may need to rename or delete sections and add building blocks. Open the resume you created in this chapter and use the copy and paste commands to simplify entering the text. Select a theme you like best for the finished resume.

•• 3: Create a Memo Using a Template from the Web

As assistant director of programs at a local park, you are responsible for soliciting ideas from employees regarding future programs and activities. In the New Document dialog box, click Memos in the Microsoft Office Online area to create a memo. Select a template you like. Use the following information to complete the memo: the memo should go to all staff members; the meeting will be held in room A42 on March 14, 2008 at 3:00 p.m.; attendees should be prepared to discuss their ideas for spring and summer activities; and attendance is mandatory. Mention that if anyone is to be on vacation or unavailable, he or she should contact you prior to the meeting to arrange for submission of activities lists.

•• 4: Create Your Resume and Cover Letter for a Potential Job

Make It Personal

Assume you are graduating this semester and need to find a job immediately after graduation. Check a local newspaper or online employment source to find an advertisement for a job relating to your major or a job for which you believe you are qualified. Use the techniques you learned in this chapter to create your resume and a cover letter. Tailor your cover letter and your resume to fit the job description. Make sure you include an objective, education, and work experience section. Also include any other pertinent sections. Use the copy and paste commands on the Office Clipboard to copy your name and address information from one document to the other.

Continued >

Cases and Places *continued*

•• 5: Create Documents Using Templates from the Web

Working Together

As active members of your school's Travel and Leisure Club, you have been assigned the task of publicizing the club's upcoming activities and soliciting new memberships. Assign each team member one of the following tasks: create a calendar listing various club activities for a three-month period, including any scheduled trips, parties, or meetings; design an award or certificate for excellence or other recognition presented to your club by another campus group; compose a letter of thanks from a past member; and create an invitation to join the Travel and Leisure Club. Visit Microsoft Office Online to obtain templates for awards and certificates, calendars, and invitations. Then, as a group, write a cover letter soliciting memberships and listing the reasons why students should join the club. Include a table or bulleted list similar to those used in this chapter. Make the package attractive and eye-catching.

Web Feature
Creating a Web Page Using Word

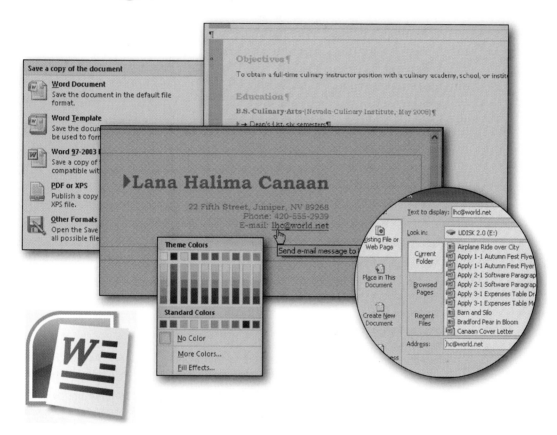

Objectives

You will have mastered the material in this feature when you can:

- Save a Word document as a Web page

- Insert a hyperlink

- Add a background color with a pattern

- Use Windows Explorer to view a Web page

Web Feature Introduction

Many people have personal Web pages, allowing them to share personal information with users around the world. Job seekers often post their resume on the Web so that potential employers can search for and view their resumes online. With Word, you easily can save any existing document as a Web page. You then can post your Web page to a Web server.

Project — Web Page

Personal Web pages contain text, documents, images, links, videos, and audio. If you have created a document using an Office program, such as Word, you can save it in a format that can be opened by a Web browser.

The project in this feature illustrates how to save the resume created in Chapter 3 as a Web page (Figure 1a). The resume itself contains an e-mail address formatted as a hyperlink. When you click the e-mail address, Word starts your e-mail program automatically with the recipient's address (lhc@world.net) already filled in. You simply type a subject and message (Figure 1b) and then click the Send button. Clicking the Send button places the message in the Outbox or sends it if you are connected to an e-mail server.

Overview

As you read through this feature, you will learn how to create the resume Web page shown in Figure 1a by performing these general tasks:

- Save a Word document as a Web page.
- Format the Web page.
- Use Windows Explorer to view a Web page.

Plan Ahead

> **General Project Guidelines**
>
> When creating a resume Web page, the actions you perform and decisions you make will affect the appearance and characteristics of the finished document. As you create a resume Web page, such as the project shown in Figure 1a, you should follow these general guidelines:
>
> 1. **Craft a successful resume.** Your resume should present, at a minimum, your contact information, objective, educational background, and work experience to a potential employer. It should honestly present all your positive points. Ask someone else to proofread your resume and give you suggestions for improvements.
>
> 2. **Create a resume Web page from your resume Word document.** Save the Word document as a Web page. Improve the usability of the resume Web page by making your e-mail address a link to an e-mail program. Enhance the look of the Web page by adding, for example, a background color. Be sure to test your finished Web page document in at least one browser program to be sure it looks and works as you intended.
>
> 3. **Publish your resume Web page.** Once you have created a Web page, you can publish it. **Publishing** is the process of making a Web page available to others on a network, such as the Internet or a company's intranet. In Word, you can publish a Web page by saving it to a Web server or to an FTP site. Many Internet access providers offer storage space on their Web servers at no cost to their subscribers. The procedures for using Microsoft Office to publish a Web page are discussed in Appendix D.
>
> This Web Feature focuses on the second guideline, identifying the actions you perform and the decisions you make during the creation of the resume Web page shown in Figure 1a.

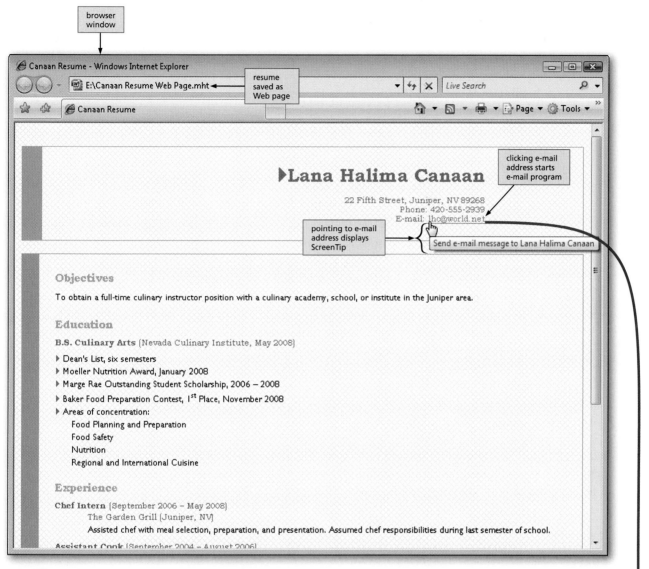

(a) Web Page Displaying Resume

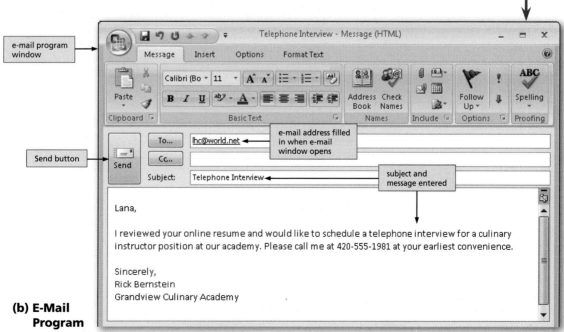

(b) E-Mail Program

Figure 1

Saving a Word Document as a Web Page

Once you have created a Word document, you can save it as a Web page so that it can be published and then viewed in a Web browser, such as Internet Explorer. When you save a file as a Web page, Word converts the contents of the document into **HTML** (hypertext markup language), which is a language that browsers can interpret. Some of Word's formatting features are not supported by Web pages. Thus, your Web page may look slightly different from the original Word document.

When saving a document as a Web page, you have three choices in Word:

- The **single file Web page format** saves all of the components of the Web page in a single file that has an .mht extension. This format is particularly useful for e-mailing documents in HTML format.

- The **Web Page format** saves some of the components of the Web page in a folder, separate from the Web page. This format is useful if you need access to the individual components, such as images, that make up the Web page.

- The **filtered Web Page format** saves the file in Web page format and then reduces the size of the file by removing specific Microsoft Office formats. This format is useful if you want to speed up the time it takes to download a Web page that contains many graphics, video, audio, or animations.

The Web page in this feature uses the single file Web page format.

BTW

Saving as a Web Page
Because you might not have access to a Web server, the Web page you create in this feature is saved on a USB flash drive rather than to a Web server.

To Save a Word Document as a Web Page

The following steps save the resume created in Chapter 3 as a Web page. If you are stepping through this feature on a computer, you will need the resume document named Canaan Resume that was created in Chapter 3. (If you did not create the resume, see your instructor for a copy of it.)

1
- Start Word and then open the file named Canaan Resume created in Chapter 3.

2
- With the resume file open in the document window, click the Office Button and then point to Save As on the Office Button menu to display the Save As submenu (Figure 2).

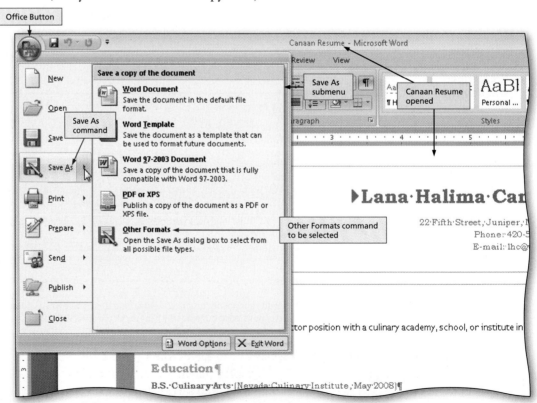

Figure 2

3

- Click Other Formats on the Save As submenu to display the Save As dialog box.

- Type `Canaan Resume Web Page` in the File name text box to change the file name. If necessary, change the Save location to UDISK 2.0 (E:). (Your USB flash drive may have a different name and letter.)

- Click the Save as type box arrow and then click Single File Web Page.

- Click the Change Title button to display the Set Page Title dialog box.

- Type `Canaan Resume` in the Page title text box (Figure 3).

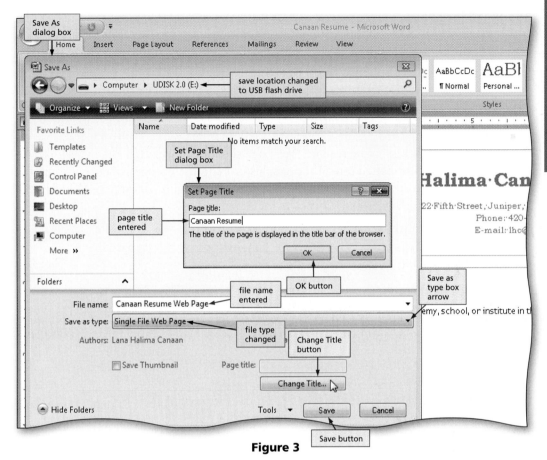

Figure 3

4

- Click the OK button in the Set Page Title dialog box.

- Click the Save button in the Save As dialog box to save the resume as a Web page and display it in the document window (Figure 4). (If Word displays a dialog box about compatibility with Web browsers, click the Continue button in the dialog box.)

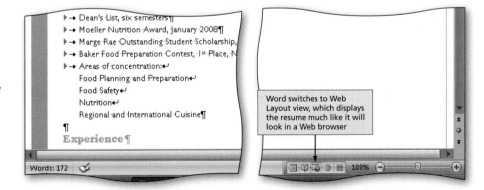

Figure 4

Other Ways
1. Press F12

Saving to a Web Server

If you have access to and can save files to a Web server, then you can save the Web page directly to the Web server by clicking the appropriate network location in the File list in the Save As dialog box. If you have access to a Web server that allows you to save to an FTP site, then you can save to the FTP site by selecting the site below FTP locations in the File list in the Save As dialog box. To learn more about saving Web pages to a Web server or FTP site using Microsoft Office programs, refer to Appendix D.

Formatting a Web Page

In this feature, the e-mail address on the Canaan Resume Web page is formatted as a hyperlink. Also, the background color of the Web page is blue. The following sections modify the Web page to include these enhancements.

To Format Text as a Hyperlink

The e-mail address in the resume Web page should be formatted as a hyperlink. When a Web page visitor clicks the hyperlink-formatted e-mail address, his or her e-mail program starts automatically and displays an e-mail window with the e-mail address already filled in (shown in Figure 1b on page WD 217). The following steps format the e-mail address as a hyperlink.

- Select the e-mail address (lhc@world.net, in this case).

- Display the Insert tab.

- Click the Insert Hyperlink button on the Insert tab to display the Insert Hyperlink dialog box (Figure 5).

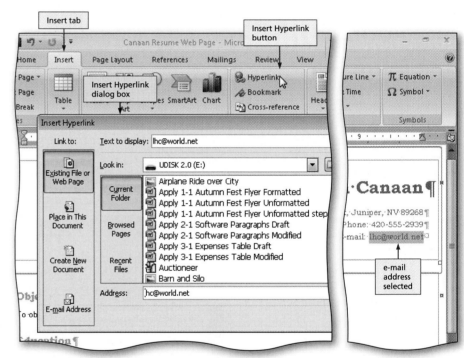

Figure 5

2

- Click E-mail Address in the Link to bar so that the dialog box displays e-mail address settings instead of Web page settings.

- In the 'Text to display' text box, if necessary, type lhc@world.net, which specifies the text that shows on the screen for the hyperlink.

- Click the E-mail address text box and then type lhc@world.net to specify the e-mail address that the Web browser uses when a user clicks the hyperlink.

- Click the ScreenTip button to display the Set Hyperlink ScreenTip dialog box.

- In the text box, type Send e-mail message to Lana Halima Canaan, which is the text that will be displayed when a user points to the hyperlink (Figure 6).

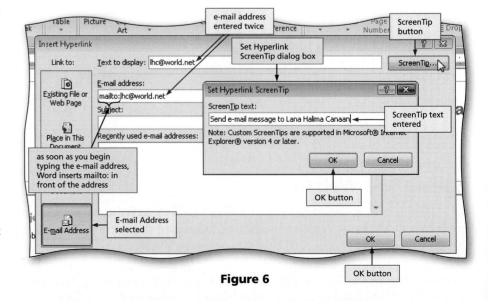

Figure 6

- Click the OK button in each dialog box to format the e-mail address as a hyperlink (Figure 7).

Q&A

How do I know if the hyperlink works?

In Word, you can test the hyperlink by holding down the CTRL key while clicking the hyperlink. In this case, CTRL+clicking the e-mail address should open an e-mail window. If you need to make a change to the hyperlink, right-click it and then click Edit Hyperlink on the shortcut menu.

e-mail address formatted as a hyperlink

Figure 7

Other Ways
1. Right-click selected text, click Hyperlink on shortcut menu 2. Select text, press CTRL+K

To Add a Background Color

The next step is to add background color to the Web page so that it looks more eye-catching. Select a color that best represents your personality. This Web page uses a light shade of blue. The following steps add a background color.

- Display the Page Layout tab.

- Click the Page Color button on the Page Layout tab to display the Page Color gallery.

- Point to the sixth color in the second row (Ice Blue, Accent 2, Lighter 80%) to display a live preview of the background color (Figure 8).

Experiment

- Point to various colors in the Page Color gallery and watch the background color change in the document window.

- Click the sixth color in the second row to change the background color to a light shade of blue.

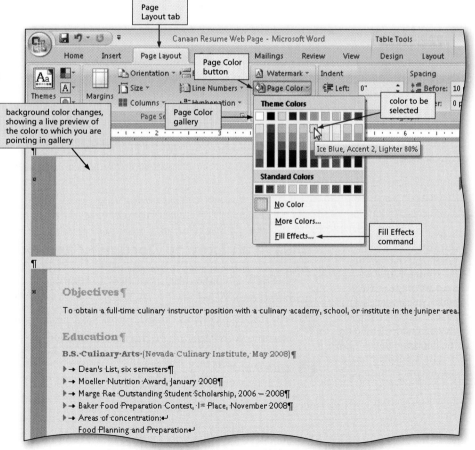

Figure 8

To Add a Pattern Fill Effect to a Background

When you changed the background color in the previous steps, Word placed a solid background color on the screen. For this resume Web page, the solid background color is a little too intense. To soften the background color, you can add patterns to it. The following steps add a pattern to the blue background.

- Click the Page Color button on the Page Layout tab (shown in Figure 8 on the previous page) to display the Page Color gallery again.
- Click Fill Effects in the Page Color gallery (shown in Figure 8) to display the Fill Effects dialog box.
- Click the Pattern tab to display the Pattern sheet in the dialog box.
- Click the Outlined diamond pattern (rightmost pattern in the fifth row) to select it (Figure 9).

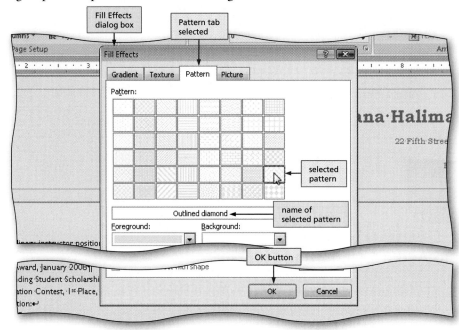

Figure 9

- Click the OK button to add the outlined diamond pattern to the blue background color (Figure 10).

Figure 10

BTW

Background Colors
When you change the background color, it appears only on-screen and in documents, such as Web pages, that are viewed online. Changing the background color has no effect on a printed document.

To Save an Existing Document and Quit Word

The Web page document now is complete. The following steps save the document again and quit Word.

1 Click the Save button on the Quick Access Toolbar to overwrite the previous Canaan Resume Web Page file on the USB flash drive.

2 Quit Word.

Testing the Web Page

After creating and saving a Web page, you will want to test it in at least one browser to be sure it looks and works the way you intended.

To Test the Web Page in a Web Browser

The following steps use Windows Explorer to display the resume Web page in the Internet Explorer Web browser.

- Click the Start button on the Windows Vista taskbar to display the Start menu.

- Click Computer on the Start menu to display the Computer window.

- If necessary, maximize the Computer window (Figure 11).

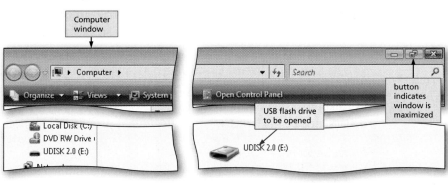

Figure 11

- Double-click the USB flash drive icon in the Computer window to display the contents of the USB flash drive (Figure 12).

- Double-click the file name, Canaan Resume Web Page, to start the Internet Explorer Web browser and display the file in the browser window (shown in Figure 1a on page WD 217).

- With the Web page document displaying in the Web browser, click the e-mail address link to ensure it displays the e-mail window, as shown in Figure 1b on page WD 217.

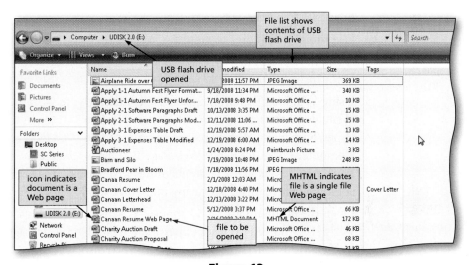

Figure 12

- Close all open windows.

BTW

Quick Reference
For a table that lists how to complete the tasks covered in this book using the mouse, Ribbon, shortcut menu, and keyboard, see the Quick Reference Summary at the back of this book, or visit the Word 2007 Quick Reference Web page (scsite.com/wd2007/qr).

Feature Summary

In this feature, you have learned how to save a Word document as a Web page, insert a hyperlink, add background color, and view a Web page. The items listed below include all the new Word skills you have learned in this feature.

1. Save a Word Document as a Web Page (WD 218)
2. Format Text as a Hyperlink (WD 220)
3. Add a Background Color (WD 221)
4. Add a Pattern Fill Effect to a Background (WD 222)
5. Test the Web Page in a Web Browser (WD 223)

If you have a SAM user profile, you may have access to hands-on instruction, practice, and assessment. Log in to your SAM account (http://sam2007.course.com) to launch any assigned training activities or exams that relate to the skills covered in this feature.

In the Lab

Design and/or create a document using the guidelines, concepts, and skills presented in this chapter. Labs are listed in order of increasing difficulty.

Lab 1: Saving a Word Document as a Web Page and in Other Formats

Problem: You created the research paper shown in Figure 2-83 on pages WD 138 and WD 139 in Chapter 2. You decide to save this research paper in a variety of formats. For each of the saved documents, be sure to change the document properties, as specified by your instructor.

Instructions:

1. Open the Lab 2-1 Computer Forensics Paper shown in Figure 2-83. (If you did not create the research paper, see your instructor for a copy.)

2. Save the research paper as a single file Web page using the file name, Lab WF-1 Computer Forensics Paper Web Page A. Print the Web page.

3. Use Internet Explorer to view the Web page.

4. If you have access to a Web server or ftp site, save the Web page to the server or site (see Appendix D for instructions).

5. Using Windows Explorer, look at the contents of the USB flash drive containing the Web page. Write down the names of the files related to Lab 2-1. Open the original Lab 2-1 Computer Forensics Paper. Save it as a Web page (not as a Single File Web Page) using the file name, Lab WF-1 Computer Forensics Paper Web Page B. That is, change the file type in the Save as type box to Web Page. Again, look at the contents of the USB flash drive using Windows Explorer. Write down any additional file names. How many more files and folders are created by the Web Page format?

6. Open the original Lab 2-1 Computer Forensics Paper. Save it as plain text using the file name, Lab WF-1 Computer Forensics Paper Plain Text. That is, change the file type in the Save as type box to Plain Text. Click the OK button if Word displays a File Conversion dialog box. Open the plain text file. *Hint:* In the Open dialog box, click the Files of type box arrow and then click All Files. Write down the difference between the plain text file and the original file.

In the Lab

Lab 2: Creating a Web Page with a Hyperlink

Problem: You created the resume shown in Figure 3-90 on page WD 211 in Chapter 3. You decide to save it as a Web page with the e-mail address as a hyperlink.

Instructions:

1. Open the Lab 3-2 Marsh Resume shown in Figure 3-90. (If you did not create the resume, see your instructor for a copy.)

2. Save the resume as a single file Web page using the file name, Lab WF-2 Marsh Resume Web Page. Change the page title to Constance Marsh. Convert the e-mail address to a hyperlink. Apply the Orange, Accent 1, Lighter 80% background color to the document. Apply the Divot pattern fill effect to the background color. Change the document properties, as specified by your instructor. Save the resume Web page again. View the Web page in Internet Explorer. Test the e-mail address hyperlink. Print the Web page.

3. If you have access to a Web server or ftp site, save the Web page to the server or site (see Appendix D).

4 Creating a Document with a Title Page, Table, Chart, and Watermark

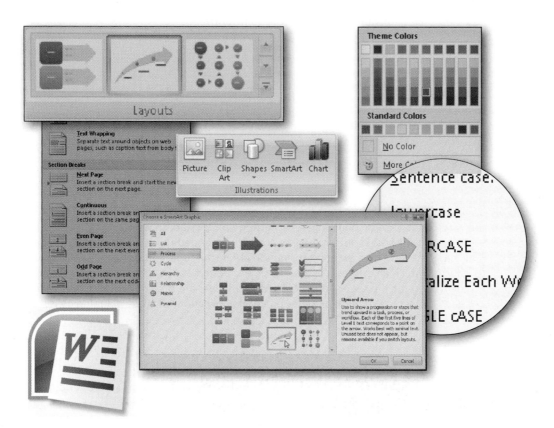

Objectives

You will have mastered the material in this project when you can:

- Border and shade a paragraph
- Insert and format a SmartArt graphic
- Insert a watermark
- Insert a section break
- Insert a Word document in an open document
- Insert headers and footers

- Modify and format a Word table
- Sum columns in a table
- Create a chart from a Word table
- Add picture bullets to a list
- Create and apply a character style
- Draw a table

4 | Creating a Document with a Title Page, Table, Chart, and Watermark

Introduction

During the course of your business and personal life, you may want or need to present a recommendation to a person or group of people for their consideration. You might suggest they purchase a product, such as vehicles or books, or contract a service, such as designing their Web page or remodeling their house. Or, you might try to convince an audience to take an action, such as signing a petition, joining a club, or donating to a cause. You may be asked to request funds for a new program or activity or to promote an idea, such as a benefits package to company employees or a budget plan to upper management. To present your recommendations, you may find yourself writing a proposal.

A proposal generally is one of three types: sales, research, or planning. A **sales proposal** sells an idea, a product, or a service. A **research proposal** usually requests funding for a research project. A **planning proposal** offers solutions to a problem or improvement to a situation.

Project Planning Guidelines

The process of developing a document that communicates specific information requires careful analysis and planning. As a starting point, establish why the document is needed. Once the purpose is determined, analyze the intended readers of the document and their unique needs. Then, gather information about the topic and decide what to include in the document. Finally, determine the document design and style that will be most successful at delivering the message. Details of these guidelines are provided in Appendix A. In addition, each project in this book provides practical applications of these planning considerations.

Project — Sales Proposal

Sales proposals describe the features and value of products and services being offered, with the intent of eliciting a positive response from the reader. Desired outcomes include the reader accepting ideas, purchasing products, volunteering time, or contributing to a cause. A well-written proposal can be the key to obtaining the desired results.

The project in this chapter follows generally accepted guidelines for writing short sales proposals and uses Word to create the sales proposal shown in Figure 4–1. The sales proposal in this chapter is designed to persuade readers to donate items or volunteer their time for a charity auction. The proposal has a colorful title page to attract readers' attention. To add impact, the sales proposal has a watermark of an auctioneer behind the text and graphics on each page. It also uses tables, a chart, and a bulleted list to summarize and highlight important data.

(a) Title Page

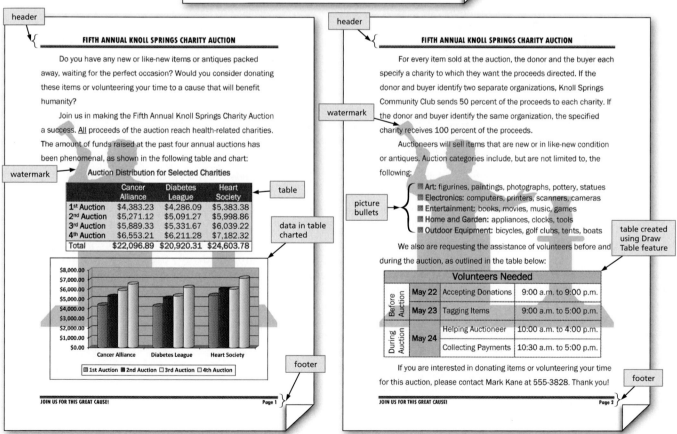

shading

border

Charity Auction

watermark

Sold

Going Twice

Going Once

SmartArt graphic

JOIN US FOR THIS GREAT CAUSE!

header

FIFTH ANNUAL KNOLL SPRINGS CHARITY AUCTION

Do you have any new or like-new items or antiques packed away, waiting for the perfect occasion? Would you consider donating these items or volunteering your time to a cause that will benefit humanity?

Join us in making the Fifth Annual Knoll Springs Charity Auction a success. All proceeds of the auction reach health-related charities. The amount of funds raised at the past four annual auctions has been phenomenal, as shown in the following table and chart:

watermark

watermark

Auction Distribution for Selected Charities

table

	Cancer Alliance	Diabetes League	Heart Society
1st Auction	$4,383.23	$4,286.09	$5,383.38
2nd Auction	$5,271.12	$5,091.27	$5,998.86
3rd Auction	$5,889.33	$5,331.67	$6,039.22
4th Auction	$6,553.21	$6,211.28	$7,182.32
Total	$22,096.89	$20,920.31	$24,603.78

data in table charted

$8,000.00
$7,000.00
$6,000.00
$5,000.00
$4,000.00
$3,000.00
$2,000.00
$1,000.00
$0.00

Cancer Alliance   Diabetes League   Heart Society

☐ 1st Auction ■ 2nd Auction ☐ 3rd Auction ☐ 4th Auction

footer

JOIN US FOR THIS GREAT CAUSE!   Page 1

(b) First Page of Body of Proposal

header

FIFTH ANNUAL KNOLL SPRINGS CHARITY AUCTION

For every item sold at the auction, the donor and the buyer each specify a charity to which they want the proceeds directed. If the donor and buyer identify two separate organizations, Knoll Springs Community Club sends 50 percent of the proceeds to each charity. If the donor and buyer identify the same organization, the specified charity receives 100 percent of the proceeds.

watermark

Auctioneers will sell items that are new or in like-new condition or antiques. Auction categories include, but are not limited to, the following:

picture bullets

■ Art: figurines, paintings, photographs, pottery, statues
■ Electronics: computers, printers, scanners, cameras
■ Entertainment: books, movies, music, games
■ Home and Garden: appliances, clocks, tools
■ Outdoor Equipment: bicycles, golf clubs, tents, boats

We also are requesting the assistance of volunteers before and during the auction, as outlined in the table below:

table created using Draw Table feature

Volunteers Needed			
Before Auction	May 22	Accepting Donations	9:00 a.m. to 9:00 p.m.
	May 23	Tagging Items	9:00 a.m. to 5:00 p.m.
During Auction	May 24	Helping Auctioneer	10:00 a.m. to 4:00 p.m.
		Collecting Payments	10:30 a.m. to 5:00 p.m.

If you are interested in donating items or volunteering your time for this auction, please contact Mark Kane at 555-3828. Thank you!

footer

JOIN US FOR THIS GREAT CAUSE!   Page 2

(c) Second Page of Body of Proposal

Figure 4–1

WD 227

Overview

As you read through this chapter, you will learn how to create the sales proposal shown in Figure 4–1 on the previous page by performing these general tasks:

- Create a title page.
- Save the title page.
- Insert a draft of the body of the sales proposal below the title page.
- Edit and enhance the draft of the body of the sales proposal.
- Save the sales proposal.
- Print the sales proposal.

Plan Ahead

General Project Guidelines

When creating a Word document, the actions you perform and decisions you make will affect the appearance and characteristics of the finished document. As you create a sales proposal, such as the project shown in Figure 4–1, you should follow these general guidelines:

1. **Identify the nature of the proposal.** A proposal may be solicited or unsolicited. If someone else requests that you develop the proposal, it is solicited. Be sure to include all requested information in a solicited proposal. When you write a proposal because you recognize a need, the proposal is unsolicited. With an unsolicited proposal, you must gather information you believe will be relevant and of interest to the intended audience.

2. **Design an eye-catching title page.** The title page should convey the overall message of the sales proposal. Use text, graphics, formats, and colors that reflect the goals of the sales proposal. Be sure to include a title.

3. **Compose the text of the sales proposal.** Sales proposals vary in length, style, and formality, but all are designed to elicit acceptance from the reader. The sales proposal should have a neat, organized appearance. A successful sales proposal uses succinct wording and includes lists for textual messages. Write text using active voice, instead of passive voice. Assume readers of unsolicited sales proposals have no previous knowledge about the topic. Be sure the goal of the proposal is clear. Establish a theme and carry it throughout the proposal.

4. **Enhance the sales proposal with appropriate visuals.** Use visuals to add interest, clarify ideas, and illustrate points. Visuals include tables, charts, and graphical images (i.e., pictures, clip art).

5. **Proofread and edit the proposal.** Carefully review the sales proposal to be sure it contains no spelling, grammar, mathematical, or other errors. Check that transitions between sentences and paragraphs are smooth. Ensure that the purpose of the proposal is stated clearly. Ask others to review the proposal and give you suggestions for improvements.

When necessary, more specific details concerning the above guidelines are presented at appropriate points in the chapter. The chapter also will identify the actions performed and decisions made regarding these guidelines during the creation of the sales proposal shown in Figure 4–1.

BTW

Certification
The Microsoft Certified Application Specialist (MCAS) program provides an opportunity for you to obtain a valuable industry credential — proof that you have the Word 2007 skills required by employers. For more information see Appendix G or visit the Word 2007 Certification Web page (scsite.com/wd2007/cert).

To Start Word

If you are using a computer to step through the project in this chapter and you want your screens to match the figures in this book, you should change your computer's resolution to 1024 × 768. For information about how to change a computer's resolution, read Appendix D.

The following steps start Word and verify Word settings.

Note: If you are using Windows XP, see Appendix F for alternate steps.

1 Click the Start button on the Windows Vista taskbar to display the Start menu.

2 Click All Programs at the bottom of the left pane on the Start menu to display the All Programs list and then click Microsoft Office in the All Programs list to display the Microsoft Office list.

3 Click Microsoft Office Word 2007 in the Microsoft Office list to start Word and display a new blank document in the Word window.

4 If the Word window is not maximized, click the Maximize button on its title bar to maximize the window.

5 If the Print Layout button is not selected, click it so that Word is in Print Layout view.

6 If your zoom level is not 100%, click the Zoom Out or Zoom In button as many times as necessary until the Zoom level button displays 100% on its face.

To Display Formatting Marks

It is helpful to display formatting marks that indicate where in the document you pressed the ENTER key, SPACEBAR, and other keys. The following steps display formatting marks.

1 If necessary, click Home on the Ribbon to display the Home tab.

2 If the Show/Hide ¶ button on the Home tab is not selected already, click it to display formatting marks on the screen.

Creating a Title Page

A **title page** is a separate cover page that contains, at a minimum, the title of the document. For a sales proposal, the title page usually is the first page of the document. Solicited proposals often have a specific format for the title page. Guidelines for the title page of a solicited proposal may stipulate the margins, spacing, layout, and required contents such as title, sponsor name, author name, date, etc. With an unsolicited proposal, by contrast, you can design the title page in a way that best presents its message.

Plan
Ahead

Design an eye-catching title page.
The title page is the first section a reader sees on the sales proposal. Thus, it is important that it appropriately reflects the goal of the sales proposal. When designing the title page, consider its text and graphics.

- **Use concise, descriptive text.** The title page should contain a short, descriptive title that accurately reflects the message of the sales proposal. The title page also may include a theme or slogan. Do not place a page number on the title page.

- **Identify appropriate fonts, font sizes, and colors for the text.** Use fonts that are easy to read. Avoid using more than two different fonts because too many fonts make the title page visually confusing. Use larger font sizes to add impact to the title page. To give the title more emphasis, its font size should be larger than any other text on the title page. Use colors that complement each other and convey the meaning of the proposal.

- **Use graphics to reinforce the goal.** Select simple graphics that clearly communicate the fundamental nature of the proposal. Possible graphics include shapes, pictures, and logos. Use colors that complement text colors. Be aware that too many graphics and colors can be a distraction. Arrange graphics with the text so that the title page is attractive and uncluttered.

The title page of the sales proposal in this project (Figure 4–1a on page WD 227) contains a colorful title that is shaded and surrounded by a border, an artistic arrow with text, a colorful slogan, and a shadow-like image of an auctioneer. The steps on the following pages create this title page.

To Change Theme Colors

Word provides document themes that contain a variety of color schemes to assist you in selecting complementary colors in a document. You should select a color scheme that reflects the goals of a sales proposal. This sales proposal uses the Verve color scheme. The following steps change theme colors.

1 Click the Change Styles button on the Home tab to display the Change Styles menu, and then point to Colors on the Change Styles menu to display the Colors gallery.

2 Click Verve in the Colors gallery to change the document theme colors to Verve.

To Format Characters

The title in the sales proposal should use a large font size, an easy-to-read font, and be the focal point on the page. The following steps enter the title, Charity Auction, centered and using 72-point Tw Cen MT Condensed Extra Bold font.

1 Click the Center button on the Home tab to center the paragraph that will contain the title.

2 Click the Font box arrow on the Home tab. Scroll to and then click Tw Cen MT Condensed Extra Bold (or a similar font) in the Font gallery, so that the text you type will use the selected font.

3 Click the Font Size box arrow on the Home tab and then click 72 in the Font Size gallery, so that the text you type will use the selected font size.

4 Type `Charity Auction` as the title.

To Border a Paragraph

When you click the Border button on the Home tab, Word applies the most recently defined border, or, if one has not been defined, it applies the default border to the current paragraph.

In this project, the title in the sales proposal has a 6-point gray border around it. You can use the Borders gallery to add borders to any or all edges of a paragraph. To specify a different point size and color, however, you use the Borders and Shading dialog box. The following steps add a 6-point gray outside border around a paragraph.

1

- With the insertion point in the paragraph to border, click the Border button arrow on the Home tab to display the Border gallery (Figure 4–2).

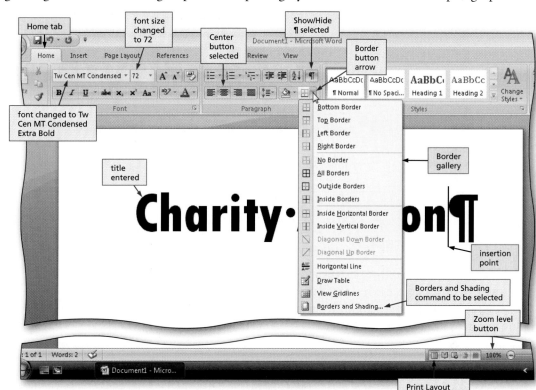

Figure 4–2

2

- Click Borders and Shading in the Border gallery to display the Borders and Shading dialog box.

- Click Box in the Setting area, which will place a border on each edge of the paragraph.

- Click the Width box arrow and then click 6 pt to make the border much thicker.

- Click the Color box arrow and then click Gray-50%, Text 2, which is the fourth color in the first row in the Color gallery (Figure 4–3).

Q&A What is the purpose of the buttons in the Preview area?

They are toggles that display and remove the top, bottom, left, and right borders from the diagram in the preview area.

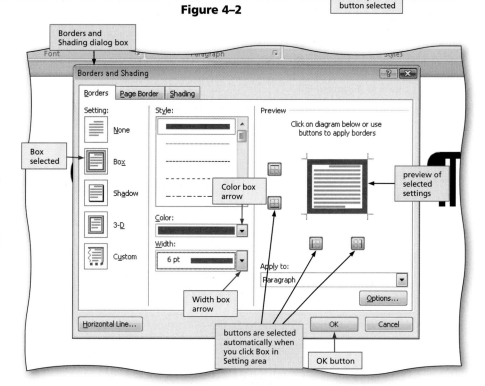

Figure 4–3

3

- Click the OK button to place a 6-point gray outside border around the title (Figure 4–4).

Q&A

How would I remove an existing border from a paragraph?

Click the Border button arrow on the Home tab and then click the border in the Border gallery that identifies the border you wish to remove.

Other Ways

1. Click Page Borders on Page Layout tab, click Borders tab in Borders and Shading dialog box, select desired border, click OK button

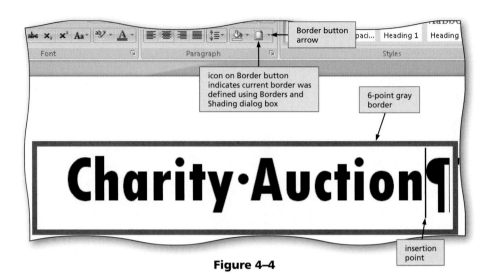

Figure 4–4

To Shade a Paragraph

To make the title of the sales proposal more eye-catching, it is shaded in a dark pink. When you shade a paragraph, Word shades the rectangular area behind any text or graphics in the paragraph from the left margin of the paragraph to the right margin. If the paragraph is surrounded by a border, Word shades inside the border. The following steps shade a paragraph.

1

- Click the Shading button arrow on the Home tab to display the Shading gallery.

- Point to Pink, Accent 2, Darker 25% (sixth color in the fifth row) to display a live preview of this color of shading (Figure 4–5).

Q&A

Why did the text color change to white in the shaded paragraph?

When the color is Automatic, it usually is black. If you select a dark shading color, Word automatically changes the text color to white so that it is easier to read.

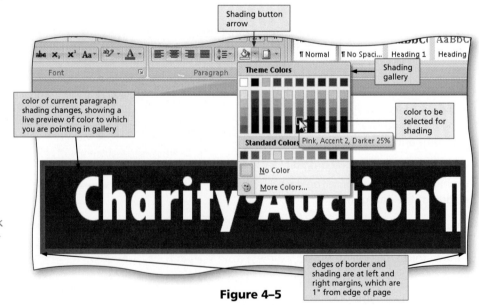

Figure 4–5

Experiment

- Point to various colors in the Shading gallery and watch the paragraph shading color change.

2

- Click Pink, Accent 2, Darker 25% to shade the current paragraph.

Other Ways

1. Click Border button arrow, click Borders and Shading, click Shading tab, click Fill   box arrow, select desired color, click OK button

To Change Left and Right Paragraph Indent

The border and shading currently extend from the left margin to the right margin (shown in Figure 4–5). In the sales proposal, the edges of the border and shading are closer to the text in the title. If you want the border and shading to start and end at a location different from the margin, change the left and right paragraph indent.

The Increase Indent and Decrease Indent buttons on the Home tab change the indent by ½-inch. To set precise indent values, use the Page Layout tab. The following steps change the left and right paragraph indent using the Page Layout tab.

1

- If the rulers are not displayed already, click the View Ruler button on the vertical scroll bar so that you can see the indent markers in relation to the margins.

- Click Page Layout on the Ribbon to display the Page Layout tab.

- With the insertion point in the paragraph to indent, click the Indent Left box up arrow three times to display 0.3" in the Indent Left box and adjust the paragraph left indent by 0.3".

- Click the Indent Right box up arrow three times to display 0.3" in the Indent Right box and adjust the paragraph right indent by 0.3" (Figure 4–6).

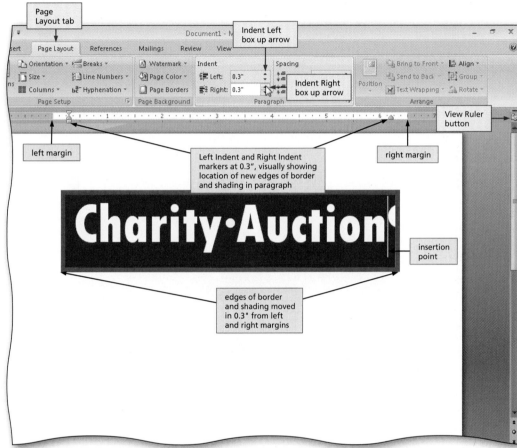

Figure 4–6

 **Experiment**

- Repeatedly click the Indent Right and Indent Left box up and down scroll arrows and watch the left and right edges of the paragraph change in the document window. When you have finished experimenting, set the left and right indent each to 0.3".

2

- Click the View Ruler button on the vertical scroll bar again to hide the ruler because you are finished using it.

Other Ways
1. Drag Left Indent and Right Indent markers on ruler   2. Click Paragraph Dialog Box Launcher on Home tab, click Indents and Spacing tab, set indentation values, click OK button   3. Right-click paragraph, click Paragraph on shortcut menu, click Indents and Spacing tab, set indentation values, click OK button

To Clear Formatting

The title is finished. When you press the ENTER key to advance the insertion point from the end of the first line to the beginning of the second line on the title page, the border and shading are carried forward to line 2, and any text you type will be 72-point Tw Cen MT Condensed Extra Bold font. The paragraphs and characters on line 2 should not have the same paragraph and character formatting as line 1. Instead, they should be formatted using the Normal style. The following steps clear formatting, which applies the Normal style formats to the location of the insertion point.

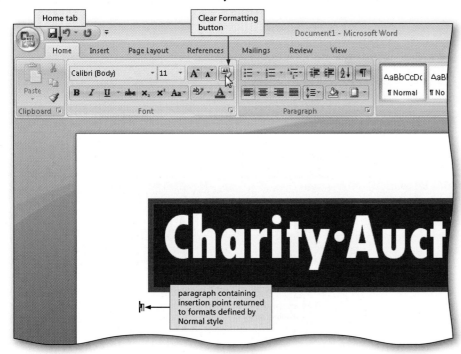

1 If necessary, position the insertion point at the end of line 1, as shown in Figure 4–6 on the previous page.

2 Press the ENTER key.

3 Display the Home tab.

4 Click the Clear Formatting button on the Home tab to apply the Normal style to the location of the insertion point (Figure 4–7).

Q&A Could I have clicked Normal in the Styles gallery instead of the Clear Formatting button?

Yes.

Figure 4–7

SmartArt Graphics

Microsoft Office 2007 includes **SmartArt graphics**, which are visual representations of ideas. Many different types of SmartArt graphics are available, allowing you to choose one that illustrates your message best. Table 4–1 identifies the purpose of some of the more popular SmartArt types. Within each type, Office provides numerous layouts. For example, you can select from more than 20 different layouts of lists.

Table 4–1 SmartArt Graphic Types

Type	Purpose
List	Shows nonsequential or grouped blocks of information
Process	Shows progression, timeline, or sequential steps in a process or workflow
Cycle	Shows continuous sequence of steps or events
Hierarchy	Illustrates organization charts, decision trees, hierarchical relationships
Relationship	Compares or contrasts connections between concepts
Matrix	Shows relationships of parts to a whole
Pyramid	Shows proportional or interconnected relationships with the largest component at the top or bottom

SmartArt graphics contain shapes. You can add text to shapes, add more shapes, or delete shapes. You also can modify the appearance of a SmartArt graphic by applying styles and changing its colors.

To Insert a SmartArt Graphic

Below the title on the title page in this project is an artistic arrow with the text, Going Once, Going Twice, Sold. You use a SmartArt graphic in Word to create this arrow. The following steps insert a SmartArt graphic centered below the title on the title page.

1
- With the insertion point on the blank paragraph below the title (shown in Figure 4–7), click the Center button on the Home tab so that the inserted SmartArt graphic will be centered below the title.

2
- Display the Insert tab.

- Click the Insert SmartArt Graphic button on the Insert tab to display the Choose a SmartArt Graphic dialog box (Figure 4–8).

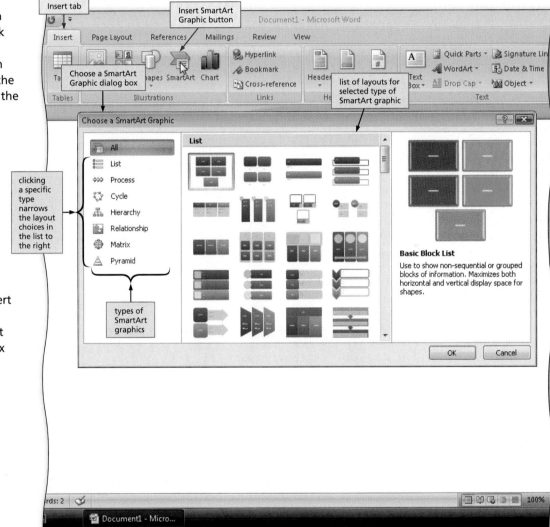

Figure 4–8

Ⓟ **Experiment**
- Click various SmartArt graphic types on the left of the dialog box and watch the related layout choices appear in the list to the right.

Ⓟ **Experiment**
- Click various layouts in the list of layouts to the right to see the preview and description of the layout appear on the far right of the dialog box.

4

- Click Process on the left of the dialog box to display the layout choices related to a process SmartArt graphic.

- If necessary, scroll through the list of layouts until Upward Arrow appears. Click Upward Arrow, which displays a preview and description of the Upward Arrow layout (Figure 4–9).

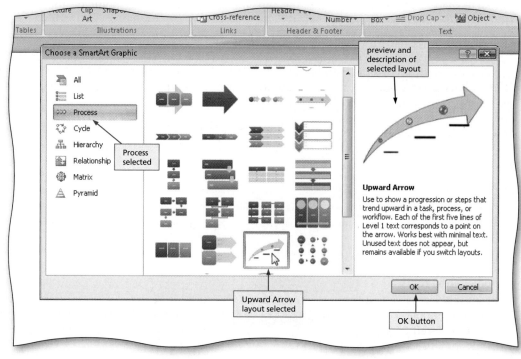

Figure 4–9

5

- Click the OK button to insert the Upward Arrow SmartArt graphic in the document at the location of the insertion point (Figure 4–10).

Q&A Can I change layout of the inserted SmartArt graphic?

Yes. Click the More button in the Layouts gallery in the SmartArt Tools Design tab to display the list of layouts.

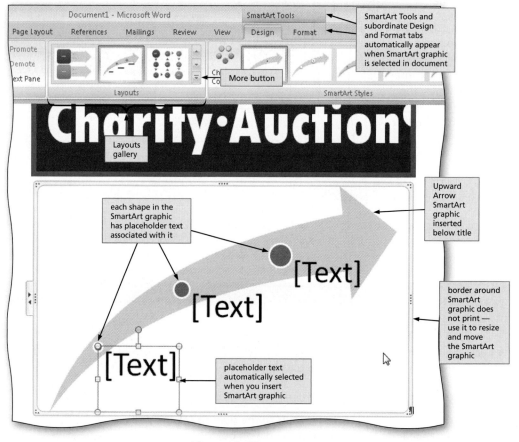

Figure 4–10

To Add Text to a SmartArt Graphic

In this title page, the graphic has the words Going Once, Going Twice, Sold, on the arrow. You can enter text in the placeholder text in the SmartArt graphic or in the Text pane. The Text pane, which is a separate window that can be displayed next to the SmartArt graphic, has placeholder text that duplicates the text in the SmartArt graphic.

The text you enter in a placeholder text wordwraps just as text wordwraps between the margins of a document. The following steps add text to the SmartArt graphic using the placeholder text in the graphic.

1

- Type Going Once in the selected lower-left placeholder text.

Q&A What if my placeholder text is no longer selected?
Click it to select it.

Q&A What if the Text pane appears next to the SmartArt graphic?
Close the Text pane by clicking its Close button or clicking the Text Pane button on the Design tab.

2

- Click the middle placeholder text to select it. Type Going Twice and then click the upper-right placeholder text to select it.

- Type Sold as the final text in the graphic (Figure 4–11).

Q&A How do I edit placeholder text if I make a mistake?
Click the placeholder text to select it and then correct the entry.

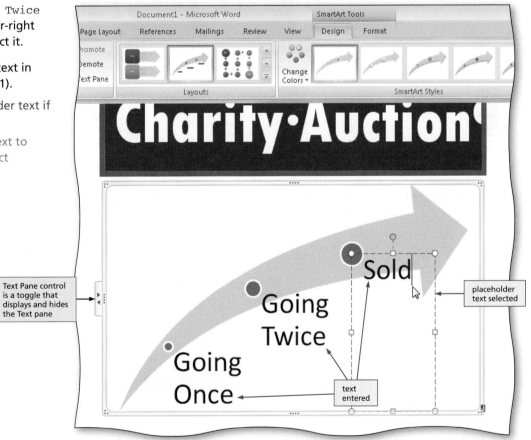

Figure 4–11

Other Ways	
1. Click Text Pane control, enter text in Text pane, close Text pane	2. Click Text Pane button on SmartArt Tools Design tab, enter text in Text pane, click Text Pane button again

To Change Colors of a SmartArt Graphic

In this project, the arrow on the title page is blue instead of pink. Word provides a variety of colors for a SmartArt graphic and the shapes in the graphic. The following steps change the colors of the SmartArt graphic.

1

• With the SmartArt graphic selected, click the Change Colors button on the Design tab to display the Change Colors gallery.

Q&A

What if the Design tab in the SmartArt Tools tab no longer is the active tab?

Click the SmartArt graphic to select it and then click Design on the Ribbon.

2

• Scroll to and then point to Colored Outline - Accent 5 in the Change Colors gallery to display a live preview of that color applied to the SmartArt graphic in the document (Figure 4–12).

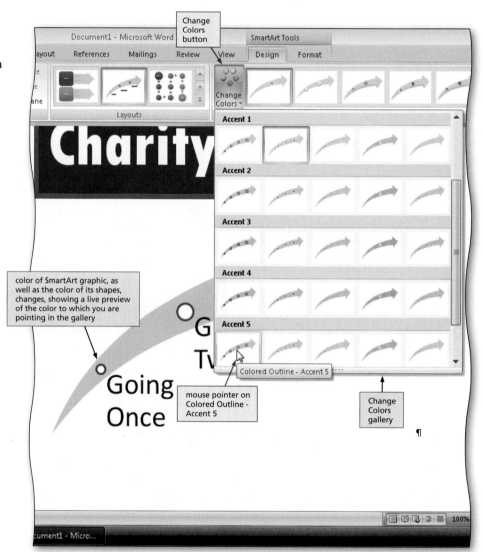

Figure 4–12

Experiment

• Point to various colors in the Change Colors gallery and watch the colors of the graphic change in the document window.

- Click Colored Outline - Accent 5 in the Change Colors gallery to apply the selected color to the SmartArt graphic (Figure 4–13).

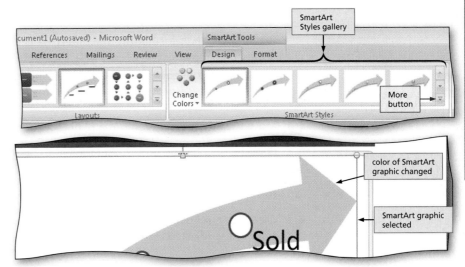

Figure 4–13

To Apply a SmartArt Style

The next step is to apply a SmartArt style to the SmartArt graphic. Word provides a SmartArt Styles gallery, allowing you to change the SmartArt graphic's format to a more visually appealing style. The following steps apply a SmartArt style to the SmartArt graphic.

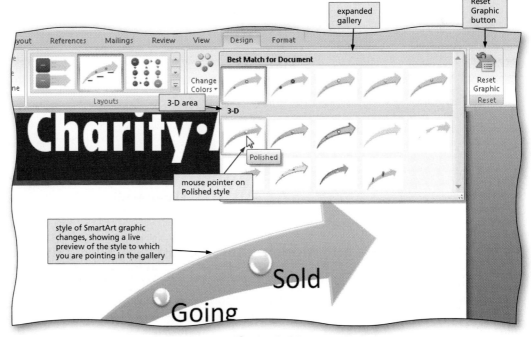

1
- With the SmartArt graphic still selected, click the More button in the SmartArt Styles gallery (shown in Figure 4–13) to expand the SmartArt Styles gallery.

2
- Point to Polished in the 3-D area of the SmartArt Styles gallery to display a live preview of that style applied to the graphic in the document (Figure 4–14).

Figure 4–14

Experiment
- Point to various SmartArt styles in the SmartArt Styles gallery and watch the style of the graphic change in the document window.

3
- Click Polished in the SmartArt Styles gallery to apply the selected style to the SmartArt graphic.

BTW

Resetting Graphics
If you want to remove all formats from a SmartArt graphic and start over, you would click the Reset Graphic button on the SmartArt Tools Design tab (Figure 4-14 on the previous page).

To Format Text Using the Mini Toolbar

The last step in formatting the SmartArt is to make the word, Sold, stand out more. The following steps use the Mini toolbar to increase the font size of the word, Sold, to 44 point, bold it, and change its color to dark pink.

1 Double-click the word, Sold, to select it.

2 Move the mouse pointer into the Mini toolbar, so that it changes to a bright toolbar.

3 Click the Bold button on the Mini toolbar to bold the selected text.

4 Click the Font Size box arrow on the Mini toolbar and then click 44 in the Font Size gallery to change the font size of the selected text.

5 Click the Font Color button arrow and then click Pink, Accent 2, Darker 25% to change the color of the selected text (Figure 4–15).

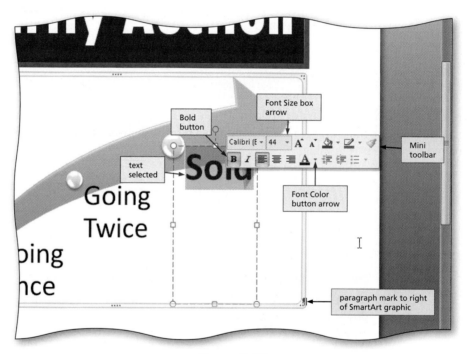

Figure 4–15

To Format Characters and Modify Character Spacing Using the Font Dialog Box

In this project, the next step is to enter and format the text at the bottom of the title page. This text is the theme of the proposal and is formatted so that it is noticeable. Its characters are 48-point bold, italic, and dark pink. Each letter in this text displays a shadow. A **shadow** is a light gray duplicate image that appears on the lower-right edge of a character or object. Also, you want extra space between each character so that the text spans across the width of the page.

You could use buttons on the Home tab to apply some of these formats. The shadow effect and expanded spacing, however, are applied using the Font dialog box. Thus, the next steps apply all above-mentioned formats using the Font dialog box.

1

- Position the insertion point on the paragraph mark to the right of the SmartArt graphic and then press the ENTER key to position the insertion point centered below the SmartArt graphic.

- Type Join us for this great cause!

- Select the sentence you just typed and then click the Font Dialog Box Launcher on the Home tab to display the Font dialog box. If necessary, click the Font tab in the dialog box.

- Click Bold Italic in the Font style list.

- Scroll through the Size list and then click 48.

- Click the Font color box arrow and then click Pink, Accent 2, Darker 25% in the Font color gallery.

- Click Shadow in the Effects area so that each character displays a shadow on its lower-right edge (Figure 4–16).

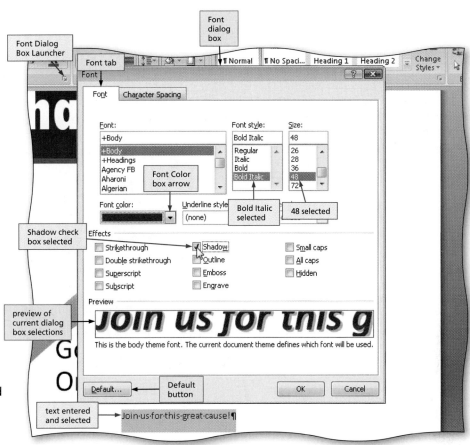

Figure 4–16

2

- Click the Character Spacing tab to display the Character Spacing sheet in the dialog box.

- Click the Spacing box arrow and then click Expanded to increase the amount of space between characters by 1 pt, which is the default.

- Click the Spacing By box up arrow until the box displays 5 pt so that 5 points of blank space are displayed between each character (Figure 4–17).

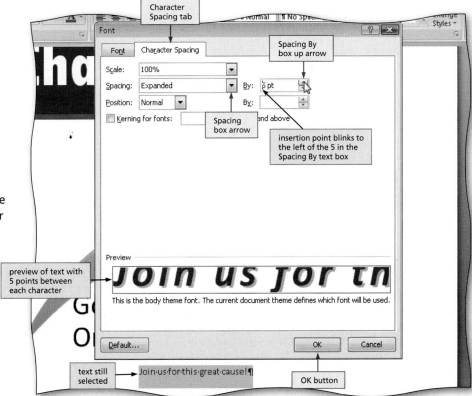

Figure 4–17

- Click the OK button to apply font changes to the selected text. If necessary, scroll so that the selected text is displayed completely in the document window (Figure 4–18). (Leave the text selected for the next set of steps.)

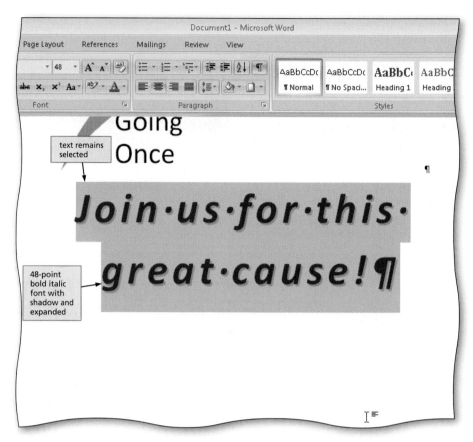

Figure 4–18

Other Ways

1. Right-click selected text, click Font on shortcut menu, select formats, click OK button

TO MODIFY THE DEFAULT FONT SETTINGS

You can change the default font so that the current document and all future documents use the new font settings. That is, if you quit Word, restart the computer, and restart Word, documents you create will use the new default font.

If you wanted to change the default font from 11-point Calibri to another font, font style, font size, font color, and/or font effects, you would perform the following steps.

1. Display the Font dialog box.

2. Make desired changes to the font settings in the Font dialog box.

3. Click the Default button (shown in Figure 4–16 on the previous page).

4. When the Microsoft Word dialog box is displayed, click the Yes button.

TO RESET THE DEFAULT FONT SETTINGS

To change the font settings back to the default, you would follow the above steps, using the default font settings when performing Step 2. If you do not remember the default settings, you would perform the following steps to restore the original Normal style settings.

1. Quit Word.

2. Use Windows Explorer to locate the normal.dotm file (be sure that hidden files and folders are displayed and include system and hidden files in your search).

3. Rename the normal.dotm file to oldnormal.dotm file so that the normal.dotm file no longer exists.

4. Start Word, which will recreate a normal.dotm file using the original default settings.

Character Effects

In addition to a shadow, the Font sheet in the Font dialog box (Figure 4–16 on page WD 241) contains many other character effects you can add to text in a document. Table 4–2 illustrates the result of each of these effects.

Type of Effect	Plain Text	Formatted Text
Strikethrough	Auction	~~Auction~~
Double strikethrough	Auction	~~Auction~~
Superscript	1st	1ST
Subscript	H2O	H_2O
Shadow	Auction	Auction
Outline	Auction	Auction
Emboss	Auction	Auction
Engrave	Auction	Auction
Small caps	Auction	Auction
All caps	Auction	AUCTION
Hidden	Auction	

Table 4–2 Character Effects Available in the Font Dialog Box

The last entry in Table 4–2 shows the hidden format. **Hidden text** does not print but is part of the document. When the Show/Hide ¶ button on the Home tab is not selected, hidden text does not appear on the screen. When the Show/Hide ¶ button is selected, Word displays hidden text on the screen.

To Change Case of Text

To make the title text at the bottom of the sales proposal more pronounced, it is formatted in all capital letters. The following steps capitalize all letters in selected text.

1
- With the text still selected, click the Change Case button on the Home tab to display the Change Case gallery (Figure 4–19).

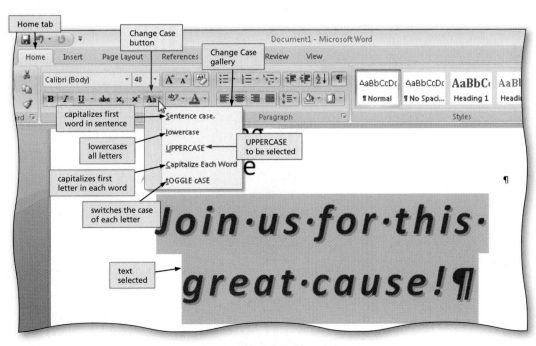

Figure 4–19

2

- Click UPPERCASE to change the characters in the selected text to all capital letters.

- Press the END key to deselect the text and position the insertion point at the end of the document (Figure 4–20).

Q&A

Could I have used the All caps check box in the Effects area of the Font dialog box to format this text in all capital letters?

Yes, but because the dialog box was closed already, the Change Case button was used.

Figure 4–20

Other Ways

1. Right-click selected text, click Font on shortcut menu, click Font tab, click All caps check box, click OK button
2. Press SHIFT+F3 repeatedly until text displays all caps

To Zoom One Page

The next step in creating the title page is to place the auctioneer graphic on it. You want to see the entire page while inserting this graphic. Thus, you zoom so that the entire page is displayed in the document window. Instead of using the Zoom slider to set the zoom, you can use the One Page button to quickly display the entire page in the document window. The following step zooms one page.

1

- Click View on the Ribbon to display the View tab.

- Click the One Page button on the View tab to display the entire page centered in the document window (Figure 4–21).

Other Ways

1. Click Zoom level button on status bar, click Whole page in the Zoom dialog box, click OK button

Figure 4–21

To Create a Watermark

A **watermark** is text or a graphic that is displayed on top of or behind the text in a document. For example, a catalog may print the words, Sold Out, on top of sold-out items. The first draft of a five-year-plan may have the word, Draft, printed behind the text of the document. Some companies use their logos or other graphics as watermarks on documents to add visual appeal to the document.

In this project, a picture of an auctioneer is displayed behind all text and graphics as a watermark. The auctioneer picture is located on the Data Files for Students. See the inside back cover of this book for instructions on downloading the Data Files for Students, or contact your instructor for information about accessing the required files. The following steps create a picture watermark.

1

- Display the Page Layout tab.

- Click the Watermark button on the Page Layout tab to display the Watermark gallery (Figure 4–22).

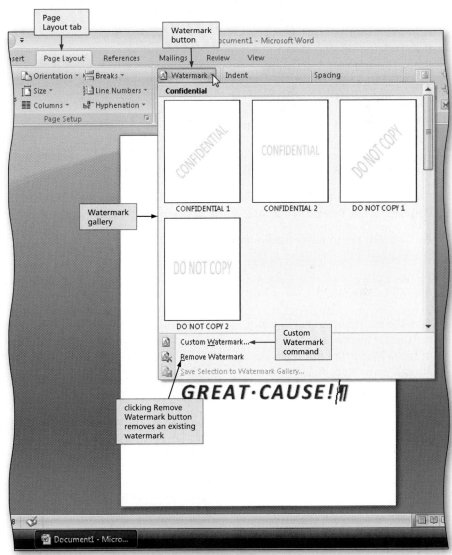

Figure 4–22

- Click Custom Watermark to display the Printed Watermark dialog box.

- With your USB flash drive connected to one of the computer's USB ports, click Picture watermark and then click the Select Picture button to display the Insert Picture dialog box.

- If the Folders list is displayed below the Folders button, click the Folders button to remove the Folders list.

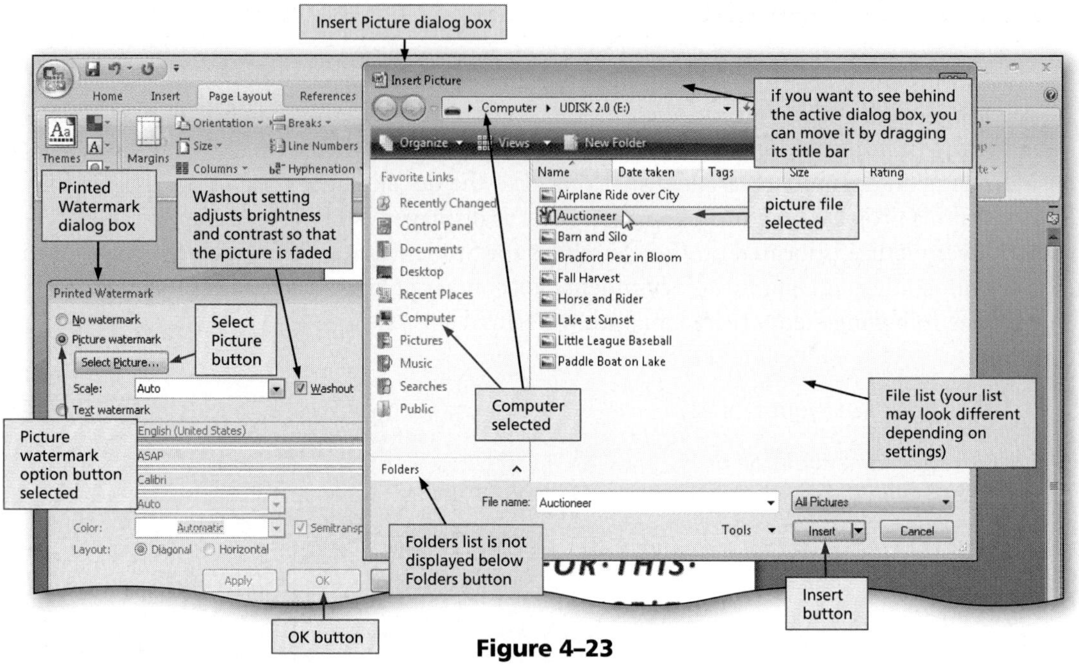

Figure 4–23

- Click Computer in the Favorite Links section and then double-click UDISK 2.0 (E:) to select the USB flash drive, Drive E in this case, as the device that contains the picture.

- Click Auctioneer to select the file name (Figure 4–23).

Q&A What if the picture is not on a USB flash drive?

Use the same process, but select the device containing the picture in the Favorite Links section.

❸

- Click the Insert button to insert the Auctioneer file name to the right of the Select Picture button in the Printed Watermark dialog box.

- Click the OK button in the Printed Watermark dialog box to insert the watermark in the document, faded behind the text and SmartArt graphic (Figure 4–24).

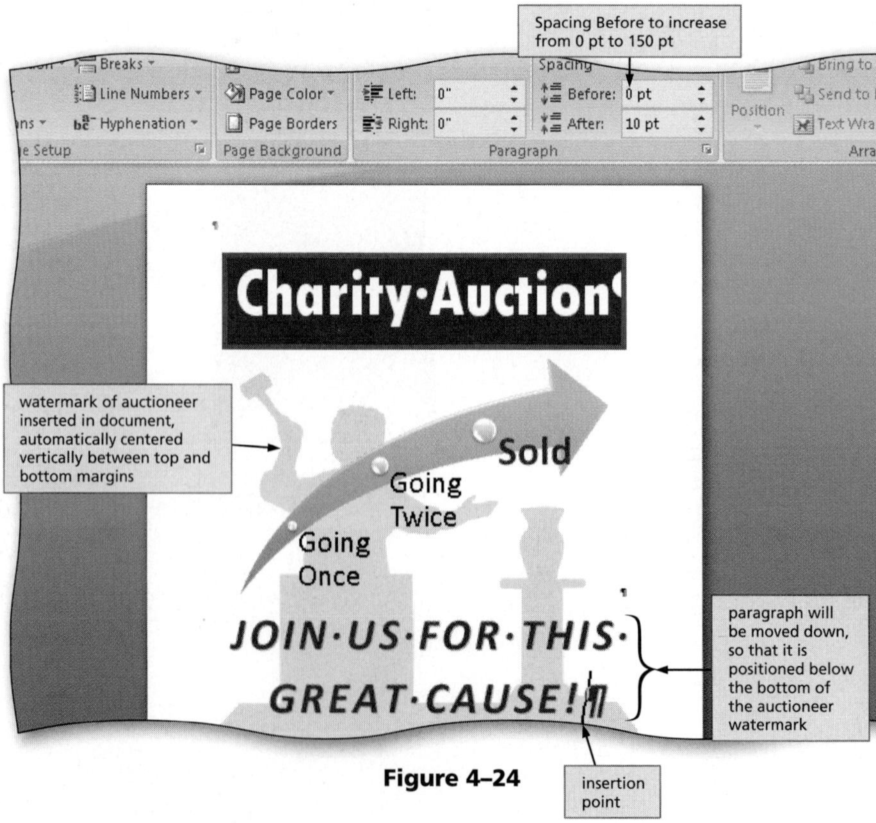

Q&A How would I remove a watermark from a document?

Click the Watermark button on the Page Layout tab and then click Remove Watermark, or click No watermark in the Printed Watermark dialog box (Figure 4–23).

Q&A How would I create a text watermark?

Click Text watermark in the Printed Watermark dialog box (Figure 4–23), select the text for the watermark or enter your own text, select formats for the text, and then click the OK button.

Figure 4–24

To Change Spacing Above a Paragraph and Set Zoom Level

To make the text, JOIN US FOR THIS GREAT CAUSE!, stand out more, this project positions it below the bottom of the auctioneer watermark. Currently, the Spacing Before this paragraph is 0 pt (shown in Figure 4–24). The following steps change the Spacing Before to 150 points and then change the zoom level back to 100% because you are finished with the title page.

1 With the insertion point in the paragraph to adjust, click the Spacing Before box up arrow on the Page Layout tab as many times as necessary until 150 pt is displayed in the Spacing Before box (Figure 4–25).

2 Change the zoom level to 100%.

Figure 4–25

To Reveal Formatting

Sometimes, you want to know what formats were applied to certain text items in a document. For example, you may wonder what font, font size, font color, and other effects were applied to the last paragraph of the title page. To display formatting applied to text, use the Reveal Formatting task pane. The next step illustrates how to reveal formatting.

- With the insertion point in the text for which you want to reveal formatting, press SHIFT+F1 to show formatting applied to the location of the insertion point in the Reveal Formatting task pane (Figure 4–26).

Experiment

- Click the Font collapse button to hide the Font formats. Click the Font expand button to redisplay the Font formats.

Q&A

Why do some of the formats in the Reveal Formatting task pane appear as links?

Clicking a link in the Reveal Formatting task pane displays an associated dialog box, allowing you to change the format of the current text. For example, clicking the Font link in the Reveal Formatting task pane displays the Font dialog box. If you make changes in the Font dialog box and then click the OK button, Word changes the format of the current text.

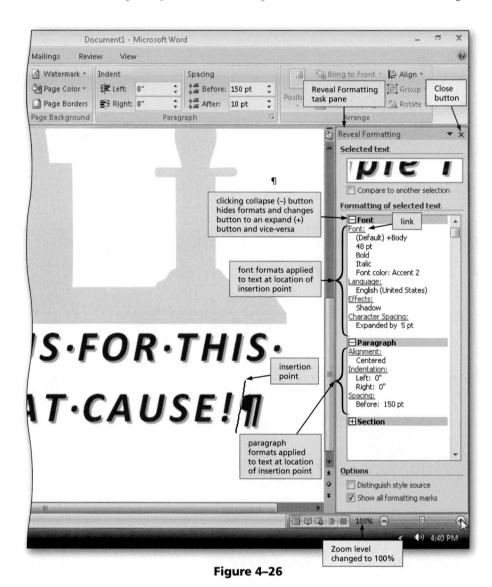

- Close the Reveal Formatting task pane by clicking its Close button.

Figure 4–26

To Save a Document

The title page for the sales proposal is complete. Thus, the next step is to save it.

1. With a USB flash drive connected to one of the computer's USB ports, click the Save button on the Quick Access Toolbar to display the Save As dialog box.

2. Type `Charity Auction Title Page` in the File name text box to change the file name.

3. If Computer is not displayed in the Favorite Links section, drag the top or bottom edge of the Save As dialog box until Computer is displayed.

④ Click Computer in the Favorite Links section, and then double-click your USB flash drive in the list of available drives.

⑤ Click the Save button in the Save As dialog box to save the document on the USB flash drive with the file name, Charity Auction Title Page.

Inserting an Existing Document in an Open Document

Assume you already have prepared a draft of the body of the proposal and saved it with the file name, Charity Auction Draft. You would like the draft to display on a separate page following the title page. Once the two documents are displayed on the screen together as one document, you save this active document with a new name so that each of the original documents remains intact.

Compose the sales proposal.
Be sure to include basic elements in your sales proposal:

• **Include an introduction, body, and conclusion.** The introduction could contain the subject, purpose, statement of problem, need, background, or scope. The body may include costs, benefits, supporting documentation, available or required facilities, feasibility, methods, timetable, materials, or equipment. The conclusion summarizes key points or requests an action.

• **Use headers and footers.** Headers and footers help to identify every page. A page number should be in either the header or footer. If the sales proposal is disassembled, the reader can use the headers and footers to determine the order and pieces of your proposal.

In the following pages, you will insert the draft of the proposal below the title page and then edit the draft as follows: customize its font set, delete a page break, and cut some text.

Sections

All Word documents have at least one section. A Word document can be divided into any number of sections. During the course of creating a document, you will create a new **section** if you need to change the top margin, bottom margin, page alignment, paper size, page orientation, page number position, or contents or position of headers, footers, or footnotes in just a portion of the document.

The next two pages of the sales proposal require page formatting different from that of the title page. The title page will not have a header or footer and the next two pages will have a header and footer.

When you want to change page formatting for a portion of a document, you create a new section in the document. Each section then may be formatted differently from the others. Thus, the title page formatted with no header or footer will be in one section, and the next two pages of the proposal that will have a header and footer will be in another section.

BTW

Reveal Formatting
When the Reveal Formatting task pane is displayed, you can click any text in the document window and the contents of the Reveal Formatting task pane will change to show formatting applied to the location of the insertion point. If you want to format selected text similarly to the text that surrounds it, select the text in the document, click the 'Selected text' text box in the Reveal Formatting task pane, click the 'Selected text' box arrow, and then click Apply Formatting of Surrounding Text.

Plan Ahead

BTW

Section Numbers
If you want to display the current section number on the status bar, right-click the status bar to display the Customize Status Bar menu and then click Section on the Customize Status Bar menu. The section number appears at the left edge of the status bar. To remove the section number from the status bar, perform the same steps.

To Insert a Next Page Section Break

The next two pages of the sales proposal have a header, but the title page does not. One way to specify different headers in a document is to divide it into sections. When you insert a section break, you specify whether the new section should begin on a new page.

In this project, the title page is separate from the next two pages. Thus, the section break should contain a page break. The following steps insert a next page section break, which instructs Word to begin the new section on a new page in the document.

1

- With the insertion point at the end of the title page, click the Breaks button on the Page Layout tab to display the Breaks gallery (Figure 4–27).

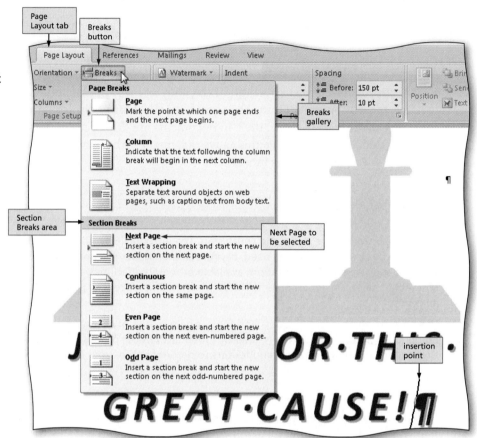

Figure 4–27

2

- Click Next Page in the Section Breaks area of the Breaks gallery to insert a next page section break in the document at the location of the insertion point. If necessary, scroll so that your screen matches Figure 4–28.

 Q&A

Why is the watermark in the new page?

A watermark is a page format that automatically is carried forward to subsequent pages.

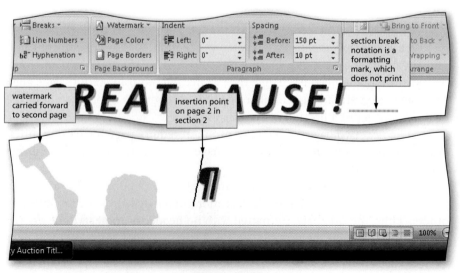

Figure 4–28

To Delete a Section Break

Word stores all section formatting in the section break. If you wanted to delete a section break and all associated section formatting, you would perform the following tasks.

1. Select the section break notation by dragging through it.

2. Right-click the selection and then click Cut on the shortcut menu.

or

1. Position the insertion point immediately to the left or right of the section break notation.

2. Press the DELETE key to delete a section break to the right of the insertion point or press the BACKSPACE key to delete a section break to the left of the insertion point.

To Clear Formatting

When you create a section break, Word carries forward any formatting at the location of the insertion point to the next section. Thus, the current paragraph has 150 points of spacing before the paragraph and the text is formatted the same as the last line of the title page. In this project, the paragraphs and characters on the second page should return to the Normal style. Thus, the following steps clear formatting.

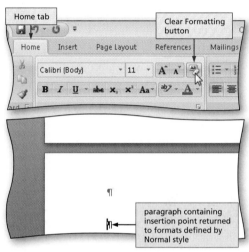

1 Display the Home tab.

2 With the insertion point positioned on the paragraph mark on the second page (shown in Figure 4–28), click the Clear Formatting button on the Home tab to apply the Normal style to the location of the insertion point (Figure 4–29).

Figure 4–29

To Insert a Word Document in an Open Document

The next step is to insert the draft of the sales proposal at the top of the second page of the document. The draft is located on the Data Files for Students. See the inside back cover of this book for instructions on downloading the Data Files for Students, or contact your instructor for information about accessing the required files. The following steps insert the draft of the proposal in the open document.

- Be sure the insertion point is positioned on the paragraph mark at the top of page 2.

- Display the Insert tab.

- With your USB flash drive connected to one of the computer's USB ports, click the Object button arrow to display the Object menu (Figure 4–30).

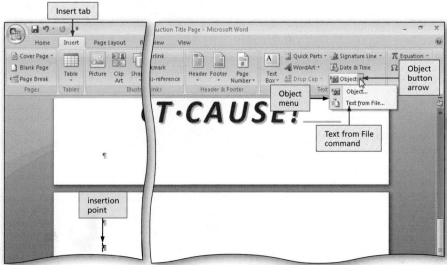

Figure 4–30

2

- On the Object menu, click Text from File to display the Insert File dialog box.

- If the Folders list is displayed below the Folders button, click the Folders button to remove the Folders list.

- If necessary, click Computer in the Favorite Links section and select the USB flash drive, Drive E in this case, in the list of files.

- Click Charity Auction Draft to select the file name (Figure 4–31).

Q&A How do I open the file if I am not using a USB flash drive?

Use the same process, but be certain to select your device in the Computer list.

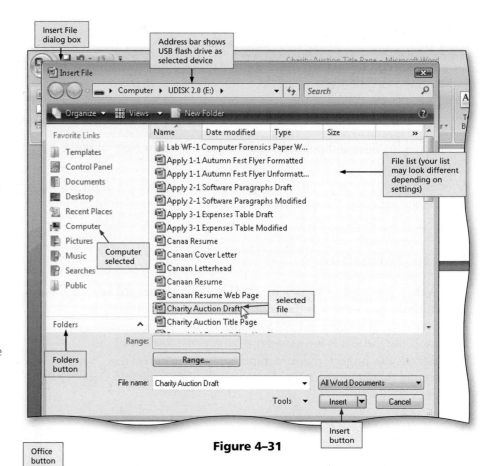

Figure 4–31

3

- Click the Insert button in the dialog box to insert the file, Charity Auction Draft, in the open document at the location of the insertion point.

Q&A Where is the insertion point?

When you insert a file in an open document, Word positions the insertion point at the end of the inserted document.

- Press SHIFT+F5 to position the insertion point on line 1 of page 2, which was its location prior to inserting the new Word document (Figure 4–32).

Q&A What is the purpose of SHIFT+F5?

The shortcut key, SHIFT+F5, positions the insertion point at your last editing location. Word remembers your last three editing locations, which means you can press this shortcut key repeatedly to return to one of your three most recent editing locations.

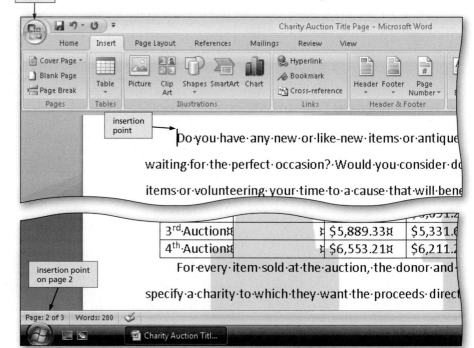

Figure 4–32

To Save an Active Document with a New File Name

BTW

Inserting Documents
When you insert a Word document in another Word document, the entire inserted document is placed at the location of the insertion point. If the insertion point, therefore, is positioned in the middle of the open document when you insert another Word document, the open document continues after the last character of the inserted document.

The current file name on the title bar is Charity Auction Title Page, yet the active document contains both the title page and the draft of the sales proposal. To keep the title page as a separate document called Charity Auction Title Page, you should save the active document with a new file name. If you save the active document by clicking the Save button on the Quick Access Toolbar, Word will assign it the current file name. You want the active document to have a new file name. The following steps save the active document with a new file name.

1 With the USB flash drive containing the Charity Auction Title Page connected to one of the computer's USB ports, click the Office Button and then click Save As on the Office Button menu to display the Save As dialog box.

2 Type `Charity Auction Proposal` in the File name text box to change the file name.

3 If Computer is not displayed in the Favorite Links section, drag the top or bottom edge of the Save As dialog box until Computer is displayed.

4 If necessary, click Computer in the Favorite Links section, and then double-click your USB flash drive in the list of available drives.

5 Click the Save button in the Save As dialog box to save the document on the USB flash drive with the file name, Charity Auction Proposal.

To Print Specific Pages in a Document

The title page is the first page of the proposal. The body of the proposal spans the second and third pages. The next steps print a hard copy of only the body of the proposal.

1

• Ready the printer.

• Click the Office Button to display the Office Button menu.

• Point to Print on the Office Button menu and then click Print on the submenu to display the Print dialog box.

• Click Pages in the Page range area of the dialog box and then type 2-3 in the Pages text box (Figure 4–33).

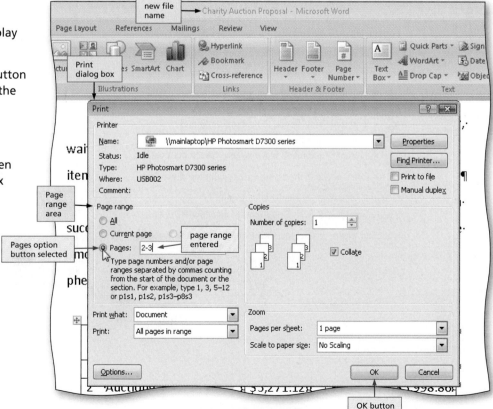

Figure 4–33

2

● Click the OK button to print the inserted draft of the sales proposal (Figure 4–34).

Q&A

What if I wanted to print pages from a certain point to the end of a document?

You would enter the page number followed by a dash in the Pages text box. For example, 5- will print from page 5 to the end of the document. To print up to a certain page, put the dash first (e.g., -5 will print pages 1 through 5).

Q&A

Why does my document wrap on different words than Figure 4–34?

Differences in wordwrap are related to the printer used by your computer.

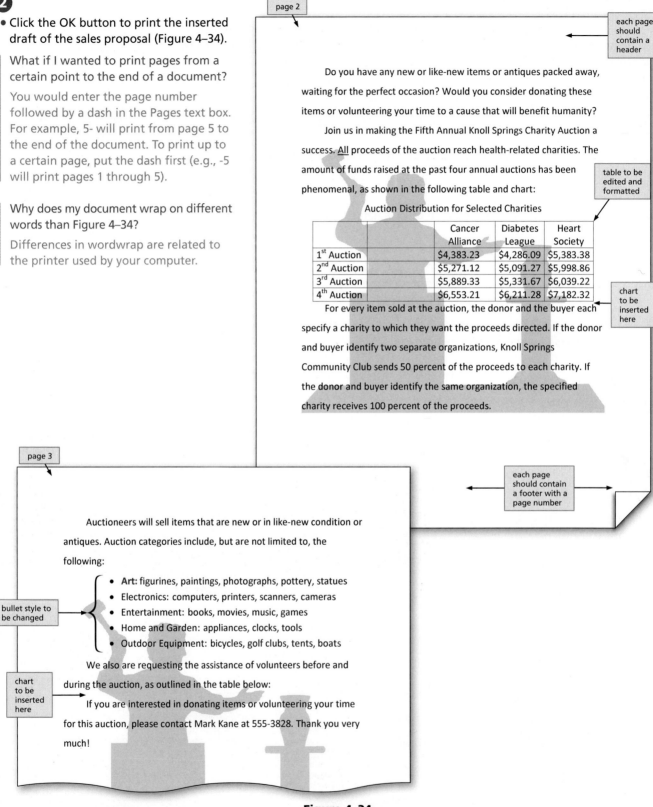

page 2

each page should contain a header

Do you have any new or like-new items or antiques packed away, waiting for the perfect occasion? Would you consider donating these items or volunteering your time to a cause that will benefit humanity?

Join us in making the Fifth Annual Knoll Springs Charity Auction a success. All proceeds of the auction reach health-related charities. The amount of funds raised at the past four annual auctions has been phenomenal, as shown in the following table and chart:

Auction Distribution for Selected Charities

table to be edited and formatted

		Cancer Alliance	Diabetes League	Heart Society
1st Auction		$4,383.23	$4,286.09	$5,383.38
2nd Auction		$5,271.12	$5,091.27	$5,998.86
3rd Auction		$5,889.33	$5,331.67	$6,039.22
4th Auction		$6,553.21	$6,211.28	$7,182.32

chart to be inserted here

For every item sold at the auction, the donor and the buyer each specify a charity to which they want the proceeds directed. If the donor and buyer identify two separate organizations, Knoll Springs Community Club sends 50 percent of the proceeds to each charity. If the donor and buyer identify the same organization, the specified charity receives 100 percent of the proceeds.

page 3

each page should contain a footer with a page number

Auctioneers will sell items that are new or in like-new condition or antiques. Auction categories include, but are not limited to, the following:

bullet style to be changed

● **Art:** figurines, paintings, photographs, pottery, statues
● Electronics: computers, printers, scanners, cameras
● Entertainment: books, movies, music, games
● Home and Garden: appliances, clocks, tools
● Outdoor Equipment: bicycles, golf clubs, tents, boats

We also are requesting the assistance of volunteers before and during the auction, as outlined in the table below:

chart to be inserted here

If you are interested in donating items or volunteering your time for this auction, please contact Mark Kane at 555-3828. Thank you very much!

Figure 4–34

Other Ways

1. Press CTRL+P

To Customize Theme Fonts

After reviewing the draft in Figure 4–34, you notice its text is based on the Office font set, which uses Cambria for headings and Calibri for body text. You prefer different fonts for the sales proposal, specifically Tw Cen MT Condensed Extra Bold for headings and Franklin Gothic Book for body text. These two fonts are not defined in a font set. Thus, the following steps create a customized theme font set for this document.

1

- Display the Home tab. Click the Change Styles button on the Home tab to display the Change Styles menu.

- Point to Fonts on the Change Styles menu to display the Fonts gallery.

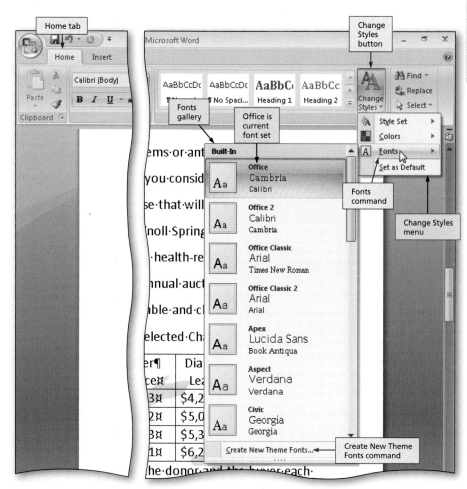

Figure 4–35

2

- Click Create New Theme Fonts in the Fonts gallery to display the Create New Theme Fonts dialog box.

- Click the Heading font box arrow; scroll to and then click Tw Cent MT Condensed Extra Bold (or a similar font).

- Click the Body font box arrow; scroll to and then click Franklin Gothic Book (or a similar font).

- Enter Charity Auction Proposal as the name for the new theme font (Figure 4–36).

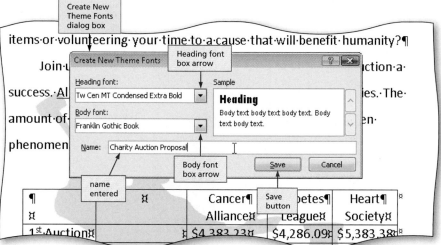

Figure 4–36

- Click the Save button in the dialog box to create the customized theme font with the name, Charity Auction Proposal, and apply the new heading and body fonts in the current document (Figure 4–37).

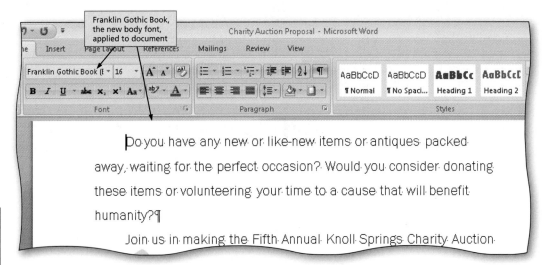

Figure 4–37

Other Ways

1. Click Theme Fonts button arrow on Page Layout tab, click Create New Theme Fonts, select fonts, click OK button

---

To Delete a Page Break

After reviewing the draft in Figure 4–34 on page WD 254, you notice it contains a page break below the third paragraph. This page break should not be in the document. The following steps delete a page break.

- Scroll to the bottom of page 2 to display the page break notation in the document window.

- To select the page break notation, position the mouse pointer to the left of the page break and then click when the mouse pointer changes to a right-pointing arrow (Figure 4–38).

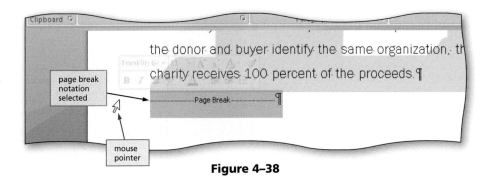

Figure 4–38

- Press the DELETE key to remove the page break from the document (Figure 4–39).

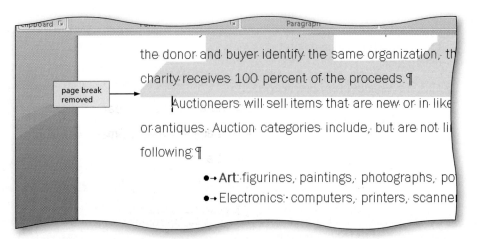

Figure 4–39

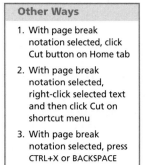

Other Ways

1. With page break notation selected, click Cut button on Home tab

2. With page break notation selected, right-click selected text and then click Cut on shortcut menu

3. With page break notation selected, press CTRL+X or BACKSPACE

To Cut Text

The last line of the draft document contains the phrase, Thank you very much! You decide to shorten it simply to say, Thank you! The following steps cut text from a document.

- Scroll to the end of the document and select the words, very much (Figure 4–40).

text to be deleted is selected

If you are interested in donating items or volunteering your ti for this auction, please contact Mark Kane at 555-3828. Thank yo very much!¶

Figure 4–40

- Click the Cut button on the Home tab to remove the selected text from the document (Figure 4–41).

When you cut items, are they placed on the Clipboard?

Yes. You then can paste items from the Clipboard in the document by clicking the Paste button on the Home tab or by using the Clipboard task pane.

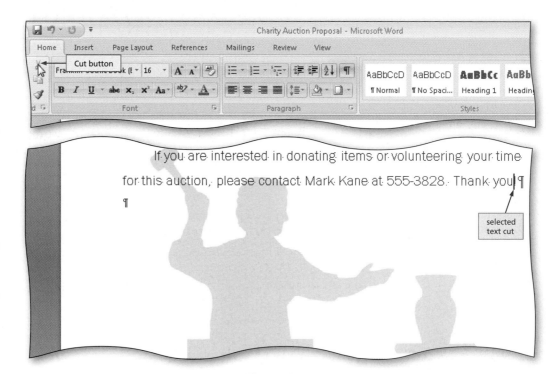

If you are interested in donating items or volunteering your time for this auction, please contact Mark Kane at 555-3828. Thank you ¶

selected text cut

Figure 4–41

Creating Headers and Footers

A **header** is text that prints at the top of each page in the document. A **footer** is text that prints at the bottom of each page. In this proposal, you want the header and footer to display on each page after the title page; that is, you do not want the header and footer on the title page. Recall that the title page is in a separate section from the rest of the sales proposal. Thus, the header and footer should not be in section 1, but they should be in section 2. The steps on the following pages explain how to create a header and footer in section 2 only.

To Go To a Section

Because the header and footer should be only on the pages in section 2 of the document, you should be sure the insertion point is in section 2 when you create the header and footer. The following steps position the insertion point in section 2, specifically, the beginning of section 2.

1

• Click the 'Page number in document' button on the status bar to display the Find and Replace dialog box.

 Experiment

• Scroll through the 'Go to what' list in the dialog box to see the many areas you can go to in a document.

2

• Click Section in the 'Go to what' area to select it.

• Type 2 in the 'Enter section number' text box (Figure 4–42).

3

• Click the Go To button in the dialog box to position the insertion point at the beginning of section 2 in the document.

• Click the Close button in the dialog box.

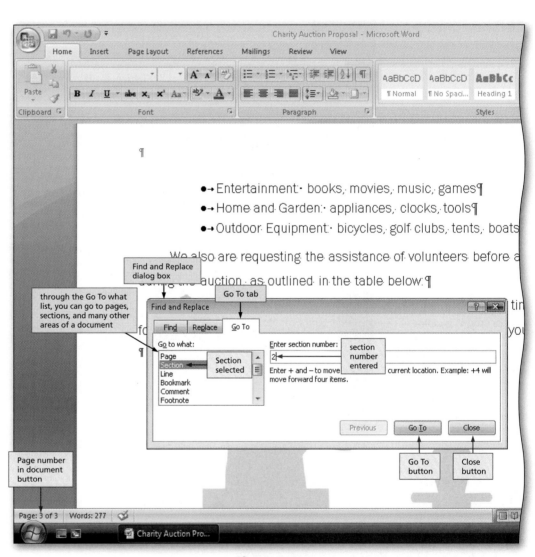

Figure 4–42

Other Ways

1. Click Select Browse Object button on vertical scroll bar, click Browse by Section

2. Click Find button arrow on Home tab, click Go To

3. Press CTRL+G

To Create a Header Different from the Previous Section Header

The next step is to instruct Word that the header and footer to be added should be in only the current (second) section of the document so that the header and footer do not appear on the title page.

1

- Display the Insert tab.

- Click the Header button on the Insert tab and then click Edit Header in the Header gallery to switch to the header for section 2 (Figure 4–43).

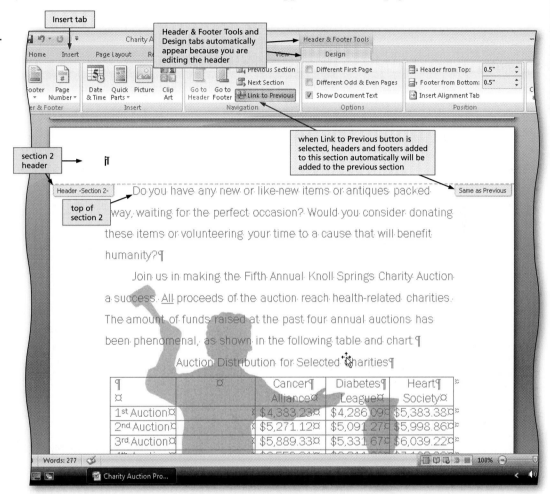

Figure 4–43

2

- If the header displays the tab, Same as Previous, in its lower-right corner, click the Link to Previous button on the Design tab to remove the Same as Previous tab, which means that the headers and footers entered in section 2 will not be copied to section 1.

Q&A What if I wanted a header and footer to appear in all sections?

You would leave the Link to Previous button selected on the Design tab.

BTW

Sections
To see formatting associated with a section, double-click the section break notation to display the Page Setup dialog box. You can change margin settings and page orientation for a section in the Margins tab. To change paper sizes for a section, click the Paper tab. The Layout tab allows you to change header and footer specifications and vertical alignment for the section. To add a border to a section, click the Borders button in the Layout sheet.

To Insert a Formatted Header

Word provides several built-in preformatted header designs for you to insert in documents. The following steps insert a formatted header in section 2 of the sales proposal.

1

- Click the Header button on the Design tab to display the Header gallery (Figure 4–44).

Experiment

- Scroll through the list of built-in headers to see the variety of available formatted header designs.

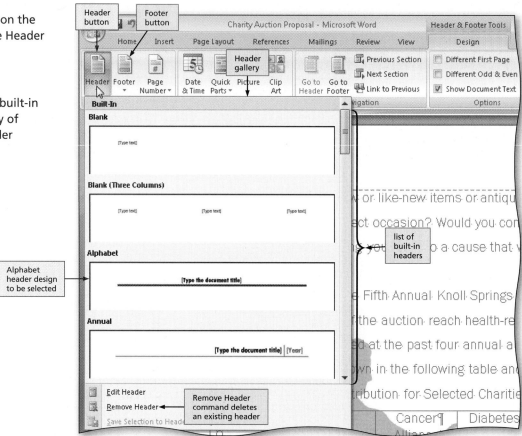

Figure 4–44

2

- Scroll to and then click the Alphabet header design to insert it in the header of section 2.

- Click the content control, Type the document title, and then type FIFTH ANNUAL KNOLL SPRINGS CHARITY AUCTION as the header text (Figure 4–45).

Q&A What if I wanted to delete a header?

You would click Remove Header in the Header gallery (Figure 4–44).

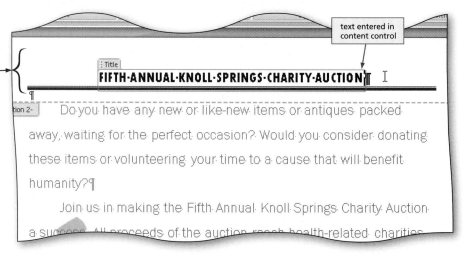

Figure 4–45

Other Ways

1. Click Header button on Insert tab, select desired header in list

To Insert a Formatted Footer

The next step is to insert the footer. Word provides the same built-in preformatted footer designs as header designs. The footer design that corresponds to the header just inserted contains text at the left margin and a page number at the right margin. The following steps insert a formatted footer in section 2 of the sales proposal that corresponds to the header just inserted.

1 Click the Go to Footer button on the Design tab to display the footer in the document window.

2 Click the Footer button on the Design tab to display the Footer gallery.

3 Click the Alphabet footer design to insert it in the footer of section 2.

4 Click the content control, Type text, and then type JOIN US FOR THIS GREAT CAUSE! as the text (Figure 4–46).

Q&A Why is the page number a 2?

The page number is 2 because, by default, Word begins numbering pages from the beginning of the document.

BTW

Headers and Footers
If a portion of a header or footer does not print, it may be in a nonprintable area. Check the printer manual to see how close the printer can print to the edge of the paper. Then, click the Page Setup Dialog Box Launcher on the Page Layout tab, click the Layout tab in the dialog box, adjust the From edge text box to a value that is larger than the printer's minimum margin setting, click the OK button, and then print the document again.

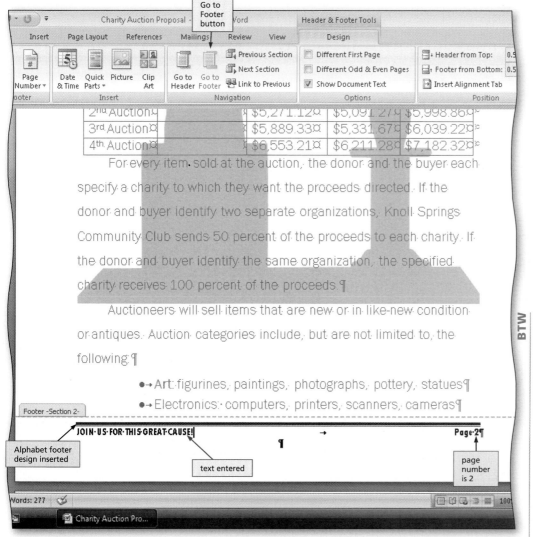

Figure 4–46

BTW

Page Numbers
If Word displays {PAGE} instead of the actual page number, press ALT+F9 to turn off field codes. If Word prints {PAGE} instead of the page number, click the Office Button, click the Word Options button, click Advanced in the left pane, scroll to the Print area, remove the check mark from the 'Print field codes instead of their values' check box, and then click the OK button.

To Format Page Numbers to Start at a Different Number

On the page after the title page in the proposal, you want to begin numbering with a number 1, instead of a 2 as shown in Figure 4–46 on the previous page. Thus, you need to instruct Word to begin numbering the pages in section 2 with the number 1. The following steps format the page numbers so they start at a different number.

- Click the Insert Page Number button on the Design tab to display the Insert Page Number menu (Figure 4–47).

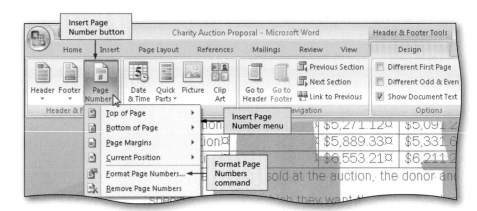

Figure 4–47

- Click Format Page Numbers on the Insert Page Number menu to display the Page Number Format dialog box.

- Click Start at in the Page numbering area (Figure 4–48).

Q&A

Can I also change the look of the page number?

Yes. Click the Number format box arrow for a list of page number variations.

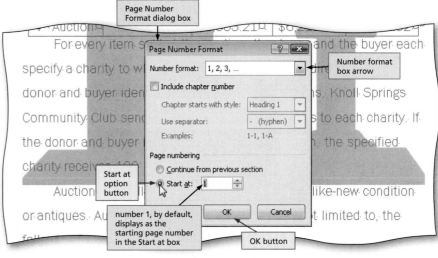

Figure 4–48

- Click the OK button to change the starting page number for section 2 to the number 1 (Figure 4–49).

- Click the Close Header and Footer button to close the header and footer.

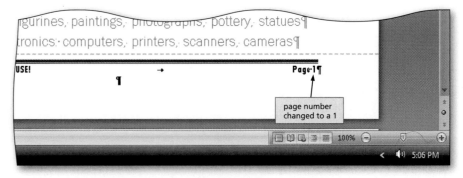

Figure 4–49

Other Ways

1. Click Insert Page Number button on Insert tab, click Format Page Numbers, set page formats, click OK button

Editing and Formatting a Table

The sales proposal draft contains a Word table (shown in Figure 4–34 on page WD 254) that was created using the Table button on the Home tab. This table contains five rows and five columns. The first row identifies the names of charities; the remaining rows show the proceeds for previous auctions. The first column identifies the auction, and the remaining columns show the proceeds for the charity.

> **Enhance the sales proposal with appropriate visuals.**
> Studies have shown that most people are visually oriented, preferring images to text. Use tables and charts to clarify ideas and illustrate points. Use pictures to break the flow of reading or emphasize a concept. Be aware, however, that too many visuals can clutter a document.

Plan Ahead

The following pages explain how to make these modifications to the table before charting it:

1. Delete the blank column between the first and third columns.
2. Add a row to the bottom of the table that shows total dollar amounts.
3. Apply a table style and then add a border to the table.
4. Change the alignment of dollar amounts.

To Format Characters

The title above the table in the sales proposal is bold and dark pink, so that it clearly identifies the table. The following steps format the table title.

1 If necessary, scroll to display the table in the document window.

2 Select the table title, Auction Distribution for Selected Charities.

3 Bold the title and then change its font color to Pink, Accent 2, Darker 25%.

To Delete a Column

The table in the draft of the proposal contains a blank column that should be deleted. The following steps delete a column from the middle of a table.

1

• Position the mouse pointer at the top of the column to be deleted and click when the mouse pointer changes to a downward-pointing arrow, which selects the entire column below the mouse pointer (Figure 4–50).

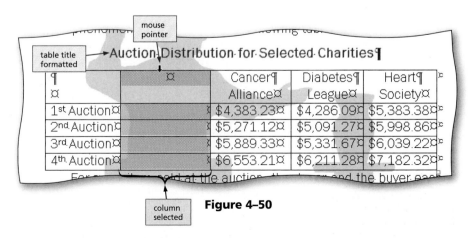

Figure 4–50

2

- Right-click the selected column to display a shortcut menu (Figure 4–51).

3

- Click Delete Columns on the shortcut menu to delete the selected column.

Q&A

How would I delete a row?

You would select the row to delete and then click Delete Rows on the shortcut menu. The Delete Columns command on the shortcut menu changes to a Delete Rows command when you select rows instead of columns in the table.

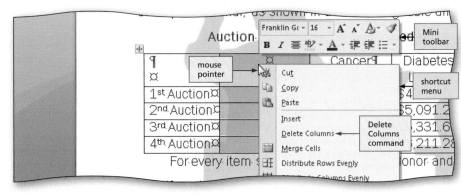

Figure 4–51

Other Ways

1. With the insertion point in column, click Delete button on Layout tab, click Delete Columns

To Add a Row to a Table

The next step is to add a row to the bottom of the table that shows totals of the dollar amounts in the second, third, and fourth columns.

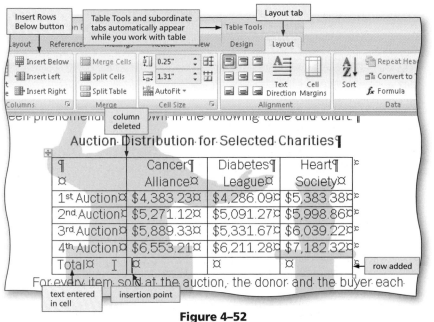

Figure 4–52

1 Position the insertion point somewhere in the bottom (fifth) row of the table.

2 Display the Layout tab in the Table Tools tab.

3 Click the Insert Rows Below button on the Layout tab to add a row below the current row.

Q&A Do I always have to insert rows below the current row?

No. You can insert above the current row by clicking the Insert Rows Above button on the Layout tab.

4 In the first cell in the last row, type Total and then press the TAB key (Figure 4–52).

To Add Columns

If you wanted to add a column to a table, you would perform the following steps.

1. Position the insertion point where you want to insert the column.

2. Click the Insert Columns to the Left button on the Layout tab to add a column to the left of the current column, or click the Insert Columns to the Right button to add a column to the right of the current column.

To Sum Columns in a Table

The last row should display the sum of the values in each column. Word can calculate the totals of each column. The following steps sum the columns in the table.

1

• With the insertion point in the cell to contain the sum (last row, second column), click the Formula button on the Layout tab to display the Formula dialog box (Figure 4–53).

Can I change the formula Word enters in the Formula text box?

Yes. If Word displays the wrong formula, simply type the correct formula in the text box. You also use the Formula dialog box to enter a formula in a cell other than summing.

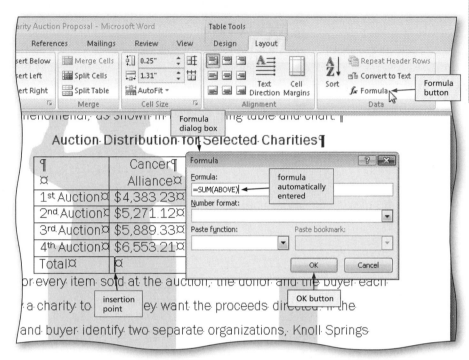

Figure 4–53

2

• Click the OK button in the Formula dialog box to place the sum of the numbers in the column in the current cell.

3

• Press the TAB key. Click the Formula button on the Layout tab to display the Formula dialog box and then click the OK button to place a sum in the third column.

• Press the TAB key. Click the Formula button on the Layout tab to display the Formula dialog box and then click the OK button to place a sum in the last column (Figure 4–54).

Can I sum a row instead of a column?

Yes. You would position the insertion point in an empty cell at the right edge of the row before clicking the Formula button.

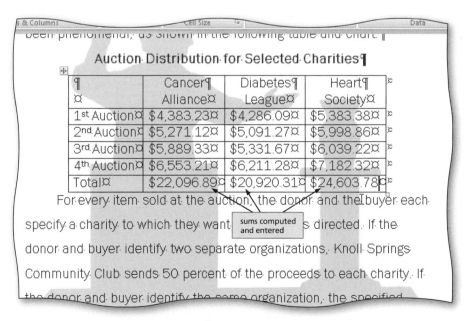

Figure 4–54

To Apply a Table Style

The table in the document looks dull. The following steps apply a table style to the table.

1 Display the Design tab.

2 With the insertion point in the table, be sure just these check boxes contain check marks in the Design tab: Header Row, Total Row, and First Column.

3 Click the More button in the Table Styles gallery to expand the Table Styles gallery.

4 Scroll to and then click Colorful List in the Table Styles gallery to apply the Colorful List style to the table (Figure 4–55).

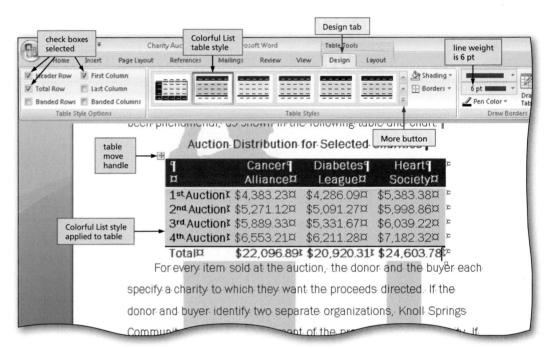

Figure 4–55

To Center a Table

The next step is to center the table horizontally between the page margins.

1 Position the mouse pointer in the table so that the table move handle appears (shown in Figure 4–55).

Q&A What if the table move handle does not appear?

You can select the table by clicking the Select Table button on the Layout tab and then clicking Select Table in the menu.

2 Click the table move handle to select the table.

3 Move the mouse pointer into the Mini toolbar and then click the Center button on the Mini toolbar, or click the Center button on the Home tab, to center the selected table between the left and right margins. (Leave the table selected for the next set of steps.)

To Border a Table

The table in this project has a 1-point, gray border. Earlier in this chapter when you created the title page, the border line weight was changed to 6 point and the border color changed to gray. Because the table border should be 1 point, you will change the line weight before adding the border to the table. The following steps add a border to a table.

1

- With the table still selected, click the Line Weight box arrow on the Design tab and then click 1 pt in the Line Weight gallery.

- Click the Borders button arrow on the Design tab to display the Borders gallery (Figure 4–56).

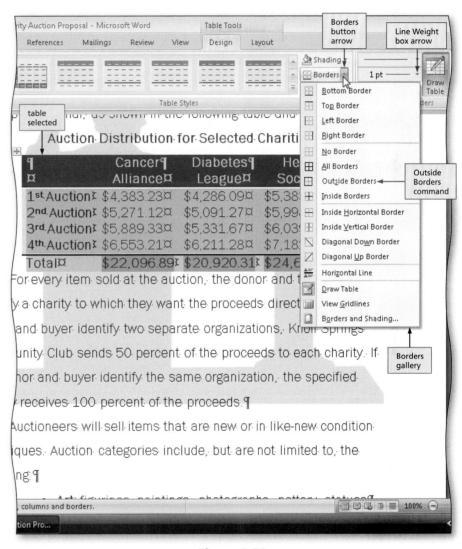

Figure 4–56

2

- Click Outside Borders to add a 1-point, gray border to the selected table.

- Click in the table to remove the selection.

Tables
If you wanted to move a table to a new location, you would point to the upper-left corner of the table until the table move handle appears (shown in Figure 4-55), point to the table move handle, and then drag it to move the entire table to a new location.

To Align Data in Cells

The next step is to change the alignment of the data in cells that contain the dollar amounts. In addition to aligning text horizontally in a cell (left, center, or right), you can align it vertically within a cell (top, center, bottom). When the height of the cell is close to the same height as the text, however, differences in vertical alignment are not readily apparent, which is the case for this table. Later in this chapter, you will align cell contents in a table that clearly will show variations in the vertical alignment. The following step right-aligns data in cells.

1

- Select the cells containing dollar amounts by dragging through them.

- Display the Layout tab.

- Click the Align Top Right button on the Layout tab to right-align the contents of the selected cells (Figure 4–57).

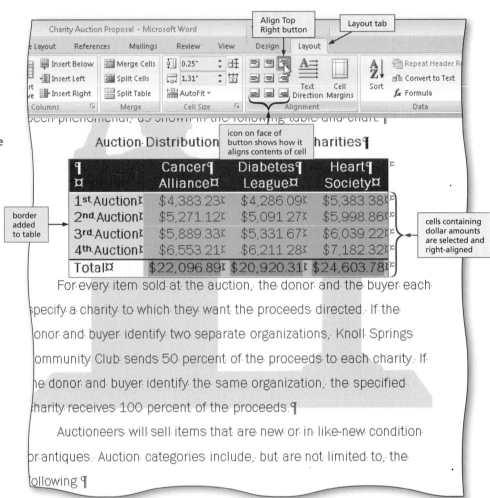

Figure 4–57

BTW

Charts
If Microsoft Excel is installed on your computer and you wanted to create a chart from an Excel worksheet, you would click the Insert Chart button on the Insert tab. If Microsoft Excel is not installed on your computer, clicking the Insert Chart button starts the Microsoft Graph program.

Charting a Word Table

When you create a Word table, you easily can chart its data using an embedded charting program called **Microsoft Graph**. Graph has its own menus and commands because it is a program embedded in Word. Using Graph commands, you can modify the appearance of the chart once you create it.

To create a chart from a Word table, the first row and left column of the selected cells in the table must contain text labels, and the other cells in the selected cells must contain numbers. The table in the Charity Auction Proposal meets these criteria. In the following pages, you will chart a table, move the legend to a different location, resize the chart, and change the chart type.

To Chart a Table

To chart a Word table, first select the rows and columns in the table to be charted. In this project, you do not want to chart the last row in the table that contains the totals. Thus, you will select the first five rows in the table and then chart the selected cells. The following steps chart a table.

- Point to the left of, or outside, the first row in the table (the column headings) until the mouse pointer changes to a right-pointing arrow and then drag downward until the first five rows in the table are selected. (Do not select the Total row.)

- Display the Insert tab.

- Click the Object button arrow to display the Object menu (Figure 4–58).

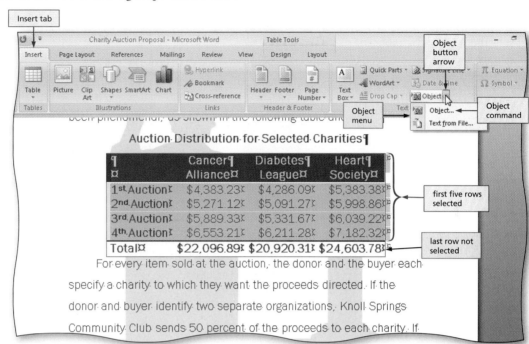

Figure 4–58

- Click Object on the Object menu to display the Object dialog box.

- If necessary, click the Create New tab. Select Microsoft Graph Chart in the Object type list (Figure 4–59).

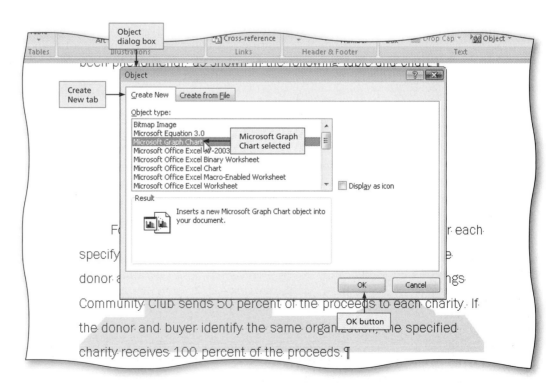

Figure 4–59

- Click the OK button to start the Microsoft Graph program, which creates a chart of the selected rows in the table (Figure 4–60).

- Close the Datasheet window by clicking its Close button.

Q&A

What is the Datasheet window?

Graph places the contents of the table in a **Datasheet window**, also called a **datasheet**. Graph then charts the contents of the datasheet. Although you can modify the contents of the datasheet, it is not necessary in this project. Thus, the datasheet is closed.

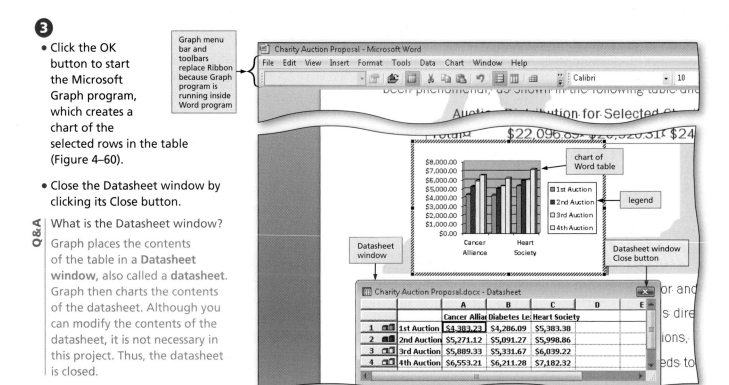

Figure 4–60

To Move Legend Placement in a Chart

The first step in changing the chart is to move the legend so that it displays below the chart instead of to the right of the chart. The **legend** is a box that identifies the colors assigned to categories in the chart. The following steps move the legend in the chart.

- If necessary, scroll to display the chart in the document window.

- Right-click the legend in the chart to display a shortcut menu related to legends (Figure 4–61).

Q&A

What if Microsoft Graph is no longer active; that is, what if the Word Ribbon is displayed instead of the Graph menus and toolbars?

While working in Graph, you may inadvertently click somewhere outside the chart, which exits Graph and returns to Word. If this occurs, simply double-click the chart to return to Graph.

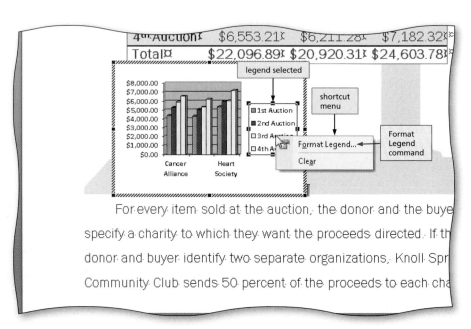

Figure 4–61

- Click Format Legend on the shortcut menu to display the Format Legend dialog box.

- Click the Placement tab, if necessary.

- Click Bottom in the Placement area (Figure 4–62).

- Click the OK button to place the legend below the chart.

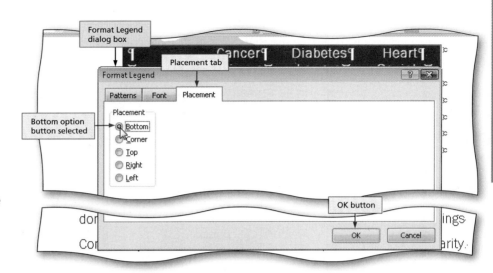

Figure 4–62

To Resize a Chart

The next step is to resize the chart so that it is bigger. You resize a chart the same way you resize any other graphical object. That is, you drag the chart's sizing handles. The following steps resize the chart.

①
- Point to the bottom-right sizing handle on the chart and drag downward and to the right as shown in Figure 4–63.

②
- Release the mouse button to resize the chart (shown in Figure 4–64 on the next page).

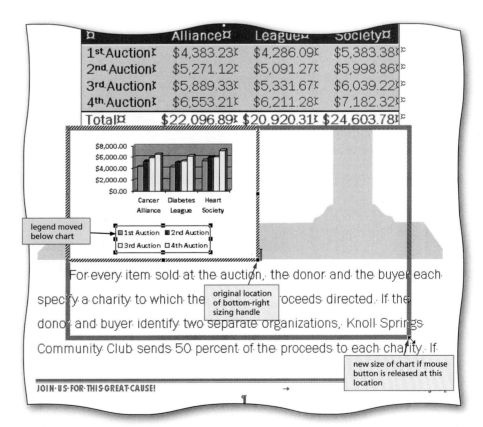

Figure 4–63

To Change the Chart Type

The next task is to change the chart type so that the columns have a cylindrical shape instead of a rectangular shape. The following steps change the chart type.

- Right-click an area of white space in the chart to display a shortcut menu (Figure 4–64).

Q&A

What if my shortcut menu differs from the one shown in the figure?

Right-click a different area of white space in the chart.

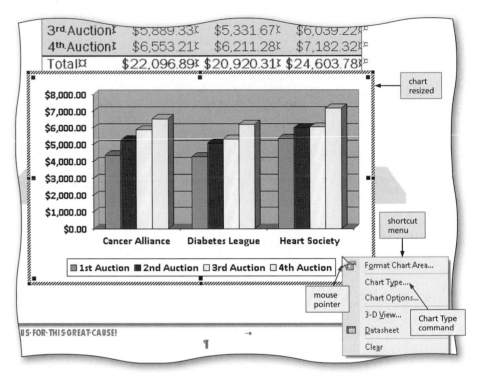

Figure 4–64

- Click Chart Type on the shortcut menu to display the Chart Type dialog box.

- If necessary, click the Standard Types tab. In the Chart type list, scroll to and then select Cylinder (Figure 4–65).

❸

- Click the OK button to change the shape of the columns to cylinders (shown in Figure 4–66).

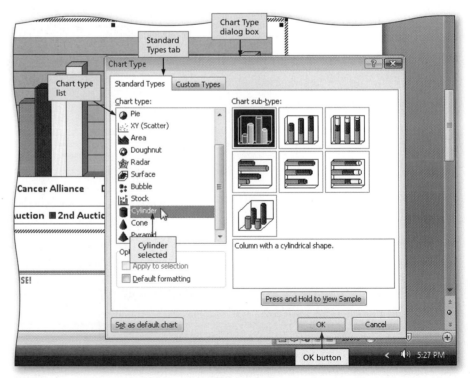

Figure 4–65

To Exit Graph and Return to Word

The modified chart is finished. The next step is to exit Graph and return to Word. In Word, you place an outside border on the chart to give it a finished look and add a blank line above the chart to separate it from the table.

1

• Click somewhere outside the chart to close the Graph program and return to Word.

• If necessary, scroll to display the chart in the document window.

Q&A | What if I want to modify an existing chart after I close Graph?

You would double-click the chart to reopen the Graph program. When you are finished making changes to the chart, click anywhere outside the chart to return to Word.

2

• Display the Home tab.

• Click the chart to select it. Click the Border button arrow on the Home tab and then click Outside Borders in the Border gallery to place the same border around the chart that is around the table.

• Click the Line spacing button on the Home tab and then click Add Space Before Paragraph to place a blank line above the chart.

• Click to the right of the chart to deselect it (Figure 4–66).

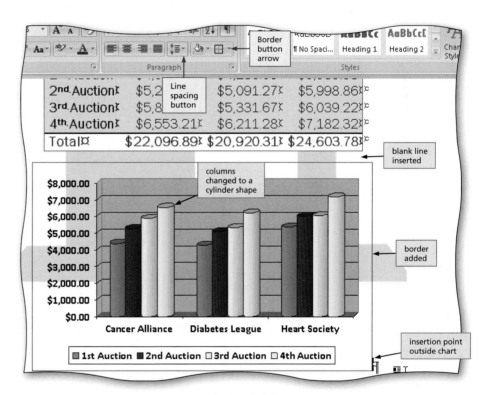

Figure 4–66

Working with Formats, Styles, and Bulleted Lists

On the last page of the sales proposal, the auction categories at the beginning of each bulleted item are emphasized. The draft of the sales proposal formatted the first auction category, Art, in bold and dark pink. All the remaining auction categories should use this format. Also, the bullet character at the beginning of each category is a picture bullet, instead of the standard dot. The following pages illustrate steps used to format the text and bullets in the auction categories:

1. Find the bold, dark pink format.
2. Create a character style for the format.
3. Select the auction categories to be formatted.
4. Apply the style.
5. Customize bullets in a list.

To Find a Format

The last page of the proposal has a bulleted list. The text at the beginning of each bulleted paragraph identifies a specific auction category. The first bullet, identified with the text, Art, has been formatted as bold and dark red. To find this text in the document, you could scroll through the document until it is displayed on the screen. A more efficient way is to find the bold, dark red format using the Find and Replace dialog box. The following steps find a format.

- Click the Find button on the Home tab to display the Find and Replace dialog box.

- If Word displays a More button in the Find and Replace dialog box, click it so that it changes to a Less button and expands the dialog box.

- Click the Format button to display the Format menu (Figure 4–67).

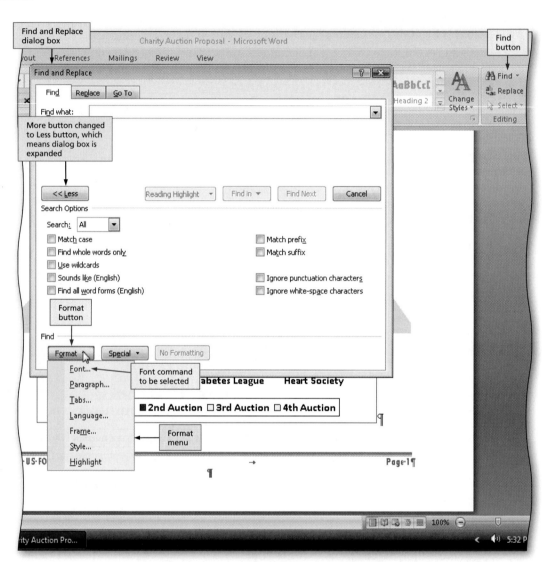

Figure 4–67

2

- Click Font on the Format menu to display the Find Font dialog box. If necessary, click the Font tab.

- In the dialog box, click Bold in the Font style list.

- In the dialog box, click the Font color box arrow and then click Pink, Accent 2, Darker 25% (Figure 4–68).

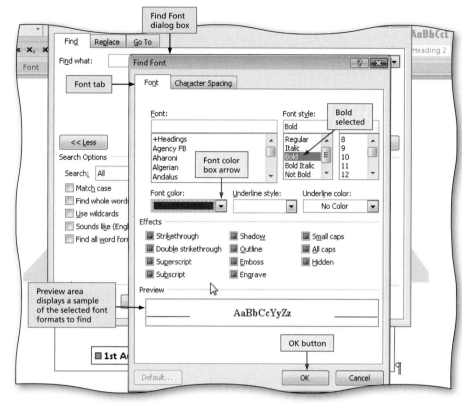

Figure 4–68

3

- Click the OK button to close the Find Font dialog box.

- When the Find and Replace dialog box is active again, click its Find Next button to locate and high-light in the document the first occurrence of the specified format (Figure 4–69).

 How do I remove a find format?

You would click the No Formatting button in the Find and Replace dialog box.

4

- Click the Cancel button in the Find and Replace dialog box because the located occurrence is the one you wanted to find.

Can I search for (find) special characters such as page breaks?

Yes. To find special characters, you would click the Special button in the Find and Replace dialog box.

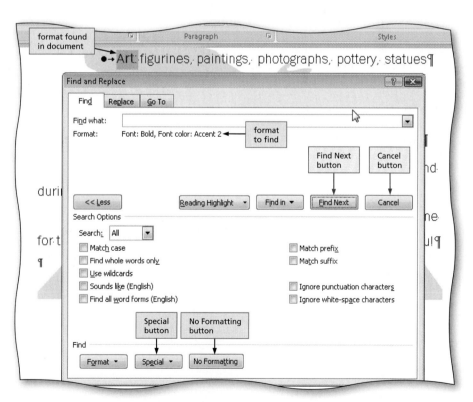

Figure 4–69

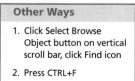

Other Ways

1. Click Select Browse Object button on vertical scroll bar, click Find icon

2. Press CTRL+F

To Create a Character Style

In this sales proposal, the auction categories at the beginning of the second, third, fourth, and fifth bulleted paragraphs are to have the same character format as the auction category at the beginning of the first bulleted paragraph (bold and dark pink). Character formats emphasize certain characters, words, and phrases to improve readability of a document.

You could select each of the auction categories and then format them. A more efficient technique is to create a character style. If you decide to modify the formats of the auction categories at a later time, you simply change the formats assigned to the style. All characters in the document based on that style will change automatically. The following steps create a character style called Categories.

- Right-click the selected auction category, Art:, and then point to Styles on the shortcut menu.

- Click Save Selection as a New Quick Style in the Styles sub-menu to display the Create New Style from Formatting dialog box (Figure 4–70).

Figure 4–70

- Type Categories in the Name text box as the name of the new style.

- Click the Modify button to display another Create New Style from Formatting dialog box.

- Click the Style type box arrow and then click Character so that the new style does not contain any paragraph formats (Figure 4–71).

- Click the OK button to create the new character style, Categories, and insert it as a Quick Style in the Styles gallery.

Other Ways

1. Click More button in Styles gallery on Home tab, click Save Selection as a New Quick Style, enter name of new style, click Modify button

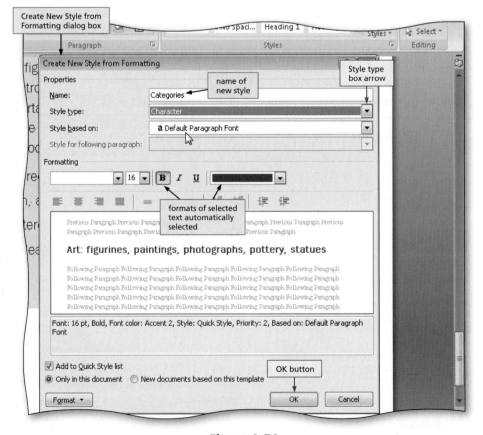

Figure 4–71

To Select Nonadjacent Text

The next step is to select the auction categories in the second, third, fourth, and fifth bulleted paragraphs so that you can apply the Categories style to the categories. Word provides a method of selecting nonadjacent or noncontiguous text, which are segments of text that are not next to each other on the right or the left. When you select nonadjacent text, you can format all occurrences of the text at once. The following steps select nonadjacent text.

1
- Drag through the first item to select, Electronics:, in this case.

2
- While holding down the CTRL key, drag through the next item to select, Entertainment:, in this case, to select the nonadjacent text.

- While holding down the CTRL key, drag through the next item to select, Home and Garden:, in this case, to select the nonadjacent text.

- While holding down the CTRL key, drag through the next item to select, Outdoor Equipment:, in this case, to select the nonadjacent text.

Q&A Does adjacent only include text to the right or left?

Yes. Text above or below a selection is considered nonadjacent in Word.

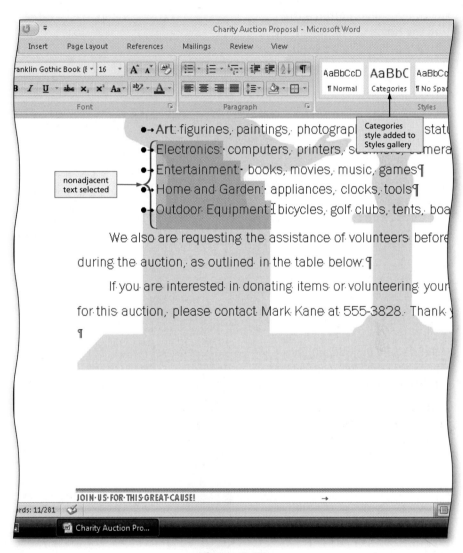

Figure 4–72

To Apply a Quick Style

The following step applies the Categories style to the selected auction categories in the bulleted list.

1 Click Categories in the Styles gallery to apply the Categories character style to the current paragraph.

To Customize Bullets in a List

The bulleted list in the sales proposal draft uses default bullet characters. You want to use a more visually appealing picture bullet. The following steps change the bullets in the list from the default to picture bullets.

- Select all the paragraphs in the bulleted list.

- Click the Bullets button arrow on the Home tab to display the Bullets gallery (Figure 4–73).

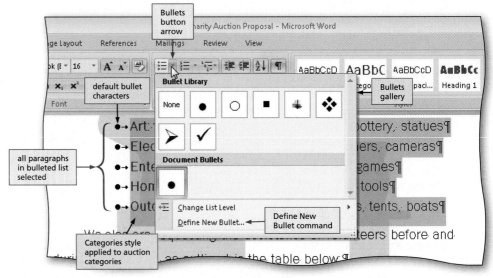

Figure 4–73

2

- Click Define New Bullet in the Bullets gallery to display the Define New Bullet dialog box.

- Click the Picture button in the Define New Bullet dialog box to display the Picture Bullet dialog box.

- Scroll through the list of picture bullets and then select the picture bullet shown in Figure 4–74 (or a similar picture bullet).

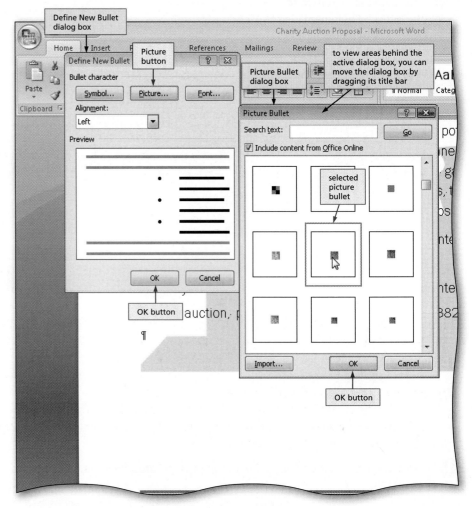

Figure 4–74

3

- Click the OK button in the Picture Bullet dialog box.

- Click the OK button in the Define New Bullet dialog box to change the bullets in the selected list to picture bullets.

- When the Word window is visible again, click in the selected list to remove the selection (Figure 4–75).

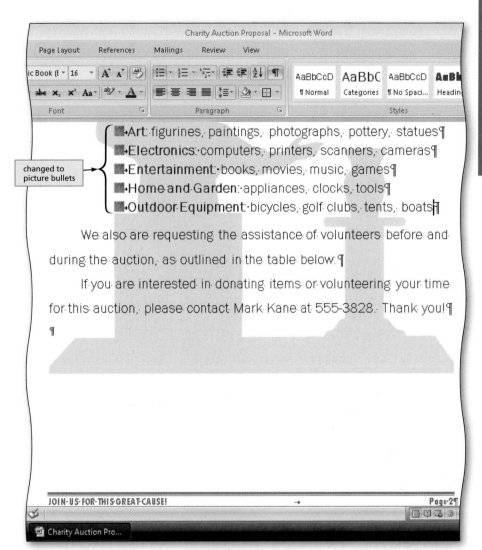

Figure 4–75

Drawing a Table

The next step is to insert a table above the last paragraph of the proposal (shown in Figure 4–1 on page WD 227). As previously discussed, a Word table is a collection of rows and columns; the intersection of a row and a column is called a cell. Cells are filled with data.

When you want to create a simple table, one with the same number of rows and columns, select the dimension of the table in the Table gallery. To create a more complex table, use Word's **Draw Table feature**. The table to be created at this point in the project is a complex table because it contains a varying number of columns per row. The following pages discuss how to use Word's Draw Table feature.

BTW

Page Breaks and Tables

If you do not want a page break to occur in the middle of a table, position the insertion point in the table, click the Table Properties button on the Table Tools Layout tab, click the Row tab in the dialog box, remove the check mark from the 'Allow row to break across pages' check box, and then click the OK button.

To Draw an Empty Table

The first step is to draw an empty table in the document. To draw the boundary, rows, and columns of the table, you drag a pencil pointer on the screen. Do not try to make the rows and columns evenly spaced as you draw them. After you draw the table, you will instruct Word to space them evenly. If you make a mistake while drawing the table, you can click the Undo button on the Quick Access Toolbar to undo your most recent action(s). The following steps draw an empty table.

- Display the Insert tab.

- Click the Table button on the Insert tab to display the Table gallery (Figure 4–76).

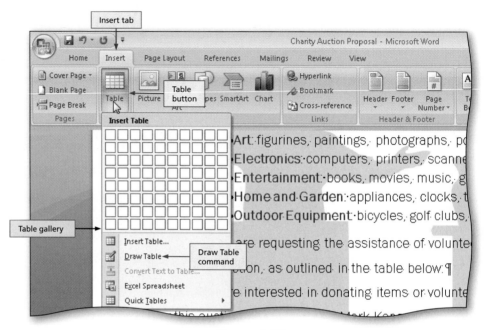

Figure 4–76

- Click Draw Table in the Table gallery.

- Position the mouse pointer, which has a pencil shape, where you want the upper-left corner of the table, as shown in Figure 4–77.

- Verify the insertion point is positioned exactly as shown in Figure 4–77.

Figure 4–77

- Drag the pencil pointer downward and to the right until the dotted rectangle, which indicates the proposed table's size, is positioned similarly to the one shown in Figure 4–78.

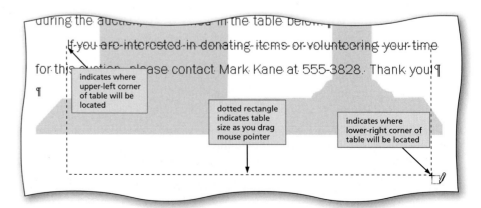

Figure 4–78

4

- Release the mouse button to draw the table border.

Q&A

What if Word wraps the text around the table?

Right-click the table, click Table Properties on the shortcut menu, click the Table tab, click None in the Text wrapping area, and then click the OK button.

Q&A

What if the table is not positioned as shown in Figure 4–79?

Click the Undo button on the Quick Access Toolbar and then repeat Steps 1 through 4.

- Position the pencil pointer in the table as shown in Figure 4–79.

Q&A

What if I do not have a pencil pointer?

Click the Draw Table button on the Design tab.

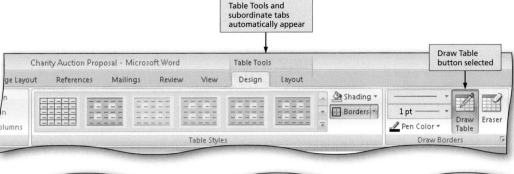

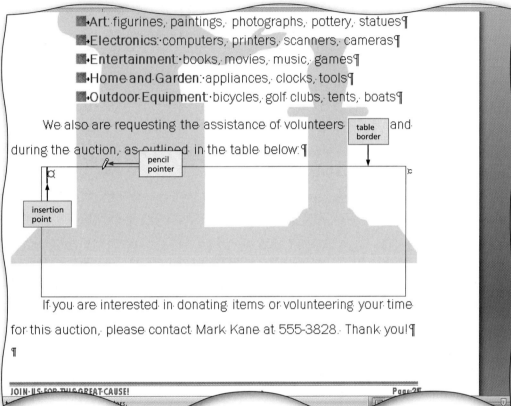

Figure 4–79

5

- Drag the pencil pointer down to the bottom of the table border to draw a vertical line.

- Drag the pencil pointer from top to bottom of the table border two more times to draw two more vertical lines, as shown in Figure 4–80.

- Position the pencil pointer in the table as shown in Figure 4–80.

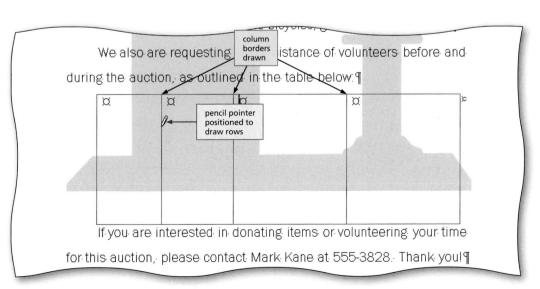

Figure 4–80

- Draw three horizontal lines to form the row borders, similarly to those shown in Figure 4–81.

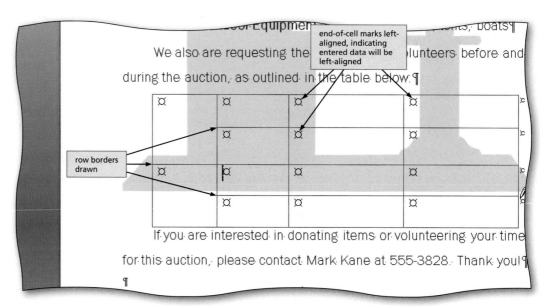

Figure 4–81

To Erase Lines in a Table

After drawing rows and columns in the table, you may want to remove a line. In this table, one line needs to be removed (shown in Figure 4–82). The following step erases a line in a table.

- Click the Eraser button on the Design tab, which causes the mouse pointer to change to an eraser shape.

- Click the line you wish to erase (Figure 4–82).

- Click the Eraser button on the Design tab to turn off the eraser.

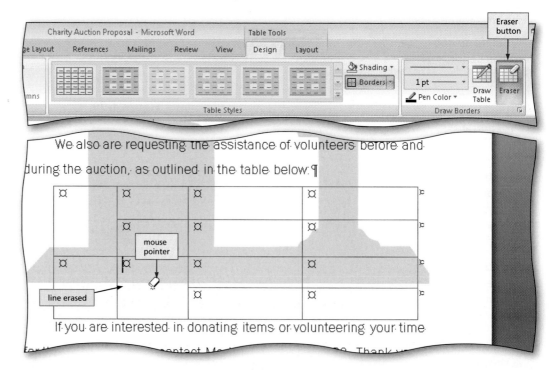

Figure 4–82

To Distribute Rows

Because you drew the table borders with the mouse, some of the rows may be varying heights. The following step spaces the row heights evenly.

1

- Display the Layout tab.

- Click the Select Table button on the Layout tab and then click Select Table on the menu to select the table.

- Click the Distribute Rows button on the Layout tab to make the height of the rows uniform (Figure 4–83).

Q&A

Can I make the columns even too?

Yes. You would click the Distribute Columns button on the Layout tab.

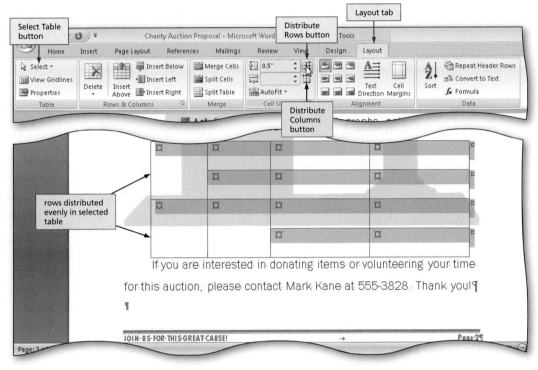

Figure 4–83

To Single-Space Table Contents

You want the data you type within the cells to be single-spaced, instead of 1.15 spacing. That is, you want any data that wraps within a cell to be single-spaced. The following steps single-space the table cells.

1 With the table still selected, press CTRL+1.

To Enter Data in a Table

The next step is to enter the data in the table. To advance from one column to the next, press the TAB key. When the insertion point is in the rightmost column, also press the TAB key to advance to the next row; do not press the ENTER key. The following steps enter the data in this table.

1 Click in the first cell of the table. Type `Before Auction` and then press the TAB key.

2 Type `May 22` and then press the TAB key. Type `Accepting Donations` and then press the TAB key. Type `9:00 a.m. to 9:00 p.m.` and then press the TAB key.

3 Press the TAB key. Type `May 23` and then press the TAB key. Type `Tagging Items` and then press the TAB key. Type `9:00 a.m. to 5:00 p.m.` and then press the TAB key.

BTW

Deleting Table Contents
If you wanted to delete the contents of a table and leave an empty table in the document, select the table contents and then press the DELETE key.

④ Type During Auction and then press the TAB key. Type May 24 and then press the TAB key. Type Helping Auctioneer and then press the TAB key. Type 10:00 a.m. to 4:00 p.m. and then press the TAB key.

⑤ Press the TAB key two times. Type Collecting Payments and then press the TAB key. Type 10:30 a.m. to 5:00 p.m. to complete the table entries (Figure 4–84).

Table Wrapping
If you wanted text to wrap around a table, instead of displaying above and below the table, do the following: right-click the table, click Table Properties on the shortcut menu, click the Table tab, click Around in the Text wrapping area, and then click the OK button.

Before Auction¤	May 22¤	Accepting Donations¤	9:00 a.m. to 9:00 p.m.¤
	May 23¤	Tagging Items¤	9:00 a.m. to 5:00 p.m.¤
During Auction¤	May 24¤	Helping Auctioneer¤	10:00 a.m. to 4:00 p.m.¤
		Collecting Payments¤	10:30 a.m. to 5:00 p.m.¤

table data entered

If you are interested in donating items or volunteering your time for this auction, please contact Mark Kane at 555-3828. Thank you!¶

Figure 4–84

To Display Text in a Cell Vertically

The data you enter in cells displays horizontally. You can rotate the text so that it displays vertically. Changing the direction of text adds variety to your tables. The following step displays text in table cells vertically.

①

• Select the cells containing the words, Before Auction and During Auction.

• Click the Text Direction button on the Layout tab twice so that the text reads from bottom to top in each cell (Figure 4-85).

Why do you click the Text Direction button twice?

The first time you click the Text Direction button, the text in the cell reads from top to bottom. The second time you click it, the text displays so it reads from bottom to top (Figure 4–85). If you would click the button a third time, the text would display horizontally again.

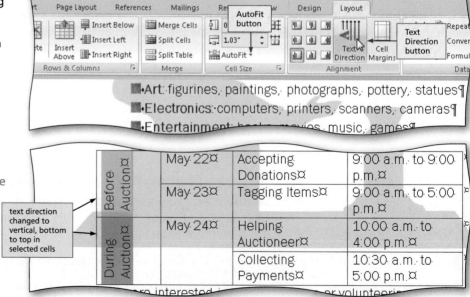

Figure 4–85

To Resize Table Columns to Fit Table Contents

Each table cell should be as wide as the longest entry in the table. The following step instructs Word to fit the width of the columns to the contents of the table.

 With the insertion point in the table, click the AutoFit button on the Layout tab and then click AutoFit Contents on the AutoFit menu, so that Word automatically adjusts columns based on the text in the table.

To Change Column Width

The AutoFit Contents command did not fit the vertical text correctly. Notice in Figure 4–86 that the column containing the Before Auction and After Auction text is not wide enough to fit the contents. Thus, you will manually make this table column wider. When the insertion point is in a table, the ruler displays column markers that indicate the beginning and ending of columns. The following steps use the ruler to change column width.

1
- Click the View Ruler button on the vertical scroll bar to display the rulers on the screen.
- Position the mouse pointer on the first Move Table Column marker on the ruler (Figure 4–86).

2
- Drag the Move Table Column marker rightward until the word, Auction, appears in the table cells (shown in Figure 4–87 on the next page).

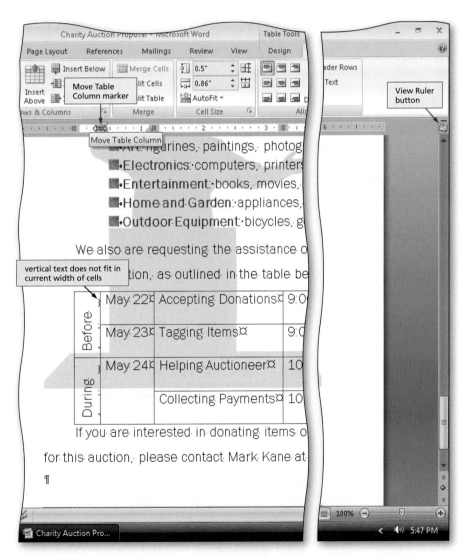

Figure 4–86

Other Ways
1. Drag column boundary (vertical gridline to right of column in table)
2. Click Properties button on Layout tab, click Column tab, enter width, click OK button

Table Columns
If you hold down the ALT key while dragging a column marker on the ruler or a column boundary in the table, the width measurements of all columns appear on the ruler as you drag the column marker or boundary.

To Align Data in Cells

The next step is to change the alignment of the data in cells. All text that displays horizontally should be centered vertically. The dates and tasks should be left-aligned, and the times should be right-aligned. The following steps align data in cells.

1 Select the cells containing the dates and the tasks.

2 Click the Align Center Left button on the Layout tab to center the selected text vertically at the left edge of the cells (Figure 4–87).

3 Select the cells containing the times (the rightmost column).

4 Click the Align Center Right button on the Layout tab to center the selected text vertically at the right edge of the cells.

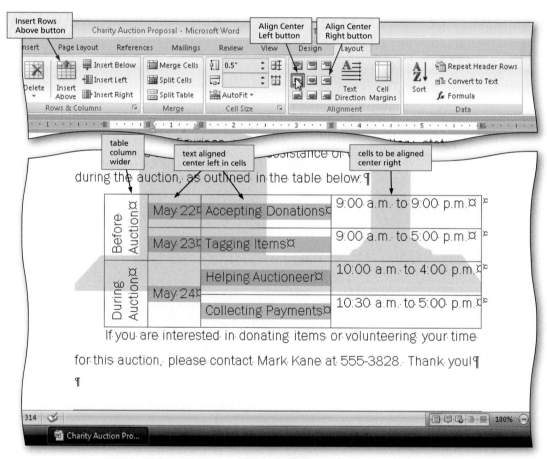

Figure 4–87

To Add a Row to a Table

The next step is to add a row to the top of the table for the table title. The following steps add a row to a table.

1 Position the insertion point somewhere in the first row of the table.

2 Click the Insert Rows Above button on the Layout tab to add a row above the current row.

To Merge Cells

The top row of the table is to contain the table title, which should be centered above the columns of the table. The row just added has one cell for each column, in this case, four cells. The title of the table, however, should be in a single cell that spans across all rows. Thus, the following steps merge the four columns into a single column.

1

- Verify the cells to merge are selected, in this case, the entire first row (Figure 4–88).

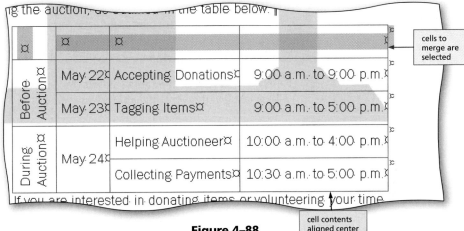

Figure 4–88

2

- Click the Merge Cells button on the Layout tab to merge the four cells into one cell (Figure 4–89).

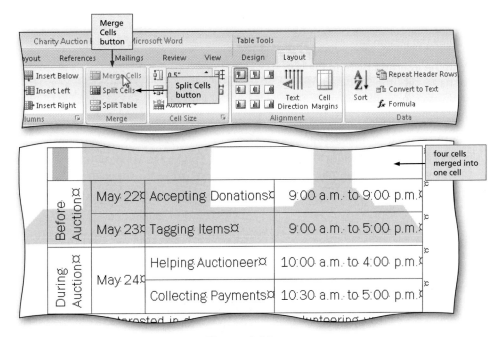

Figure 4–89

Other Ways

1. Right-click selected cells, click Merge Cells on shortcut menu

To Split Table Cells

Instead of merging multiple cells into a single cell, sometimes you want to split a single cell into multiple cells. If you wanted to split cells, you would perform the steps below and at the top of the next page.

1. Position the insertion point in the cell to split.

2. Click the Split Cells button on the Layout tab, or right-click the cell and then click Split Cells on the shortcut menu.

3. When Word displays the Split Cells dialog box, enter the number of columns and rows into which you want the cell split.

4. Click the OK button.

To Enter and Format Text in a Table Cell

The next task is to format and enter the title in the merged cell. The cell uses the formats that were in the leftmost cell, which means its contents are aligned vertically bottom to top. The following steps format and enter text in the merged cell.

1 With the first row of the table still selected, click the Text Direction button so that the text will be displayed horizontally in the merged cell.

2 Click the Align Center button so that the text will be centered in the cell.

3 Type Volunteers Needed as the table title.

To Shade a Table Cell

The next step is to shade the cell containing the title, Volunteers Needed, in gray. The following steps shade a cell.

1

• Display the Design tab.

• With the insertion point in the cell to shade, click the Shading button arrow on the Design tab to display the Shading gallery.

• Point to Gray-50%, Text 2, Lighter 60% in the Shading gallery to display a live preview of that shading color applied to the current cell in the table (Figure 4–90).

Experiment

• Point to various colors in the Shading gallery and watch the shading color of the current cell change.

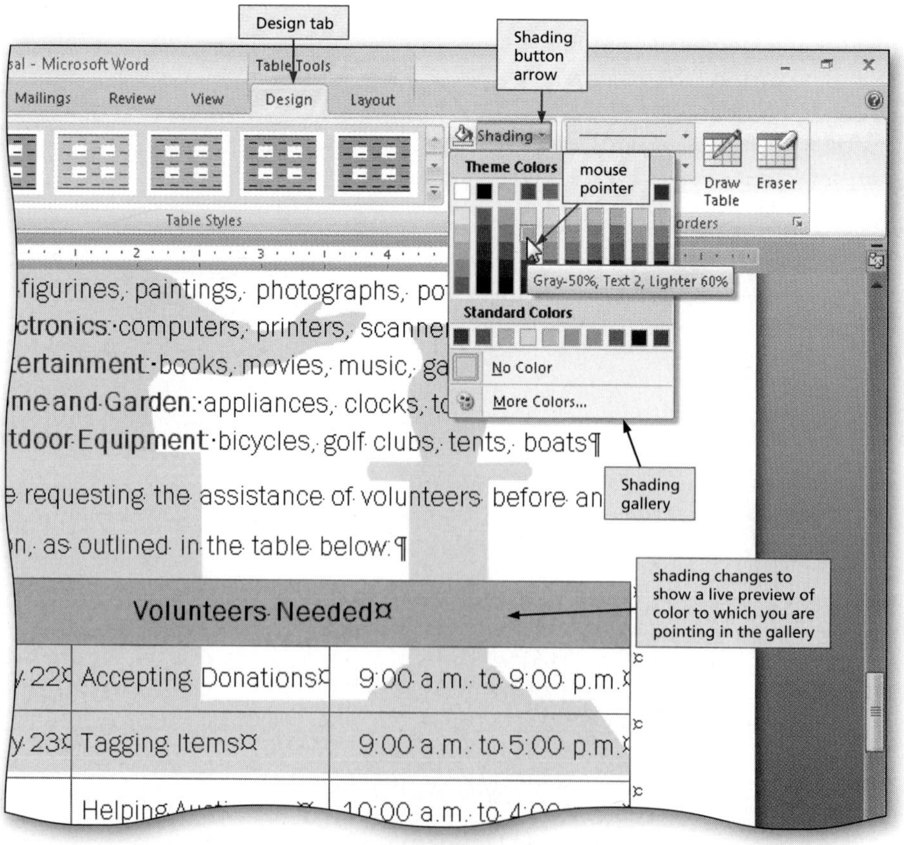

2

• Click Gray-50%, Text 2, Lighter 60% in the Shading gallery to apply the selected style to the current cell.

Q&A How would I remove shading from a cell?

Click the Shading button arrow and then click No Color in the Shading gallery.

Figure 4–90

To Format and Shade More Cells and Change Table Border Color

With the title shaded gray, the text is a little difficult to read. Thus, you will increase the font size and bold the text. Also, the date cells should be bold and shaded the same color as the title cell.

1 Select the table title, Volunteers Needed, and then bold it. Change its font size to 20 point.

2 Select the dates (May 22, May 23, May 24) and bold them.

3 Shade the date cells Gray-50%, Text 2, Lighter 60%.

4 Select the entire table. Click the Border button arrow on the Design tab and then click Borders and Shading in the Border gallery to display the Borders and Shading dialog box.

5 If necessary, click All in the Setting area so that all borders in the table are formatted.

6 Click the Color box arrow and then click Pink, Accent 2, Darker 25% in the Color gallery to change the border colors in the preview area (Figure 4–91).

7 Click the OK button to change border colors in the selected table.

8 Click outside the table to remove the selection.

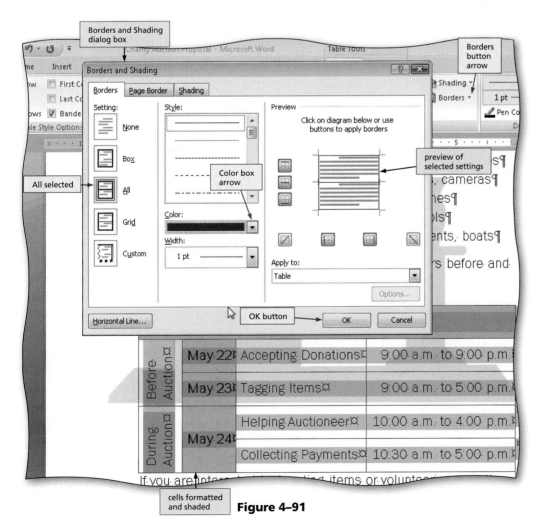

Figure 4–91

BTW

Conserving Ink and Toner
You can instruct Word to print draft quality documents to conserve ink or toner by clicking the Office Button, clicking the Word Options button, clicking Advanced in the left pane of the Word Options dialog box, scrolling to the Print area, placing a check mark in the 'Use draft quality' check box, and then clicking the OK button. Click the Office Button, point to Print, and then click Quick Print.

To Change Row Height

The next step is to narrow the height of the row containing the table title. The steps below change a row's height.

- Point to the bottom border of the first row. When the mouse pointer changes to a double-headed arrow, drag up until the proposed row border looks like Figure 4–92.

- Release the mouse button to resize the row at the location of the dotted line.

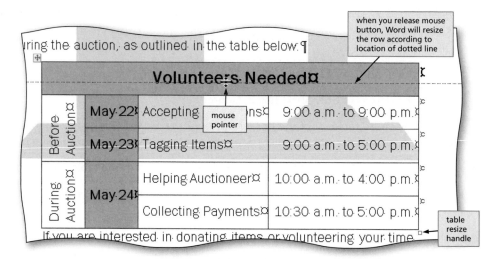

Figure 4–92

Other Ways

1. Click Table Properties button on Layout tab, click Row tab, enter row height in Specify height box, click OK button
2. Right-click row, click Table Properties on shortcut menu, click Row tab, enter row height in Specify height box, click OK button

To Add a Blank Line Above a Paragraph

The table is complete. The next step is to add a blank line above the last paragraph to put a space between the table and the paragraph.

1. Position the insertion point in the last paragraph of the proposal and then press CTRL+0 (the numeral zero) to add a blank line above the paragraph (Figure 4–93).

Q&A What if the last paragraph spills onto the next page?

You can make the table smaller so the paragraph fits at the bottom of the page. To do this, drag the table resize handle (shown in Figure 4–92) that appears in the lower-right corner of the table inward.

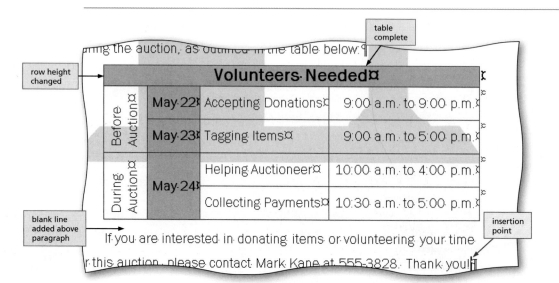

Figure 4–93

To Check Spelling, Save, Print, and Quit Word

The following steps check the spelling of the document, save the document, and then print the document.

1 Click the Spelling & Grammar button on the Review tab. Correct any misspelled words.

2 Save the sales proposal again with the same file name.

3 Print the sales proposal (shown in Figure 4–1 on page WD 227).

4 Quit Word.

BTW

Quick Reference
For a table that lists how to complete the tasks covered in this book using the mouse, Ribbon, shortcut menu, and keyboard, see the Quick Reference Summary at the back of this book, or visit the Word 2007 Quick Reference Web page (scsite.com/wd2007/qr).

Chapter Summary

In this chapter, you learned how to add a border and shading to a paragraph, insert and format a SmartArt graphic, insert a watermark, insert a Word document in an open document, insert formatted headers and footers, modify and format an existing Word table, chart a Word table using Microsoft Graph, and use the Draw Table feature. The items listed below include all the new Word skills you have learned in this chapter.

1. Border a Paragraph (WD 231)
2. Shade a Paragraph (WD 232)
3. Change Left and Right Paragraph Indent (WD 233)
4. Insert a SmartArt Graphic (WD 235)
5. Add Text to a SmartArt Graphic (WD 237)
6. Change Colors of a SmartArt Graphic (WD 238)
7. Apply a SmartArt Style (WD 239)
8. Format Characters and Modify Character Spacing Using the Font Dialog Box (WD 240)
9. Modify the Default Font Settings (WD 242)
10. Reset the Default Font Settings (WD 242)
11. Change Case of Text (WD 243)
12. Zoom One Page (WD 244)
13. Create a Watermark (WD 245)
14. Reveal Formatting (WD 248)
15. Insert a Next Page Section Break (WD 250)
16. Delete a Section Break (WD 251)
17. Insert a Word Document in an Open Document (WD 251)
18. Print Specific Pages in a Document (WD 253)
19. Customize Theme Fonts (WD 255)
20. Delete a Page Break (WD 256)
21. Cut Text (WD 257)
22. Go To a Section (WD 258)
23. Create a Header Different from the Previous Section Header (WD 259)
24. Insert a Formatted Header (WD 260)
25. Insert a Formatted Footer (WD 261)
26. Format Page Numbers to Start at a Different Number (WD 262)
27. Delete a Column (WD 263)
28. Add Columns (WD 264)
29. Sum Columns in a Table (WD 265)
30. Border a Table (WD 267)
31. Align Data in Cells (WD 268)
32. Chart a Table (WD 269)
33. Move Legend Placement in a Chart (WD 270)
34. Resize a Chart (WD 271)
35. Change the Chart Type (WD 272)
36. Exit Graph and Return to Word (WD 273)
37. Find a Format (WD 274)
38. Create a Character Style (WD 276)
39. Select Nonadjacent Text (WD 277)
40. Customize Bullets in a List (WD 278)
41. Draw an Empty Table (WD 280)
42. Erase Lines in a Table (WD 282)
43. Distribute Rows (WD 283)
44. Display Text in a Cell Vertically (WD 284)
45. Change Column Width (WD 285)
46. Merge Cells (WD 287)
47. Split Table Cells (WD 287)
48. Shade a Table Cell (WD 288)
49. Change Row Height (WD 290)

If you have a SAM user profile, you may have access to hands-on instruction, practice, and assessment. Log in to your SAM account (http://sam2007.course.com) to launch any assigned training activities or exams that relate to the skills covered in this chapter.

Learn It Online

Test your knowledge of chapter content and key terms.

Instructions: To complete the Learn It Online exercises, start your browser, click the Address bar, and then enter the Web address scsite.com/wd2007/learn. When the Word 2007 Learn It Online page is displayed, click the link for the exercise you want to complete and then read the instructions.

Chapter Reinforcement TF, MC, and SA
A series of true/false, multiple choice, and short answer questions that test your knowledge of the chapter content.

Flash Cards
An interactive learning environment where you identify chapter key terms associated with displayed definitions.

Practice Test
A series of multiple choice questions that test your knowledge of chapter content and key terms.

Who Wants To Be a Computer Genius?
An interactive game that challenges your knowledge of chapter content in the style of a television quiz show.

Wheel of Terms
An interactive game that challenges your knowledge of chapter key terms in the style of the television show *Wheel of Fortune*.

Crossword Puzzle Challenge
A crossword puzzle that challenges your knowledge of key terms presented in the chapter.

Apply Your Knowledge

Reinforce the skills and apply the concepts you learned in this chapter.

Working with a Complex Table
Instructions: Start Word. Open the document, Apply 4-1 Awesome Antiques Draft, from the Data Files for Students. See the inside back cover of this book for instructions on downloading the Data Files for Students, or contact your instructor for information about accessing the required files.

The document contains a Word table that you are to modify. The modified table is shown in Figure 4–94.

AWESOME ANTIQUES					
SECOND QUARTER SALES REPORT					
		APRIL	MAY	JUNE	TOTAL
ZONE 1	BOSTON	98,764	102,987	110,864	312,615
	CHICAGO	76,432	69,075	87,952	233,459
	DETROIT	68,064	71,536	70,443	210,043
ZONE 2	DENVER	100,987	98,221	103,416	302,624
	HOUSTON	64,842	69,844	70,009	204,695
	SEATTLE	88,513	87,990	92,752	269,255
TOTAL SALES		497,602	499,653	535,436	1,532,691

Figure 4–94

Perform the following tasks:

1. Use the Split Cells command or the Split Cells button on the Table Tools Layout tab to split the first row into two rows (one column). In the new cell below the company name, type **Second Quarter Sales Report** as the subtitle.

2. Add a row to the bottom of the table. In the newly added bottom row, use the Merge Cells command or the Merge Cells button on the Layout tab to merge the first two cells into a single cell. Type **Total Sales** in the merged cell.

3. Use the Formula button on the Layout tab to place totals in the bottom row for the April, May, and June columns.

4. Use the Formula button to place totals in the right column. Start in the bottom-right cell and work your way up the table. *Hint:* The formula should be =SUM(LEFT).

5. Select the cells containing the row headings, Zone 1 and Zone 2. Use the Text Direction button on the Layout tab to position the text vertically from bottom to top. Change the alignment of these two cells to Align Center. Click in the table to remove the selection.

6. Change the width of the column containing the Zone 1 and Zone 2 text so that it is narrower.

7. Create a customized theme font set that uses the Copperplate Gothic Bold font for both headings and body fonts. Save the theme font with the name Awesome Antiques.

8. Apply the Light List – Accent 3 table style to the table.

9. Use the Distribute Rows button to make all the rows the same size.

10. Select all the cells in the columns containing the April, May, and June sales and then use the Distribute Columns button to make these columns evenly spaced.

11. Align top center the first two rows of the table.

12. Align center the cells containing the column headings, April, May, June, and Total.

13. Align center right the cells containing numbers.

14. Align center left the cells containing these labels: Boston, Chicago, Detroit, Denver, Houston, Seattle, and Total Sales.

15. Center the entire table across the width of the page.

16. Shade the bottom row and the rightmost column Olive Green, Accent 3, Lighter 80%.

17. Shade the bottom-right cell Olive Green, Accent 3.

18. Change the font size of the first row title to 18 point.

19. Shade the first row Red, Accent 2, Darker 50%.

20. Change the document properties as specified by your instructor.

21. Save the modified file with the file name, Apply 4-1 Awesome Antiques Modified.

22. Print the revised table.

23. Position the insertion point in the first row of the table. Display the Reveal Formatting task pane. On your printout, write down all the formatting assigned to this row.

Extend Your Knowledge

Extend the skills you learned in this chapter and experiment with new skills. You may need to use Help to complete the assignment.

Embedding an Excel Chart in a Word Document

Instructions: Start Word. Open the document, Extend 4-1 Housing Table, from the Data Files for Students. See the inside back cover of this book for instructions on downloading the Data Files for Students, or contact your instructor for information about accessing the required files.

You will use Excel to create a chart of a Word table. If you do not have Excel on your computer, do not follow the steps below; instead, use Microsoft Graph to create a chart of the table and format the chart.

Perform the following tasks:

1. Use Help to learn about adding an Excel chart to a Word document. (*Hint:* Press the F1 key while pointing to the Insert Chart button on the Insert tab.)

2. Copy the first five rows of the Word table to the Clipboard (all rows except for the total row).

3. Position the insertion point below the Word table because Excel positions the chart at the location of the insertion point. Click the Insert Chart button on the Insert tab. Select the 3-D Column chart in the Insert Chart dialog box.

4. In Excel, use Help to learn about working in Excel and pasting.

5. Paste the Word table data from the Office Clipboard with cell A1 of Excel worksheet being the upper-left corner for the pasted table. Drag the lower-right corner of the range so that it does not include column D. Close the Excel window.

6. Move the legend to the bottom of the chart (Figure 4–95).

7. Right-click the chart and change the chart type to a type other than 3-D Column.

8. Use the Chart Styles gallery on the Chart Tools Design tab on the Ribbon to change the style of the chart so that it is not Style 2.

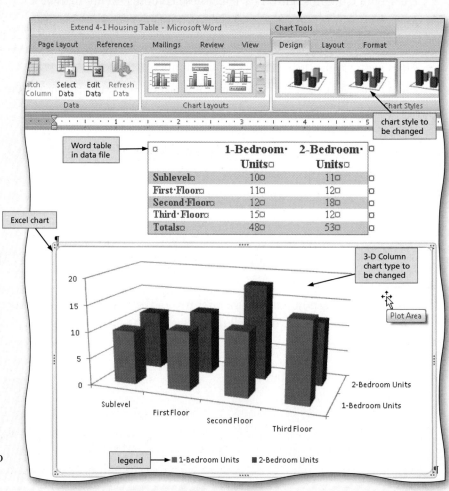

Figure 4–95

9. Use the buttons on the Chart Tools Layout tab on the Ribbon to add a title to the chart, the x-axis, and the y-axis.

10. Change the document properties, as specified by your instructor. Save the revised document using a new file name and then submit it in the format specified by your instructor.

Make It Right

Analyze a document and correct all errors and/or improve the design.

Formatting a Title Page

Instructions: Start Word. Open the document, Make It Right 4-1 Title Page Draft, from the Data Files for Students. See the inside back cover of this book for instructions on downloading the Data Files for Students, or contact your instructor for information about accessing the required files.

The document is a title page that is missing elements and that is not formatted ideally (Figure 4–96). You are to remove the header and edit the border, shading, SmartArt, watermark, and text.

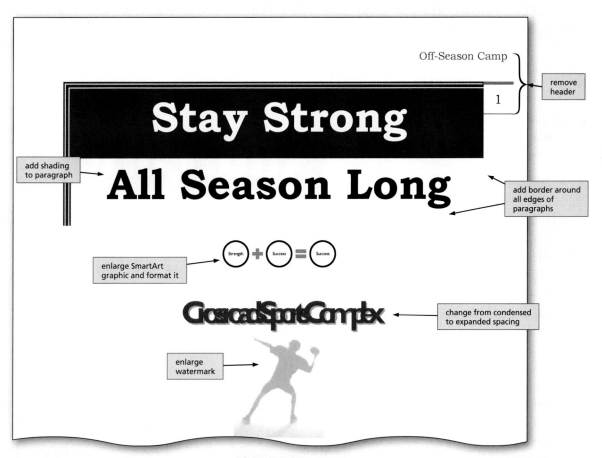

Figure 4–96

Perform the following tasks:

1. Remove the header from the title page.

2. Modify the border so that it surrounds all edges of the title.

3. Modify the paragraph shading in the title so that both lines of the title are shaded.

Continued >

Make It Right *continued*

4. Increase the size of the SmartArt graphic on the title page. The text in the middle shape in the SmartArt is not correct. Change the word, Success, to Dedication in the middle shape. Change the colors of the SmartArt graphic and then change the SmartArt style.

5. Change the zoom to one page. Increase the size of the watermark so that it fills the page.

6. Change the character spacing of the last line on the title page from condensed to expanded.

7. Add or remove space above or below paragraphs so that all contents of the title page fit on a single page. Change the zoom back to 100%.

8. Increase fonts so they are easy to read. Use the Change Font Case button to change capitalization.

9. Change the document properties, as specified by your instructor. Save the revised document with a new file name and then submit it in the format specified by your instructor.

In the Lab

Design and/or create a document using the guidelines, concepts, and skills presented in this chapter. Labs are listed in order of increasing difficulty.

Lab 1: Creating a Proposal that has a SmartArt Graphic and Uses the Draw Table Feature

Problem: The owner of the Clean Fleet Auto has hired you to prepare a sales proposal describing their services, which will be mailed to local businesses.

Perform the following tasks:

1. Change the theme colors to the Metro color scheme.

2. Create the title page as shown in Figure 4–97a. Be sure to do the following:

    (a) Insert the SmartArt graphic, add text to it, and change its colors and style as specified in the figure.

    (b) Change the fonts, font sizes, font colors, and font effects. Add the borders and paragraph shading. Indent the left and right edges of the title paragraph by 0.4 inches. Expand the characters in the text, ON-SITE CLEANING, by 5 points. In the company name at the bottom of the title page, add a shadow to the characters.

Figure 4–97 (a)

(c) Create the picture watermark. The picture is called Car Wash and is available on the Data Files for Students. See the inside back cover of this book for instructions on downloading the Data Files for Students, or contact your instructor for information about accessing the required files.

3. At the bottom of the title page, insert a next page section break. Clear formatting.

4. Create a customized theme font set that uses the Broadway font for headings and Verdana font for body text. Save the theme font with the name Clean Fleet. Increase the font size of the body text on the second page to 14 point.

5. Create the second page of the proposal as shown in Figure 4–97b.

(a) Insert the formatted header using the Pinstripes design. The header should appear only on the second page (section) of the proposal. Format the header text as shown in the figure.

(b) Change the bullets in the bulleted list to gold picture bullets.

(c) Draw the table with the Draw Table feature. The border should have a 1-point line weight with a color of Gold, Accent 3, Darker 25%. Distribute rows in the table so that they are all the same height. Center the table. Single-space the contents of the table and change spacing after paragraphs to 0 point. Change the direction of the row title, Cars; make the column width of this column narrower; and align center the text. Change the alignment of the title and column headings to align center; the second column to align center left; and the cells with numbers to align center right. Distribute the columns with numbers so that they are the same width. Shade the table cells as specified in the figure.

(d) Create a character style for the first word in the products list of bold with the color Gold, Accent 3, Darker 25%. Apply the character style to the first word in each paragraph in the bulleted list.

6. Check the spelling. Change the document properties, as specified by your instructor. Save the document with Lab 4-1 Clean Fleet Auto Proposal as the file name.

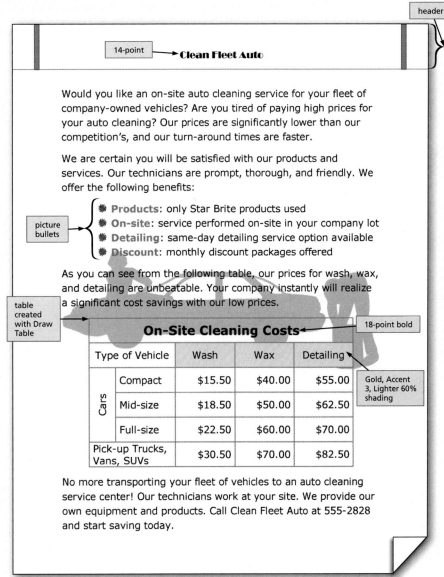

Figure 4–97 (b)

In the Lab

Lab 2: Creating a Proposal that Includes a SmartArt Graphic, a Table and a Chart

Problem: The owner of the Deli Express has hired you to prepare a sales proposal describing their foods and services, which will be mailed to all community residents.

Perform the following tasks:

1. Change the theme colors to the Opulent color scheme.

2. Create the title page as shown in Figure 4–98a. Be sure to do the following:

   (a) Insert the SmartArt graphic, add text to it, insert the pictures, and change its colors and style as specified in the figure. The three picture files are called Sub Sandwich, Salad, and Soup and are available on the Data Files for Students. See the inside back cover of this book for instructions on downloading the Data Files for Students, or contact your instructor for information about accessing the required files. (*Hint:* To insert a picture, double-click the picture placeholder to display the Insert Picture dialog box, locate the picture file, and then click the Insert button.)

   (b) Change the fonts, font sizes, font colors, and font effects. Include the border and paragraph shading around the company name. Add a shadow to and expand the characters in the text, Let us feed your crowd!, by 5 points.

   (c) Create a horizontal text watermark that says, Great Food.

3. At the bottom of the title page, insert a next page section break. Clear formatting.

4. Create a customized theme font set that uses the Cooper Black font for headings and Berlin Sans FB Demi font for body text. Save the theme font with the name Deli Express. Increase the font size of the body text on the second page to 14 point.

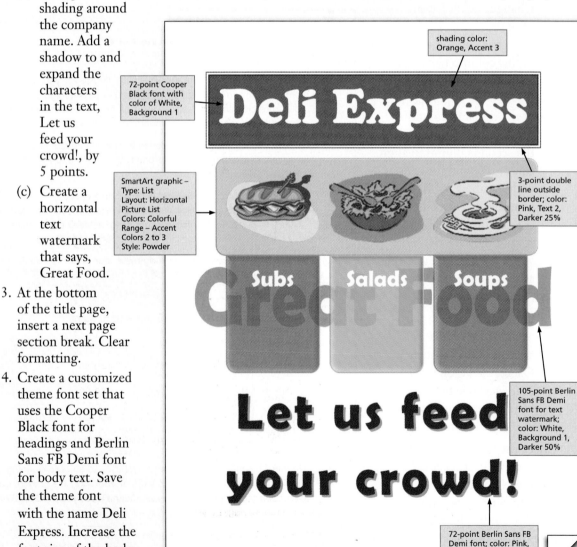

shading color: Orange, Accent 3

72-point Cooper Black font with color of White, Background 1

3-point double line outside border; color: Pink, Text 2, Darker 25%

SmartArt graphic – Type: List Layout: Horizontal Picture List Colors: Colorful Range – Accent Colors 2 to 3 Style: Powder

105-point Berlin Sans FB Demi font for text watermark; color: White, Background 1, Darker 50%

72-point Berlin Sans FB Demi font; color: Pink, Text 2, Darker 25%

Figure 4–98 (a)

5. Create the second page of the proposal as shown in Figure 4–98b.

   (a) Insert the formatted header using the Alphabet design. The header should appear only on the second page of the proposal. Format the header text as shown in the figure.

   (b) Insert the formatted footer using the Alphabet design. The footer should appear only on the second page of the proposal. Replace the page number with the telephone number.

   (c) The bulleted list has pink picture bullets.

   (d) Create a 4 × 4 table. Apply the table style indicated in the figure. Align top center the column headings and the numbers. Center the table between the page margins.

   (e) Chart the table. Resize the chart so that it is wider. Change the chart type to cylinder. Move the legend. Add a ½-point outline with a color of Black, Text 1, Lighter 50% around the chart. Insert a blank line above the chart.

   (f) Create a character style for the first word in the menu items list of underlined with the color Lavender, Background 2, Darker 50%. Apply the character style to the first word in each paragraph in the bulleted list.

6. Check the spelling. Change the document properties, as specified by your instructor. Save the document with Lab 4-2 Deli Express Proposal as the file name.

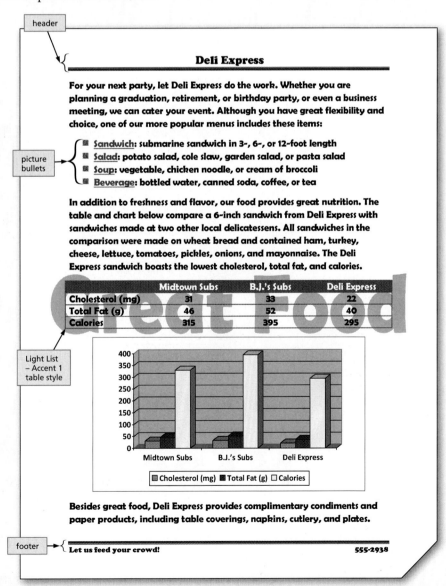

Figure 4–98 (b)

In the Lab

Lab 3: Enhancing a Draft of a Proposal

Problem: You work in the district office of Ashton Community School District. Your boss has prepared a draft of a proposal requesting voters pass the upcoming referendum. You decide to enhance the proposal by adding picture bullets, another table, and a chart. You also prepare a title page that includes a SmartArt graphic.

Perform the following tasks:

1. Change the theme colors to the Solstice color scheme.

2. Create a title page similar to the one shown in Figure 4–99a. The picture for the watermark is called School and is available on the Data Files for Students. See the inside back cover of this book for instructions on downloading the Data Files for Students, or contact your instructor for information about accessing the required files. The SmartArt graphic has been resized so that it is wider and also each individual chevron in the graphic was selected and flipped vertically. Use Help to learn how to flip a graphic.

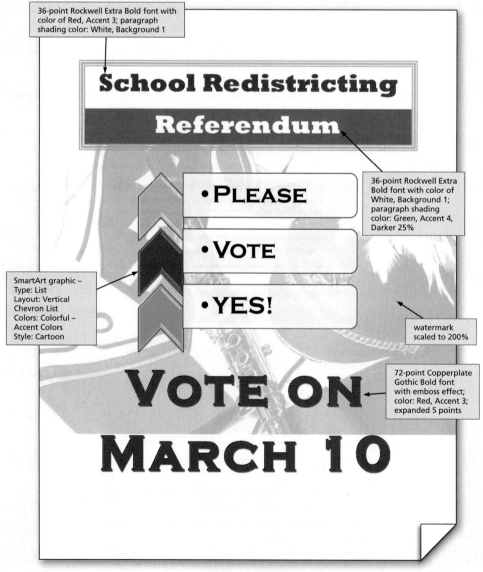

Figure 4–99 (a)

3. Insert a next page section break. Clear formatting. Insert the draft of the body of the proposal below the title page. The draft is called Lab 4-3 School Proposal Draft on the Data Files for Students (shown in Figure 4–99b).

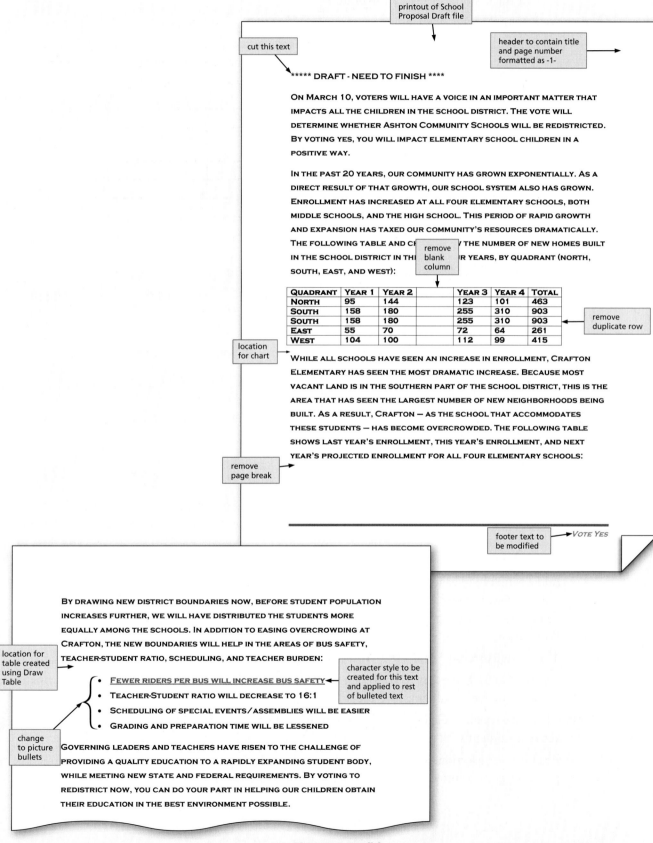

printout of School Proposal Draft file

cut this text

header to contain title and page number formatted as -1-

***** DRAFT - NEED TO FINISH ****

ON MARCH 10, VOTERS WILL HAVE A VOICE IN AN IMPORTANT MATTER THAT IMPACTS ALL THE CHILDREN IN THE SCHOOL DISTRICT. THE VOTE WILL DETERMINE WHETHER ASHTON COMMUNITY SCHOOLS WILL BE REDISTRICTED. BY VOTING YES, YOU WILL IMPACT ELEMENTARY SCHOOL CHILDREN IN A POSITIVE WAY.

IN THE PAST 20 YEARS, OUR COMMUNITY HAS GROWN EXPONENTIALLY. AS A DIRECT RESULT OF THAT GROWTH, OUR SCHOOL SYSTEM ALSO HAS GROWN. ENROLLMENT HAS INCREASED AT ALL FOUR ELEMENTARY SCHOOLS, BOTH MIDDLE SCHOOLS, AND THE HIGH SCHOOL. THIS PERIOD OF RAPID GROWTH AND EXPANSION HAS TAXED OUR COMMUNITY'S RESOURCES DRAMATICALLY. THE FOLLOWING TABLE AND CHART SHOW THE NUMBER OF NEW HOMES BUILT IN THE SCHOOL DISTRICT IN THE LAST FOUR YEARS, BY QUADRANT (NORTH, SOUTH, EAST, AND WEST):

remove blank column

QUADRANT	YEAR 1	YEAR 2		YEAR 3	YEAR 4	TOTAL
NORTH	95	144		123	101	463
SOUTH	158	180		255	310	903
SOUTH	158	180		255	310	903
EAST	55	70		72	64	261
WEST	104	100		112	99	415

remove duplicate row

location for chart

WHILE ALL SCHOOLS HAVE SEEN AN INCREASE IN ENROLLMENT, CRAFTON ELEMENTARY HAS SEEN THE MOST DRAMATIC INCREASE. BECAUSE MOST VACANT LAND IS IN THE SOUTHERN PART OF THE SCHOOL DISTRICT, THIS IS THE AREA THAT HAS SEEN THE LARGEST NUMBER OF NEW NEIGHBORHOODS BEING BUILT. AS A RESULT, CRAFTON — AS THE SCHOOL THAT ACCOMMODATES THESE STUDENTS — HAS BECOME OVERCROWDED. THE FOLLOWING TABLE SHOWS LAST YEAR'S ENROLLMENT, THIS YEAR'S ENROLLMENT, AND NEXT YEAR'S PROJECTED ENROLLMENT FOR ALL FOUR ELEMENTARY SCHOOLS:

remove page break

footer text to be modified → VOTE YES

BY DRAWING NEW DISTRICT BOUNDARIES NOW, BEFORE STUDENT POPULATION INCREASES FURTHER, WE WILL HAVE DISTRIBUTED THE STUDENTS MORE EQUALLY AMONG THE SCHOOLS. IN ADDITION TO EASING OVERCROWDING AT CRAFTON, THE NEW BOUNDARIES WILL HELP IN THE AREAS OF BUS SAFETY, TEACHER-STUDENT RATIO, SCHEDULING, AND TEACHER BURDEN:

location for table created using Draw Table

- FEWER RIDERS PER BUS WILL INCREASE BUS SAFETY
- TEACHER-STUDENT RATIO WILL DECREASE TO 16:1
- SCHEDULING OF SPECIAL EVENTS/ASSEMBLIES WILL BE EASIER
- GRADING AND PREPARATION TIME WILL BE LESSENED

character style to be created for this text and applied to rest of bulleted text

change to picture bullets

GOVERNING LEADERS AND TEACHERS HAVE RISEN TO THE CHALLENGE OF PROVIDING A QUALITY EDUCATION TO A RAPIDLY EXPANDING STUDENT BODY, WHILE MEETING NEW STATE AND FEDERAL REQUIREMENTS. BY VOTING TO REDISTRICT NOW, YOU CAN DO YOUR PART IN HELPING OUR CHILDREN OBTAIN THEIR EDUCATION IN THE BEST ENVIRONMENT POSSIBLE.

Figure 4–99 (b)

Continued >

In the Lab *continued*

4. On the first page of the body of the draft, do the following:

   (a) Cut the first line of text in the draft.

   (b) Delete the page break at the bottom of the first page.

   (c) Below the third paragraph, use the Draw Table button to create a table that is similar to the following. Select appropriate fonts and font colors, shade important cells, add a colorful border around the table, and align data in the cells as shown.

	Enrollment Figures per School		
School	Last Year	This Year	Next Year (Projected)
Crafton	342	418	475
Grover Cleveland	200	212	220
Cummings	240	252	267
Idlewild	210	233	260

(VOTE YES appears vertically at left of table)

   (d) Change the style of bullet characters in the list to picture bullets.

   (e) Use the Find and Replace dialog box to find the font format of underlined with a color of Gold, Accent 2, Darker 50%. Create a character style for this format. Apply the character style to each of the remaining bulleted paragraphs of text.

5. On the table on the second page of the body of the proposal, do the following:

   (a) Delete the duplicate row for South.

   (b) Delete the blank column.

   (c) Add a row to the top of the table for a title, merge the cells, and enter an appropriate title.

   (d) Align right all numbers.

   (e) Apply a table style to the table.

   (f) Center the table.

6. Chart the first four columns of the last five rows of the table (all but the title row and the total column). Enlarge the chart so that it is wider. Move the legend to the left of the chart. Change the chart type to cylinder bar. Add the title, Number of New Homes, to the z-axis. *Hint*: Use the Chart Options command.

7. Add a formatted header using the Stacks design. Enter an appropriate document title. Change the starting page number to 1. Format the page number so that it has dashes on each side (e.g., -1-). Select the formatted page number and change it to the Body font: 11-point Copperplate Gothic Bold font.

8. The footer currently has the text, Vote Yes. Edit the footer so that its text reads: Vote on March 10!

9. Use the Go to dialog box to go to section 1 and then to section 2. Make any additional formatting changes you feel would improve the document.

10. Check the spelling. Change the document properties, as specified by your instructor. Save the active document with the file name, Lab 4-3 School Redistricting Proposal.

11. Position the insertion point in the first line of the title page. Display the Reveal Formatting task pane. On your printout, write down all formatting assigned to this paragraph.

Cases and Places

Apply your creative thinking and problem solving skills to design and implement a solution.

• Easier   •• More Difficult

• 1: Create a Sales Proposal for a Veterinarian's Office

You are participating in an internship this summer at a local veterinarian's office. Because it is a fairly new practice, business is not as brisk as the veterinarian would like. She has asked you to design a sales proposal that will be sent to area residents; data for the table is shown below. The title page is to contain the name, PetCare Animal Hospital, formatted with a border and shading. Include an appropriate SmartArt graphic and a watermark. Include the slogan, Full-Service Care for Pets. The second page of the proposal should contain the following: first paragraph — We know you love your pets. When they need medical attention, you can be confident when you turn to us. Pet Care Animal Hospital offers full-service care, 24 hours a day, 365 days a year for the following types of animals:; list with picture bullets — Cats, Dogs, Birds, Small pocket pets; next paragraph — Accredited by the American Veterinary Group, PetCare Animal Hospital meets strict guidelines in patient care, surgery, and sanitation. Our staff is dedicated to providing your pet with the highest quality of care and state-of-the-art medical treatment. The table below lists some of our general practice services and surgeries:; paragraph below table — You are invited to tour our new facilities and to meet with our staff at any time. Stop by our office at 22 West Barrington in Stillwater anytime, or call us at 555-9092 for an appointment. We look forward to serving you and your faithful friend.

General Practice	Wellness checkups
	Immunizations
	Dental care
	Parasite control
Treatments and Surgery	Emergency surgery
	Spaying and neutering
	Oral surgery
	Chemotherapy

•• 2: Create a Planning Proposal for a Property Management Group

Your boss at Stefanson Property Management has asked you to create a planning proposal for a potential new client, Crescent Apartments. The apartment complex consists of 12 buildings, with between 20 to 30 units per building, a pool area, a clubhouse, and extensive grounds and parking. Typically, outside contractors are hired to perform maintenance duties at a cost of more than $130,000 per year. Signing a yearly contract with Stefanson Property Management can save Crescent Apartments nearly half their yearly maintenance costs. Included in Stefanson's yearly cost are groundskeeping ($23,000), snow removal ($12,300), electrical ($10,500), HVAC (heating, ventilation, and air conditioning) ($18,500), and plumbing ($8,000). General maintenance and repairs are charged at a per job basis. For additional charges, Stefanson can complete other tasks, such as painting, replacing flooring, installing cabinets, and removing wallpaper. Create a proposal for your boss to present to the owner of Crescent Apartments that outlines the services provided, the cost, and other key information. Place the company name, appropriate SmartArt graphic, and the company slogan ("Efficient property management") on the title page. Be sure the body of the proposal includes the following items: a list with picture bullets, a table, a chart, a watermark, a header, and a footer.

Continued >

Cases and Places *continued*

•• 3: Create a Proposal for an Alumni Club

To satisfy part of the community service requirements for your scholarship, you have volunteered in the Alumni Club office on your campus. Part of your new duties involves informing members of the many benefits to which they are entitled as alumni. Create a proposal that alerts alumni to the benefits of membership. Some of the benefits include staying in touch with other alumni; receiving a free monthly magazine; access to the campus Career and Opportunity Center; automobile, health, and life insurance plans; credit card with no annual fee; various discounts on airfare, car rental, and hotel rooms; club-sponsored outings; and discount event tickets. The Alumni Club has a Web site where members can look up other members, visit the campus store, register for outings, or obtain information about promotions and discounts for alumni. Several events have been scheduled, including a spring dance, a 20-year reunion dinner, a seminar about using the Web effectively in job searches, and a dinner and silent auction for charity. Use the techniques you learned in this chapter to create a sales proposal, selling the idea of membership to recent alumni. Place the club name, appropriate SmartArt graphic, and the slogan "Join the Circle!" on the title page. Be sure the proposal includes the following items: a list with picture bullets, a table with totals, a chart, a watermark, a header with a page number, and a footer.

•• 4: Create a Proposal for a Club or Event at your School

Make It Personal

As a college student, you are aware of the many clubs, activities, and events on your campus. Some students join clubs that let them interact with like-minded students; others engage in activities that will help them in their area of study. While most students like the college they attend, improvements always can be made. For example, you might be a nursing student who sees a need for a forum for other student nursing majors to get together and discuss their clinical experiences. You could be a business major who thinks a club on campus would provide a good outlet for business majors. Maybe you subscribe to a cause or idea that is not represented on your campus. If you are a music buff, you might want to organize and schedule musical gatherings. Keeping your major or area of interest in mind, create a proposal for a new club or event for your campus that solicits members or attendees. Provide information about the club or event, including its name, meeting/event location and time, and purpose. Include a title page with appropriate SmartArt graphic, the club or event name, and a suitable slogan. Be sure the proposal contains the following items: a list with picture bullets, a table, a chart, a header with a page number, a footer, and a watermark.

•• 5: Create a Research Proposal for New Computers

Working Together

Wayfield Industries is a food service provider with a main office and a staff of five salespeople. The sales staff covers a 300-mile area around River Oaks, selling primarily to restaurants, schools, and hotels. Increasingly, it has become apparent that the salespeople need constant computer access in order to service their accounts efficiently. Your boss at Wayfield Industries has asked you to create a research proposal that outlines the cost of providing each of the five salespeople with a notebook computer. He wants at least three different brands of computers to compare, and each must meet the following minimum requirements: 2 GB RAM, 17-inch display, 120 GB hard disk, and an Intel Core Duo processor. It is vital that the notebook computers have a built-in wireless connection for accessing the Internet, at least three USB 2.0 ports, and a CD/DVD drive. In addition, he has asked that you list any features the different brands might include that are desirable, such as built-in fingerprint scanners, additional USB ports, second battery, preinstalled software, or free upgrades. Assign each team member a computer brand to research. Gather information about the required features and capabilities listed above. As a team, compile the information about each type of computer researched and prepare a proposal. Create an appropriate title page that includes a formatted title and appropriate SmartArt graphic. Be sure the proposal contains a watermark, a list with picture bullets, a table, a chart, a header, a footer, and page numbers.

5 | Generating Form Letters, Mailing Labels, and Directories

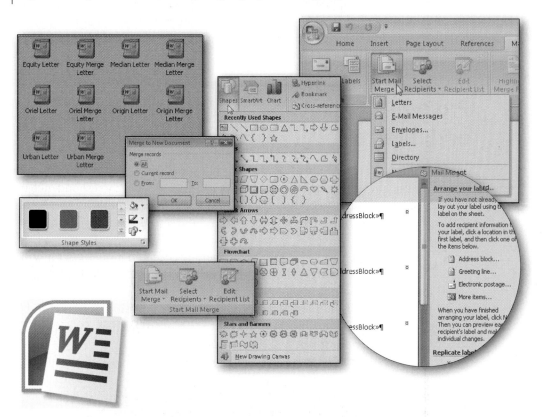

Objectives

You will have mastered the material in this chapter when you can:

- Explain the merge process
- Use the Mail Merge task pane and the Mailings tab on the Ribbon
- Use a letter template as the main document for a mail merge
- Insert and format a shape on a drawing canvas
- Create and edit a data source
- Insert merge fields in a main document
- Create a multilevel list

- Use an IF field in a main document
- Merge and print form letters
- Sort data records
- Address and print mailing labels and envelopes
- Merge all data records to a directory
- Change page orientation
- Modify table properties

5 | Generating Form Letters, Mailing Labels, and Directories

Introduction

People are more likely to open and read a personalized letter than a letter addressed as Dear Sir, Dear Madam, or To Whom It May Concern. Typing individual personalized letters, though, can be a time-consuming task. Thus, Word provides the capability of creating a form letter, which is an easy way to generate mass mailings of personalized letters. The basic content of a group of form letters is similar. Items such as name and address, however, vary from one letter to the next. With Word, you also easily can address and print mailing labels or envelopes for the form letters.

Project — Form Letters, Mailing Labels, and Directories

Both businesses and individuals regularly use form letters to communicate via the postal service or e-mail with groups of people. Types of form letter correspondence include announcements of sales to customers, notices of benefits to employees, invitations to the public to participate in a sweepstakes giveaway, and letters of job application to potential employers.

The project in this chapter follows generally accepted guidelines for writing form letters and uses Word to create the form letters shown in Figure 5–1. The form letters inform health club members of club improvements and notifies members of a monthly rate increase. Each form letter states the club member's membership type and his or her new monthly amount due. The new rate for the Standard Plan is $75 per month, and the new rate for the Premium Plan is $105 per month.

To generate form letters, such as the ones shown in Figure 5–1, you create a main document for the form letter (Figure 5–1a), create or specify a data source (Figure 5–1b), and then merge, or *blend*, the main document with the data source to generate a series of individual letters (Figure 5–1c). In Figure 5–1a, the main document represents the portion of the form letter that repeats from one merged letter to the next. In Figure 5–1b, the data source contains the name, address, and membership type for different club members. To personalize each letter, you merge the member data in the data source with the main document for the form letter, which generates or prints and an individual letter for each club member listed in the data source.

Word provides two methods of merging documents: the Mail Merge task pane and the Mailings tab on the Ribbon. The Mail Merge task pane displays a wizard, which is a step-by-step progression that guides you through the merging process. The Mailings tab provides buttons and boxes you use to merge documents. This chapter illustrates both techniques.

Picture Tools | Table Tools

ew | View | Format | Design | Layout

(a) Main Document for the Form Letter

(b) Data Source

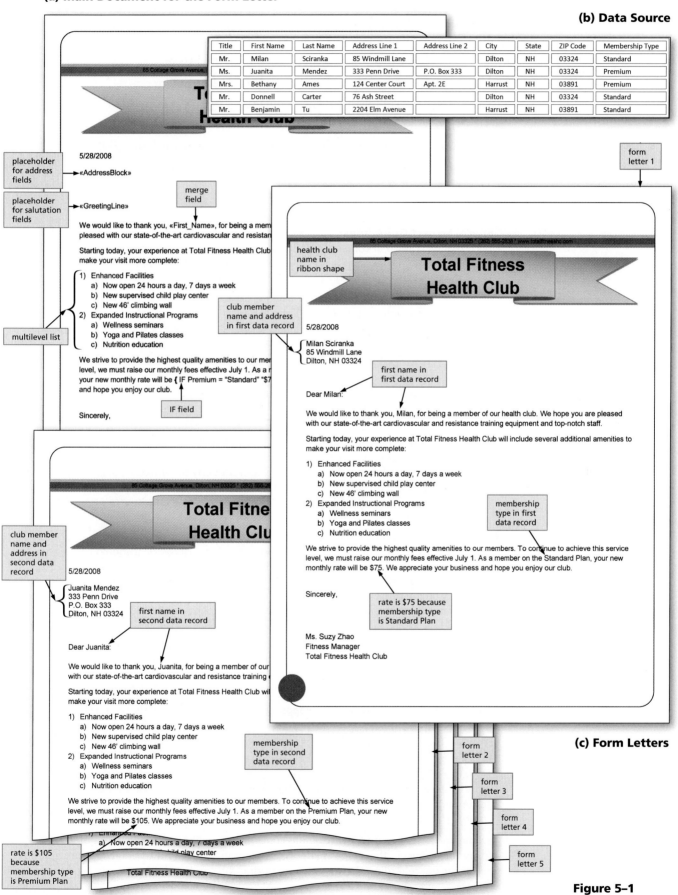

Title	First Name	Last Name	Address Line 1	Address Line 2	City	State	ZIP Code	Membership Type
Mr.	Milan	Sciranka	85 Windmill Lane		Dilton	NH	03324	Standard
Ms.	Juanita	Mendez	333 Penn Drive	P.O. Box 333	Dilton	NH	03324	Premium
Mrs.	Bethany	Ames	124 Center Court	Apt. 2E	Harrust	NH	03891	Premium
Mr.	Donnell	Carter	76 Ash Street		Dilton	NH	03324	Standard
Mr.	Benjamin	Tu	2204 Elm Avenue		Harrust	NH	03891	Standard

form letter 1

placeholder for address fields → «AddressBlock»

placeholder for salutation fields → «GreetingLine»

merge field

We would like to thank you, «First_Name», for being a memb... pleased with our state-of-the-art cardiovascular and resistan...

Starting today, your experience at Total Fitness Health Club... make your visit more complete:

1) Enhanced Facilities
   a) Now open 24 hours a day, 7 days a week
   b) New supervised child play center
   c) New 46' climbing wall
2) Expanded Instructional Programs
   a) Wellness seminars
   b) Yoga and Pilates classes
   c) Nutrition education

multilevel list

We strive to provide the highest quality amenities to our mer... level, we must raise our monthly fees effective July 1. As a r... your new monthly rate will be { IF Premium = "Standard" "$7... and hope you enjoy our club.

Sincerely,

IF field

5/28/2008

**Total Fitness
Health Club**

health club name in ribbon shape

club member name and address in first data record

5/28/2008

Milan Sciranka
85 Windmill Lane
Dilton, NH 03324

first name in first data record

Dear Milan:

We would like to thank you, Milan, for being a member of our health club. We hope you are pleased with our state-of-the-art cardiovascular and resistance training equipment and top-notch staff.

Starting today, your experience at Total Fitness Health Club will include several additional amenities to make your visit more complete:

1) Enhanced Facilities
   a) Now open 24 hours a day, 7 days a week
   b) New supervised child play center
   c) New 46' climbing wall
2) Expanded Instructional Programs
   a) Wellness seminars
   b) Yoga and Pilates classes
   c) Nutrition education

membership type in first data record

We strive to provide the highest quality amenities to our members. To continue to achieve this service level, we must raise our monthly fees effective July 1. As a member on the Standard Plan, your new monthly rate will be $75. We appreciate your business and hope you enjoy our club.

Sincerely,

rate is $75 because membership type is Standard Plan

Ms. Suzy Zhao
Fitness Manager
Total Fitness Health Club

club member name and address in second data record

**Total Fitne...
Health Clu...**

5/28/2008

Juanita Mendez
333 Penn Drive
P.O. Box 333
Dilton, NH 03324

first name in second data record

Dear Juanita:

We would like to thank you, Juanita, for being a member of our... with our state-of-the-art cardiovascular and resistance training...

Starting today, your experience at Total Fitness Health Club wi... make your visit more complete:

1) Enhanced Facilities
   a) Now open 24 hours a day, 7 days a week
   b) New supervised child play center
   c) New 46' climbing wall
2) Expanded Instructional Programs
   a) Wellness seminars
   b) Yoga and Pilates classes
   c) Nutrition education

We strive to provide the highest quality amenities to our members. To continue to achieve this service level, we must raise our monthly fees effective July 1. As a member on the Premium Plan, your new monthly rate will be $105. We appreciate your business and hope you enjoy our club.

membership type in second data record

rate is $105 because membership type is Premium Plan

1) Enhanced Fac...
   a) Now open 24 hours a day, 7 days a week
   ...hild play center

Total Fitness Health Club

form letter 2

form letter 3

form letter 4

form letter 5

(c) Form Letters

Figure 5–1

Overview

As you read through this chapter, you will learn how to create and generate the form letters shown in Figure 5–1 on the previous page, along with mailing labels, envelopes, and a directory, by performing these general tasks:

- Identify a template as the main document for the form letter.
- Create a letterhead for the main document.
- Type the contents of the data source.
- Compose the remainder of the main document, below the letterhead.
- Address and print mailing labels and envelopes using the data source.
- Create a directory, which displays the contents of the data source.

Plan Ahead

General Project Guidelines

When creating a Word document, the actions you perform and decisions you make will affect the appearance and characteristics of the finished document. As you create form letters, such as the project shown in Figure 5–1, and related documents, you should follow these general guidelines:

1. **Identify the main document for the form letter.** When creating form letters, you either can type the letter from scratch in a blank document window or use a letter template. A letter template saves time because the word processing program prepares a letter with text and/or formatting common to all letters. Then, you customize the resulting letter by selecting and replacing prewritten text.

2. **Design a creative letterhead.** Use text, graphics, formats, and colors that reflect you or your business. Include a name, postal mailing address, and telephone number. If you have an e-mail address and Web address, include those as well.

3. **Create or specify the data source.** The **data source** contains the variable, or changing, values for each letter. A data source can be an Access database table, an Outlook contacts list, or an Excel worksheet. If the necessary and properly organized data already exists in one of these Office programs, you can instruct Word to use the existing file as the data source for the mail merge. Otherwise, you can create a new data source using one of these programs.

4. **Compose the main document for the form letter.** A **main document** contains the constant, or unchanging, text, punctuation, spaces, and graphics. It should reference the data in the data source properly. The finished main document letter should look like a symmetrically framed picture with evenly spaced margins, all balanced below an attractive letterhead. The content of the main document for the form letter should contain proper grammar, correct spelling, logically constructed sentences, flowing paragraphs, and sound ideas. Be sure to proofread it carefully.

5. **Merge the main document with the data source to create the form letters.** **Merging** is the process of combining the contents of a data source with a main document. You can print the merged letters on the printer or place them in a new document, which you later can edit. You also have the option of merging all data in a data source, or just merging a portion of it.

6. **Generate mailing labels and envelopes.** To generate mailing labels and envelopes for the form letters, follow the same process as for the form letters. That is, determine the appropriate data source, create the label or envelope main document, and then merge the main document with the data source to generate the mailing labels and envelopes.

7. **Create a directory of the data source.** A **directory** is a listing of the contents of the data source. To create a directory, follow the same process as for the form letters. That is, determine the appropriate data source, create the directory main document, and then merge the main document with the data source to create the directory.

When necessary, more specific details concerning the above guidelines are presented at appropriate points in the chapter. The chapter also will identify the actions performed and decisions made regarding these guidelines during the creation of the form letters shown in Figure 5–1, and related documents.

To Start Word

If you are using a computer to step through the project in this chapter and you want your screens to match the figures in this book, you should change your computer's resolution to 1024 × 768. For information about how to change a computer's resolution, read Appendix D.

The following steps start Word and verify Word settings.

1 Start Word.

2 If the Word window is not maximized, click its Maximize button.

3 If the Print Layout button is not selected, click it so that Word is in Print Layout view.

4 If your zoom level is not 100%, click the Zoom Out or Zoom In button as many times as necessary until the Zoom level button displays 100% on its face.

5 If the Show/Hide ¶ button on the Home tab is not selected already, click it to display formatting marks on the screen.

Identifying the Main Document for Form Letters

The first step in the mail merge process is to identify the type of document you are creating for the main document. Typical installations of Word support five types of main documents: letters, e-mail messages, envelopes, labels, and a directory. In this section of the chapter, you create letters as the main document. Later in this chapter, you will specify labels, envelopes, and a directory as the main document.

Identify the main document for the form letter. Be sure the main document for the form letter includes all essential business letter elements. All business letters should contain a date line, inside address, message, and signature block. Many business letters contain additional items such as a special mailing notation(s), an attention line, a salutation, a subject line, a complimentary close, reference initials, and an enclosure notation.	**Plan Ahead**

To Identify the Main Document for the Form Letter Using the Task Pane

This project uses a letter template as the main document for the form letter. Word provides five styles of merge letter templates: Equity, Median, Oriel, Origin, and Urban. The following steps use the Mail Merge task pane to identify the Equity Merge Letter template as the main document for a form letter.

1

• Click Mailings on the Ribbon to display the Mailings tab.

• Click the Start Mail Merge button on the Mailings tab to display the Start Mail Merge menu (Figure 5–2).

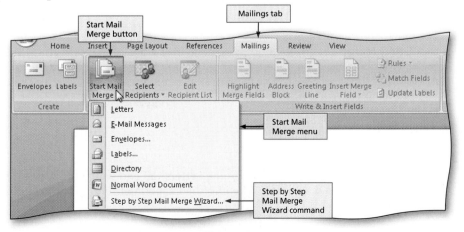

Figure 5–2

- Click Step by Step Mail Merge Wizard on the Start Mail Merge menu to display the Mail Merge wizard in the Mail Merge task pane (Figure 5–3).

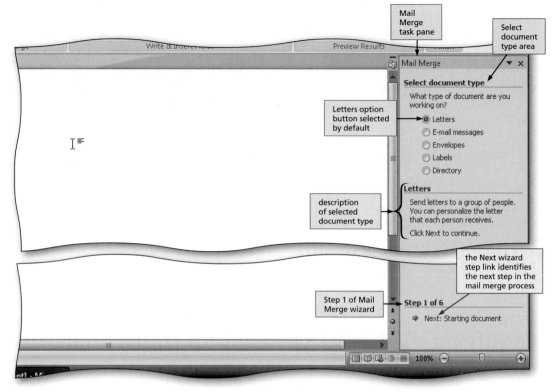

Figure 5–3

- Click the 'Next wizard step' link at the bottom of the Mail Merge task pane to display Step 2 of the Mail Merge wizard.

- Click 'Start from a template' in the 'Select starting document' area and then click the 'Select mail merge template' link to display the Select Template dialog box.

- Click the Letters tab in the dialog box and then click Equity Merge Letter, which shows a preview of the selected template in the Preview area (Figure 5–4).

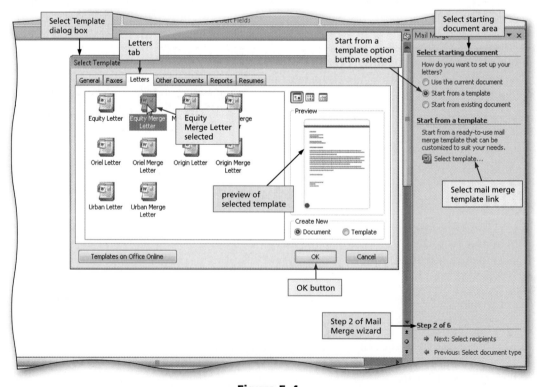

Figure 5–4

🔍 **Experiment**

- Click various Merge Letter templates in the Letters tab and watch the preview display at the right edge of the dialog box. When finished experimenting, click the Equity Merge Letter template.

4

- Click the OK button to display a letter in the document window that is based on the Equity Merge Letter template (Figure 5–5).

5

- Click the Close button in the upper-right corner of the Mail Merge task pane title bar to close the Mail Merge wizard.

Q&A

Why am I closing the Mail Merge task pane?

You temporarily are stopping the merge process while you create the letterhead for the form letter. When you are ready to continue with the merge process, you will redisplay the Mail Merge task pane.

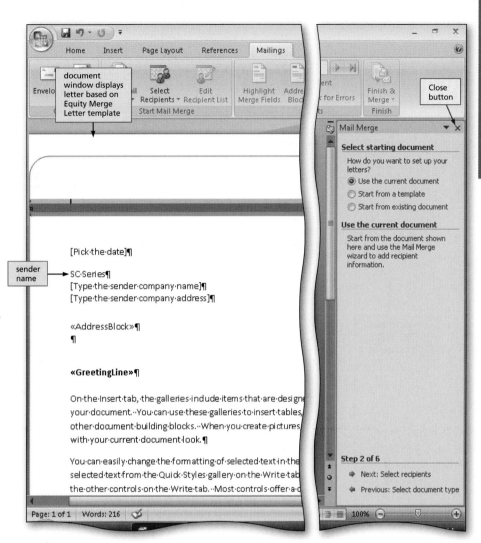

Figure 5–5

Other Ways

1. Click Office Button, click New, click Installed Templates, click Equity Merge Letter, click Create button. Click Start Mail Merge button on Mailings tab, click Letters

To Print the Document

The next step is to print the letter that Word generated, which is based on the Equity Merge Letter template.

1 Ready the printer. Display the Office Button menu, point to Print, and then click Quick Print to print the document that is based on the Equity Merge Letter template (Figure 5–6 on the next page).

What are the content controls in the document?

A content control contains instructions for filling in areas of the document. To select a content control, click it. Later in this chapter, you will personalize the content controls.

Why does SC Series display as the sender name?

Word places the user name associated with your copy of Microsoft Word as the sender name. SC Series, which stands for Shelly Cashman Series, is the user name associated with this copy of Word.

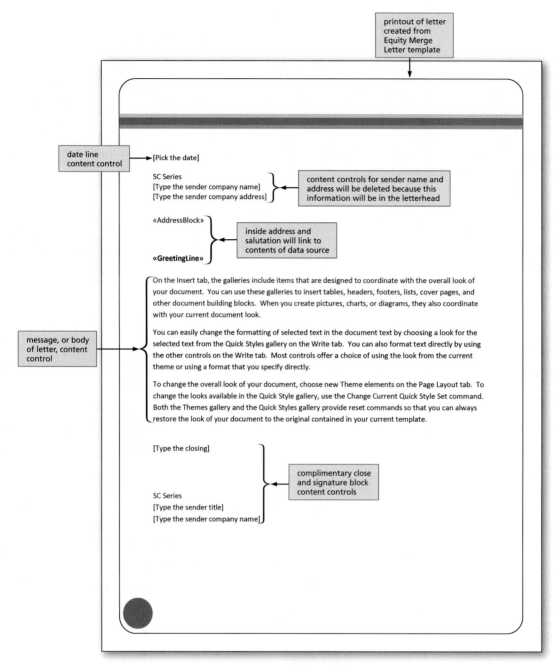

Figure 5–6

To Change the User Name and Initials

If you wanted to change the user name and initials associated with your copy of Microsoft Word, you would perform the following steps.

1. Display the Office Button menu and then click the Word Options button to display the Word Options dialog box.

2. Click Popular in the left pane.

3. Enter your name in the User name text box.

4. Enter your initials in the Initials text box.

5. Click the OK button.

To Change Theme Colors and Fonts

The form letter in this project uses the Equity color scheme and Office Classic 2 font set. The following steps change theme colors and the font set.

1 Display the Home tab. Click the Change Styles button on the Home tab, point to Colors on the Change Styles menu, and then click Equity in the Colors gallery to change the document theme colors to Equity.

2 Click the Change Styles button on the Home tab; point to Fonts on the Change Styles menu; if necessary, scroll to Office Classic 2 in the Fonts gallery; and then click Office Classic 2 to change the document theme fonts to Office Classic 2.

BTW

Changing Margins
If you want to see the current margin settings, display the ruler and then hold down the ALT key while pointing to the margin boundary (where the blue meets the white on the ruler). To see the numeric margin settings while changing the margins, hold down the ALT key while dragging the margin boundary on the ruler.

To Change the Margin Settings

Word is preset to use standard 8.5-by-11-inch paper, with 1-inch top, bottom, left, and right margins. If you change the default margin settings, the new margin settings affect every page in the document. If you wanted the margins to affect just a portion of the document, you would divide the document into sections as discussed in Chapter 4, which would enable you to specify different margin settings for each section.

The form letter in this chapter has .75-inch left and right margins and 1-inch top and bottom margins, so that more text can fit from left to right on the page. The following steps change margin settings.

1

- Display the Page Layout tab.

- Click Margins button on the Page Layout tab to display the Margins gallery (Figure 5–7).

2

- Click Moderate in the Margins gallery to change the left and right margins to .75-inches.

Q&A What if the margin settings I want are not in the Margins gallery?

You can click the Custom Margins command in the Margins gallery and then enter your desired margin values in the top, bottom, left, and right text boxes in the dialog box.

Q&A Why does my document wrap on different words?

Differences in wordwrap relate to the printer used by your computer. Thus, it is possible that the same document could wordwrap differently if associated with a different printer.

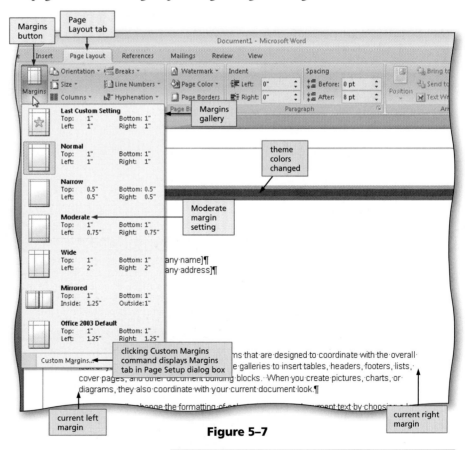

Figure 5–7

Other Ways	
1. Position mouse pointer on margin boundary on ruler; when mouse pointer	changes to two-headed arrow, drag margin boundary on ruler

Working with Shapes and the Drawing Canvas

The letterhead for the form letter consists of the company address, telephone number, and Web site information in a line above the company name, which is surrounded by a ribbon-like shape (Figure 5–1 on page WD 307). Word has a variety of predefined shapes, which are a type of drawing object, that you can insert in documents. A **drawing object** is a graphic that you create using Word. The following pages create the letterhead for the form letter.

To Enter Text in a Table Row

The orange bar at the top of the form letter is actually a three-row table, with each row containing a different shading color. The following steps enter the company address, telephone number, and Web site information in the second row of the table.

1 Click the dark orange bar to position the insertion point in the second row of the table.

2 Center the insertion point in the cell.

3 Type 85 Cottage Grove Avenue, Dilton, NH 03324 * (282) 555-2838 * www.totalfitnesshc.com in the table cell (Figure 5–8).

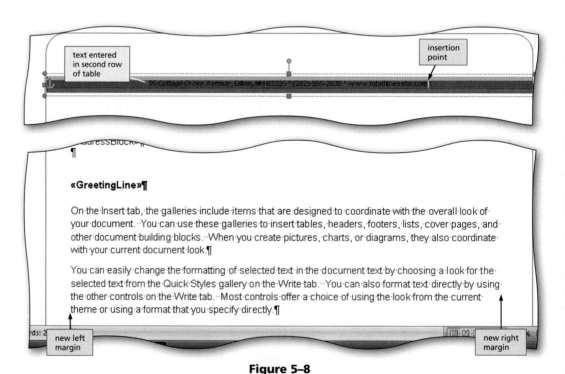

Drawing Canvas
If you want the drawing canvas to be displayed automatically when you insert a shape, click the Office Button; click the Word Options button on the Office Button menu; click Advanced in the left pane; if necessary, scroll to the Editing options area; place a check mark in the Automatically create drawing canvas when inserting AutoShapes check box; and then click the OK button. With this check box selected, you would skip the steps on page WD 315.

Figure 5–8

To Insert a Drawing Canvas

The next step is to insert the ribbon-like shape that will contain the company name. When you insert shapes, it is recommended you insert them in a drawing canvas. A **drawing canvas** is a rectangular boundary between your shape and the rest of the document; it also is a container that helps you to resize and arrange shapes on the page. The next steps insert a drawing canvas in a document.

1

- With the insertion point in the second row of the table, display the Insert tab.

- Click the Shapes button on the Insert tab to display the Shapes gallery (Figure 5–9).

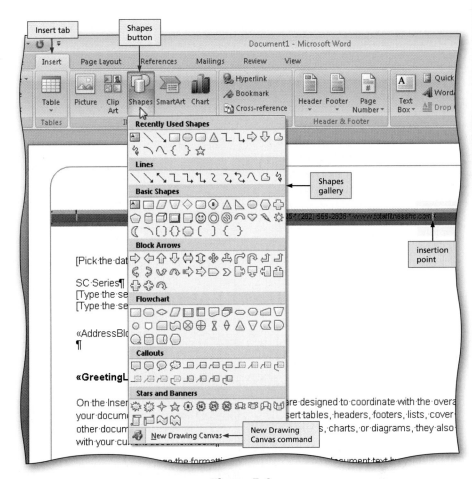

Figure 5–9

2

- Click New Drawing Canvas in the Shapes gallery to insert a drawing canvas at the location of the insertion point (Figure 5–10).

Q&A What is the patterned rectangle around the drawing canvas?

It indicates the drawing canvas is selected. You also can use it to resize or move the drawing canvas and its contents.

Q&A Can I change the colors of the drawing canvas?

Yes. You can use the Drawing Tools Format tab to change colors and other formats of the drawing canvas.

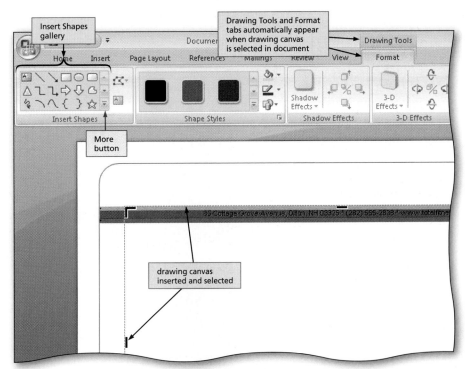

Figure 5–10

To Insert a Shape

The next step is to draw a ribbon shape in the drawing canvas. Examples of predefined shapes in Word include rectangles, circles, triangles, arrows, flowcharting symbols, stars, banners, and callouts. The following steps insert a ribbon shape in the drawing canvas.

- Click the More button in the Insert Shapes gallery on the Format tab (shown in Figure 5–10 on the previous page), which shows more gallery options (Figure 5–11).

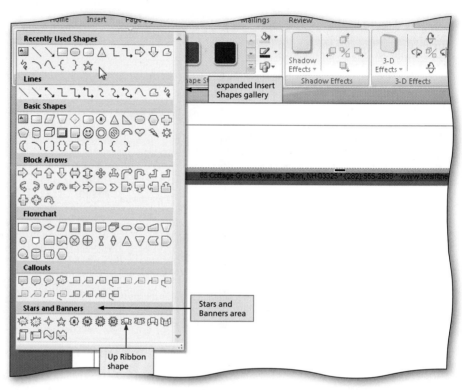

Figure 5–11

- Click the Up Ribbon shape in the Stars and Banners area of the Insert Shapes gallery, which removes the gallery and changes the mouse pointer to the shape of a crosshair.

- Position the mouse pointer (a crosshair) on the left of the drawing canvas below the shaded table, as shown in Figure 5–12.

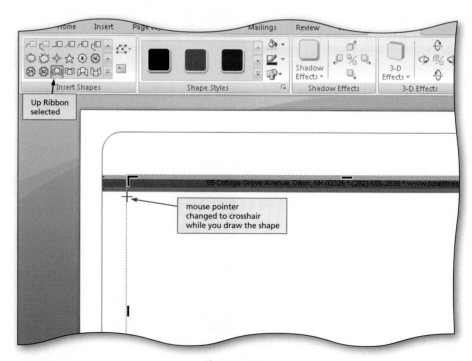

Figure 5–12

3

- Drag the mouse, as shown in Figure 5–13, to the right and downward to form the ribbon shape.

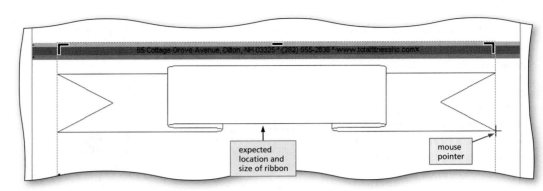

Figure 5–13

4

- Release the mouse button so that Word draws the shape in the drawing canvas. If your shape is not the same approximate height and width as shown in Figure 5–14, drag the shape's sizing handles to resize it, or enter the appropriate values in the Shape Height and Shape Width text boxes on the Format tab.

What is the purpose of the rotate and adjustment handles?

When you drag an object's **rotate handle**, which is the green circle, Word rotates the object in the direction you drag the mouse. When you drag an object's **adjustment handle**, which is the yellow diamond, Word changes the object's shape.

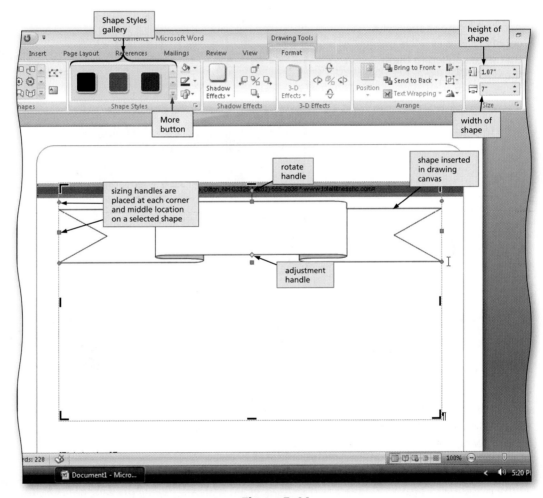

Figure 5–14

What if I wanted to delete a shape and start over?

With the shape selected, press the DELETE key.

Other Ways

1. Click Shapes button on Insert tab, select desired shape

To Apply a Shape Style

The next step is to apply a style to the shape, so that it is more colorful. Word provides a Shape Styles gallery, allowing you to change the look of the shape to a more visually appealing style. The following steps apply a style to the shape.

- With the shape still selected, click the More button in the Shape Styles gallery (shown in Figure 5–14 on the previous page) to expand the Shape Styles gallery.

- Point to Diagonal Gradient - Accent 2 in the Shape Styles gallery to display a live preview of that style applied to the shape in the document (Figure 5–15).

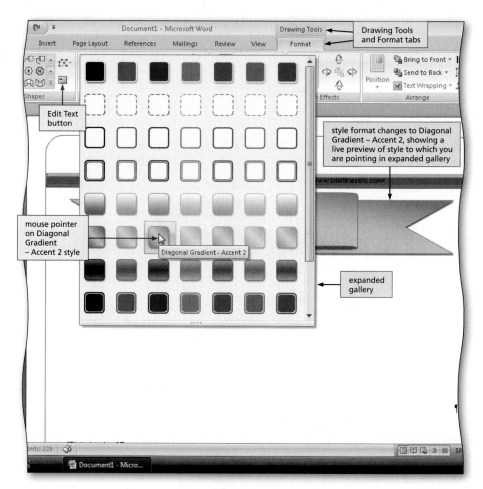

Figure 5–15

Experiment

- Point to various styles in the Shape Styles gallery and watch the style of the shape change in the drawing canvas.

- Click Diagonal Gradient - Accent 2 in the Shape Styles gallery to apply the selected style to the shape.

Other Ways

1. Click Advanced Tools Dialog Box Launcher in Shape Styles group, select desired colors, click OK button
2. Right-click shape, click Format AutoShape on shortcut menu, select desired colors, click OK button

To Add Formatted Text to a Shape

The next step is to add the company name to the shape, centered with a 26-point bold font. The following steps add text to a shape.

1

- Click the Edit Text button on the Drawing Tools Format tab (shown in Figure 5–15) to place an insertion point in the shape and display the Text Box Tools and its subordinate Format tab on the Ribbon (Figure 5–16).

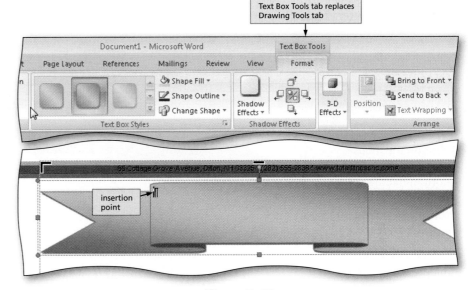

Figure 5–16

2

- Display the Home tab.

- Click the Center button on the Home tab.

- Click the Bold button on the Home tab.

- Change the font size to 26 point.

- Type Total Fitness and then press SHIFT+ENTER to insert a line break character.

- Type Health Club on the second line of the shape (Figure 5–17). (If all the letters in the company name do not fit in the shape, drag the sizing handles on the shape until all text is displayed in the shape.)

 Why insert a line break instead of pressing the ENTER key?

The default space after a paragraph is 8 points. To suppress paragraph spacing between lines, insert a line break.

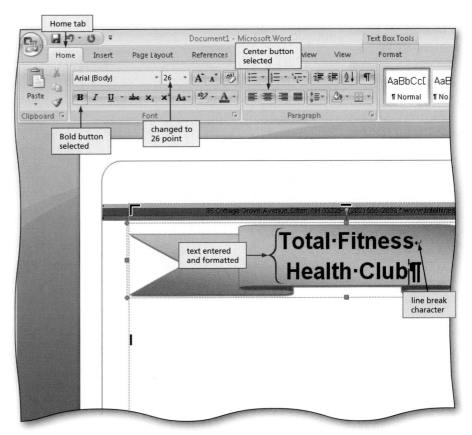

Figure 5–17

Other Ways
1. Right-click shape, click Add Text on shortcut menu

To Resize a Drawing Canvas

Recall that you drew the ribbon shape in a drawing canvas. The height of the drawing canvas is almost four inches, which is too tall for this letter. You want the drawing canvas to touch the bottom of the shape, to leave plenty of room for the letter. The following steps resize a drawing canvas.

- Click in the drawing canvas in an area outside the shape to select the drawing canvas.

- Position the mouse pointer on the bottom-middle sizing handle until the mouse pointer shape changes to a T.

- Drag the bottom-middle sizing handle upward, as shown in Figure 5–18, until the dotted line touches the bottom of the shape.

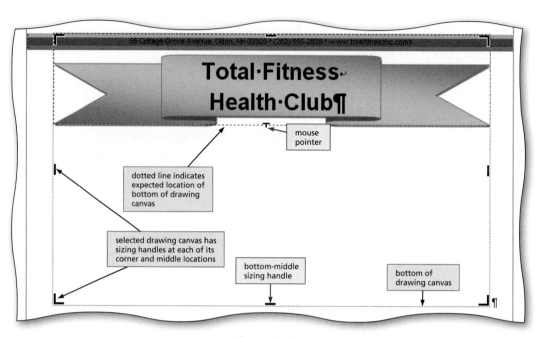

Figure 5–18

- Release the mouse button to resize the drawing canvas (Figure 5–19).

Can I move the shape around in the drawing canvas?

Yes. You can drag the shape to any location in the drawing canvas.

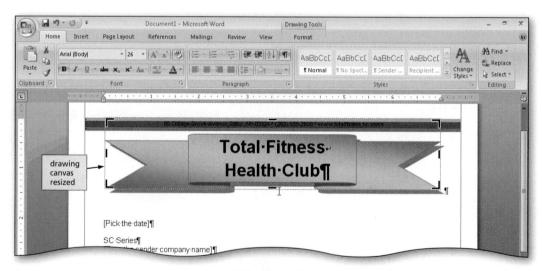

Figure 5–19

Other Ways

1. Enter new values in Shape Width and Shape Height text boxes on Format tab

2. Right-click drawing canvas, click Format Drawing Canvas on shortcut menu, click Size tab, enter height and width values in text boxes, click OK button

To Create a Folder while Saving

You have performed several tasks while creating this project and should save it. You want to save this and all other documents created in this chapter in a folder called Total Fitness. This folder does not exist, so you must create it. Rather than creating the folder in Windows, you can create folders in Word, which saves time. The following steps create a folder during the process of saving a document.

- With a USB flash drive connected to one of the computer's USB ports, click the Save button on the Quick Access Toolbar to display the Save As dialog box.

- Type `Health Club Form Letter` in the File name text box to change the file name.

- If Computer is not displayed in the Favorite Links section, drag the top or bottom edge of the Save As dialog box until Computer is displayed.

- Click Computer in the Favorite Links section, and then double-click your USB flash drive in the list of available drives.

- Click the 'Create a new, empty folder' button in the Save As dialog box to display a folder with the name New Folder selected in the dialog box (Figure 5–20).

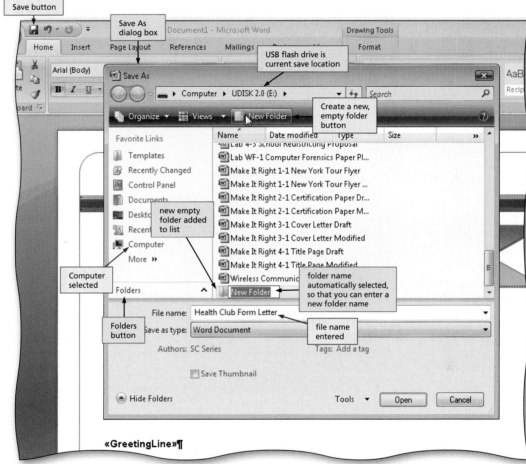

Figure 5–20

- Type `Total Fitness` as the new folder name and then press the ENTER key to create the new folder on the USB flash drive.

- Click the Save button in the Save As dialog box to save the Health Club Form Letter in the Total Fitness folder on the USB flash drive.

Q&A

Can I create a folder in any other dialog box?

Yes. Any dialog box that displays a File list, such as the Open and Insert File dialog boxes, also has the 'Create a new, empty folder' button, allowing you to create a new folder in Word instead of using Windows Vista for this task.

Other Ways

1. Press F12

Creating a Data Source

A data source is a file that contains the data that changes from one merged document to the next. As shown in Figure 5–21, a data source often is shown as a table that consists of a series of rows and columns. Each row is called a **record**. The first row of a data source is called the **header record** because it identifies the name of each column. Each row below the header row is called a **data record**. Data records contain the text that varies in each copy of the merged document. The data source for this project contains five data records. In this project, each data record identifies a different club member. Thus, five form letters will be generated from this data source.

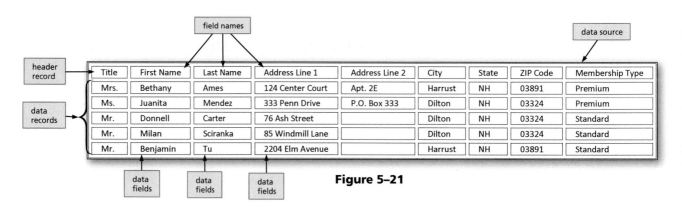

Figure 5–21

Each column in the data source is called a **data field**. A data field represents a group of similar data. Each data field must be identified uniquely with a name, called a **field name**. For example, First Name is the name of the data field (column) that contains the first names of club members. In this project, the data source contains nine data fields with the following field names: Title, First Name, Last Name, Address Line 1, Address Line 2, City, State, ZIP Code, and Membership Type.

Plan Ahead

Create the data source.
When you create a data source, you will need to determine the fields it should contain. That is, you will need to identify the data that will vary from one merged document to the next. Following are a few important points about fields:

- For each field, you may be required to create a field name. Because data sources often contain the same fields, some programs create a list of commonly used field names that you may use.

- Field names must be unique; that is, no two field names may be the same.

- Fields may be listed in any order in the data source. That is, the order of fields has no effect on the order in which they will print in the main document.

- Organize fields so that they are flexible. For example, break the name into separate fields: title, first name, and last name. This arrangement allows you to print a person's title, first name, and last name (e.g., Mr. Roger Bannerman) in the inside address but only the title and last name in the salutation (Dear Mr. Bannerman).

To Create a New Data Source

Word provides a list of 13 commonly used field names. This project uses 8 of the 13 field names supplied by Word: Title, First Name, Last Name, Address Line 1, Address Line 2, City, State, and ZIP Code. This project does not use the other five field names supplied by Word: Company Name, Country or Region, Home Phone, Work Phone, and E-mail Address. Thus, you will delete these five field names. Then, you will add one new field name (Membership Type) to the data source. The following steps create a new data source for a mail merge.

- Display the Mailings tab.

- Click the Start Mail Merge button on the Mailings tab and then click Step by Step Mail Merge Wizard to redisplay the Mail Merge task pane.

- Click 'Type a new list' in the Select recipients area, which displays the 'Type a new list' area.

- Click the 'Create new recipient list' link to display the New Address List dialog box (Figure 5–22).

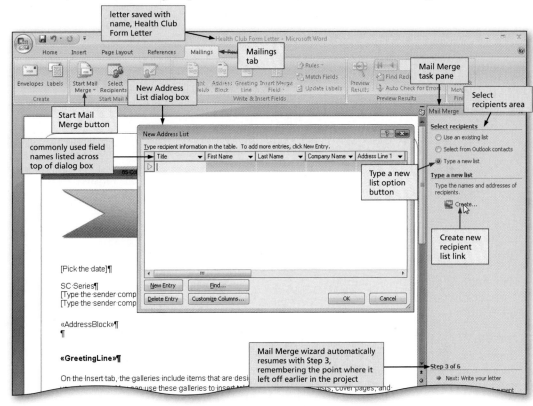

Figure 5–22

Q&A

When would I use the other two option buttons in the Select recipients area?

If you had a data source already created, you would use the first option: Use an existing list. If you wanted to use your Outlooks contacts list as the data source, you would choose the second option.

- Click the Customize Columns button to display the Customize Address List dialog box (Figure 5–23).

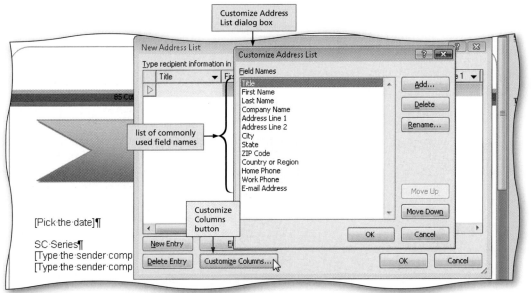

Figure 5–23

- Click Company Name in the Field Names list and then click the Delete button to display a dialog box asking if you are sure you want to delete the selected field (Figure 5–24).

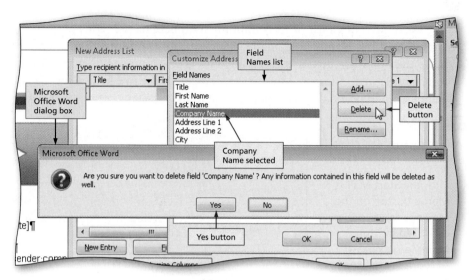

Figure 5–24

- Click the Yes button in the Microsoft Office Word dialog box.

- Click Country or Region in the Field Names list. Click the Delete button. Click the Yes button to remove the field.

- Click Home Phone in the Field Names list. Click the Delete button. Click the Yes button to remove the field.

- Use this same procedure to delete the Work Phone and E-mail Address fields (Figure 5–25).

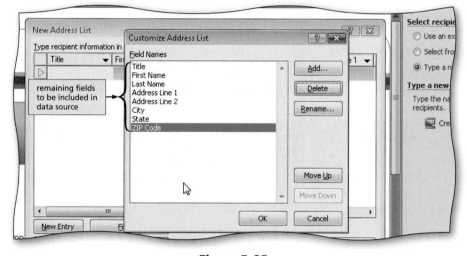

Figure 5–25

- Click the Add button to display the Add Field dialog box.

- Type Membership Type in the 'Type a name for your field' text box (Figure 5–26).

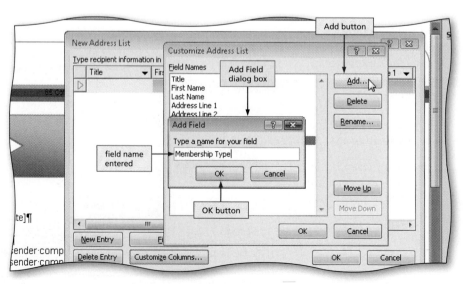

Figure 5–26

6

- Click the OK button to close the Add Field dialog box and add the Membership Type field name to the bottom of the Field Names list (Figure 5–27).

Q&A Can I change the name of a field?

Yes. Select the field, click the Rename button, type the new name, and then click the OK button.

Q&A Could I add more field names to the list?

Yes. You would click the Add button for each field name you want to add.

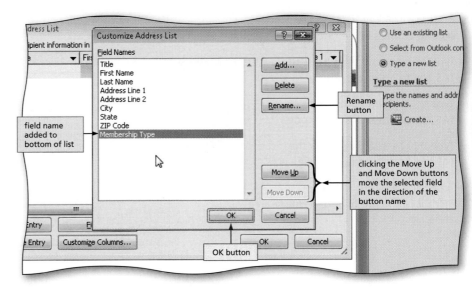

Figure 5–27

7

- Click the OK button to close the Customize Address List dialog box, which positions the insertion point in the Title text box for the first record (row) in the New Address List dialog box (Figure 5–28).

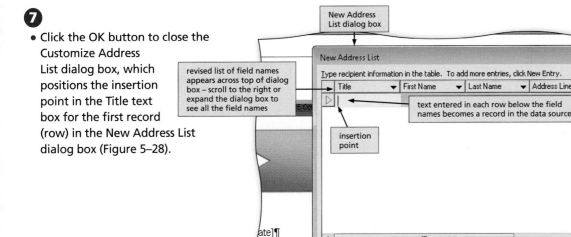

Figure 5–28

8

- Type Mr. and then press the TAB key to enter the title for the first data record.

- Type Milan and then press the TAB key to enter the first name.

- Type Sciranka and then press the TAB key to enter the last name.

- Type 85 Windmill Lane and then press the TAB key to enter the first address line (Figure 5–29).

Q&A What if I notice an error in an entry?

Click the entry and then correct the error as you would in the document window.

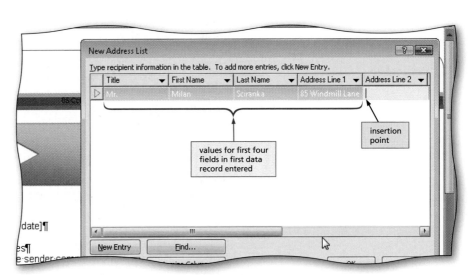

Figure 5–29

- Press the TAB key to leave the second address line empty.

- Type `Dilton` and then press the TAB key to enter the city.

- Type `NH` and then press the TAB key to enter the state code.

- Type `03324` and then press the TAB key to enter the ZIP code.

- Type `Standard` to enter the membership type (Figure 5–30).

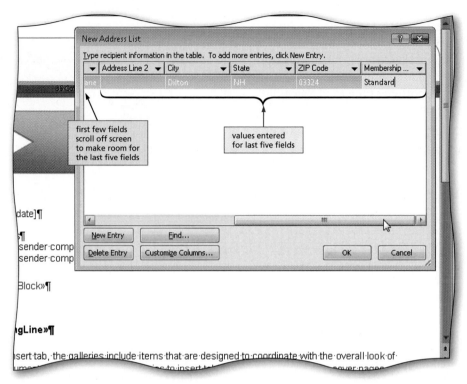

Figure 5–30

- Click the New Entry button to add a new blank record and position the insertion point in the Title field of the new record (Figure 5–31).

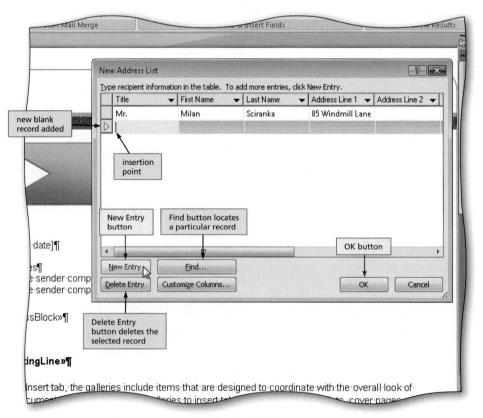

Figure 5–31

To Enter More Records

The following steps enter the remaining four records in the New Address List dialog box.

1 Type Ms. and then press the TAB key. Type Juanita and then press the TAB key. Type Mendez and then press the TAB key.

2 Type 333 Penn Drive and then press the TAB key. Type P.O. Box 333 and then press the TAB key.

3 Type Dilton and then press the TAB key. Type NH and then press the TAB key. Type 03324 and then press the TAB key.

4 Type Premium and then click the New Entry button.

Q&A Instead of clicking the New Entry button, can I press the TAB key at the end of one row to add a new blank record?

Yes. Pressing the TAB key at the end of a row has the same function as clicking the New Entry button.

5 Type Mrs. and then press the TAB key. Type Bethany and then press the TAB key. Type Ames and then press the TAB key.

6 Type 124 Center Court and then press the TAB key. Type Apt. 2E and then press the TAB key.

7 Type Harrust and then press the TAB key. Type NH and then press the TAB key. Type 03891 and then press the TAB key.

8 Type Premium and then click the New Entry button.

9 Type Mr. and then press the TAB key. Type Donnell and then press the TAB key. Type Carter and then press the TAB key.

10 Type 76 Ash Street and then press the TAB key twice.

11 Type Dilton and then press the TAB key. Type NH and then press the TAB key. Type 03324 and then press the TAB key.

12 Type Standard and then click the New Entry button.

13 Type Mr. and then press the TAB key. Type Benjamin and then press the TAB key. Type Tu and then press the TAB key.

14 Type 2204 Elm Avenue and then press the TAB key twice.

15 Type Harrust and then press the TAB key. Type NH and then press the TAB key. Type 03891 and then press the TAB key.

16 Type Standard and then click the OK button (shown in Figure 5–31), which displays the Save Address List dialog box (shown in Figure 5–32 on the next page).

BTW

Certification
The Microsoft Certified Application Specialist (MCAS) program provides an opportunity for you to obtain a valuable industry credential — proof that you have the Word 2007 skills required by employers. For more information see Appendix G or visit the Word 2007 Certification Web page (scsite.com/wd2007/cert).

To Save the Data Source when Prompted by Word

When you click the OK button in the New Address List dialog box, Word displays the Save Address List dialog box so that you can save the data source. The following steps save the data source in the Total Fitness folder created earlier in this project.

- Type Health Club Members in the File name text box.

- If necessary, locate and select the USB flash drive and then double-click the Total Fitness folder to open the folder (Figure 5–32).

Q&A

What is a Microsoft Office Address Lists file type?

It is a Microsoft Access database file. If you are familiar with Microsoft Access, you can open the Health Club Members file in Access. You do not have to be familiar with Access or have Access installed on your computer, however, to continue with this mail merge process. Word simply stores a data source as an Access table because it is an efficient method of storing a data source.

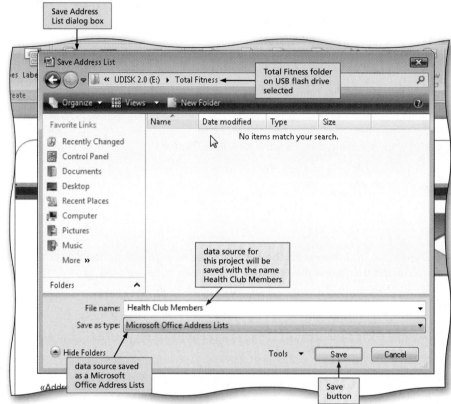

Figure 5–32

- Click the Save button in the Save Address List dialog box to save the data source in the Total Fitness folder on the USB flash drive using the file name, Health Club Members, and then display the Mail Merge Recipients dialog box (Figure 5–33).

- Click the OK button to close the Mail Merge Recipients dialog box.

- Click the Close button on the Mail Merge task pane title bar because you are finished with the wizard.

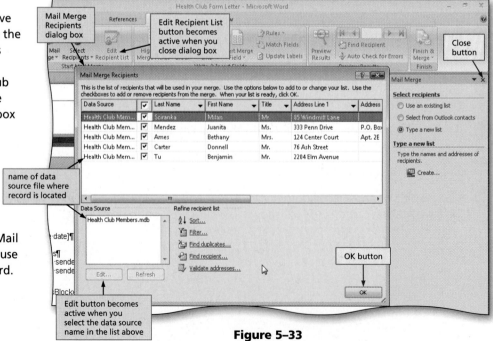

Figure 5–33

Editing Records in the Data Source

All of the data records have been entered in the data source and saved with the file name, Health Club Members. To add or edit data records in the data source, you would click the Edit Recipient List button on the Mailings tab to display the Mail Merge Recipients dialog box (shown in Figure 5–33). Click the data source name in the Data Source list and then click the Edit button in the Mail Merge Recipients dialog box to display the data records in a dialog box similar to the one shown in Figure 5–31 on page WD 326. Then, add or edit records as described in the previous steps. If you want to edit a particular record and the list of data records is long, you can click the Find button to locate an item, such as the first name, quickly in the list.

To delete a record, select it using the same procedure described in the previous paragraph. Then, click the Delete Entry button in the dialog box (Figure 5–31 on page WD 326).

Composing the Main Document for the Form Letters

The next step is to enter and format the text and fields in the main document for the form letters (shown in Figure 5–1a on page WD 307). With the letterhead for the form letters complete, you will follow these steps to compose the remainder of the main document for the form letter.

1. Format the date line and enter the date
2. Delete the company content controls
3. Edit the greeting line (salutation)
4. Enter text and insert merge fields
5. Create a multilevel list
6. Insert an IF field
7. Merge the letters

To Change Spacing Before Paragraphs

The default amount of space above (before) the date line paragraph is 36 points. In this project, it is reduced to 24 points to be sure the entire letter fits on a single page. The following steps change the spacing before to 24 point.

1 Click the date content control to select it.

2 Display the Page Layout tab.

3 Click the Spacing Before box down arrow on the Page Layout tab as many times as necessary until 24 pt is displayed in the Spacing Before text box.

BTW

Saving Data Sources
Word, by default, saves a data source in the My Data Sources folder on your hard disk. Likewise, when you open a data source, Word initially looks in the My Data Sources folder for the file. The default file type for a new data source created in Word is called Microsoft Office Address Lists. If you are familiar with Microsoft Access, you can open and view these file types in Access using the Microsoft Office Access file type.

To Enter the Date

The next step is to enter the date. You can click the date content control and type the correct date, or you can click the box arrow and select the date from a calendar. The following steps use the calendar to enter the date.

- With the date content control selected, click its box arrow to display a calendar.

- Scroll through the calendar months until May, 2008 is displayed (Figure 5–34).

- Click 28 in the calendar to display 5/28/2008 in the date line of the form letter (shown in Figure 5-35).

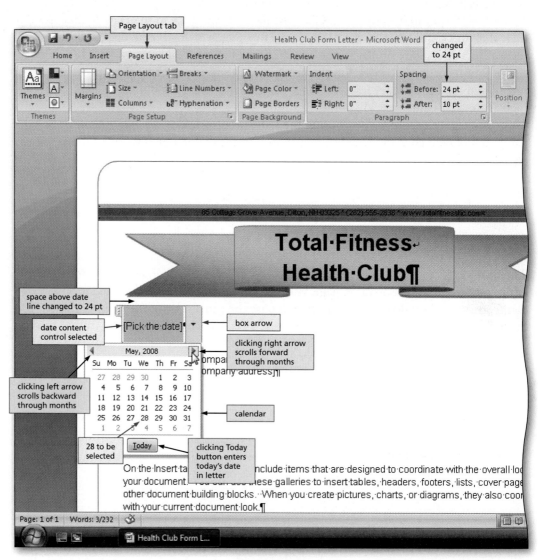

Figure 5–34

Other Ways

1. Type date in date content control

To Delete Content Controls

Earlier in this chapter, you created the letterhead for the main document for the form letter. Thus, the letter does not require the company content controls below the date. The following steps delete these content controls.

1. Select the three lines of company content controls by dragging through them (Figure 5–35).

2. Press the DELETE key to delete the selected content controls.

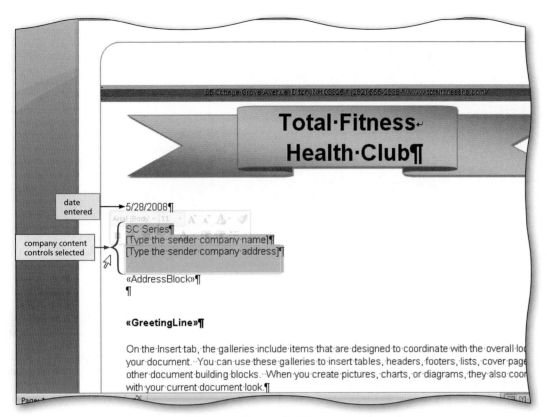

Figure 5–35

Merge Fields

In this form letter, the inside address appears below the date line, and the salutation is below the inside address. The contents of the inside address and salutation are located in the data source. To link the data source to the main document, you insert the field names from the data source in the main document.

In the main document, field names linked to the data source are called **merge fields** because they merge, or combine, the main document with the contents of the data source. When a merge field is inserted in the main document, Word surrounds the field name with merge field characters (shown in Figure 5–36 on the next page). The **merge field characters**, which are chevrons, mark the beginning and ending of a merge field. Merge field characters are not on the keyboard; therefore, you cannot type them directly in the document. Word automatically displays them when a merge field is inserted in the main document.

Most letters contain an address and salutation. For this reason, Word provides an AddressBlock merge field and a GreetingLine merge field. The **AddressBlock merge field** contains several fields related to an address: title, first name, middle name, last name, suffix, company, street address 1, street address 2, city, state, and ZIP code. When Word uses the AddressBlock merge field, it automatically looks for any fields in the associated data source that are related to an address and then formats the address block properly when you merge the data source with the main document. For example, if your inside address does not use a middle name, suffix, or company, Word omits these items from the inside address and adjusts the spacing so that the address prints correctly.

The Mail Merge template automatically inserted the AddressBlock and GreetingLine merge fields in the form letter. If you wanted to insert these merge fields in a document, you would click the Address Block button or the Greeting Line button on the Mailings tab.

BTW

Fields
When you insert fields in a document, the displayed fields may be surrounded by braces instead of chevrons and extra instructions may appear between the braces. If this occurs, then field codes have been turned on. To turn off field codes so that they do not display, press ALT+F9.

To Edit the GreetingLine Merge Field

The **GreetingLine merge field** contains text and fields related to a salutation. The default greeting for the salutation is in the format, Dear Joshua, followed by a comma. In this letter, you want a more formal ending to the salutation — a colon. Also, the GreetingLine merge field is formatted in bold. You do not want the salutation to print in bold. The following steps edit the GreetingLine merge field.

1

• Select the GreetingLine merge field by clicking to its left.

Q&A

Why does the GreetingLine merge field turn gray?

Word, by default, shades a field in gray when the insertion point is in the field. The shading displays on the screen to help you identify fields; the shading does not print on a hard copy. To select an entire field, double-click it.

• Display the Home tab. Click the Bold button on the Home tab to remove the bold format from the GreetingLine merge field.

• Right-click the GreetingLine merge field (Figure 5–36).

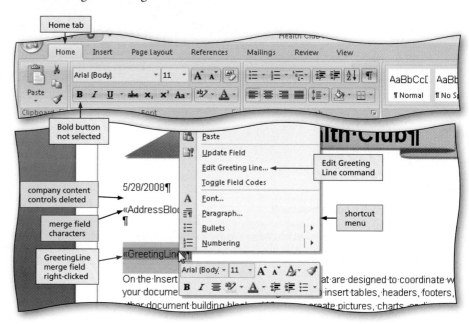

Figure 5–36

2

• Click Edit Greeting Line on the shortcut menu to display the Modify Greeting Line dialog box.

• Click the rightmost 'Greeting line format' box arrow and then click the colon (:) in the list (Figure 5–37).

3

• Click the OK button to modify the greeting line format.

Q&A

Will I notice a change in the GreetingLine merge field?

No. The new format will be displayed later in this chapter when you merge the form letter to the data source.

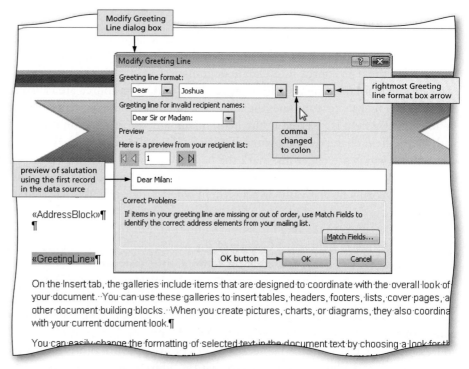

Figure 5–37

To Begin Typing the Body of the Form Letter

The next step is to begin typing the message, or body of the letter, which is to be located where Word has the content control, Type the body of the letter. The following steps begin typing the letter in the location of the content control.

1 Click the body of the letter to select the content control (Figure 5–38).

2 With the content control selected, type We would like to thank you, and then press the SPACEBAR.

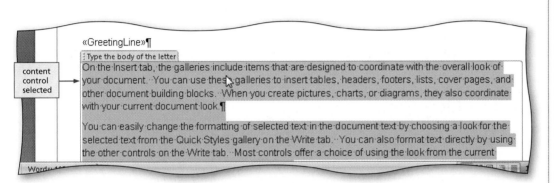

Figure 5–38

BTW

Insert Merge Field Button
If you click the Insert Merge Field button instead of the Insert Merge Field button (Figure 5–39), Word displays the Insert Merge Field dialog box instead of the Insert Merge Field menu. To insert fields from the dialog box, click the field name and then click the Insert button. The dialog box remains open so that you can insert multiple fields, if necessary. When finished inserting fields, click the Close button in the dialog box.

To Insert a Merge Field in the Main Document

The first sentence in the first paragraph of the letter states the first name of the member. To instruct Word to use data fields from the data source, you insert merge fields in the main document for the form letter. The following steps insert a merge field at the location of the insertion point.

1

- Display the Mailings tab.

- Click the Insert Merge Field button arrow on the Mailings tab to display the Insert Merge Field menu (Figure 5–39).

Q&A

Why is the underscore character in some of the field names?

Word places an underscore character in place of the space in merge fields.

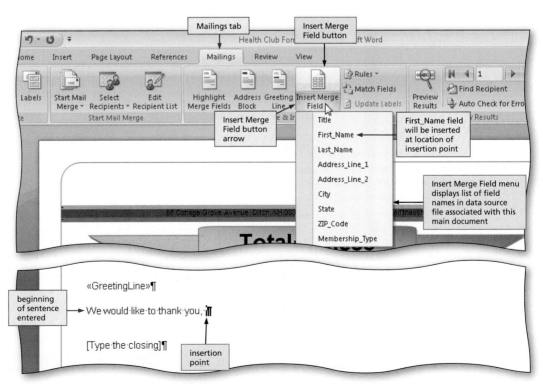

Figure 5–39

2

- Click First_Name to insert the selected merge field in the document at the location of the insertion point (Figure 5–40).

Q&A

Will First_Name print when I merge the form letters?

No. When you merge the data source with the main document, the first name (e.g., Milan) will print at the location of the merge field, First_Name.

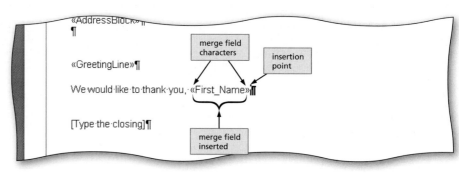

Figure 5–40

Other Ways

1. Click Insert Merge Field button on Mailings tab, click desired field, click Insert button, click Close button

---

To Enter More Text

The next step is to enter the remainder of the first paragraph and the beginning of the second paragraph.

1 With the insertion point at the location shown in Figure 5–40, type a comma, press the SPACEBAR, and then type `for being a member of our health club. We hope you are pleased with our state-of-the-art cardiovascular and resistance training equipment and top-notch staff.`

2 Press the ENTER key. Type `Starting today, your experience at Total Fitness Health Club will include several additional amenities to make your visit more complete:` and then press the ENTER key (Figure 5–41).

Figure 5–41

To Create a Multilevel List

The next step is to enter a multilevel list in the form letter (shown in Figure 5–1a on page WD 307). A **multilevel list** is a list that contains several levels of items, with each level displaying a different numeric, alphabetic, or bullet symbol.

To ensure that no existing formatting will affect the multilevel list, the first step in creating the list is to clear formatting. The following steps create a multilevel list.

1

- Scroll to display the insertion point higher in the document window.

- Display the Home tab and then click the Clear Formatting button to remove any existing formatting.

- Click the Multilevel List button on the Home tab to display the Multilevel List gallery.

- Position the mouse pointer in the second style in the first row in the List Library area to see a preview of the style (Figure 5–42).

 Experiment

- Point to various list styles in the gallery to see the list style previews.

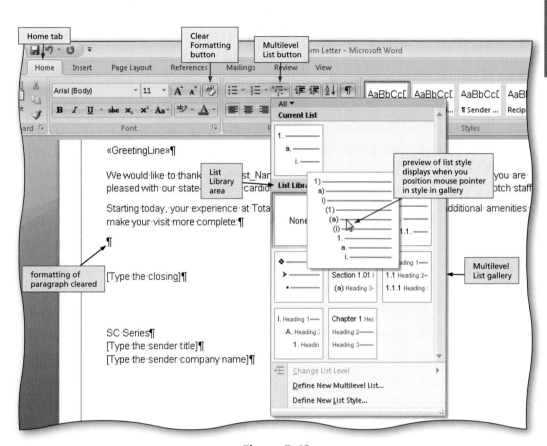

Figure 5–42

2

- Click the desired list style (second style in the first row in List Library area) to apply the selected multilevel list style to the current paragraph.

- Type Enhanced Facilities and then press the ENTER key to enter this first-level list item (Figure 5–43).

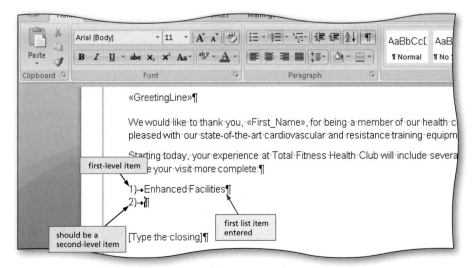

Figure 5–43

❸

- Press the TAB key to demote the current list item to a second-level list item that is indented below the first list item.

- Type Now open 24 hours a day, 7 days a week and then press the ENTER key to enter a second-level list item.

- Type New supervised child play center and then press the ENTER key to enter a second-level list item.

- Type New 46' climbing wall and then press the ENTER key to enter a second-level list item (Figure 5–44).

Q&A Can I adjust the level of a list item after it is typed?

Yes. With the insertion point in the item to adjust, click the Increase Indent or Decrease Indent button on the Home tab, press TAB or SHIFT+TAB, or right-click the list item and then click the desired command on the shortcut menu.

«Greeting_...¶

We would like to thank you, «First_Name», for being a member of our health pleased with our state-of-the-art cardiovascular and resistance training equipm

Starting today, your experience at Total Fitness Health Club will include sever make your visit more complete:¶

1)→Enhanced Facilities¶
 a)→Now open 24 hours a day, 7 days a week¶
 b)→New supervised child play center¶
 c)→New 46' climbing wall¶
 d)→¶

should be promoted to a first-level item, aligned below the number one

second-level items entered

[Type the closing]¶

SC Series¶
[Type the sender title]¶
[Type the sender company name]¶

Figure 5–44

❹

- Press SHIFT+TAB to promote the current list item.

- Type Expanded Instructional Programs and then press the ENTER key.

- Press the TAB key to demote the current list item, which will be Wellness seminars.

- Type Wellness seminars and then press the ENTER key.

- Type Yoga and Pilates classes and then press the ENTER key.

- Type Nutrition education and then press the ENTER key three times to end the numbered list (Figure 5–45).

Q&A Why did the automatic numbering stop?

Word turns off automatic numbering when you press the ENTER key without entering text next to a numbered or bulleted list item. Another way to stop automatic numbering is to click the Numbering button on the Home tab.

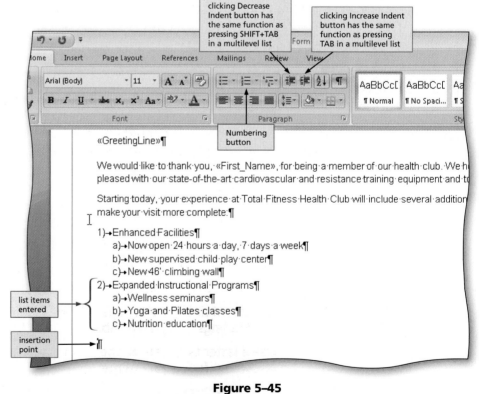

clicking Decrease Indent button has the same function as pressing SHIFT+TAB in a multilevel list

clicking Increase Indent button has the same function as pressing TAB in a multilevel list

Numbering button

«GreetingLine»¶

We would like to thank you, «First_Name», for being a member of our health club. We h pleased with our state-of-the-art cardiovascular and resistance training equipment and to

Starting today, your experience at Total Fitness Health Club will include several additio make your visit more complete:¶

1)→Enhanced Facilities¶
 a)→Now open 24 hours a day, 7 days a week¶
 b)→New supervised child play center¶
 c)→New 46' climbing wall¶
2)→Expanded Instructional Programs¶
 a)→Wellness seminars¶
 b)→Yoga and Pilates classes¶
 c)→Nutrition education¶

list items entered

insertion point

Figure 5–45

To Enter More Text and a Merge Field

The next paragraph states the member's membership type, which is a merge field. The following step enters the beginning of the next paragraph with the merge field.

1 Type `We strive to provide the highest quality amenities to our members. To continue to achieve this service level, we must raise our monthly fees effective July 1. As a member on the` and then press the SPACEBAR.

2 Display the Mailings tab. Click the Insert Merge Field button arrow on the Mailings tab and then click Membership_Type on the Insert Merge Field menu.

3 Press the SPACEBAR and then type `Plan, your new monthly rate will be` and then press the SPACEBAR.

IF Fields

In addition to merge fields, you can insert Word fields that are designed specifically for a mail merge. An **IF field** is an example of a Word field. One form of the IF field is called an **If...Then:** If a condition is true, then perform an action. For example, If Mary owns a house, then send her information about homeowner's insurance. Another form of the IF field is called an **If...Then...Else:** If a condition is true, then perform an action; else perform a different action. For example, If John has an e-mail address, then send him an e-mail message; else send him the message via the postal service.

In this project, the form letter checks the club member's membership type. If the membership type is Standard, then the new monthly rate is $75; else if the membership type is Premium, then the new monthly rate is $105. Thus, you will use an If...Then... Else: If the membership type is equal to Standard, then print $75 on the form letter, else print $105.

The phrase that appears after the word If is called a rule or a condition. A **condition** consists of an expression, followed by a comparison operator, followed by a final expression.

Expression The expression in a condition can be a merge field, a number, a series of characters, or a mathematical formula. Word surrounds a series of characters with quotation marks ("). To indicate an empty, or null, expression, Word places two quotation marks together ("").

Comparison Operator The comparison operator in a condition must be one of six characters: = (equal to or matches the text), <> (not equal to or does not match text), < (less than), <= (less than or equal to), > (greater than), >= (greater than or equal to).

If the result of a condition is true, then Word evaluates the **true text**. If the result of the condition is false, Word evaluates the **false text** if it exists. In this project, the first expression in the condition is a merge field (Membership_Type); the comparison operator is equal to (=); and the second expression is the text "Standard". The true text is "$75". The false text is "$105". The complete IF field is as follows:

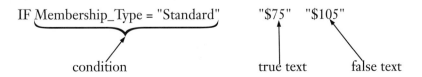

To Insert an IF Field in the Main Document

The following steps insert this IF field in the form letter: If the membership type is Standard, then the new monthly rate is $75; else if the membership type is Premium, then the new monthly rate is $105.

1

- With the insertion point positioned as shown in Figure 5–46, click the Rules button on the Mailings tab to display the Rules menu (Figure 5–46).

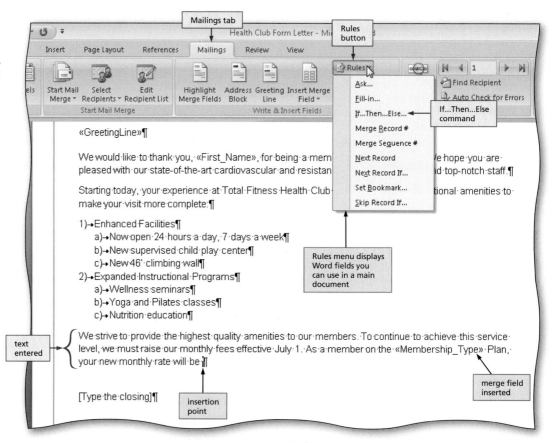

Figure 5–46

2

- Click If...Then...Else on the Rules menu to display the Insert Word Field: IF dialog box (Figure 5–47).

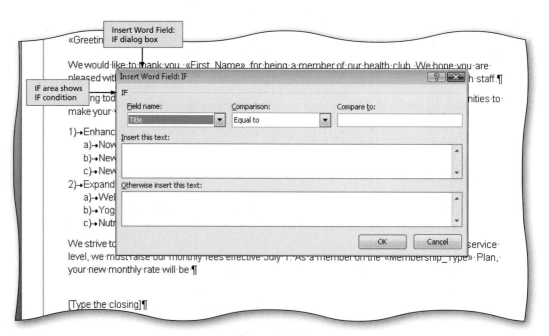

Figure 5–47

3

- Click the Field name box arrow to display the list of fields in the data source.

- Scroll through the list of fields in the Field name list and then click Membership_Type.

- Position the insertion point in the Compare to text box and then type Standard as the comparison text.

- Press the TAB key and then type $75 as the true text.

- Press the TAB key and then type $105 as the false text (Figure 5–48).

Does the capitalization matter in the comparison text?

Yes. The text, Standard, is different from the text, standard, in a comparison. Be sure to enter the text exactly as you entered it in the data source.

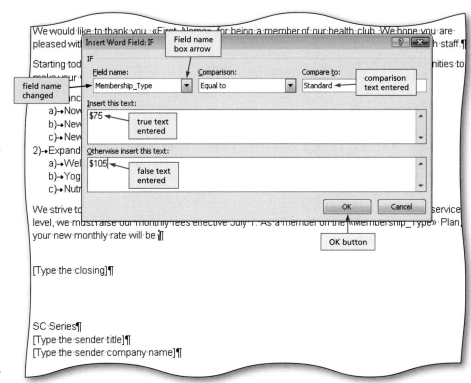

Figure 5–48

4

- Click the OK button to insert the IF field at the location of the insertion point (Figure 5–49).

Why does the main document display $75 instead of the IF field instructions?

The $75 is displayed because the first record in the data source has a membership type of Standard. Word, by default, evaluates the IF field using the current record and displays the results, called the **field results**, in the main document instead of displaying the IF field instructions. Later in the chapter, you will view the IF field instructions.

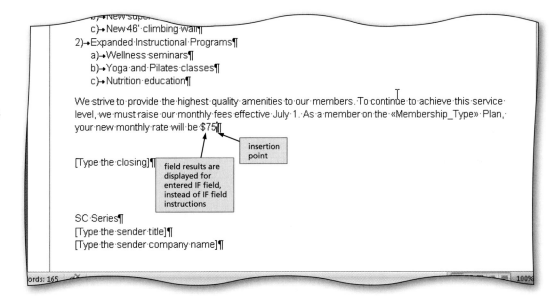

Figure 5–49

BTW

Word Fields
In addition to the IF field, Word provides other fields that may be used in form letters. For example, the ASK and FILLIN fields prompt the user to enter data for each record in the data source. The SKIP RECORD IF field instructs the mail merge not to generate a form letter for a data record if a specific condition is met.

To Enter More Text in Content Controls

The following steps enter the text in the remainder of the form letter.

1 Type a PERIOD and then press the SPACEBAR. Type `We appreciate your business and hope you enjoy our club.`

2 If necessary, scroll to display the closing and signature block in the document window.

3 Select the closing content control and then type `Sincerely,` as the closing.

4 Select the sender name content control. (If your sender name content control already displays a name, drag through the name to select it also.) Type `Ms. Suzy Zhao` as the sender name.

5 Select the sender title content control and then type `Fitness Manager` as the sender title.

6 Select the sender company name content control and then type `Total Fitness Health Club` as the sender company name (Figure 5–50).

BTW

Opening Main Document Files
When you open a main document, Word attempts to open the associated data source file too. If the data source is not in the same location (i.e., drive and folder) as it was when it originally was saved, Word may display a dialog box indicating that it could not find the data source. When this occurs, click the Find Data Source button in the dialog box to display the Open Data Source dialog box, which is where you can locate the data source file. If Word does not display a dialog box with the Find Data Source button, then the data source is not associated with the main document. To associate the data source with the main document, click the Select Recipients button on the Mailings tab, click Use Existing List, and then locate the data source file. When you save the main document, Word will associate the data source with the main document.

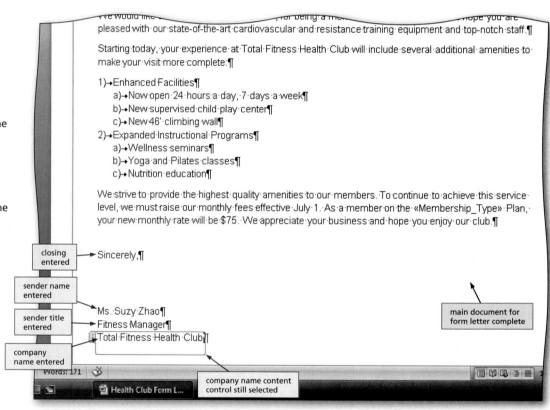

Figure 5–50

To Save a Document Again

The main document for the form letter now is complete. Thus, you should save it again.

1 Save the main document for the form letter again with the same file name, Health Club Form Letter.

To Display a Field Code

The instructions in the IF field are not displayed in the document; instead, the field results are displayed for the current record (Figure 5–51). The instructions of an IF field are called as **field codes**, and the default for Word is for field codes not to be displayed. Thus, field codes do not print or show on the screen unless you turn them on. You use one procedure to show field codes on the screen and a different procedure to print them on a hard copy.

You might want to turn on a field code to verify its accuracy or to modify it. Field codes tend to clutter the screen. Thus, most Word users turn them off after viewing them. The following steps show a field code on the screen.

1

- Right-click the dollar amount, $75, to display a shortcut menu (Figure 5–51).

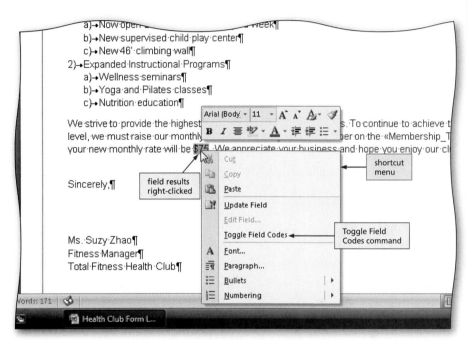

Figure 5–51

2

- Click Toggle Field Codes on the shortcut menu to display the field code instead of the field results for the IF field (Figure 5–52).

Q&A Will displaying field codes affect the merged documents?

No. Displaying field codes has no effect on the merge process.

Q&A What if I wanted to display all field codes in a document?

You would press ALT+F9. Then, to hide all the field codes, press ALT+F9 again.

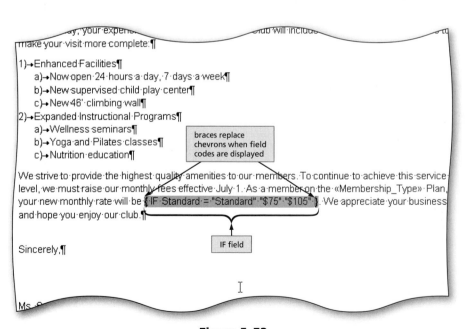

Figure 5–52

Other Ways
1. With insertion point in field, press SHIFT+F9

To Print Field Codes in the Main Document

When you merge or print a document, Word automatically converts field codes that show on the screen to field results. You may want to print the field codes version of the form letter, however, so that you have a hard copy of the field codes for future reference. When you print field codes, you must remember to turn off the field codes option so that merged documents print field results instead of field codes. The following steps print the field codes in the main document and then turn off the print field codes option.

1

• Display the Office Button menu and then click the Word Options button to display the Word Options dialog box.

• Click Advanced in the left pane to display advanced options in the right pane. Scroll to the Print area in the right pane of the dialog box.

• Place a check mark in the 'Print field codes instead of their values' check box (Figure 5–53).

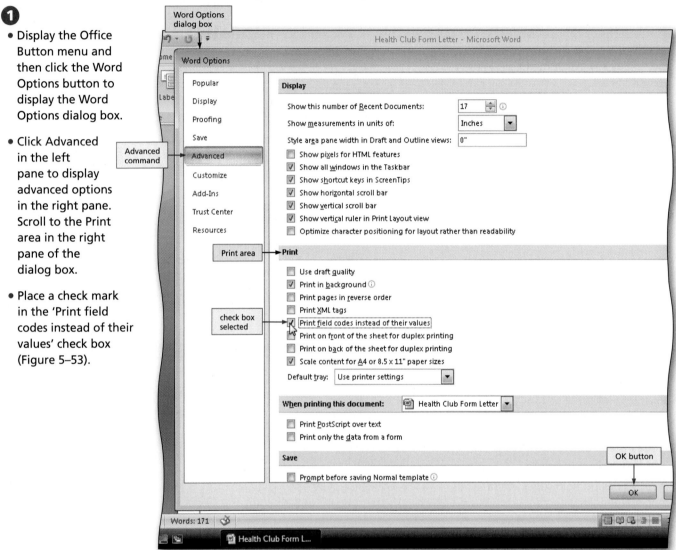

Figure 5–53

2

• Click the OK button to instruct Word to show field codes when the document prints.

3

- Display the Office Button menu, point to Print, and then click Quick Print to print the main document with all field codes showing (Figure 5–54).

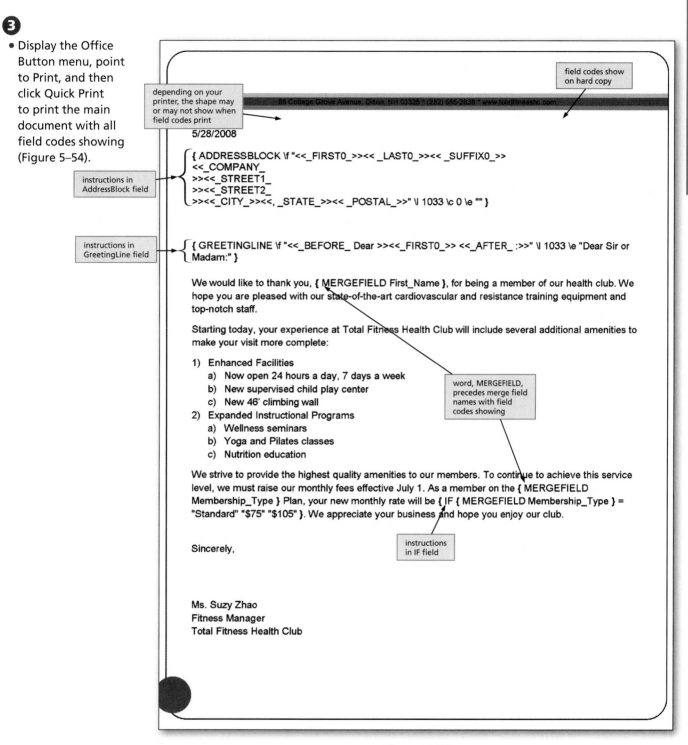

field codes show on hard copy

depending on your printer, the shape may or may not show when field codes print

86 Cottage Grove Avenue, Dilton, NH 03325 * (282) 555-2838 * www.totalfitnesshc.com

5/28/2008

{ ADDRESSBLOCK \f "<<_FIRST0_>><< _LAST0_>><< _SUFFIX0_>>
<<_COMPANY_
>><<_STREET1_
>><<_STREET2_
>><<_CITY_>><<, _STATE_>><< _POSTAL_>>" \l 1033 \c 0 \e "" }

instructions in AddressBlock field

{ GREETINGLINE \f "<<_BEFORE_ Dear >><<_FIRST0_>> <<_AFTER_ :>>" \l 1033 \e "Dear Sir or Madam:" }

instructions in GreetingLine field

We would like to thank you, { MERGEFIELD First_Name }, for being a member of our health club. We hope you are pleased with our state-of-the-art cardiovascular and resistance training equipment and top-notch staff.

Starting today, your experience at Total Fitness Health Club will include several additional amenities to make your visit more complete:

1) Enhanced Facilities
   a) Now open 24 hours a day, 7 days a week
   b) New supervised child play center
   c) New 46' climbing wall
2) Expanded Instructional Programs
   a) Wellness seminars
   b) Yoga and Pilates classes
   c) Nutrition education

word, MERGEFIELD, precedes merge field names with field codes showing

We strive to provide the highest quality amenities to our members. To continue to achieve this service level, we must raise our monthly fees effective July 1. As a member on the { MERGEFIELD Membership_Type } Plan, your new monthly rate will be { IF { MERGEFIELD Membership_Type } = "Standard" "$75" "$105" }. We appreciate your business and hope you enjoy our club.

Sincerely,

instructions in IF field

Ms. Suzy Zhao
Fitness Manager
Total Fitness Health Club

Figure 5–54

4

- Display the Office Button menu and then click the Word Options button to display the Word Options dialog box.

- Click Advanced in the left pane to display advanced options in the right pane. Scroll to the Print area in the right pane of the dialog box.

- Remove the check mark in the 'Print field codes instead of their values' check box.

- Click the OK button to instruct Word to print field results the next time you print.

To Merge the Form Letters to the Printer

The data source and main document for the form letter are complete. The next step is to merge them to generate the individual form letters. The following steps merge the form letters, sending the merged letters to the printer.

- Click the Finish & Merge button on the Mailings tab to display the Finish & Merge menu (Figure 5–55).

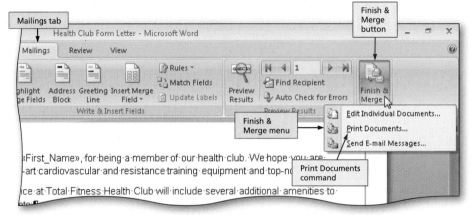

Figure 5–55

2

- Click Print Documents to display the Merge to Printer dialog box.

- If necessary, click All to select it (Figure 5–56).

Q&A

Do I have to merge all records?

No. Through this dialog box you can merge the current record or a range of record numbers.

3

- Click the OK button to display the Print dialog box.

- Click the OK button in the Print dialog box to print five separate letters, one for each club member in the data source, as shown in Figure 5–1c on page WD 307. (If Word displays a message about locked fields, click its OK button.)

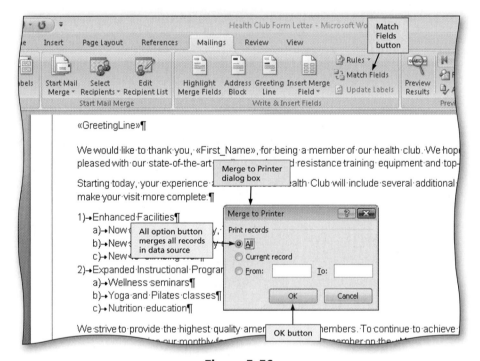

Figure 5–56

Correcting Errors in Merged Documents

If you notice errors in the printed form letters, edit the main document the same way you edit any other document. Then, save the changes and merge again. If the wrong field results print, Word may be mapping the fields incorrectly. To view fields, click the Match Fields button on the Mailings tab (Figure 5–56). Then, review the list of fields in the list. For example, the Last Name should map to the Last Name field in the data source. If it does not, click the box arrow to change the name of the data source field.

To MERGE TO A NEW DOCUMENT WINDOW

Instead of immediately printing the merged form letters, you could send them to a new document window, where you can view the merged form letters on the screen to verify their accuracy before printing them. When you are finished viewing the merged form letters, you can print them as you print any other Word document.

In addition, you can edit the contents of individual merged letters. You also can save the merged form letters in a file or close the document window without saving them.

If you wanted to merge to a new document window, you would perform the following steps.

1. Click the Finish & Merge button on the Mailings tab and then click Edit Individual Documents to display the Merge to New Document dialog box.

2. Click All.

3. Click the OK button to merge the form letters to a new document window.

BTW

Locking Fields
If you wanted to lock a field so that its field results cannot be changed, click the field and then press CTRL+F11. To subsequently unlock a field so that it may be updated, click the field and then press CTRL+SHIFT+F11.

To Select Records to Merge

Instead of merging and printing all of the records in the data source, you can choose which records will merge, based on a condition you specify. The dialog box in Figure 5–56 allows you to specify by record number which records to merge. Often you merge based on the contents of a specific field. For example, you may want to merge and print only those club members whose membership type is Premium. The following steps select records for a merge.

1

- Click the Edit Recipient List button on the Mailings tab to display the Mail Merge Recipients dialog box (Figure 5–57).

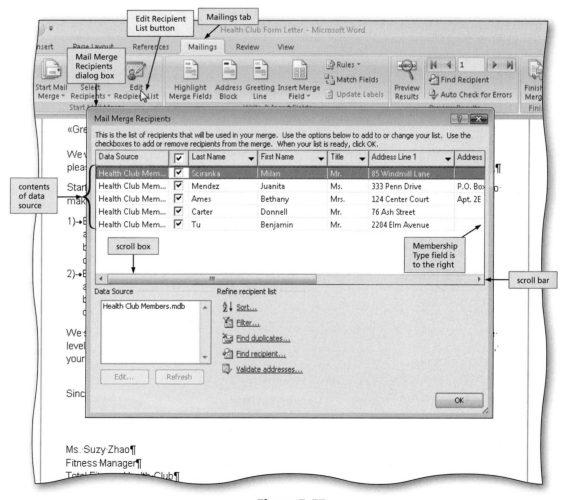

Figure 5–57

2

- Drag the scroll box to the right edge of the scroll bar in the Mail Merge Recipients dialog box so that the Membership Type field appears in the dialog box.

- Click the box arrow to the right of the field name, Membership Type, to display sort and filter criteria for the Membership Type field (Figure 5–58).

Q&A

What are the filter criteria in the parenthesis?

The (All) option clears any previously set filter criteria. The (Blanks) option selects records that contain blanks in that field, and the (Nonblanks) option selects records that do not contain blanks in that field. The (Advanced) option displays the Filter and Sort dialog box, which allows you to perform more advanced record selection operations.

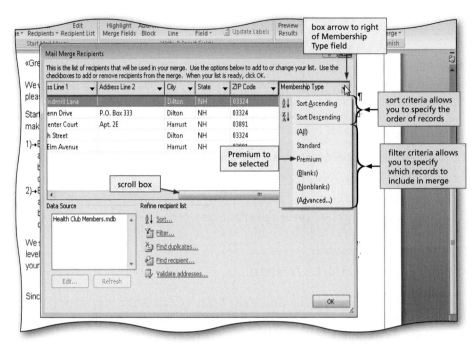

Figure 5–58

3

- Click Premium to reduce the number of data records displayed in the Mail Merge Recipients dialog box to two, because two club members have a membership type of Premium (Figure 5–59).

- Click the OK button to close the Mail Merge Recipients dialog box.

Q&A

What happened to the other three records that did not meet the criteria?

They still are part of the data source, just not appearing in the Mail Merge Recipients dialog box. When you clear the filter, all records will reappear.

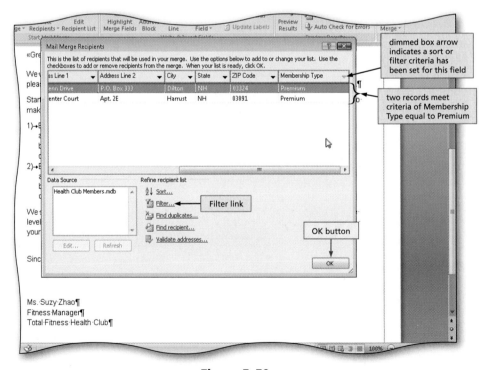

Figure 5–59

Other Ways

1. Click Filter link in Mail Merge Recipients dialog box, click Filter Records tab, enter filter criteria, click OK button

To Merge the Form Letters to the Printer

The next step is to merge the selected records. To do this, you follow the same steps described earlier. The difference is that Word will merge only those records that meet the criteria specified, that is, just those with a membership type of Premium.

1 Click the Finish & Merge button on the Mailings tab to display the Finish & Merge menu.

2 Click Print Documents to display the Merge to Printer dialog box. If necessary, click All in the dialog box.

3 Click the OK button to display the Print dialog box.

4 Click the OK button in the Print dialog box to print two separate letters, one for each club member whose membership type is Premium (Figure 5–60). (If Word displays a message about locked fields, click its OK button.)

BTW

Conserving Ink and Toner

You can instruct Word to print draft quality documents to conserve ink or toner by clicking the Office Button, clicking the Word Options button, clicking Advanced in the left pane of the Word Options dialog box, scrolling to the Print area, placing a check mark in the 'Use draft quality' check box, and then clicking the OK button. Click the Office Button, point to Print, and then click Quick Print.

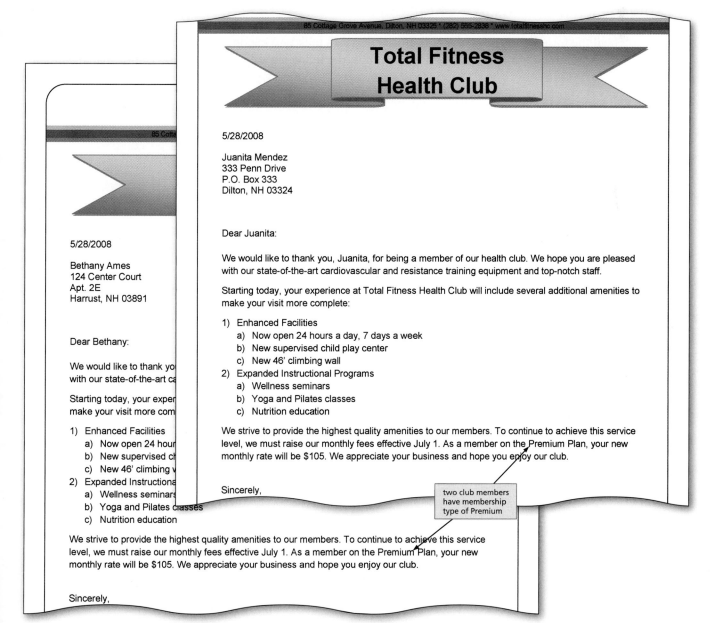

Figure 5–60

To Remove a Merge Condition

You should remove the merge condition so that future merges will not be restricted to club members with a membership type of Premium.

1 Click the Edit Recipient List button on the Mailings tab to display the Mail Merge Recipients dialog box.

2 Click the Filter link in the dialog box (shown in Figure 5–59 on page WD 346) to display the Filter and Sort dialog box.

3 If necessary, click the Filter Records tab.

4 Click the Clear All button in the dialog box. Click the OK button in each of the two open dialog boxes.

To Sort the Data Records in a Data Source

If you mail the form letters using the U.S. Postal Service's bulk rate mailing service, the post office requires that you sort and group the form letters by ZIP code. Thus, the following steps sort the data records by ZIP code.

1

- Click the Edit Recipient List button on the Mailings tab to display the Mail Merge Recipients dialog box.

- Scroll to the right until the ZIP Code field shows in the dialog box.

- Position the mouse pointer on the ZIP Code field name (Figure 5–61).

BTW

Validating Addresses
If you have installed address validation software, you can click the Validate addresses link in the Mail Merge Recipients dialog box to validate your recipients' addresses. If you would like information about installing address validation software and have not yet installed the software, click the Validate addresses link in the Mail Merge Recipients dialog box and then click the Yes button in the Microsoft Office Word dialog box to display a related Microsoft Office Web page.

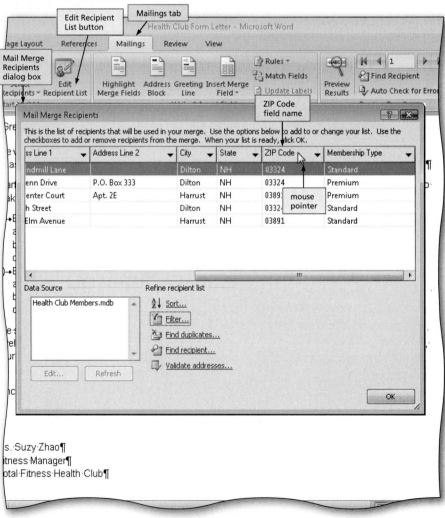

Figure 5–61

2

- Click the ZIP Code field name to sort the data source records in ascending (smallest to largest) order by ZIP Code (Figure 5–62).

- Click the OK button to close the Mail Merge Recipients dialog box.

Q&A

In what order would the form letters print if I merged them again now?

Word would print them in ZIP code order; that is, the records with ZIP Code 03324 would print first, and the records with ZIP Code 03891 would print last.

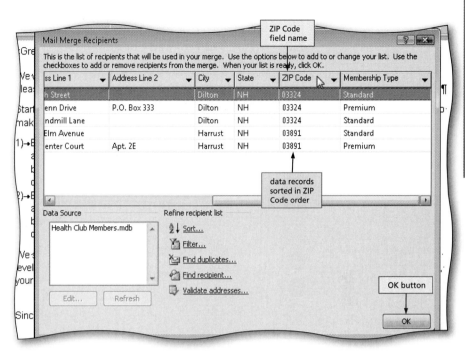

Figure 5–62

To View Merged Data in the Main Document

You can verify the order of the data records without printing them by viewing field results instead of merge fields. The following steps view merged data.

1

- If necessary, scroll up to display the AddressBlock merge field in the document window.

- Click the View Merged Data button on the Mailings tab to display the values in the first data record, instead of the merge fields (Figure 5–63).

2

- Click the View Merged Data button on the Mailings tab again to display the merge fields in the main document, instead of the field values.

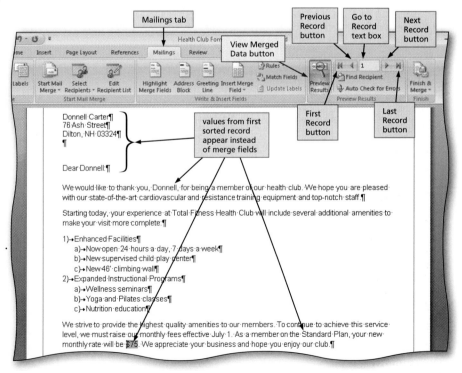

Figure 5–63

Displaying Data Source Records in the Main Document

When you are viewing merged data in the main document (the View Merged Data button is selected), you can click the Last Record button (Figure 5–63 on the previous page) on the Mailings tab to display the values from the last record in the data source, the First Record button to display the values in record one, the Next Record button to display the values in the next consecutive record number, or the Previous Record button to display the values from the previous record number. You also can display a specific record by clicking the Go to Record text box, typing the record number you would like to be displayed in the main document, and then pressing the ENTER key.

BTW

Closing Main Document Files
Word always asks if you want to save changes when you close a main document, even if you just saved the document. If you are sure that no additional changes were made to the document, click the No button; otherwise, click the Yes button — just to be safe.

To Close a Document

The health club form letter is complete. Thus, the next step is to close the document.

1 Display the Office Button menu and then click Close.

2 If a Microsoft Office Word dialog box is displayed, click the Yes button to save the changes.

Addressing and Printing Mailing Labels and Envelopes

Now that you have merged and printed the form letters, the next step is to print addresses on mailing labels to be affixed to envelopes for the form letters. The mailing labels will use the same data source as the form letter, Health Club Members. The format and content of the mailing labels will be exactly the same as the inside address in the main document for the form letter. That is, the first line will contain the club member's title and first name followed by the last name. The second line will contain his or her street address, and so on. Thus, you will use the AddressBlock merge field in the mailing labels.

Plan Ahead

> **Generate mailing labels and envelopes.**
> An envelope should contain the sender's full name and address in the upper-left corner of the envelope. It also should contain the addressee's full name and address, positioned approximately in the vertical and horizontal center of the envelope. The address can be typed directly on the envelope or on a mailing label that is affixed to the envelope.

You follow the same basic steps to create the main document for the mailing labels as you did to create the main document for the form letters. The major difference is that the data source already exists because you created it earlier in this project.

To Address and Print Mailing Labels Using an Existing Data Source

To address mailing labels, you specify the type of labels you intend to use. Word will request the label information, including the label vendor and product number. You can obtain this information from the box of labels. For illustration purposes in addressing these labels, the label vendor is Avery and the product number is J8158. The next steps address and print mailing labels using an existing data source.

1

- Display the Office Button menu. Click New on the Office Button menu to display the New Document dialog box. With Blank document selected, click the Create button to open a new blank document window.

- Display the Mailings tab.

- Click the Start Mail Merge button on the Mailings tab and then click Step by Step Mail Merge Wizard to display Step 1 of the Mail Merge wizard in the Mail Merge task pane.

- Specify labels as the main document type by clicking Labels in the 'Select document type' area (Figure 5–64).

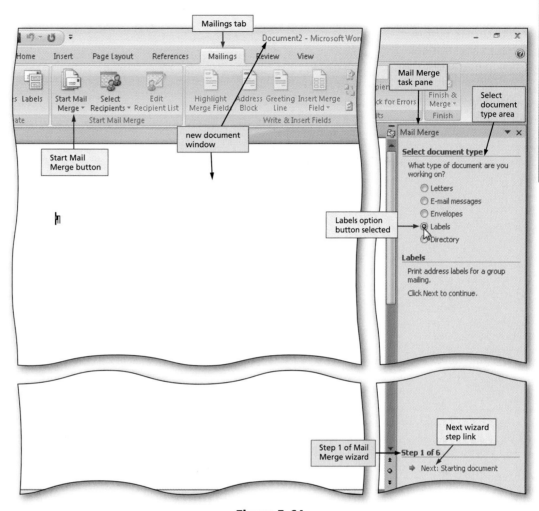

Figure 5–64

2

- Click the 'Next wizard step' link at the bottom of the Mail Merge task pane to display Step 2 of the Mail Merge wizard.

- In the Mail Merge task pane, click the 'Select label size' link to display the Label Options dialog box.

- Select the label vendor and product number (in this case, Avery A4/A5 and J8158), as shown in Figure 5–65.

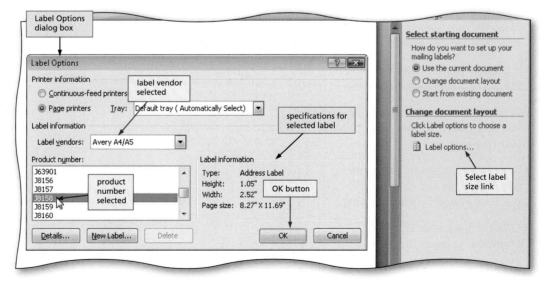

Figure 5–65

- Click the OK button in the Label Options dialog box to display the selected label layout as the main document (Figure 5–66).

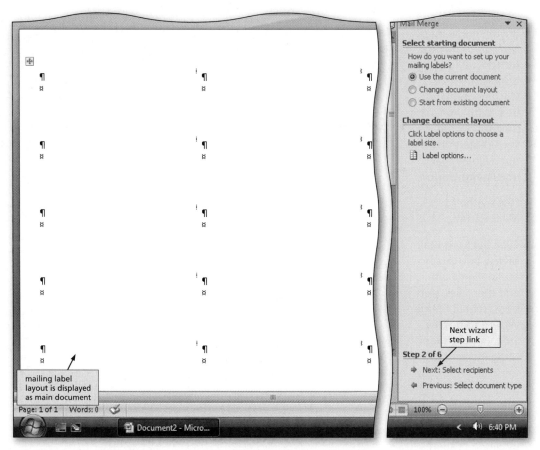

Figure 5–66

- Click the 'Next wizard step' link at the bottom of the Mail Merge task pane to display Step 3 of the Mail Merge wizard, which allows you to select the data source.

- If necessary, click 'Use an existing list' in the Select recipients area.

- Click the 'Select recipient list file' link to display the Select Data Source dialog box.

- If necessary, locate and select the USB flash drive and then double-click the Total Fitness folder to select it.

- Click the file name, Health Club Members, to select the data source you created earlier in the chapter (Figure 5–67).

Q&A Why did Word initially open the All Data Sources folder in the Select Data Source dialog box?

The All Data Sources folder is the default folder for storing data source files. Word looks in that folder first for an existing data source.

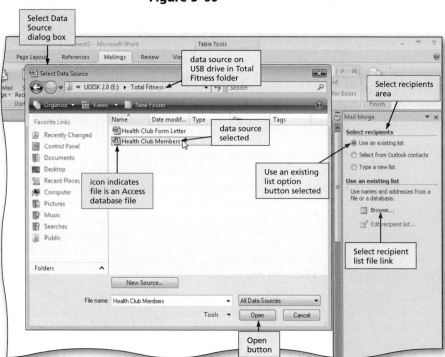

Figure 5–67

5

- Click the Open button to display the Mail Merge Recipients dialog box (Figure 5–68).

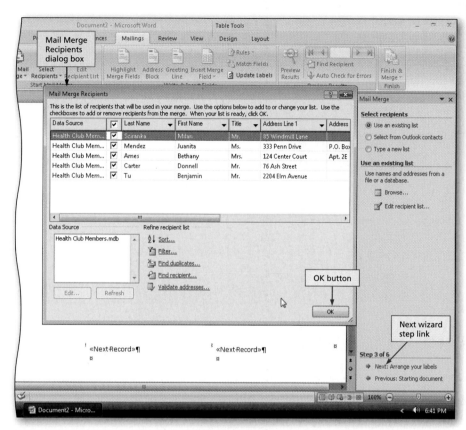

Figure 5–68

6

- Click the OK button to close the dialog box.

- At the bottom of the Mail Merge task pane, click the 'Next wizard step' link to display Step 4 of the Mail Merge wizard in the Mail Merge task pane.

- In the Mail Merge task pane, click the 'Insert formatted address' link to display the Insert Address Block dialog box (Figure 5–69).

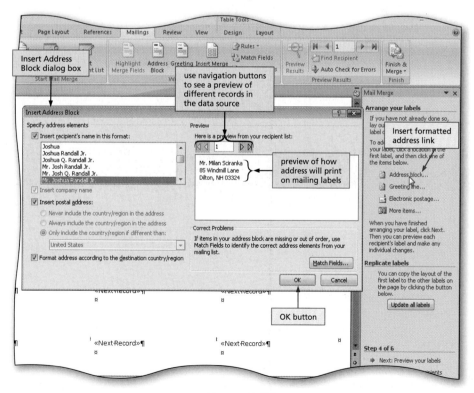

Figure 5–69

- Click the OK button to close the dialog box and insert the AddressBlock mail merge field in the first label of the main document (Figure 5–70).

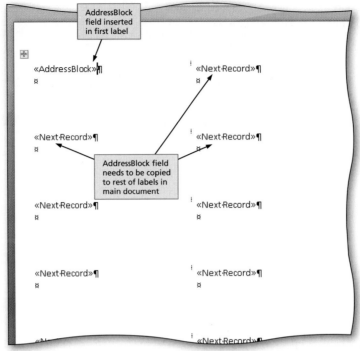

Figure 5–70

- Click the 'Update all labels' button to copy the layout of the first label to the remaining label layouts in the main document (Figure 5–71).

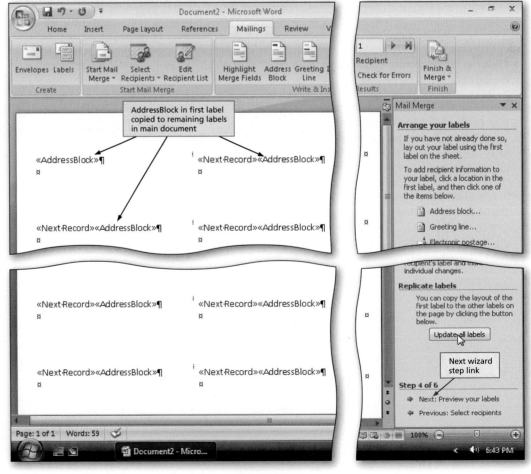

Figure 5–71

9

- Click the 'Next wizard step' link at the bottom of the Mail Merge task pane to display Step 5 of the Mail Merge wizard, which shows a preview of the mailing labels in the document window (Figure 5–72).

Q&A

What if I do not want a blank space between each line in the printed mailing addresses?

You would select all the mailing labels by pressing CTRL+A and then change the Spacing Before to 0 pt on the Page Layout tab.

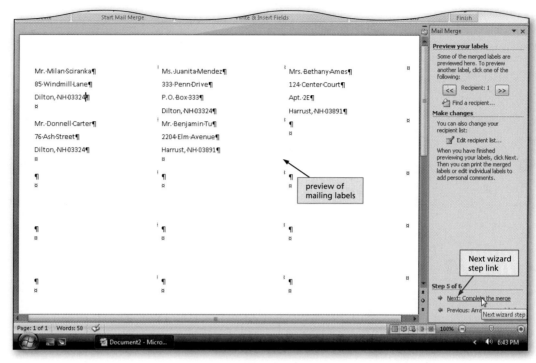

Figure 5–72

10

- Click the 'Next wizard step' link at the bottom of the Mail Merge task pane to display Step 6 of the Mail Merge wizard.

- In the Mail Merge task pane, click the 'Merge to printer' link to display the Merge to Printer dialog box (Figure 5–73).

- If necessary, click All in the dialog box so that all records in the data source will be included in the merge.

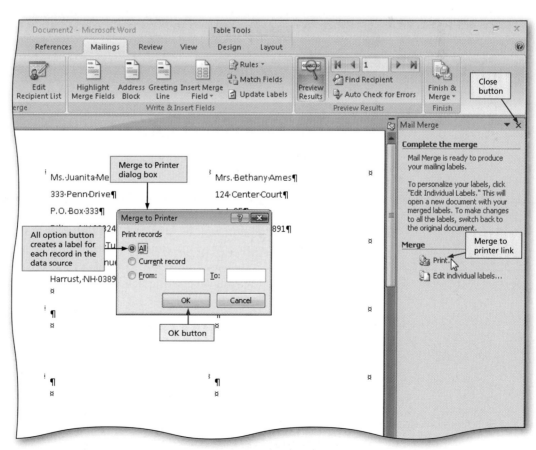

Figure 5–73

- If necessary, insert a sheet of blank mailing labels in the printer.

- Click the OK button to display the Print dialog box.

- Click the OK button in the Print dialog box to print the mailing labels (Figure 5–74).

- Click the Close button at the right edge of the Mail Merge task pane.

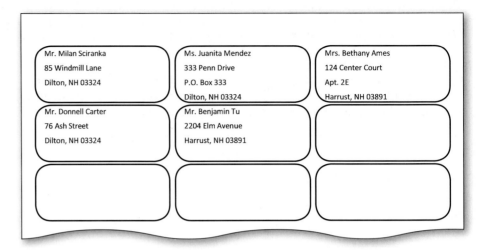

Mr. Milan Sciranka
85 Windmill Lane
Dilton, NH 03324

Ms. Juanita Mendez
333 Penn Drive
P.O. Box 333
Dilton, NH 03324

Mrs. Bethany Ames
124 Center Court
Apt. 2E
Harrust, NH 03891

Mr. Donnell Carter
76 Ash Street
Dilton, NH 03324

Mr. Benjamin Tu
2204 Elm Avenue
Harrust, NH 03891

Figure 5–74

To Save the Mailing Labels

The following steps save the mailing labels.

1 With a USB flash drive connected to one of the computer's USB ports, click the Save button on the Quick Access Toolbar to display the Save As dialog box.

2 Type `Health Club Mailing Labels` in the File name text box to change the file name.

3 If necessary, locate and select your USB flash drive in the list of available drives and then double-click the Total Fitness folder to open the folder.

4 Click the Save button in the Save As dialog box to save the document in the Total Fitness folder on the USB flash drive with the file name, Health Club Mailing Labels.

To Address and Print Envelopes Using an Existing Data Source

Instead of addressing mailing labels to affix to envelopes, your printer may have the capability of printing directly on envelopes. To print the address information directly on envelopes, follow the same basic steps as you did to address the mailing labels. The following steps address envelopes using an existing data source.

Note: If your printer does not have the capability of printing envelopes, skip these steps and proceed to the next section titled, Merging All Data Records to a Directory. If you are in a laboratory environment, ask your instructor if you should perform these steps or skip them.

1 Display the Office Button menu. Click New on the Office Button menu to display the New Document dialog box. With Blank document selected, click the Create button to open a new blank document window.

2 Click the Start Mail Merge button on the Mailings tab and then click Step by Step Mail Merge Wizard to display Step 1 of the Mail Merge wizard in the Mail Merge task pane. Specify envelopes as the main document type by clicking Envelopes in the 'Select document type' area.

3 Click the 'Next wizard step' link at the bottom of the Mail Merge task pane to display Step 2 of the Mail Merge wizard. In the Mail Merge task pane, click the Set Envelope Options link to display the Envelope Options dialog box.

4 Select the envelope size and then click the OK button in the Envelope Options dialog box, which displays the selected envelope layout as the main document.

5 If your envelope does not have a pre-printed return address, position the insertion point in the upper-left corner of the envelope layout and then type a return address.

6 Click the 'Next wizard step' link at the bottom of the Mail Merge task pane to display Step 3 of the Mail Merge wizard, which allows you to select the data source. If necessary, click 'Use an existing list' in the Select recipients area. Click the 'Select recipient list file' link to display the Select Data Source dialog box. If necessary, locate and select the USB flash drive and then double-click the Total Fitness folder to select it. Click the file name, Health Club Members, to select the data source you created earlier in the chapter. Click the Open button, which displays the Mail Merge Recipients dialog box, and then click the OK button to close the dialog box. At the bottom of the Mail Merge task pane, click the 'Next wizard step' link to display Step 4 of the Mail Merge wizard in the Mail Merge task pane.

7 Position the insertion point in the middle of the envelope. In the Mail Merge task pane, click the 'Insert formatted address' link to display the Insert Address Block dialog box. Click the OK button to close the dialog box and insert the AddressBlock mail merge field in the envelope layout of the main document (Figure 5–75).

8 Click the 'Next wizard step' link at the bottom of the Mail Merge task pane to display Step 5 of the Mail Merge wizard, which shows a preview of an envelope in the document window.

9 Click the 'Next wizard step' link at the bottom of the Mail Merge task pane to display Step 6 of the Mail Merge wizard. In the Mail Merge task pane, click the 'Merge to printer' link to display the Merge to Printer dialog box. If necessary, click All in the dialog box so that all records in the data source will be included in the merge.

10 If necessary, insert blank envelopes in the printer. Click the OK button to display the Print dialog box. Click the OK button in the Print dialog box to print the address on the envelopes. Click the Close button at the right edge of the Mail Merge task pane.

BTW

AddressBlock Merge Field
Another way to insert the AddressBlock merge field in a document is to click the Address Block button on the Mailings tab.

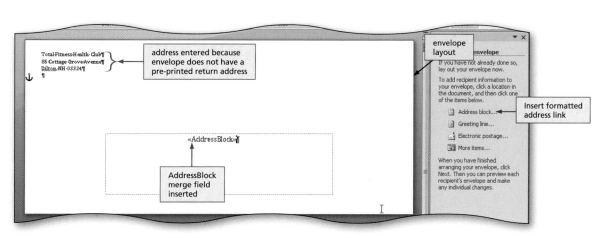

Figure 5–75

To Save the Envelopes

The following steps save the envelopes.

1 With a USB flash drive connected to one of the computer's USB ports, click the Save button on the Quick Access Toolbar to display the Save As dialog box.

2 Type `Health Club Envelopes` in the File name text box to change the file name.

3 If necessary, locate and select your USB flash drive in the list of available drives and then double-click the Total Fitness folder to open the folder.

4 Click the Save button in the Save As dialog box to save the document in the Total Fitness folder on the USB flash drive with the file name, Health Club Envelopes.

Merging All Data Records to a Directory

You may want to print the data records in the data source. Recall that the data source is saved as a Microsoft Access database table. Thus, you cannot open the data source in Word. To view the data source, you click the Edit Recipient List button on the Mailings tab, which displays the Mail Merge Recipients dialog box. This dialog box, however, does not have a Print button.

When you merge to a directory, the default organization of a directory places each record one after next, similar to the look of entries in a telephone book. The directory in this chapter is more organized with the rows and columns divided and field names placed above each column (shown in Figure 5–1b on page WD 307). To accomplish this look, the following steps are required:

1. Create a directory, placing a separating character between each merge field.
2. Convert the directory to a table, using the separator character as the identifier for each new column.
3. Change the page orientation from portrait to landscape, so that all records fit across one row.
4. Merge the directory to a new document, which creates a table of all records in the data source.
5. Format the table containing the directory.
6. Sort the table by last name, so that it is easy to locate a particular record.

To Merge to a Directory

One way to print the contents of the data source is to merge all data records in the data source into a single document, called a **directory**. That is, a directory does not merge each data record to a separate document; instead, a directory lists all records together in a single document. The next steps merge the data records in the data source to a directory. For illustration purposes, these steps use the buttons on the Mailings tab rather than using the Mail Merge task pane.

- Display the Office Button menu and then click New to display the New Document dialog box. With Blank document selected, click the Create button to open a new blank document window.

- Display the Mailings tab.

- Click the Start Mail Merge button on the Mailings tab to display the Start Mail Merge menu (Figure 5–76).

2

- Click Directory as the main document type.

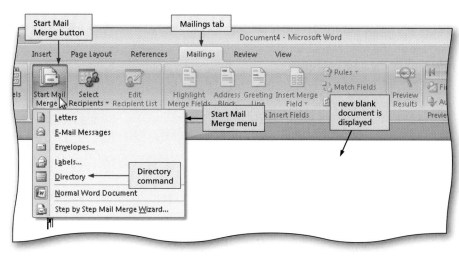

Figure 5–76

3

- Click the Select Recipients button on the Mailings tab to display the Select Recipients menu (Figure 5–77).

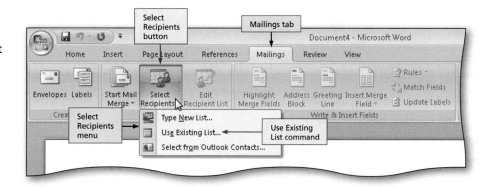

Figure 5–77

- Click Use Existing List on the Select Recipients menu to display the Select Data Source dialog box.

- If necessary, locate and select the USB flash drive and then double-click the Total Fitness folder to select it.

- Click the file name, Health Club Members, to select the data source you created earlier in the chapter (Figure 5–78).

5

- Click the Open button to associate the selected data source with the current main document.

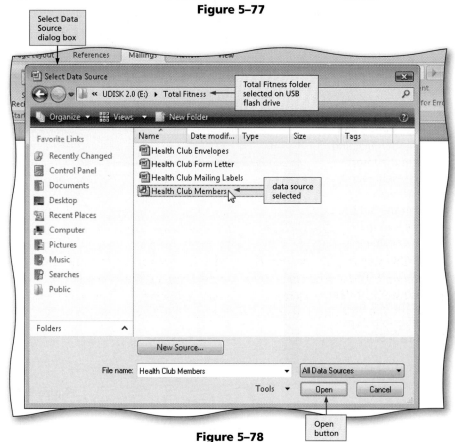

Figure 5–78

6

- Click the Insert Merge Field button arrow on the Mail Merge toolbar to display the Insert Merge Field menu (Figure 5–79).

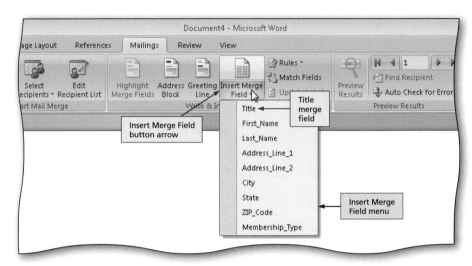

Figure 5–79

7

- Click Title on the Insert Merge Field menu to insert the merge field in the document.

- Press the HYPHEN (-) key to place the hyphen character after the inserted merge field (Figure 5–80).

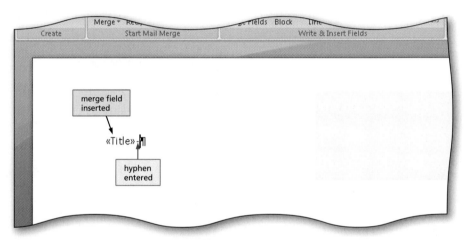

Figure 5–80

8

- Repeat Steps 6 and 7 for each remaining field in the Insert Merge Field menu, so that every field in the data source is in the main document separated by a hyphen, except do not put a hyphen after the last field: Membership_Type (Figure 5–81).

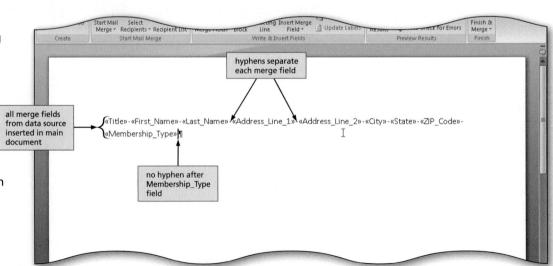

Figure 5–81

To Convert Text to a Table

If you merge the records now, they will print in one long list, one record below the next. Instead of a long list, you want each data record to be in a single row and each merge field to be in a column. That is, you want the directory to be in a table form. The following steps convert the text containing the merge fields to a table.

1

- Press CTRL+A to select the entire document, because you want all document contents to be converted to a table.

- Display the Insert tab.

- Click the Table button on the Insert tab to display the Table gallery (Figure 5–82).

Q&A

Can I convert a section of a document to table?

Yes, simply select the characters, lines, or paragraphs to be converted before displaying the Convert Text to Table dialog box.

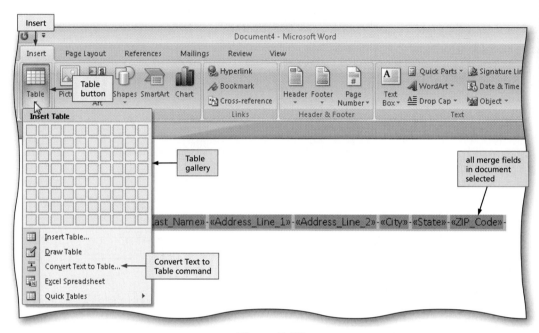

Figure 5–82

2

- Click Convert Text to Table to display the Convert Text to Table dialog box.

- If necessary, type 9 in the Number of columns box because the resulting table should have 9 columns.

- If necessary, click Other in the 'Separate text at' area and then type a hyphen (-) in the text box (Figure 5–83).

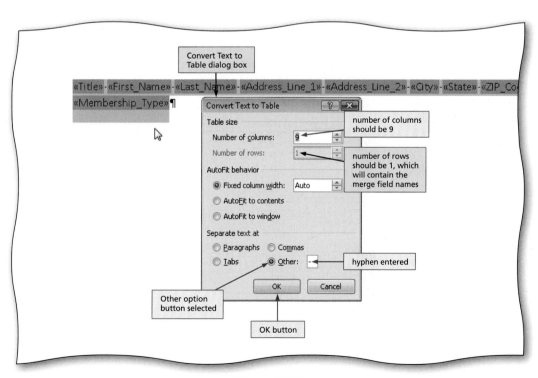

Figure 5–83

3

- Click the OK button to convert the selected text (the merge fields) to a table (Figure 5–84).

Q&A

Can I format the table?

Yes. You can use any of the commands on the Table Tools subordinate tabs to change the look of the table.

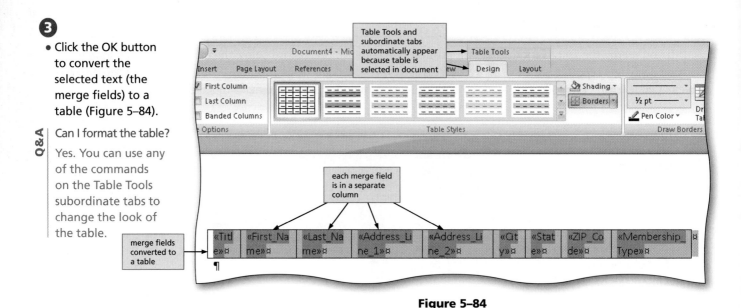

Figure 5–84

To Change Page Orientation

Notice in Figure 5–84 that none of the merge field names fit across the width of their columns. That is, they wrap to a second line. This is because the contents of the cells are too wide to fit on a piece of paper in portrait orientation. When a document is in **portrait orientation**, the short edge of the paper is the top of the document. You can instruct Word to layout a document in **landscape orientation**, so that the long edge of the paper is the top of the document. The following steps change the orientation of the document from portrait to landscape.

1

- Display the Page Layout tab.

- Click the Page Orientation button on the Page Layout tab to display the Page Orientation gallery (Figure 5–85).

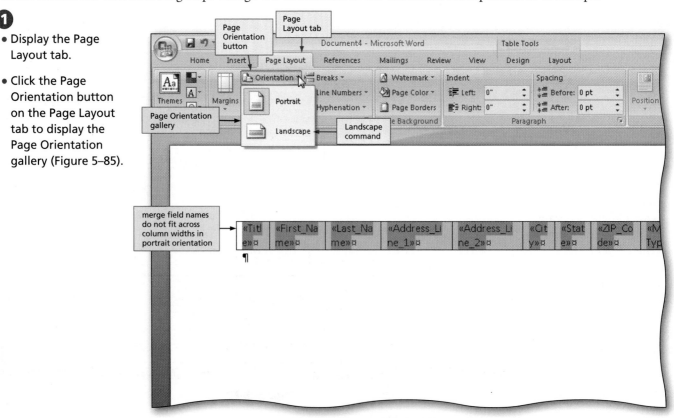

Figure 5–85

2

- Click Landscape in the Page Orientation gallery to change the page orientation to landscape (Figure 5–86).

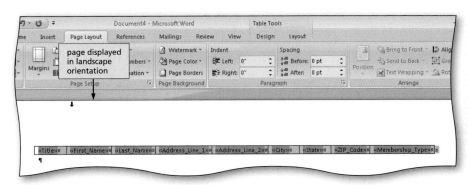

Figure 5–86

To Merge to a New Document Window

The next step is to merge the data source and the directory main document to a new document window, so that you can edit the resulting document. The following steps merge to a new document window.

1

- Display the Mailings tab.

- Click the Finish & Merge button on the Mailings tab to display the Finish & Merge menu (Figure 5–87).

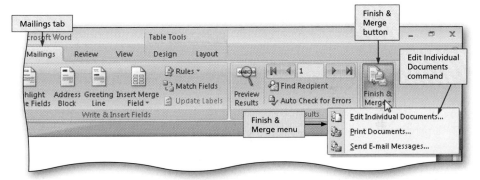

Figure 5–87

2

- Click Edit Individual Documents on the Finish & Merge menu to display the Merge to New Document dialog box.

- If necessary, click All in the dialog box.

- Click the OK button to merge the data records to a directory in a new document window (Figure 5–88).

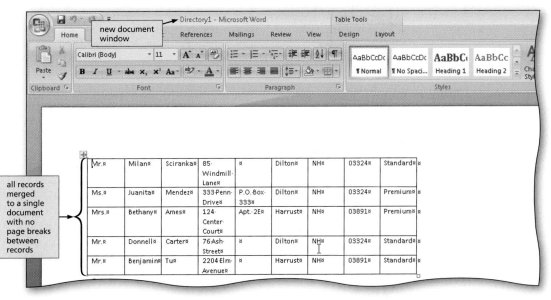

Figure 5–88

To Modify and Format a Table

The table would be more descriptive if the field names were displayed in a row above the actual data. The following steps add a row to the top of a table and format the data in the new row.

1 Add a row to the top of the table by positioning the insertion point in the first row of the table and then clicking the Insert Rows Above button on the Layout tab.

2 Click in the first (leftmost) cell of the new row. Type `Title` and then press the TAB key. Type `First Name` and then press the TAB key. Type `Last Name` and then press the TAB key. Type `Address Line 1` and then press the TAB key. Type `Address Line 2` and then press the TAB key. Type `City` and then press the TAB key. Type `State` and then press the TAB key. Type `ZIP Code` and then press the TAB key. Type `Membership Type` as the last entry in the row.

3 Make all columns as wide as their contents using the AutoFit Contents command.

To Modify Table Properties

The next step is to increase the left and right margin in each cell of the table and place a .05-inch space between each cell, so that the table is easier to read. To make these changes, you use the Table Properties dialog box. You also can center the table between the left and right margins in this dialog box. The following steps use the Table Properties dialog box.

- Click the Table Properties button on the Layout tab to display the Table Properties dialog box.

- Click the Options button to display the Table Options dialog box.

- Click the Left box up arrow until 0.15" is displayed in the Left text box.

- Click the Right box up arrow until 0.15" is displayed in the Right text box.

- Place a check mark in the 'Allow spacing between cells' check box and then click the up arrow until 0.05" is displayed in this text box (Figure 5–89).

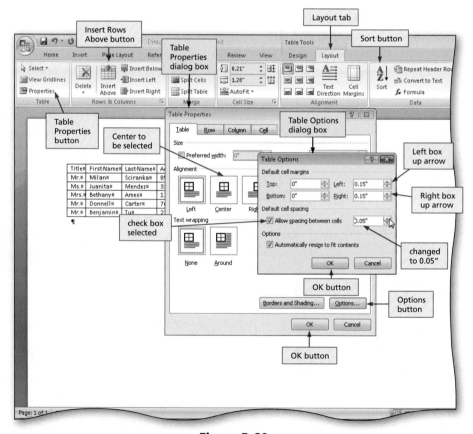

Figure 5–89

2

- Click the OK button to close the Table Options dialog box.

- Click Center in the Alignment area.

- Click the OK button to apply the modified properties to the table (Figure 5–90).

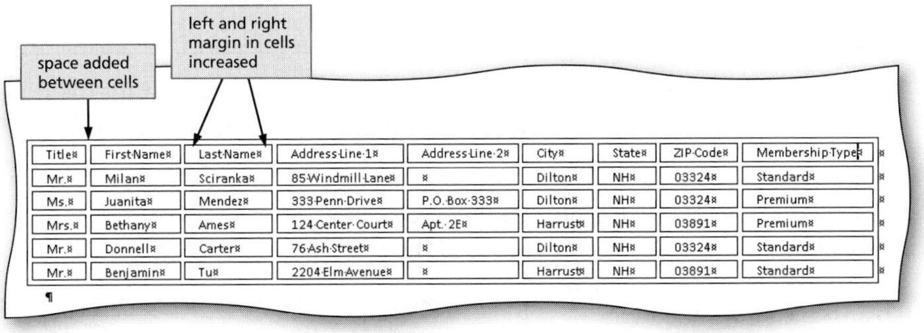

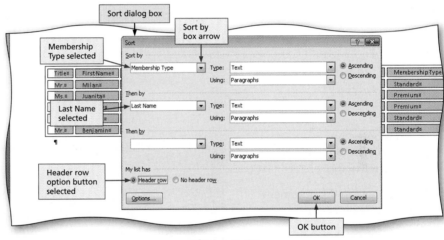

Figure 5–90

Other Ways

1. Right-click table, click Table Properties on shortcut menu

To Sort a Table

The next step is to sort the table. In this project, the table records are displayed in membership type order. Within each membership type, the records should be sorted by club member last name. The following steps sort a table.

1

- Click the Sort button on the Layout tab (shown in Figure 5–89) to display the Sort dialog box.

- Click Header row so that the first row is left in its current location when the table is sorted.

- Click the Sort by box arrow; scroll to and then click Membership Type.

- Click the first Then by box arrow and then click Last Name (Figure 5–91).

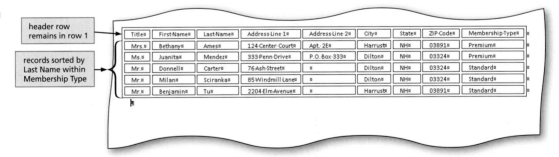

Figure 5–91

2

- Click the OK button to sort the records in the table in ascending Last Name order within ascending Membership Type order (Figure 5–92).

Q&A

What does ascending mean?

With the Last Name and Membership Type data, ascending means alphabetical. With the dates, ascending means the earliest date is at the top of the list, and for numbers, ascending order puts the smallest numbers first.

Figure 5–92

To Format Text as Hidden

You want to add a note to the top of this table, but do not want the note to print. To do this, you format the text as hidden. The following steps enter text and then format it as hidden.

1

- Click in the top-left corner of the table and then press the ENTER key to position the insertion point on a blank line above the table.

- Type `Table last updated on May 28.`

- Select the text just entered above the table.

- Click Font Dialog Box Launcher to display the Font dialog box. If necessary, click the Font tab.

- In the Effects area, click Hidden (Figure 5–93).

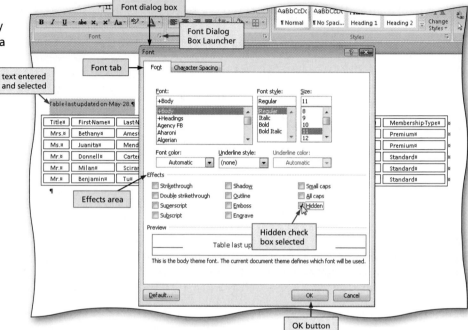

Figure 5–93

2

- Click the OK button to apply the hidden effect to the selected text.

- Click anywhere in the document to remove the highlight (Figure 5–94).

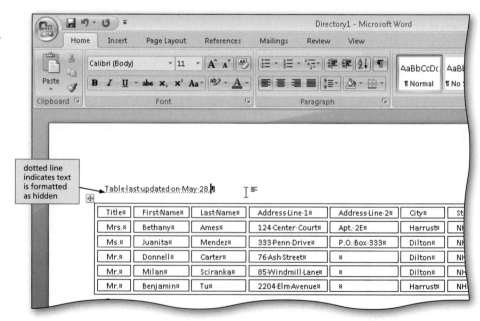

Figure 5–94

Other Ways

1. Right-click selected text, click Font on shortcut menu, click Font tab, click Hidden, click OK button

To Hide Hidden Text

Hidden text appears on the screen only when the Show/Hide ¶ button on the Home tab is selected. The following step hides text formatted as hidden.

1

- If the Show/Hide ¶ button on the Home tab is selected, click it to deselect it (Figure 5–95).

How do I show the hidden text again?

Click the Show/Hide ¶ button on the Home tab again.

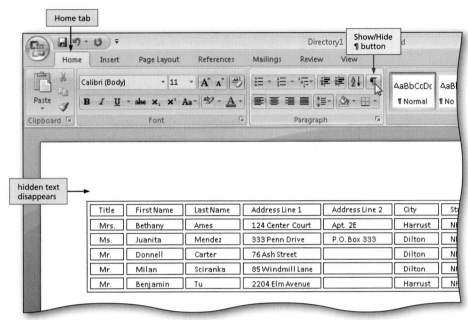

Figure 5–95

Other Ways

1. Press CTRL+SHIFT+*

To Print a Document

The following step prints the directory in landscape orientation.

1 Display the Office Button menu, point to Print, and then click the Quick Print button on the Home tab to print the directory in landscape orientation (Figure 5–96).

If Microsoft Access is installed on my computer, can I use that to print the data source?

As an alternative to merging to a directory and printing the results, if you are familiar with Microsoft Access and it is installed on your computer, you can open and print the data source in Access.

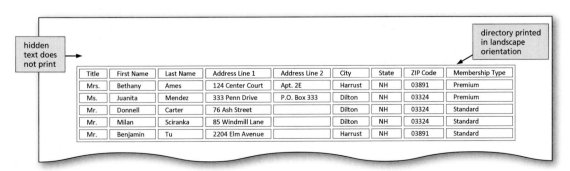

Figure 5–96

To Save the Directory

The following steps save the directory.

1 With a USB flash drive connected to one of the computer's USB ports, click the Save button on the Quick Access Toolbar to display the Save As dialog box.

2 Type `Health Club Member Directory` in the File name text box to change the file name.

3 If necessary, locate and select your USB flash drive in the list of available drives and then double-click the Total Fitness folder to open the folder.

4 Click the Save button in the Save As dialog box to save the document in the Total Fitness folder on the USB flash drive with the file name, Health Club Member Directory.

To Quit Word

The following steps close all open documents and quit Word.

1 Display the Office Button menu and then click the Exit Word button to close all open documents and quit Word.

2 When Word asks if you want to save the document used to create the directory, click the No button. For all other documents, click the Yes button to save the changes.

Opening a Main Document

You open a main document as you open any other Word document (i.e., clicking Open on the Office Button menu). If Word displays a dialog box indicating it will run an SQL command, click the Yes button (Figure 5–97).

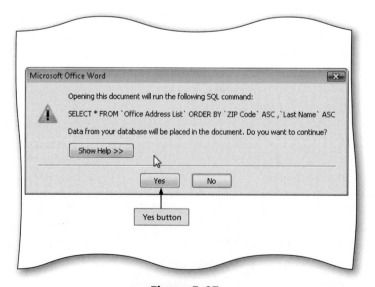

Figure 5–97

Converting Main Document Files
If you wanted to convert a mail merge main document to a regular Word document, you would open the main document, click the Start Mail Merge button on the Mailings tab, and then click Normal Word Document on the Start Mail Merge menu.

When you open a main document, Word attempts to open the associated data source file, too. If the data source is not in exactly the same location (i.e., drive and folder) as when it originally was saved, Word displays a dialog box indicating that it could not find the data source (Figure 5–98). When this occurs, click the Find Data Source button to display the Open Data Source dialog box, which allows you to locate the data source file.

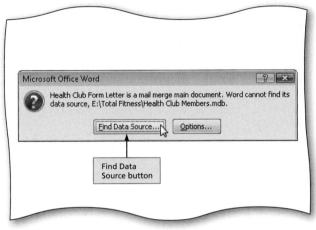

Figure 5–98

Chapter Summary

In this chapter, you have learned how to create and print form letters, create a data source, insert and format shapes, create a multilevel list, address mailing labels and envelopes from a data source, and merge to a directory. The items listed below include all the new Word skills you have learned in this chapter.

1. Identify the Main Document for the Form Letter Using the Task Pane (WD 308)
2. Change the User Name and Initials (WD 312)
3. Change the Margin Settings (WD 313)
4. Insert a Drawing Canvas (WD 314)
5. Insert a Shape (WD 316)
6. Apply a Shape Style (WD 318)
7. Add Formatted Text to a Shape (WD 319)
8. Resize a Drawing Canvas (WD 320)
9. Create a Folder while Saving (WD 321)
10. Create a New Data Source (WD 323)
11. Save the Data Source when Prompted by Word (WD 328)
12. Enter the Date (WD 330)
13. Edit the GreetingLine Merge Field (WD 332)
14. Insert a Merge Field in the Main Document (WD 333)
15. Create a Multilevel List (WD 335)
16. Insert an IF Field in the Main Document (WD 338)
17. Display a Field Code (WD 341)
18. Print Field Codes in the Main Document (WD 342)
19. Merge the Form Letters to the Printer (WD 344)
20. Merge to a New Document Window (WD 345, WD 363)
21. Select Records to Merge (WD 345)
22. Remove a Merge Condition (WD 348)
23. Sort the Data Records in a Data Source (WD 348)
24. View Merged Data in the Main Document (WD 349)
25. Address and Print Mailing Labels Using an Existing Data Source (WD 350)
26. Address and Print Envelopes Using an Existing Data Source (WD 356)
27. Merge to a Directory (WD 358)
28. Convert Text to a Table (WD 361)
29. Change Page Orientation (WD 362)
30. Modify Table Properties (WD 364)
31. Sort a Table (WD 365)
32. Format Text as Hidden (WD 366)
33. Hide Hidden Text (WD 367)

Learn It Online

Test your knowledge of chapter content and key terms.

Instructions: To complete the Learn It Online exercises, start your browser, click the Address bar, and then enter the Web address `scsite.com/wd2007/learn`. When the Word 2007 Learn It Online page is displayed, click the link for the exercise you want to complete and then read the instructions.

Chapter Reinforcement TF, MC, and SA
A series of true/false, multiple choice, and short answer questions that test your knowledge of the chapter content.

Flash Cards
An interactive learning environment where you identify chapter key terms associated with displayed definitions.

Practice Test
A series of multiple choice questions that test your knowledge of chapter content and key terms.

Who Wants To Be a Computer Genius?
An interactive game that challenges your knowledge of chapter content in the style of a television quiz show.

Wheel of Terms
An interactive game that challenges your knowledge of chapter key terms in the style of the television show *Wheel of Fortune*.

Crossword Puzzle Challenge
A crossword puzzle that challenges your knowledge of key terms presented in the chapter.

Apply Your Knowledge

Reinforce the skills and apply the concepts you learned in this chapter.

Working with a Form Letter
Instructions: Start Word. Open the document, Apply 5-1 Green Grove Form Letter, from the Data Files for Students. See the inside back cover of this book for instructions on downloading the Data Files for Students, or contact your instructor for information about accessing the required files. When you open the main document, if Word displays a dialog box about an SQL command, click the Yes button. If Word prompts for the name of the data source, select Apply 5-1 Green Grove Customers on the Data Files for Students.

The document is a main document for a Green Grove form letter. You are to edit the greeting line field, print the form letter with field codes displaying, add a record to the data source, and then merge the form letters to a file.

Perform the following tasks:
1. Edit the date content control so that it contains the date 1/15/2008.
2. Edit the GreetingLine merge field so that the salutation ends with a colon (:).
3. Save the modified main document for the form letter with the name Apply 5-1 Green Grove Format Letter Modified.
4. View merged data in the document. Use the navigation buttons in the Preview Results group to display merged data from various records in the data source. What is the last name of the first record? The third record? The fifth record?
5. Print the form letter by clicking the Office Button, pointing to Print, and then clicking Quick Print (Figure 5–99).

Green Grove Nursery

1/15/2008   *Order online at www.greengrove.com today!*

«AddressBlock»

«GreetingLine»

Thank you for your order from our early spring catalog. Your «Item» will be delivered in time for spring planting in zone «Zone».

Your shipment will include all items ordered, detailed planting and care instructions, and – because you ordered before February 1 – your free gift. Also enclosed is a spring/summer catalog that contains a $10 coupon for use on your next order.

Green Grove Nursery strives to provide the highest-quality specimens available commercially. If for any reason you are unhappy with your order, contact us for replacement plants or a full refund.

Sincerely,

Keesha Wills
Customer Order Specialist

Figure 5–99

6. Print the form letter with field codes, that is, with the 'Print field codes instead of their values' check box selected. Be sure to deselect this check box after printing the field codes version of the letter. How does this printout differ from the one in Instruction #5?

Continued >

Apply Your Knowledge *continued*

7. Add a record to the data source that contains your personal information. Type hostas in the Item field and 2 in the Zone field. *Hint*: Click the Edit Recipient List button; click the data source name, Apply 5-1 Green Grove Customers in the Data Source area of the Mail Merge Recipients dialog box; and then click the Edit button in the Mail Merge Recipients dialog box.

8. In the data source, change Regina Herrera's last name to Gonzales.

9. Sort the data source by the Last Name field.

10. Save the main document for the form letter again.

11. Use the navigation buttons in the Preview Results group to display merged data from various records in the data source. What is the last name of the first record? The third record? The fifth record?

12. Merge the form letters to a new document. Save the new document with the name Apply 5-1 Green Grove Merged Form Letters. Print the document containing the merged form letters.

13. Merge the form letters directly to the printer.

Extend Your Knowledge

Extend the skills you learned in this chapter and experiment with new skills. You may need to use Help to complete the assignment.

Working with Word Fields and Multilevel Lists

Instructions: Start Word. Open the document, Extend 5-1 Far Horizons Form Letter, from the Data Files for Students. See the inside back cover of this book for instructions on downloading the Data Files for Students, or contact your instructor for information about accessing the required files. When you open the main document, if Word displays a dialog box about an SQL command, click the Yes button. If Word prompts for the name of the data source, select Extend 5-1 Far Horizons Customers on the Data Files for Students.

The document is a main document for a Far Horizons form letter (Figure 5–100). You will change the margins, change the shape, change the numbering format in the multilevel list, add a field to the data source, modify an IF field, and add a Fill-in field.

Perform the following tasks:

1. Use Help to learn about margins, shapes, multilevel lists, mail merge, IF fields, and Fill-in fields.

2. Change the top margin to 0.5" (one-half inch).

3. Change the shape at the top of the letter. *Hint*: Click the Change Shape button on the Text Box Tools Format tab.

4. Change the color of the shape. Add a shadow effect to the shape. Change the color of the shadow.

5. Change the numbering format of the multilevel list.

6. Add a field to the data source called Cruise Type. Enter field values for each record, i.e., Alaskan, Caribbean, etc.

7. In the first sentence and also in the last sentence of the main document, insert the new field called Cruise Type, just before the word, cruise.

8. Edit the IF field so that two-berth cabins cost $700. *Hint*: Display the IF field code in the document window and edit the IF field directly in the document.

9. At the bottom of the document, just above the horizontal line, insert a Fill-in field, so that you can type a different personalized note to each customer. When you merge the letters, type an appropriate note to each customer. The notes should be meaningful to the recipient, such as related to their local sports team, weather, a recent telephone call, etc.

10. Print the form letter by clicking the Office Button, pointing to Print, and then clicking Quick Print.

11. Print the form letter with field codes, that is, with the 'Print field codes instead of their values' check box selected. Be sure to deselect this check box after printing the field codes version of the letter. How does this printout differ from the one in Instruction #10?

12. Change the document properties, as specified by your instructor. Save the revised document using a new file name.

13. Merge the form letters to a new document and then submit it in the format specified by your instructor.

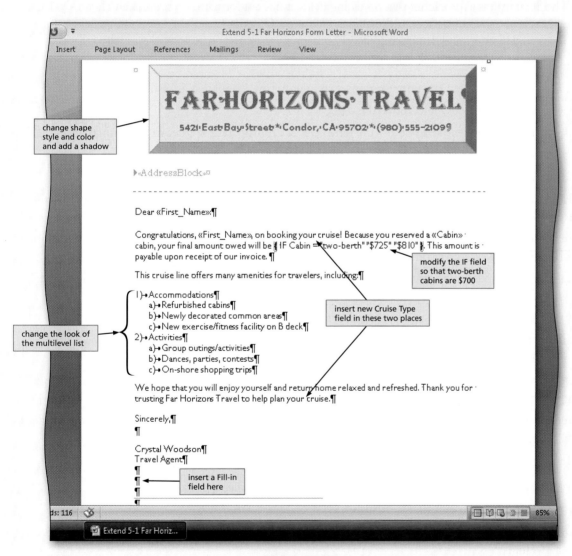

Figure 5–100

Make It Right

Analyze a document and correct all errors and/or improve the design.

Working with a Form Letter and Multilevel List

Instructions: Start Word. Open the document, Make It Right 5-1 Arrow Appliance Form Letter, from the Data Files for Students. See the inside back cover of this book for instructions on downloading the Data Files for Students, or contact your instructor for information about accessing the required files. When you open the main document, if Word displays a dialog box about an SQL command, click the Yes button. If Word prompts for the name of the data source, select Make It Right 5-1 Arrow Appliance Customers on the Data Files for Students.

The document is a form letter that is missing fields and is not formatted appropriately (Figure 5–101). You are to resize the shape, insert an AddressBlock field and a GreetingLine field, insert merge fields, switch merge fields, and promote and demote multilevel list items.

Perform the following tasks:

1. Resize the shape so that the entire company name, Arrow Appliance, is visible.
2. Insert the AddressBlock field above the date.
3. Insert the GreetingLine field below the date. Use an appropriate salutation and punctuation.
4. The end of the first sentence is missing the merge field, Appliance.
5. In the second sentence, remove the ZIP Code field.
6. In the third sentence of the first paragraph, the two merge fields for Term and Appliance should be reversed.
7. Format the multilevel list so that it is more organized. It should have two levels. You will need to demote some levels and promote others. Sort the list within each level.
8. In the data source, find the record whose last name is Franc. Fix the State and ZIP Code entries in this record.
9. In the data source, find the misspelling dryr and correct its spelling to dryer.
10. Change the document properties, as specified by your instructor. Save the revised document using a new file name.
11. Specify that only customers who purchased a refrigerator should be included in a merge. Merge these form letters to the printer. Clear the filter.
12. Identify another type of filter for this data source and merge those form letters to a new document. On the printout, write down the filter you used.
13. Merge all the records to a new document in last name order.

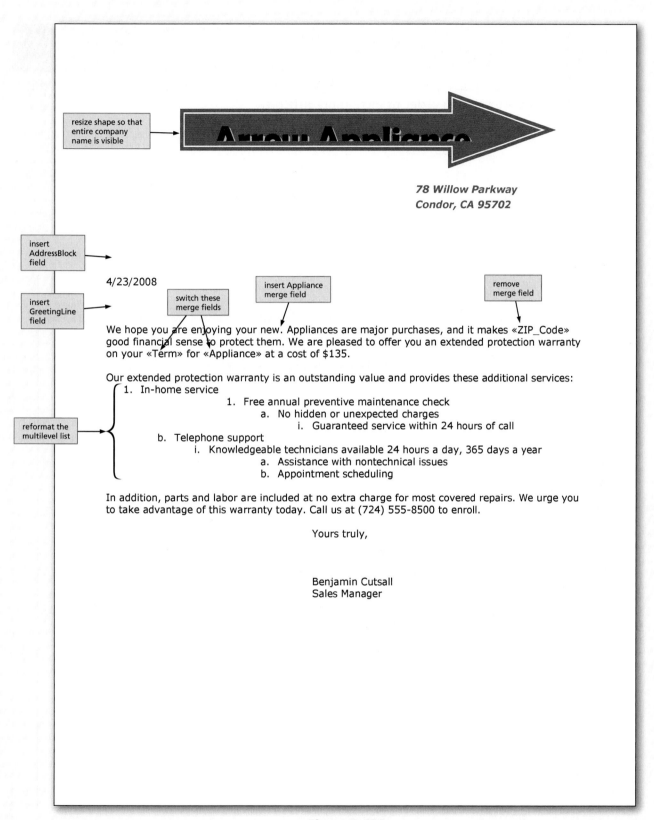

resize shape so that entire company name is visible

Arrow Appliance

78 Willow Parkway
Condor, CA 95702

insert AddressBlock field

4/23/2008

insert GreetingLine field

switch these merge fields

insert Appliance merge field

remove merge field

We hope you are enjoying your new. Appliances are major purchases, and it makes «ZIP_Code» good financial sense to protect them. We are pleased to offer you an extended protection warranty on your «Term» for «Appliance» at a cost of $135.

Our extended protection warranty is an outstanding value and provides these additional services:

reformat the multilevel list

1. In-home service
    1. Free annual preventive maintenance check
        a. No hidden or unexpected charges
            i. Guaranteed service within 24 hours of call
    b. Telephone support
        i. Knowledgeable technicians available 24 hours a day, 365 days a year
            a. Assistance with nontechnical issues
            b. Appointment scheduling

In addition, parts and labor are included at no extra charge for most covered repairs. We urge you to take advantage of this warranty today. Call us at (724) 555-8500 to enroll.

Yours truly,

Benjamin Cutsall
Sales Manager

Figure 5–101

In the Lab

Design and/or create a document using the guidelines, concepts, and skills presented in this chapter. Labs are listed in order of increasing difficulty.

Lab 1: Creating a Form Letter Using a Template, a Data Source, Mailing Labels, and a Directory

Problem: The owner of Diamond Eye Care has asked you to send a letter to patients that are due for an eye exam. You decide to create the form letter shown in Figure 5–102a.

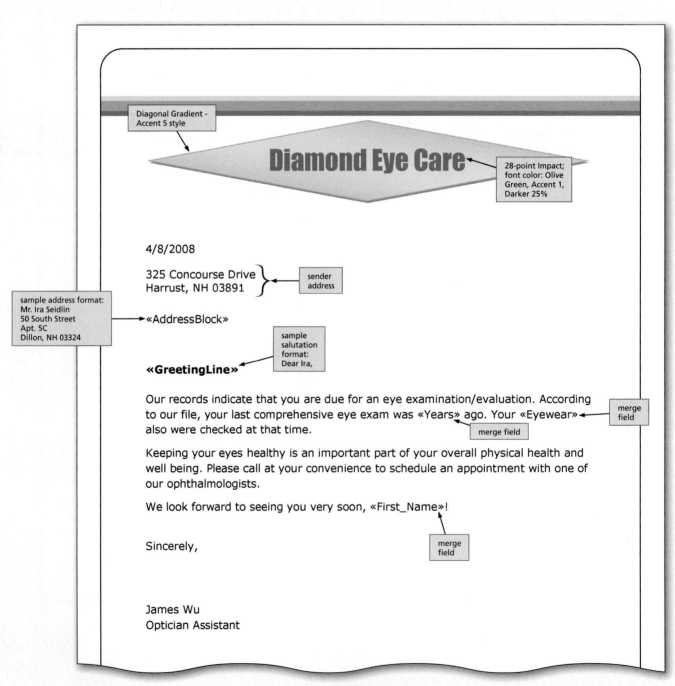

Figure 5–102 (a)

Perform the following tasks:

1. Use the Equity Merge Letter template to create a form letter.

2. Insert a drawing canvas and then a diamond shape inside the drawing canvas. Add text to and format the shape as shown in Figure 5-102a.

3. Type a new data source using the data shown in Figure 5–102b. Delete field names not used, and add two field names: Years and Eyewear. Save the data source with the file name, Lab 5-1 Diamond Eye Care Patients, in a folder called Lab 5-1 Diamond Eye Care. *Hint:* You will need to create the folder while saving.

Title	First Name	Last Name	Address Line 1	Address Line 2	City	State	ZIP Code	Years	Eyewear
Mr.	Ira	Seidlin	50 South Street	Apt. 5C	Dillon	NH	03324	two years	contacts
Mr.	Roberto	Abela	909 Pillston Ct.		Dillon	NH	03324	three years	glasses
Ms.	Leslie	Gerhard	2328 N. 128 Blvd.	Apt. 410	Harrust	NH	03891	two years	glasses
Ms.	Matilda	Jung	876 O'Toole Drive		Harrust	NH	03891	four years	contacts
Ms.	Emily	Stefanson	62 Harbor Ct.		Dillon	NH	03324	three years	contacts

Figure 5–102 (b)

4. Save the main document for the form letter with the file name, Lab 5-1 Diamond Eye Care Form Letter, in the folder called Lab 5-1 Diamond Eye Care. Compose the form letter for the main document as shown in Figure 5–102a. Insert the merge fields as shown in Figure 5–102a. Change the theme colors to Paper. Change the theme fonts to the Aspect font set.

5. Save the main document for the form letter again. Print the main document.

6. Merge the form letters to the printer.

7. In a new document window, address mailing labels using the same data source you used for the form letters. Save the mailing labels with the name, Lab 5-1 Diamond Eye Care Labels, in the Lab 5-1 Diamond Eye Care folder.

8. In a new document window, specify the main document type as a directory. Insert all merge fields in the document. Convert the list of fields to a Word table (the table will have 10 columns). Change the page layout to landscape orientation. Merge the directory layout to a new document window. Add a row to the top of the table and insert field names in the empty cells. Bold the text in the first row. Resize the columns so that the table columns look like Figure 5–102b. Add 0.05" between each table cell and center the table using the Table Properties dialog box.

9. Insert your name as text above the table. Format your name as hidden text. Hide the text on the screen. Then, reveal the text on the screen.

10. Save the directory with the name, Lab 5-1 Diamond Eye Care Directory, in the folder named Lab 5-1 Diamond Eye Care. Print the directory (your name should not print because it is hidden).

11. Sort the table in the directory by the Last Name field. Print the sorted directory.

STUDENT ASSIGNMENTS

In the Lab

Lab 2: Creating a Form Letter with an IF Field and a Multilevel List

Problem: As the president of the Athletic Booster Club, you send a letter to new members, thanking them for their support. You create the form letter shown in Figure 5–103a. The membership type will vary, depending on the donation amount.

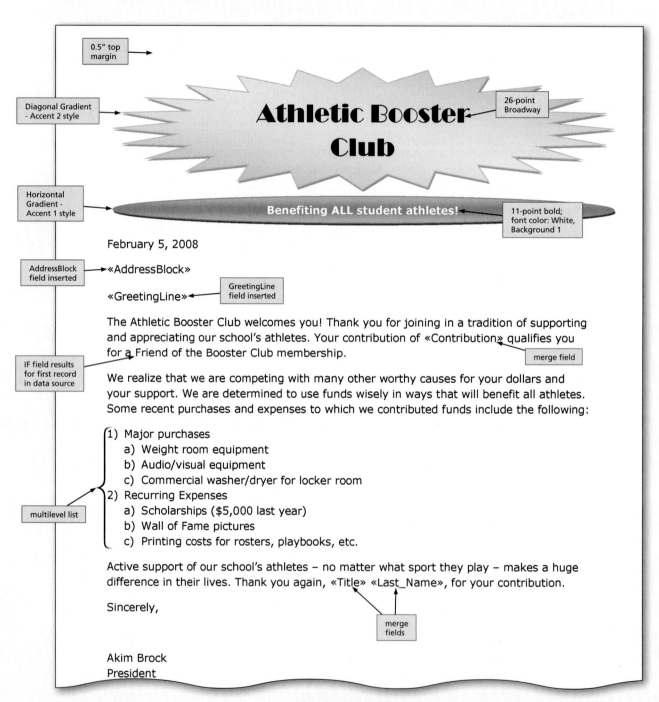

Figure 5–103 (a)

Perform the following tasks:

1. Do not use a template to create this form letter. Select 'Use the current document', which should be a blank document in the document window.

2. Insert a drawing canvas and then a 24-point star shape inside the drawing canvas. Also insert an oval shape in the drawing canvas below the star shape. Add text to and format the shapes as shown in Figure 5-103a.

3. Change the margins to Moderate (1-inch top and bottom; .75-inch left and right). Then, use the Custom Margins command to change the top margin to .5-inch.

4. Type a new data source using the data shown in Figure 5–103b. Delete field names not used, and add one field name: Contribution. Save the data source with the file name, Lab 5-2 Booster Club Members, in a folder called Lab 5-2 Booster Club. *Hint*: You will need to create the folder while saving.

Title	First Name	Last Name	Address Line 1	Address Line 2	City	State	ZIP Code	Contribution
Mr.	Adam	Willis	2445 Saren Lane	Apt. 402	Blackburg	TX	77490	$50.00
Ms.	Maxine	Tremain	8950 Treeway Ct.		Blackburg	TX	77490	$50.00
Ms.	Kim	Chung	5056 E. Fourth St.	Apt. 1A	Blackburg	TX	77490	$200.00
Mr.	David	Goldberg	17 South Street		Delman	TX	79006	$100.00
Mr.	Apurv	Patel	32 Fountain Square		Delman	TX	79006	$50.00

Figure 5–103 (b)

5. Save the main document for the form letter with the file name, Lab 5-2 Booster Club Form Letter, in the folder named Lab 5-2 Booster Club. Compose the form letter for the main document as shown in Figure 5–103a. Edit the GreetingLine field so that it shows a colon at the end of the salutation (e.g., Dear Mr. Willis:). Insert the merge fields as shown in the figure. Create the multilevel list as shown in the figure. Change the theme colors to Oriel. Change the theme fonts to the Aspect font set. The IF field tests if Contribution is less than or equal to 50; if it is, then print the text, Friend of the Booster Club; otherwise print the text, Super Booster.

6. Save the main document for the form letter again. Print the main document twice: once with field codes displaying and once without field codes.

7. Merge the form letters to the printer.

8. In a new document window, address mailing labels using the same data source you used for the form letters. Save the mailing labels with the name, Lab 5-2 Booster Club Labels, in the Lab 5-2 Booster Club folder. Merge and print the mailing labels.

9. If your printer allows and your instructor requests it, in a new document window, address envelopes using the same data source you used for the form letters. Save the envelopes with the file name, Lab 5-2 Booster Club Envelopes, in the folder named Lab 5-2 Booster Club. Merge and print the envelopes.

Continued >

STUDENT ASSIGNMENTS

In the Lab *continued*

10. In a new document window, specify the main document type as a directory. Insert all merge fields in the document. Convert the list of fields to a Word table (the table will have nine columns). Change the page layout to landscape orientation. Merge the directory layout to a new document window. Add a row to the top of the table and insert field names in the empty cells. Bold the text in the first row. Change the top, bottom, left, and right page margins to Narrow (one-half inch). Resize the columns so the table looks like Figure 5–103b on the previous page. Add 0.1" above and below each table cell and between each cell using the Table Properties dialog box. Center the table between the margins.

11. Insert your name as text above the table. Format your name as hidden text.

12. Save the directory with the name, Lab 5-2 Booster Club Directory, in the folder named Lab 5-2 Booster Club. Print the directory (your name should not print because it is hidden).

13. Sort the table in the directory by the Last Name field within the ZIP Code field. Print the sorted directory.

14. Save the directory again.

In the Lab

Lab 3: Designing a Data Source, Form Letter, and Mailing Labels from Sample Letters

Problem: The circulation manager at Squireman Publications would like to send a thank-you letter to magazine subscribers. Sample drafted letters are shown in Figure 5–104a and Figure 5-104b on page WD 382.

Perform the following tasks:

1. Decide which fields should be in the data source. Write the field names down on a piece of paper.

2. In Word, identify a main document for the letters.

3. Create a data source containing five records, which consists of data from the two letters shown in Figure 5–104 and then add three more records with your own data. Save the data source with the file name, Lab 5-3 Squireman Publications Address List, in a folder named Lab 5-3 Squireman Publications.

4. Save the main document for the form letter with the file name, Lab 5-3 Squireman Publications Form Letter. Enter the shape in the document and enter text and fields of the main document for the form letter shown in Figure 5–104.

5. Print the main document twice, once with field codes displaying and once without field codes.

6. Merge and print the form letters.

7. Merge the data source to a directory. Convert it to a Word table. Add an attractive border to the table and apply any other formatting you feel necessary. Print the table. Save the file using the name Lab 5-3 Squireman Publications Directory.

Squireman Publications

202 West Squire Boulevard * Micheltown, DE 19722 * squireman@link.net

Matthew Mason
7676 Independence Parkway
Rocktown, AR 71672

2/19/2008

Dear Mr. Mason:

Thank you for your recent subscription. Your first issue of *Off-Roading Journal* will be delivered to you next month. As a premium for your one-year subscription, we have enclosed a calendar and memo pad as your free gift.

We appreciate your business and hope that you will enjoy every issue of *Off-Roading Journal*. Should you have any questions, please feel free to contact us at the address or e-mail address above. Thank you again, Matthew!

Yours truly,

Dashuan Titus
Circulation Manager

Figure 5–104 (a)

Continued >

In the Lab *continued*

Squireman Publications

202 West Squire Boulevard * Micheltown, DE 19722 * squireman@link.net

Lee Sun
42 W. 18th Street
Apt. 9C
Ponrolet, MI 49155

2/19/2008

Dear Mr. Sun:

Thank you for your recent subscription. Your first issue of *Aspiring Gourmet* will be delivered to you next month. As a premium for your two-year subscription, we have enclosed a slimline calculator as your free gift.

We appreciate your business and hope that you will enjoy every issue of *Aspiring Gourmet*. Should you have any questions, please feel free to contact us at the address or e-mail address above. Thank you again, Lee!

Yours truly,

Dashuan Titus
Circulation Manager

Figure 5–104 (b)

Cases and Places

Apply your creative thinking and problem solving skills to design and implement a solution.

● EASIER   ●● MORE DIFFICULT

● 1: Create a Form Letter for a Charitable Organization

Charitable Outreach is a local organization that contributes volunteers, money, and other donations to area charities. As a volunteer, you have been asked by the director to send letters to past donors thanking them for their donation and alerting them to the organization's current needs. Create a form letter using the following information: Insert a shape of your choice in a drawing canvas, and insert the text Charitable Outreach within the shape. Format the shape and the text using the Styles button on the Ribbon. The organization's address is 75 Welton Plaza, Twister, OK 74519 and their telephone is (217) 555-6542. Create the data source shown in Figure 5–105. After the salutation, the first paragraph should read: Thank you for your recent contribution of «amount». As you know, Charitable Outreach is a nonprofit organization dedicated to improving the quality of life for all residents in a three-county region. Donors like you, «first name», have made possible the following fundraisers:. Create a multilevel list for the following items: 1) Spring events - Dinner dance, Golf outing, Garden tour; 2) Fall events - Harvest Ball, Bonfire, Football weekend trip. Last paragraph: Our tradition of community outreach would not be possible without donors like you. We thank you for your support and look forward to seeing you at our next event. Use your name in the signature block. Address and print accompanying labels or envelopes for the form letters.

Title	First Name	Last Name	Address Line 1	Address Line 2	City	State	Zip Code	Amount
Ms.	Lucy	Song	4483 W. 119th Street	Apt. 12L	Twister	OK	74519	$100.00
Mr.	Arnold	Green	15 N. Commerce Street		Twister	OK	74519	$75.00
Mr.	Miguel	Arroyo	P. O. Box 244	125 Main Street	Sandfly	OK	74877	$25.00
Ms.	Joseph	Ipolito	709 Placid Way		Twister	OK	74519	$100.00
Ms.	LaToya	Carrothers	323 Eaton Parkway		Sandfly	OK	74877	$200.00

Figure 5–105

●● 2: Create a Memo Form Letter for Company Training

You work part-time at HomeCare, a home health care service. Your boss has just announced that all company computers are being upgraded to run Windows Vista and Office 2007. He needs to schedule training sessions for employees in the two departments he oversees, accounting and communications. He has asked you to create a memo that can be sent to both departments and gives the pertinent information. If your instructor approves, change the user name and initials associated with your copy of Word to your name and initials. Then, use a suitable memo template and include the following information: The memo should be sent to both departments. The accounting department should be informed that they are going to receive training on Microsoft Excel 2007, and the communications department will receive training on Microsoft Word 2007 (use an IF field in the To: portion of the memo template to accomplish this). The training session for Accounting will be held on March 26 from 1:00 - 4:00 p.m.; the training session for Communications will be held on the same day from 8:00 - 11:00 a.m. Both sessions will meet in Conference Room G. Merge and print the memos, then merge the data source to a directory. Convert the directory to a Word table and apply formatting to make the table more attractive and readable.

Continued >

Cases and Places *continued*

•• 3: Create a Form Letter for a Mail-Order Company

Nature Pride Naturals, where you work part-time, is a mail-order company specializing in vitamins, herbal remedies, and organic foods and beverages. Your boss has asked you to design a form letter that can be sent to customers thanking them for their orders and listing the new specials. This month, organic teas and multivitamins are featured items. The teas are 100 percent organic, handpicked, and are caffeine- and pesticide-free. The multivitamins are available in 50-, 100-, and 200-caplet bottles (use a multilevel list for this). You also must inform the customers that you have enclosed a coupon for their next order. If they spent less than $50.00, they received a 10 percent off coupon; if they spent more than $50.00, they received a 15 percent off coupon (use an IF field for this). Obtain the names and addresses of at least five classmates, friends, or family members and use them as records in the data source. Create a directory of the data source records. Address accompanying labels or envelopes for the form letters.

•• 4: Create a Form Letter as the Cover Letter for your Resume

Make It Personal

Whether it is now or after graduation, at some point in your life you will need to search for a job. Suppose you already have your resume prepared and want to send it to a group of potential employers. Design an accompanying cover letter for your resume using the skills and techniques you learned in this chapter. Obtain a recent newspaper and cut out at least three classified advertisements for jobs in which you are interested or are in your current field of study. Also, find two job listings on the Web. Create a cover letter for your resume that can be sent as a form letter. Make sure it contains your name, address, telephone number, and e-mail address (if you have one). Use the information in the advertisements you found to create the data source. The data source should contain the five employers' names, addresses, and the job title for which you are applying. Address accompanying labels or envelopes for the cover letters. Also, create a directory of the data source records and format it as a Word table. Use the concepts and skills you learned in this chapter to format the form letter and directory. Submit the want ads with your printouts.

•• 5: Create Form Letters Using Different Types of Data Sources

Working Together

This chapter illustrated using one type of data source for merging form letters. Other types of data sources, however, can be used for a merge operation. As a starting point for this assignment, select either the form letter created in this chapter, the Apply Your Knowledge letter, or any of the other assignments completed and the data source. Divide into teams, then create and merge form letters as follows:

1. One or more team members should merge the contents of the data source to e-mail addresses. It may be necessary to use Help in Word to accomplish this.

2. One or more team members should use Microsoft Office Access 2007 to view, format, and print the contents of a data source created in Word. It may be necessary to use Help in Access.

3. One or more team members should use Microsoft Office Excel 2007 to create a table and then use that table as the data source in the merge document. It may be necessary to use Help in both Word and in Excel for instructions on creating and saving a worksheet in the proper format for a mail merge.

4. One or more team members should use Microsoft Office Outlook recipients as a data source in a mail merge document. It may be necessary to use Help in both Word and in Outlook.

Then, as a team, develop a PowerPoint slide show that outlines the steps required to complete the four tasks listed above. Present the slide show to your classmates.

6 Creating a Professional Newsletter

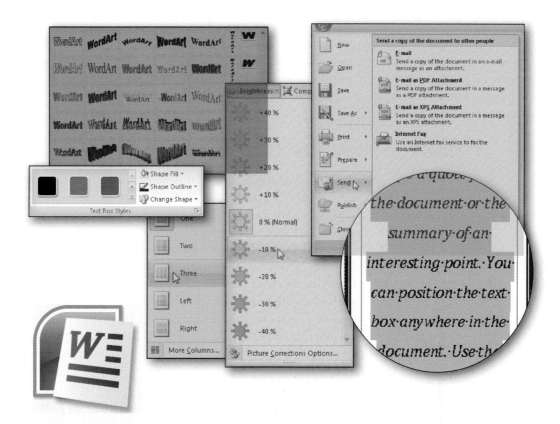

Objectives

You will have mastered the material in this chapter when you can:

- Create and format WordArt
- Insert a symbol in a document
- Insert and format a floating graphic
- Format a document in multiple columns
- Format a character as a drop cap
- Insert a column break
- Modify a style

- Place a vertical rule between columns
- Insert and format a text box
- Copy and paste using a split window
- Balance columns
- Modify and format a SmartArt graphic
- Add a page border

6 | Creating a Professional Newsletter

Introduction

Professional looking documents, such as newsletters and brochures, often are created using desktop publishing software. With desktop publishing software, you can divide a document in multiple columns, wrap text around diagrams and other graphical images, change fonts and font sizes, add color and lines, and so on, to create an attention-grabbing document. Desktop publishing software, such as Adobe PageMaker or QuarkXpress, enables you to open an existing word processing document and enhance it through formatting not provided in your word processing software. Word, however, provides many of the formatting features that you would find in a desktop publishing program. Thus, you can use Word to create eye-catching newsletters and brochures.

Project — Newsletter

A newsletter is a publication geared for a specific audience that is created on a recurring basis, such as weekly, monthly, or quarterly. The audience may be subscribers, club members, employees, customers, patrons, etc.

The project in this chapter uses Word to produce the two-page newsletter shown in Figure 6–1. The newsletter is a monthly publication, called Health Bits, which is for members of Health Bits Group. Each issue of Health Bits contains a feature article and announcements. This month's feature article discusses health concerns related to computer use. The feature article spans the first two columns of the first page of the newsletter and then continues on the second page. The announcements, located in the third column of the first page, remind members about the upcoming meeting, inform them about member discounts, and advise them of the topic of the next month's feature article.

Overview

As you read through this chapter, you will learn how to create the newsletter shown in Figure 6–1 by performing these general tasks:

- Create the nameplate on the first page of the newsletter.
- Format the first page of the body of the newsletter.
- Create a pull-quote on the first page of the newsletter.
- Create the nameplate on the second page of the newsletter.
- Format the second page of the body of the newsletter.
- Print the newsletter.

The project in this chapter involves several steps requiring you to drag the mouse. If you drag to the wrong location, you may want to cancel an action. Remember that you always can click the Undo button on the Quick Access Toolbar to cancel your most recent action.

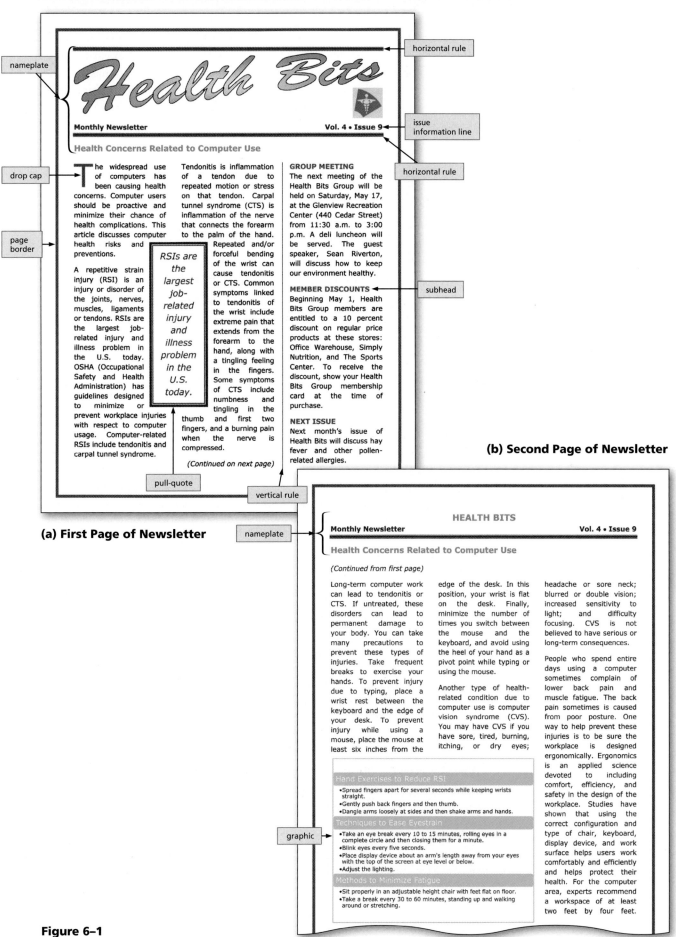

(b) Second Page of Newsletter

(a) First Page of Newsletter

Figure 6–1

The Health Bits newsletter incorporates the desktop publishing features of Word. The body of each page of the newsletter is divided in three columns. A variety of fonts, font sizes, and colors add visual appeal to the document. The first page has text wrapped around a pull-quote, and the second page has text wrapped around a graphic. Horizontal and vertical lines separate distinct areas of the newsletter, including a page border around the perimeter of each page.

Desktop Publishing Terminology

As you create professional looking newsletters and brochures, you should be familiar with several desktop publishing terms. Figure 6–1 on the previous page identifies these terms:

- A **nameplate**, or **banner**, is the portion of a newsletter that contains the title of the newsletter and usually an issue information line.
- The **issue information line** identifies the specific publication.
- A **ruling line**, usually identified by its direction as a **horizontal rule** or **vertical rule**, is a line that separates areas of the newsletter.
- A **subhead** is a heading within the body of the newsletter.
- A **pull-quote** is text that is *pulled*, or copied, from the text of the document and given graphical emphasis.

Plan Ahead

> **General Project Guidelines**
> When creating a Word document, the actions you perform and decisions you make will affect the appearance and characteristics of the finished document. As you create a newsletter, such as the project shown in Figure 6–1, you should follow these general guidelines:
>
> 1. **Create the nameplate.** The nameplate visually identifies the newsletter. Usually, the nameplate is positioned horizontally across the top of the newsletter, although some nameplates are vertical. The nameplate typically consists of text, graphics, and ruling lines.
>
> 2. **Determine content for the body of the newsletter.** Newsletters typically have one or more articles that begin on the first page. Include articles that are interesting to the audience. Incorporate color, appropriate fonts and font sizes, and alignment to provide visual interest. Use pull-quotes, graphics, and ruling lines to draw the reader's attention to important points. Avoid overusing visual elements — too many visuals can give the newsletter a cluttered look.
>
> 3. **Bind and distribute the newsletter.** Many newsletters are printed and mailed to recipients. Some are placed in public locations, free for interested parties. Others are e-mailed or posted on the Web for users to download. Printed newsletters typically are stapled at the top, along the side, or on a fold. For online newsletters, be sure the newsletter is in a format that most computer users will be able to open.

When necessary, more specific details concerning the above guidelines are presented at appropriate points in the chapter. The chapter also will identify the actions performed and decisions made regarding these guidelines during the creation of the newsletter shown in Figure 6–1.

To Start Word

If you are using a computer to step through the project in this chapter and you want your screens to match the figures in this book, you should change your computer's resolution to 1024 × 768. For information about how to change a computer's resolution, read Appendix D.

The following steps start Word and verify Word settings.

1 Start Word.

2 If the Word window is not maximized, click its Maximize button.

3 If the Print Layout button on the status bar is not selected, click it so that Word is in Print Layout view.

4 If your zoom level is not 100%, click the Zoom Out or Zoom In button as many times as necessary until the Zoom level button displays 100% on its face.

5 If the Show/Hide ¶ button on the Home tab is not selected already, click it to display formatting marks on the screen.

6 If the rulers are not displayed already, click the View Ruler button on the vertical scroll bar because you will use the rulers to perform tasks in this project.

To Set Custom Margins

Recall that Word is preset to use standard 8.5-by-11-inch paper, with 1-inch top, bottom, left, and right margins. In Chapter 5, you changed the margins by selecting predefined settings in the Margins gallery. For the newsletter in this chapter, all margins (left, right, top, and bottom) are .75 inches, which is not a predefined setting in the Margins gallery. Thus, the following steps set custom margins.

1

• Display the Page Layout tab.

• Click the Margins button on the Page Layout tab to display the Margins gallery (Figure 6–2).

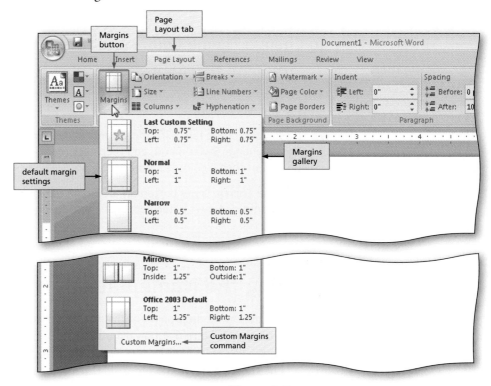

Figure 6–2

- Click Custom Margins in the Margins gallery to display the Page Setup dialog box. If necessary, click the Margins tab in the dialog box.

- Type .75 in the Top text box to change the top margin setting and then press the TAB key to position the insertion point in the Bottom text box.

- Type .75 in the Bottom text box to change the bottom margin setting and then press the TAB key.

- Type .75 in the Left text box to change the left margin setting and then press the TAB key.

- Type .75 in the Right box to change the right margin setting (Figure 6–3).

❸

- Click the OK button to set the custom margins for this document.

Other Ways

1. Position mouse pointer on margin boundary on ruler; when mouse pointer changes to two-headed arrow, drag margin boundaries on ruler

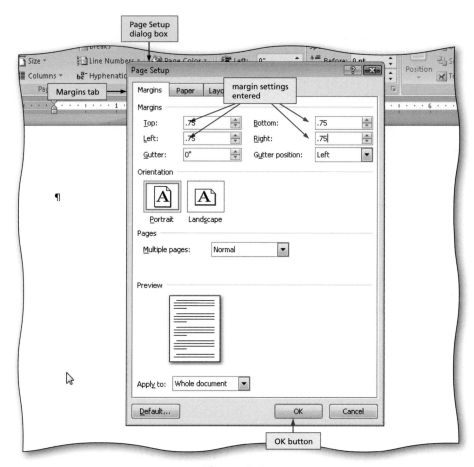

Figure 6–3

BTW

Saving Modified Themes
If you want to save a modified theme so that you can use it again in another document, modify the theme colors or fonts (as described in the steps to the right), click the Themes button on the Page Layout tab, click Save Current Theme in the Themes gallery, enter a theme name in the File name text box, and then click the Save button.

To Change Theme Colors and Fonts

The newsletter in this chapter uses the Metro color scheme and Aspect font set. The following steps change the theme colors to the Metro color scheme and the theme fonts to the Aspect font set.

❶ Display the Home tab. Click the Change Styles button on the Home tab, point to Colors on the Change Styles menu, and then click Metro in the Colors gallery to change the document theme colors to Metro.

❷ Click the Change Styles button on the Home tab, point to Fonts on the Change Styles menu, and then click Aspect in the Fonts gallery to change the document theme fonts to Aspect.

Creating the Nameplate

The nameplate on the first page of this newsletter consists of the information above the multiple columns (Figure 6–1a on page WD 387). In this project, the nameplate includes the newsletter title, Health Bits, the issue information line, and the title of the feature article. The steps on the following pages create the nameplate for the first page of the newsletter in this project.

Create the nameplate.
The nameplate should catch the attention of readers, enticing them to read the newsletter. The nameplate typically consists of the title of the newsletter and the issue information line. Some also include a subtitle, a slogan, and a graphical image or logo. Guidelines for the newsletter title and other elements in the nameplate are as follows:

- Compose a title that is short, yet conveys the contents of the newsletter. In the newsletter title, eliminate unnecessary words such as these: the, newsletter. Use a decorative font in as large a font size as possible so that the title stands out on the page.

- Other elements on the nameplate should not compete in size with the title. Use colors that complement the title. Select easy-to-read fonts.

- Arrange the elements of the nameplate so that it does not have a cluttered appearance. If necessary, use ruling lines to visually separate areas of the nameplate.

The following pages use the steps outlined below to create the nameplate for the newsletter in this chapter.

1. Enter and format the newsletter title using WordArt.

2. Add a horizontal rule above the newsletter title.

3. Enter the issue information line.

4. Add a horizontal rule below the issue information line.

5. Insert and format an appropriate clip art image.

6. Enter the feature article title.

To Insert WordArt

In Chapter 5, you added a shape drawing object to a document. Recall that a drawing object is a graphic you create using Word. Another type of drawing object, called **WordArt**, enables you to create special effects such as shadowed, rotated, stretched, skewed, and wavy text.

This project uses WordArt for the newsletter title, Health Bits, to draw the reader's attention to the nameplate. The following steps insert WordArt.

- Display the Insert tab.

- Click the WordArt button on the Insert tab to display the WordArt gallery (Figure 6–4).

Q&A

Why will I choose WordArt style 1?

You want to add your own special text effects to the WordArt, and WordArt style 1 is the most basic style.

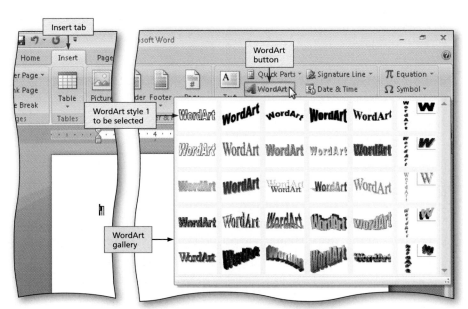

Figure 6–4

● Click WordArt style 1, the style in the upper-left corner of the WordArt gallery, to display the Edit WordArt Text dialog box.

● Type Health Bits in the Text text box, as the WordArt text.

● Click the Font box arrow in the dialog box; scroll to and then click Brush Script MT, or a similar font, to change the font of the WordArt text.

● Click the Size box arrow in the dialog box; scroll to and then click 72 to change the font size of the WordArt text (Figure 6–5).

Figure 6–5

● Click the OK button to display the WordArt text in the document window (Figure 6–6).

How do I correct a mistake in the WordArt text?

Click the Edit Text button on the WordArt Tools Format tab, or right-click the WordArt and then click Edit Text on the shortcut menu, to redisplay the Edit WordArt Text dialog box.

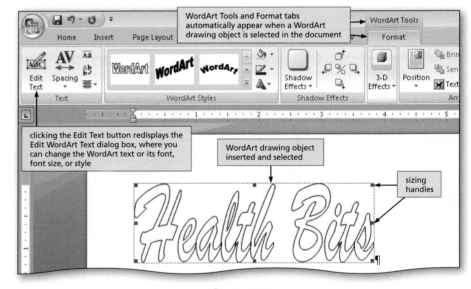

Figure 6–6

To Resize WordArt

You resize WordArt the same way you resize any other graphic. That is, you can drag its sizing handles or enter values in the Shape Height and Shape Width text boxes. The next steps resize the WordArt.

1 Drag the bottom-right sizing handle to the right and slightly downward until the WordArt size is similar to Figure 6–7.

2 If the values in the Shape Height and Shape Width text boxes are not approximately equal to 1.4" and 7", respectively, change their values so that the WordArt is similar in size to Figure 6–7.

Figure 6–7

To Change the WordArt Fill Color

The next step is to change the color of the WordArt so that it displays a green to yellow to green gradient color effect. **Gradient** means the colors blend into one another. In this newsletter, the yellow color is in the middle of the WordArt text, which blends into the green color to the edges of the WordArt text. The following steps change the fill color of the WordArt.

1

- With the WordArt selected, click the Shape Fill button arrow on the WordArt Tools Format tab to display the Shape Fill gallery.

Q&A The Shape Fill gallery did not display. Why not?

Be sure you click the Shape Fill button arrow, which is to the right of the Shape Fill button. If you mistakenly click the Shape Fill button, Word places a default fill in the selected WordArt instead of displaying the Shape Fill gallery.

- Point to Gradient in the Shape Fill gallery to display the Gradient gallery (Figure 6–8).

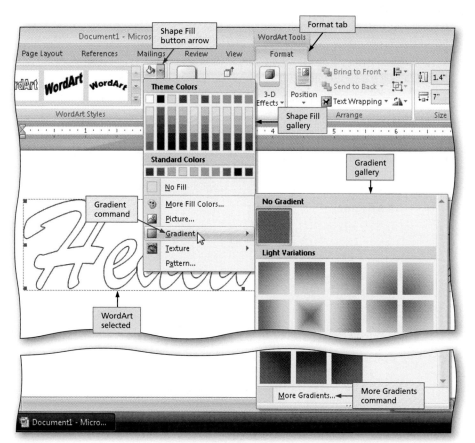

Figure 6–8

2

- Click More Gradients in the Gradient gallery to display the Fill Effects dialog box. If necessary, click the Gradient tab in the dialog box.

- In the Colors area, click Two colors, which causes two separate color text boxes to appear in the dialog box (Figure 6–9).

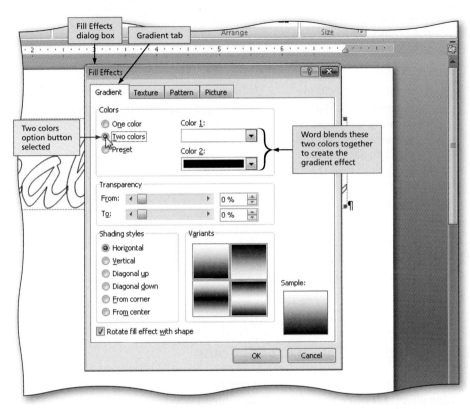

Figure 6–9

3

- Click the Color 1 box arrow and then click Gold, Accent 3, Lighter 60% (third row, seventh column) in the color gallery.

- Click the Color 2 box arrow and then click Green, Accent 1, Darker 25% (fifth row, fifth column) in the color gallery.

- Click From center in the Shading styles area and then, if necessary, click the left variant in the Variants area (Figure 6–10).

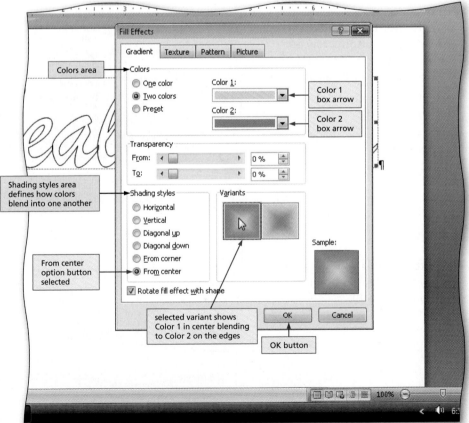

Figure 6–10

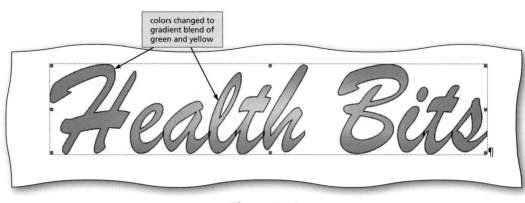

4

- Click the OK button to change the colors of the WordArt (Figure 6–11).

> **Other Ways**
>
> 1. Right-click WordArt, click Format WordArt on shortcut menu, click Fill Effects button, select desired options, click OK button in each dialog box

colors changed to gradient blend of green and yellow

Figure 6–11

To Change the WordArt Shape

Word provides a variety of shapes to make your WordArt more interesting. For the newsletter in this chapter, the WordArt slants at an upward angle to make room for a graphic on the right edge of the nameplate. The following steps change the WordArt to a cascade up shape.

 1

- Click the Change WordArt Shape button on the Format tab to display the WordArt Shape gallery (Figure 6–12).

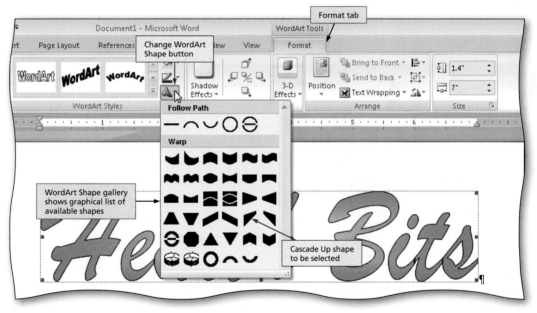

Format tab

Change WordArt Shape button

WordArt Shape gallery shows graphical list of available shapes

Cascade Up shape to be selected

Figure 6–12

2

- Click the Cascade Up shape in the WordArt Shape gallery to instruct Word to form itself into the Cascade Up shape (Figure 6–13).

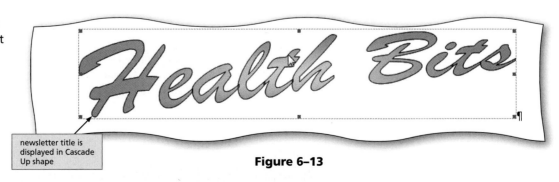

newsletter title is displayed in Cascade Up shape

Figure 6–13

BTW

Deleting WordArt Graphics
If you want to delete a WordArt graphic, you would right-click it and then click Cut on the shortcut menu, or click it and then press the DELETE key.

To Center the Newsletter Title

The next step is to center the paragraph containing the WordArt.

1 Click the paragraph mark to the right of the WordArt text to deselect the WordArt and position the insertion point in the paragraph containing the WordArt.

2 If necessary, display the Home tab, and then click the Center button on the Home tab to center the paragraph containing the WordArt.

Q&A Will I notice a change after centering the WordArt?

Because the WordArt object extends from the left to the right margins, you may not notice a difference in its position after clicking the Center button.

To Border One Edge of a Paragraph

In Word, you use borders to create ruling lines. As discussed in previous projects, Word can place borders on any edge of a paragraph; that is, Word can place a border on the top, bottom, left, and right edges of a paragraph.

In this project, the title of the newsletter has a 3-point, decorative, dark-pink border above it. The following steps place a border above a paragraph.

- Click the Border button arrow on the Home tab and then click Borders and Shading in the Border gallery to display the Borders and Shading dialog box.

2

- Click Custom in the Setting area because you are setting just a top border.

- Scroll through the style list and click the style shown in Figure 6–14, which has a thick middle line between two thin lines.

- Click the Color button arrow and then click Pink, Accent 2, Darker 50% (sixth column in the last row of Theme Colors) in the Color gallery.

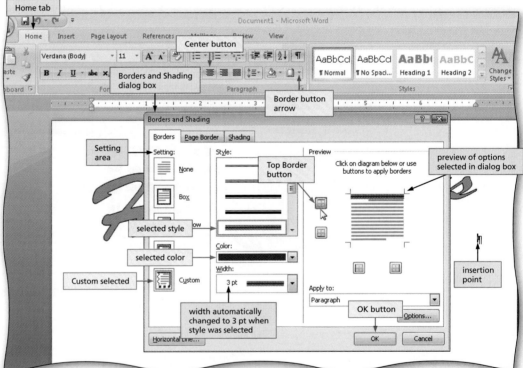

Figure 6–14

- Click the Top Border button in the Preview area of the dialog box to show a preview of the selected border style (Figure 6–14).

Q&A What is the purpose of the buttons in the Preview area?

They are toggles that display and remove the top, bottom, left, and right borders from the diagram in the Preview area.

3

- Click the OK button to place the defined border above the newsletter title (Figure 6–15).

How would I change an existing border?

First, you remove the border by clicking the Border button arrow on the Home tab, and then click the border in the Border gallery that identifies the border you wish to remove. Then, add a new border as described in these steps.

Figure 6–15

Other Ways

1. Click Page Borders on Page Layout tab, click Borders tab in Borders and Shading dialog box, select desired border, click OK button

To Clear Formatting

When you press the ENTER key at the end of the newsletter title to advance the insertion point to the next line, Word carries forward formatting. You do not want the paragraphs and characters on line 2 to have the same formatting as line 1. Instead, you clear formatting so that the characters on line 2 use the Normal style. The following steps clear formatting after pressing the ENTER key.

1 With the insertion point positioned at the end of line 1 (shown in Figure 6–15), press the ENTER key.

2 Click the Clear Formatting button on the Home tab to remove any existing formatting.

To Set a Right-Aligned Tab Stop

The issue information line in this newsletter contains the text, Monthly Newsletter, at the left margin and the volume and issue number at the right margin (shown in Figure 6–1a on page WD 387). A paragraph cannot be formatted as both left-aligned and right-aligned. To place text at the right margin of a left-aligned paragraph, you must set a tab stop at the right margin. The steps on the next page set a right-aligned tab stop at the right margin.

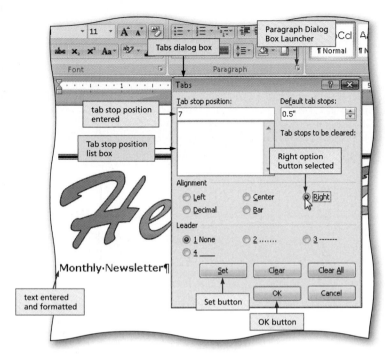

tab stop position entered

Tab stop position list box

text entered and formatted

Tabs dialog box

Paragraph Dialog Box Launcher

Right option button selected

Set button

OK button

Figure 6–16

1 Click the Bold button on the Home tab. Click the Font Color button arrow on the Home tab and change the font color to Pink, Accent 2, Darker 50%. Type `Monthly Newsletter` on line 2 of the newsletter.

2 Click the Paragraph Dialog Box Launcher to display the Paragraph dialog box and then click the Tabs button in the Paragraph dialog box to display the Tabs dialog box.

3 Type `7` in the Tab stop position text box, which is the location of the right margin.

4 Click Right in the Alignment area to specify alignment for text at the tab stop (Figure 6–16).

5 Click the Set button in the Tabs dialog box to set a right-aligned custom tab stop, which places the entered tab stop position, the number 7 in this case, in the Tab stop position list box.

6 Click the OK button to place a right tab marker at the 7" mark on the ruler.

To Insert a Symbol

In the newsletter in this chapter, a large round dot is between the volume number and issue number. This special symbol (the large round dot) is not on the keyboard. You insert dots and other symbols, such as letters in the Greek alphabet and mathematical characters, using the Symbol dialog box.

The following steps insert a dot symbol between the volume and issue numbers in the issue information line of the newsletter.

1

• Press the TAB key. Type `Vol. 4` and then press the SPACEBAR.

• Display the Insert tab.

• Click the Symbol button on the Insert tab (Figure 6–17).

Q&A

What if the symbol I want to insert already appears in the Symbol gallery?

You can click any symbol shown in the Symbol gallery to insert it in the document.

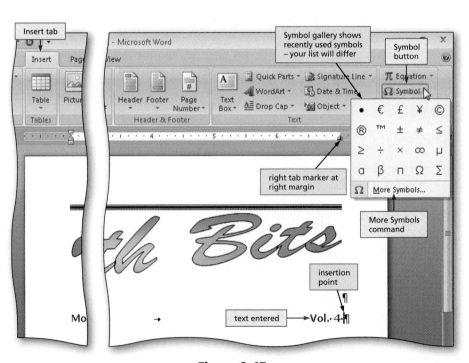

Insert tab

Symbol gallery shows recently used symbols – your list will differ

Symbol button

right tab marker at right margin

More Symbols command

insertion point

text entered

Figure 6–17

2

- Click More Symbols in the Symbol gallery to display the Symbol dialog box.

- If Symbol is not the Font displayed in the Font box, click the Font box arrow in the dialog box and then scroll to Symbol and click it.

- In the list of symbols, if necessary, scroll to and then click the dot symbol shown in Figure 6–18.

- Click the Insert button to place the dot symbol in the document to the left of the insertion point (Figure 6–18).

Why is the Symbol dialog box still open?

The Symbol dialog box remains open, allowing you to insert additional symbols.

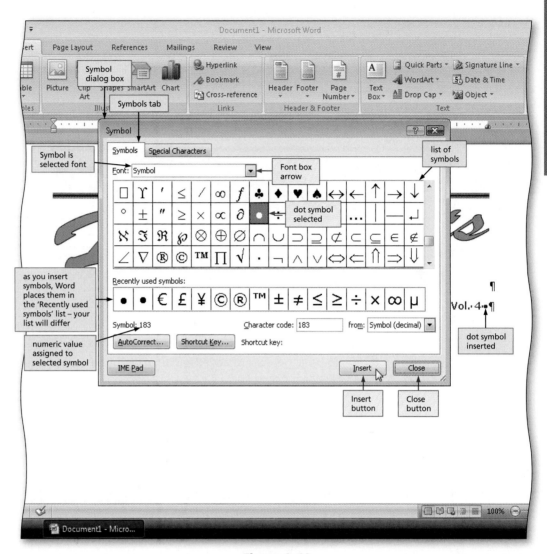

Figure 6–18

3

- Click the Close button in the Symbol dialog box.

Other Ways

1. While holding ALT key, with the NUM LOCK key on, use numeric keypad to type ANSI character code for symbol

To Enter Text and Add a Border

The next step is to finish entering text in the issue information line and then place a border immediately below the issue information line. The border has the same format as the one above the newsletter title. The steps on the next page enter text and add the border.

Inserting Special Characters
In addition to symbols, you can insert a variety of special characters including dashes, hyphens, spaces, apostrophes, and quotation marks. Click the Special Characters tab in the Symbols dialog box, click the desired character in the Character list, click the Insert button, and then click the Close button.

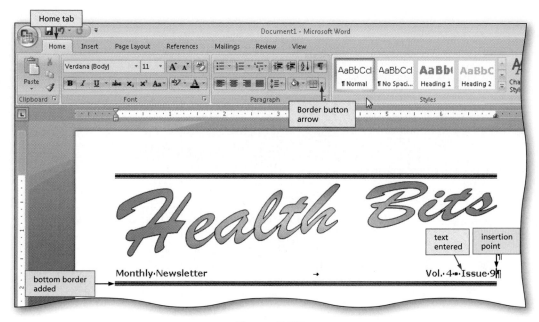

Figure 6–19

① Press the SPACEBAR. Type Issue 9 at the end of the issue information line.

② Display the Home tab. Click the Border button arrow on the Home tab and then click Bottom Border in the Border gallery to place a bottom border on the current paragraph using the same formats as the previously defined border (Figure 6–19).

Q&A What if my border is not the same as the one above the title?

Remove the border just added and then define a new bottom border using the Borders and Shading dialog box.

To Save a Document

The next step is to save the newsletter because you have performed many steps thus far.

① With a USB flash drive connected to one of the computer's USB ports, click the Save button on the Quick Access Toolbar to display the Save As dialog box.

② Save the document on a USB flash drive with the file name, Health Bits Newsletter.

To Insert Clip Art from the Web

Note: The following steps assume your computer is connected to the Internet. If it is not, go directly to the shaded steps on the next page that are titled To Insert a Graphic File from the Data Files for Students.

The next step is to insert an image of a caduceus (a symbol often associated with health care) from the Web in the nameplate.

① Display the Insert tab. Click the Clip Art button on the Insert tab to display the Clip Art task pane.

② In the Clip Art task pane, type caduceus in the Search for text box.

③ Click the Go button to display a list of clips that match the description, caduceus.

④ Scroll to and then click the clip art of the caduceus that matches the one in Figure 6–20. (If the clip art image does not appear in the task pane, click the Close button on the Clip Art task pane and then proceed to the shaded steps on the next page.)

⑤ Click the Close button on the Clip Art task pane title bar to close the task pane.

Q&A What if my clip art image is not in the same location as in Figure 6–20?

The clip art image may be in a different location, depending on the position of the insertion point when you inserted the image. In a later section, you will move the image to a different location.

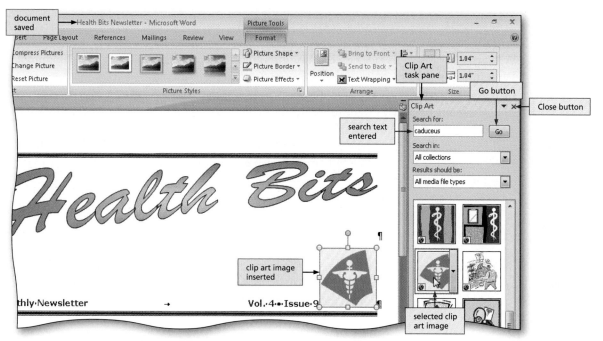

Figure 6–20

To Insert a Graphic File from the Data Files for Students

If you do not have access to the Internet, you can insert the clip art file in the Word document from the Data Files for Students. See the inside back cover of this book for instructions on downloading the Data Files for Students, or contact your instructor for information about accessing the required files. Only perform these steps if you were not able to insert the caduceus clip art from the Web in the steps at the bottom of the previous page.

1 Display the Insert tab. Click the Insert Picture from File button on the Insert tab to display the Insert Picture dialog box.

2 With your USB flash drive connected to one of the computer's USB ports, locate and then click the file called Caduceus on the USB flash drive to select the file.

3 Click the Insert button in the dialog box to insert the picture at the location of the insertion point in the document (shown in Figure 6–20).

To Resize the Clip Art Image

The clip art image is too big. It should be about one-quarter of its current size. The following steps resize the clip art image.

1 Drag the top-right sizing handle inward until the size of the clip art image is similar to Figure 6–21.

2 If necessary, double-click the clip art image to display the Picture Tools Format tab. If the values in the Shape Height and Shape Width text boxes are not approximately equal to .67 each, change their values so that the clip art image size is similar to Figure 6–21.

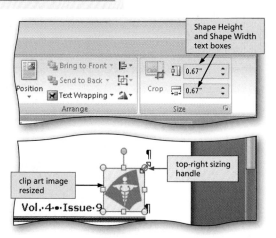

Figure 6–21

Floating vs. Inline Objects

When you insert an object, such as a clip art image, in a paragraph in a document, Word inserts it as an inline object. An **inline object** is an object that is part of a paragraph. With inline objects, you change the location of the object by setting paragraph options, such as centered, right-aligned, and so on.

In many cases, you want more flexibility in positioning objects. That is, you want to position the object at a specific location in a document. To do this, the object must be floating. A **floating object** is an object that can be positioned at a specific location in a document or in a layer over or behind text in a document. You can position a floating object anywhere on the page.

To Format a Graphic as Floating

In the nameplate of the newsletter in this chapter, the caduceus image is positioned at the right edge of the nameplate between the newsletter title and the issue information line. The following steps change the image from an inline object to a floating object, which will enable you to move the graphic to any location on the page.

1

- If necessary, double-click the clip art image to display the Picture Tools Format tab.

- Click the Text Wrapping button on the Format tab to display the Text Wrapping menu (Figure 6–22).

Q&A

Does Word have different types of floating formats?

Yes. Square wraps text in a box around an object; Tight wraps text around the shape of the object; Behind Text places the object behind the text without wrapping; In Front of Text places the object in front of the text without wrapping; Top and Bottom places text above and below the object; and Through runs text through the object.

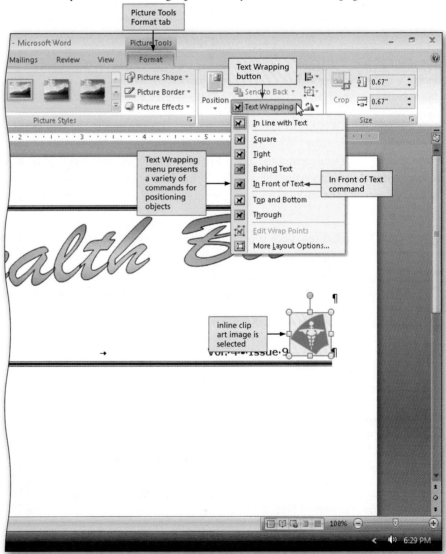

Figure 6–22

● In the Text Wrapping menu, click
In Front of Text so that the image
changes to a floating object that
can be positioned in front of text
on the page (Figure 6–23).

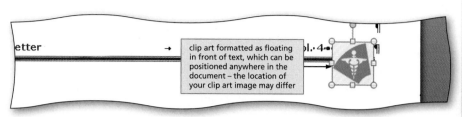

Figure 6–23

To Move a Graphic

The next step is to move the clip art image up so that it is positioned between the
newsletter title and the issue information line.

❶ Point to the middle of the graphic, and when the mouse pointer has a four-headed arrow
attached to it, drag the graphic to the location shown in Figure 6–24.

Figure 6–24

To Flip a Graphic

The next step is to flip the clip art image so that the arc is facing the opposite direction. The following steps
flip a graphic horizontally.

● With the graphic still
selected, click the
Rotate button on the
Format tab to display
the Rotate gallery
(Figure 6–25).

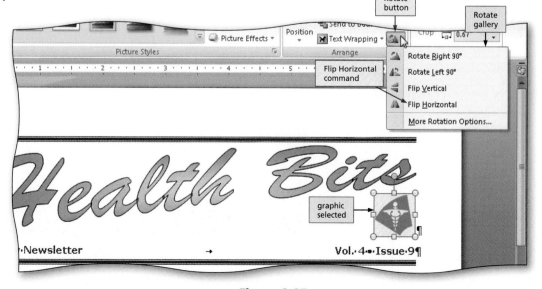

Figure 6–25

- Click Flip Horizontal on the Rotate gallery, so that Word flips the graphic to display its mirror image (Figure 6–26).

Can I flip a graphic vertically?

Yes, you would click the Flip Vertical command in the Rotate gallery.

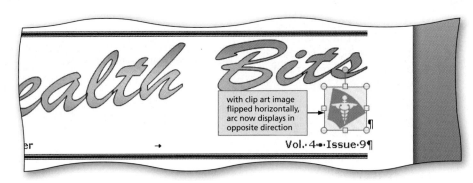

Figure 6–26

To Adjust the Brightness of a Graphic

In this newsletter, the clip art image is a bit darker so that its colors blend more with the colors in the newsletter title. In Word, you can increase or decrease the brightness of a graphic. The following steps adjust a graphic's brightness.

1

- Click the Brightness button on the Format tab to display the Brightness gallery.

- Point to -10 % in the Brightness gallery to display a live preview of that decrease in brightness applied to the selected clip art image (Figure 6–27).

Experiment

- Point to various percentages in the Brightness gallery and watch the clip art image colors lighten and darken.

- Click -10 % in the Brightness gallery to darken the clip art image.

Can I remove all formatting applied to a graphic and start over?

Yes, you would click the Reset Picture button on the Format tab to return a graphic to its original settings.

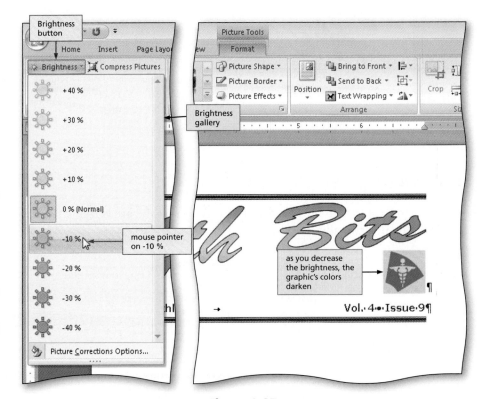

Figure 6–27

Other Ways

1. Right-click image, click Format Picture on shortcut menu, click Picture in left pane, drag Brightness slider, click Close button

To Clear Formatting

The next step is to enter the title of the feature article below the horizontal rule. To do this, you position the insertion point at the end of the issue information line (after the 9 in Issue 9) and then press the ENTER key. Recall that the issue information line has a bottom border. When you press the ENTER key in a bordered paragraph, Word carries forward any borders to the next paragraph. Thus, after you press the ENTER key, you should clear formatting to format the new paragraph to the Normal style. The following steps clear formatting.

1 Click at the end of line 2 (the issue information line) so that the insertion point is immediately after the 9 in Issue 9. Press the ENTER key.

2 Display the Home tab. Click the Clear Formatting button on the Home tab to apply the Normal style to the location of the insertion point.

To Enter Text as a Heading Style

Below the bottom border in the nameplate is the title of the feature article, Health Concerns Related to Computer Use, which is formatted in a Heading 2 style. The following steps enter text using the Heading 2 style.

1 Click Heading 2 on the Home tab.

2 Type `Health Concerns Related to Computer Use` to enter the feature title in the Heading 2 style.

To Modify a Style Using the Modify Style Dialog Box

The Heading 2 style is uses a bright green color. In this newsletter, you would like the Heading 2 style to be one shade darker. The following steps modify a style.

1

- Right-click Heading 2 on the Home tab to display a shortcut menu (Figure 6–28).

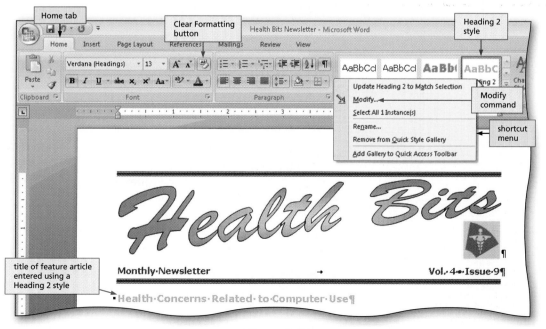

Figure 6–28

- Click Modify on the shortcut menu to display the Modify Style dialog box.

- Click the Color box arrow and then click Green, Accent 1, Darker 25% to change the color to a darker shade of green.

- Place a check mark in the Automatically update check box so that any additional changes you make to the Heading 2 style will automatically modify the style (Figure 6–29).

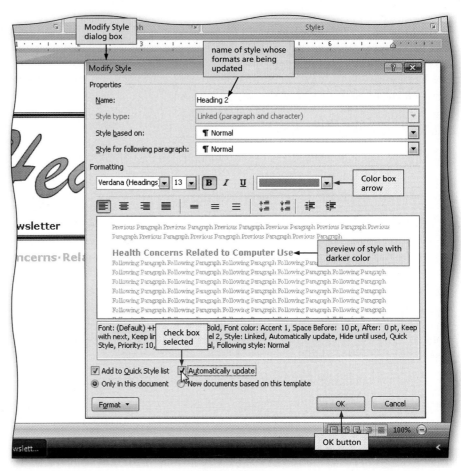

Figure 6–29

- Click the OK button to update the Heading 2 style (Figure 6–30).

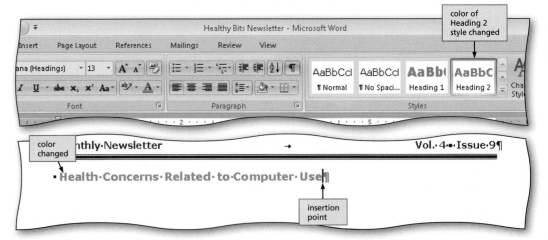

Figure 6–30

Other Ways

1. Click Styles Dialog Box Launcher, point to style name in list, click box arrow next to style name, click Modify in menu, change settings, click OK button

2. Click Styles Dialog Box Launcher, click Manage Styles button, select style name in list, click Modify button, change settings, click OK button in each dialog box

To Save a Document Again

The nameplate for the newsletter is complete. You should save the newsletter again.

 Save the newsletter again with the same file name, Health Bits Newsletter.

Formatting the First Page of the Body of the Newsletter

The next step is to format the first page of the body of the newsletter. The body of the newsletter in this chapter is divided in three columns (Figure 6–1a on page WD 387). The first two columns contain the feature article and the third column contains announcements. The characters in the paragraphs are aligned on both the right and left edges — similar to newspaper columns. The first letter in the first paragraph is much larger than the rest of the characters in the paragraph. A vertical rule separates the second and third columns. The steps on the following pages format the first page of the body of the newsletter using these desktop publishing features.

Plan Ahead

Determine the content for the body of the newsletter.
While content and subject matter of newsletters may vary, the procedures used to create newsletters is similar:

- **Write the body copy.** Newsletters should contain articles of interest and relevance to readers. Some share information, while others promote a product or service. Use active voice in body copy, which is more engaging than passive voice. Proofread the body copy to be sure it is errorfree. Check all facts for accuracy.

- **Organize body copy in columns.** Most newsletters divide body copy in columns. The body copy in columns, often called **snaking columns** or newspaper-style columns, flows from the bottom of one column to the top of the next column.

- **Format the body copy.** Begin the feature article on the first page of the newsletter. If the article spans multiple pages, use a continuation line, called jump or jump line, to guide the reader to the remainder of the article. The message at the end of the article on the first page of the newsletter is called a **jump-to line**, and a **jump-from line** marks the beginning of the continuation, which is usually on a subsequent page.

- **Maintain consistency.** Be consistent with placement of body copy elements in newsletter editions. If the newsletter contains announcements, for example, position them in the same location in each edition so that readers easily can find them.

- **Maximize white space.** Allow plenty of space between lines, paragraphs, and columns. Tightly packed text is difficult to read. Separate the text adequately from graphics, borders, and headings.

- **Incorporate color.** Use colors that complement those in the nameplate. Be careful not to overuse color. Restrict color below the nameplate to drop caps, subheads, graphics, and ruling lines. If you do not have a color printer, still change the colors because the colors will print in shades of black and gray. These shades add variety to the newsletter.

(continued)

Plan
Ahead

(continued)

- **Select and format subheads.** Develop subheads with as few words as possible. Readers should be able to identify content of the next topic by glancing at a subhead. Subheads should be emphasized in the newsletter but should not compete with text in the nameplate. Use a larger, bold, or otherwise contrasting font for subheads so that they stand apart from the body copy. Use this same format for all subheads for consistency. Leave a space above subheads to visually separate their content from the previous topic. Be consistent with spacing above and below subheads throughout the newsletter.

- **Divide sections with vertical rules.** Use vertical rules to guide the reader through the newsletter.

- **Enhance the document with visuals.** Add energy to the newsletter and emphasis to important points with graphics, pull-quotes, and other visuals such as drop caps to mark beginning of an article. Use these elements sparingly, however, so that the newsletter does not look crowded. Fewer, large visuals are more effective several smaller ones. If you use a graphic that you did not create, be sure to obtain permission to use it in the newsletter and give necessary credit to the creator of the graphic.

Columns

When you begin a document in Word, it has one column. You can divide a portion of a document or the entire document in multiple columns. Within each column, you can type, modify, or format text.

To divide a portion of a document in multiple columns, you use section breaks. Word requires that a new section be created each time you alter the number of columns in a document. Thus, if a document has a nameplate (one column) followed by an article of three columns followed by an article of two columns, the document would be divided in three separate sections.

Plan
Ahead

Organize body copy in columns.
Be consistent from page to page with number of columns. Narrow columns generally are easier to read than wide ones. Columns, however, can be too narrow. A two- or three-column layout generally is appealing and offers a flexible design. Try to have between five and fifteen words per line. To do this, you may need to adjust the column width, the font size, or the leading (line spacing). Font size of text in columns should be no larger than 12 point but not so small that readers must strain to read the text.

BTW

Certification
The Microsoft Certified Application Specialist (MCAS) program provides an opportunity for you to obtain a valuable industry credential — proof that you have the Word 2007 skills required by employers. For more information see Appendix G or visit the Word 2007 Certification Web page (scsite.com/wd2007/cert).

To Insert a Continuous Section Break

In this chapter, the nameplate is one column and the body of the newsletter is three columns. Thus, you must insert a continuous section break below the nameplate. The term, continuous, means the new section should be on the same page as the previous section, which, in this case, means that the three columns of body copy will be positioned directly below the nameplate on the first page of the newsletter. The following steps insert a continuous section break.

1

- With the insertion point at the end of the feature article title (shown in Figure 6–30 on page WD 406), press the ENTER key to position the insertion point below the article title.

- Display the Page Layout tab.

- Click the Insert Page and Section Breaks button on the Page Layout tab to display the Insert Page and Section Breaks gallery (Figure 6–31).

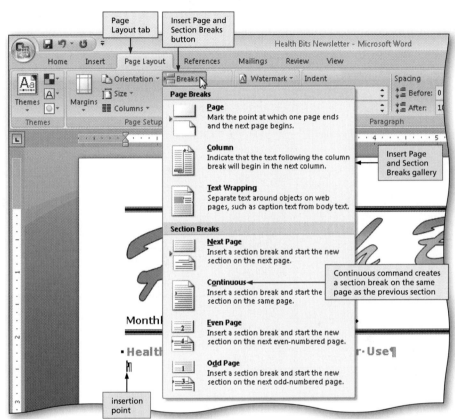

Figure 6–31

2

- Click Continuous in the Insert Page and Section Breaks gallery to insert a continuous section break above the insertion point (Figure 6–32).

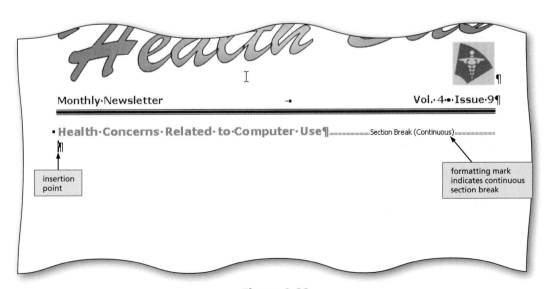

Figure 6–32

To Change the Number of Columns

The document now has two sections. The nameplate is in the first section, and the insertion point is in the second section. The second section should be formatted to three columns. Thus, the following steps format the second section in the document to three columns.

1

- Click the Columns button on the Page Layout tab to display the Columns gallery (Figure 6–33).

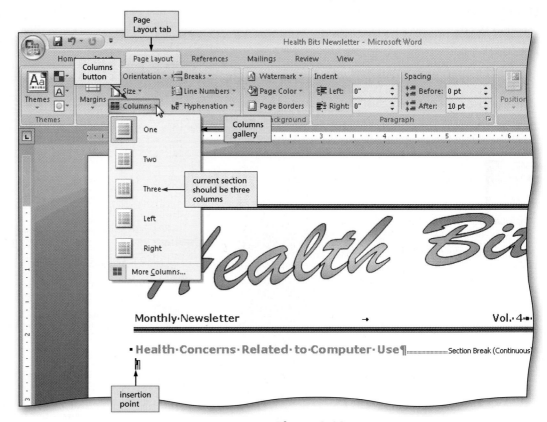

Figure 6–33

2

- Click Three in the Columns gallery to divide the section containing the insertion point in three evenly sized and spaced columns (Figure 6–34).

Q&A What if I want columns of different widths?

You would click the More Columns command in the Columns gallery, which displays the Columns dialog box. In this dialog box, you can specify varying column widths and spacing.

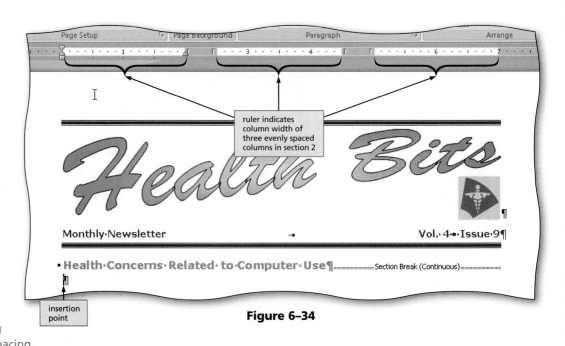

Figure 6–34

To Justify a Paragraph

The text in the paragraphs of the body of the newsletter is **justified**, which means that the left and right margins are aligned, like the edges of newspaper columns. The following step enters the first paragraph of the feature article using justified alignment.

- Display the Home tab.

- Click the Justify button on the Home tab so that Word aligns both the left and right margins of typed text.

- Type the first paragraph of the feature article (Figure 6–35): The widespread use of computers has been causing health concerns. Computer users should be proactive and minimize their chance of health complications. This article discusses computer health risks and preventions.

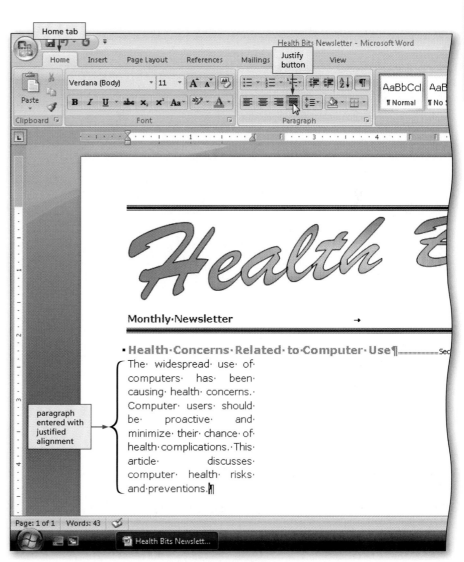

Figure 6–35

Q&A

Why do some words have extra space between them?

When a paragraph is formatted to justified alignment, Word places extra space between words so that the left and right edges of the paragraph are aligned. To remedy big gaps, sometimes called rivers, you can add or rearrange words, change the column width, change the font size, and so on.

Other Ways

1. Right-click paragraph, click Paragraph on shortcut menu, click Indents and Spacing tab, click Alignment box arrow, click Justified, click OK button

2. Click Paragraph Dialog Box Launcher, click Indents and Spacing tab, click Alignment box arrow, click Justified, click OK button

3. Press CTRL+J

To Insert a File in a Column of the Newsletter

Instead of typing the rest of the feature article in the newsletter in this chapter, the next step is to insert a file named Health Bits Main Article in the newsletter. This file, which contains the remainder of the feature article, is located on the Data Files for Students. See the inside back cover of this book for instructions on downloading the Data Files for Students, or contact your instructor for information about accessing the required files.

The following steps insert the Health Bits Main Article file in a column of the newsletter.

- Press the ENTER key.

- Display the Insert tab.

- Click the Insert Object button arrow on the Insert tab to display the Object menu.

- Click Text from File on the Object menu to display the Insert File dialog box.

- With your USB flash drive connected to one of the computer's USB ports, locate and then click the file called Health Bits Main Article on the USB flash drive to select the file (Figure 6–36).

Figure 6–36

2

- Click the Insert button to insert the file, Health Bits Main Article, in the file Health Bits Newsletter at the location of the insertion point.

- Scroll so that the bottom of the first page appears in the document window so that you can see how the article fills the three columns on the first and second pages (Figure 6–37).

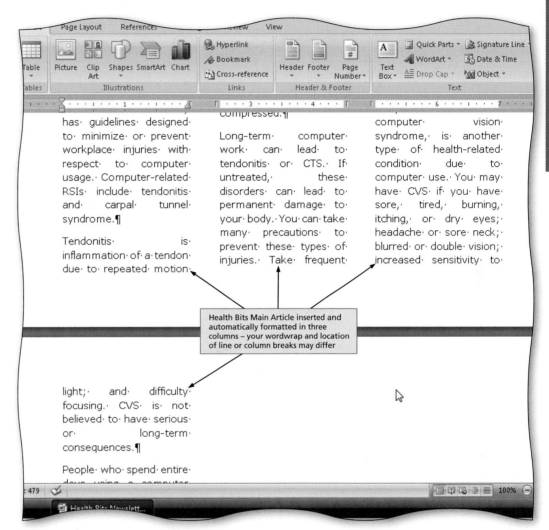

Health Bits Main Article inserted and automatically formatted in three columns – your wordwrap and location of line or column breaks may differ

Figure 6–37

To Change Spacing below a Paragraph

The space between the feature article title and the text in the feature article is tight. To improve readability, this newsletter has additional white space below the feature article title. The following steps increase the spacing below the paragraph containing the feature article title.

1 Scroll to the top of the document and then position the insertion point in the paragraph to be adjusted, in this case, the paragraph containing the article title.

2 Display the Page Layout tab.

3 Click the Spacing After box up arrow on the Page Layout tab as many times as necessary until 12 pt is displayed in the Spacing After text box (Figure 6–38 on the next page).

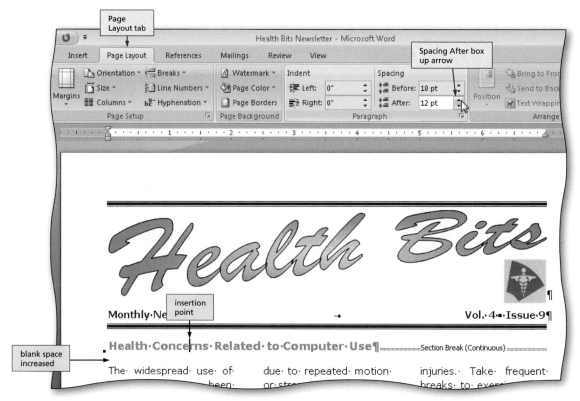

Figure 6–38

To Increase Column Width

The columns in the newsletter currently contain many rivers due to the justified alignment in the narrow column width. To eliminate some of the rivers, you increase the size of the columns slightly in this newsletter. The following steps increase column widths.

- Position the insertion point somewhere in the feature article text.

- Click the Columns button on the Page Layout tab to display the Columns gallery (Figure 6–39).

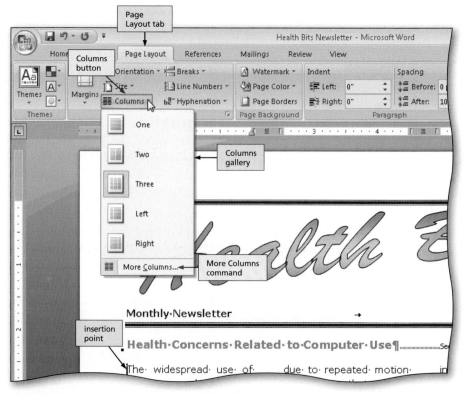

Figure 6–39

2

- Click More Columns in the Columns gallery to display the Columns dialog box.

- In the 'Width and spacing' area, click the Width box up arrow as many times as necessary until the Width box reads 2.1" (Figure 6–40).

Q&A

How would I make the columns different widths?

You would remove the check mark from the 'Equal column width' check box and then set the individual column widths in the dialog box.

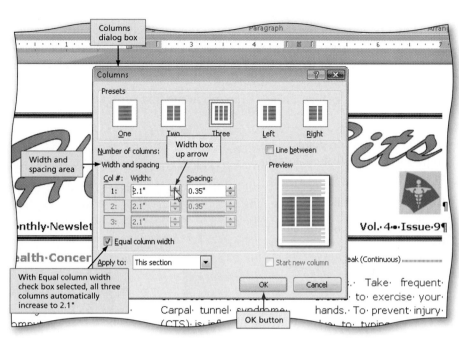

Figure 6–40

3

- Click the OK button to make the columns slightly wider (Figure 6–41).

Figure 6–41

Other Ways
1. Double-click space between columns on ruler, enter column width in dialog box, click OK button
2. Drag column boundaries on ruler

To Format a Letter as a Drop Cap

The first letter in the feature article in this newsletter is formatted as a drop cap. A **drop cap** is a capital letter whose font size is larger than the rest of the characters in the paragraph. In Word, the drop cap can sink into the first few lines of text, or it can extend into the left margin, which often is called a stick-up cap. In this newsletter, the paragraph text wraps around the drop cap.

The following steps create a drop cap in the first paragraph of the feature article in the newsletter.

- Position the insertion point somewhere in the first paragraph of the feature article.

- Display the Insert tab.

- Click the Drop Cap button on the Insert tab to display the Drop Cap gallery (Figure 6–42).

Experiment

- Point to various commands in the Drop Cap gallery to see a live pre-view of the drop cap formats in the document.

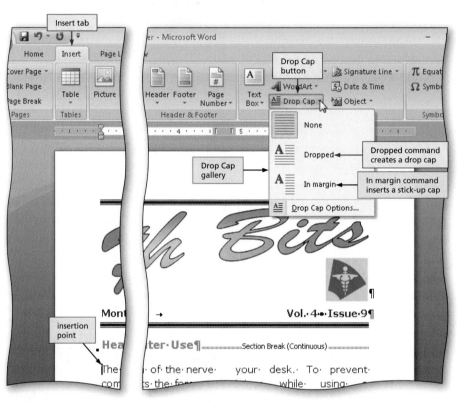

Figure 6–42

- Click Dropped in the Drop Cap gallery to format the T in the word, The, as a drop cap and wrap subsequent text in the paragraph around the drop cap (Figure 6–43).

Q&A

What is the outline around the drop cap in the document?

When you format a letter as a drop cap, Word places a frame around it. A **frame** is a container for text that allows you to position the text anywhere on the page. Word formats a frame for the drop cap so that text wraps around it. The frame also contains a paragraph mark nonprinting character to the right of the drop cap, which may or may not be visible on your screen.

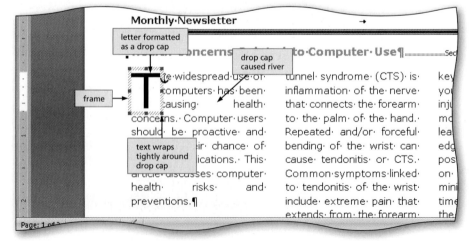

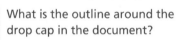

Figure 6–43

To Format the Drop Cap

The drop cap caused a river in the third line of the paragraph, and the drop cap also is too close to the text in the first line of the paragraph. You will resize the frame around the drop cap to remedy these two problems. Also, the drop cap is to be a gold color. The following steps apply these formats to the drop cap.

- Drag the right-middle sizing handle on the frame slightly rightward until the text in the first three lines of the paragraph looks like Figure 6–44.

Q&A
What if my frame no longer is displayed?

Click the drop cap to select it. Then, click the blue selection rectangle to display the frame.

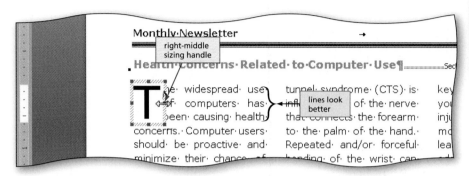

Figure 6–44

Q&A
What if the drop cap moves on the page?

Position the mouse pointer on an edge of the drop cap frame and when the mouse pointer has a four-headed arrow attached to it, drag the drop cap to the correct location.

- Triple-click inside the frame to select the drop cap.

- Right-click the selected drop cap to display the Mini toolbar. Click the Font Color button arrow on the Mini toolbar to display the Font Color gallery (Figure 6–45).

3

- Click Gold, Accent 3, Darker 50% (seventh color in the last row of Theme Colors) to change the color of the drop cap.

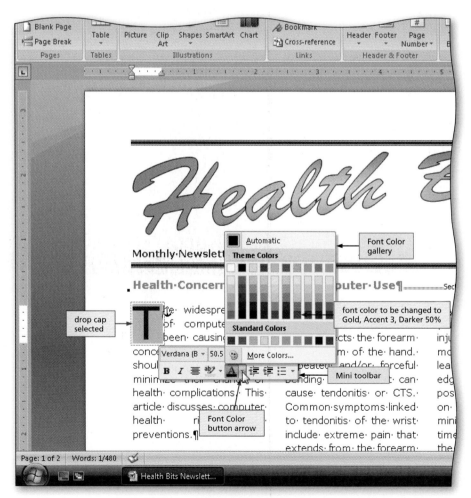

Figure 6–45

To Insert a Next Page Section Break

The third column on the first page of the newsletter is not a continuation of the feature article. The third column, instead, contains several member announcements. The feature article continues on the second page of the newsletter (shown in Figure 6–1b on page WD 387). Thus, you must insert a next page section break at the bottom of the second column so that the remainder of the feature article moves to the second page. The following steps insert a next page section break at the bottom of the second column.

- Scroll to display the bottom of the second column of the first page of the newsletter in the document window. Position the insertion point to the left of the L in the paragraph beginning with the word, Long-term.

- Display the Page Layout tab.

- Click the Insert Page and Section Breaks button on the Page Layout tab to display the Insert Page and Section Breaks gallery (Figure 6–46).

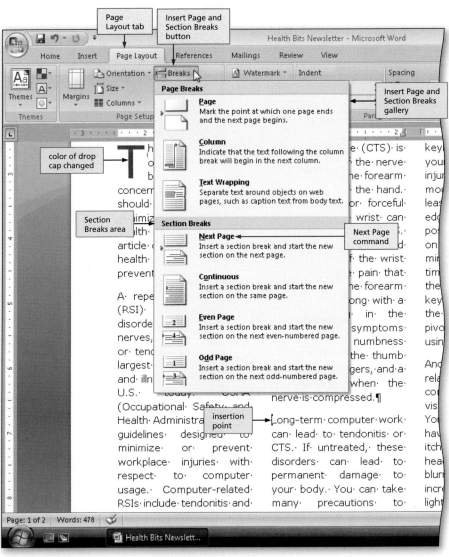

Figure 6–46

2

• In the Section Breaks area in the gallery, click Next Page to insert a section break and position the insertion point on the next page (Figure 6–47).

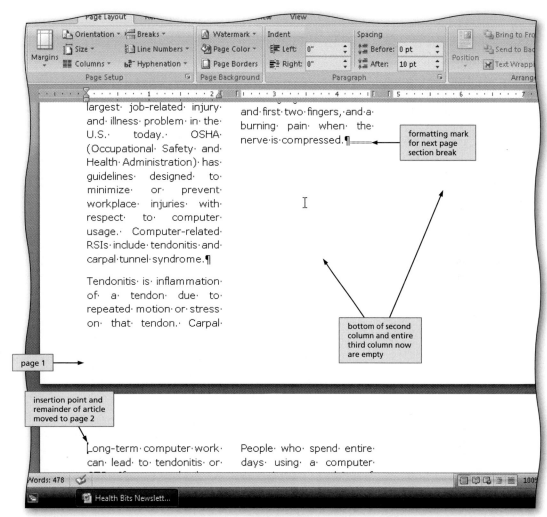

Figure 6–47

To Enter Text

The next step is to insert a jump-to line at the end of the second column, informing the reader where to look for the rest of the feature article. The following steps insert text at the bottom of the second column.

1 Scroll to display the bottom of the second column of the first page of the newsletter in the document window and then position the insertion point between the paragraph mark and the section break notation.

2 Press the ENTER key twice to insert a blank line for the jump-to text above the section break notation.

3 Press the UP ARROW key to position the insertion point on the blank line.

4 Press CTRL+R to right align the paragraph mark. Press CTRL+I to turn on the italic format. Type (Continued on next page) as the jump-to text and then press CTRL+I again to turn off the italic format.

BTW

Quick Reference
For a table that lists how to complete the tasks covered in this book using the mouse, Ribbon, shortcut menu, and keyboard, see the Quick Reference Summary at the back of this book, or visit the Word 2007 Quick Reference Web page (scsite.com/wd2007/qr).

To Insert a Column Break

In the Health Bits newsletters, for consistency, the member announcements always begin at the top of the third column. If you insert the Health Bits Announcements at the current location of the insertion point, however, they will begin at the bottom of the second column.

For the member announcements to be displayed in the third column, you insert a **column break** at the bottom of the second column, which places the insertion point at the top of the next column. Thus, the next step is to insert a column break at the bottom of the second column.

- Position the insertion point to the left of the paragraph mark of the line containing the next page section break, which is the location where the column break should be inserted.

- Click the Insert Page and Section Breaks button on the Page Layout tab to display the Insert Page and Section Breaks gallery (Figure 6–48).

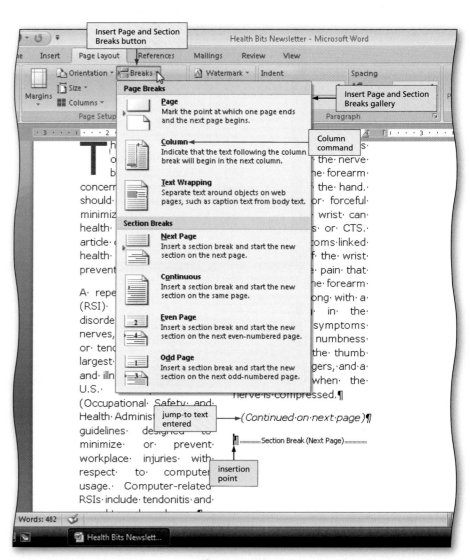

Figure 6–48

2

- Click Column in the Insert Page and Section Breaks gallery to insert a column break at the bottom of the second column on page 1 and move the insertion point to the top of the third column (Figure 6–49).

Q&A

What if I wanted to remove a column break?

You would double-click it to select it and then click the Cut button on the Home tab or press the DELETE key.

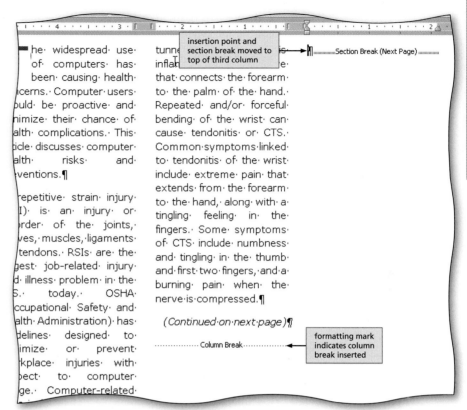

Figure 6–49

Other Ways
1. Press CTRL+SHIFT+ENTER

To Save a Document Again

You have performed several steps since the last save. Thus, you should save the newsletter again.

1 Save the newsletter again with the same file name, Health Bits Newsletter.

To Insert a File in a Column of the Newsletter

So that you do not have to enter the entire third column of announcements in the newsletter, the next step in the project is to insert the file named Health Bits Announcements in the third column of the newsletter. This file contains the three announcements: the first about a group meeting, the second about member discounts, and the third about the topic of the next newsletter issue.

The Health Bits Announcements file is located on the Data Files for Students. See the inside back cover of this book for instructions on downloading the Data Files for Students, or contact your instructor for information about accessing the required files. The steps below and at the top of the next page insert a file in a column of the newsletter.

1 With the insertion point at the top of the third column, display the Insert tab.

2 Click the Insert Object button arrow on the Insert tab to display the Object menu and then click Text from File on the Object menu to display the Insert File dialog box.

③ With your USB flash drive connected to one of the computer's USB ports, locate and then click the file called Health Bits Announcements on the USB flash drive to select the file.

④ Click the Insert button to insert the file, Health Bits Announcements, in the file Health Bits Newsletter in the third column of the newsletter.

Q&A What if text from the announcements column spills onto the second page of the newsletter?

You will format text in the announcements column so that all of its text fits in the third column of the first page.

⑤ Press SHIFT+F5 to return the insertion point to the last editing location, that is, the top of the third column on the first page of the newsletter.

To Format Text as a Heading Style

The announcements in the third column contain three subheads that need to be formatted so that they better identify their respective messages. The following steps apply the Heading 3 style to the first subhead in the announcements column.

① Position the insertion point somewhere in the subhead, GROUP MEETING.

② Display the Home tab.

③ Click the More button in the Styles gallery to expand the gallery. Click Heading 3 in the expanded Styles gallery to apply the Heading 3 style to the paragraph containing the insertion point (Figure 6–50).

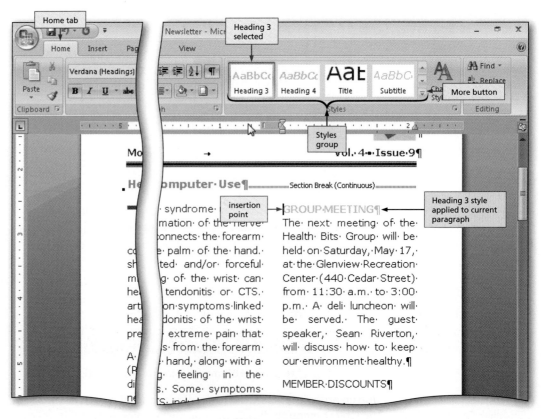

Figure 6–50

To Format More Text as a Heading Style

The following steps apply the Heading 3 style to the second and third subhead in the announcements column.

1 Position the insertion point somewhere in the subhead, MEMBER DISCOUNTS.

2 Click Heading 3 in the Styles gallery to apply the Heading 3 style to the second subhead in the announcements column.

3 Position the insertion point somewhere in the subhead, NEXT ISSUE, and then apply the Heading 3 style to this third subhead in the announcements column.

4 If an extra blank paragraph mark along with the next page section break is on the second page of the newsletter instead of the first page, position the insertion point on the paragraph mark at the end of the paragraph below the NEXT ISSUE subhead and then press the DELETE key so that the second page of the newsletter contains the remainder of the feature article (Figure 6–51).

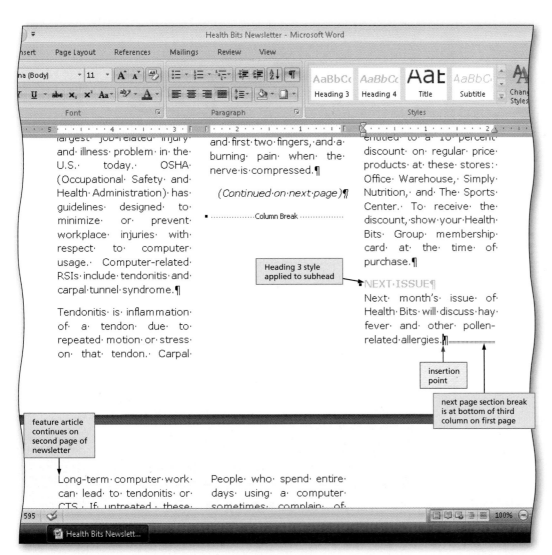

Figure 6–51

To Update a Style to Match a Selection

Instead of bright green, the subheads in this newsletter are the same gold color as the drop cap. The following steps change the color of the characters in the first subhead and then update the Heading 3 style so that all other subheads match this modified text.

1

- Scroll to and then select the line containing the subhead, GROUP MEETING.

- Right-click the selected subhead text to display the Mini toolbar and shortcut menu.

- Click the Font Color button on the Mini toolbar to change the color of the selected subhead to Gold, Accent 3, Darker 50%.

Q&A What if my Font Color button does not display the correct color?

Click the Font Color button arrow and select the correct color in the Font Color gallery.

2

- Right-click the selected subhead text again and then point to Styles on the shortcut menu to display the Styles menu (Figure 6–52).

3

- On the Styles menu, click Update Heading 3 to Match Selection, which modifies the Heading 3 style to match the formats of the selected text and changes all other Heading 3 text in the document to the updated style.

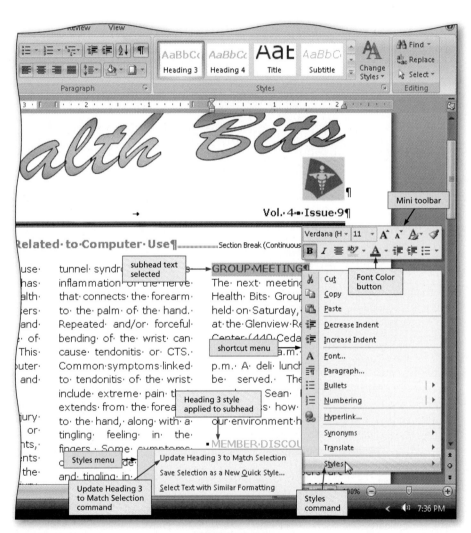

Figure 6–52

Other Ways

1. Right-click style name in Styles gallery on Home tab, click Update [style name] to Match Selection on shortcut menu

Vertical Rules

In newsletters, you often see a vertical rule separating columns. The newsletter in this chapter has a vertical rule between the second and third columns, that is, between the feature article and the announcements.

Divide sections with vertical rules.
If a multi-column newsletter contains a single article, place a vertical rule between every column. If different columns present different articles, place a vertical rule between each article.

Plan Ahead

To Place a Vertical Rule between Columns

In Word, a vertical rule is created with a left or right border that is spaced several points from the text. A point is approximately 1/72 of an inch. The following steps place a vertical rule between the second and third columns of the newsletter.

- Change the zoom level to 70% and then scroll through the document so that the entire third column is displayed in the document window.

- Drag through all of the text in the third column of the newsletter to select it.

- With the third column of page 1 in the newsletter still selected, click the Borders button arrow on the Home tab and then click Borders and Shading in the Borders gallery to display the Borders and Shading dialog box.

- If necessary, click the Borders tab in the dialog box.

- Click the Left Border button in the Preview area (Figure 6–53).

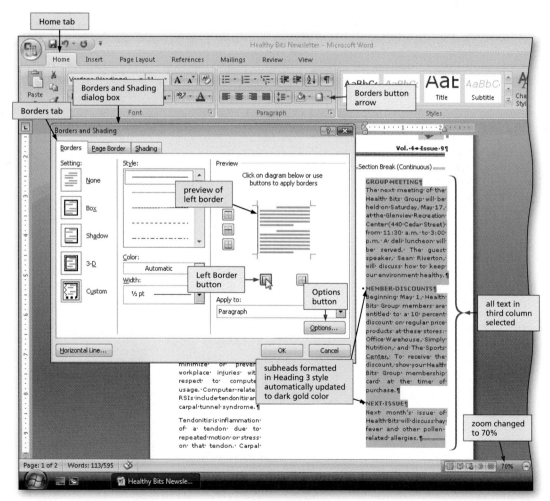

Figure 6–53

2

- Click the Options button to display the Border and Shading Options dialog box.

- In the dialog box, change the Left text box to 10 pt, which instructs Word to move the left border 10 points from the edge of the paragraph (Figure 6–54).

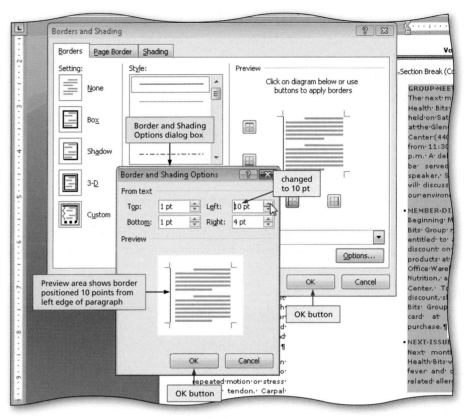

Figure 6–54

3

- Click the OK button in each open dialog box to draw a left border that is positioned 10 points from the edge of the text.

- Click in the document to remove the selection from the third column (Figure 6–55).

 Q&A

How would I place a vertical rule between every column in a newsletter?

You would click the Columns button on the Page Layout tab, click the More Columns command in the Columns gallery, place a check mark in the Line between check box, and then click the OK button.

- Change the zoom level to 100% so that the newsletter text is easier to read.

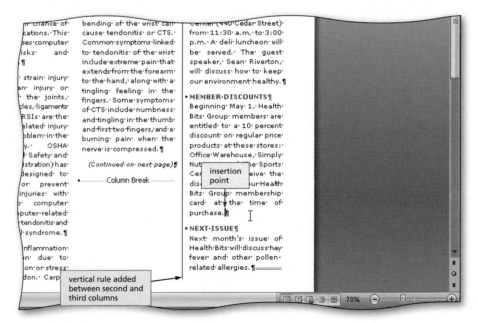

Figure 6–55

Other Ways
1. Click Page Borders button on Page Layout tab, click Borders tab in Borders and Shading dialog box, select desired border, click Options button, adjust border from text, click OK button in each dialog box

Creating a Pull-Quote

A pull-quote is text pulled, or copied, from the text of the document and given graphical emphasis so that it stands apart and commands the reader's attention. The newsletter in this project has a pull-quote on the first page between the first and second columns (Figure 6–1a on page WD 387).

> **Enhance the document with pull-quotes.**
> Because of their bold emphasis, pull-quotes should be used sparingly in a newsletter. Pull-quotes are useful for breaking the monotony of long columns of text. Typically, quotation marks are used only if you are quoting someone directly. If you use quotation marks, use curly (or smart) quotation marks instead of straight quotation marks.

Plan Ahead

To create the pull-quote in this newsletter, follow this general procedure:

1. Create a **text box**, which is a container for text that allows you to position the text anywhere on the page.
2. Copy the text from the existing document to the Clipboard and then paste the text from the Clipboard to the text box.
3. Resize the text box.
4. Move the text box to the desired location.

To Insert a Text Box

The first step in creating the pull-quote is to insert a text box. A text box is like a frame; the difference is that a text box has more graphical formatting options than does a frame. Word provides a variety of built-in text boxes, saving you the time of formatting the text box. The following steps insert a built-in text box.

1

- Scroll to display the top portion of the newsletter in the document window and position the insertion point at an approximate location for the pull-quote (you will position the pull-quote at the exact location in a later step).

- Display the Insert tab.

- Click the Text Box button on the Insert tab to display the Text Box gallery (Figure 6–56).

🔍 **Experiment**

- Scroll through the Text Box gallery to see the variety of text box styles available.

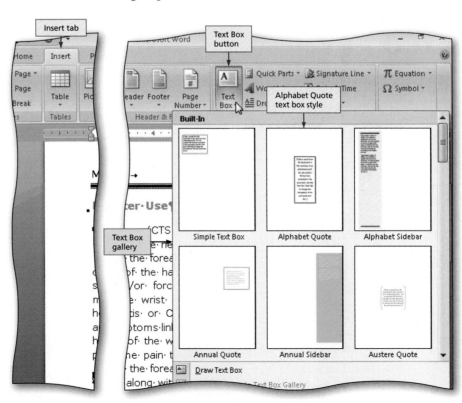

Figure 6–56

- Click Alphabet Quote in the Text Box gallery to insert that text box style in the document (Figure 6–57).

Q&A Does my text box need to be in the same location as Figure 6–57?

No. You will move the text box later.

Q&A The layout of the first page is all messed up because of the text box. What do I do?

You will enter text in the text box and then position it in the correct spot. At that time, the layout of the first page will be fixed.

Other Ways

1. Click Quick Parts button on Insert tab, click Building Blocks Organizer on Quick Parts menu, select desired text box name in Building blocks list, click Insert button

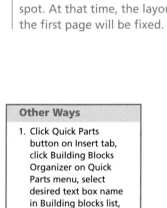

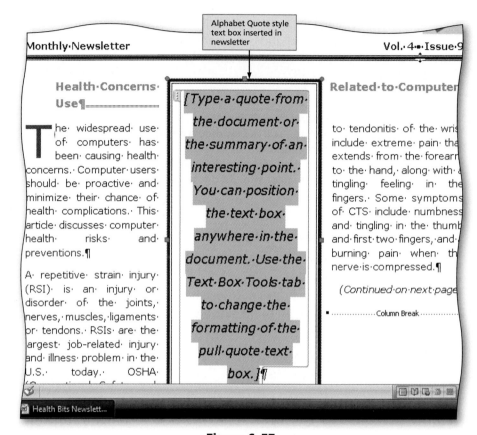

Figure 6–57

To Copy and Paste

The next step in creating the pull-quote is to copy text from the newsletter to the Clipboard and then paste the text into the text box. The item being copied is called the **source object**. The object to which you are pasting is called the **destination object**. Thus, the source object is a sentence in the body copy of the newsletter, and the destination object is the text box. The following steps copy and then paste the sentence.

- If necessary, scroll to display the second paragraph in the newsletter and then select its second sentence, which is the text for the pull-quote: RSIs are the largest job-related injury and illness problem in the U.S. today.

- If necessary, display the Home tab.

- With the sentence to be copied selected, click the Copy button on the Home tab (Figure 6–58).

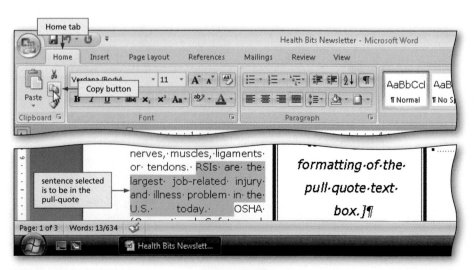

Figure 6–58

2

- If necessary, scroll to display the text box in the document window. Click the text in the text box to select it.

- Click the Paste button on the Home tab to paste the contents of the Clipboard in the text box, which replaces the selected text.

Q&A   Why did the Paste menu appear below the Paste button?
You clicked the Paste button arrow instead of the Paste button.

3

- Because you want the pasted text to use the formats that were in the text box (the destination) instead of the formats of the copied text (the source), click the Paste Options button to display the Paste Options menu (Figure 6–59).

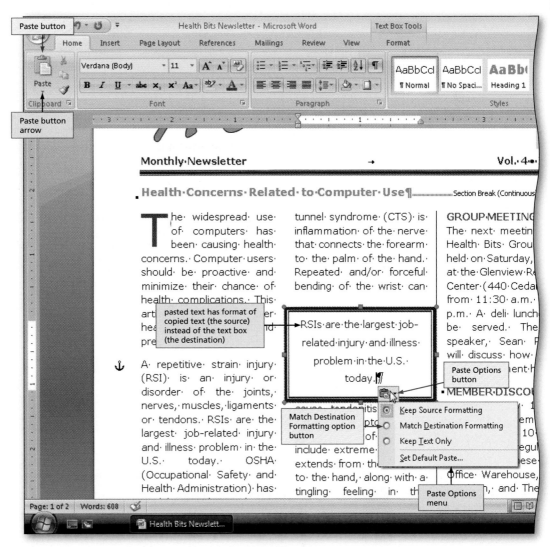

Figure 6–59

Q&A   What if the Paste Options button does not appear?
Format the text in the text box to italic with a font size of 14 point and then skip Step 4 on the next page.

Q&A   What if my pasted text already is formatted like the destination (i.e., looks like Figure 6–60 on the next page)?
Skip steps 3 and 4.

4

- Click Match Destination Formatting on the Paste Options menu to format the pasted text the same as the destination, which in this case, is the text box contents (Figure 6–60).

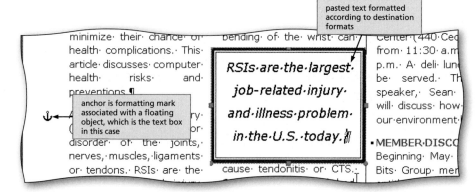

pasted text formatted according to destination formats

anchor is formatting mark associated with a floating object, which is the text box in this case

Figure 6–60

To Format Text

The next steps format the text in the pull-quote to color the text and change line spacing to 1.15.

1 Triple-click the pull-quote text to select it.

2 Use the Font Color button arrow to change the pull-quote's font color to Pink, Accent 2, Darker 50%.

3 Click in the pull-quote text to remove the selection.

4 Click the Line spacing button and then click 1.15 in the Line spacing gallery to change the line spacing of the pull-quote (Figure 6–61).

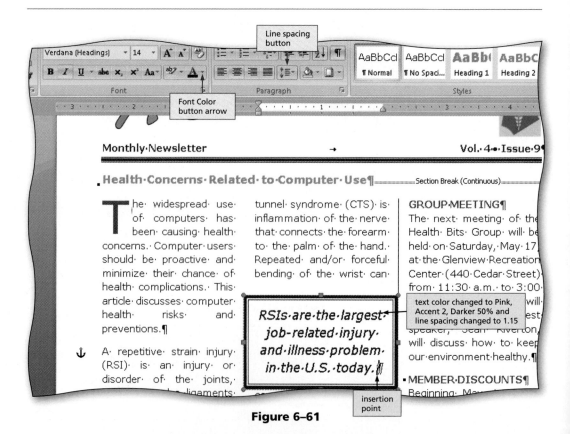

Figure 6–61

To Resize a Text Box

The next step in formatting the pull-quote is to resize the text box. You resize a text box the same way as any other object. That is, you drag its sizing handles. The following steps resize the text box.

1 If necessary, click the edge of the text box to select it.

2 Drag the right-middle sizing handle inward about one inch to make the pull-quote narrower so that the pull-quote text looks like Figure 6–62.

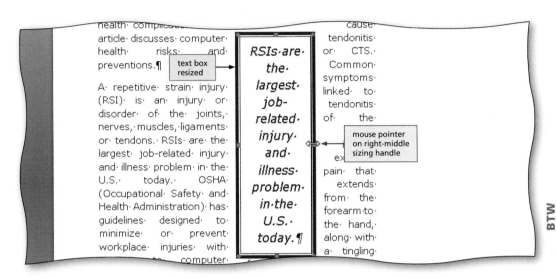

Figure 6–62

BTW

Moving Text Boxes
To move a text box using the keyboard, select the text box and then press the arrow keys on the keyboard. For example, each time you press the DOWN ARROW key, the selected text box moves down one line.

To Position a Text Box

The final step is to position the pull-quote text box between the first and second columns of the newsletter. The following step moves the text box to the desired location.

1

- With the text box still selected, drag the text box to its new location (Figure 6–63). You may need to drag and/or resize the text box a couple of times so that it looks similar to this figure.

- Click outside the text box to remove the selection.

Q&A

Why does my text wrap differently around the text box?

Differences in wordwrap relate to the printer used by your computer. Thus, your document may wordwrap around the text box differently.

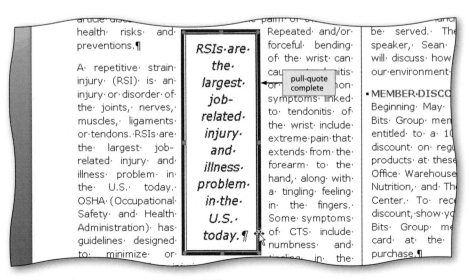

Figure 6–63

To Save a Document Again

You have performed several steps since the last save. You should save the newsletter again.

 Save the newsletter again with the same file name, Health Bits Newsletter.

Formatting the Second Page of the Newsletter

The second page of the newsletter (Figure 6–1b on page WD 387) continues the feature article that began in the first two columns on the first page. The nameplate on the second page is simpler than the one on the first page of the newsletter. In addition to the text in the feature article, page two contains a graphic. The following pages format the second page of the newsletter in this project.

<table>
<tr><td>Plan
Ahead</td><td>**Create the nameplate.**
The top of the inner pages of a newsletter may or may not have a nameplate. If you choose to create one for your inner pages, it should not be the same as, or compete with, the one on the first page. Inner page nameplates usually contain only a portion of the nameplate from the first page of a newsletter.</td></tr>
</table>

To Change Column Formatting

The document currently is formatted in three columns. The nameplate at the top of the second page, however, should be in a single column. The next step, then, is to change the number of columns at the top of the second page from three to one.

As discussed earlier in this project, Word requires a new section each time you change the number of columns in a document. Thus, you first must insert a continuous section break and then format the section to one column so that the nameplate can be entered on the second page of the newsletter. The following steps insert a continuous section break and then change the column format.

- Scroll through the document and then position the mouse pointer at the upper-left corner of the second page of the newsletter (to the left of L in Long-term).

- Display the Page Layout tab.

- Click the Insert Page and Section Breaks button on the Page Layout tab to display the Insert Page and Section Breaks gallery (Figure 6–64).

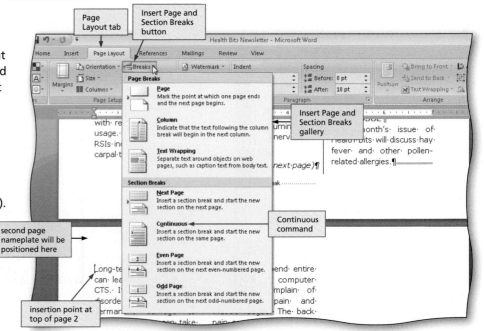

Figure 6–64

2

- Click Continuous in the Insert Page and Section Breaks gallery to insert a continuous section break above the insertion point.

- Press the UP ARROW key to position the insertion point to the left of the continuous section break just inserted.

- Click the Columns button on the Page Layout tab to display the Columns gallery (Figure 6–65).

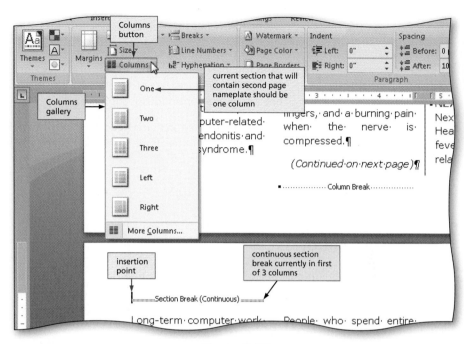

Figure 6–65

3

- Click the One in the Columns gallery to format the current section to one column, which now is ready for the second page nameplate (Figure 6–66).

Can I change the column format of existing text?

Yes. If you already have typed text and would like it to be formatted in a different number of columns, select the text, click the Columns button on the Page Layout tab, and then click the number of columns desired in the Columns gallery. Word automatically creates a new section for the newly formatted columns.

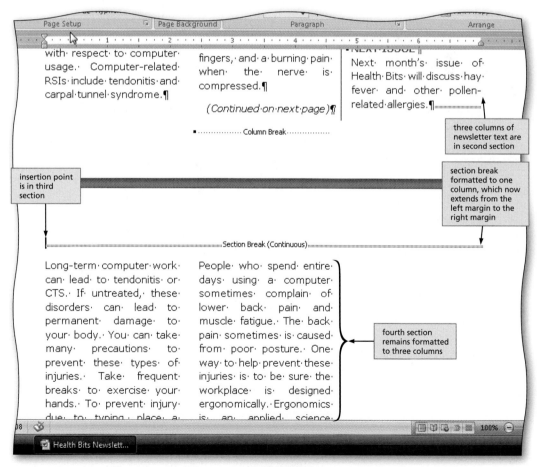

Figure 6–66

To Format and Enter Text

The following steps describe how to enter the newsletter title at the top of the second page in the third section.

1 With the insertion point to the left of the section break notation in the third section, press the ENTER key twice. Press the UP ARROW key to position the insertion point on the blank line above the continuous section break.

2 Display the Home tab. Click Heading 1 in the Styles gallery on the Home tab. Click the Center button on the Home tab to center the paragraph mark and insertion point.

3 Type HEALTH BITS as the newsletter title and then press the ENTER key.

To Split the Window

The rest of the nameplate on the second page is identical to the nameplate on the first page. That is, the issue information line is below the newsletter title, followed by a horizontal rule, which is followed by the title of the feature article. The next step is to copy these lines from the nameplate on the first page and then paste them on the second page.

To simplify this process, you would like to view the nameplate on the first page and the nameplate on the second page on the screen at the same time. Word allows you to split the window in two separate panes, each containing the current document and having its own scroll bar. This enables you to scroll to and view two different portions of the same document at the same time. The following steps split the Word window.

- Position the mouse pointer on the split box at the top of the vertical scroll bar, which changes the mouse pointer to a resize pointer (Figure 6–67).

Q&A What does the resize pointer look like?

The **resize pointer** consists of two small horizontal lines each with a vertical arrow.

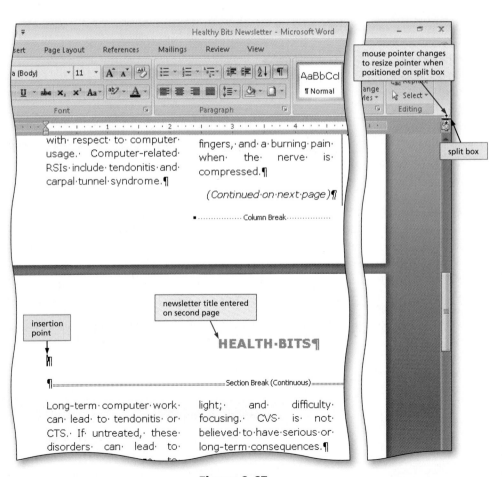

Figure 6–67

2

- Double-click the resize pointer to divide the document window in two separate panes - both the upper and lower panes display the current document (Figure 6–68).

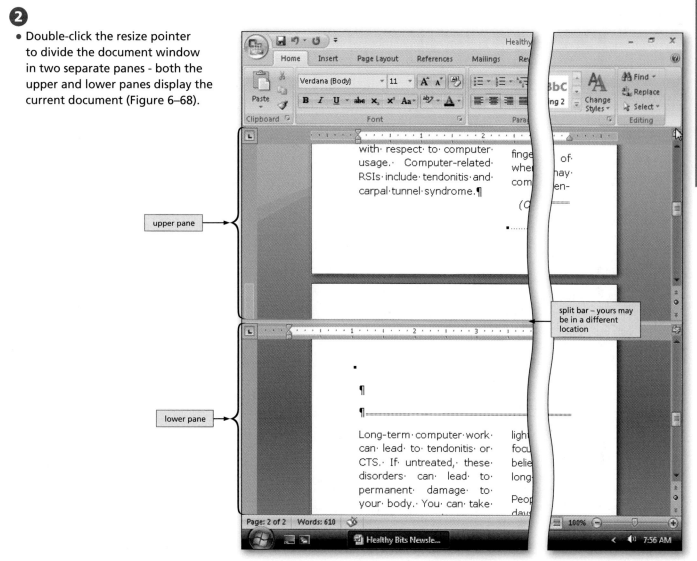

Figure 6–68

Other Ways

1. Click Split on View tab, click at desired split location in window
2. Press ALT+CTRL+S, then ENTER

TO ARRANGE ALL OPEN WORD DOCUMENTS ON THE SCREEN

If you have multiple Word documents open and want to view all of them at the same time on the screen, you can instruct Word to arrange all the open documents on the screen from top to bottom. If you wanted to arrange all open Word documents on the same screen, you would perform the following steps.

1. Click Arrange All on the View tab to display each open Word document on the screen.
2. To make one of the arranged documents fill the entire screen again, maximize the window by clicking its Maximize button or double-clicking its title bar.

To Copy and Paste Using Split Windows

The next step is to copy the bottom of the nameplate from the first page to the second page nameplate using the split window. The following steps copy and then paste using the split window.

1

- In the upper pane, scroll to display the nameplate on page 1.

- In the lower pane, scroll to display the nameplate on page 2.

- Select the issue information line and the feature article title on page 1.

- Click the Copy button on the Home tab to copy the selected text to the Clipboard (Figure 6–69).

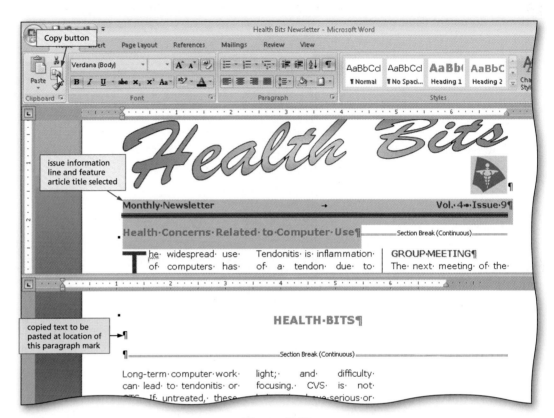

Figure 6–69

2

- Position the insertion point in the lower pane on the paragraph mark below the newsletter title.

- Click the Paste button on the Home tab to paste the issue information line and feature article title on the second page of the newsletter.

- If an extra paragraph mark appears below the feature article title, remove it (Figure 6–70).

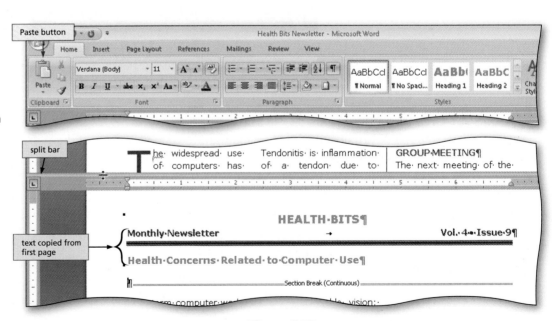

Figure 6–70

To Remove a Split Window

The next step is to remove the split window so that you can continue formatting the second page of the newsletter. The following step removes a split window.

1 Double-click the split bar, or click the Remove Split button on the View tab, or press ALT+SHIFT+C, to remove the split window and return to a single Word window on the screen.

To Enter Text

The second page of the feature article on the second page of this newsletter begins with a jump-from line (the continued message) immediately below the nameplate. The following steps enter the jump-from line.

1 With the insertion point on the line immediately below the pasted text, press CTRL+I to turn on the italic format. Type (Continued from first page) and then press CTRL+I to turn off the italic format.

2 If the continuous section break is on the line below the jump-from line, press the DELETE key to move it up to the same line as the jump-from line (Figure 6–71).

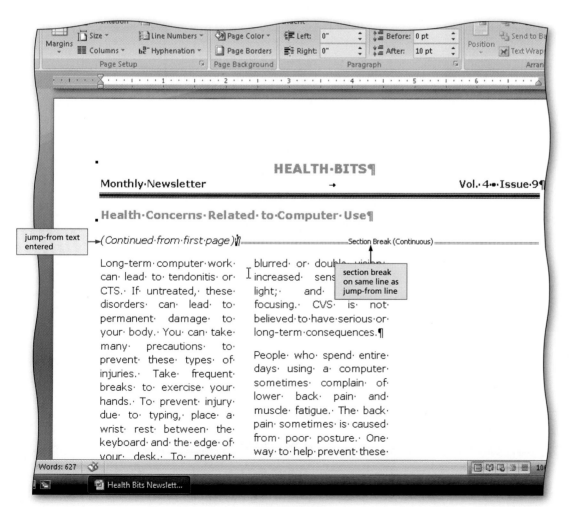

Figure 6–71

To Balance Columns

Currently, the text on the second page of the newsletter completely fills up the first column and almost fills the second column. The third column is empty. The text in the three columns should consume the same amount of vertical space. That is, the three columns should be balanced. To balance columns, you insert a continuous section break at the end of the text. The following steps balance columns.

- Scroll to the bottom of the text in the second column on the second page of the newsletter and then position the insertion point at the end of the text.

- If an extra paragraph mark is below the last line of text, press the DELETE key to remove the extra paragraph mark.

- Display the Page Layout tab.

- Click the Insert Page and Section Breaks button on the Page Layout tab to display the Insert Page and Section Breaks gallery (Figure 6–72).

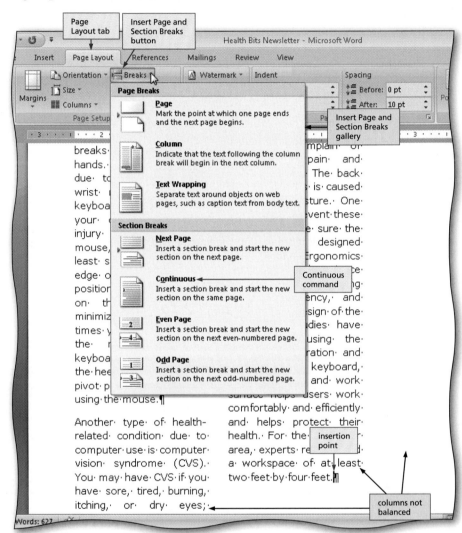

Figure 6–72

- Click Continuous in the Insert Page and Section Breaks gallery to insert a continuous section break, which balances the columns on the second page of the newsletter (Figure 6–73).

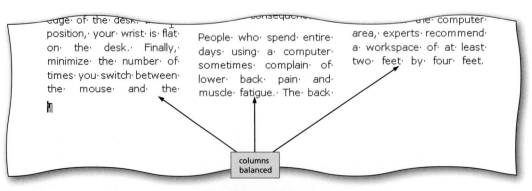

Figure 6–73

To Save a Document Again

You have performed several steps since the last save. Thus, you should save the newsletter again.

1 Save the newsletter again with the same file name, Health Bits Newsletter.

Modifying and Formatting a SmartArt Graphic

Recall from Chapter 4 that Microsoft Office 2007 includes **SmartArt graphics**, which are visual representations of ideas. Many different types of SmartArt graphics are available, allowing you to choose one that illustrates your message best.

In this newsletter, a SmartArt graphic is positioned in the lower-left corner of the second page, just below the first and second columns. Because the columns are small in the newsletter, it is best to work with a SmartArt graphic in a separate document window so that you easily can see all of its components. When finished editing the graphic, you can copy and paste it in the newsletter. You will follow these steps for the SmartArt graphic in this newsletter:

1. Open the document that contains the SmartArt graphic for the newsletter.
2. Modify the layout of the graphic. Add a shape and text to the graphic.
3. Copy and paste the graphic in the newsletter.
4. Resize the graphic and add a border to it.

To Open a Document from Word

The first draft of the SmartArt graphic is in a file called Hand and Eye Chart on the Data Files for Students. See the inside back cover of this book for instructions on downloading the Data Files for Students, or contact your instructor for information about accessing the required files. The following steps open the Hand and Eye Chart file from the USB flash drive.

1 With your USB flash drive connected to one of the computer's USB ports, click the Office Button and then click Open on the Office Button menu to display the Open dialog box.

2 Locate and select the Hand and Eye Chart file on the USB flash drive. Click the Open button to open the selected file and display its contents in the Word window.

3 Click the graphic to select it and display the SmartArt Tools tab and its subordinate tabs on the Ribbon (Figure 6–74).

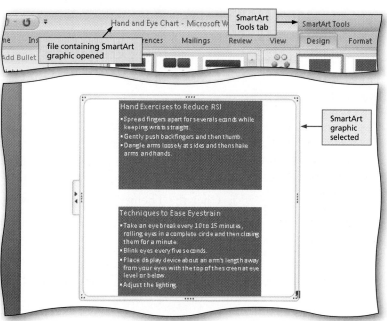

Figure 6–74

To Change the Layout of a SmartArt Graphic

The SmartArt graphic currently uses the Basic Block List layout. This newsletter uses the Vertical Bullet List layout. The following step changes the layout of an existing SmartArt graphic.

- If necessary, display the SmartArt Tools Design tab.

- With the SmartArt graphic selected, locate and click the Vertical Bullet List layout in the Layouts gallery to change the layout of the SmartArt graphic (Figure 6–75).

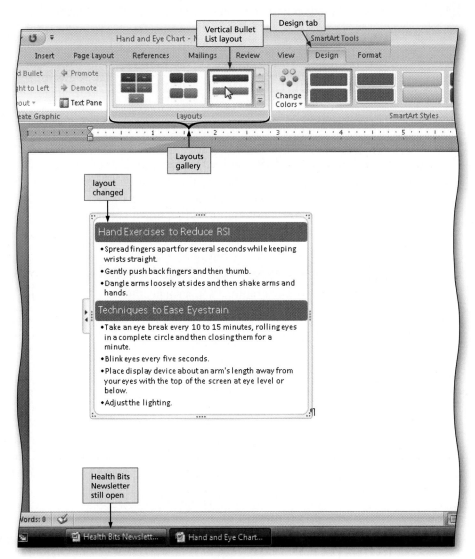

Figure 6–75

Other Ways

1. Right-click the selected graphic, click Change Layout on shortcut menu, select desired layout, click OK button

TO MODIFY THEME EFFECTS

If you wanted to change the theme effects, which would change the look of graphics such as SmartArt graphics, you would perform the following steps.

1. Click the Theme Effects button on the Page Layout tab.
2. Click the desired effect in the Theme Effects gallery.

To Add a Shape to a SmartArt Graphic

The current SmartArt graphic has two shapes — one for hand exercises and one for easing eyestrain. This newsletter has a third shape that outlines methods to minimize fatigue. The following step adds a shape to a SmartArt graphic.

1

• With the diagram selected, click the Add Shape button on the Design tab to add a shape to the SmartArt graphic (Figure 6–76).

Q&A Why did my screen display a menu instead of adding a shape?

You clicked the Add Shape button arrow instead of the Add Shape button. Clicking the Add Shape button adds the shape automatically; clicking the Add Shape button arrow displays a menu allowing you to specify the location of the shape.

Q&A How do I delete a shape?

Select the shape by clicking it and then press the DELETE key, or right-click the shape and then click Cut on the shortcut menu.

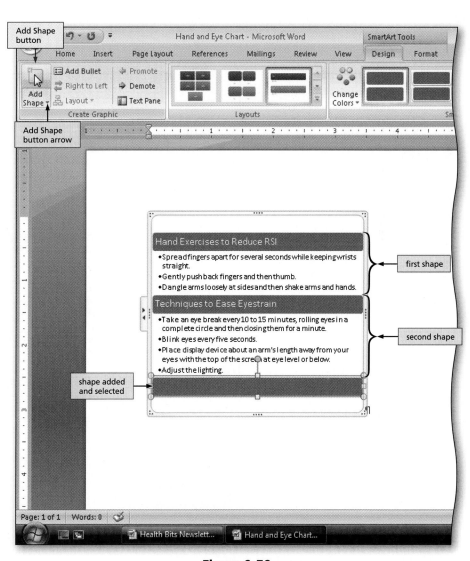

Figure 6–76

To Save Customized Themes

When you modify the theme effects, theme colors, or theme fonts, you can save the modified theme for future use. If you wanted to save a customized theme, you would perform the following steps.

1. Click the Themes button on the Page Layout tab to display the Themes gallery.

2. Click Save Current Theme in the Themes gallery.

3. Enter a theme name in the File name text box.

4. Click the Save button to add the saved theme to the Themes gallery.

To Add Text to a SmartArt Graphic through the Text Pane

In Chapter 4, you added text directly to the shapes in the SmartArt graphic. In this project, you enter the text through the Text pane. The following step uses the Text pane to add text to a shape.

1

- Click the Text Pane button on the Design tab to display the Text pane to the left of the SmartArt graphic.

- Scroll to the bottom of the Text pane and then, if necessary, position the insertion point to the right of the bullet that has no text to its right.

- Type Methods to Minimize Fatigue as the text for the shape (Figure 6–77).

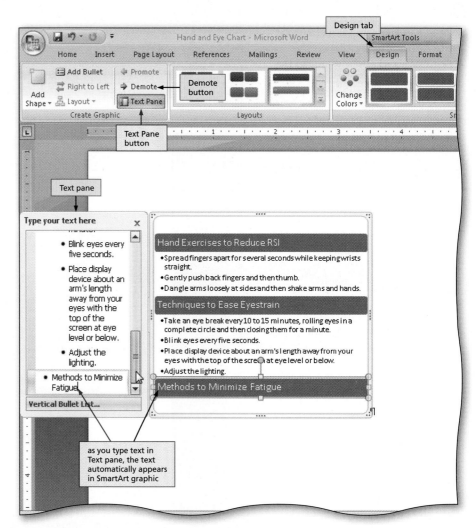

Figure 6–77

BTW

Demoting Text Pane Text
Instead of pressing the TAB key in the Text pane, you could click the Demote button on the Design tab to increase the indent for a bullet. You also can click the Promote button to decrease the indent for a bullet.

To Enter More Text to a SmartArt Graphic

The following steps enhter the remaining text in the SmartArt graphic.

1 Press the ENTER key to add a new bullet and then press the TAB key to indent the bullet.

2 Type Sit properly in an adjustable height chair with feet flat on floor.

3 Press the ENTER key to add a new bullet.

4 Type Take a break every 30 to 60 minutes, standing up and walking around or stretching. (Figure 6–78).

5 Click the Close button on the Text Pane title bar to close the Text pane.

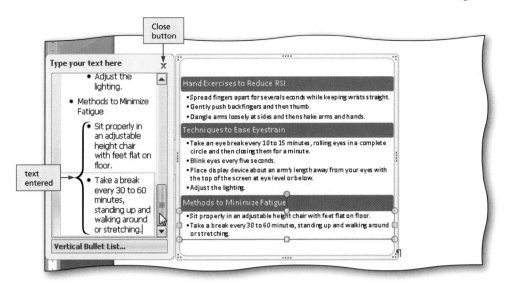

Figure 6–78

To Save an Active Document with a New File Name

To preserve the contents of the original Hand and Eye Chart file, you should save the active document with a new file name. The following steps save the active document with a new file name.

1 With the USB flash drive containing the Hand and Eye Chart file connected to one of the computer's USB ports, click the Office Button and then click Save As on the Office Button menu to display the Save As dialog box.

2 Save the document on the USB flash drive with the file name, Hand and Eye Chart Modified.

To Copy and Paste a SmartArt Graphic

The next step is to copy the SmartArt graphic from this document window and then paste it in the newsletter. The following steps use the Clipboard task pane to copy the graphic and then paste it in the second page of the newsletter.

- Display the Home tab.

- Click the Clipboard Dialog Box Launcher on the Home tab to display the Clipboard task pane.

- If the Office Clipboard in the Clipboard task pane is not empty, click the Clear All button in the Clipboard task pane.

- If necessary, click the SmartArt graphic to select it.

- Click the Copy button on the Home tab to copy the selected SmartArt graphic to the Office Clipboard (Figure 6–79).

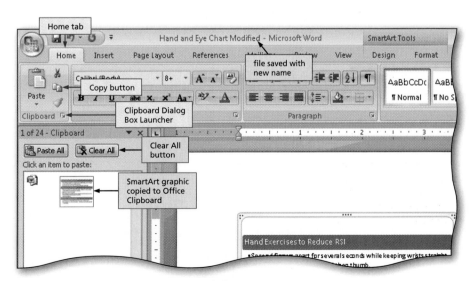

Figure 6–79

2

- Click Health Bits Newsletter - Microsoft Word program button on the Windows Vista taskbar to display the newsletter document.

- Position the insertion point at the bottom of the second page of the newsletter and then click the Paste button on the Home tab to paste the SmartArt graphic in the newsletter (Figure 6–80).

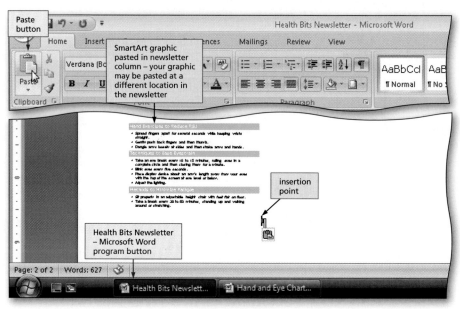

Figure 6–80

To Format a Graphic as Floating

The text in the newsletter should wrap around the graphic in a square shape. Thus, the next step is to change the graphic from inline to floating with a wrapping style of square. Perform the following steps to format the graphic as floating with square wrapping.

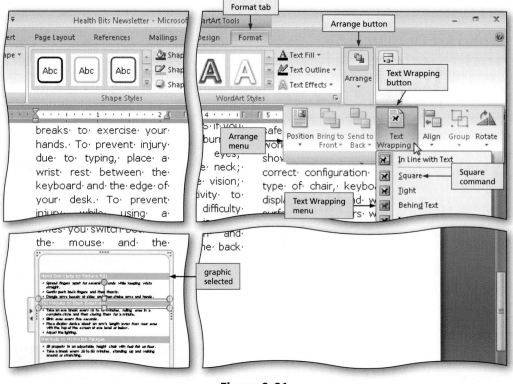

Figure 6–81

1 If necessary, double-click the SmartArt graphic to select it.

2 Display the SmartArt Tools Format tab on the Ribbon.

3 With the SmartArt graphic selected, click the Arrange butthon on the Format tab and then click the Text Wrapping button on the Arrange menu to display the Text Wrapping menu (Figure 6–81).

4 Click Square on the Text Wrapping menu to change the graphic from inline to floating with square wrapping.

To Resize and Position the SmartArt Graphic

The next task is to increase the size of the SmartArt graphic so that it is as wide as the first two columns in the newsletter and then position it in the bottom left corner of the second page. The following steps resize and then position the graphic.

1 Drag the upper-right corner sizing handle outward until the graphic is approximately the same size as shown in Figure 6–82.

2 Point to the frame on the graphic and when the mouse has a four-headed arrow attached to it, drag the graphic to the location shown in Figure 6–82. You may have to drag the graphic a couple of times to position it similarly to the figure.

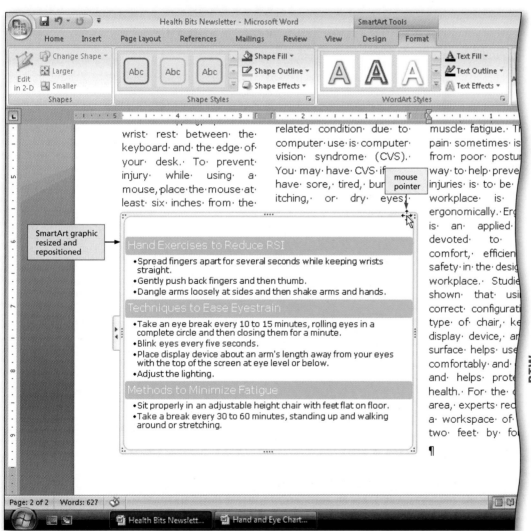

Figure 6–82

BTW

Space Around Graphics
The space between a graphic and the text, which sometimes is called the **run-around** should be at least 1/8" and should be the same for all graphics in a document. Adjust the run-around of a selected floating graphic by doing the following: click the Arrange button on the SmartArt Tools Format tab, click the Position button on the Arrange menu, click the More Layout Options on the Position menu, adjust the values in the 'Distance from text' text boxes, and then click the OK button.

To Add an Outline to a SmartArt Graphic

The SmartArt graphic in this newsletter has a green outline around it. The following steps add an outline to a SmartArt graphic.

- Click the Shape Outline button arrow on the Format tab to display the Shape Outline gallery.

- Point to Green, Accent 1 in the Shape Outline gallery to display a live preview of that color outline applied to the SmartArt graphic in the document (Figure 6–83).

Experiment

- Point to various colors in the Shape Outline gallery and watch the outline color around the SmartArt graphic change.

- Click Green, Accent 1 in the Shape Outline gallery to apply the selected outline color to the SmartArt graphic.

Q&A

Can I change other aspects of a graphic?

Yes. Through the Design and Format tabs, you can change the size of a shape, fill and outline colors, text styles and colors, and more.

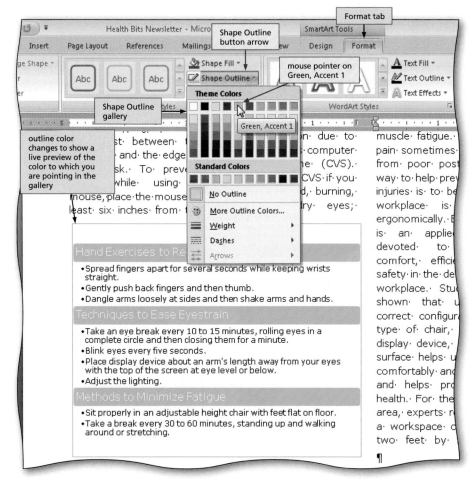

Figure 6–83

- Click outside the graphic so that it is no longer selected.

Other Ways

1. Right-click selected graphic, click Format Object on shortcut menu, click Line Color in left pane, click Solid line, select color, click Close button

---

Finishing and Distributing the Newsletter

With the text and graphics in the newsletter entered and formatted, the next step is to look at the newsletter as a whole and determine if it looks finished in its current state. To give the newsletter a finished look, you will add a border to its edges.

Then, you will distribute the newsletter via e-mail. When you e-mail the newsletter, however, you cannot be certain that it will print correctly for the recipients because printers wordwrap text differently. To ensure that the newsletter will look the same on the recipients as on your computer, you will save the newsletter in a special format that allows others to view the document as you see it.

The following pages finish the document and then distribute it via e-mail.

To Zoom Two Pages

The last step in formatting the newsletter is to place a border around its edges. You can place both pages in the document window at once so that you can see all the page borders applied. The following steps zoom two pages.

1 Display the View tab.

2 Click the Two Pages button on the View tab to display both entire pages of the newsletter in the document window (Figure 6–84).

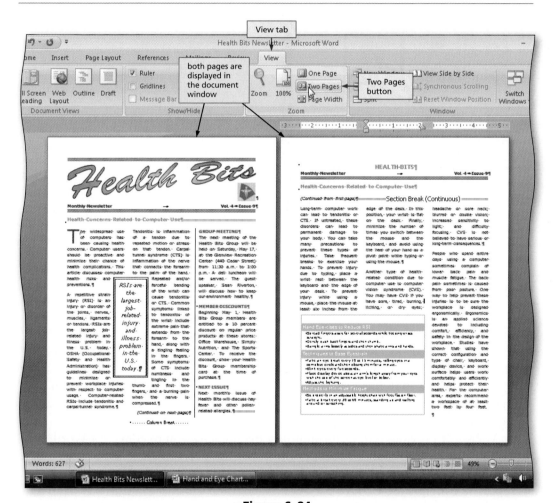

Figure 6–84

To Add a Page Border

This newsletter has a 4 ½ point gold border around the perimeter of each page. The steps below and on the next page add a page border around the pages of the newsletter.

1 Display the Page Layout tab.

2 Click the Page Borders button on the Page Layout tab to display the Borders and Shading dialog box. If necessary, click the Page Border tab.

Q&A What if I cannot select the Page Borders button because it is dimmed?

Click somewhere in the newsletter to make the newsletter the active document and then redo Step 2.

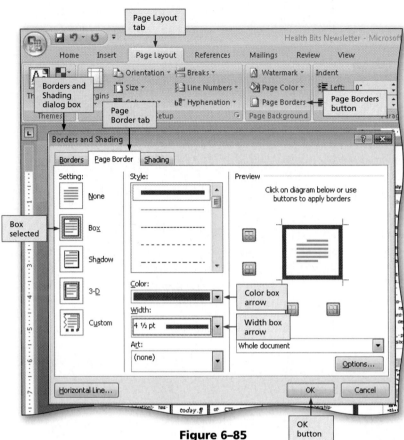

Figure 6–85

③ Click Box in the Setting area to specify a border on all four sides.

④ Click the Color box arrow and then click Gold, Accent 3, Darker 50% in the Color gallery.

⑤ Click the Width box arrow and then click 4 ½ pt (Figure 6–85).

⑥ Click the OK button to place the defined border on each page of the newsletter.

BTW

Printing Borders
In Word, page borders are positioned 24 points from the edge of the page. Many printers cannot print text and graphics that close to the edge of the page. To alleviate this problem, you may need to change the Measure from setting in the Borders and Shading Options dialog box so that the border is positioned from the edge of the text, instead of the edge of the page.

PDF

PDF, which stands for Portable Document Format, is a file format created by Adobe Systems that shows all elements of a printed document as an electronic image. Users can view a PDF document without the software that created the original document. Thus, the PDF format enables users easily to share documents with others. To view, navigate, and print a PDF file, you use a program called **Acrobat Reader**, which can be downloaded free from Adobe's Web site. Figure 6–86 shows the newsletter in this chapter opened in an Acrobat Reader window.

Microsoft provides a free add-in utility that enables you to convert a Word document to a PDF format. To check if the utility has been downloaded to your computer, click the Office Button menu and then point to Save As. If your Save As submenu contains the PDF or XPS command, then the add-in utility has been installed. If your Save As submenu contains the 'Find add-ins for other file formats' command, then the add-in utility has not been installed. To download the add-in utility, click 'Find add-ins for other file formats' on the Save As submenu to display the 'Enable support for other file formats, such as PDF and XPS' Help window. Scroll through the Help window and then click the Microsoft Save as PDF or XPS Add-in for 2007 Microsoft Office Programs command, which displays a Web page on Microsoft's site. Follow the instructions at that Web page to download and install the add-in utility.

With the PDF add-in utility installed on your computer, you can save your documents as PDF files or e-mail the document to others as a PDF file.

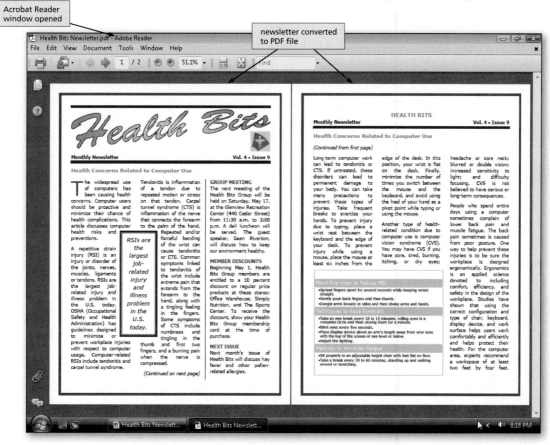

Figure 6–86

To E-Mail a Document as a PDF

If the PDF add-in utility is installed on your computer, you can e-mail the document displayed in the Word window as a PDF file. The original Word document remains intact — Word creates a copy of the file in a PDF format and attaches the PDF file to the e-mail message using your default e-mail program. The following steps e-mail a PDF of the current document, assuming you use Outlook as your default e-mail program.

1

- Click the Office Button and then point to Send on the Office Button menu (Figure 6–87).

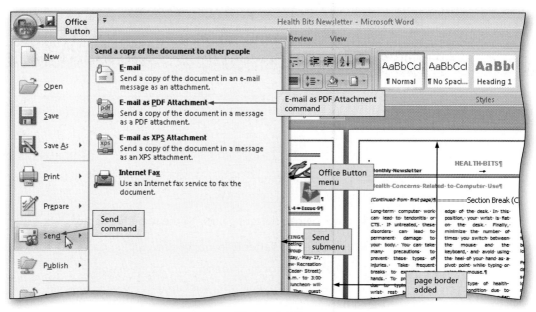

Figure 6–87

2

● Click E-mail as PDF Attachment on the Send submenu, which converts the current document to a PDF file, starts your default e-mail program, and attaches the PDF file to the e-mail message.

Q&A

What if the E-mail as PDF Attachment command is not on my Send submenu?

The PDF add-in utility has not been installed on your computer. See the discussion in the previous section for information about installing the PDF add-in utility.

● If necessary, maximize the e-mail window.

● Fill in the To text box with the recipient's e-mail address.

● Fill in the message (Figure 6–88).

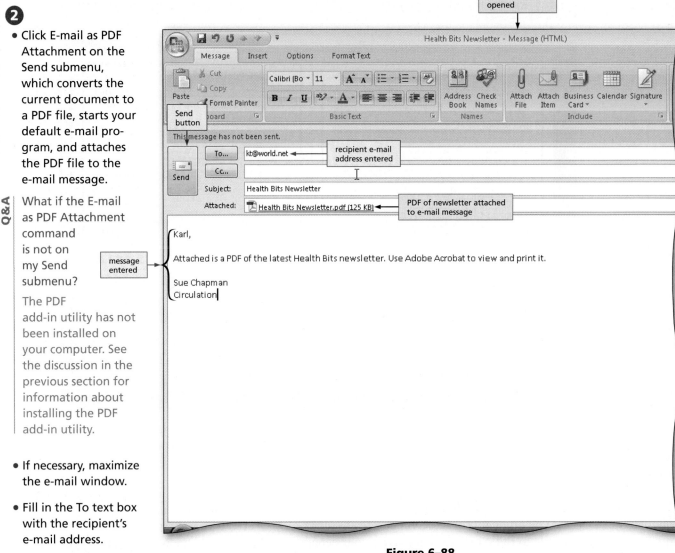

Figure 6–88

3

● Click the Send button to send the e-mail message along with the PDF attachment to the recipient named in the To text box.

To Save, Print, and Quit Word

The newsletter now is complete. You should save the document, print the document, and then quit Word.

1 Save the newsletter again with the same file name.

2 Print the newsletter (shown in Figure 6–1 on page WD 387).

Q&A

What if an error message appears about margins?

Depending on the printer you are using, you may need to set the margins differently for this project.

Q&A What if one or more of the borders do not print?

Click the Page Borders button on the Page Layout tab, click the Options button in the dialog box, click the Measure from box arrow and click Text, change the four text boxes to 15 pt, and then click the OK button in each dialog box. Try printing the document again. If the borders still do not print, adjust the text boxes in the dialog box to a number smaller than 15 point.

3 Quit Word, closing all open documents.

BTW **Conserving Ink and Toner**
You can instruct Word to print draft quality documents to conserve ink or toner by clicking the Office Button, clicking the Word Options button, clicking Advanced in the left pane of the Word Options dialog box, scrolling to the Print area, placing a check mark in the 'Use draft quality' check box, and then clicking the OK button. Click the Office Button, point to Print, and then click Quick Print.

Chapter Summary

In this chapter, you have learned how to create a professional looking newsletter using Word's desktop publishing features such as WordArt, columns, horizontal and vertical rules, and pull-quotes. The items listed below include all the new Word skills you have learned in this chapter.

1. Set Custom Margins (WD 389)
2. Insert WordArt (WD 391)
3. Change the WordArt Fill Color (WD 393)
4. Change the WordArt Shape (WD 395)
5. Border One Edge of a Paragraph (WD 396)
6. Insert a Symbol (WD 398)
7. Format a Graphic as Floating (WD 402)
8. Move a Graphic (WD 403)
9. Flip a Graphic (WD 403)
10. Adjust the Brightness of a Graphic (WD 404)
11. Modify a Style Using the Modify Style Dialog Box (WD 405)
12. Insert a Continuous Section Break (WD 409)
13. Change the Number of Columns (WD 410)
14. Justify a Paragraph (WD 411)
15. Insert a File in a Column of the Newsletter (WD 412)
16. Increase Column Width (WD 414)
17. Format a Letter as a Drop Cap (WD 416)
18. Format the Drop Cap (WD 417)
19. Insert a Next Page Section Break (WD 418)
20. Insert a Column Break (WD 420)
21. Update a Style to Match a Selection (WD 424)
22. Place a Vertical Rule between Columns (WD 425)
23. Insert a Text Box (WD 427)
24. Copy and Paste (WD 428)
25. Position a Text Box (WD 431)
26. Change Column Formatting (WD 432)
27. Split the Window (WD 434)
28. Arrange All Open Word Documents on the Screen (WD 435)
29. Copy and Paste Using Split Windows (WD 436)
30. Remove a Split Window (WD 437)
31. Balance Columns (WD 438)
32. Change the Layout of a SmartArt Graphic (WD 440)
33. Modify Theme Effects (WD 440)
34. Add a Shape to a SmartArt Graphic (WD 441)
35. Save Customized Themes (WD 441)
36. Add Text to a SmartArt Graphic through the Text Pane (WD 442)
37. Copy and Paste a SmartArt Graphic (WD 443)
38. Add an Outline to a SmartArt Graphic (WD 446)
39. E-Mail a Document as a PDF (WD 449)

If you have a SAM user profile, you may have access to hands-on instruction, practice, and assessment. Log in to your SAM account (http://sam2007.course.com) to launch any assigned training activities or exams that relate to the skills covered in this chapter.

Learn It Online

Test your knowledge of chapter content and key terms.

Instructions: To complete the Learn It Online exercises, start your browser, click the Address bar, and then enter the Web address `scsite.com/wd2007/learn`. When the Word 2007 Learn It Online page is displayed, click the link for the exercise you want to complete and then read the instructions.

Chapter Reinforcement TF, MC, and SA
A series of true/false, multiple choice, and short answer questions that test your knowledge of the chapter content.

Flash Cards
An interactive learning environment where you identify chapter key terms associated with displayed definitions.

Practice Test
A series of multiple choice questions that test your knowledge of chapter content and key terms.

Who Wants To Be a Computer Genius?
An interactive game that challenges your knowledge of chapter content in the style of a television quiz show.

Wheel of Terms
An interactive game that challenges your knowledge of chapter key terms in the style of the television show *Wheel of Fortune*.

Crossword Puzzle Challenge
A crossword puzzle that challenges your knowledge of key terms presented in the chapter.

Apply Your Knowledge

Reinforce the skills and apply the concepts you learned in this chapter.

Working with Desktop Publishing Elements of a Newsletter
Instructions: Start Word. Open the document, Apply 6-1 Totally Toned Newsletter Draft, from the Data Files for Students. See the inside back cover of this book for instructions on downloading the Data Files for Students, or contact your instructor for information about accessing the required files.

The document contains a newsletter that you are to modify. The modified newsletter is shown in Figure 6–89.

Perform the following tasks:
1. Change the column width of the columns in the body of the newsletter to 2.1".
2. Change the WordArt shape to Chevron Up.
3. Move the graphic of the weight lifter to the location shown in Figure 6–89.
4. Adjust the brightness of the graphic of the weight lifter to +20 %.
5. In the issue information line, insert a dot symbol between the volume and issue.
6. Change the alignment of the paragraph containing the drop cap from left-aligned to justified.
7. Change the color of the subhead, Weight Room Makeover, to Red, Accent 3, Darker 25%. Select the subhead and then update all Heading 3 styles to match the selection.
8. Add a shape to the bottom of the SmartArt graphic and then insert the text, Nutrition, in the bottom shape. Be sure the inserted text is formatted the same as the text in the other two shapes.
9. If necessary, move the SmartArt graphic so that it is positioned similarly to the one in Figure 6–89.
10. If necessary, move the pull-quote so that it is positioned similarly to the one shown in Figure 6–89.
11. Change the document properties as specified by your instructor.

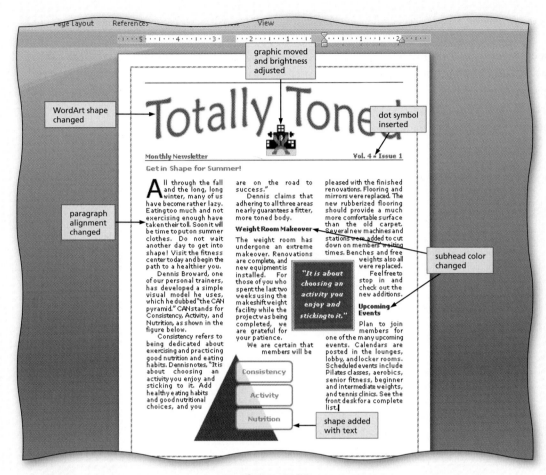

Figure 6–89

12. Save the modified file with the file name, Apply 6-1 Totally Toned Newsletter Modified.

13. Submit the revised newsletter in the format specified by your instructor.

Extend Your Knowledge

Extend the skills you learned in this chapter and experiment with new skills. You may need to use Help to complete the assignment.

Adding a Table to a Newsletter and Enhancing a Nameplate

Instructions: Start Word. Open the document, Extend 6-1 Park Department Newsletter Draft, from the Data Files for Students. See the inside back cover of this book for instructions on downloading the Data Files for Students, or contact your instructor for information about accessing the required files.

You will add a table to the bottom of the newsletter, change the format of the WordArt, change the look of the horizontal rules, change the symbol in the issue information line, add a drop cap, and place vertical rules between each column in the newsletter.

Perform the following tasks:

1. Use Help to review how to create and format a table, if necessary, and to learn about WordArt options, borders, symbols, drop caps, lines between columns, and tabs.

Continued >

Extend Your Knowledge *continued*

2. Insert a continuous section break at the end of the third column of the newsletter to balance the columns. Change the number of columns in the new section from three to one. Change the style of the paragraph in the new section to No Spacing. Use the Table command on the Insert menu to insert a table that has eight rows and three columns. Enter the data in the table as shown in Figure 6–90. Format the table using a table style of your preference.

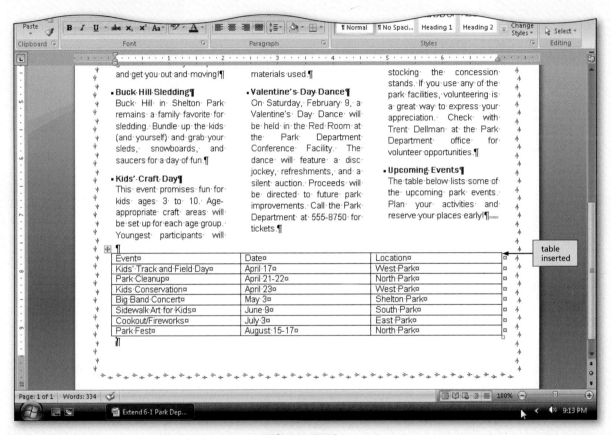

Figure 6–90

3. Change the WordArt to a style other than WordArt style 1. Add a fill texture to the WordArt. Add a Shadow Effect to the WordArt.

4. Remove the horizontal rules (top and bottom borders). Add decorative, colored ruling lines in the same position that are different from the default.

5. Change the symbol between the volume and issue in the information line to a symbol other than the dot.

6. Add a drop cap to the first paragraph in the body of the newsletter. Change the number of lines to drop from three to two lines.

7. Place a vertical line between the three columns in the body of the newsletter.

8. If the newsletter flows to two pages, reduce the size of elements such as WordArt or clip art or the table, or adjust spacing above or below paragraphs so that the newsletter fits on a single page. Make any other necessary adjustments to the newsletter.

9. Clear all tabs in the issue information line in the nameplate. Insert a right-aligned tab stop at the 7" mark. Fill the tab space with a leader character of your choice.

10. Change the document properties as specified by your instructor.

11. Save the revised document with a new file name and then submit it in the format specified by your instructor.

Make It Right

Analyze a document and correct all errors and/or improve the design.

Formatting a Newsletter

Instructions: Start Word. Open the document, Make It Right 6-1 Spring Projects Newsletter Draft, from the Data Files for Students. See the inside back cover of this book for instructions on downloading the Data Files for Students, or contact your instructor for information about accessing the required files.

The document is a newsletter whose elements are not formatted properly (Figure 6–91). You are to edit and format the WordArt, format the clip art image and columns, add a drop cap, format the SmartArt graphic, and add a border.

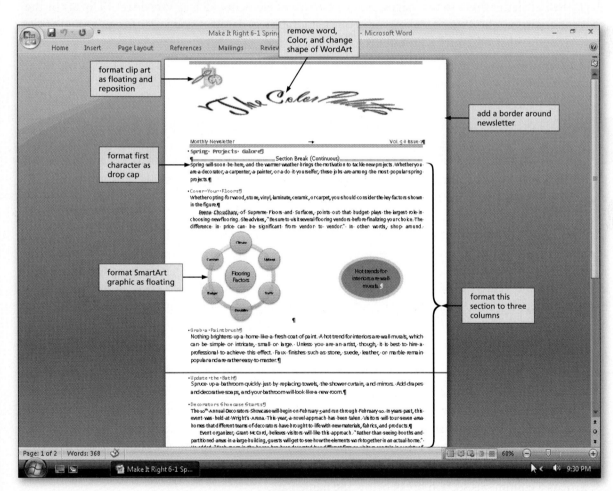

Figure 6–91

Perform the following tasks:

1. Change the theme colors to a color scheme other than Verve.

2. Remove the word, Color, from the WordArt, so that the newsletter title is The Palette. Change the shape of the WordArt so that the text is more readable.

3. Format the clip art image of the color palette to floating (In Front of Text) and then position the image in an open space on the nameplate. If necessary, adjust the size of the WordArt and the clip art image so that they have a pleasing appearance in the nameplate.

Continued >

Make It Right *continued*

4. Change the number of columns in the body of the newsletter from one to three.

5. Format the first letter in the first paragraph of text as a drop cap. Color the drop cap.

6. If necessary, insert a column break so that the subhead, Decorators Showcase Starts, begins at the top of the third column.

7. Format the SmartArt graphic as floating with a Tight wrapping style. Move the SmartArt graphic to the bottom-left corner of the newsletter. Change the theme effects to one other than Office. Save the modified theme.

8. Position the pull-quote near the Grab a Paintbrush section of the newsletter.

9. Add an attractive border around the edge of the newsletter. Do not use the default single line, black border.

10. If the newsletter flows to two pages, reduce the size of elements such as WordArt or clip art or the pull-quote, or adjust spacing above or below paragraphs so that the newsletter fits on a single page. Make any other necessary adjustments to the newsletter.

11. Change the document properties, as specified by your instructor. Save the revised document with a new file name and then submit it in the format specified by your instructor.

In the Lab

Design and/or create a document using the guidelines, concepts, and skills presented in this chapter. Labs are listed in order of increasing difficulty.

Lab 1: Creating a Newsletter with a Pull-Quote and an Article on File

Problem: You are an editor of the newsletter, Memory Lane. The next edition is due out in one week. This issue's article will discuss the new exhibit (Figure 6–92). The text for the feature articles in the newsletter is in a file on the Data Files for Students. See the inside back cover of this book for instructions on downloading the Data Files for Students, or contact your instructor for information about accessing the required files. You need to create the nameplate and the pull-quote.

Perform the following tasks:

1. Change all margins to .75 inches. Depending on your printer, you may need different margin settings.

2. Create the nameplate using the formats identified in Figure 6–92. Create the title using WordArt. Insert the dot symbol between the volume and issue on the issue information line. Use the Clip Art task pane to locate the image shown, or use a similar graphic (or you can insert the picture called Clock, which is on the Data Files for Students). Resize the image to the size shown in the figure. Format the image as floating and then position it as shown.

3. Create a continuous section break below the nameplate.

4. Format section 2 to three columns.

5. Insert the Lab 6-1 Memory Lane Articles, which is located on the Data Files for Students, in section 2 below the nameplate.

6. Format the newsletter according to Figure 6–92. Columns should have a width of 2" with spacing of 0.5". Resize the drop cap so that it is not so close to the text. Position the border between the second and third column 15 points from the left edge of the text.

7. Insert a continuous section break at the end of the document to balance the columns.

8. Format the subheads, New Artifacts and Next Month's Issue, using the Heading 2 style. Be sure the New Artifacts subhead starts at the top of the third column. If necessary, insert a column break.

9. Insert a Pinstripes Quote text box for the pull-quote. The text for the pull-quote is in the second column of the article. Copy the text and then paste it in the text box. Change the style of the text box to Diagonal Gradient - Accent 5. Resize the text box so that it is similar in size to Figure 6–92. Position the text box as shown in Figure 6–92.

10. Add the page border as shown in the figure. (*Hint:* Use the Art box arrow in the Page Border tab of the Borders and Shading dialog box.)

11. View the document in print preview. If it does not fit on a single page, click the Shrink to Fit button on the Print Preview tab or reduce the size of the WordArt or adjust spacing above and below paragraphs.

12. Save the document with Lab 6-1 History Museum Newsletter as the file name and then submit it in the format specified by your instructor.

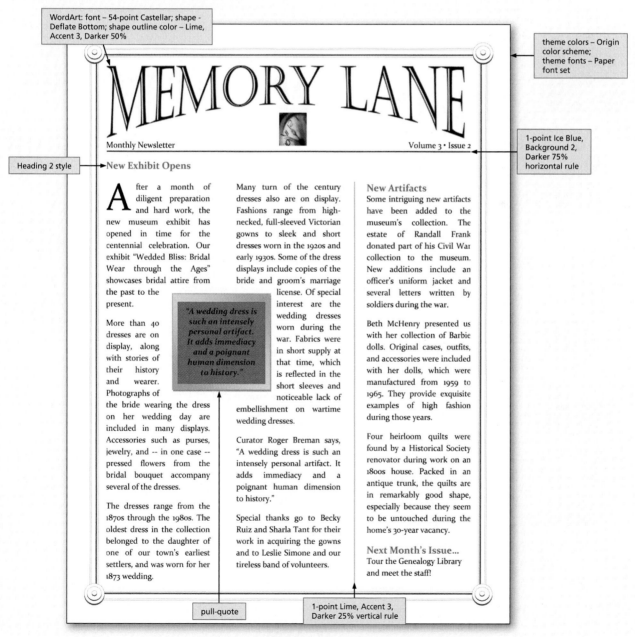

Figure 6–92

In the Lab

Lab 2: Creating a Newsletter with a SmartArt Graphic and an Article on File

Problem: You are responsible for the monthly preparation of The Free Press, a newsletter for community members. The next edition discusses upcoming community activities (Figure 6–93). This article already has been prepared and is on the Data Files for Students. See the inside back cover of this book for instructions on downloading the Data Files for Students, or contact your instructor for information about accessing the required files. You need to create the nameplate and the SmartArt graphic.

Perform the following tasks:

1. Change all margins to .75 inches. Depending on your printer, you may need different margin settings.

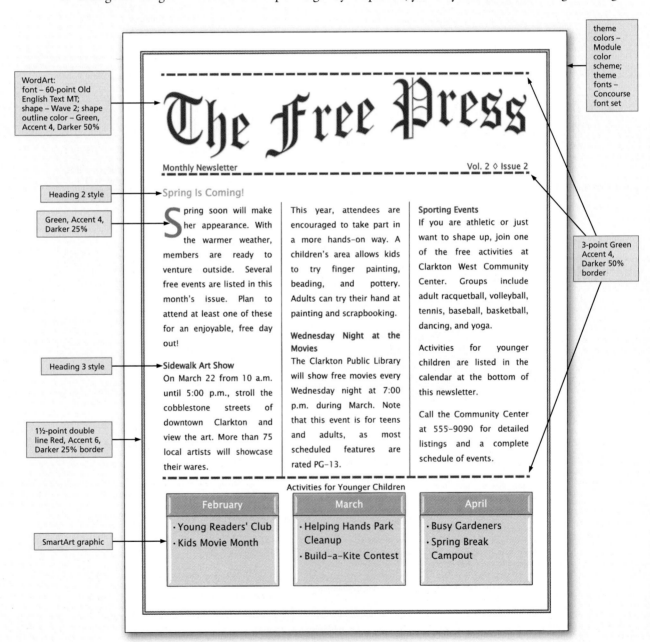

WordArt:
font – 60-point Old English Text MT; shape – Wave 2; shape outline color – Green, Accent 4, Darker 50%

theme colors – Module color scheme; theme fonts – Concourse font set

Heading 2 style

Green, Accent 4, Darker 25%

3-point Green Accent 4, Darker 50% border

Heading 3 style

1½-point double line Red, Accent 6, Darker 25% border

SmartArt graphic

The Free Press

Monthly Newsletter   Vol. 2 ◊ Issue 2

Spring Is Coming!

Spring soon will make her appearance. With the warmer weather, members are ready to venture outside. Several free events are listed in this month's issue. Plan to attend at least one of these for an enjoyable, free day out!

Sidewalk Art Show
On March 22 from 10 a.m. until 5:00 p.m., stroll the cobblestone streets of downtown Clarkton and view the art. More than 75 local artists will showcase their wares.

This year, attendees are encouraged to take part in a more hands-on way. A children's area allows kids to try finger painting, beading, and pottery. Adults can try their hand at painting and scrapbooking.

Wednesday Night at the Movies
The Clarkton Public Library will show free movies every Wednesday night at 7:00 p.m. during March. Note that this event is for teens and adults, as most scheduled features are rated PG-13.

Sporting Events
If you are athletic or just want to shape up, join one of the free activities at Clarkton West Community Center. Groups include adult racquetball, volleyball, tennis, baseball, basketball, dancing, and yoga.

Activities for younger children are listed in the calendar at the bottom of this newsletter.

Call the Community Center at 555-9090 for detailed listings and a complete schedule of events.

Activities for Younger Children

February	March	April
• Young Readers' Club • Kids Movie Month	• Helping Hands Park Cleanup • Build-a-Kite Contest	• Busy Gardeners • Spring Break Campout

Figure 6–93

2. Create the nameplate using the formats identified in Figure 6–93. Create the title using WordArt. Insert the diamond symbol between the volume and issue on the issue information line.

3. Create a continuous section break below the nameplate.

4. Format section 2 to three columns.

5. Insert the Lab 6-2 Free Press Articles, which is located on the Data Files for Students, in section 2 below the nameplate.

6. Format the newsletter according to Figure 6–93. Columns should have a width of 2.1" with spacing of 0.35". Format the subheads using the Heading 3 style. Change the Heading 3 style to Red, Accent 6, Darker 25%. Save this new format as part of the Heading 3 style.

7. Insert a continuous section break at the end of the document to balance the columns.

8. Add the page border as shown in the figure.

9. Open a new document window and create the SmartArt graphic shown in Figure 6–93. Use the Horizontal Bullet List layout. Add text shown in the figure. Apply the Cartoon SmartArt style. Save the graphic with the file name, Lab 6-2 Activities for Children Graphic. Use the Office Clipboard to copy and paste the SmartArt graphic to the bottom section of the newsletter. Change its color to Colored Fill - Accent 1. Add the title and border above the SmartArt graphic.

10. Arrange both documents (the graphic and the newsletter) on the screen. Scroll through both open windows. Maximize the newsletter window.

11. View the document in print preview. If it does not fit on a single page, click the Shrink to Fit button on the Print Preview tab or reduce the size of the WordArt or adjust spacing above and below paragraphs.

12. Save the newsletter using Lab 6-2 Free Press Newsletter as the file name and submit it in the format specified by your instructor.

In the Lab

Lab 3: Creating a Newsletter from Scratch

Problem: You work part-time for Bowl-a-Rama Lanes, which publishes a monthly newsletter. Figure 6–94 on the next page shows the contents of the next issue.

Perform the following tasks:

1. Change all margins to .75 inches. Depending on your printer, you may need different margin settings.

2. Create the nameplate using the formats identified in Figure 6–94. Create the title using WordArt. Insert the diamond symbol between the volume and issue on the issue information line. Use the Clip Art task pane to locate the images shown or similar images (or you can insert the pictures called Bowling Ball and Bowling Pins, which are on the Data Files for Students). Resize the images and position them as shown in the figure. Flip the image of the bowling ball.

3. Create a continuous section break below the nameplate. Format section 2 to two columns. Enter the text in section 2 using justified paragraph formatting. Place a vertical rule between the columns in section 2.

4. Insert a Braces Quote 2 text box for the pull-quote. Copy the text for the pull-quote from the newsletter and then paste it in the text box. Change the fill of the text box to Tan, Background 2, Darker 50% and the outline to Orange, Accent 1, Darker 25%. Resize and position the text box so that it is similar in size and location to Figure 6–94.

5. Insert a continuous section break at the end of the second column in section 2. Format section 3 to one column. Create the table as shown at the bottom of the newsletter in section 3.

Continued >

In the Lab *continued*

6. Make any additional formatting required in the newsletter so that it looks like the figure. The entire newsletter should fit on a single page.

7. Save the document with Lab 6-3 Eleventh Frame Newsletter as the file name and then submit it in the format specified by your instructor.

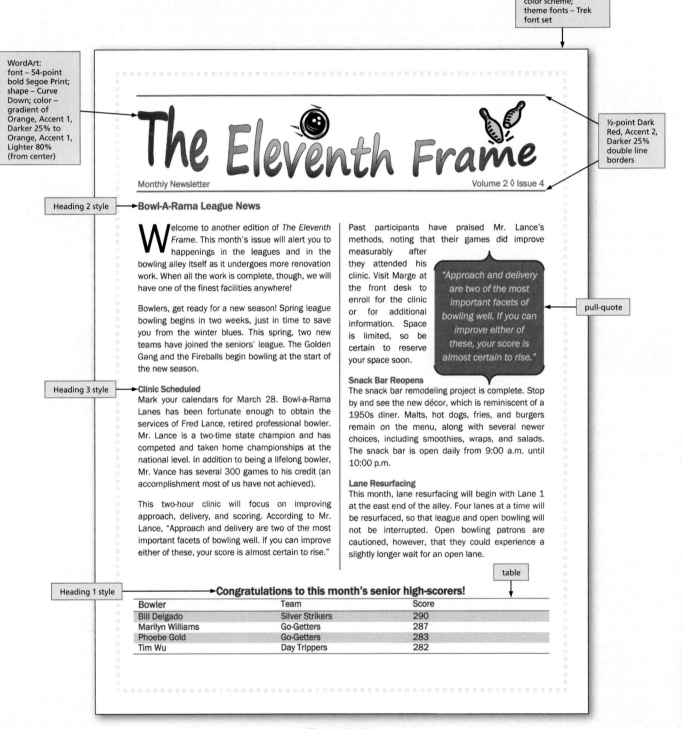

theme colors – Equity color scheme; theme fonts – Trek font set

WordArt: font – 54-point bold Segoe Print; shape – Curve Down; color – gradient of Orange, Accent 1, Darker 25% to Orange, Accent 1, Lighter 80% (from center)

½-point Dark Red, Accent 2, Darker 25% double line borders

The Eleventh Frame

Monthly Newsletter   Volume 2 ◊ Issue 4

Heading 2 style → **Bowl-A-Rama League News**

Welcome to another edition of *The Eleventh Frame*. This month's issue will alert you to happenings in the leagues and in the bowling alley itself as it undergoes more renovation work. When all the work is complete, though, we will have one of the finest facilities anywhere!

Bowlers, get ready for a new season! Spring league bowling begins in two weeks, just in time to save you from the winter blues. This spring, two new teams have joined the seniors' league. The Golden Gang and the Fireballs begin bowling at the start of the new season.

Heading 3 style → **Clinic Scheduled**

Mark your calendars for March 28. Bowl-a-Rama Lanes has been fortunate enough to obtain the services of Fred Lance, retired professional bowler. Mr. Lance is a two-time state champion and has competed and taken home championships at the national level. In addition to being a lifelong bowler, Mr. Vance has several 300 games to his credit (an accomplishment most of us have not achieved).

This two-hour clinic will focus on improving approach, delivery, and scoring. According to Mr. Lance, "Approach and delivery are two of the most important facets of bowling well. If you can improve either of these, your score is almost certain to rise."

Past participants have praised Mr. Lance's methods, noting that their games did improve measurably after they attended his clinic. Visit Marge at the front desk to enroll for the clinic or for additional information. Space is limited, so be certain to reserve your space soon.

pull-quote → *"Approach and delivery are two of the most important facets of bowling well. If you can improve either of these, your score is almost certain to rise."*

Snack Bar Reopens

The snack bar remodeling project is complete. Stop by and see the new décor, which is reminiscent of a 1950s diner. Malts, hot dogs, fries, and burgers remain on the menu, along with several newer choices, including smoothies, wraps, and salads. The snack bar is open daily from 9:00 a.m. until 10:00 p.m.

Lane Resurfacing

This month, lane resurfacing will begin with Lane 1 at the east end of the alley. Four lanes at a time will be resurfaced, so that league and open bowling will not be interrupted. Open bowling patrons are cautioned, however, that they could experience a slightly longer wait for an open lane.

table →

Heading 1 style → **Congratulations to this month's senior high-scorers!**

Bowler	Team	Score
Bill Delgado	Silver Strikers	290
Marilyn Williams	Go-Getters	287
Phoebe Gold	Go-Getters	283
Tim Wu	Day Trippers	282

Figure 6–94

Cases and Places

Apply your creative thinking and problem solving skills to design and implement a solution.

• EASIER   •• MORE DIFFICULT

• 1: Create a Page in this Textbook

For the final project in your computer concepts class, you have been assigned the task of creating page WD 452 in this textbook. The page contains many desktop publishing elements: nameplate, horizontal rules, columns of text, balanced columns, and a variety of font sizes, font colors, and shading. Use WordArt for the text in the nameplate. Split the Word window and copy the Learn It Online nameplate to the location for the Apply Your Knowledge nameplate in the middle of the page. Then, edit the WordArt text in the pasted nameplate to Apply Your Knowledge. Use the concepts and techniques presented in this chapter to format your Word document so that it looks as much like page WD 452 as possible.

•• 2: Create a Newsletter for Residents of an Active Adult Community

As a part-time office assistant at an active adult community, you have been asked to produce a monthly newsletter to help residents get better acquainted with each other and with the many activities and events available at the social center. The community has individual patio homes, several common areas, a park, and a social center. The social center has one large and three smaller rooms available at no cost to residents for events such as showers, parties, reunions, lunches, lectures, and so on. Several events have been scheduled for the next month. For example, on July 3, residents are invited to a cookout and fireworks in the park area. On August 21 and 22, a community garage sale will be set up in the east commons area. The social center events include a free blood pressure screening in Room B, a senior Pilates class in Room A, and a Civil War lecture in Room A. The newsletter should welcome the three new residents that recently moved into the community. Use your library, the Internet, personal experiences, or other resources to obtain more information about active adult communities so that you can elaborate on the information presented here. Organize the information and create a newsletter. The newsletter should contain at least two of these graphic elements: clip art image, picture, SmartArt graphic, pull-quote. Enhance the newsletter with a drop cap, WordArt, color, ruling lines, and a page border.

•• 3: Create a Newsletter about Library Happenings

As a part-time library assistant, you have been asked by the director to create a monthly newsletter. The director wants the first issue to publicize the new technology center and to alert patrons to the many events scheduled at the library this month. Especially important, he believes, are the children's reading program, the used book sale, and upcoming author lectures. He also wants you to list the new releases in both fiction and nonfiction. Use your library, the Internet, personal experiences, or other resources to assist you with elaborating on information presented here. Organize the information and create a newsletter. The newsletter should contain at least two of these graphic elements: clip art image, picture, SmartArt graphic, pull-quote. Enhance the newsletter with a drop cap, WordArt, color, ruling lines, and a page border. Use leader characters to fill the tab space in the issue information line.

Continued >

Cases and Places *continued*

•• 4: Create a Newsletter about a Topic that Interests You

Make It Personal

What are your interests and hobbies? How do you pass the time? Do you belong to any clubs or organizations? In this assignment, you are to create a newsletter that discusses or highlights an activity or interest of yours. If you are an avid traveler, you could create a newsletter highlighting recent or upcoming trips. If you belong to a club or organization, create a newsletter that covers club activities and members. Perhaps you have a hobby that you can translate into a newsletter, such as photography, quilting, scuba diving, gardening, or sports. Students with jobs could write a newsletter about company happenings and fellow employees, and music or movie buffs could write reviews and news as articles in the newsletter. Organize the information and create a newsletter. The newsletter should contain at least two of these graphic elements: clip art image, picture, SmartArt graphic, pull-quote. Enhance the newsletter with a drop cap, WordArt, color, ruling lines, and a page border.

•• 5: Create a Newsletter that Highlights an Aspect of Your School or Community

Working Together

Find a group, club, event, or facility at your school or organization that you believe could be better publicized or utilized. For example, you could compile a newsletter about the career center, the library, or recreation facility at your school. If your school has a drama or choir department, you could create a newsletter about past and upcoming performances, student actors/singers, and so on. If your school does not have these facilities, find an organization in your community. One team member should gather information for a feature article that highlights the facility or group's purpose or history. Another member should interview its president, director, resource person, or other willing party. Another team member should compile a list of features or upcoming events and activities. Copy all team members' text to the Office Clipboard and then use the Paste All command to compile all the gathered information into a single newsletter. The newsletter should contain at least one clip art image, a picture, a SmartArt graphic, and a pull-quote. Enhance the newsletter with a drop cap, WordArt, color, ruling lines, and a page border.

Integration Feature

Linking an Excel Worksheet and Chart to a Word Document

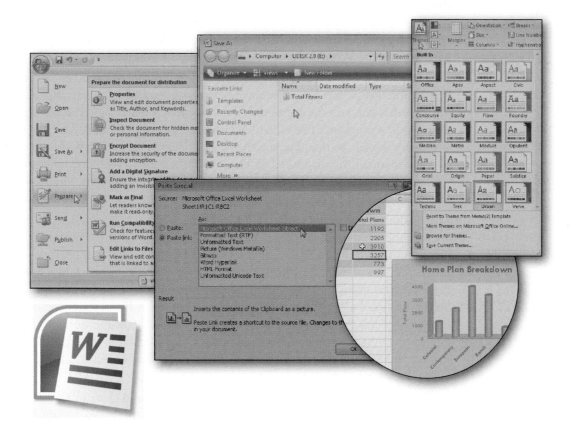

Objectives

You will have mastered the material in this feature when you can:

- Apply a theme to a document
- Update the body text style
- Link an Excel worksheet to a Word document
- Link an Excel chart to a Word document
- Break links
- Save a document so that it is compatible with a previous version of Word
- E-mail a document

Integration Feature Introduction

With Microsoft Office, you can copy part or all of a project created in one Office program to a project created in another Office program. The item being copied is called the **object**. For example, you could copy an Excel worksheet (the object) that is located in an Excel workbook (the source document) to a Word document (the destination document). That is, an object can be copied from a source document to a destination document.

Project — Document Containing Linked Objects

You can use one of three techniques to copy objects from one program to another: copy and paste, embed, or link.

- **Copy and paste**. When you copy an object and then paste it, the object becomes part of the destination document. You edit a pasted object using editing features of the destination program. For example, when you select an Excel worksheet in an Excel workbook, click the Copy button on Excel's Home tab, and then click the Paste button on Word's Home tab, each row in the Excel worksheet becomes a separate paragraph in the Word document and each column is separated by a tab character.

- **Embed**. When you embed an object, like a pasted object, it becomes part of the destination document. The difference between an embedded object and a pasted object is that you edit the contents of an embedded object using the editing features of the source program. The embedded object, however, contains static data; that is, any changes made to the object in the source program are not reflected in the destination document. If you embed an Excel worksheet in a Word document, the Excel worksheet remains as an Excel worksheet in the Word document. When you edit the Excel worksheet from within the Word document, you will use Excel editing features.

- **Link**. A linked object, by contrast, does not become a part of the destination document even though it appears to be a part of it. Rather, a connection is established between the source and destination documents so that when you open the destination document, the linked object appears as part of it. When you edit a linked object, the source program starts and opens the source document that contains the linked object. For example, when you edit a linked worksheet, Excel starts and displays the Excel workbook that contains the worksheet; you then edit the worksheet in Excel. Unlike an embedded object, if you open the Excel workbook that contains the Excel worksheet and then edit the Excel worksheet, the linked object will be updated in the Word document, too.

The project in this feature links an Excel worksheet and chart to a Word document (a memo). Because the worksheet and chart are inserted in the Word document as a link, any time you open the memo in Word, the latest version of the Excel worksheet data is displayed in the memo. Figure 1a shows the memo draft (without any links to Excel); Figure 1b shows the Excel worksheet and chart; and Figure 1c shows the final copy of the memo linked to the Excel worksheet and chart.

BTW

Linked Objects
When you open a document that contains linked objects, Word displays a dialog box asking if you want to update the Word document with data from the linked file. Click the Yes button only if you are certain the linked file is from a trusted source; that is, you should be confident that the source file does not contain a virus or other potentially harmful program before you instruct Word to link the source file to the destination document.

(a) Draft of Word Document (containing no links)

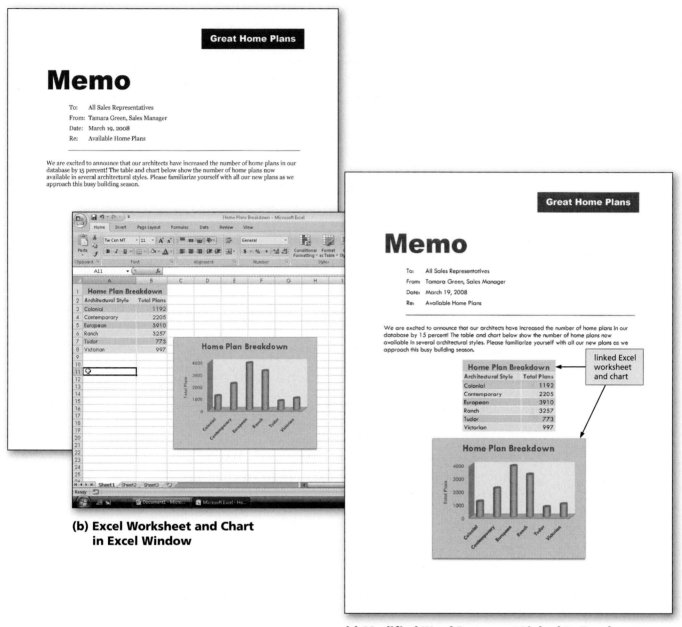

**(b) Excel Worksheet and Chart
in Excel Window**

**(c) Modified Word Document Linked to Excel
Worksheet and Chart**

Figure 1

Overview

As you read through this feature, you will learn how to create the document with the links shown in Figure 1c and then e-mail a copy of the document without links by performing these general tasks:

- Open and re-format the memo.
- Link the Excel worksheet and chart to the memo.
- Edit the Excel worksheet and update the Word document.
- Prepare the memo to be e-mailed to users who may have earlier versions of Word.

Plan
Ahead

General Project Guidelines

When creating a Word document that contains an object created in another Office program, the actions you perform and decisions you make will affect the appearance and characteristics of the finished document. When you create a document that is to contain another Office program's object, such as the project shown in Figure 1 on the previous page, you should follow these general guidelines:

1. **Determine how to copy the object.** You can copy and paste, embed, or link an object created in another Office program to the Word document.

   * If you simply want to use the object's data and have no desire to use the object in the source program, then copy and paste the object.

   * If you want to use the object in the source program but you want the object's data to remain static if it changes in the source document, then embed the object.

   * If you want to ensure that the most current version of the object appears in the destination document, then link the object. If the source file is large, such as a video clip or a sound clip, link the object to keep the size of the destination document smaller.

2. **Be certain files from others are virus free.** When using objects created by others, do not use the source document until you are certain it does not contain a virus or other malicious program. Use an antivirus program to verify that any files you use are free of viruses and other potentially harmful programs.

To Open a Word Document and Save It with a New File Name

The first step in this integration feature is to open the draft of the memo that is to contain links to the Excel worksheet and chart objects. The memo file, named Home Plans Memo Draft, is located on the Data Files for Students. See the inside back cover of this book for instructions on downloading the Data Files for Students, or contact your instructor for information about accessing the required files.

To preserve the contents of the original Home Plans Memo Draft file, you will save it with a new file name. The following steps open the memo in Word and save it with a new file name.

1 Start Word and then open the file named Home Plans Memo Draft from the Data Files for Students.

2 Click the Office Button and then click Save As on the Office Button menu to display the Save As dialog box.

3 Type `Home Plans Memo Modified` in the File name text box to change the file name.

4 Locate and select your USB flash drive in the list of available drives.

5 Click the Save button in the Save As dialog box to save the document on the USB flash drive with the new file name, Home Plans Memo Modified.

6 If the zoom level is not 100%, change it to 100%.

BTW

Certification
The Microsoft Certified Application Specialist (MCAS) program provides an opportunity for you to obtain a valuable industry credential — proof that you have the Word 2007 skills required by employers. For more information see Appendix G or visit the Word 2007 Certification Web page (scsite.com/wd2007/cert).

To Change the Document Theme

The projects in previous chapters have used a color scheme from one document theme and a font set from another document theme. In this feature, the modified memo uses the Median color scheme and Median font set. Instead of changing the color scheme and font set individually, Word provides a means of changing the entire document theme (color scheme, font set, and effects) at once. The following steps change the document theme.

1

• Display the Page Layout tab.

• Click the Themes button on the Page Layout tab to display the Themes gallery (Figure 2).

🔍 **Experiment**

• Point to various themes in the Themes gallery and watch the color scheme and font set change in the document window.

2

• Click Median in the Themes gallery to change the document theme to Median.

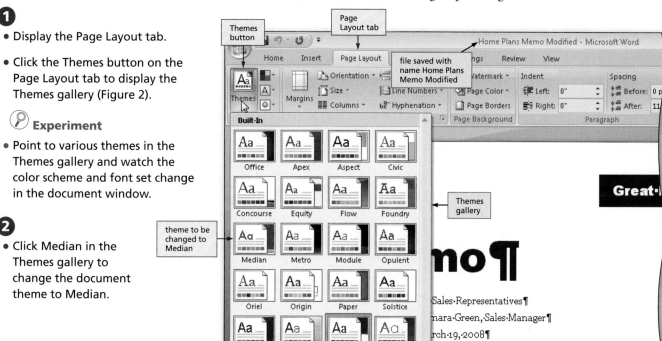

Figure 2

To Update the Body Text Style

The font size of the body text in the memo document is a little small, making it difficult for some people to read. The following steps increase the font size by one point and then update the Body Text style to reflect this change.

1 Triple-click the paragraph of text in the memo to select it. Right-click the selected text to display the Mini toolbar and shortcut menu.

2 Click the Grow Font button on the Mini toolbar to increase the font size of the selected text to 12 point.

3 Right-click the selected text again and then point to Styles on the shortcut menu to display the Styles menu (Figure 3 on the next page).

4 On the Styles menu, click Update Body Text to Match Selection, which modifies the Body Text style to match the formats of the selected text and then changes all other text formatted using the Body Text style in the document to the updated style.

Figure 3

Linking an Excel Worksheet and Chart

The next step in this integration feature is to link the Excel worksheet and chart (the objects), which are located in the Excel workbook called Home Plans Breakdown (the source document), to the Home Plans Memo Modified file (the destination document). To link the worksheet to the memo in this feature, you will follow these general steps:

1. Start Excel and open the Excel workbook that contains the objects (worksheet and chart) to be linked.
2. Select the object (worksheet or chart) in Excel and then copy the selected object to the Clipboard.
3. Switch to Word and link the copied object using the Paste Special command.

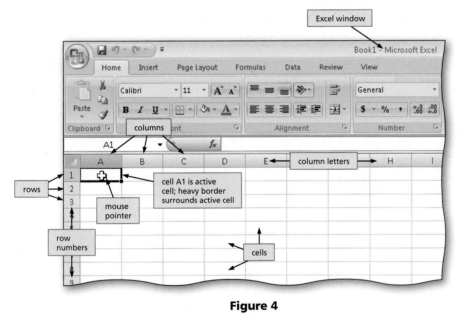

Figure 4

Excel Basics

The Excel window contains a rectangular grid that consists of columns and rows. A column letter above the grid identifies each column. A row number on the left side of the grid identifies each row. The intersection of each column and row is a cell. A cell is referred to by its unique address, which is the coordinates of the intersection of a column and a row. To identify a cell, specify the column letter first, followed by the row number. For example, cell reference A1 refers to the cell located at the intersection of column A and row 1 (Figure 4).

To Start Excel and Open an Excel Workbook

The Excel worksheet to be linked to the memo is in an Excel workbook called Home Plans Breakdown, which is located on the Data Files for Students. See the inside back cover of this book for instructions on downloading the Data Files for Students, or contact your instructor for information about accessing the required files.

The next steps start Excel and open the workbook called Home Plans Breakdown. (Do not quit Word or close the open Word document before starting these steps.)

1 Click the Start button on the Windows Vista taskbar to display the Start menu.

2 Point to All Programs on the Start menu, click Microsoft Office in the All Programs list, and then click Microsoft Office Excel 2007 in the Microsoft Office list to start Excel and display a new blank workbook in the Excel window.

3 If the Excel window is not maximized, click the Maximize button on its title bar to maximize the window.

4 With your USB flash drive connected to one of the computer's USB ports, click the Office Button in the Excel window to display the Office Button menu and then click Open on the Office Button menu to display the Open dialog box.

5 Locate and select your USB flash drive in the list of available drives.

6 Click Home Plans Breakdown to select the file name and then click the Open button to open the selected file and display the Home Plans Breakdown workbook in the Excel window.

BTW

Opening Word Documents
When you open a document that contains a linked object, Word attempts to locate the source file associated with the link. If Word cannot find the source file, click the Office Button, point to Prepare, and then click Edit Links to Files to display the Links dialog box. Next, select the appropriate source file in the list, click the Change Source button, locate the source file, and then click the OK button.

To Link an Excel Worksheet to a Word Document

The next step is to copy the Excel worksheet to the Clipboard and then use the Paste Link command in Word to link the Excel worksheet from the Clipboard to the Word document. The following steps link the Excel worksheet to the Word document.

1

- In the Excel window, drag through cells in the range A1 through B8 to select them.

- In the Excel window, click the Copy button on the Home tab to copy the selected cells to the Clipboard (Figure 5).

Q&A

What is the dotted line around the selected cells?

Excel surrounds copied cells with a moving marquee to help you visually identify the copied cells.

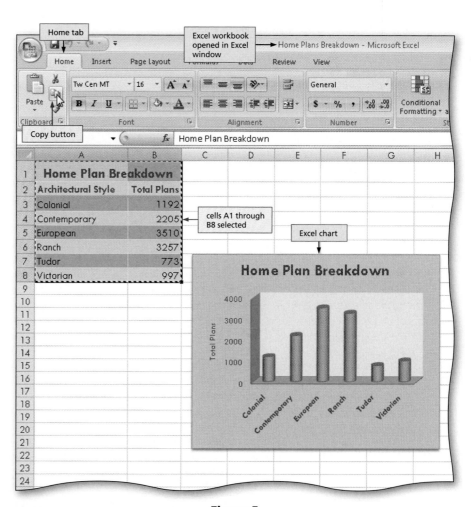

Figure 5

2

- Click the Home Plans Memo Modified - Microsoft Word program button on the taskbar to switch to the Word window.

- Position the insertion point at the end of the paragraph of text and then press the ENTER key. Center the paragraph mark below the paragraph of text so that the linked worksheet will be centered on the page.

- Scroll so that the paragraph in the memo is near the top of the document window.

- In Word, click the Paste button arrow on the Home tab to display the Paste menu (Figure 6).

Q&A The Paste menu did not display on my screen. Why not?

You clicked the Paste button instead of the Paste button arrow. Click the Undo button on the Quick Access Toolbar and then click the Paste button arrow.

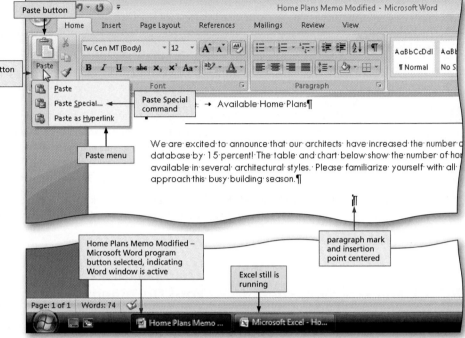
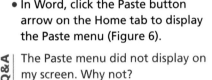

Figure 6

3

- Click the Paste Special command on the Paste menu to display the Paste Special dialog box.

- Click Paste link to select the option button.

- Select Microsoft Office Excel Worksheet Object in the As list (Figure 7).

Q&A What if the Paste link option button is dimmed?

Click the Microsoft Excel – Home Plans Breakdown program button on the taskbar, select cells A1 through B8 again, click the Copy button in Excel again, click the Home Plans Memo Modified - Microsoft Word program button again, click the Paste button arrow, and then repeat Step 3.

Q&A What if I wanted to embed an object instead of link it?

You would select the Paste option button in the dialog box instead of the Paste link option button.

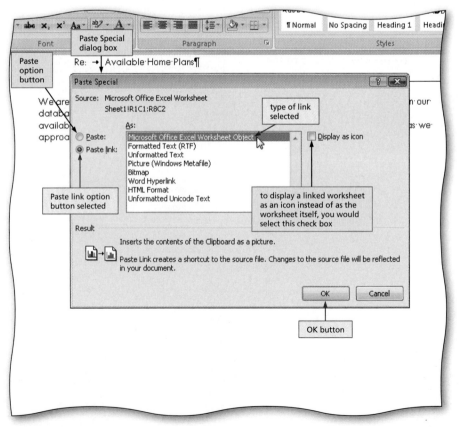

Figure 7

4

- Click the OK button to insert the Excel worksheet as a linked object at the location of the insertion point (Figure 8).

Q&A

What if I wanted to delete the linked worksheet?

You would select the linked worksheet and then press the DELETE key.

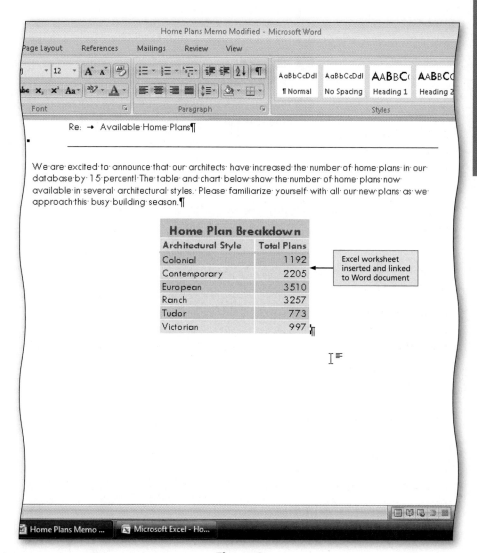

Figure 8

Other Ways

1. To link an entire source file, click the Object button on the Insert tab, click Create from File tab, locate file, click 'Link to file' check box, click OK button

To Link an Excel Chart to a Word Document

The next step is to copy the Excel chart to the Clipboard and then use the Paste Special command in Word to link the Excel chart from the Clipboard to the Word document. The following steps link the Excel chart to the Word document.

1 Click the Microsoft Excel - Home Plans Breakdown program button on the taskbar to switch to the Excel window.

2 In the Excel window, click an edge of the chart to select the chart. Click the Copy button on the Home tab to copy the selected Excel chart to the Clipboard.

3 Click the Home Plans Memo Modified - Microsoft Word program button on the taskbar to switch to the Word window. With the insertion point to the right of the linked worksheet, press the ENTER key.

4 In Word, click the Paste button arrow on the Home tab to display the Paste menu and then click the Paste Special command on the Paste menu to display the Paste Special dialog box.

5 Click Paste link to select the option button.

6 Select Microsoft Office Excel Chart Object in the As list.

7 Click the OK button to insert the Excel chart as a linked object at the location of the insertion point (Figure 9).

8 Switch back to Excel. Quit Excel by clicking the Close button on the upper-right corner of the title bar.

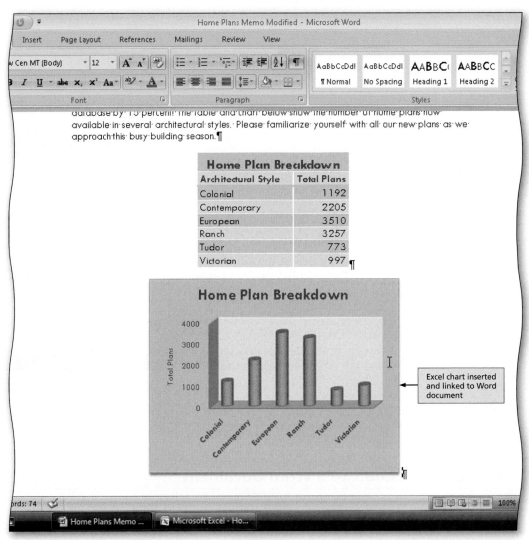

Figure 9

To Copy and Paste Excel Data

If you wanted to copy and paste the chart data, instead of link it, you would perform the following steps.

1. Start Excel.

2. In Excel, select the worksheet cells and then click the Copy button on the Home tab to copy the selected cells to the Clipboard.

3. Switch to Word. Click the Paste button on the Home tab in Word to paste the contents of the Clipboard in the Word document at the location of the insertion point.

To Save a Document Again

You have performed several modifications to this memo file. Thus, you should save it again.

1 Click the Save button on the Quick Access Toolbar to save the document again with the same file name, Home Plans Memo Modified.

Editing a Linked Worksheet

At a later time, you may find it necessary to change the data in the Excel worksheet. Any changes you make to the Excel worksheet while in Excel will be reflected in the Excel worksheet and chart in the Word document because the objects are linked to the Word document.

To Edit a Linked Object

The following steps change the number of European home plans from 3510 to 3910 in the Excel worksheet.

1

- In the Word document, double-click the Excel worksheet to start the Excel program and open the source document that contains the linked worksheet.

- If necessary, maximize the Excel window.

- With the Excel worksheet displaying on the screen, click cell B5 to select it.

- Type 3910 and then press the ENTER key to change the value in cell B5, which also automatically updates the associated bar in the chart (Figure 10).

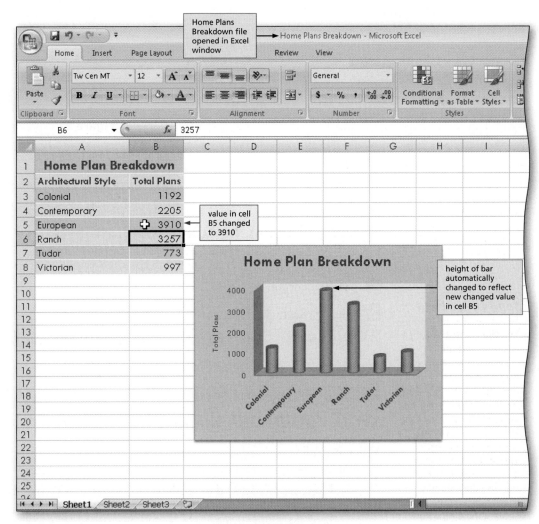

Figure 10

- Click the Save button on the Quick Access Toolbar to save the changes.
- Quit Excel.

- With the Word window redisplaying on the screen, if necessary, scroll to display the worksheet and chart in the document window.

- To update the worksheet with the edited Excel data, click the worksheet in the Word document and then press the F9 key (Figure 11).

4

- To update the chart with the edited Excel data, click the chart in the Word document and then press the F9 key.

Q&A

Do I always need to press the F9 key to update linked objects?

No. When you open a Word document containing links, Word asks if you want to update the document with the linked files. If you click the Yes button, Word automatically updates links in the opened document.

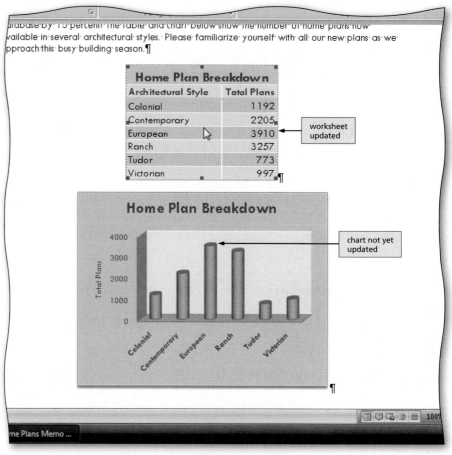

Figure 11

Other Ways

1. To open link, right-click link, point to Linked Worksheet Object, click Edit Link on shortcut menu; to update link, right-click link, click Update Link on shortcut menu

BTW

Conserving Ink and Toner
You can instruct Word to print draft quality documents to conserve ink or toner by clicking the Office Button, clicking the Word Options button, clicking Advanced in the left pane of the Word Options dialog box, scrolling to the Print area, placing a check mark in the 'Use draft quality' check box, and then clicking the OK button. Click the Office Button, point to Print, and then click Quick Print.

To Save a Document Again and Print It

You are finished with the memo. Thus, you should save it again and then print it.

1   Save the document again with the same file name, Home Plans Memo Modified.

2   Print the memo (Figure 1c on page WD 465).

Preparing the Memo To Be E-Mailed to Users with Earlier Versions of Word

When e-mailing a Word document to others, you want to ensure they will be able to open it and use it. Before e-mailing this memo, take these two steps:

1. **Convert any linked or embedded objects to Word objects.** If you send a Word document that contains a linked Excel object, users will be asked by Word if they want to update the links when they open the Word document. If users are unfamiliar with links, they will not know how to answer the question. Further, if

they do not have the source program, such as Excel, they may not be able to open the Word document.

2. **Save the Word 2007 document in an earlier version of Word.** If you send a document created in Word 2007 to users that have an earlier version of Word, such as Word 2003, they will not be able to open the Word 2007 document. This is because Word 2007 saves documents in a format that is not backward compatible. Word 2007 documents have a file type of .docx, and previous versions of Word have a .doc file type.

The following pages explain these procedures and then e-mail the document.

To Break Links

To convert a linked or embedded object to a Word object, you break the link. That is, you break the connection between the source document and the destination document. When you break a linked Excel worksheet or chart (each of which is an object), the linked worksheet or chart becomes a Word object, a graphic in this case. The following steps break the links to the Excel worksheet and chart.

1

- Click the Office Button and then point to Prepare on the Office Button menu (Figure 12).

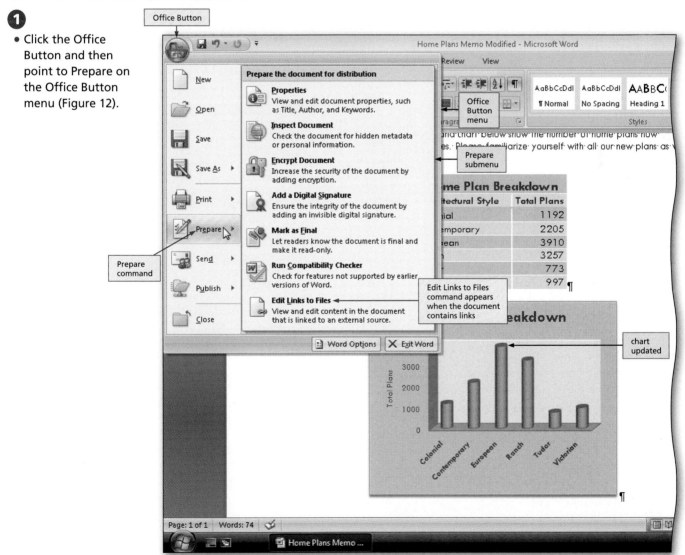

Figure 12

- Click Edit Links to Files on the Prepare submenu to display the Links dialog box.

- If necessary, click the first source file listed in the dialog box to select it.

- Click the Break Link button, which displays a dialog box asking if you are sure you want to break the selected links (Figure 13).

- Click the Yes button in the dialog box to remove the source file from the list (break the link).

- Click the remaining source file listed in the dialog box, if necessary. Click the Break Link button and then click the Yes button in the Microsoft Office Word dialog box to break the remaining link.

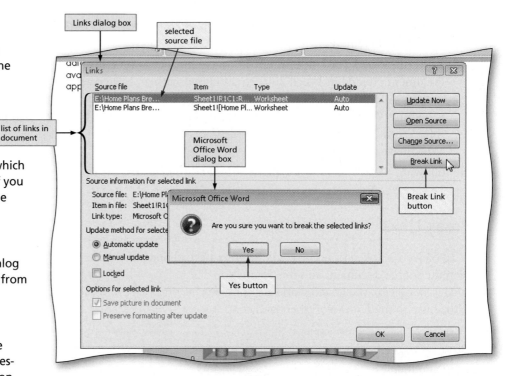

Figure 13

- Use the Save As command on the Office Button menu to save the file with the name, Home Plans Memo Modified Without Links.

- Double-click the worksheet object in the Word document to be sure that the link has been broken (Figure 14).

Q&A

Why did the Picture Tools tab appear on the Ribbon?

The worksheet now is a Word graphic. When you double-click a graphic, Word displays the Picture Tools tab so that you can edit the picture.

Other Ways

1. Right-click link, point to Linked Worksheet Object, click Links on shortcut menu, select link, click Break Link button, click Yes button, click OK button

2. Select link, press CTRL+SHIFT+F9

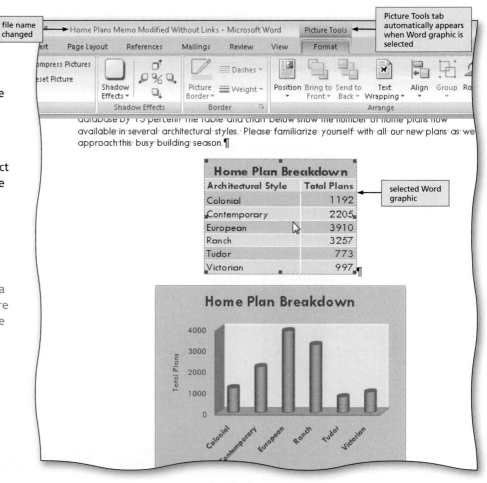

Figure 14

To Save a Word 2007 Document in a Previous Word Format

Documents saved in the Word 2007 format cannot be opened in previous versions of Word. To ensure that all Word users can open your Word 2007 document, you should save the Word 2007 document in a previous version format. The following steps save a Word 2007 document in the Word 97-2003 format.

- Click the Office Button and then point to Save As on the Office Button menu (Figure 15).

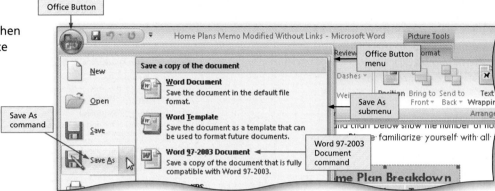

Figure 15

- Click Word 97-2003 Document on the Save As submenu to display the Save As dialog box with Word 97-2003 Document already filled in the 'Save as type' box.

- If necessary, locate and select the USB flash drive in the list of available drives (Figure 16).

3

- Click the Save button in the dialog box to save the file in a Word 97-2003 format.

Q&A

How can I tell a Word 2007 file from a Word 97-2003 file?

For files saved in the Word 97-2003 format, the Word title bar displays the text, [Compatibility Mode], next to the file name. The file properties also show the file type. You can view the file properties when you open or save a document. Or, click the Document Properties button in the Document Information Panel, click Advanced Properties, and then click the General tab.

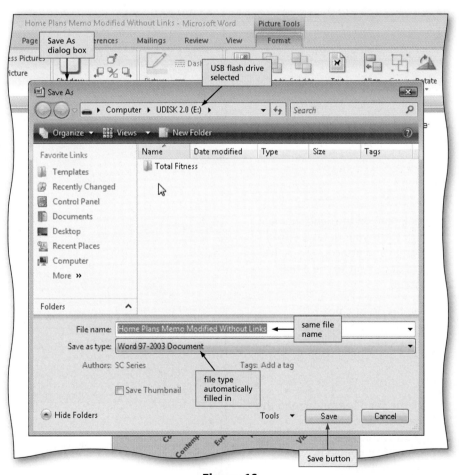

Figure 16

Other Ways
1. Click Office Button, click Save As, change file type to Word 97-2003 Document, click Save button in dialog box   2. Press F12, change file type to Word 97-2003 Document, click Save button in dialog box

To E-Mail a Document as an Attachment

The final step in this feature is to e-mail the Home Plans Memo Modified Without Links document saved in the Word 97-2003 format. The following steps e-mail a document as an attachment, assuming you use Outlook as your default e-mail program.

1

• Click the Office Button and then point to Send on the Office Button menu (Figure 17).

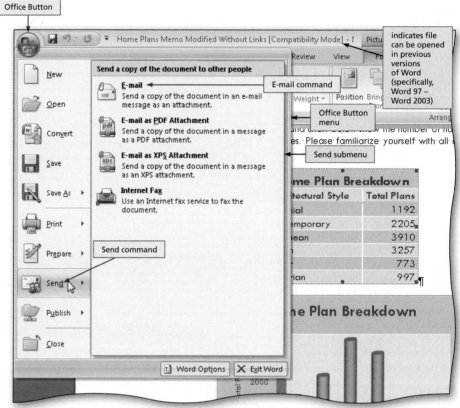

Figure 17

2

• Click E-mail on the Send submenu, which starts your default e-mail program and attaches the active Word document to the e-mail message.

• Fill in the To text box with the recipient's e-mail address.

• Fill in the message (Figure 18).

3

• Click the Send button to send the e-mail message along with the attachment to the recipient named in the To text box.

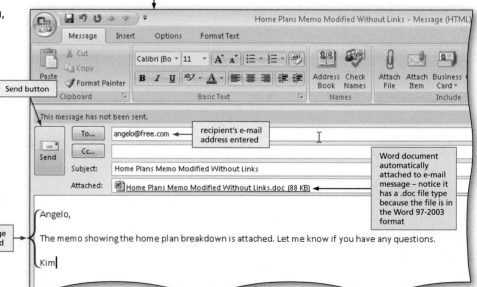

Figure 18

To Quit Word

You are finished with the project in this feature and should quit Word.

1 Quit Word.

BTW

Quick Reference
For a table that lists how to complete the tasks covered in this book using the mouse, Ribbon, shortcut menu, and keyboard, see the Quick Reference Summary at the back of this book, or visit the Word 2007 Quick Reference Web page (scsite.com/wd2007/qr).

Feature Summary

In this feature, you have learned how to apply a theme, update body text, link an Excel worksheet and chart to a Word document, break links, save a document in a previous Word format, and e-mail a document. The items listed below include all the new Word skills you have learned in this feature.

1. Change the Document Theme (WD 467)
2. Update the Body Text Style (WD 467)
3. Link an Excel Worksheet to a Word Document (WD 469)
4. Link an Excel Chart to a Word Document (WD 471)
5. Copy and Paste Excel Data (WD 472)
6. Edit a Linked Object (WD 473)
7. Break Links (WD 475)
8. Save a Word 2007 Document in a Previous Word Format (WD 477)
9. E-Mail a Document as an Attachment (WD 478)

 If you have a SAM user profile, you may have access to hands-on instruction, practice, and assessment. Log in to your SAM account (http://sam2007.course.com) to launch any assigned training activities or exams that relate to the skills covered in this feature.

In the Lab

Design and/or create a document using the guidelines, concepts, and skills presented in this chapter. Labs are listed in order of increasing difficulty. Note: These labs use files from the Data Files for Students. See the inside back cover of this book for instructions on downloading the Data Files for Students, or contact your instructor for information about accessing the required files.

Lab 1: Linking an Excel Worksheet to a Word Document

Problem: Charlotte Keyes, director at County Library, has created an Excel worksheet that lists the circulation figures for the library branches. She would like you to modify a draft memo so that it includes the Excel worksheet.

Instructions:

1. Open the memo called Lab IF-1 County Library Memo Draft from the Data Files for Students.
2. Use the Save As command to save the memo with the name, Lab IF-1 County Library Memo Modified.
3. Change the document theme to Trek.
4. Change the paragraph of body text to 12 point. Update the Body Text style.
5. Use the Copy and Paste Special commands to link the worksheet in the Lab IF-1 Circulation Figures Excel workbook, which is on the Data Files for Students, to the Word memo file.
6. Save the Word memo file again. Submit the memo in the format specified by your instructor.

In the Lab

Lab 2: Linking Data from an Excel Worksheet and an Excel Chart to a Word Document

Problem: Mario Joseph, manager at Party Palace, has created an Excel worksheet that lists the company's recent sales figures. He also has charted the data in Excel. He would like you to prepare a memo that includes the Excel table and chart.

Instructions:

1. Open the memo called Lab IF-2 Party Palace Memo Draft from the Data Files for Students.

2. Use the Save As command to save the memo with the name, Lab IF-2 Party Palace Memo Modified.

3. Change the document theme to Module.

4. Change the paragraph of body text to 12 point. Update the Body Text style.

5. Use the Copy and Paste Special commands to link the worksheet in the Lab IF-2 Party Supply Sales Excel workbook, which is on the Data Files for Students, to the Word memo file.

6. Use the Copy and Paste Special commands to link the chart in the Lab IF-2 Party Supply Sales Excel workbook, which is on the Data Files for Students, to the memo file. If necessary, resize the chart so all memo contents fit on a single page.

7. Save the Word memo file again. Submit the memo in the format specified by your instructor.

8. Break the links in the Word memo file. Save the modified file with the name, Lab IF-2 Party Palace Memo Modified Without Links. Submit the memo in the format specified by your instructor.

9. Save the memo file in the Word 97-2003 format. Submit the memo in the format specified by your instructor.

10. If your instructor approves, e-mail the file created in Step 9 to him or her.

In the Lab

Lab 3: Creating an Excel Worksheet and Linking It to a Word Document

Problem: As a part-time computer assistant at Secondhand Stories, your boss has asked you to create an Excel worksheet that lists the units sold by inventory category and then prepare a memo that links the Excel worksheet to a memo.

Instructions:

1. Create an Excel worksheet that has two columns (Item and Units Sold) and five rows (Books, 17252; Music CDs, 10256; Computer Games, 1632; Movies, 3598; Stationery, 5450). Format the worksheet. Save the Excel workbook with the name, Lab IF-3 Secondhand Stories Sales.

2. Create a memo to All Staff. Save the memo using the file name, Lab IF-3 Secondhand Stories Memo. Use this paragraph of text in the memo: Inventory finally is complete – thank you all for your hard work! The table below shows the number of items sold from inventory by category.

3. Use the Copy and Paste Special commands to link the Excel worksheet data to the Word memo file.

4. Save the Word memo file again. Submit the memo in the format specified by your instructor.

5. Quit Excel. Edit the linked worksheet. Change the number of Computer Games to 7632. Save the worksheet again.

6. Update the linked Excel worksheet in the Word memo. Save the memo again. Submit the memo in the format specified by your instructor.

7 | Working with Document Sharing Tools, a Master Document, a Table of Contents, and an Index

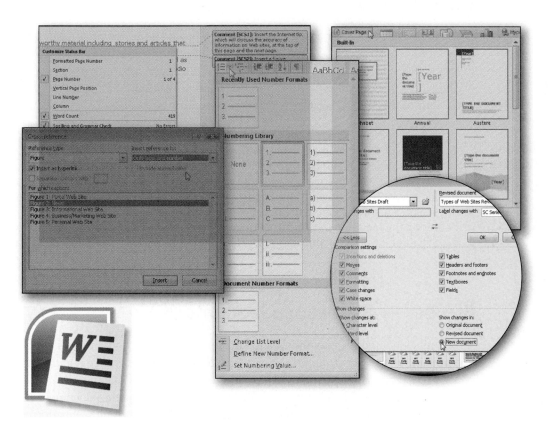

Objectives

You will have mastered the material in this chapter when you can:

- Insert comments
- Track changes
- Review tracked changes
- Compare documents and combine documents
- Add and modify a caption
- Create a cross-reference
- Use the Building Blocks Organizer
- Link text boxes

- Compress pictures
- Work with a master document and subdocuments
- Insert a cover page
- Create and modify a table of contents
- Use the Document Map
- Create a table of figures
- Build and modify an index

7 | Working with Document Sharing Tools, a Master Document, a Table of Contents, and an Index

Introduction

During the course of your academic studies and professional activities, you may find it necessary to compose a document that is many pages in length or even hundreds of pages in length. When composing a long document, you must ensure that the document is organized so that a reader easily can locate material in that document. Sometimes a document of this nature is called a **reference document**.

Project Planning Guidelines

> The process of developing a document that communicates specific information requires careful analysis and planning. As a starting point, establish why the document is needed. Once the purpose is determined, analyze the intended readers of the document and their unique needs. Then, gather information about the topic and decide what to include in the document. Finally, determine the document design and style that will be most successful at delivering the message. Details of these guidelines are provided in Appendix A. In addition, each chapter in this book provides practical applications of these planning considerations.

Project — Reference Document

A reference document is any multipage document organized so that users easily can locate material and navigate through the document. Examples of reference documents include user guides, term papers, pamphlets, manuals, proposals, and plans.

The project in this chapter uses Word to produce the reference document shown in Figure 7–1. This reference document, titled the *Internet Post*, is a multipage information guide that is distributed by Donner County Library to library patrons. Notice that the inner margin between facing pages has extra space to allow duplicated copies of the document to be bound (i.e., stapled or fastened in some manner) — without the binding covering the words.

The *Internet Post* reference document begins with a title page designed to entice the target audience to open the document and read it. Next is the table of contents, followed by an introduction. The document then discusses five types of Web sites: portal, news, informational, business/marketing, and personal. The end of this reference document has a table of figures and an index to assist readers in locating information contained within the document. A miniature version of the *Internet Post* reference document is shown in Figure 7–1; for a more readable view, visit scsite.com/wd2007/ch7.

The section of the *Internet Post* reference document that is titled, Types of Web Sites, contains content written by someone other than you. After reviewing and editing the content, you will incorporate it in the reference document. The draft of this content is located on the Data Files for Students in a file called Types of Web Sites Draft. See the inside back cover of this book for instructions on downloading the Data Files for Students, or contact your instructor for information about accessing the required files.

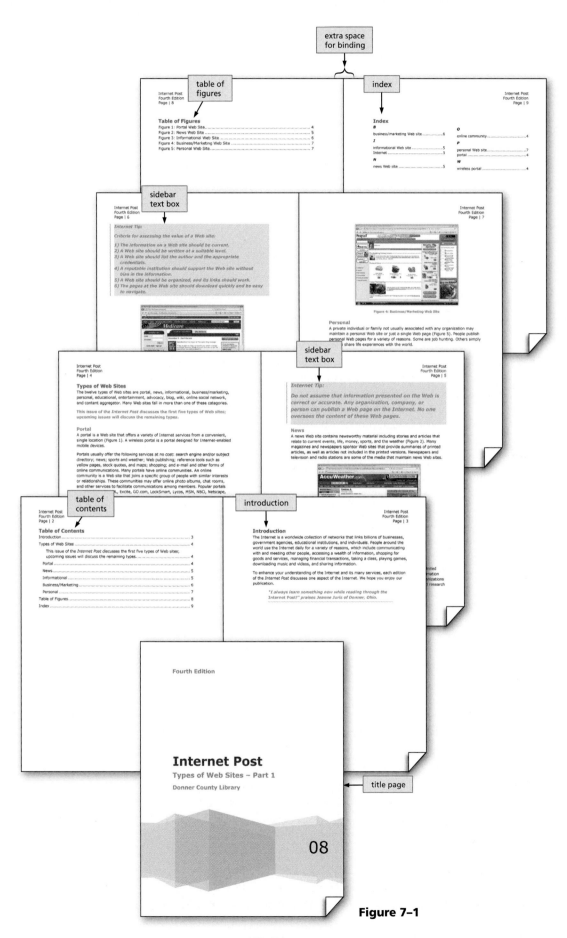

Figure 7–1

Overview

As you read through this chapter, you will learn how to create the reference document shown in Figure 7–1 on the previous page by performing these general tasks:

- Review the draft document.
- Modify the reviewed document.
- Create a master document for the reference document.
- Organize the reference document with a table of contents, a table of figures, and an index.
- Print the reference document.

Plan Ahead

General Project Guidelines

When creating a Word document, the actions you perform and decisions you make will affect the appearance and characteristics of the finished document. As you create a reference document, such as the project shown in Figure 7–1, you should follow these general guidelines:

1. **Prepare a document to be included in a longer document.** If a document contains multiple illustrations (figures), each figure should have a caption. In addition, each figure should be referenced from within the text. Any terms to be included in an index should be marked as an index entry.

2. **Include elements common to a reference document.** Most reference documents contain a title page, a table of contents, and an index. The title page entices passersby to take a copy of the document. By placing a table of contents at the beginning of the document and an index at the end, you help a reader locate topics within the document. If a document contains several illustrations, you also should include a table of figures.

3. **Prepare the document for distribution.** The reference document in Figure 7–1 prints on nine separate sheets of paper. When it is duplicated back to back, however, the document uses only five sheets of paper. The top of the first sheet of paper shows the title page, and the back of the same sheet contains the table of contents; the top of the second sheet of paper shows the introduction, and so on. The table of contents and introduction pages are called facing pages when duplicated in this manner. Be sure to allow enough room in the margins for binding (i.e., stapling) the document.

   For long documents that will be viewed online, incorporate bookmarks and/or hyperlinks so that a user can navigate quickly and easily through the document while viewing it on a computer.

   When necessary, more specific details concerning the above guidelines are presented at appropriate points in the chapter. The chapter also will identify the actions performed and decisions made regarding these guidelines during the creation of the newsletter shown in Figure 7–1.

To Start Word

If you are using a computer to step through the project in this chapter and you want your screens to match the figures in this book, you should change your computer's resolution to 1024×768. For information about how to change a computer's resolution, read Appendix D.

The following steps start Word and verify Word settings.

Note: If you are using Windows XP, see Appendix F for alternate steps.

1 Click the Start button on the Windows Vista taskbar to display the Start menu.

2 Click All Programs at the bottom of the left pane on the Start menu to display the All Programs list and then click Microsoft Office in the All Programs list to display the Microsoft Office list.

3 Click Microsoft Office Word 2007 in the Microsoft Office list to start Word and display a new blank document in the Word window.

4 If the Word window is not maximized, click the Maximize button on its title bar to maximize the window.

5 If the Print Layout button on the status bar is not selected, click it so that Word is in Print Layout view.

6 If the rulers are displayed on the screen, click the View Ruler button at the top vertical scroll bar to remove the rulers from the Word window.

Reviewing a Document

Word provides many tools that allow users to work with others, or **collaborate**, on a document. One set of collaboration tools within Word allows you to track changes in a document and review the changes. That is, one computer user can create a document and another user(s) can make changes and insert comments in the same document. Those changes then appear on the screen with options that allow the originator (author) to accept or reject the changes and delete the comments. With another collaboration tool, you can compare and/or merge two or more documents to determine the differences between them.

To illustrate Word collaboration tools, this section follows these general steps:

1. Open the document to be reviewed.
2. Insert comments in the document for the originator (author).
3. Track changes in the document.
4. Accept and reject the tracked changes and delete all comments. For illustration purposes, you assume the role of originator (author) of the document in this step.
5. Compare the reviewed document to the original to view the differences.
6. Merge the original document with the reviewed document and with another reviewer's suggestions.

To Open a Word Document and Save It with a New File Name

The first step is to open the file called Types of Web Sites Draft on the Data Files for Students, so that you can review it. See the inside back cover of this book for instructions on downloading the Data Files for Students, or contact your instructor for information about accessing the required files. To preserve the contents of the original Types of Web Sites Draft file, you will save it with a new file name. The following steps open a document and save it with a new file name.

1 Click the Office Button and then click Open to display the Open dialog box.

2 Locate and then select the file with the name, Types of Web Sites Draft, and then click the Open button to display the document in the Word window.

3 Click the Office Button and then click Save As on the Office Button menu to display the Save As dialog box.

4 Type `Types of Web Sites Reviewed` in the File name text box to change the file name.

5 Locate and select your USB flash drive in the list of available drives.

6 Click the Save button in the Save As dialog box to save the document on the USB flash drive with the new file name, Types of Web Sites Reviewed.

7 If your zoom level is not 100%, click the Zoom Out or Zoom In button as many times as necessary until the Zoom level button displays 100% on its face.

8 Display the top of page 2 in the document window because this is the page that will contain the comments and tracked changes.

To Hide White Space

To display more content on the screen in Print Layout view, you can hide the white space if it is displayed at the top and bottom of the pages and the space between pages. Because the reference document in this chapter has several short pages, you hide white space. The following steps hide white space, if your screen displays it.

1

• Position the mouse pointer in the document window above the page (in the space between pages) until the mouse pointer changes to a Hide White Space button (Figure 7–2).

Q&A

My mouse pointer will not change to show the Hide White Space button. Why not?

You may not be in Print Layout view. Click the Print Layout button on the status bar.

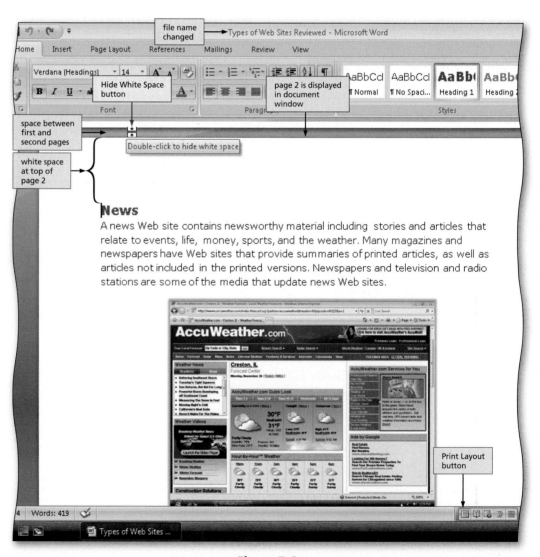

Figure 7–2

2

- Read through the comment and then click the Delete Comment button on the Review tab to remove the comment balloon from the Markup Area and comment marks in the document window (Figure 7–17).

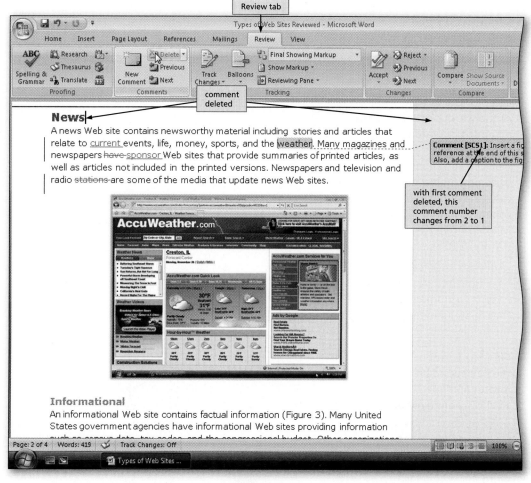

Figure 7–17

3

- Click the Next Change button on the Review tab again, so that Word locates and selects the next tracked change or comment, in this case, the inserted word, current (Figure 7–18).

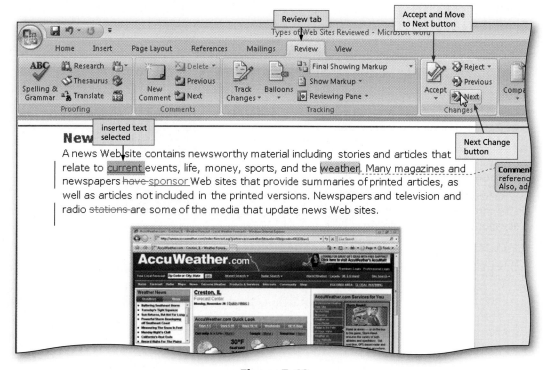

Figure 7–18

- Because you agree with this change, click the Accept and Move to Next button on the Review tab to accept the insertion of the word, current, and instruct Word to locate and select the next tracked change or comment, in this case, the remaining comment in the Markup Area (Figure 7–19).

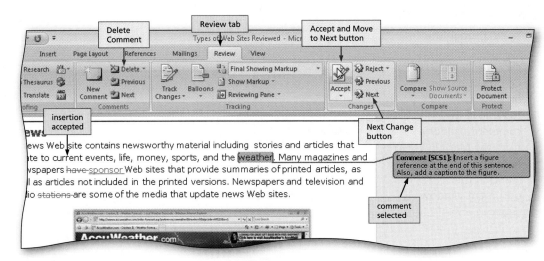

Figure 7–19

- Read the comment and then click the Delete Comment button on the Review tab.

- Click the Next Change button on the Review tab, so that Word locates and selects the next tracked change or comment.

- Click the Accept and Move to Next button on the Review tab to accept the deletion of the word, have, and instruct Word to locate and select the next tracked change or comment.

- Click the Accept and Move to Next button on the Review tab to accept the insertion of the word, sponsor, and instruct Word to locate and select the next tracked change or comment, in this case, the deletion of the word, stations (Figure 7–20).

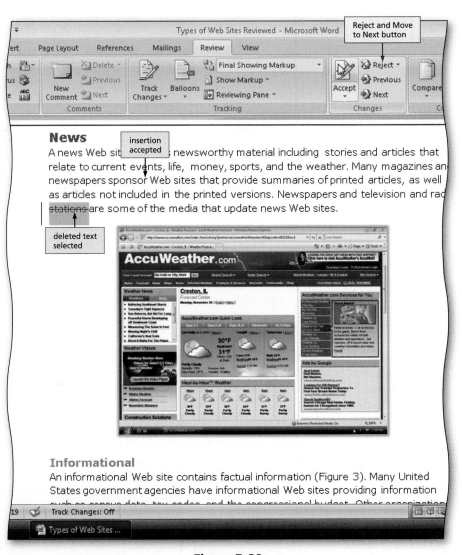

6

- Because you do not agree with this change, click the Reject and Move to Next button on the Review tab to reject the marked deletion.

- Click the OK button in the dialog box that appears, which indicates the document contains no more comments or tracked changes.

Figure 7–20

Other Ways

1. Right-click comment or tracked change, click desired command on shortcut menu

TO DELETE ALL COMMENTS

If you wanted to delete all comments in the document at once, you would perform these steps.

1. Click the Delete Comment button arrow on the Review tab to display the Delete Comment menu.

2. Click Delete All Comments in Document on the Delete Comment menu.

Changing Tracking Options

If you wanted to change the color and markings reviewers use for tracked changes and comments or change how balloons are displayed, use the Track Changes Options dialog box (Figure 7–21). To display the Track Changes Options dialog box, click the Track Changes button arrow on the Review tab and then click Change Tracking Options on the Track Changes menu.

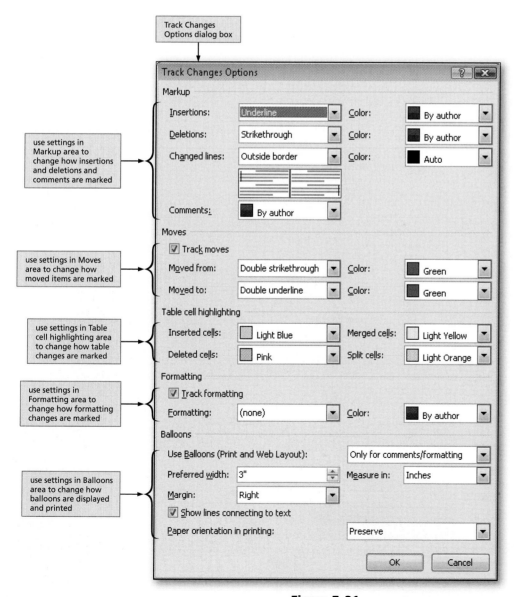

Figure 7–21

- To change how insertions and deletions are marked, modify the settings in the Markup area of the Track Changes Options dialog box.
- To change how moved items are marked, modify the settings in the Moves area of the Track Changes Options dialog box.
- To change how table changes are marked, modify the settings in the 'Table cell highlighting' area of the Track Changes Options dialog box.
- To change how formatting changes are marked, modify the settings in the Formatting area of the Track Changes Options dialog box.
- To change how balloons are displayed and printed, modify the settings in the Balloons area of the Track Changes Options dialog box.

To Save a Document Again

You have completed reviewing the document. Thus, you should save the document again.

 Save the document again with the same file name, Types of Web Sites Reviewed.

To Compare Documents

With Word, you can compare two documents to each other, which allows you easily to identify any differences between the two files. Word displays the differences between the documents as tracked changes for your review. By comparing files, you can verify that two separate files have the same or different content. If no tracked changes are found, then the two documents are identical.

Assume you want to compare the original Types of Web Sites Draft document with the Types of Web Sites Reviewed document so that you can identify the changes made to the document. The following steps compare two documents.

- Click the Compare button on the Review tab to display the Compare menu (Figure 7–22).

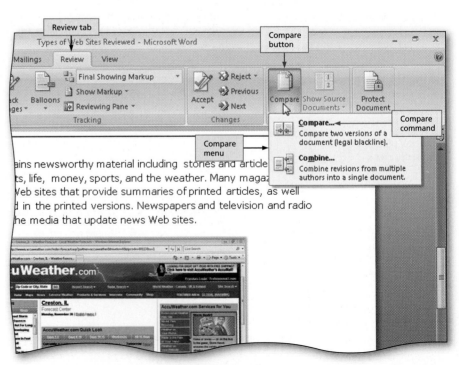

Figure 7–22

2

- Click Compare on the Compare menu to display the Compare Documents dialog box.

- Click the Original document box arrow and then click the file, Types of Web Sites Draft, in the Original document list.

Q&A
What if the file is not in the Original document list?

Click the Browse for Original button, locate the file, and then click the Open button.

- Click the Revised document box arrow and then click the file, Types of Web Sites Reviewed, in the Revised document list.

Q&A
What if the file is not in the Revised document list?

Click the Browse for Revised button, locate the file, and then click the Open button.

- If a More button appears in the dialog box, click it to expand the dialog box.

- If necessary, in the 'Show changes in' area, click New document so that tracked changes are marked in a new document. Ensure that all your settings in the expanded dialog box (below the Less button) match those in Figure 7–23.

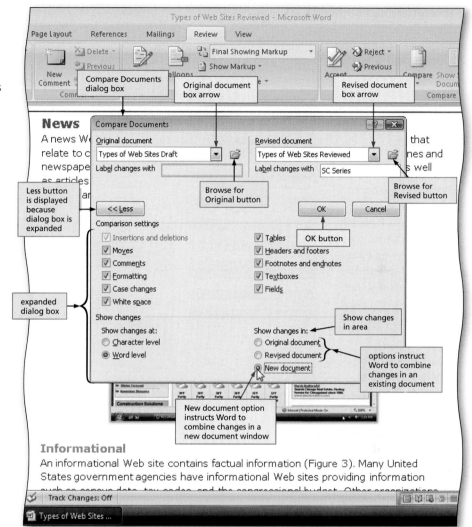

Figure 7–23

3

- Click the OK button to open a new document window and display the differences between the two documents as tracked changes in the new document window.

- Because you want to see the original document (Types of Web Sites Draft) and the revised document (Types of Web Sites Reviewed) on the screen along with the new document, verify that these documents are displayed on the

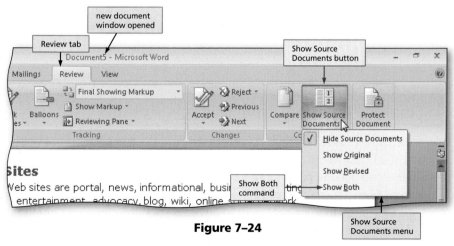

Figure 7–24

screen by clicking the Show Source Documents button on the Review tab to display the Show Source Documents menu (Figure 7–24).

Q&A
What if my screen already displays the original and revised documents?

You can skip Step 4 on the next page.

- If necessary, click Show Both on the Show Source Documents menu to display the original and revised documents, each in a separate window on the screen.

- If the Reviewing Pane does not appear automatically on your screen, click the Reviewing Pane button arrow on the Review tab and then click Reviewing Pane Vertical.

- Click the Next Change button on the Review tab to display the first tracked change in the compared document. If necessary, scroll to see the changes (Figure 7–25).

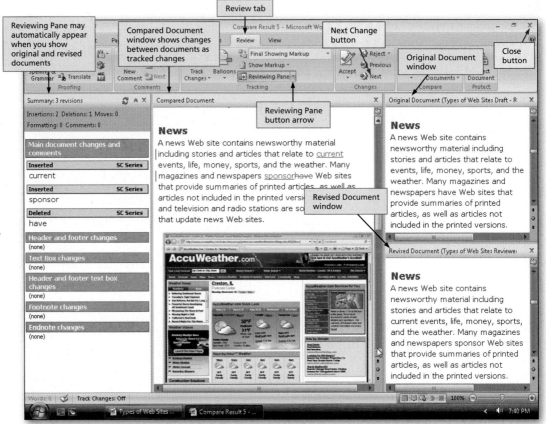

Figure 7–25

 Experiment

- Scroll through the Compared Document window and watch the Original Document window and Revised Document window scroll synchronously.

- When finished comparing the documents, click the Close button in the document window and then click the No button when Word asks if you want to save the compare results.

To Combine Revisions from Multiple Authors

Often, you have multiple reviewers that send you their markups (tracked changes) for the same original documents. Using Word, you can combine the tracked changes from multiple reviewers' documents into a single document, two documents at a time, until all documents are combined. Combining documents allows you to review all markups from a single document, from which you can accept and reject changes and read comments. Each reviewer's markups are shaded in a different color to help you visually differentiate among multiple reviewers' markups.

Assume you want to combine the original Types of Web Sites Draft document with the Types of Web Sites Reviewed document and also with a document called Types of Web Sites Reviewed by R. Smith, which is on the Data Files for Students. See the inside back cover of this book for instructions on downloading the Data Files for Students, or contact your instructor for information about accessing the required files. The next steps combine the three documents, two at a time.

1

- Click the Compare button on the Review tab to display the Compare menu (Figure 7–26).

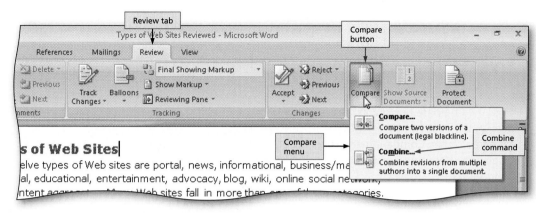

Figure 7–26

2

- Click Combine on the Compare menu to display the Combine Documents dialog box.

- Click the Original document box arrow and then click the file, Types of Web Sites Draft, in the Original document list.

Q&A What if the file is not in the Original document list?

Click the Browse for Original button, locate the file, and then click the Open button.

- Click the Revised document box arrow and then click the file, Types of Web Sites Reviewed, in the Revised document list.

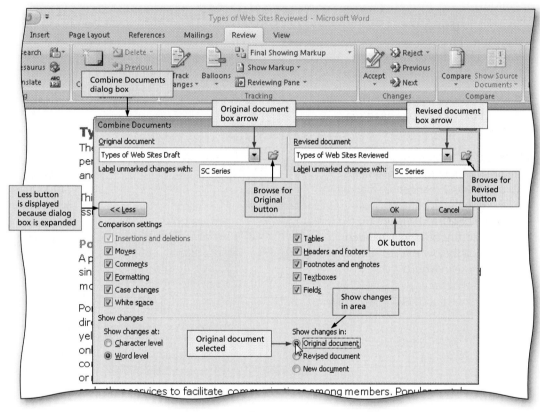

Figure 7–27

Q&A What if the file is not in the Revised document list?

Click the Browse for Revised button, locate the file, and then click the Open button.

- If a More button appears in the dialog box, click it to expand the dialog box.

- In the 'Show changes in' area, click Original document so that tracked changes are marked in the original document (Types of Web Sites Draft). Ensure that all your settings in the expanded dialog box (below the Less button) match those in Figure 7–27.

3

• Click the OK button to combine the Types of Web Sites Reviewed document with the Types of Web Sites Draft document and display the differences between the two documents as tracked changes in the Types of Web Sites Draft document.

4

• Click the Compare button on the Review tab again and then click Combine on the Compare menu to display the Combine Documents dialog box.

• Locate and display the file name, Types of Web Sites Draft, in the Original document text box.

• Locate and display the file name, Types of Web Sites Reviewed by R. Smith, in the Revised document text box.

• If a More button appears in the dialog box, click it to expand the dialog box.

• If necessary, in the 'Show changes in' area, click Original document so that tracked changes are marked in the original document (Types of Web Sites Draft). Ensure that all your settings in the expanded dialog box (below the Less button) match those in Figure 7–28.

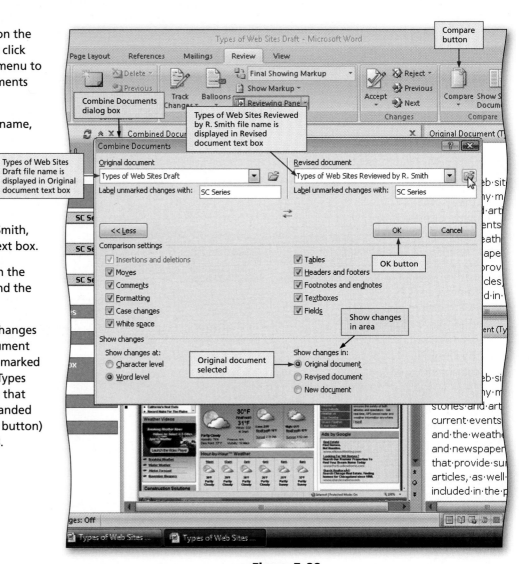

Figure 7–28

5

- Click the OK button to combine the Types of Web Sites Reviewed by R. Smith document with the currently combined document and display the differences between the three documents as tracked changes in the Types of Web Sites Draft document.

- If the source documents are displayed in the document window, click the Show Source Documents button on the Review tab to display the Show Source Documents menu (Figure 7–29).

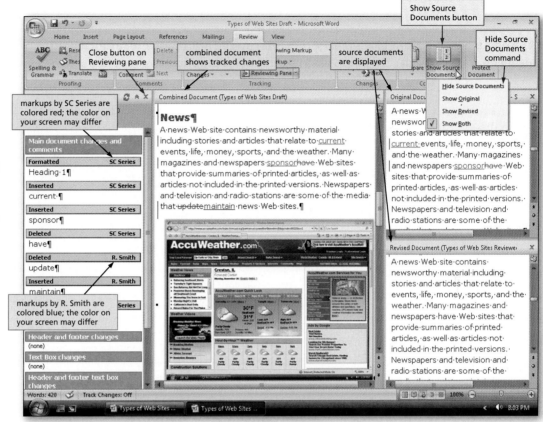

Figure 7–29

6

- Click the Hide Source Documents to close the Original Document window and the Revised Document window.

- If the Reviewing Pane is displayed, click its Close button.

To Show Tracked Changes and Comments by a Single Reviewer

In the documents just combined, you previously have seen all the SC Series (red) markups. R. Smith had this additional markup (in blue): replace the word, update, with the word, maintain. Instead of looking through a document for a particular reviewer's markups, you can show markups by reviewer. The following steps show the markups by the reviewer named R. Smith.

1

- Click the Show Markup button on the Review tab and then point to Reviewers on the Show Markup menu to display the Reviewers submenu (Figure 7–30).

Q&A What if my Reviewers submenu differs?

Your submenu may have additional or different reviewer names or colors, depending on your Word settings.

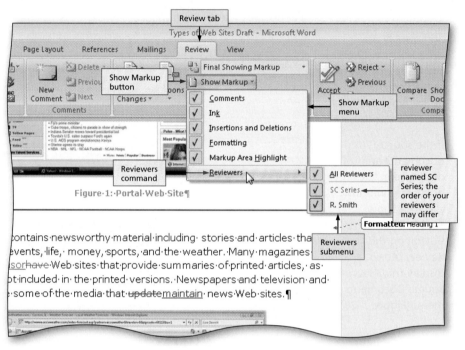

Figure 7–30

2

- Click SC Series on the Reviewers submenu to hide SC Series markups, which leaves markups by R. Smith displaying on the screen.

Q&A Are the SC Series reviewer markups deleted?

No. They are hidden from view.

- If necessary, scroll to redisplay the remaining markups in the document window (Figure 7–31).

3

- Redisplay all reviewer comments by clicking the Show Markup button on the Review tab, pointing to Reviewers, and then clicking All Reviewers on the Reviewers submenu.

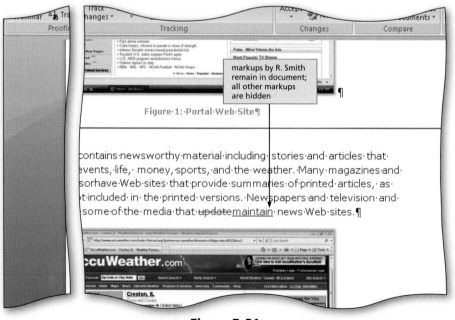

Figure 7–31

To Accept All Changes in a Document

If you are certain you plan to accept all changes in a document that contains tracked changes, you can accept all the changes at once. Doing this instructs Word that you agree with all changes in the combined document. Thus, the following steps reject the first change and then accept all remaining changes in a document.

- Click the Next Change button on the Review tab to locate the next change in the document (the formatting change) and then click the Reject and Move to Next button to reject the change.

- Click the Accept and Move to Next button arrow on the Review tab to display the Accept and Move to Next menu (Figure 7–32).

❸

- Click Accept All Changes in Document, which instructs Word to accept all changes.

Q&A

Can I reject all changes in a document?

Yes. You would click the Reject and Move to Next button arrow and then click Reject All Changes in Document.

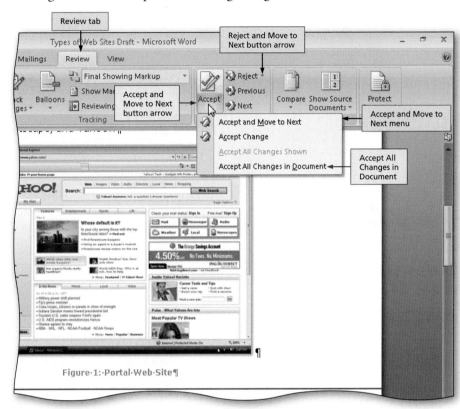

Figure 7–32

To Customize the Status Bar

You are finished working with tracked changes in this chapter. The following steps remove the Tracking Changes button from the status bar.

❶ Right-click anywhere on the status bar to display the Customize Status Bar menu.

❷ Remove the check mark beside the Track Changes command, which removes the Tracking Changes button from the status bar.

❸ Press the ESCAPE key to remove the Customize Status Bar menu from the screen.

To Save a Document with a New File Name and Close It

The next step is to save the draft document with a new file name.

❶ Click the Office Button and then click Save As on the Office Button menu to display the Save As dialog box.

❷ Type `Types of Web Sites Combined` in the File name text box to change the file name.

3 Locate and select your USB flash drive in the list of available drives.

4 Click the Save button in the Save As dialog box to save the document on the USB flash drive with the new file name, Types of Web Sites Combined.

5 Close any open documents.

Preparing a Document To Be Included in a Reference Document

Before including the Types of Web Sites document in a longer document, you will make several modifications to the document:

1. Open the document to be modified.
2. Add a caption to the figure in the News section.
3. Insert a reference to the figure in the text.
4. Mark an index entry.
5. Insert text boxes that contain Internet tips.
6. Compress the pictures.

The following pages outline these changes.

Plan Ahead

> **Prepare a document to be included in a longer document.**
> Ensure that reference elements in a document, such as captions and index entries, are formatted properly and entered consistently.
>
> • **Captions.** A **caption** is text that appears outside of an illustration, usually below it. If the illustration is identified with a number, the caption may include the word, Figure, along with the illustration number (i.e., Figure 1). In the caption, separate the figure number from the text of the figure by a space or punctuation mark such as a period or colon (Figure 1: Portal Web Site).
>
> • **Index Entries.** If your document will include an index, read through the document and mark any terms or headings that you want to appear in the index. Include any term that the reader may want to locate quickly. Omit figures from index entries if the document will have a table of figures; otherwise, include figures in the index if appropriate.

To Open a Word Document and Save It with a New File Name

The first step is to open the file called Types of Web Sites Draft 2 on the Data Files for Students, so that you can modify it. See the inside back cover of this book for instructions on downloading the Data Files for Students, or contact your instructor for information about accessing the required files. To preserve the contents of the original Types of Web Sites Draft 2 file, you will save it with a new file name. The following steps open a document and save it with a new file name.

1 Click the Office Button and then click Open to display the Open dialog box.

2 Locate and then select the file with the name Types of Web Sites Draft 2 and then click the Open button to display the document in the Word window.

③ Click the Office Button and then click Save As on the Office Button menu to display the Save As dialog box.

④ Type `Types of Web Sites Final` in the File name text box to change the file name.

⑤ Locate and select your USB flash drive in the list of available drives.

⑥ Click the Save button in the Save As dialog box to save the document on the USB flash drive with the new file name, Types of Web Sites Final.

⑦ If your zoom level is not 100%, click the Zoom Out or Zoom In button as many times as necessary until the Zoom level button displays 100% on its face.

⑧ Display the top of page 2 in the document window because this is the page that will contain the modifications.

To Add a Caption

In this reference document, the captions contain the word, Figure, followed by the figure number, followed by a figure description. In Word, you can add a caption to an equation, a figure, and a table. If you move, delete, or add captions in a document, Word renumbers remaining captions in the document automatically. In the Types of Web Sites document, the illustration in the News section is missing its caption. The following steps add a caption to the illustration.

①

- Click the graphic to select it.

- Display the References tab.

- Click the Insert Caption button on the References tab to display the Caption dialog box with a figure number automatically assigned to the selected graphic (Figure 7–33).

Q&A Why is the figure number a 2?

The document already contains a Figure 1 as a caption. When you insert a new caption, or move or delete items containing captions, Word automatically updates caption numbers throughout the document.

Q&A What if the Caption text box has the label Table or Equation instead of Figure?

Click the Label box arrow in the Caption dialog box and then click Figure.

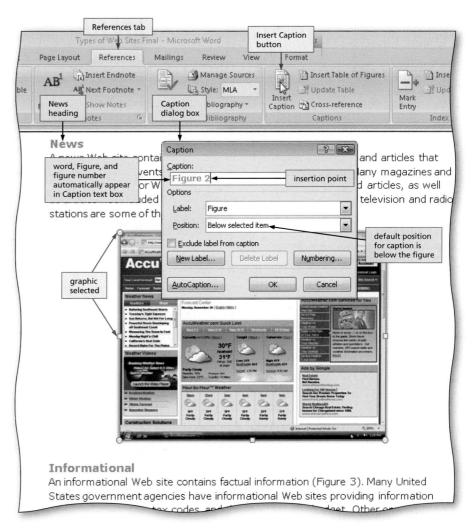

Figure 7–33

2

- Press the COLON (:) key and then press the SPACEBAR.

- Type News as the caption description (Figure 7–34).

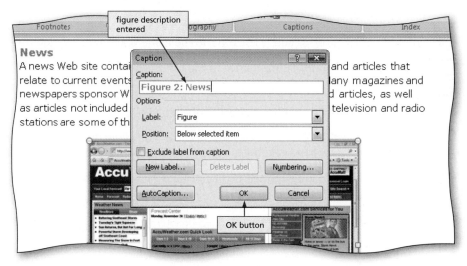

Figure 7–34

3

- Click the OK button to insert the caption below the selected graphic.

- If necessary, scroll to display the caption in the document window (Figure 7–35).

BTW

Captions
If a caption appears with extra characters inside curly braces {}, Word is displaying field codes instead of field results. Press ALT+F9 to display captions correctly as field results. If Word prints fields codes for captions, click the Office Button, click the Word Options button, click Advanced in the left pane, scroll to the Print section, remove the check mark from the 'Print field codes instead of their values' check box, click the OK button, and then print the document again.

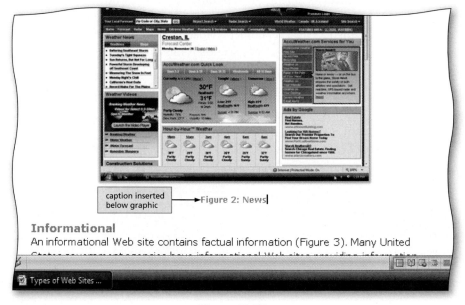

Figure 7–35

Caption Numbers

Each caption number contains a field. In Word, a **field** is a placeholder for data that might change in a document. Examples of fields you have used in previous projects are page numbers, merge fields, IF fields, form fields, and the current date. You update caption numbers using the same technique used to update any other field. That is, to update all caption numbers, select the entire document and then press the F9 key or right-click the field and click Update Field on the shortcut menu. When you print a document, Word updates the caption numbers automatically, regardless of whether the document window displays the updated caption numbers.

To Create a Cross-Reference

In reference documents, the text should reference a particular figure and explain the contents of the figure. The next step in this project is to add a reference to the new Figure 2. Because figures may be inserted, deleted, or moved, you may not know the actual figure number in the final document. For this reason, Word provides a method of creating a **cross-reference**, which is a link to an item such as a heading, caption, or footnote in a document. By creating a cross-reference to the caption, the text that mentions the figure will be updated whenever the caption to the figure is updated. The following steps create a cross-reference.

- At the end of the first sentence below the News heading, position the insertion point to the left of the period, press the SPACEBAR, and then press the LEFT PARENTHESIS key.

- Click the Cross-reference button on the References tab to display the Cross-reference dialog box (Figure 7–36).

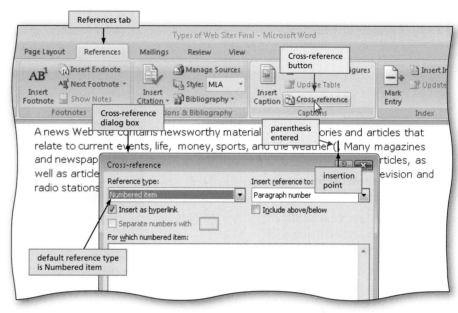

Figure 7–36

- Click the Reference type box arrow; scroll to and then click Figure, which displays a list of figures from the document in the 'For which caption' list.

- In the 'For which caption' list, click Figure 2: News.

- Click the 'Insert reference to' box arrow and then click 'Only label and number' to instruct Word that the cross-reference in the document should list just the label, Figure, followed by the number 2 (Figure 7–37).

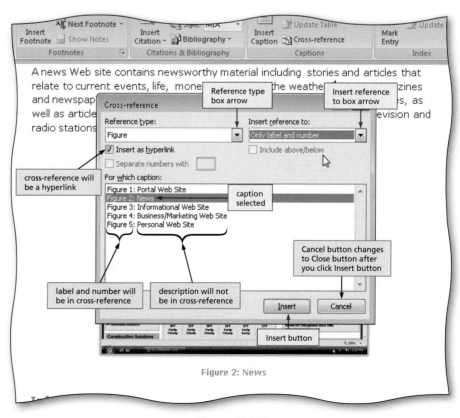

Figure 2: News

Figure 7–37

• Click the Insert button to insert the cross-reference in the document at the location of the insertion point.

Q&A

What if my cross-reference is shaded gray?

The cross-reference is a field. Depending on your Word settings, fields may appear shaded in gray to help you identify them on the screen.

• Click the Close button in the Cross-reference dialog box.

• Press the RIGHT PARENTHESIS key to close off the cross-reference (Figure 7–38).

Q&A

How do I update a cross-reference if a caption is added, deleted, or moved?

In many cases, Word automatically updates cross-references in a document if the item it refers to changes. To update a cross-reference manually, select the cross-reference and then press the F9 key, or right-click the cross-reference and then click Update Field on the shortcut menu.

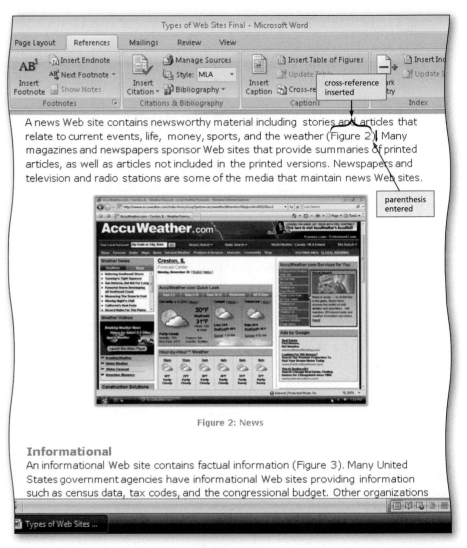

Figure 7–38

To Mark an Index Entry

The last page of the reference document in this project is an index, which lists important terms discussed in the document along with each term's corresponding page number. For Word to generate the index, you first must mark any text you wish to appear in the index. When you mark an index entry, Word creates a field that it uses to build the index. Index entry fields are hidden and are displayed on the screen only when you show formatting marks, that is, when the Show/Hide ¶ button on the Home tab is selected.

In this document, you want the text, news Web site, in the first sentence below the News heading to be marked as an index entry. The next steps mark an index entry.

1

- Select the text you wish to appear in the index (the words, news Web site, in this case).

- Click the Mark Entry button on the References tab to display the Mark Index Entry dialog box (Figure 7–39).

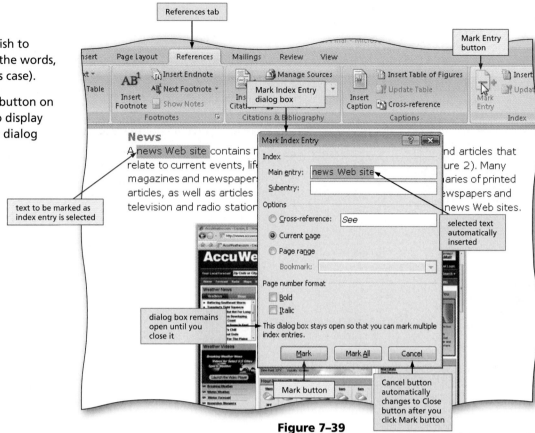

Figure 7–39

2

- Click the Mark button to mark the selected text in the document as an index entry (Figure 7–40).

- Click the Close button in the Mark Index Entry dialog box.

Q&A

Why do formatting marks now appear on the screen?

When you mark an index entry, Word automatically shows formatting marks so that you can see the index entry field. To hide the formatting marks, click the Show/Hide ¶ button on the Home tab.

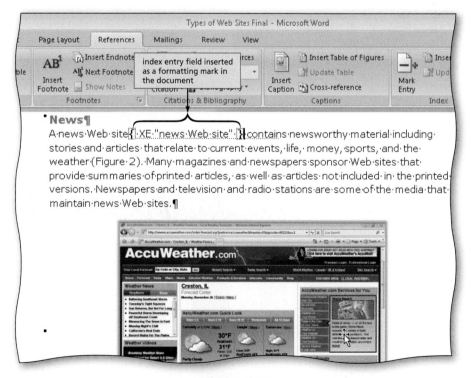

Figure 7–40

Other Ways

1. Select text, press ALT+SHIFT+X

Index Entries

Index entries may include a switch, which is a slash followed by a letter inserted after the field text. Switches include \b to apply bold formatting to the entry's page number, \f to define an entry type, \i to make the entry's page number italic, \r to insert a range of pages numbers, \t to insert specified text in place of a page number, and \y to specify that the subsequent text defines the pronunciation for the index entry. A colon in an index entry precedes a subentry keyword in the index.

To Mark Multiple Index Entries

Word leaves the Mark Index Entry dialog box open until you close it, which allows you to mark multiple index entries without having to reopen the dialog box repeatedly. To mark multiple index entries, you would perform the following steps.

1. With the Mark Index Entry dialog box displayed, click in the document window; scroll to and select the next index entry.

2. If necessary, click the Main entry text box in the Mark Index Entry dialog box to display the selected text in the Main entry text box.

3. Click the Mark button.

4. Repeat Steps 1 through 3 for all entries. When finished, click the Close button in the dialog box.

To Search for and Highlight Specific Text

This document contains several marked index entries. Notice that the marked index entry begins with the letters, XE. You could scroll through the document, scanning for all occurrences of XE, to locate all the index entries. Or, you could use Word to highlight all occurrences of XE in the document so that you easily can locate them. The following steps search for and highlight all occurrences of XE in the document.

1

- Display the Home tab.

- Click the Find button on the Home tab to display the Find and Replace dialog box.

- Type XE in the Find what text box.

- Click the Reading Highlight button to display the Reading Highlight menu (Figure 7–41).

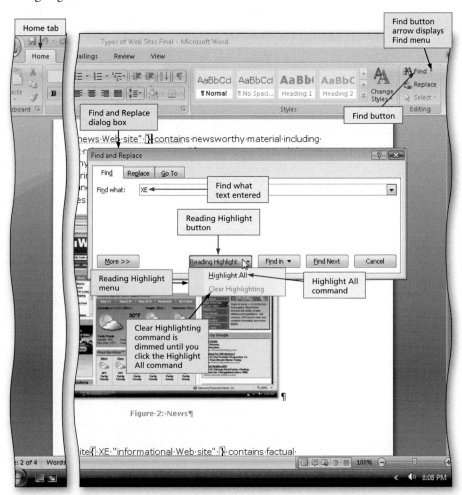

Figure 2: News

Figure 7–41

2

- Click Highlight All on the Reading Highlight menu to highlight in yellow all occurrences of the text, XE, in the document (Figure 7–42).

🔎 **Experiment**

- Scroll through the document to see other occurrences of the highlighted text.

3

- Turn off the highlighting by clicking the Reading Highlight button again and then clicking Clear Highlighting on the Reading Highlight menu (shown in Figure 7–41).

- Close the Find and Replace dialog box.

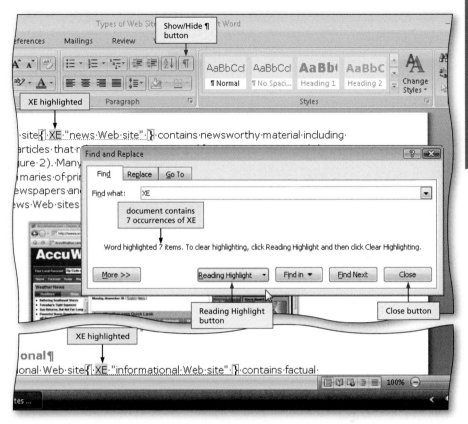

Figure 7–42

Other Ways

1. Click Select Browse Object button on vertical scroll bar, click Find icon
2. Press CTRL+F

To Hide Formatting Marks

To remove the clutter of index entry fields from the document, you should hide formatting marks.

1 If the Show/Hide ¶ button on the Home tab is selected, click it to hide formatting marks.

Q&A What if the index entries still appear after clicking the Show/Hide ¶ button?

Click the Office Button, click the Word Options button, click Display in the left pane, remove the check mark from the Hidden text check box, and then click the OK button.

Building Blocks

Word includes many predefined **building blocks**, which are reusable formatted objects that are stored in galleries. Examples of building blocks include cover pages, headers, footers, page numbers, and text boxes. When you inserted a formatted header, for instance, you are working with a building block.

You can see a list of every available building block in the **Building Blocks Organizer**. From the Building Blocks Organizer, you can sort building blocks, change their properties, or insert them in a document. The project in this chapter uses a text box building block, specifically the Sideline Sidebar building block. The next pages follow these general steps to insert and format the building block.

1. Sort the building blocks in the Building Block Organizer.
2. Insert the Sideline Sidebar text box building block in the document.
3. Enter text in the text box.
4. Insert another Sideline Sidebar text box building block in the document.
5. Link the two text boxes together so that the text flows automatically from one text box to the other.

To Sort Building Blocks and Insert a Sidebar Text Box Building Block Using the Building Blocks Organizer

A **sidebar text box** is a text box that runs across the top or bottom of a page or along the edge of the right or left of a page. As an alternative to inserting a text box using the Text Box gallery, you can insert a text box (or any building block) using the Building Blocks Organizer.

To easily locate building blocks in the Building Blocks Organizer, you can sort its contents by name, gallery, category, template, behavior, or description. The following steps sort the Building Blocks Organizer by gallery, so that all the text box building blocks are grouped together, and then insert the Sideline Sidebar building block in the document on the current page.

- Be sure the insertion point is on page 2 of the document; building blocks are inserted on the current page.

- Display the Insert tab.

- Click the Quick Parts button on the Insert tab to display the Quick Parts menu (Figure 7–43).

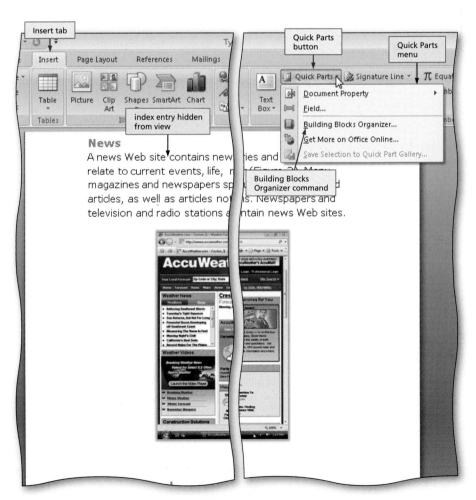

Figure 7–43

- Click Building Blocks Organizer on the Quick Parts menu to display the Building Blocks Organizer dialog box.

Experiment

- Drag the horizontal scroll bar in the Building Blocks Organizer dialog box to the right so that you can look at all the columns. When finished, drag the horizontal scroll bar back to the left in the Building Blocks Organizer dialog box.

3

- Click the Gallery heading in the Building blocks list to sort the building blocks by gallery (Figure 7–44).

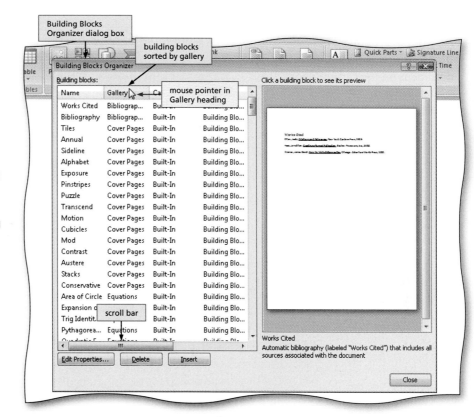

Figure 7–44

- Position the mouse pointer between the Name and Gallery column headings and double-click when the mouse pointer changes to a two-headed arrow, so that you can see the entire name in the first column of the list.

Experiment

- Click various names in the Building blocks list and notice a preview of the selected building block appears in the dialog box.

- Scroll through the Building blocks list to the Text Boxes group in the Gallery column and then click Sideline Sidebar to select it (Figure 7–45).

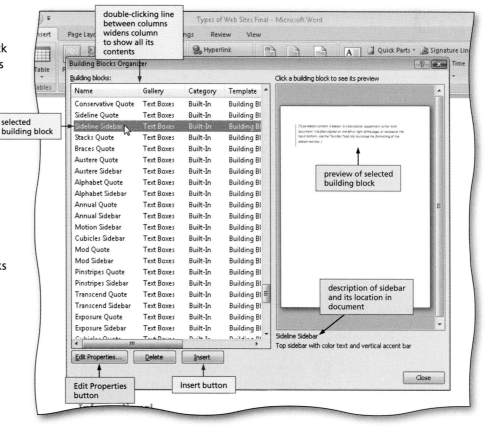

Figure 7–45

6
- Click the Insert button to insert the selected building block in the document on the current page (Figure 7–46).

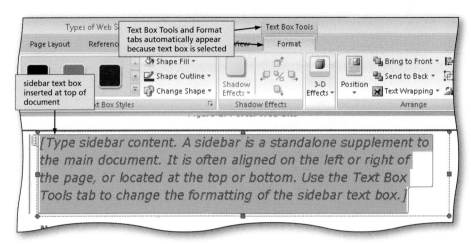

Figure 7–46

Equations

Word includes several predefined mathematical equations that you can insert in a document and then edit, if desired. You insert an equation, such as the quadratic equation, using the Building Blocks Organizer. Or, you can click the Equation button on the Insert tab to display the Equation Tools Design tab, which enables you to insert and customize equations.

TO EDIT PROPERTIES OF BUILDING BLOCK ELEMENTS

Properties of a building block include its name, gallery, category, description, location where it is saved, and how it is inserted in the document. If you wanted to change any of these building block properties for a particular building block, you would perform these steps.

1. Click the Quick Parts button on the Insert tab to display the Quick Parts menu.
2. Click Building Blocks Organizer on the Quick Parts menu to display the Building Blocks Organizer dialog box.
3. Select the building block you wish to edit.
4. Click the Edit Properties button (shown in Figure 7–45 on the previous page) to display the Modify Building Block dialog box.
5. Edit any property in the dialog box and then click the OK button. Close the Building Blocks Organizer dialog box.

To Enter Text in the Sidebar Text Box

The next step is to enter the text in the sidebar text box, up to the numbered list.

1 If necessary, click the sidebar text box to select it.

2 Press the DELETE key to delete the current content of the sidebar text box.

3 In a 14-point bold italic font, type Internet Tip: and then press the ENTER key.

4 Type the following paragraph: Do not assume that information presented on the Web is correct or accurate. Any organization, company, or person can publish a Web page on the Internet. No one oversees the content of these Web pages.

5 Press the ENTER key. Use the buttons on the Home tab to change the font size to 12 point. Type Internet Tip: and then press the ENTER key.

6 Type Criteria for assessing the value of a Web site: and then press the ENTER key (Figure 7–47).

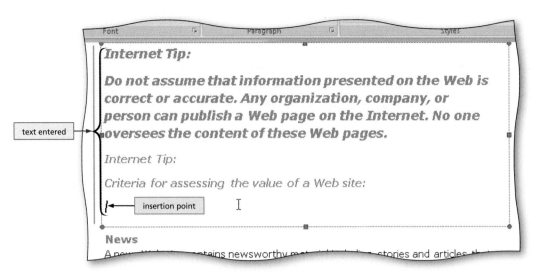

 text entered

insertion point

Figure 7–47

To Enter and Format a Numbered List

The last part of the text in the text box is a numbered list. After entering the numbered list, you change the format of the numbers so that they are followed by parentheses instead of periods. Also, a numbered list, by default, is indented. Because the sidebar text box has a vertical line along its left edge, you remove the indent so that the vertical line is not broken. The following steps enter and format a numbered list.

1

- If necessary, display the Home tab.

- Click the Numbering button on the Home tab to turn on numbering, which automatically displays a number 1 followed by a period.

- Type The information on a Web site should be current. and then press the ENTER key.

- Enter the remaining text for numbers 2 through 6, as shown in Figure 7–48, pressing the ENTER key at the end of each line, except for the last one.

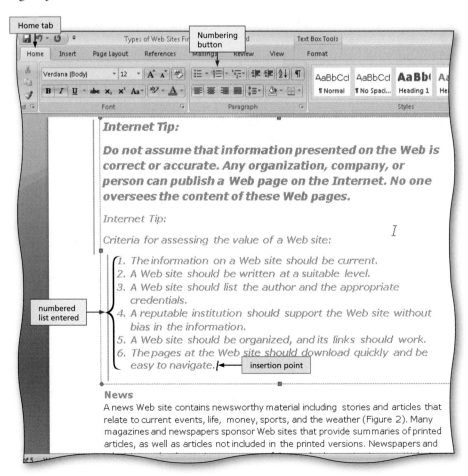

Figure 7–48

- Select the numbered list by dragging through it.

- Click the Numbering button arrow on the Home tab to display the Numbering gallery (Figure 7–49).

- Select Number alignment: Left (third format in first row in Numbering Library area) to change the numbering format of the selected text.

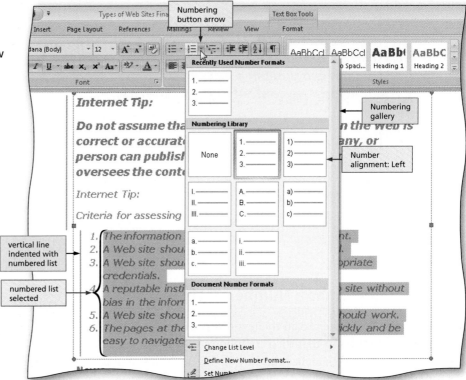

Figure 7–49

- Click the View Ruler button on the vertical scroll bar to display the rulers.

- Drag the Left Indent marker from the ½" mark on the ruler to the ¼" mark, so that the vertical line to the left of the numbered list is aligned with the rest of the text box vertical line (Figure 7–50).

- Click the View Ruler button on the vertical scroll bar to hide the rulers.

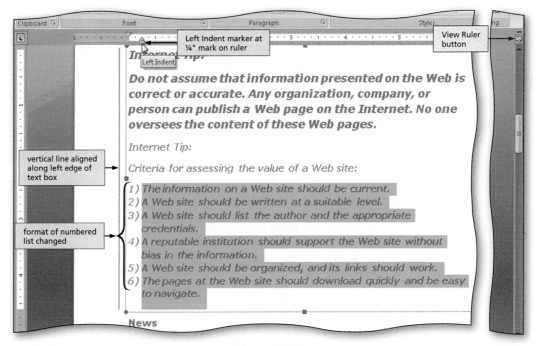

Figure 7–50

To Link Text Boxes

The text box above the News heading is too long. Instead of one long text box, this project splits the text box across the top of two pages. Word allows you to link two separate text boxes, so that the text automatically flows from one text box into the other. The following steps link text boxes.

1

- Display Figure 3 in the document window.

- Position the insertion point to the left of the figure and then press the ENTER key.

- Position the insertion point on the blank line above the figure.

- If necessary, display the Insert tab.

- Click the Quick Parts button on the Insert tab to display the Quick Parts menu.

- Click Building Blocks Organizer on the Quick Parts menu to display the Building Blocks Organizer dialog box.

- Locate the Sideline Sidebar building block and then click the Insert button to insert the sideline text box in the document.

- If necessary, click the text box to select it and then press the DELETE key to delete its contents (Figure 7–51).

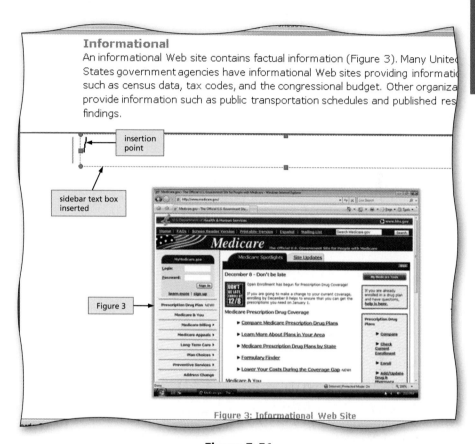

Figure 7–51

2

- Scroll to display the first text box in the document window.

- Click the text box to select it.

- Click the Create Link button on the Format tab (Figure 7–52).

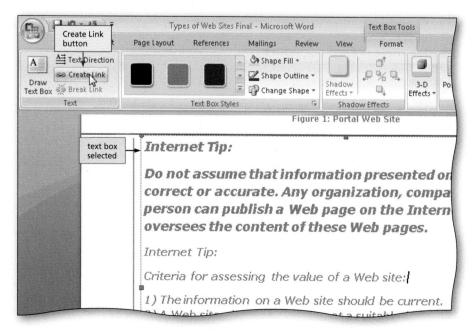

Figure 7–52

- Scroll to display the second (empty) text box in the document window, noticing that the mouse pointer now has the shape of a cup.

- Position the mouse pointer in the empty text box, so that the mouse pointer shape changes to a pouring cup (Figure 7–53).

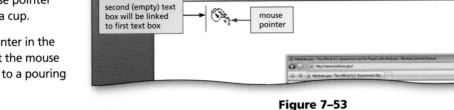

Figure 7–53

- Click the empty text box to link it to the first text box, which causes text from the first text box to flow into the second (linked) text box (Figure 7–54).

Q&A

How would I remove a link?

Select the text box in which you created the link and then click the Break Link button on the Format tab.

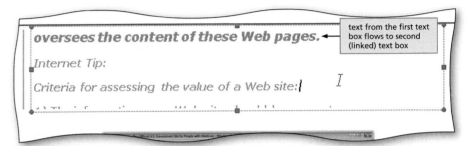

Figure 7–54

- Display the first text box in the document window and then select the text box.

- Resize the text box by dragging its bottom-middle sizing handle until the amount of text that is displayed in the text box is similar to Figure 7–55.

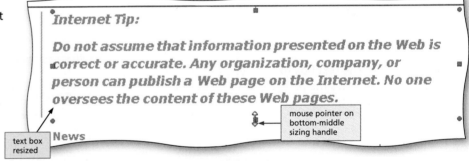

Figure 7–55

- Display the second text box in the document window and then select the text box.

- Resize the text box by dragging its bottom-middle sizing handle until the amount of text that is displayed in the text box is similar to Figure 7–56.

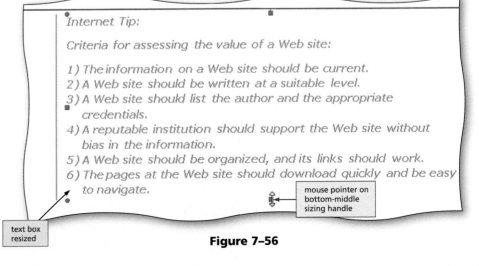

Figure 7–56

To Fill Text Boxes with Color

To make the sidebar text boxes more eye-catching, they are filled with a light orange color. The following steps fill a text box.

1

- With the second text box selected, click the Shape Fill button arrow on the Format tab to display the Shape Fill gallery.

What if the Format tab is not active?

Click Format on the Ribbon to display the Format tab.

- Point to Orange, Accent 1, Lighter 80% (fifth color in the second row) to display a live preview of this fill color (Figure 7–57).

2

 Experiment

- Point to various colors in the Shape Fill gallery and watch the text box fill color change in the document window.

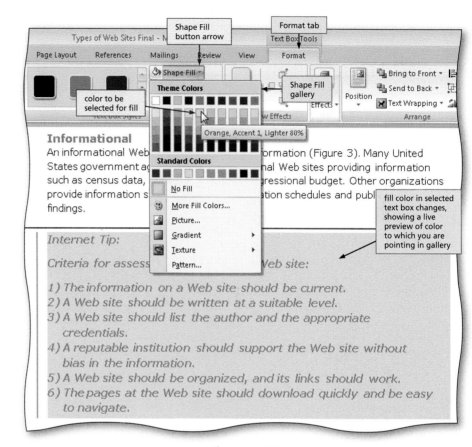

Figure 7–57

3

- Click Orange, Accent 1, Lighter 80% (fifth color in second row) to change fill color of the text box.

4

- Display the first text box in the document window and then click the text box to select it.

- Click the Shape Fill button to fill this text box with the most recently defined fill color (Orange, Accent 1, Lighter 80%), as shown in Figure 7–58.

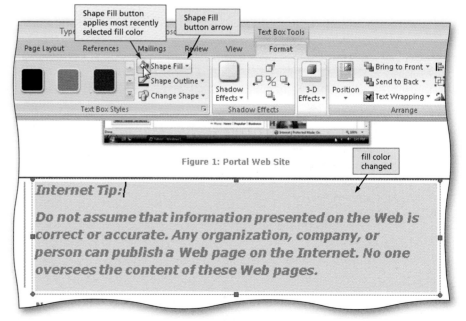

Figure 7–58

To Compress Pictures

Pictures and other illustrations in documents can increase the size of your Word documents. If you plan to e-mail a document or post it for downloading, you may want to reduce its file size to speed up file transmission time. In Word, you can compress pictures, which reduces the size of the Word document. Compressing the pictures in Word does not cause any loss in their quality. The following steps compress pictures in the document.

1

- Click any figure in the document to select it, so that the Picture Tools and Format tabs appear. If necessary, click Format to display the Format tab.

- Click the Compress Pictures button on the Format tab to display the Compress Pictures dialog box.

- If the 'Apply to selected pictures only' check box contains a check mark, click the check box to remove the check mark.

- Click the Options button to display the Compression Settings dialog box.

- If necessary, select the first two check boxes in the Compression options area.

- If necessary, select Print in the Target output area (Figure 7–59).

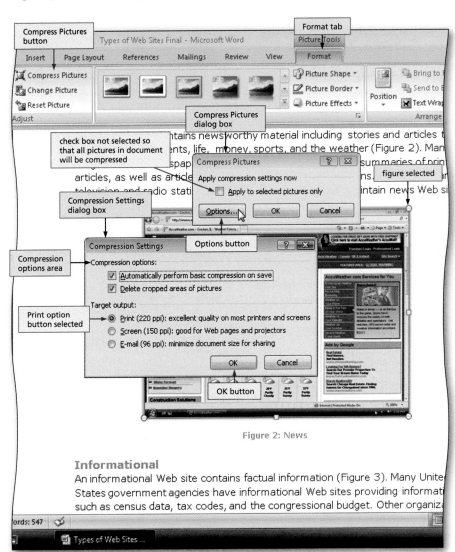

Figure 7–59

2

- Click the OK button in each dialog box to compress all pictures in the document.

Q&A Can I compress a single picture?

Yes. Select the picture and then place a check mark in the 'Apply to selected pictures only' check box.

- Save the document again with the same file name.

Other Ways

1. Click the Tools button in the Save As dialog box, click Compress Pictures on the Tools menu

To Close a Document

You are finished modifying the Types of Web Sites Final document. Thus, you close it.

1 Click the Office Button and then click Close on the Office Button menu.

Working with a Master Document

When you are creating a document that includes other files, you may want to create a master document to organize the documents. A **master document** is simply a document that contains links to one or more other documents, each of which are called a **subdocument**. In addition to subdocuments, a master document can contain its own text and graphics.

In this project, the master document file is named Internet Post - Fourth Edition. This master document file contains a link to one subdocument: the Types of Web Sites Final file. The master document also contains other items: a title page, a table of contents, a table of figures, and an index. The following pages create this master document and insert the necessary elements in the document to create the finished Internet Post - Fourth Edition document.

Outlines

To create a master document, you must be in Outline view. You then enter the headings of the document as an outline using Word's built-in heading styles. In an outline, the major heading is displayed at the left margin with each subordinate, or lower-level, heading indented. In Word, the built-in Heading 1 style is displayed at the left margin in outline view. Heading 2 style is indented below Heading 1 style, Heading 3 style is indented further, and so on.

You do not want to use a built-in heading style for the paragraphs of text within the document because when you create a table of contents, Word places all lines formatted using the built-in heading styles in the table of contents. Thus, the text below each heading is formatted using the Body Text style.

Each heading should print at the top of a new page. Because you might want to format the pages within a heading differently from those pages in other headings, you insert next page section breaks between each heading.

To Create an Outline

The Internet Post - Fourth Edition document contains these four major headings: Overview (which later is changed to Introduction), Types of Web Sites, Table of Figures, and Index. The heading, Types of Web Sites, is not entered in the outline; instead, it is part of the subdocument inserted in the master document.

The Overview section contains three paragraphs of body text, which you enter directly in the outline. The Types of Web Sites content is inserted from the subdocument. You will instruct Word to create the content for the Table of Figures and Index later in this chapter. The steps on the next pages create an outline that contains headings and body text to be used in the master document.

BTW

Master Documents
Master documents can be used when multiple people prepare different sections of a document or when a document contains separate elements such as the chapters in a book. If multiple people in a network need to work on the same document simultaneously, individual people each can work on a section (subdocument), all of which can be stored together collectively in a master document on the network server.

- To display a new blank document window, click the Office Button, click New on the Office Button menu, click Blank document in the New Document dialog box, if necessary, and then click the Create button.

- To switch to Outline view, click the Outline button on the status bar, which displays the Outlining tab on the Ribbon.

- Be sure the Show Text Formatting check box is selected on the Outlining tab.

- Type Overview as the first heading in the outline and then press the ENTER key.

- Click the Demote to Body Text button, so that you can enter the Overview paragraphs of text (Figure 7–60).

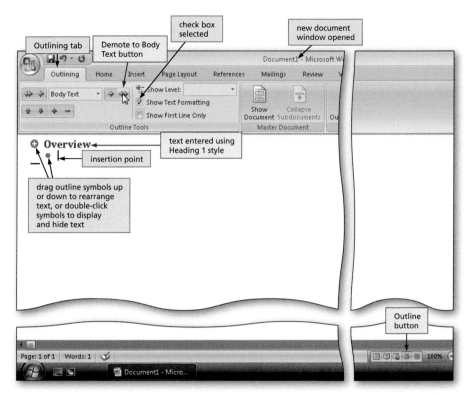

Figure 7–60

- Type the first overview paragraph shown in Figure 7–61 and then press the ENTER key.

Q&A Why is only my first line of text in the paragraph displayed?

Remove the check mark from the Show First Line Only check box on the Outlining tab.

- Type the second overview paragraph shown in Figure 7–61 and then press the ENTER key.

- Type the third overview paragraph shown in Figure 7–61 and then press the ENTER key.

- Click the Promote to Heading 1 button on the Outlining tab because you are finished entering body text and will enter the remaining headings in the outline.

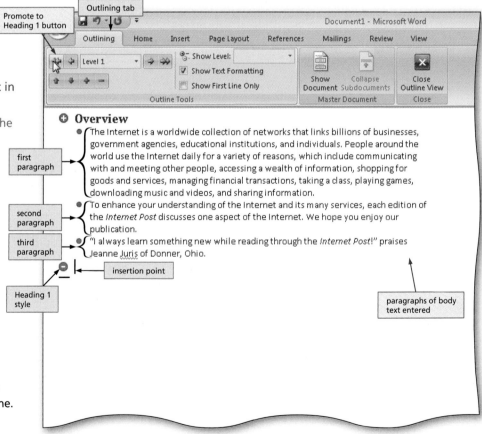

Figure 7–61

- Display the Page Layout tab.

- To enter a next page section break before the next heading, click the Breaks button on the Page Layout tab and then click Next Page on the Breaks menu.

- Type Table of Figures and then press the ENTER key.

- Repeat Step 3.

- Type Index as the last entry (Figure 7–62).

Q&A

Why do some outline symbols contain a plus and others a minus?

The plus means the outline level has subordinate levels; the minus means the outline level does not have any subordinate levels.

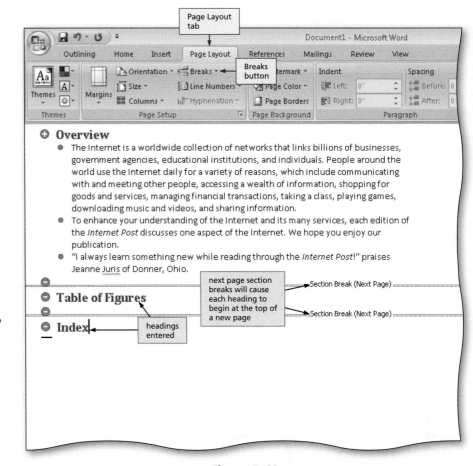

Figure 7–62

Other Ways

1. Click Outline View button on View tab

To Show First Line Only

With the Show First Line only button not selected, the content of each paragraph of body text is displayed in outline view. To make the outline more readable, users often instruct Word to display just the first line of each paragraph of body text. The following step displays only the first line of body text paragraphs.

- Display the Outlining tab.

- Place a check mark in the Show First Line Only check box on the Outlining tab, so that Word displays only the first line of each paragraph (Figure 7–63).

Q&A

How would I redisplay all lines of the paragraphs of body text?

Remove the check mark from the Show First Line Only check box.

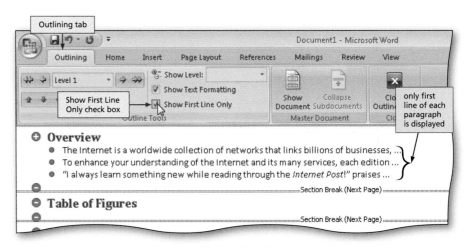

Figure 7–63

To Insert a Subdocument

The next step is to insert a subdocument in the master document. Word places the first line of text in the subdocument at the first heading level because it is defined using the Heading 1 style. The subdocument to be inserted is the Types of Web Sites Final file you modified earlier in this chapter. The following steps insert a subdocument in a master document.

- If formatting marks do not appear, click the Show/Hide ¶ button on the Home tab.

- Position the insertion point where you want to insert the subdocument (on the section break between the Overview and Table of Figures headings).

- Click the Show Document button on the Outlining tab so that all commands in the Master Document group appear.

- With the USB flash drive that contains the Types of Web Sites Final file connected to one of the computer's USB ports, click the Insert Subdocument button on the Outlining tab.

- When Word displays the Insert Subdocument dialog box, locate and select your USB flash drive in the list of available drives and then click the Types of Web Sites Final file (Figure 7–64).

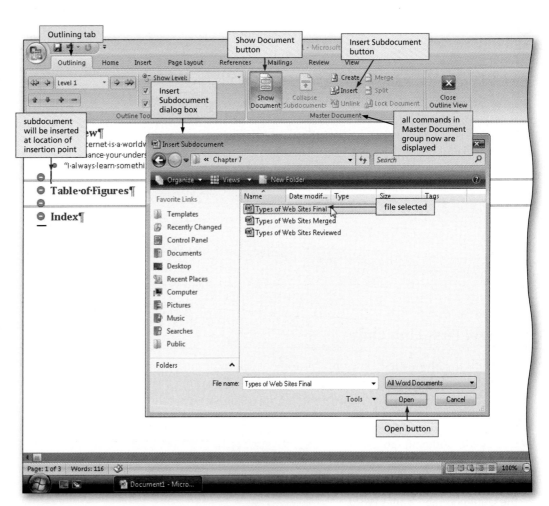

Figure 7–64

3

- Click the Open button in the dialog box to insert the selected file as a subdocument.

- If Word displays a dialog box about styles, click the No to All button.

- Press CTRL+HOME to position the insertion point at the top of the document (Figure 7–65).

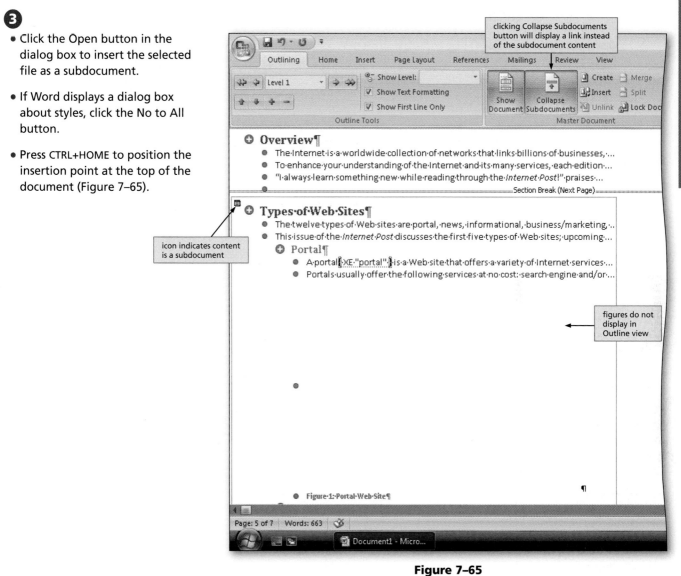

Figure 7–65

To Save a Document

With the headings entered and subdocument inserted, you are finished in Outline view with the master document. When you save a master document, Word also saves any subdocument files on the disk. Thus, the Types of Web Sites Final file automatically will be saved along with the master document. The following steps save the master document.

1 Click the Save button on the Quick Access Toolbar to display the Save As dialog box.

2 Type `Internet Post - Fourth Edition` in the File name text box to change the file name.

3 Locate and select your USB flash drive in the list of available drives.

4 Click the Save button in the Save As dialog box to save the document on the USB flash drive with the new file name, Internet Post - Fourth Edition.

Master Documents and Subdocuments

When you open the master document, the subdocuments initially are collapsed, that is, displayed as hyperlinks (Figure 7–66). To work with the contents of a master document after you open it, switch to Outline view and then expand the subdocuments by clicking the Expand Subdocuments button.

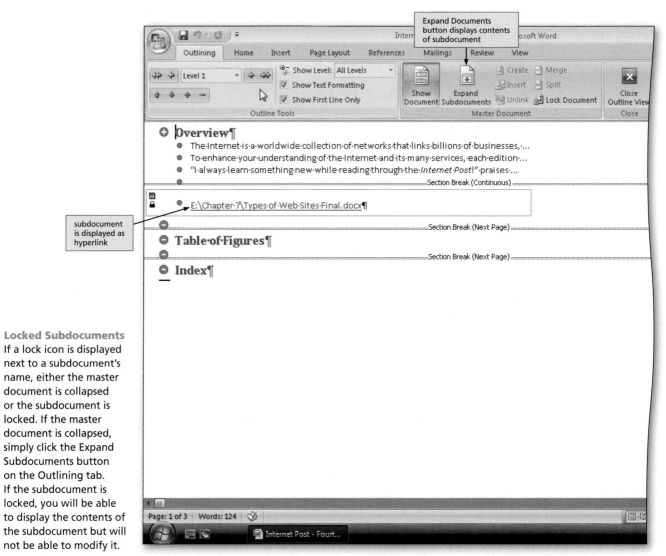

Figure 7–66

You can open a subdocument in a separate document window and modify it. To open a collapsed subdocument, click the hyperlink. To open an expanded subdocument, double-click the subdocument icon to the left of the document heading (shown in Figure 7-65 on the previous page).

If, for some reason, you wanted to remove a subdocument from a master document, you would expand the subdocuments, click the subdocument icon to the left of the subdocument's first heading, and then press the DELETE key. Although Word removes the subdocument from the master document, the subdocument file remains on disk.

Occasionally, you may want to convert a subdocument to part of the master document — breaking the connection between the text in the master document and the subdocument. To do this, expand the subdocuments, click the subdocument icon, and then click the Remove Subdocument button on the Outlining tab.

Organizing a Reference Document

Reference documents are organized and formatted so that users easily can navigate through and read the document. The reference document in this chapter includes the following elements: a formatted quotation, a title page, a table of contents, a table of figures, an index, alternating headers, and a gutter margin. This section illustrates the tasks required to include these elements.

Include elements common to a reference document.

Plan Ahead

Be sure to include all essential information on the title page, table of contents, table of figures or list of tables (if one exists), and index.

- **Title Page.** A title page should contain, at a minimum, the title of the document and name of the author. Some also contain a subtitle, edition or volume number, and date written.

- **Table of Contents.** The table of contents should list the title (heading) of each chapter or section and the starting page number of the chapter or section. You may use a leader character, such as a dot or hyphen, to fill the space between the heading and the page number. Sections prior to the table of contents are not listed in it — only list material that follows the table of contents.

- **Table of Figures or List of Tables.** If you have multiple figures or tables in a document, consider identifying all of them in a table of figures or a list of tables. The format of the table of figures or list of tables should match the table of contents.

- **Index.** The index normally is set in two columns, although one column is acceptable. The index can contain any item a reader might want to look up, such as a heading or a key term. If the document does not have a table of figures or list of tables, also include figures and tables in the index.

To Change the View and the Document Theme

The first step in this section is to switch to Print Layout view and change the document theme to Aspect.

1 Click the Print Layout button on the status bar so that Word switches from Outline view to Print Layout view.

2 Display the Page Layout tab.

3 Click the Themes button on the Page Layout tab and then click Aspect in the Themes gallery to change the document theme to Aspect.

4 Display the Home tab. If formatting marks are showing, click the Show/Hide ¶ button to hide them.

BTW

Readability Statistics
You can instruct Word to display readability statistics when it has finished a spelling and grammar check on a document. Three readability statistics presented are the percent of passive sentences, the Flesch Reading Ease score, and the Flesch-Kincaid Grade Level score. The Flesch Reading Ease score uses a 100-point scale to rate the ease with which a reader can understand the text in a document. A higher score means the document is easier to understand. The Flesch-Kincaid Grade Level score rates the text in a document on a U.S. school grade level. For example, a score of 10.0 indicates a student in the tenth grade can understand the material. To show readability statistics when the spelling check is complete, click the Office Button, click the Word Options button, click Proofing in the left pane, place a check mark in the 'Show readability statistics' check box, and then click the OK button.

To Apply a Quote Style

Word provides two different styles for quotations (Quote and Intense Quote), so that a reader easily can identify a quotation. In the Overview section of this document, the last paragraph is a quotation. The following steps format the paragraph using the Intense Quote style.

- Position the insertion point somewhere in the paragraph containing the quotation.

- If necessary, display the Home tab.

- Click the More button in the Styles group to display the Styles gallery (Figure 7–67).

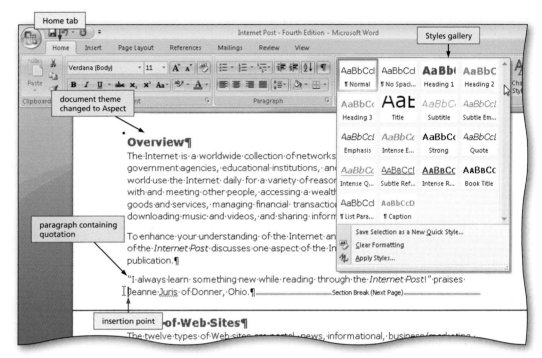

Figure 7–67

- Point to Intense Quote in the Styles gallery to display a live preview in the document of the Intense Quote style (Figure 7–68).

Experiment

- Point to Quote in the Styles gallery and watch the paragraph containing the insertion point (the quotation) show a live preview of the Quote style, so that you can see the differences between the Intense Quote and Quote styles.

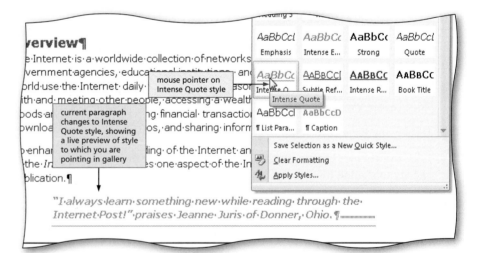

Figure 7–68

- Click Intense Quote in the Styles gallery to apply the Intense Quote style to the paragraph containing the quotation.

Other Ways
1. Click Styles Dialog Box Launcher, click Intense Quote or Quote style in Styles task pane	2. Press CTRL+SHIFT+S, click Style Name box arrow in Apply Styles task pane, click Intense Quote or Quote in the list

To Change the Format of Text

The name of a publication, such as the *Internet Post*, usually is italicized. Because the Intense Quote style italicizes the text in the quotation, the name of the publication in the quote no longer is set apart. In this situation, you use a contrafont for the publication; that is, you remove the italic from the publication name. The following steps remove the italic format from text.

1 Select the text, Internet Post, in the quotation.

2 Click the Italic button on the Home tab to remove the italic format from the selected text.

To Insert a Cover Page

The reference document in this chapter includes a title page. Word has many predefined cover page formats that you can use for the title page in a document. The following steps insert a cover page.

1

- Display the Insert tab.

- Click the Cover Page button on the Insert tab to display the Cover Page gallery (Figure 7–69).

 Experiment

- Scroll through the Cover Page gallery to see the variety of available predefined cover pages.

Q&A

Does it matter where I position the insertion point?

No. By default, Word inserts the cover page as the first page in a document.

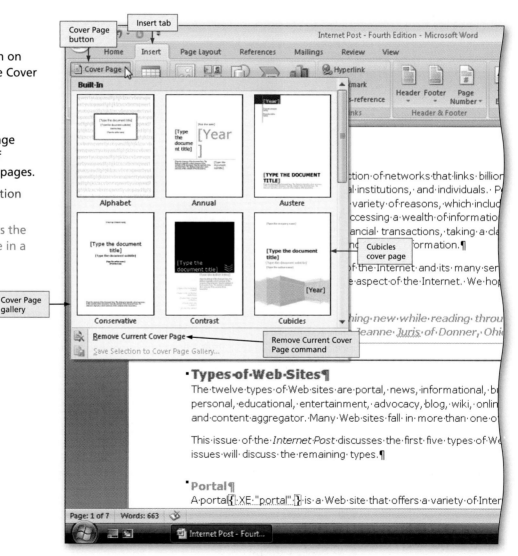

Figure 7–69

2

- Click Cubicles in the Cover Page gallery to insert the Cubicles cover page as the first page in the current document.

- Change the zoom level to 60% so that the entire cover page is displayed in the document window (Figure 7–70).

Q&A Does the cover page have to be the first page?

No. You can right-click the desired cover page and then click the desired location from the submenu.

Q&A How would I delete a cover page?

You would click the Cover Page button on the Insert tab and then click Remove Current Cover Page in the Cover Page gallery.

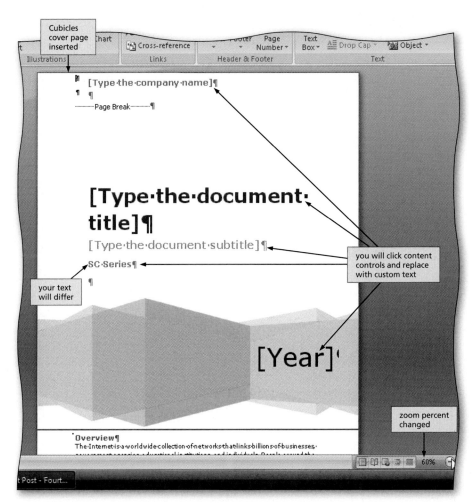

Figure 7–70

To Enter Text in Content Controls

The next step is to select content controls on the cover page and replace their instructions or text with the title page information. Keep in mind that the content controls present suggested text. You can enter any appropriate text in any content control. The following steps enter title page text on the cover page.

1 Because formatting marks clutter the title page, if necessary, click the Show/Hide ¶ button on the Home tab to turn off formatting marks.

2 Click the content control with the instruction, Type the company name. Type `Fourth Edition` in the content control.

3 Click the content control with the instruction, Type the document title. Type `Internet Post` in the content control.

4 Click the content control with the instruction, Type the document subtitle. Type `Types of Web Sites - Part 1` in the content control.

5 Replace the text in the user name content control, SC Series in this case, with the text `Donner County Library`.

6 Type `08` in the Year content control (Figure 7–71).

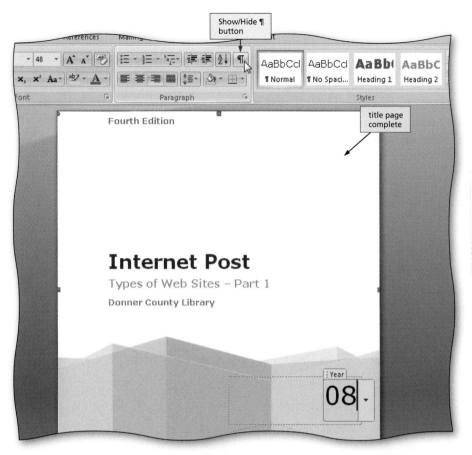

Figure 7–71

To Insert a Blank Page

In the reference document in this chapter, the table of contents is on a page between the title page and the Overview page. Thus, the next step inserts a blank page before the current second page.

- Change the zoom back to 100%.

- Position the insertion point to the left of the word, Overview, on page 2.

- Display the Insert tab.

- Click the Blank Page button on the Insert tab to insert a blank page at the location of the insertion point.

- If necessary, hide white space again by positioning the mouse pointer above the page (in the space between pages) and double-clicking when the mouse pointer changes to a Hide White Space button.

- If necessary, scroll to display the blank page in the document window (Figure 7–72).

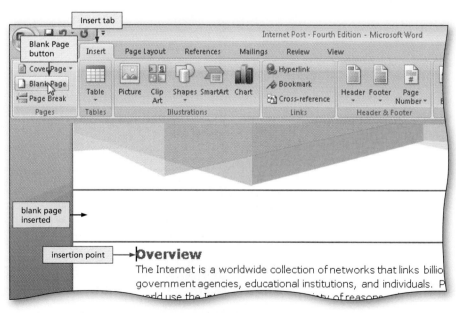

Figure 7–72

To Create a Table of Contents

A table of contents lists all headings in a document and their associated page numbers. When you use Word's built-in heading styles (for example, Heading 1, Heading 2, and so on), you can instruct Word to create a table of contents from these headings. In the reference document in this chapter, the heading of each section uses the Heading 1 style, and subheadings use the Heading 2 style.

Word has many predefined table of contents formats. The following steps use a predefined building block to create a table of contents.

1
• Position the insertion point at the top of the blank page 2, which is the location for the table of contents.

• Display the References tab.

• Ensure that formatting marks do not show.

Q&A
Why should I hide formatting marks?
Formatting marks, especially those for index entries, sometimes can cause wrapping to occur on the screen that will be different from how the printed document will wrap. These differences could cause a heading to move to the next page. To ensure that the page references in the table of contents reflect the printed pages, be sure that formatting marks are hidden when you create a table of contents.

2
• Click the Table of Contents button on the References tab to display the Table of Contents gallery (Figure 7–73).

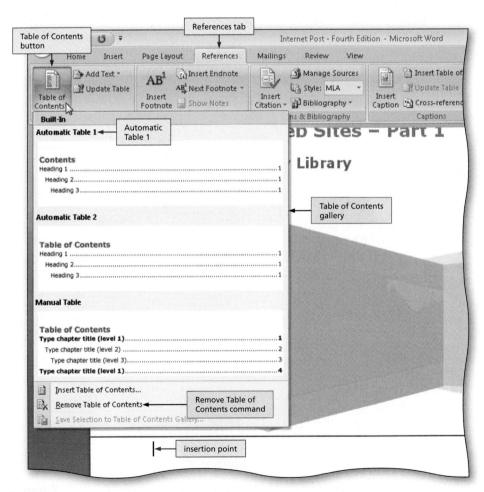

Figure 7–73

- Click Automatic Table 1 in the Table of Contents gallery to insert the table of contents at the location of the insertion point (Figure 7–74).

Q&A How would I delete a table of contents?

You would click the Table of Contents button on the References tab and then click Remove Table of Contents in the Table of Contents gallery.

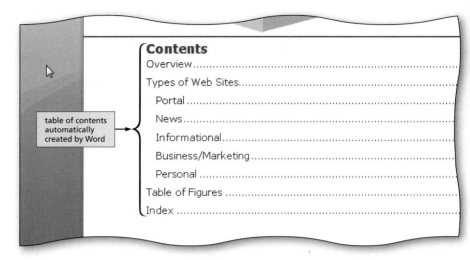

Figure 7–74

Other Ways	
1. Click Table of Contents button on References tab, click Insert Table of	Contents, select table of contents options, click OK button

To Use the Document Map

When you use Word's built-in heading styles in a document, you can use the Document Map to navigate quickly through the document. The Document Map is a pane at the left edge of the Word window that displays in an outline format any text formatted using Word's heading styles. When you click a heading in the Document Map, Word displays the page associated with that heading in the document window. The following steps show the Document Map and then navigate to a heading using the Document Map.

- Display the View tab.

- Place a check mark in the Document Map check box on the View tab to display the Document Map in a separate pane at the left edge of the Word window (Figure 7–75).

Q&A What if all the headings do not display?

Right-click the Document Map and then click All on the shortcut menu to ensure that all headings are displayed. If a heading still does not display, verify that the heading is formatted with a heading style. To display subheadings below a heading in the Document Map, click the plus sign (+) to the left of the heading. Likewise, to hide subheadings, click the minus sign (–) to the left of the heading.

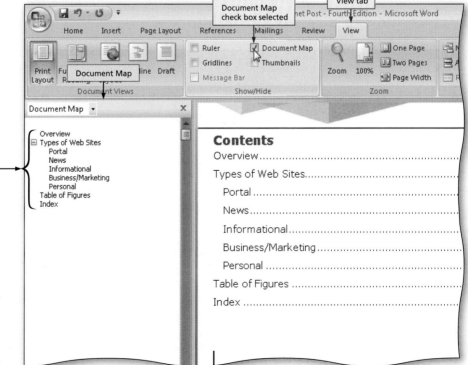

Figure 7–75

• Click the heading, Types of Web Sites, in the Document Map to display the page containing the Types of Web Sites heading in the Word window (Figure 7–76).

Q&A Can I adjust the width of the Document Map?

Yes. You can change the width of the Document Map by dragging its resize bar to the left or right. If a heading is too wide for the Document Map, you can point to the heading to display a ScreenTip that shows the complete title.

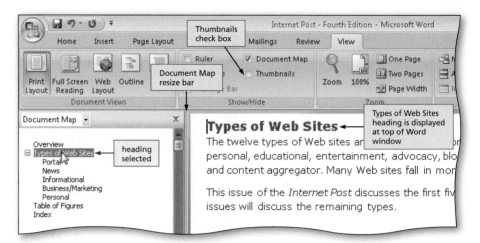

Figure 7–76

TO DISPLAY THUMBNAILS

Instead of headings, you can display **thumbnails**, which are miniature images of each page, on the left side of the Word window. You then can scroll through and click any thumbnail to display the associated page in the document window. If you wanted to display thumbnails, you would perform these steps.

1. Display the View tab.
2. Place a check mark in the Thumbnails check box (shown in Figure 7–76) to display the Thumbnails pane.

To Add Text to the Table of Contents

Occasionally, you may want to add a paragraph of text, which normally is not formatted using a heading style, to a table of contents. The following steps add a paragraph of text to the table of contents by formatting it as Level 3.

• Position the insertion point in the paragraph of text that you want to add to the table of contents, as shown in Figure 7–77.

• Display the References tab.

• Click the Add Text button on the References tab to display the Add Text menu (Figure 7–77).

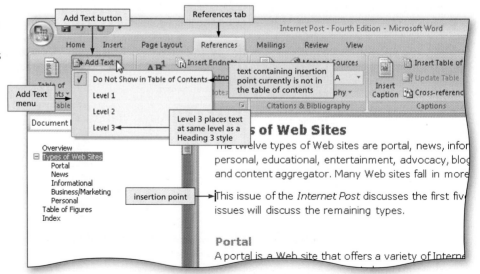

Figure 7–77

2

- Click Level 3 in the Add Text menu, which changes the format of the current paragraph to a Heading 3 style and adds the paragraph of text to the table of contents (Figure 7–78).

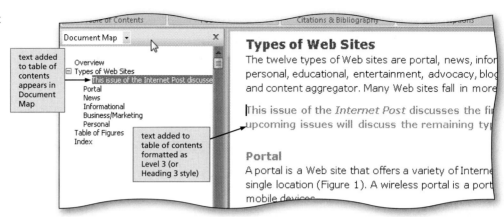

Figure 7–78

To Modify Heading Text

Instead of the term, Overview, you decide to use the term, Introduction, as the heading for the page that follows the table of contents. The following steps modify the heading text.

1 Click the heading, Overview, in the Document Map to display the Overview heading in the document window.

2 Replace the word, Overview, with the word, Introduction (Figure 7–79).

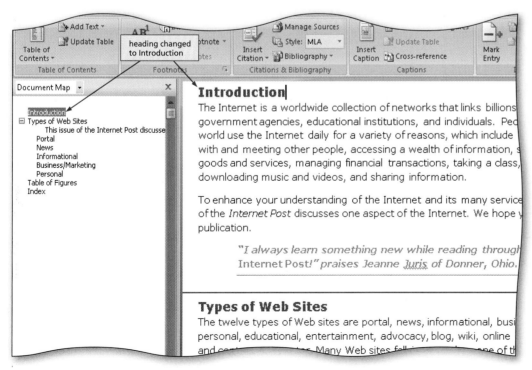

Figure 7–79

To Update a Table of Contents

When you change headings or text in a document, you should update the associated table of contents. You have made two changes that will affect the table of contents: changed a heading and added a paragraph of text. Thus, the following steps update the table of contents.

- Display the table of contents in the document window.

- Click the table of contents to select it (Figure 7–80).

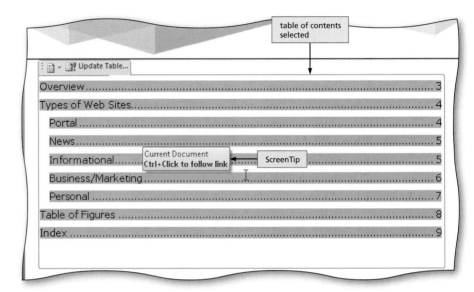

Figure 7–80

- Click the Update Table button that is attached to the table to update the table of contents (Figure 7–81).

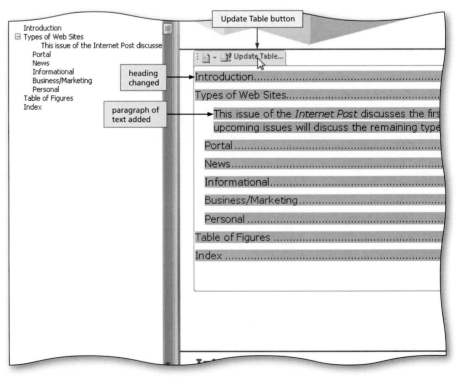

Figure 7–81

Other Ways

1. Select table, click Update Table button on References tab
2. Select table, press F9 key

To Change the Format of a Table of Contents

You can change the format of the table of contents to any of the predefined table of contents styles. The following steps change the table of contents to the Automatic Table 2 style.

- Click the Table of Contents button that is attached to the selected table of contents, which displays the Table of Contents gallery (Figure 7–82).

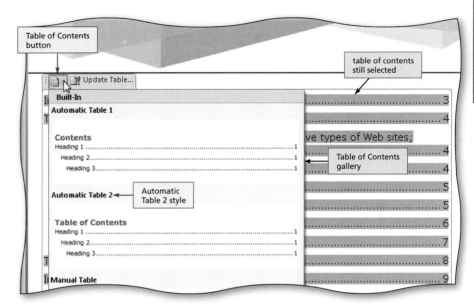

Figure 7–82

- Click Automatic Table 2 in the Table of Contents gallery to change the table of contents style (Figure 7–83).

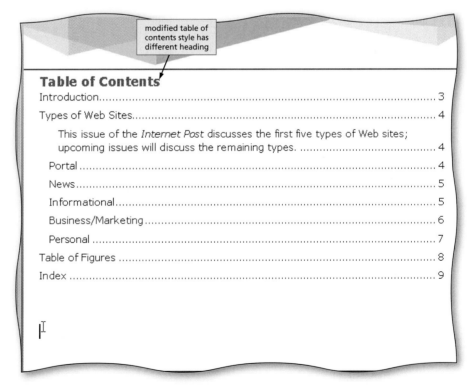

Figure 7–83

Other Ways
1. Click Table of Contents button on References tab

To Create a Table of Figures

At the end of the reference document is a table of figures, which lists all figures and their corresponding page numbers. Word generates this table of figures from the captions in the document. The following steps create a table of figures.

- Ensure that formatting marks are not displayed.

- Click the heading, Table of Figures, in the Document Map to display the Table of Figures heading in the document window.

- Position the insertion point at the end of the Table of Figures heading and then press the ENTER key, so that the insertion point is on the line below the heading.

- Click the Insert Table of Figures button on the References tab to display the Table of Figures dialog box.

- Be sure that all settings in your dialog box match those in Figure 7–84.

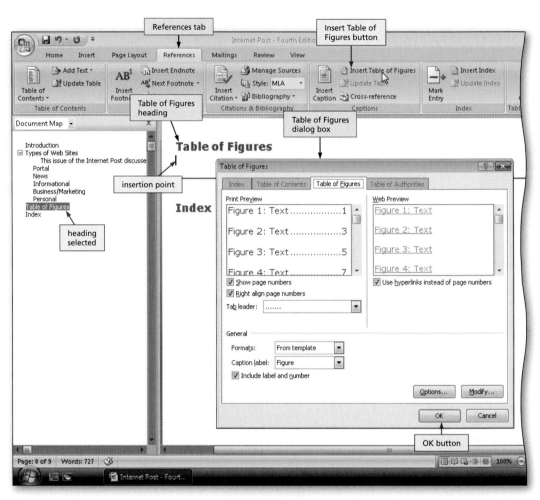

Figure 7–84

- Click the OK button to create a table of figures at the location of the insertion point (Figure 7–85).

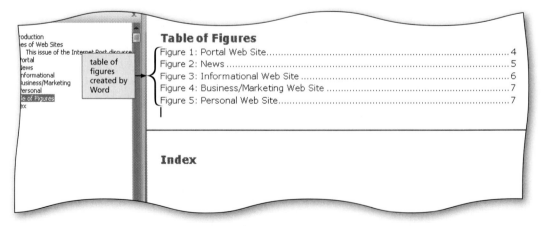

Figure 7–85

To Change the Format of the Table of Figures

If you wanted to change the format of the table of figures, you would perform the following steps.

1. Click the table of figures to select it.
2. Click the Insert Table of Figures button on the References tab to display the Table of Figures dialog box.
3. Change settings in the dialog box as desired.
4. Click the OK button to apply the changed settings.
5. Click the OK button when Word asks if you want to replace the selected table of figures.

To Edit a Caption and Update the Table of Figures

When you modify captions in a document or move illustrations to a different location in the document, you will have to update the table of figures. The following steps change the Figure 2 caption and then update the table of figures.

- Click the heading, News, in the Document Pane to display the News heading in the document window.

- Scroll to display the Figure 2 caption in the document window.

- Add the words, Web Site, to the Figure 2 caption so that it reads: News Web Site (Figure 7–86).

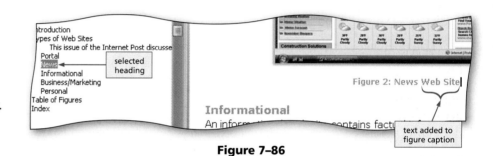

Figure 7–86

- Click the heading, Table of Figures, in the Document Map to display the Table of Figures heading in the document window.

- Click the table of figures to select it.

- Click the Update Table of Figures button on the References tab to display the Update Table of Figures dialog box.

- Click 'Update entire table', so that Word updates the contents of the entire table of figures instead of updating only the page numbers (Figure 7–87).

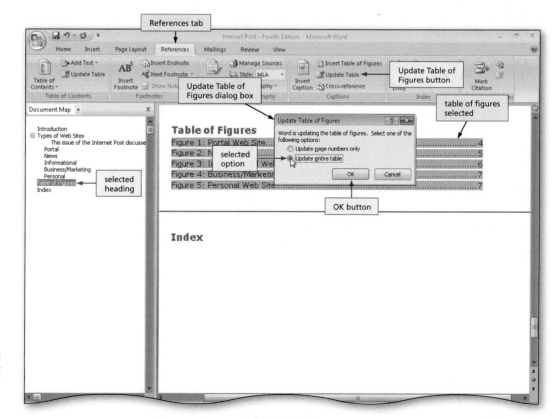

Figure 7–87

- Click the OK button to update the table of figures (Figure 7–88).

Q&A

Are the entries in the table of figures links?

Yes. As with the table of contents, you can CTRL+click any entry in the table of figures and Word will display the associated figure in the document window.

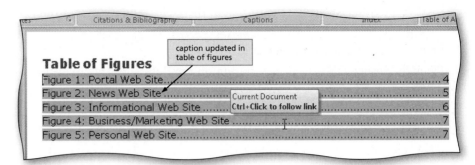

Figure 7–88

Other Ways

1. Select table, press F9 key

To Build an Index

The reference document in this chapter ends with an index. For Word to generate the index, you first must mark any text you wish to appear in the index. Earlier, this chapter showed how to mark index entries.

Once all index entries are marked, Word can build the index from the index entry fields in the document. Recall that index entry fields begin with XE, which appear on the screen when formatting marks are displayed. When index entry fields show on the screen, the document's pagination probably will be altered because of the extra text in the index entries. Thus, be sure to hide formatting marks before building an index. The following steps build an index.

- Click the heading, Index, in the Document Map to display the Index heading in the document window.

- Click to the right of the Index heading and then press the ENTER key.

- Ensure that formatting marks are not displayed.

- Click the Insert Index button on the References tab to display the Index dialog box.

- If necessary, click the Formats box arrow in the dialog box; scroll to and then click Formal in the list, to select the Formal index format (Figure 7–89).

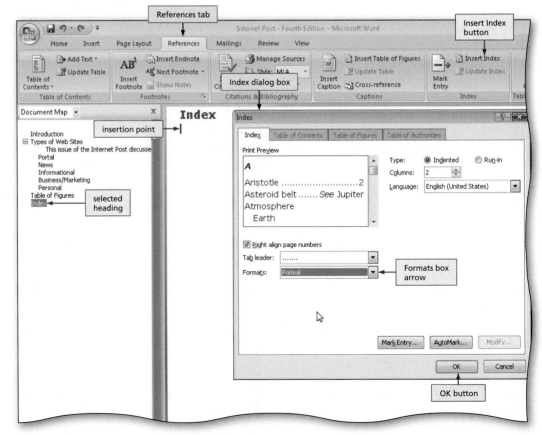

Figure 7–89

2

• Click the OK button to create an index at the location of the insertion point (Figure 7–90).

index created by Word

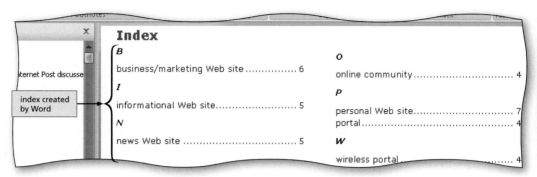

Figure 7–90

To Mark Another Index Entry

The following steps mark an index entry in the Introduction section.

1 Click the heading, Introduction, in the Document Map to display the Introduction heading in the document window.

2 Select the word, Internet, in the first sentence below the heading.

3 Click the Mark Entry button on the References tab to display the Mark Index Entry dialog box (Figure 7–91).

4 Click the Mark button to mark the entry.

5 Close the dialog box.

6 Hide formatting marks.

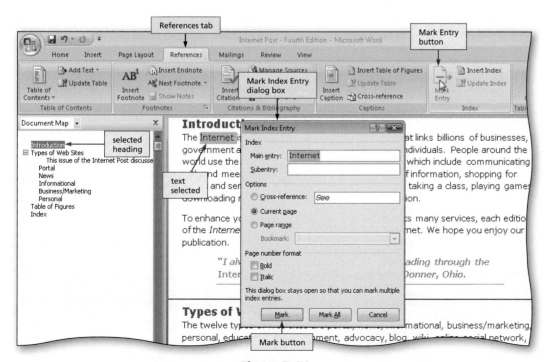

Figure 7–91

TO EDIT AN INDEX ENTRY

At some time, you may want to change an index entry. For example, the entry, online community, might need to change to the entry, online user community. If you wanted to change an index entry, you would perform the following steps.

1. Display formatting marks.
2. Locate the XE field for the index entry you wish to change (i.e., { XE "online community"}).
3. Change the text inside the quotation marks (i.e., { XE "online user community"}).
4. Update the index as described in the steps at the bottom of this page.

TO DELETE AN INDEX ENTRY

If you wanted to delete an index entry, you would perform the following steps.

1. Display formatting marks.
2. Select the XE field for the index entry you wish to delete (i.e., { XE "online community"}).
3. Press the DELETE key.
4. Update the index as described in the next steps.

To Update an Index

After marking a new index entry, you must update the index. The following step updates the index.

- Click the heading, Index, in the Document Map to display the Index heading in the document window.

- In the document window, click the index to select it.

- Click the Update Index button on the References tab to update the index (Figure 7–92).

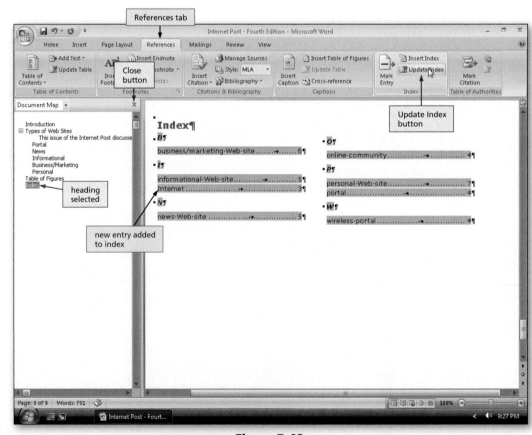

Figure 7–92

Other Ways
1. Select index, press F9 key

To Change the Format of the Index

If you wanted to change the format of the index, you would perform the following steps.

1. Click the index to select it.
2. Click the Insert Index button on the References tab to display the Index dialog box.
3. Change settings in the dialog box as desired. If you want to modify the style used for the index, click the Modify button.
4. Click the OK button to apply the changed settings.
5. Click the OK button when Word asks if you want to replace the selected index.

To Delete an Index

If you wanted to delete an index, you would perform the following steps.

1. Click the index to select it.
2. Press SHIFT+F9 to display field codes.
3. Drag through the entire field code, including the braces, and then press the DELETE key.

Table of Authorities

In addition to creating an index, table of figures, and table of contents, you can use Word to create a table of authorities. Legal documents often include a **table of authorities** to list references to cases, rules, statutes, etc. To create a table of authorities, mark the citations first and then build the table of authorities.

The procedures for marking citations, editing citations, creating the table of authorities, changing the format of the table of authorities, and updating the table of authorities are the same as those for indexes. The only difference is you use the buttons in the Table of Authorities group instead of the buttons in the Index group.

To Close the Document Map

You are finished using the Document Map. Thus, the following step closes the Document Map.

1 Click the Close button in the Document Map to close it.

BTW

Field Codes
If your index, table of contents, or table of figures displays odd characters inside curly braces {}, then Word is displaying field codes instead of field results. Press ALT+F9 to display the index or table correctly. If Word prints field codes for your index or table, click the Office Button, click the Word Options button, click Advanced in the left pane, scroll to the Print section, remove the check mark from the 'Print field codes instead of their values' check box, click the OK button, and then print the document again.

To Create Alternating Headers

The *Internet Post* documents are designed so that they can be duplicated back-to-back. That is, the document prints on nine separate pages. When they are duplicated, however, pages one and two are printed on opposite sides of the same sheet of paper. Thus, the nine-page document when printed back-to-back uses only five sheets of paper.

In many books and documents that have facing pages, the page number is on the outside edges of the pages. In Word, you accomplish this task by specifying one type of header for even-numbered pages and another type of header for odd-numbered pages. The following steps create alternating headers beginning on the second page of the document.

- Press CTRL+HOME to position the insertion point at the top of the document.

- Display the Insert tab.

- Click the Header button on the Insert tab and then click Edit Header to display the header area.

- Be sure the Different First Page check box contains a check mark.

- Place a check mark in the Different Odd & Even Pages check box, so that you can enter a different header for odd and even pages.

- Click the Next Section button to display the Even Page Header -Section 1-.

- Type Internet Post and then press the ENTER key. Type Fourth Edition and then press the ENTER key.

- Click the Insert Page Number button, point to Current Position, and then select Accent Bar 3 in the Current Position gallery. Press the ENTER key (Figure 7–93).

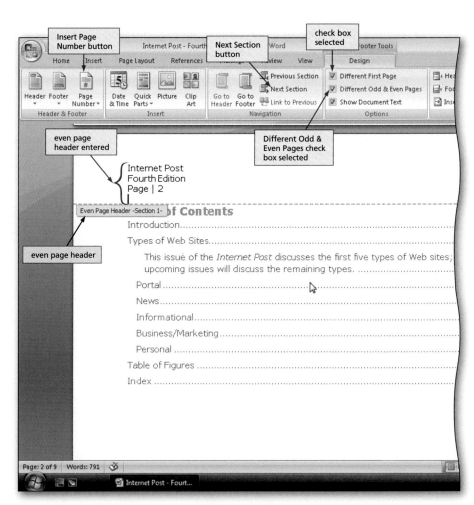

Figure 7–93

3

- Click the Next Section button to display the Odd Page Header.

- Right-align the insertion point.

- Type Internet Post and then press the ENTER key. Type Fourth Edition and then press the ENTER key.

- Click the Insert Page Number button, point to Current Position, and then select Accent Bar 3 in the Current Position gallery. Press the ENTER key (Figure 7–94).

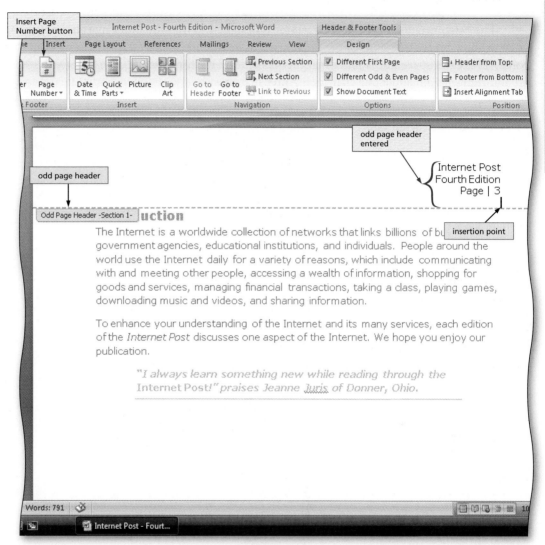

Figure 7–94

Q&A What if some pages do not have a header?

Click the header and then click the Link to Previous button on the Design tab. If a dialog box appears, click the Yes button. If the header still does not appear, re-enter the header text in that section.

4

- Click the Close Header and Footer button.

Q&A Can I create alternating footers?

Yes. Follow the same basic procedure, except enter text in the footer instead of the header.

To Set a Gutter Margin

The reference document in this chapter is designed so that the inner margin between facing pages has extra space to allow printed versions of the documents to be bound (such as stapled) — without the binding covering the words. This extra space in the inner margin is called the **gutter margin**. The following steps set a three-quarter-inch left and right margin and a one-half-inch gutter margin.

- Display the Page Layout tab.

- Click the Margins button and then click Custom Margins to display the Page Setup dialog box.

- Type .75 in the Left text box, .75 in the Right text box, and .5 in the Gutter text box.

- Click the Apply to box arrow and then click Whole document (Figure 7–95).

- Click the OK button to set the new margins for the entire document.

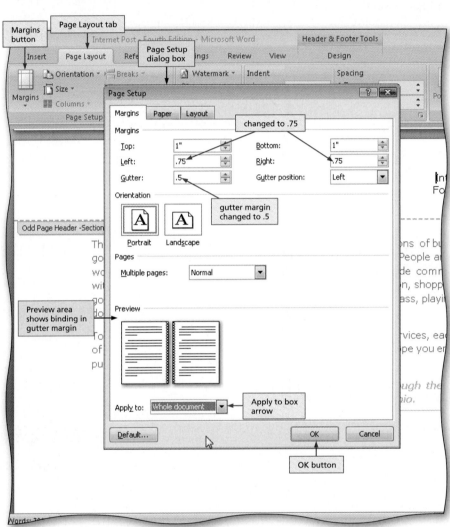

Figure 7–95

To Display the Document in Print Preview

To view the layout of all the pages in the document, the following steps display all the pages in print preview.

1. Click the Office Button, point to Print, and then click Print Preview.

2. Change the zoom level to 10% to display all the pages in the reference document, as shown in Figure 7–96.

3. Click the Close Print Preview button on the Print Preview tab.

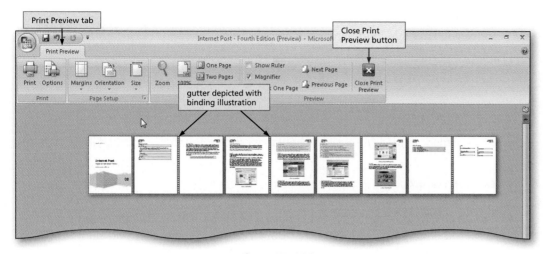

Figure 7–96

To Add Bookmarks

To assist users in navigating through a document online, you can add bookmarks. A **bookmark** is an item in a document that you name for future reference. For example, you could bookmark the headings in the document, so that users easily could jump to these areas of the document. The following steps add bookmarks.

1

- Display the Portal heading in the document window and then select the heading.

- Display the Insert tab.

- Click the Bookmark button on the Insert tab to display the Bookmark dialog box.

- Type Portal in the Bookmark name text box (Figure 7–97).

 Are there any rules for bookmark names?

Bookmark names can contain only letters, numbers, and the under-score character (_). They also must begin with a letter and cannot contain spaces.

2

- Click the Add button to add the bookmark name to the list of existing bookmarks in the document.

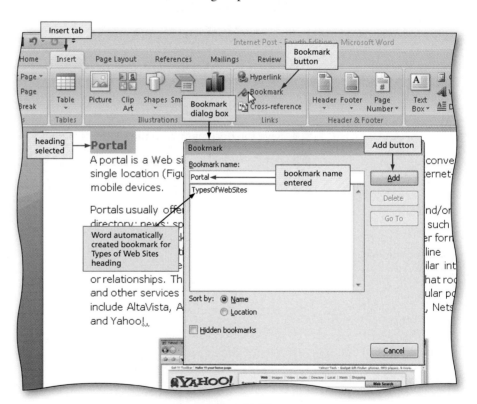

Figure 7–97

3

- Repeat Steps 1 and 2 for these headings in the document: News, Informational, Business/Marketing (note: use Business as the bookmark name because the slash is not a valid character in bookmark names), and Personal.

To Go To a Bookmark

Once you have added bookmarks, you can jump to them by performing these steps.

1. Display the Bookmark dialog box (Figure 7–97 on the previous page).
2. Click the bookmark name in the list and then click the Go To button.

or

1. Press the F5 key to display the Go To sheet in the Find and Replace dialog box.
2. Click Bookmark in the list, select the bookmark name, and then click the Go To button.

To Insert a Hyperlink

Instead of or in addition to bookmarks in online documents, you can insert hyperlinks. For example, the Types of Web Sites section lists the Web sites discussed in the paper. You could convert each of the listed Web sites to a hyperlink, so that a user could click the link to display that section of the paper in the document window. If you wanted to insert a hyperlink that links to a heading or bookmark in the document, you would follow these steps.

1. Select the text to be a hyperlink.
2. Click the Insert Hyperlink button on the Insert tab.
3. In the Link to bar, click Place in This Document, so that Word displays all the headings and bookmarks in the document.
4. Click the heading or bookmark to which you want to link.
5. Click the OK button.

To Save and Print a Document and Quit Word

The reference document for this project now is complete. Save the document, print it, and then quit Word.

1 Save the document with the same file name.

2 Print the finished document (shown in Figure 7–1 on page WD 483).

3 Quit Word.

BTW

Conserving Ink and Toner
You can instruct Word to print draft quality documents to conserve ink or toner by clicking the Office Button, clicking the Word Options button, clicking Advanced in the left pane of the Word Options dialog box, scrolling to the Print area, placing a check mark in the 'Use draft quality' check box, and then clicking the OK button. Click the Office Button, point to Print, and then click Quick Print.

Chapter Summary

In this chapter, you have learned how to insert comments, track changes, review tracked changes, compare documents and combine documents, use the Building Blocks Organizer, work with master documents and subdocuments, and create a table of contents, a table of figures, and an index. The items listed below include all the new Word skills you have learned in this chapter.

1. Hide White Space (WD 486)
2. Insert a Comment (WD 488)
3. Change Reviewer Information (WD 490)
4. Enable Tracked Changes (WD 490)
5. Track Changes (WD 491)
6. Change How Markups Are Displayed (WD 492)
7. Disable Tracked Changes (WD 492)
8. Edit a Comment in a Comment Balloon (WD 493)
9. Use the Reviewing Pane (WD 493)
10. Print Markups (WD 495)
11. Review Tracked Changes and View Comments (WD 496)
12. Delete All Comments (WD 499)
13. Compare Documents (WD 500)
14. Combine Revisions from Multiple Authors (WD 502)
15. Show Tracked Changes and Comments by a Single Reviewer (WD 506)
16. Accept All Changes in a Document (WD 507)
17. Customize the Status Bar (WD 507)
18. Add a Caption (WD 509)
19. Create a Cross-Reference (WD 511)
20. Mark an Index Entry (WD 512)
21. Mark Multiple Index Entries (WD 514)
22. Search for and Highlight Specific Text (WD 514)
23. Sort Building Blocks and Insert a Sidebar Text Box Building Block Using the Building Blocks Organizer (WD 516)
24. Edit Properties of Building Block Elements (WD 518)
25. Enter and Format a Numbered List (WD 519)
26. Link Text Boxes (WD 521)
27. Fill Text Boxes with Color (WD 523)
28. Compress Pictures (WD 524)
29. Create an Outline (WD 525)
30. Show First Line Only (WD 527)
31. Insert a Subdocument (WD 528)
32. Apply a Quote Style (WD 532)
33. Insert a Cover Page (WD 533)
34. Insert a Blank Page (WD 535)
35. Create a Table of Contents (WD 536)
36. Use the Document Map (WD 537)
37. Display Thumbnails (WD 538)
38. Add Text to the Table of Contents (WD 538)
39. Update a Table of Contents (WD 540)
40. Change the Format of a Table of Contents (WD 541)
41. Create a Table of Figures (WD 542)
42. Change the Format of the Table of Figures (WD 543)
43. Edit a Caption and Update the Table of Figures (WD 543)
44. Build an Index (WD 544)
45. Edit an Index Entry (WD 546)
46. Delete an Index Entry (WD 546)
47. Update an Index (WD 546)
48. Change the Format of the Index (WD 547)
49. Delete an Index (WD 547)
50. Create Alternating Headers (WD 548)
51. Set a Gutter Margin (WD 550)
52. Add Bookmarks (WD 551)
53. Go To a Bookmark (WD 552)
54. Insert a Hyperlink (WD 552)

 If you have a SAM user profile, you may have access to hands-on instruction, practice, and assessment. Log in to your SAM account (http://sam2007.course.com) to launch any assigned training activities or exams that relate to the skills covered in this chapter.

BTW

Quick Reference
For a table that lists how to complete the tasks covered in this book using the mouse, Ribbon, shortcut menu, and keyboard, see the Quick Reference Summary at the back of this book, or visit the Word 2007 Quick Reference Web page (scsite.com/wd2007/qr).

Learn It Online

Test your knowledge of chapter content and key terms.

Instructions: To complete the Learn It Online exercises, start your browser, click the Address bar, and then enter the Web address scsite.com/wd2007/learn. When the Word 2007 Learn It Online page is displayed, click the link for the exercise you want to complete and then read the instructions.

Chapter Reinforcement TF, MC, and SA
A series of true/false, multiple choice, and short answer questions that test your knowledge of the chapter content.

Flash Cards
An interactive learning environment where you identify chapter key terms associated with displayed definitions.

Practice Test
A series of multiple choice questions that test your knowledge of chapter content and key terms.

Who Wants To Be a Computer Genius?
An interactive game that challenges your knowledge of chapter content in the style of a television quiz show.

Wheel of Terms
An interactive game that challenges your knowledge of chapter key terms in the style of the television show *Wheel of Fortune*.

Crossword Puzzle Challenge
A crossword puzzle that challenges your knowledge of key terms presented in the chapter.

Apply Your Knowledge

Reinforce the skills and apply the concepts you learned in this chapter.

Working with Word's Collaboration Features
Instructions: Start Word. Open the document, Apply 7-1 E-Commerce Draft, from the Data Files for Students. See the inside back cover of this book for instructions on downloading the Data Files for Students, or contact your instructor for information about accessing the required files.

The document includes several paragraphs of text that contain tracked changes and comments. You are to insert additional tracked changes and comments, accept and reject tracked changes, delete comments, and compare documents.

Perform the following tasks:
1. Save the document with Apply 7-1 E-Commerce Reviewed as the file name.

2. If necessary, customize the status bar so that it displays the Tracking Changes button.

3. Enable (turn on) tracked changes.

4. If approved by your instructor, change the user name and initials so that your name and initials are displayed in the tracked changes and comments.

5. Use the Review tab to navigate to the first comment. Follow the instruction in the comment. Be sure tracked changes are on when you add the required text to the document.

6. When finished making the change, reply to the comment with a new comment that includes a message you completed the requested task. What color are the SCS markups? What color are your markups?

7. With tracked changes on, insert the words, or service, after the word, product, in the second sentence of the third paragraph so that the sentence reads: Users can purchase just about any type of product or service on the Web.

8. Insert the following comment for the word, Internet, in the first sentence: Should the word, Internet, be in all lowercase?

9. With tracked changes on, change the word, difference, in the last paragraph to the word, different.

10. Edit the comment entered in Step 8 to add the word, letters, at the end of the comment — immediately to the left of the question mark.

11. Print the document with tracked changes. *Hint*: In the Print dialog box, select 'Document showing markup' in Print what list.

12. Print just the tracked changes. *Hint*: In the Print dialog box, select 'List of markup' in Print what list.

13. Save the document again with the same name, Apply 7-1 E-Commerce Reviewed (Figure 7–98).

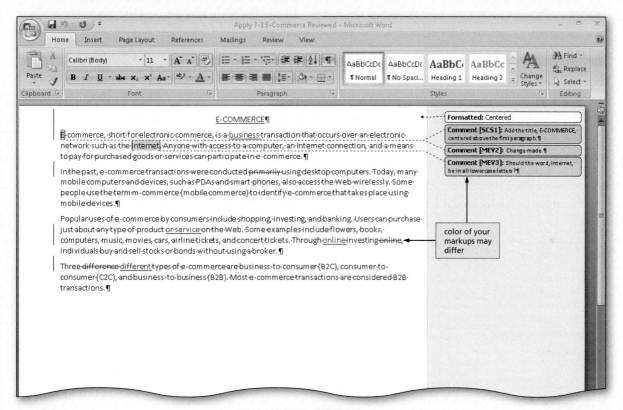

Figure 7–98

14. Reject the deletion of the word, primarily, in the second paragraph.

15. Accept all the remaining edits in the document.

16. Delete all the comments.

17. Disable (turn off) tracked changes. Remove the Tracking Changes button from the status bar.

18. Change the document properties as specified by your instructor. Save the document with a new file name, Apply 7-1 E-Commerce Final.

19. Submit the revised document in the format specified by your instructor.

20. Close all open documents.

21. Compare the Apply 7-1 E-Commerce Draft (original document) with the Apply 7-1 E-Commerce Final (revised document) file. Show changes in a new document. Show both source documents. Save the compare result document with the name, Apply 7-1 E-Commerce Compared.

22. Compare the Apply 7-1 E-Commerce Draft with the Apply 7-1 E-Commerce Final file. Show changes in the original document (Apply 7-1 E-Commerce Draft). Close the document without saving.

Extend Your Knowledge

Extend the skills you learned in this chapter and experiment with new skills. You may need to use Help to complete the assignment.

Working with a Reference Document

Instructions: Start Word. Open the document, Extend 7-1 Certification Draft, from the Data Files for Students. See the inside back cover of this book for instructions on downloading the Data Files for Students, or contact your instructor for information about accessing the required files.

You will change the format of the cover page, change the format of and update the table of contents, change the format of and update the index, change the format of and update the table of figures, insert a sidebar, link text boxes, and format text boxes.

Perform the following tasks:

1. Use Help to review and expand your knowledge about these topics: cover page, table of contents, index, table of figures, and text boxes.

2. Display the Document Map. Use the Document Map to navigate to areas of the reference document for the tasks in this exercise.

3. Change the title page to a cover page format other than Pinstripes.

4. Change the format of the table of contents to Automatic Table 1.

5. Change the leader character in the table of contents to hyphens (Figure 7–99).

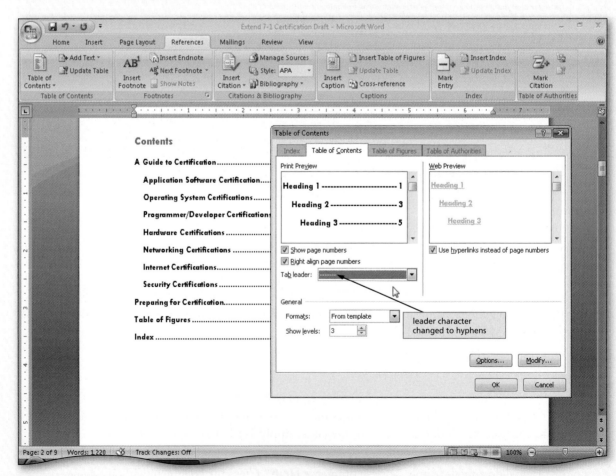

Figure 7–99

6. Change the format of the table of figures to a format other than the From template format. Change the leader character in the table of figures to hyphens.

7. Change the format of the index to a format other than From template.

8. The document currently has eight terms marked as index entries. Read through the document and mark 10 more terms as index entries.

9. Change the index entry, software certifications, to read as follows: application software certifications.

10. Update the index.

11. Modify the caption for Figure 5 to insert the word, usually, between the words, certifications test, so that it reads as follows: Networking certifications usually test knowledge of a company-specific network.

12. Update the table of figures.

13. Change the heading, Application Software Certification, to Application Software Certifications (add an s to Certification).

14. Update the table of contents.

15. Display the Building Blocks Organizer. Sort the building blocks by category. Sort the building blocks by gallery.

16. Use the Building Blocks Organizer to insert a second Exposure Sidebar text box in the document on a page other than page 3.

17. Link the two text boxes together. Resize the text boxes so that the text in the first paragraph is in the first text box and the text in the second paragraph is in the second text box.

18. Format the text boxes using a style other than the default.

19. Make any other necessary formatting changes to the document.

20. Change the document properties as specified by your instructor.

21. Save the revised document with a new file name and then submit it in the format specified by your instructor.

Make It Right

Analyze a document and correct all errors and/or improve the design.

Formatting a Reference Document

Instructions: Start Word. Open the document, Make It Right 7-1 IT Job Descriptions Draft, from the Data Files for Students. See the inside back cover of this book for instructions on downloading the Data Files for Students, or contact your instructor for information about accessing the required files.

The document is a reference document whose elements are not formatted properly (Figure 7–100 on the next page). You are to insert a page break, delete a section break, reformat headings for the table of contents, add text to the table of contents, format a quote, insert bookmarks, and add a header and footer with a page number.

Continued >

Make It Right *continued*

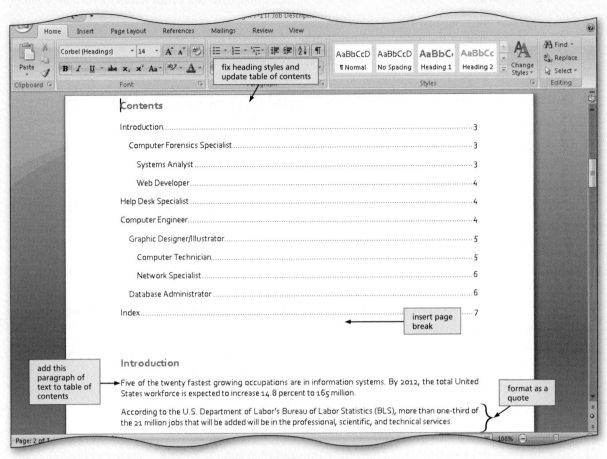

Figure 7–100

Perform the following tasks:

1. Hide white space between pages.

2. Insert a page break between the table of contents and the introduction.

3. Delete the next page section break above the Graphic Designer/Illustrator heading.

4. All entries in the table of contents should be a Heading 1. Reformat all headings to Heading 1.

5. Add the first paragraph in the Introduction as text in the table of contents. Convert it to a Level 3.

6. Update the table of contents.

7. In the Introduction section, format the second paragraph that begins with the word, According, to either the Quote Style or the Intense Quote Style.

8. The index currently contains 3 entries. Mark at least 15 more entries and then update the index. Change the index to a format of your choice.

9. Search for and highlight all occurrences of the word, degree. How many occurrences were located? Clear the highlighting.

10. Insert a bookmark for each heading in the document.

11. Use the Go To command to practice locating bookmarks in the document.

12. Add a built-in header to the document. Add the same style of built-in footer to the document. Fill in the appropriate text in the header and footer. Be sure to include a page number.

13. Change the document properties, as specified by your instructor. Save the revised document with a new file name and then submit it in the format specified by your instructor.

In the Lab

Design and/or create a document using the guidelines, concepts, and skills presented in this chapter. Labs are listed in order of increasing difficulty.

Lab 1: Working with a Cover Page, a Table of Contents, and an Index

Problem: As a computer technician in the Computer Systems department at your school, you have been asked to prepare a guide outlining backup procedures. A miniature version of this document is shown in Figure 7–101. For a more readable view, visit scsite.com/wd2007/ch7 or see your instructor.

A draft of the body of the document is on the Data Files for Students. See the inside back cover of this book for instructions on downloading the Data Files for Students, or contact your instructor for information about accessing the required files.

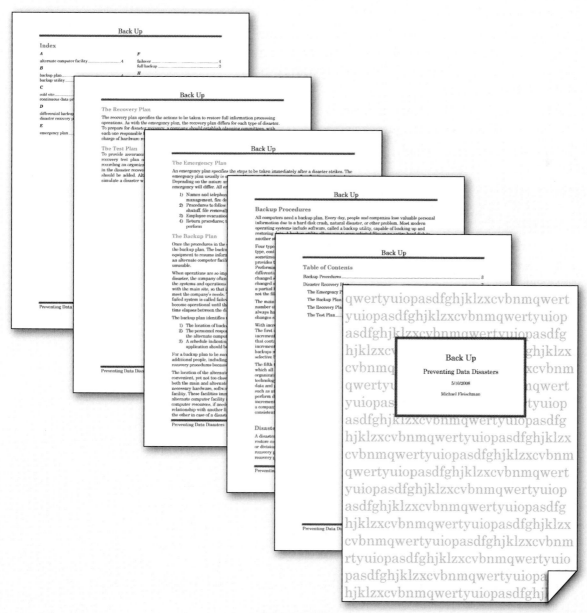

Figure 7–101

Continued >

Perform the following tasks:

1. Open the document, Lab 7-1 Backup Procedures Draft, from the Data Files for Students. Save the document with a new file name, Lab 7-1 Backup Procedures Final.

2. Create a title page by inserting the Alphabet style cover page. Use the following information on the title page: title - Back Up; subtitle - Preventing Data Disasters; date - *use today's date*; author - *use your name*.

3. Insert a blank page between the title page and the heading, Backup Procedures.

4. Create a table of contents on the blank page using the Automatic Table 2 style.

5. Change the format of the numbered lists in the Emergency Plan and Backup Plan sections to Number alignment: Left.

6. Insert the Alphabet header on all pages but the title page.

7. Insert the Alphabet footer on all pages but the title page. Replace the content control with the text, Preventing Data Disasters.

8. Mark the following terms in the document as index entries: alternate computer facility, backup plan, backup utility, cold site, continuous data protection, differential backup, disaster recovery plan, emergency plan, failover, full backup, hot site, incremental backup, recovery plan, selective backup, test plan.

9. Build an index for the document. Remember to hide formatting marks prior to building the index. Use the Formal format, with right-aligned page numbers.

10. Save the document again and then submit it in the format specified by your instructor.

In the Lab

Lab 2: Working with a Cover Page, a Table of Contents, a Table of Figures, and an Index

Problem: As a laboratory assistant for the computer department at your school, you have been asked to prepare a guide outlining the basics of software use. A miniature version of this document is shown in Figure 7–102. For a more readable view, visit scsite.com/wd2007/ch7 or see your instructor.

A draft of the body of the document is on the Data Files for Students. See the inside back cover of this book for instructions on downloading the Data Files for Students, or contact your instructor for information about accessing the required files.

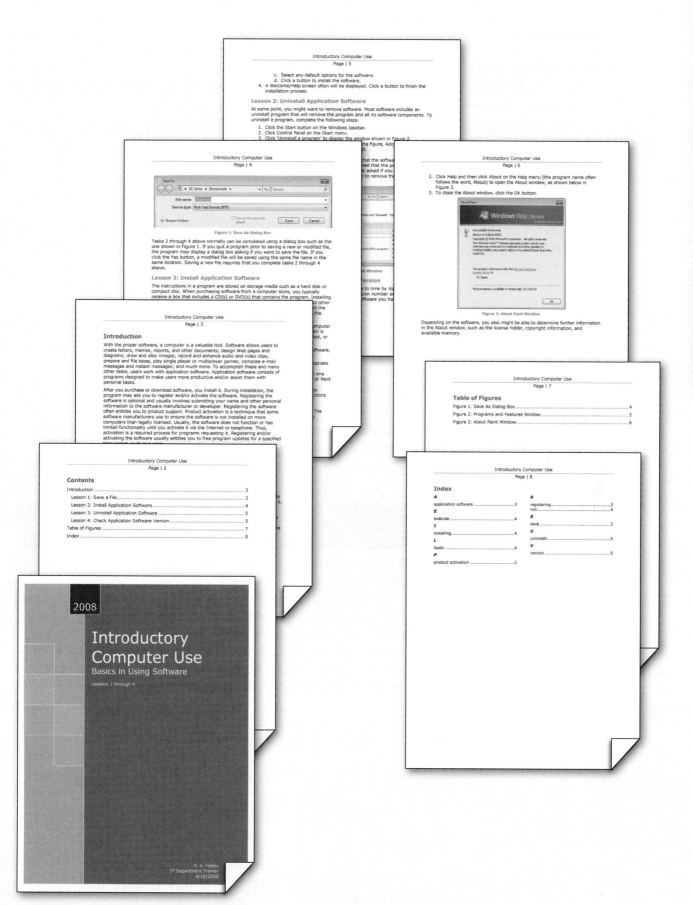

Figure 7–102

Continued >

In the Lab *continued*

Perform the following tasks:

1. Open the document, Lab 7-2 Using Software Draft, from the Data Files for Students. Save the document with a new file name, Lab 7-2 Using Software Final.

2. Create a title page by inserting the Puzzle style cover page. Use the following information on the title page: year - *use current year*; title - Introductory Computer Use; subtitle - Basics in Using Software; abstract - Lessons 1 through 4; author - *use your name*; company - *use your instructor's name*; date - *use today's date*. If necessary, reduce the size of the year so that it fits on a single line.

3. Insert a blank page between the title page and the heading, Introduction.

4. Create a table of contents on the blank page using the Automatic Table 1 style.

5. Insert the Conservative header on all pages but the title page. Delete the date and replace it with the page number. Use the Accent Bar 3 page number style.

6. Add the following caption to the figures: first figure - Figure 1: Save As Dialog Box; second figure - Figure 2: Programs and Features Window; third figure - Figure 3: About Paint Window.

7. Replace the occurrences of xx in the document with cross-references to the figure captions.

8. At the end of the document, create a table of figures on a separate page. Use the From template format.

9. Mark the following terms in the document as index entries: application software, execute, installing, loads, product activation, registering, run, save, uninstall, version.

10. Build an index for the document. Remember to hide formatting marks prior to building the index. Use the Formal format, with right-aligned page numbers.

11. Save the document again and then submit it in the format specified by your instructor.

In the Lab

Lab 3: Working with a Linked Text Box, a Master Document, a Cover Page, a Table of Contents, a Table of Figures, and an Index

Problem: As part of your Computer Concepts class, your instructor has asked you to prepare a reference document about detailed analysis. A miniature version of this document is shown in Figure 7–103. For a more readable view, visit scsite.com/wd2007/ch7 or see your instructor.

The document is a master document with one subdocument. The subdocument is on the Data Files for Students. See the inside back cover of this book for instructions on downloading the Data Files for Students, or contact your instructor for information about accessing the required files.

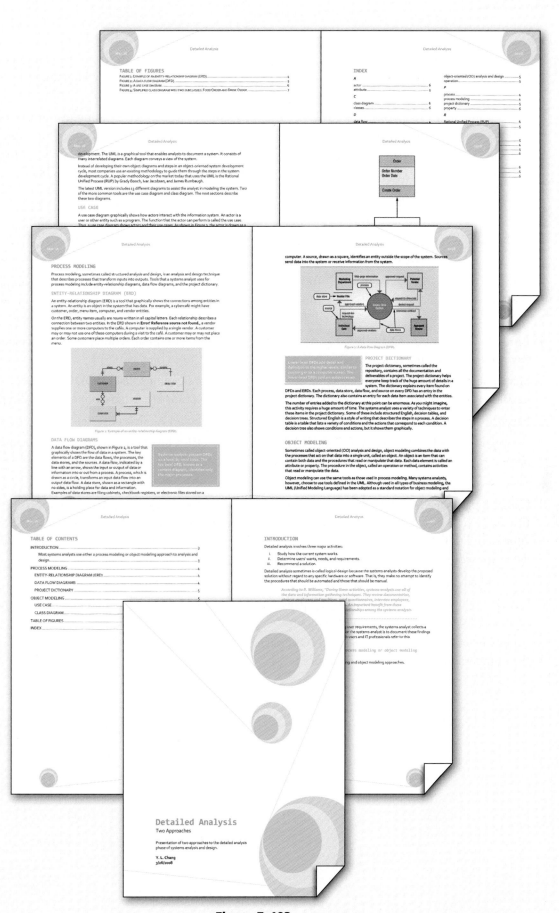

Figure 7–103

Continued >

Perform the following tasks:

1. Open the file Lab 7-3 Process and Object Modeling Subdocument Draft, from the Data Files for Students. Save the document with the name, Lab 7-3 Process and Object Modeling Subdocument Final.

2. Insert a simple text box to the right of the DATA FLOW DIAGRAMS heading. Enter this text in the text box: `Systems analysts prepare DFDs on a level-by-level basis. The top level DFD, known as a context diagram, identifies only the major processes.` Press the ENTER key. Continue entering this text in the text box: `Lower-level DFDs add detail and definition to the higher levels, similar to zooming in on a computer screen. The lower-level DFDs contain subprocesses.` Format the text box using the Solid Fill, Compound Outline - Accent 1 style. Change the font color of the text to white in the text box and bold the text. Change its wrapping style to Square.

3. On the next page, to the left of the PROJECT DICTIONARY heading, insert another simple text box. Format it using the Solid Fill, Compound Outline - Accent 1 style. Change its wrapping style to Square.

4. Link the two text boxes together. Resize each text box so that each one contains just one paragraph. Save and close the document.

5. Start a new document. In Outline view, enter the following headings: INTRODUCTION, TABLE OF FIGURES, and INDEX. Insert a next page section break between each heading.

6. Save the master document with the file name, Lab 7-3 Detailed Analysis Master Document.

7. Between the INTRODUCTION and TABLE OF FIGURES headings, insert the subdocument named Lab 7-3 Process and Object Modeling Subdocument Final.

8. Switch to Print Layout view.

9. Create a title page by inserting the Mod style cover page. Use the following information on the title page: title - Detailed Analysis; subtitle - Two Approaches; abstract - Presentation of two approaches to the detailed analysis phase of systems analysis and design.; author - *use your name*; date - *use today's date*.

10. Insert a blank page between the title page and the heading, Introduction.

11. Create a table of contents on the blank page using the Automatic Table 2 style. Change the heading to all uppercase using the Change Case button on the Ribbon.

12. Enter the text for the INTRODUCTION page as shown in Figure 7–104. Change the format of the numbered list as shown in the figure.

Detailed analysis involves three major activities:

i.   Study how the current system works.
ii.   Determine users' wants, needs, and requirements.
iii. Recommend a solution.

Detailed analysis sometimes is called logical design because the systems analysts develop the proposed solution without regard to any specific hardware or software. That is, they make no attempt to identify the procedures that should be automated and those that should be manual.

According to R. Williams, "During these activities, systems analysts use all of the data and information-gathering techniques. They review documentation, observe employees and machines, send questionnaires, interview employees, conduct JAD sessions, and do research. An important benefit from these activities is that they build valuable relationships among the systems analysts and users."

While studying the current system and identifying user requirements, the systems analyst collects a great deal of data and information. A major task for the systems analyst is to document these findings in a way that can be understood by everyone. Both users and IT professionals refer to this documentation.

Most systems analysts use either a process modeling or object modeling approach to analysis and design.

The following sections discuss the process modeling and object modeling approaches.

Figure 7–104

13. On the INTRODUCTION page, format the quotation paragraph using the Intense Quote style.

14. Add the text in the second to last paragraph on the INTRODUCTION page to the table of contents, as a Level 3.

15. Update the table of contents.

16. At the end of the document, create a table of figures on the page with the TABLE OF FIGURES heading. Use the Formal format.

17. Build an index for the document. Remember to hide formatting marks prior to building the index. Use the Formal format with right-aligned page numbers.

18. Beginning on the second page (the table of contents), create alternating headers and footers. Use the Mod (Even Page) header style for the even page header. Use the Mod (Odd Page) header style for the odd page header. Use the current date in the header. Use the Mod (Even Page) footer style for the even page footer. Use the Mod (Odd Page) footer style for the odd page footer. The title page does not have a header or footer.

19. For the entire document, set the left and right margins to .75" and set a gutter margin of .5".

20. Insert a bookmark for each Heading 1 in the document.

21. Compress the pictures in the document.

22. Save the document again and then submit it in the format specified by your instructor.

23. Make any additional adjustments so that the document looks like Figure 7–103 on page WD 563.

24. Save the document again. Print the document. If you have access to a copy machine, duplicate the document back-to-back.

Cases and Places

Apply your creative thinking and problem solving skills to design and implement a solution.

• Easier •• More Difficult

• 1: Create the Next Edition of this Chapter's Master Document and Subdocument

As an assistant at the public library, you have been asked to create a series of documents for distribution to patrons in the computer laboratory. The IT director asked you to create handouts that discuss various types of Web sites. The first document you created is shown in Figure 7–1 on page WD 483. The next reference document will be a continuation of this topic. Use the file named, Case 1 - Other Types of Web Sites, as the subdocument. This file is on the Data Files for Students. See the inside back cover of this book for instructions on downloading the Data Files for Students, or contact your instructor for information about accessing the required files. For each section in the subdocument, insert the appropriate figure. The figures are on the Data Files for Students, and their file names reflect the section in which they should be inserted. For example, the file named, Case 1 - Types of Web Sites - Blog, contains the figure that should be inserted in the Blog section; the file named, Case 1 - Types of Web Sites - Advocacy, contains the figure that should be inserted in the Advocacy section; and so on. Insert an appropriate caption below each figure, and then insert a cross-reference to each figure. At a minimum, mark the following terms as index entries: educational Web site, entertainment Web site, advocacy Web site, blog, vlog, vlogosphere, vlogger, wiki, online social networks, social networking Web site, and content aggregator. Once the figures are inserted and the index entries marked, close the subdocument file. Create a master document that contains the subdocument file. The master document also should have a title page (cover page), an introduction, a table of contents, a table of figures, and an index. Format the document with alternating headers and a gutter margin. Compress the pictures. Use the concepts and techniques presented in this chapter to organize and format the document.

• 2: Create a Reference Document about Using Word (No Master Document)

As a laboratory assistant at your school's computer facility, your supervisor has asked you to create a document for distribution to students in the lab that outlines some of the features of Microsoft Office Word 2007. To compose the document, you can use any text in this textbook. The document should contain at least three figures, which can be created by capturing screen shots. To capture a screen shot, display the screen on your computer and then press the PRINT SCREEN key. Use Paint or another graphic program to paste the screen shot and then save it. Insert the graphic files (screen shots) in the Word document. Use Word's Callouts shapes to add bubbles to the figures, if necessary. Add captions to the figures. Insert cross-references to the figures. The finished document should have a title page, an introduction, a table of contents, a table of figures, and an index. Format the document with alternating headers and a gutter margin. Compress the pictures. The entire document should be at least nine pages in length. Use the concepts and techniques presented in this chapter to organize and format the document.

•• 3: Create a Legal Reference Document (No Master Document)

Your aunt has hired you this summer to work as an office assistant for her law firm. The firm is expanding, and your aunt has found what she believes to be an ideal location, complete with a suitable building that needs minor repair and remodeling. She has asked you to help her create a document she will present to the other partners. The document must outline the various considerations involved in expanding to a second location on the city's west side. In addition to an introduction, she needs four additional sections included: need/reason for expansion, location, building contractor estimates, and inspector findings. You must obtain estimates, reports, and expert input using public records from building contractors and the inspectors. In addition, you will need to obtain legal documents from the city containing zoning restrictions and a description of the property. Use Word to create a reference document with an introduction section and headings for each of the four additional sections. The town's legal documents, along with the building contractor's and inspector's reports, should be cited as authorities so that you can generate a table of authorities in the final document. Once you have created the table of authorities, practice changing its format and updating its content. Also include a title page, a table of contents, an index, and — if you use digital photographs, charts, SmartArt graphics, or tables — a table of figures. Use the concepts and techniques presented in this chapter to format the document.

• • 4: Create a Reference Document from your Experiences (No Master Document)

Make It Personal

For this assignment, you will create a reference document that highlights a recent trip you took, an event you attended, or an activity in which you participate (or just enjoy). For example, you could create a document that lists your last vacation's destination, itinerary, and pictures. If you play a sport, the document might discuss the sport in general or your team in particular. Create subheadings for pertinent areas about your topic. For instance, if football is your chosen sport, you could include sections about history of the game, favorite team, players, owner, division, statistics, draft picks, and so forth. If you recently took a trip to Spain, you could include a section about the country's geography, your itinerary, sites you visited, hotel accommodations, food, etc. The document should have a minimum of four figures. For the figures, you can use digital photographs, scanned images, SmartArt graphics, tables, or charts. Include a title page, a table of contents, a table of figures, and an index. Format the document with alternating headers and a gutter margin. Compress the pictures. Use the concepts and techniques presented in this chapter to organize and format the document.

• • 5: Create a Master Document that contains Subdocuments Reviewed by Classmates

Working Together

Virtually every student has spent hours pouring over school course catalogues trying to determine which classes to take. Sometimes it is helpful to talk to someone who has taken the class you are considering, for a more personal perspective. For this assignment, do the following:

1. Assign each team member an area or category of classes to describe (i.e., have one member write about math classes, another about English or literature classes, another history classes, another science classes, etc.). Each member should write course descriptions for three classes he or she currently is taking or has taken in the past in his or her assigned area. For each class, include a section about class description, credit hours, topics/material covered, likes/dislikes, and a recommendation for taking (or not taking) the class.

2. Each team member should use tracked changes to review the other's documents. Change your reviewer's ink colors for all markup options: insertions, deletions, formatting, changed lines, comments, and moves. Also, change the width of the balloons to 2". On each document, make at least five tracked changes and insert at least two comments. Then, obtain the files from your teammates containing tracked changes for the document you wrote. Compare the documents. Then, combine them into your document. Show reviewer markups one at a time. Accept and reject that reviewer's changes, as you deem appropriate. Save the final document.

3. Each of the final documents from your teammates should become a subdocument in a master document. The master document should include a title page (cover page), a table of contents, an index, and if appropriate, a table of figures. Insert a hyperlink to each heading in the document. Use the concepts and techniques presented in this chapter to format the document.

8 Creating an Online Form

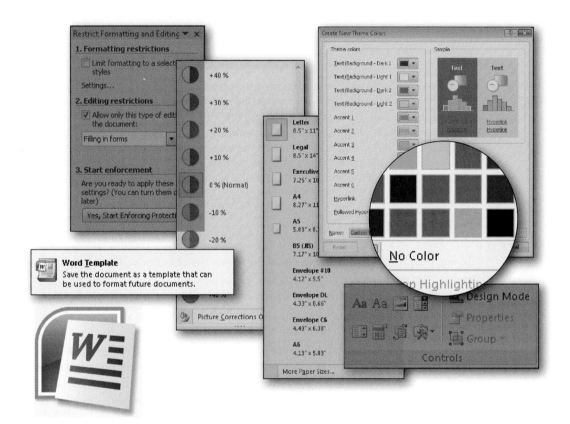

Objectives

You will have mastered the material in this chapter when you can:

- Design an online form
- Change paper size
- Save a document as a template
- Insert a borderless table in a form
- Insert plain text, drop-down list, combo box, date, and rich text content controls
- Edit placeholder text
- Change properties of content controls

- Use the Format Painter
- Insert and format a rectangle shape
- Modify a theme
- Protect a form
- Open a new document based on a template
- Fill in a form

8 | Creating an Online Form

Introduction

During your personal and professional life, you undoubtedly have filled in countless forms. Whether a federal tax form, a time card, a job application, an order, a deposit slip, or a survey, a form is designed to collect information. In the past, forms were printed; that is, you received the form on a piece of paper, filled it in with a pen or pencil, and then returned it manually. With an **online form**, you use a computer to access, fill in, and then return the form. In Word, you easily can create an online form for distribution electronically; you also can fill in that same form using Word.

Project Planning Guidelines

> The process of developing a document that communicates specific information requires careful analysis and planning. As a starting point, establish why the document is needed. Once the purpose is determined, analyze the intended readers of the document and their unique needs. Then, gather information about the topic and decide what to include in the document. Finally, determine the document design and style that will be most successful at delivering the message. Details of these guidelines are provided in Appendix A. In addition, each chapter in this book provides practical applications of these planning considerations.

Project — Online Form

Today, people are concerned with using resources efficiently. To minimize paper waste, protect the environment, enhance office efficiency, and improve access to data, many businesses have moved toward a paperless office. Thus, online forms have replaced many paper forms. You access online forms at a Web site, on your company's intranet, or from your inbox if you receive the form via e-mail.

The project in this chapter uses Word to produce the online form shown in Figure 8–1. Universal Travel is a travel agency that offers weekly specials to its customers. Instead of receiving the specials via the postal service, Universal Travel will e-mail the specials to customers who would like to receive them electronically. To request the weekly specials, customers fill out the form shown in Figure 8–1, save it, and then e-mail it back to Universal Travel.

Figure 8–1a shows how the form is displayed on a user's screen initially; Figure 8–1b shows the form partially filled in by one user; and Figure 8–1c shows how the user filled in the entire form.

The data entry area of the form contains four text boxes (First Name, Last Name, E-Mail Address, and Favorite Destinations), one drop-down list box (Preferred Airline Ticket), a combination text box/drop-down list box (Preferred Rental Vehicle), and a date (Today's Date).

The form is designed so that it fits completely within a Word window that is set at a predefined zoom level — without a user having to scroll while filling in the form. The data entry area of the form is enclosed by a rectangle that is outlined with a dotted gray line. The rectangle also has a shadow on its bottom and right edges. The line of text above the data entry area is covered with the color gray, giving it the look of text that has been marked with a highlighter pen.

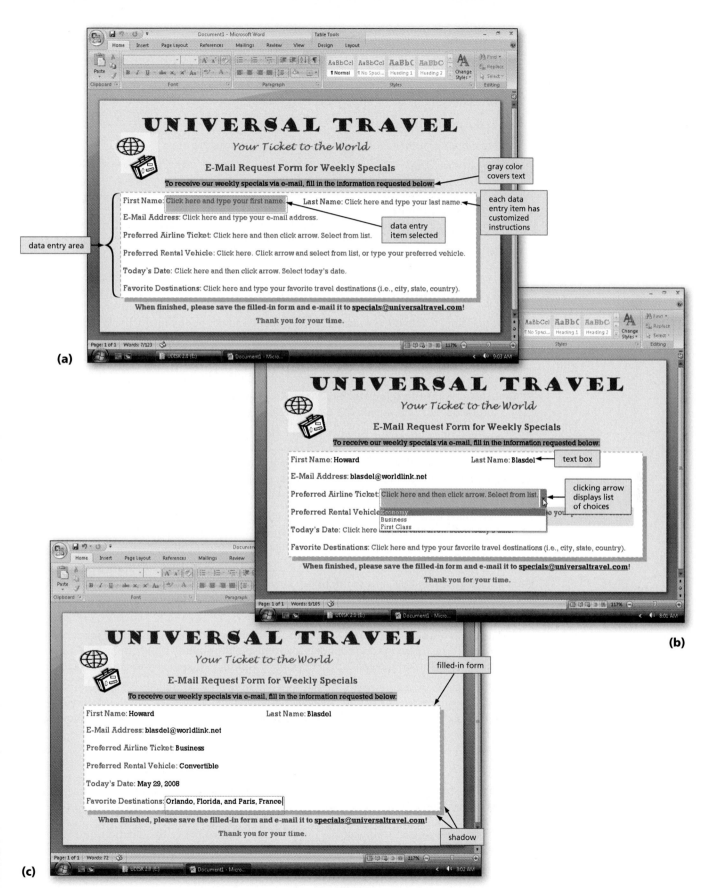

Figure 8–1

Overview

As you read through this chapter, you will learn how to create the online form shown in Figure 8–1 on the previous page by performing these general tasks:

- Save a document as a template.
- Set document formats.
- Enter text, graphics, and content controls in the form.
- Protect the form.

**Plan
Ahead**

General Project Guidelines

When creating a Word document, the actions you perform and decisions you make will affect the appearance and characteristics of the finished document. As you create an online form, such as the project shown in Figure 8–1, you should follow these general guidelines:

1. **Design the form.** To minimize the time spent creating a form while at the computer, you should sketch the form on a piece of paper first. Design a well-thought-out draft of the form — being sure to include all essential form elements. These elements include the form's title, text and graphics, data entry fields, and data entry instructions. A **data entry field** is a placeholder for data that a user enters in the form.

2. **Determine the correct field type for each data entry field.** For each data entry field, decide its specifications, such as its type and/or a list of possible values that it can contain.

3. **Save the form as a template.** By saving a form as a Word template, instead of as a Word document, you will simplify the data entry process for users of the form.

4. **Create a functional and visually appealing form.** Use colors that complement one another. Draw the user's attention to important sections. Arrange data entry fields in logical groups on the form and in an order that users would expect. Data entry instructions should be succinct and easy to understand. Ensure that users can change and enter data only in designated areas of the form.

5. **Determine how the form data will be analyzed.** If the data entered in the form will be analyzed by a program outside of Word, create the data entry fields so that the entries are stored in separate fields that can be shared with other programs.

6. **Test the form.** Be sure that the form works as you intended. Fill in the form as if you are a user. Have others fill in the form to be sure it is organized in a logical manner and is easy to understand and complete. If any errors or weaknesses in the form are identified, correct them and test the form again.

7. **Publish or distribute the form.** Not only does an online form reduce the need for paper, it saves the time spent making copies of the form and distributing it. When the form is complete, post it on the Web or your company's intranet, or e-mail it to targeted recipients.

When necessary, more specific details concerning the above guidelines are presented at appropriate points in the chapter. The chapter also will identify the actions performed and decisions made regarding these guidelines during the creation of the online form shown in Figure 8–1.

To Start Word

If you are using a computer to step through the project in this chapter and you want your screens to match the figures in this book, you should change your computer's resolution to 1024 × 768. For information about how to change a computer's resolution, read Appendix D.

The following steps start Word and verify Word settings.

1 Start Word.

2 If the Word window is not maximized, click its Maximize button.

3 If the Print Layout button on the status bar is not selected, click it so that Word is in Print Layout view.

4 If your zoom level is not 100%, click the Zoom Out or Zoom In button as many times as necessary until the Zoom level button displays 100% on its face.

5 If the rulers are displayed, click the View Ruler button on the vertical scroll bar because you will not use the rulers to perform tasks in this project.

To Display Formatting Marks

It is helpful to display formatting marks that indicate where in the online form you pressed the ENTER key, SPACEBAR, and other keys. The following steps display formatting marks.

1 If necessary, display the Home tab.

2 If the Show/Hide ¶ button on the Home tab is not selected already, click it to display formatting marks on the screen.

Saving a Document as a Template

A **template** is a file that contains the definition of the appearance of a Word document, including items such as default font, font size, margin settings, and line spacing; available styles; and even placement of text. Every Word document you create is based on a template. When you select Blank document in the New Document dialog box, Word creates a document based on the Normal template. Word also provides other templates for more specific types of documents such as memos, letters, and fax cover sheets. Creating a document based on these templates can improve your productivity because Word has defined much of the document's appearance for you.

In this chapter, you create an online form. If you create and save an online form as a Word document, users will be required to open that Word document to display the form on the screen. Next, they will fill in the form. Then, to preserve the content of the original form, they will have to save the form with a new file name. If they accidentally click the Save button on the Quick Access Toolbar during the process of filling in the form, Word will replace the original blank form with a filled-in form.

If you create and save the online form as a template instead, users will open a new document window that is based on that template. This displays the form on the screen as a brand new Word document; that is, the document does not have a file name. Thus, the user fills in the form and then clicks the Save button to save his or her filled-in form. By creating a Word template for the form, instead of a Word document, the original template for the form remains intact when the user clicks the Save button.

To Save a Document as a Template

The following steps save a document as a template, which will be used for the online form.

- If necessary, display a new blank document in the Word window.

- With a USB flash drive connected to one of the computer's USB ports, click the Office Button and then point to Save As on the Office Button menu to display the Save As submenu (Figure 8–2).

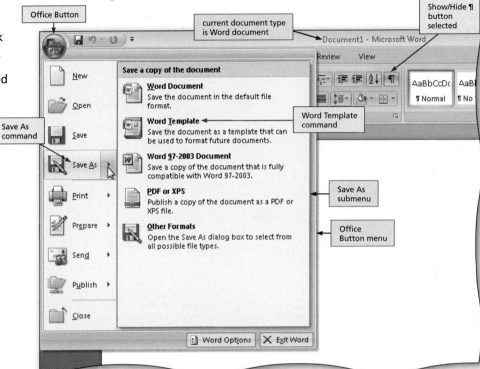

Figure 8–2

- Click Word Template on the Save As submenu to display the Save As dialog box with the file type automatically changed to Word Template (Figure 8–3).

Q&A

How does Word differentiate between a saved Word template and a saved Word document?

Files typically have a file name and a file extension. The file extension identifies the file type. The source program often assigns a file type to a file. A Word document has an extension of .docx, whereas a Word template has an extension of .dotx. Thus, a file named July Report.docx is a Word document, and a file named Fitness Form.dotx is a Word template.

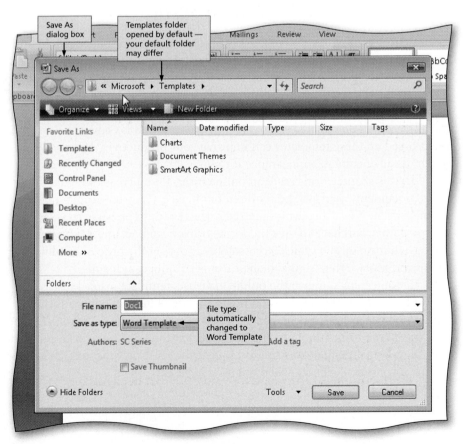

Figure 8–3

3

- Type Universal Travel in the File name text box to change the file name.

- Change the save location to the USB flash drive (Figure 8–4).

4

- Click the Save button in the Save As dialog box to save the document as a Word template with the name Universal Travel.

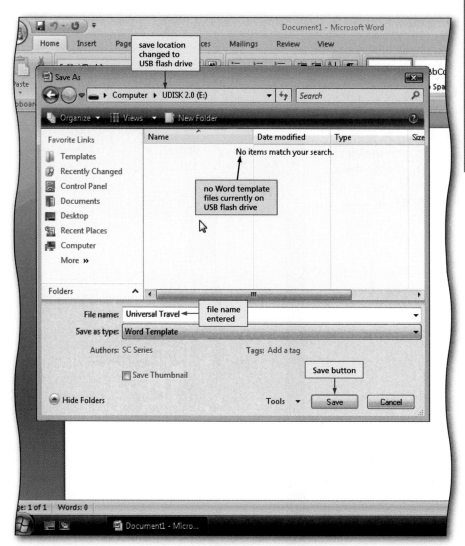

Figure 8–4

Other Ways

1. Press F12; change document type to Word Template

Changing Document Settings

To enhance the look of the form, you change several default settings in Word:

1. Display the page as wide as possible in the document window to maximize the amount of space for text and graphics on the form.

2. Change the size of the paper so that it fits completely within the document window.

3. Adjust the margins so that as much text as possible will fit in the document.

4. Change the document theme to Foundry.

5. Change the page color to light blue.

The following pages make these changes to the document.

To Zoom Page Width

In the online form in this chapter, the form is to appear as wide as possible in the document window. When you change the zoom to page width, Word extends the edges of the page to the edge of the document window. The following step zooms page width.

1

- Display the View tab.

- Click the Page Width button on the View tab to change the zoom to page width (Figure 8–5).

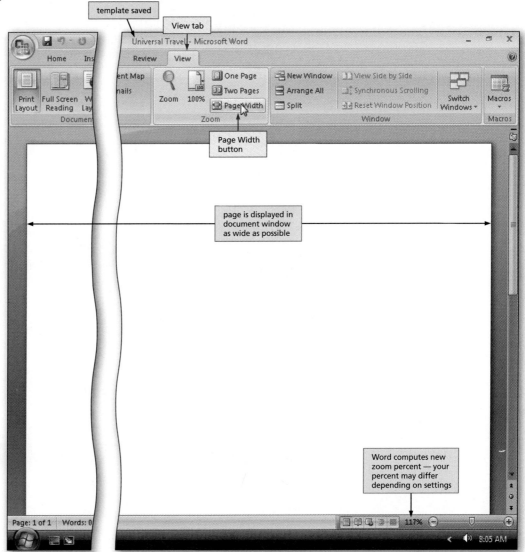

Figure 8–5

BTW

Certification
The Microsoft Certified Application Specialist (MCAS) program provides an opportunity for you to obtain a valuable industry credential — proof that you have the Word 2007 skills required by employers. For more information see Appendix G or visit the Word 2007 Certification Web page (scsite.com/wd2007/cert).

To Change Paper Size

For the online form in this chapter, all edges of the paper appear in the document window. Currently, the top, left, and right edges are displayed in the document window. To display the bottom edge also, change the height of the paper from 11 inches to 4.75 inches. The following steps change paper size.

- Display the Page Layout tab.

- Click the Page Size button on the Page Layout tab to display the Page Size gallery (Figure 8–6).

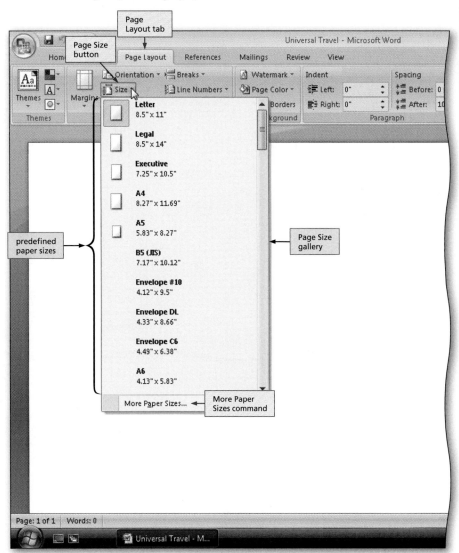

Figure 8–6

2

- Click More Paper Sizes in the Page Size gallery to display the Paper sheet in the Page Setup dialog box.

- In the Height text box, type 4.75 as the new height (Figure 8–7).

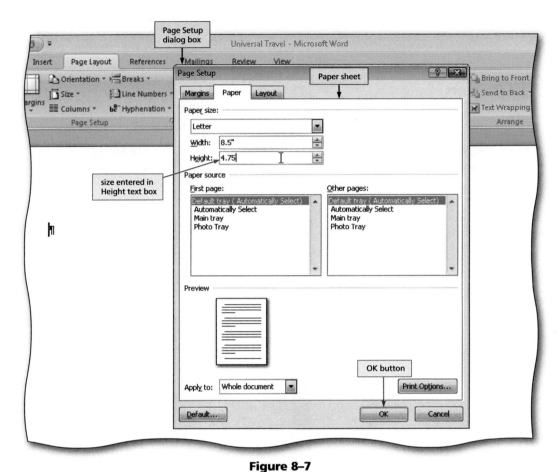

Figure 8–7

3

- Click the OK button to change the paper size to 8.5 inches wide by 4.75 inches tall (Figure 8–8).

Q&A

What if the height of my document does not match the figure?

It is possible that you need to show white space. Position the mouse pointer above the top of the page below the Ribbon and then double-click when the mouse pointer changes to a Show White Space button.

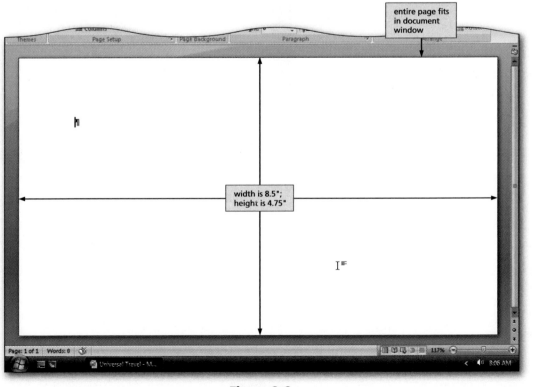

Figure 8–8

To Set Custom Margins

Recall that Word is preset to use 1-inch top, bottom, left, and right margins. To maximize the space for the contents of the form, this chapter sets the left and right margins to .5 inches, the top margin to .25 inches, and the bottom margin to 0 inches. The following steps set custom margins.

1 Click the Margins button on the Page Layout tab to display the Margins gallery.

2 Click Custom Margins in the Margins gallery to display the Margins sheet in Page Setup dialog box.

3 Type .25 in the Top text box to change the top margin setting and then press the TAB key to position the insertion point in the Bottom text box.

4 Type 0 (zero) in the Bottom text box to change the bottom margin setting and then press the TAB key.

Q&A Why set the bottom margin to zero?

This allows you to place form contents at the bottom of the page, if necessary.

5 Type .5 in the Left text box to change the left margin setting and then press the TAB key.

6 Type .5 in the Right box to change the right margin setting (Figure 8–9).

7 Click the OK button to set the custom margins for this document.

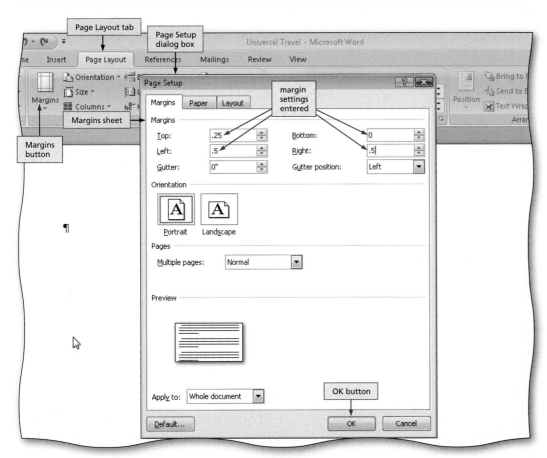

Figure 8–9

To Change the Document Theme

The next step in this section is to change the document theme to Foundry.

1 Click the Themes button on the Page Layout tab and then click Foundry in the Themes gallery to change the document theme to Foundry, which causes the face of the buttons in the Themes group to show colors, fonts, and effects associated with the Foundry theme.

To Change the Page Color

The next step is to change the page color of the online form so that it is visually appealing. This online form uses a light shade of blue. The following steps change the page color.

1 Click the Page Color button on the Page Layout tab to display the Page Color gallery.

2 Point to the seventh color in the second row (Sky Blue, Accent 3, Lighter 80%) to display a live preview of the selected page color (Figure 8–10).

3 Click the seventh color in the second row to change the page color to a light shade of blue.

Q&A Do page colors print?

When you change the page color, it appears only on screen. Changing the background color has no effect on a printed document.

4 If the rulers appear on the screen, click the View Ruler button at the top of the vertical scroll bar to hide the rulers.

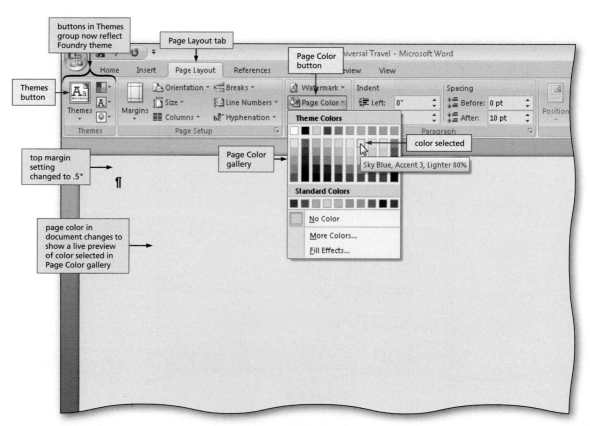

Figure 8–10

Enter Content in the Online Form

The next step in creating the online form in this chapter is to enter the text, graphics, and content controls in the document. The following pages outline this process.

To Enter Text

The next step is to enter the text at the top of the online form.

1 Type UNIVERSAL TRAVEL and then press the ENTER key.

2 Type Your Ticket to the World and then press the ENTER key.

3 Type E-Mail Request Form for Weekly Specials and then press the ENTER key.

4 Type To receive our weekly specials via e-mail, fill in the information requested below: and then press the ENTER key (Figure 8–11).

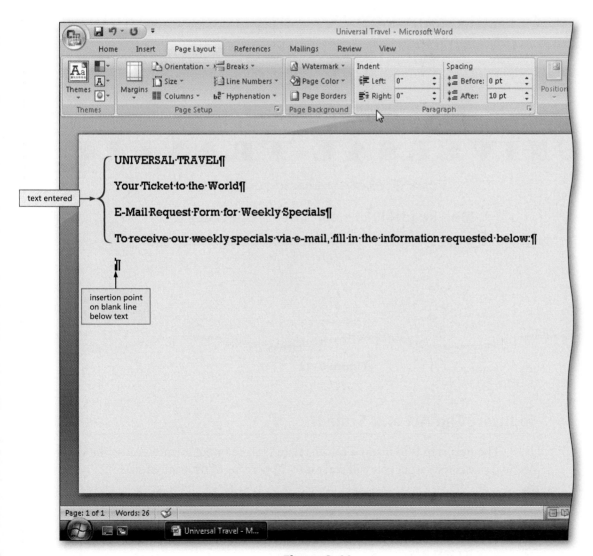

Figure 8–11

To Format Text

The following steps format the text at the top of the online form.

1 Center the four lines of text just entered.

2 Format the characters on the first line to 26-point Goudy Stout font with the color of Rose, Accent 6, Darker 50%.

3 Format the characters on the second line to 14-point bold Lucida Handwriting font with the color of Sky Blue, Accent 3, Darker 50%.

4 Format the characters on the third line to 14-point bold font with the color of Black, Text 1, Lighter 35%.

5 Change the spacing after the first line to 0 point.

6 Change the spacing after the third line to 6 point (Figure 8–12).

Figure 8–12

To Insert Clip Art and Scale It

The next step is to insert a travel-related image in the form. Because the graphic's original size is too large, you will scale it to 50 percent of its original size.

1 Display the Insert tab. Click the Clip Art button on the Insert tab to display the Clip Art task pane.

2 In the Clip Art task pane, if necessary, click the Search for text box. Type travel in the Search for text box.

3 Click the Go button to display a list of clips that match the description, travel.

4 Scroll to and then click the travel-related clip art that matches the one in Figure 8–13.

5 Close the Clip Art task pane.

Q&A What if my clip art image is not in the same location as in Figure 8–13?

The clip art image may be in a different location, depending on the position of the insertion point when you inserted the image. In a later section, you will move the image to a different location.

6 With the graphic still selected, click the Size Dialog Box Launcher on the Picture Tools Format tab to display the Size dialog box.

Q&A What if the Format tab is not the active tab on my Ribbon?

Double-click the graphic or click Format on the Ribbon to display the Format tab.

7 Change the values in the Height and Width text boxes in the Scale area to 50% (Figure 8–13).

Q&A Why does the width value change to match the height value?

When the 'Lock aspect ratio' check box is selected, Word automatically keeps the proportion of the height and width the same.

8 Click the Close button in the Size dialog box to close the dialog box.

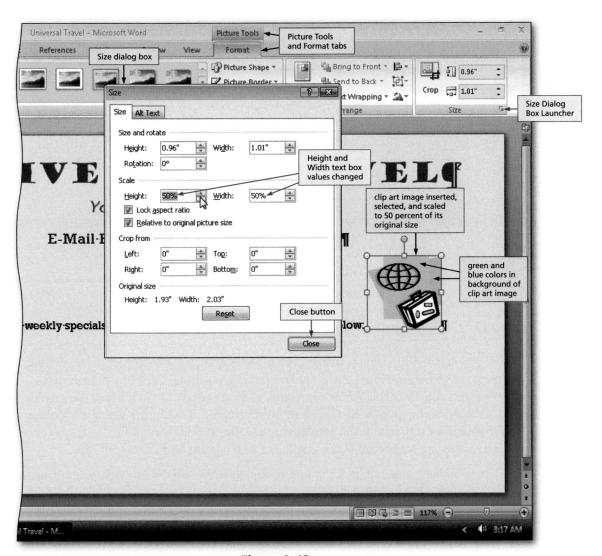

Figure 8–13

To Adjust the Contrast of a Graphic

In this online form, the blue and green background colors in the clip art image are too dark. You would like to soften the colors, that is, increase the contrast in the graphic. The following steps adjust a graphic's contrast.

- Click the Contrast button on the Format tab to display the Contrast gallery.

- Point to +40 % in the Contrast gallery to display a live preview of that contrast applied to the selected clip art image (Figure 8–14).

Experiment

- Point to various percentages in the Contrast gallery and watch the clip art image's contrast change.

- Click +40 % in the Contrast gallery to increase the contrast in the clip art image.

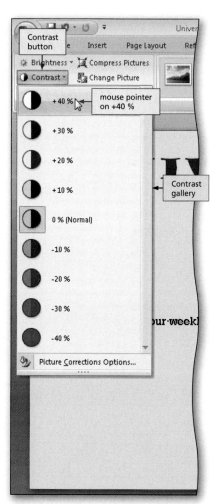

Figure 8–14

Other Ways

1. Right-click image, click Format Picture on short-cut menu, click Picture in left pane, drag Contrast slider, click Close button

To Format a Graphic's Text Wrapping

Word inserted the clip art image as an inline graphic, that is, as part of the current paragraph. In this online form, the graphic should be positioned near the bottom-left corner of the company name (shown in Figure 8–1 on page WD 571). Thus, the graphic needs to be a floating graphic instead of an inline graphic. That is, the text in the online form should not wrap around the graphic; instead, the graphic should float in front of the text. The following steps change the graphic's text wrapping to In Front of Text.

1. With the graphic selected, click the Text Wrapping button on the Format tab to display the Text Wrapping menu (Figure 8–15).

2. Click In Front of Text on the Text Wrapping menu to change the graphic from inline to floating with In Front of Text wrapping.

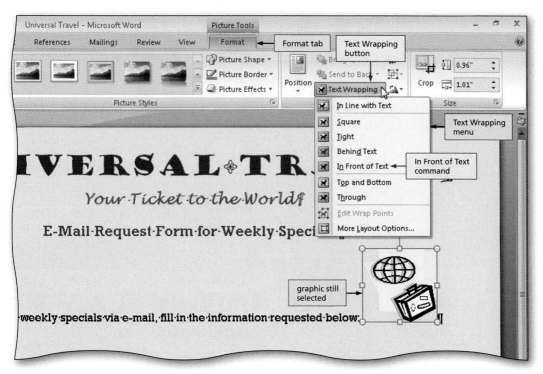

Figure 8–15

To Move a Graphic

The final step associated with the graphic is to move it so that it is positioned on the left side of the online form.

1 Point inside the selected graphic, and when the mouse pointer has a four-headed arrow attached to it, drag the graphic to the location shown in Figure 8–16.

Figure 8–16

To Highlight Text

You want to emphasize the fourth line of text that instructs the user to fill in the information in the form. To emphasize text in an online document, you can highlight it. **Highlighting** alerts a reader to online text's importance, much like a highlighter pen does in a textbook. Word provides 15 colors you can use to highlight text, including the traditional yellow and green, as well as some nontraditional highlight colors such as gray, dark blue, and dark red. The following steps highlight the fourth line of text in the color gray.

1

- Select the text to be highlighted, which, in this case, is the fourth line of text.

- Display the Home tab.

- Click the Text Highlight Color button arrow to display the Text Highlight Color gallery (Figure 8–17).

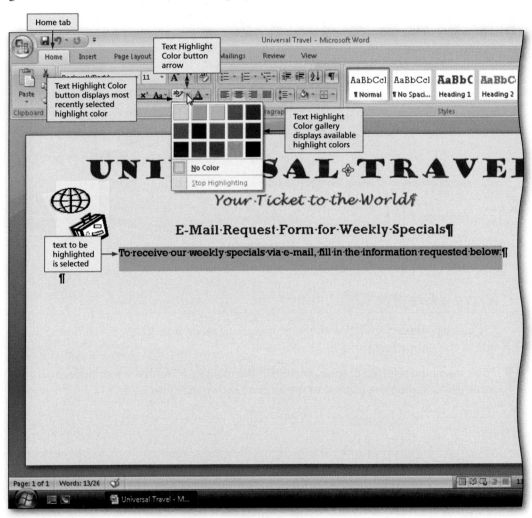

Figure 8–17

The Text Highlight Color gallery did not appear. Why not?

You clicked the Text Highlight Color button instead of the Text Highlight Color button arrow. Click the Undo button on the Quick Access Toolbar and then repeat Step 1.

What if the icon on the Text Highlight Color button already displays the color I want to use?

You can click the Text Highlight Color button instead of the button arrow.

2

• Point to Gray-25% in the Text Highlight Color gallery to display a live preview of this highlight color applied to the selected text (Figure 8–18).

⊘ Experiment

• Point to various colors in the Text Highlight Color gallery and watch the highlight color on the selected text change.

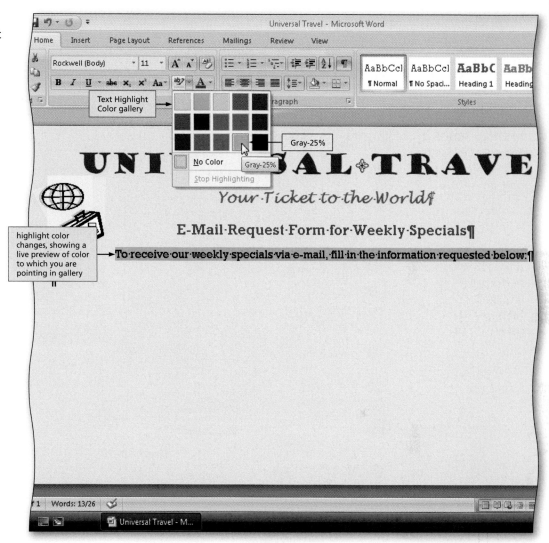

Figure 8–18

3

• Click Gray-25% in the Text Highlight Color gallery to highlight the selected text in gray.

Q&A How would I remove a highlight from text?

Select the highlighted text, click the Text Highlight Color button arrow, and then click No Color in the Text Highlight Color gallery.

Other Ways

1. Click Text Highlight Color button arrow, select desired color, select text to be highlighted in document, select any additional text to be highlighted, click Text Highlight Color button to turn off highlighting

BTW

Highlighter
If you click the Text Highlight Color button without first selecting any text, the highlighter remains active until you turn it off. This allows you to continue selecting text that you want to be highlighted. To deactivate the highlighter, click the Text Highlight Color button, click Stop Highlighting on the Text Highlight Color menu, or press the ESC key.

To Show the Developer Tab

To create a form in Word, you need to use buttons on the Developer tab. Because it allows you to perform more advanced tasks not required by everyday Word users, the Developer tab does not appear on the Ribbon by default. The following steps display the Developer tab on the Ribbon.

1

- Click the Office Button to display the Office Button menu (Figure 8–19).

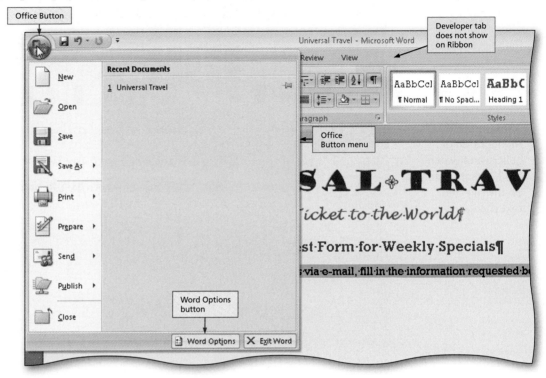

Figure 8–19

2

- Click the Word Options button on the Office Button menu to display the Word Options dialog box.

- If necessary, click Popular in the left pane.

- If it is not selected already, place a check mark in the Show Developer tab in the Ribbon check box (Figure 8–20).

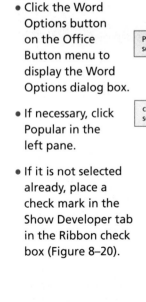

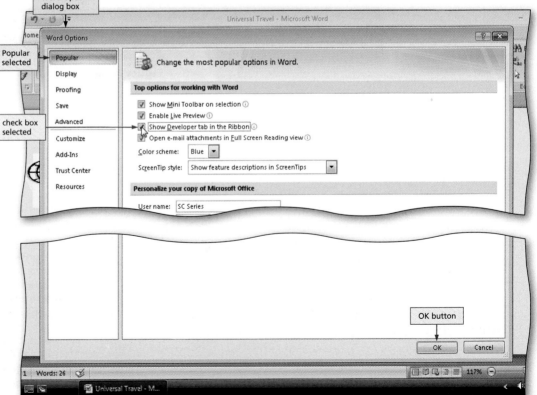

Figure 8–20

3

- Click the OK button to show the Developer tab on the Ribbon (Figure 8–21).

How do I remove the Developer tab from the Ribbon?

Follow these same steps, except remove the check mark from the Show Developer tab in the Ribbon check box in the Word Options dialog box.

Figure 8–21

To Insert a Borderless Table in a Form

The first line of data entry in the form consists of the First Name content control, which begins at the left margin, and the Last Name content control, which begins at the center point of the same line. At first glance, you might decide to set a tab stop at each content control location. This, however, can be a complex task. For example, to place two content controls evenly across a row, you must calculate the location of each tab stop. If you insert a 2 × 1 table instead, Word automatically calculates the size of two evenly spaced columns. Thus, to enter multiple content controls on a single line, insert a table.

In this online form, the line containing the First Name and Last Name content controls will be a 2 × 1 table, that is, a table with two columns and one row. By inserting a 2 × 1 table, Word automatically positions the second column at the center point.

When you insert a table, Word automatically surrounds it with a border. You do not want borders on tables in forms. Also, to maintain consistent formatting throughout the form, you also will place 10 points after the table. The steps on the next page enter a 2 × 1 table in the form, remove its border, and add space after it.

1

- If necessary, position the insertion point on the blank paragraph mark below the gray highlighted text (shown in Figure 8–21 on the previous page).

- Display the Insert tab. Click the Table button on the Insert tab to display the Table gallery.

- Point to the cell in the first row and second column of the grid to preview the desired table dimension at the location of the insertion point (Figure 8–22).

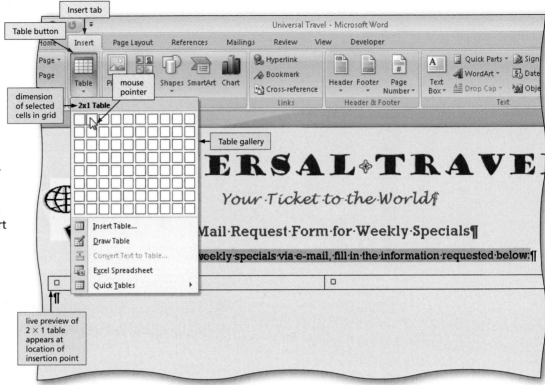

Figure 8–22

2

- Click the cell in the first row and second column of the grid to insert an empty 2 × 1 table.

3

- Point to the first cell in the table to display the table move handle.

- Click the table move handle to select the table.

- Click the Borders button arrow on the Design tab to display the Borders gallery (Figure 8–23).

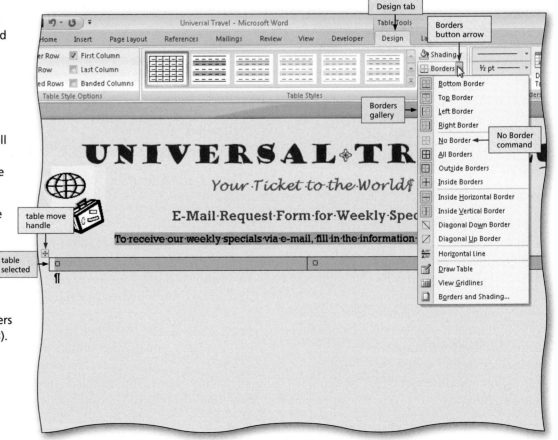

Figure 8–23

4

- Click No Border in the Borders gallery to remove the borders from the table.

- Click the first cell of the table to remove the selection.

5

- Display the Page Layout tab.

- Change the value in the Spacing After text box to 10 pt (Figure 8–24).

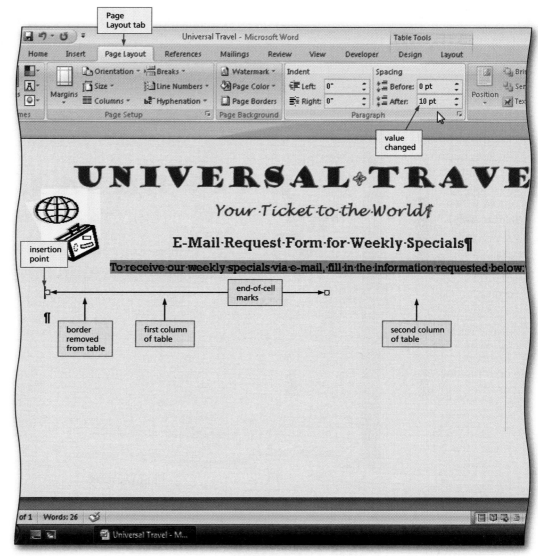

Figure 8–24

Q&A My screen does not display the end-of-cell marks. Why not?

You can display formatting marks by clicking the Show/Hide ¶ button on the Home tab.

Other Ways

1. Click Table button on Insert tab, click Insert Table in Table gallery, enter number of columns and rows, click OK button

To Show Gridlines

When you remove the borders from the table, you no longer can see the individual cells in the table. To help identify the location of cells, you can display **gridlines**, which show cell outlines on the screen. The following step shows gridlines.

- If necessary, position the insertion point in a table cell.

- Display the Layout tab.

- Click the View Table Gridlines button on the Layout tab to show table gridlines on the screen (Figure 8–25).

Q&A

Do table gridlines print?

No. Gridlines are formatting marks that show only on the screen. Gridlines help users easily identify cells, rows, and columns in borderless tables.

Figure 8–25

Content Controls

To add data entry fields in a Word form, you insert content controls. The Developer tab in Word includes seven different content controls you can insert in your online forms. Table 8–1 outlines the use of each of these controls.

Table 8–1 Content Controls	
Type	**Use**
Rich Text	User enters text, and if desired, may format the entered text.
Plain Text (or Text)	User enters text, which may not be formatted.
Picture	User inserts drawing, shape, picture, clip art, or SmartArt graphic.
Combo Box	User types text entry or selects one item from a list of choices.
Drop-Down List	User selects one item from a list of choices.
Date	User interacts with a calendar to select a date or types a date in the placeholder.
Building Block Gallery	User selects built-in building block from gallery.

Determine the correct field type for each data entry field.
Word uses content controls for data entry fields. For each data entry field, decide which content control best maps to the type of data the field will contain. The field specifications for the fields in this chapter's online form are listed below:

- The First Name, Last Name, E-Mail Address, and Favorite Destinations data entry fields will contain text. The first three will be plain text content controls and the last will be a rich text content control.

- The Preferred Airline Ticket data entry field must contain one of these three values: Economy, Business, or First Class. This field will be a drop-down list content control.

- The Preferred Rental Vehicle data entry field can contain one of these five values: Compact Car, Full-Size Car, SUV, Minivan, or All-Terrain Vehicle. In addition, users should be able to enter their own value in this data entry field if none of these five values are applicable. A combo box content control will be used for this field.

- The Today's Date data entry field should contain only a valid date value. Thus, this field will be a date content control.

The following pages insert content controls in the online form.

To Insert a Plain Text Content Control

The first item that a user enters in the E-Mail Request Form for Weekly Specials is his or her first name. Because the first name entry contains text that the user should not format, this online form uses a plain text content control for the first name data entry field. The label, First Name, displays to the left of the plain text content control. To improve readability, a colon or some other character often separates a label from the content control. The following steps enter the label, First Name:, and a plain text content control.

- With the insertion point in the first cell of the table as shown in Figure 8–25, type First Name: as the label for the content control.

- Press the SPACEBAR (Figure 8–26).

Figure 8–26

- Display the Developer tab.

- Click the Text button on the Developer tab to insert a plain text content control at the location of the insertion point (Figure 8–27).

Q&A Is the plain text content control similar to the content controls that I have used in Word installed templates, such as the memo and resume templates?

Yes. The content controls you insert through the Developer tab have the same functionality as the content controls in the Word installed templates.

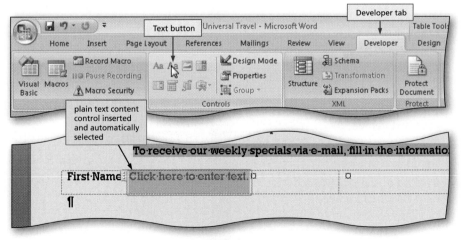

Figure 8–27

To Edit Placeholder Text

A content control displays **placeholder text**, which instructs the user how to enter values in the content control. The default placeholder text for a plain text content control is the instruction, Click here to enter text. You can change the wording in the placeholder text to be more instructional. The following steps edit the placeholder text for the plain text content control just entered.

1

- With the plain text content control selected, click the Design Mode button on the Developer tab to turn on design mode (Figure 8–28).

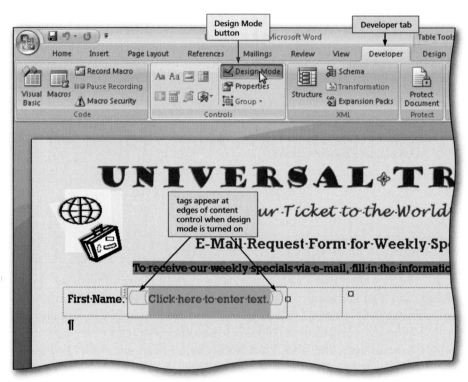

Figure 8–28

2

- If necessary, click the placeholder text to position the insertion point in it (Figure 8–29).

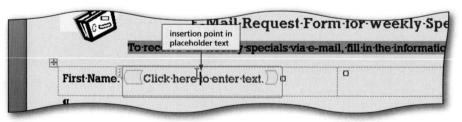

Figure 8–29

3

- Edit the placeholder text so that it contains this instruction (Figure 8–30): Click here and type your first name.

Q&A

What if the placeholder text wraps to the next line?

Because of the tags at each edge of the placeholder text, the entered text may wrap in the table cell. Once you turn off design mode, the placeholder text should fit on a single line.

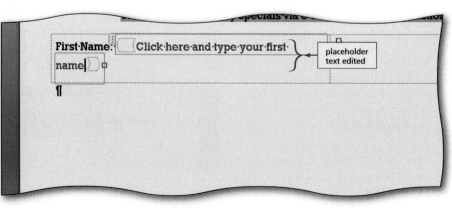

Figure 8–30

4

- Click the Design Mode button on the Developer tab to turn off design mode (Figure 8–31).

When users enter data in the content control, how will their entry be formatted?

It will look just like the placeholder text. If you want the format of data that the user enters to be different from the format of the current placeholder text, simply change the format of the place-holder text when design mode is turned on.

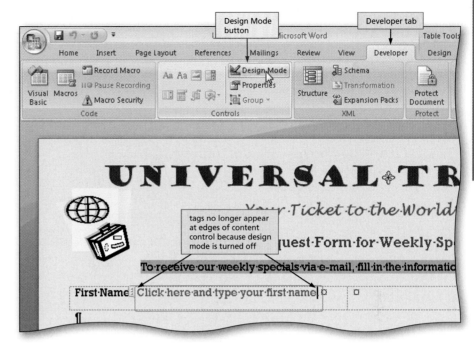

Figure 8–31

To Change the Properties of a Plain Text Content Control

When you click a content control in a Word installed template, the content control may display an identifier in its top-left corner. For templates that you create, you can instruct Word to display this identifier, called the title, by changing the properties of the content control. In addition, you can lock the content control so that a user cannot delete the content control during the data entry process. The following steps change properties of a plain text content control.

1

- With content control selected, click the Control Properties button on the Developer tab to display the Content Control Properties dialog box (Figure 8–32).

How do I know the content control is selected?

A selected content control is surrounded by a blue outline. It also may be shaded or contain the insertion point.

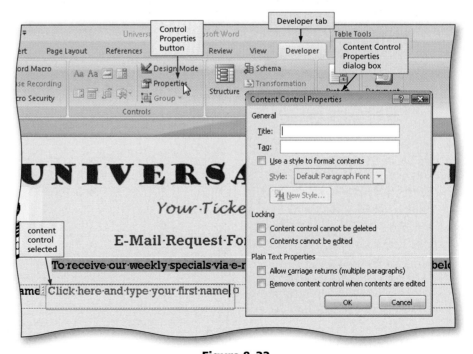

Figure 8–32

2

- Type First Name in the Title text box.

- Place a check mark in the 'Content control cannot be deleted' check box (Figure 8–33).

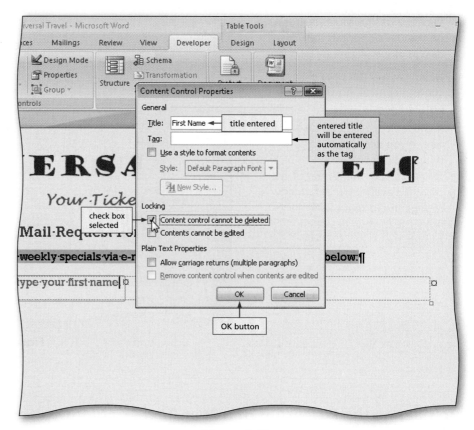

Figure 8–33

3

- Click the OK button to assign the modified properties to the content control (Figure 8–34).

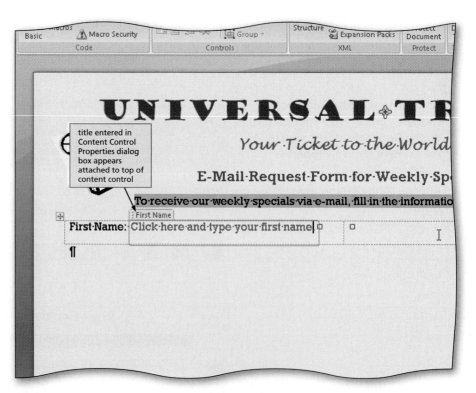

Figure 8–34

To Insert Another Plain Text Content Control and Edit Its Placeholder Text

The second item that a user enters in the E-Mail Request Form for Weekly Specials is his or her last name. The steps for entering the last name content control are similar to those for the first name because the last name also is a plain text content control. The following steps enter the label, Last Name:, and a plain text content control and edit its placeholder text.

1 Position the insertion point in the second cell (column) in the table.

2 With the insertion point in the second cell of the table, type Last Name: as the label for the content control and then press the SPACEBAR.

3 Click the Text button on the Developer tab to insert a plain text content control at the location of the insertion point.

4 With the plain text content control selected, click the Design Mode button on the Developer tab to turn on design mode.

5 If necessary, click the placeholder text to position the insertion point in it.

6 Edit the placeholder text so that it contains this instruction (Figure 8-35): Click here and type your last name.

7 Click the Design Mode button on the Developer tab to turn off design mode.

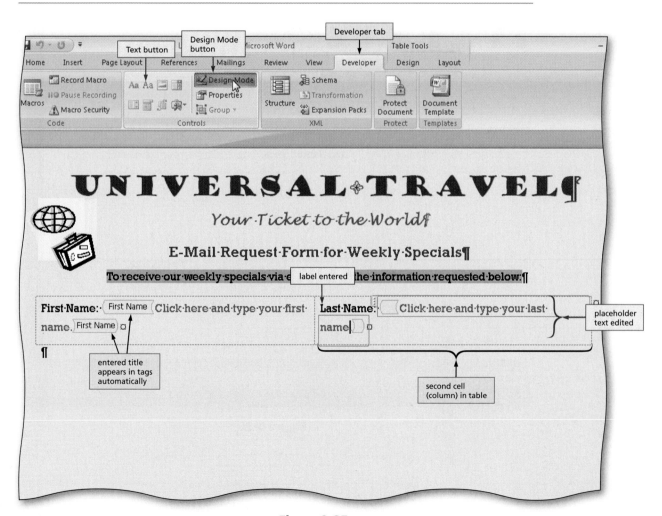

Figure 8–35

To Change the Properties of a Plain Text Content Control

The next step is to change the title and locking properties of the Last Name content control, as you did for the First Name content control. The following steps change properties of a plain text content control.

1 With content control selected, click the Control Properties button on the Developer tab to display the Content Control Properties dialog box.

2 Type Last Name in the Title text box.

3 Place a check mark in the 'Content control cannot be deleted' check box (Figure 8–36).

4 Click the OK button to assign the properties to the content control.

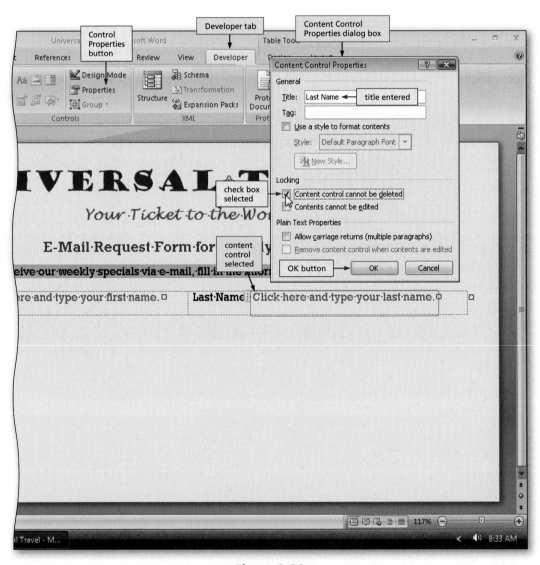

Figure 8–36

To Hide Gridlines

Because you are finished with the table in this form and will not enter any additional tables, you will hide the gridlines. The following steps hide gridlines.

1 If necessary, position the insertion point in a table cell.

2 Display the Layout tab.

3 Click the View Table Gridlines button on the Layout tab to hide table gridlines on the screen (Figure 8–37).

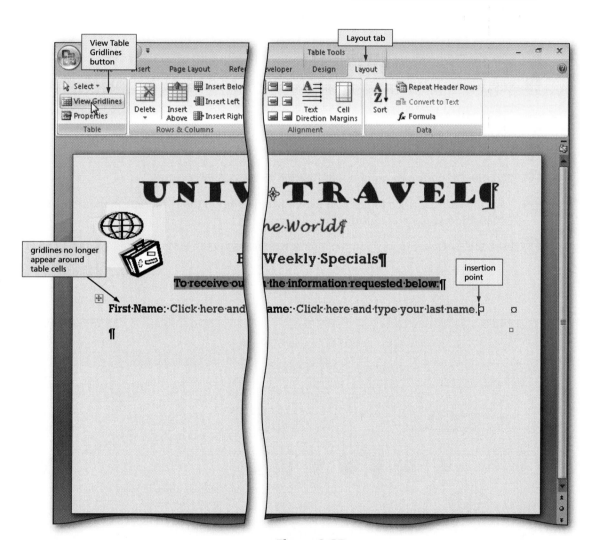

Figure 8–37

To Insert Another Plain Text Content Control, Edit Its Placeholder Text, and Change Its Properties

The third item that a user enters in the E-Mail Request Form is his or her e-mail address. You use similar steps to enter the e-mail address content control as for the first name and last name; that is, the e-mail address also is a plain text content control. The steps on the next page enter a plain text content control, edit its placeholder text, and then change its properties.

1 Position the insertion point on the blank paragraph mark below the First Name content control.

2 Type E-Mail Address: as the label for the content control and then press the SPACEBAR.

3 If necessary, display the Developer tab. Click the Text button on the Developer tab to insert a plain text content control at the location of the insertion point.

4 With the plain text content control selected, click the Design Mode button on the Developer tab to turn on design mode.

5 If necessary, click the placeholder text to position the insertion point in it.

6 Edit the placeholder text so that it contains this instruction: Click here and type your e-mail address.

7 Click the Design Mode button on the Developer tab to turn off design mode.

8 With content control selected, click the Control Properties button on the Developer tab to display the Content Control Properties dialog box.

9 Type E-Mail Address in the Title text box.

10 Place a check mark in the 'Content control cannot be deleted' check box (Figure 8–38).

11 Click the OK button to assign the properties to the content control.

12 Press the END key twice to position the insertion point on the paragraph mark after the E-Mail Address content control.

13 Press the ENTER key to position the insertion point below the E-Mail Address content control.

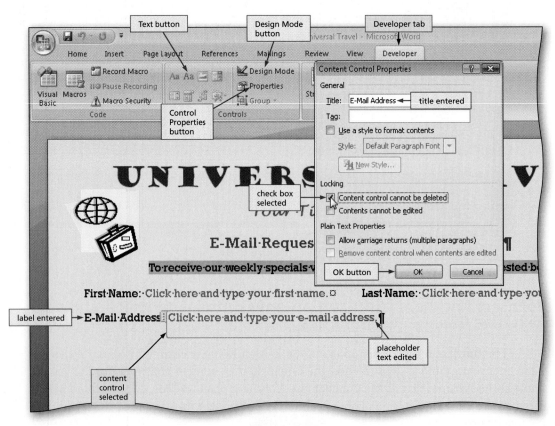

Figure 8–38

To Insert a Drop-Down List Content Control

In the online form in this chapter, the user selects from one of these three choices for the Preferred Airline Ticket content control: Economy, Business, or First Class. To present a set of choices to a user in the form of a drop-down list, from which the user selects one, insert a drop-down list content control. To view the set of choices, the user clicks the arrow at the right edge of the content control. The following steps insert a drop-down list content control.

1

- With the insertion point positioned on the blank paragraph mark below the E-Mail Address content control, type `Preferred Airline Ticket:` and then press the SPACEBAR.

2

- Click the Drop-Down List button on the Developer tab to insert a drop-down list content control at the location of the insertion point (Figure 8–39).

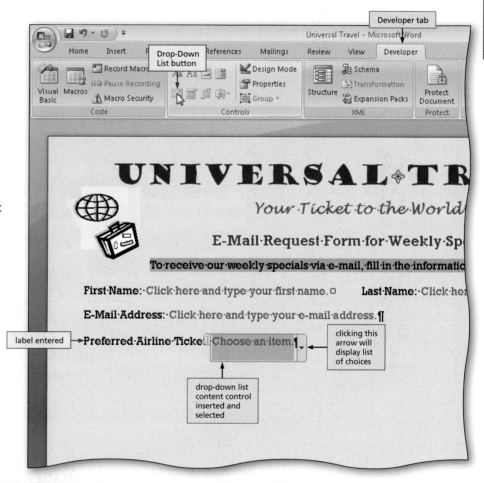

Figure 8–39

To Edit Placeholder Text

The following steps edit the placeholder text for the drop-down list content control.

1 With the drop-down list content control selected, click the Design Mode button on the Developer tab to turn on design mode.

2 If necessary, click the placeholder text to position the insertion point in it.

3 Edit the placeholder text so that it contains this instruction: Click here and then click arrow. Select from list.

4 Click the Design Mode button on the Developer tab to turn off design mode.

To Change the Properties of a Drop-Down List Content Control

In addition to identifying a title and locking the drop-down list content control, you need to specify the choices that will be displayed when a user clicks the arrow to the right of the content control. The following steps change the properties of a drop-down list content control.

- With content control selected, click the Control Properties button on the Developer tab to display the Content Control Properties dialog box.

- Type `Airline Ticket` in the Title text box.

- Place a check mark in the 'Content control cannot be deleted' check box.

- In the Drop-Down List Properties area, click 'Choose an item.' to select it (Figure 8–40).

- Click the Remove button to delete the 'Choose an item' entry.

Q&A Why delete the 'Choose an item' entry?

If you leave it in the list, it will appear as the first item in the list when the user clicks the content control arrow. You do not want it in the list, so you delete it.

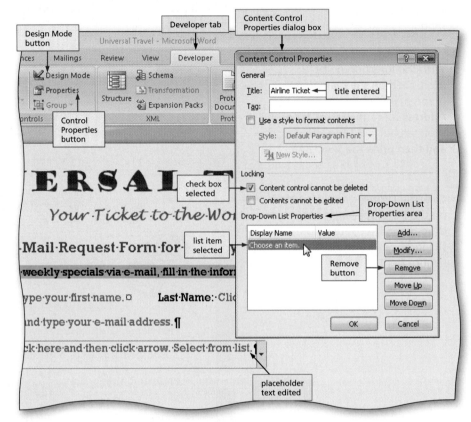

Figure 8–40

- Click the Add button to display the Add Choice dialog box.

- Type `Economy` in the Display Name text box (Figure 8–41).

Q&A What is the difference between a display name and a value?

In many cases, such as the example shown here, they are the same. Sometimes, however, you want to store a shorter or different value. For example, if the user selects a state such as Illinois as the display name, you may wish to store the value as the state code of IL. Using shorter values, such as IL, makes it easier for separate programs to analyze and interpret entered data.

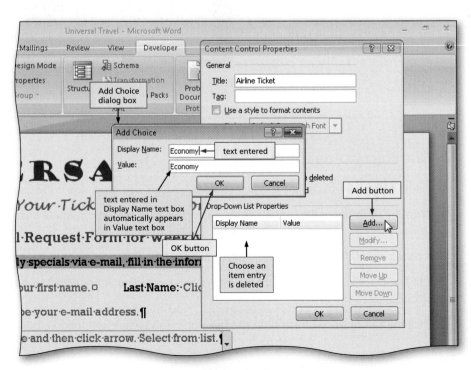

Figure 8–41

4

- Click the OK button or press the ENTER key to add the entered display name to the list of choices in the Drop-Down List Properties area in the Content Control Properties dialog box.

- Click the Add button to display the Add Choice dialog box.

- Type `Business` in the Display Name text box.

- Click the OK button or press the ENTER key to add the entry to the list.

- Click the Add button to display the Add Choice dialog box.

- Type `First Class` in the Display Name text box.

- Click the OK button or press the ENTER key to add the entry to the list (Figure 8–42).

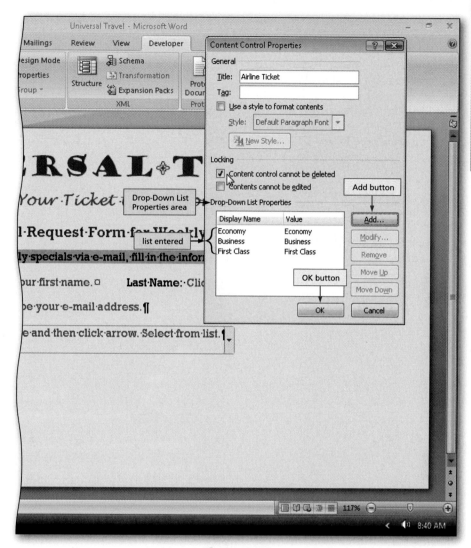

Figure 8–42

5

- Click the OK button to change the content control properties.

- Press the END key twice to position the insertion point at the end of the current line and then press the ENTER key to position the insertion point below the Preferred Airline Ticket content control.

To Insert a Combo Box Content Control

In the online form in this chapter, users can type their own entry in the Preferred Rental Vehicle content control or select from one of these five choices: Compact Car, Full-Size Car, SUV, Minivan, All-Terrain Vehicle. In Word, a combo box content control allows a user to type text or select from a list. The following steps insert a combo box content control.

1
- With the insertion point positioned on the blank paragraph mark below the Preferred Airline Ticket content control, type `Preferred Rental Vehicle:` and then press the SPACEBAR.

2
- Click the Combo Box button on the Developer tab to insert a combo box content control at the location of the insertion point (Figure 8–43).

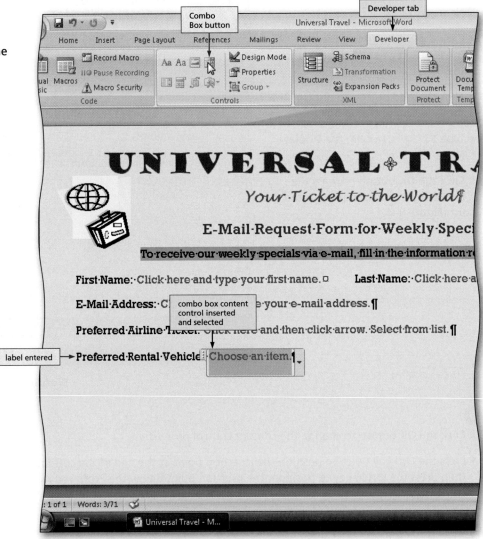

Figure 8–43

To Edit Placeholder Text

The following steps edit the placeholder text for the combo box content control.

1 With the combo box content control selected, click the Design Mode button on the Developer tab to turn on design mode.

2 If necessary, click in the placeholder text to position the insertion point in it.

3 Edit the placeholder text so that it contains this instruction: Click here. Click arrow and select from list, or type your preferred vehicle.

4 Click the Design Mode button on the Developer tab to turn off design mode.

To Change the Properties of a Combo Box Content Control

You follow similar steps to enter the list for a combo box content control as you do for the drop-down list content control. The following steps change the properties of a combo box content control.

1

- With content control selected, click the Control Properties button on the Developer tab to display the Content Control Properties dialog box.

- Type Rental Vehicle in the Title text box.

- Place a check mark in the 'Content control cannot be deleted' check box.

- In the Drop-Down List Properties area, click 'Choose an item.' to select it (Figure 8–44).

2

- Click the Remove button to delete the 'Choose an item.' entry.

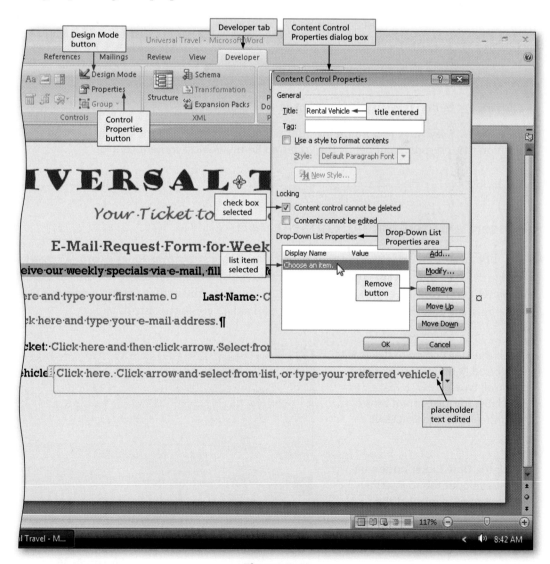

Figure 8–44

- Click the Add button to display the Add Choice dialog box.

- Type Compact Car in the Display Name text box.

- Click the OK button to add the entered display name to the list of choices in the Drop-Down List Properties area in the Content Control Properties dialog box.

- Click the Add button and add Full-Size Car to the list.

- Click the Add button and add SUV to the list.

- Click the Add button and add Minivan to the list.

- Click the Add button and add All-Terrain Vehicle to the list (Figure 8–45).

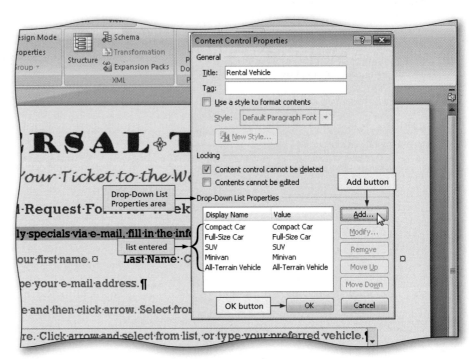

Figure 8–45

- Click the OK button to change the content control properties.

- Press the END key twice to position the insertion point at the end of the current line and then press the ENTER key to position the insertion point below the Preferred Rental Vehicle content control.

To Insert a Date Content Control

The next item that users enter in the E-Mail Request Form is today's date. To assist users with entering dates, Word provides a date picker content control, which displays a calendar when the user clicks the arrow to the right of the content control. Users also can enter a date directly in the content control without using the calendar. The following steps enter the label, Today's Date:, and a date content control.

- With the insertion point below the Preferred Rental Vehicle content control, type Today's Date: as the label for the content control and then press the SPACEBAR.

- Click the Date Picker button on the Developer tab to insert a date content control at the location of the insertion point (Figure 8–46).

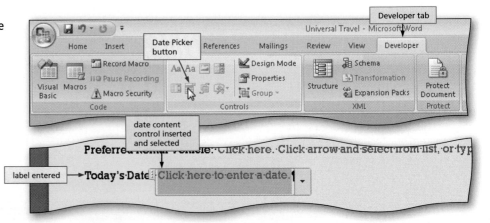

Figure 8–46

To Edit Placeholder Text

The following steps edit the placeholder text for the date content control.

1 With the date content control selected, click the Design Mode button on the Developer tab to turn on design mode.

2 If necessary, click the placeholder text to position the insertion point in it.

3 Edit the placeholder text so that it contains this instruction: Click here and then click arrow. Select today's date.

4 Click the Design Mode button on the Developer tab to turn off design mode.

To Change the Properties of a Date Content Control

In addition to identifying a title for a date content control and locking the control, you can specify how the date will be displayed when the user selects it from the calendar. The following steps change these properties of a date content control.

1

- With content control selected, click the Control Properties button on the Developer tab to display the Content Control Properties dialog box.

- Type `Today's Date` in the Title text box.

- Place a check mark in the 'Content control cannot be deleted' check box.

- In the 'Display the date like this' area, click the desired format in this list (Figure 8–47).

2

- Click the OK button to change the content control properties.

- Press the END key twice to position the

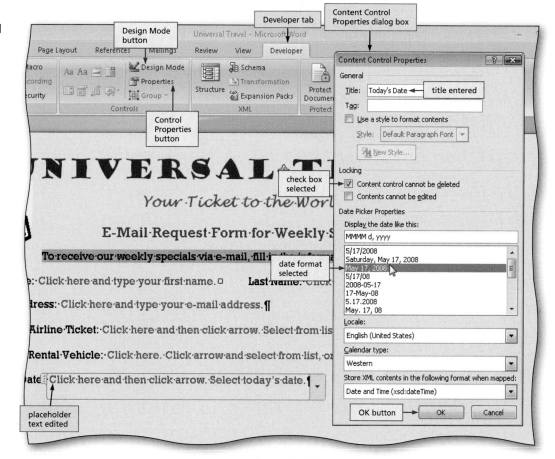

Figure 8–47

insertion point at the end of the current line and then press the ENTER key to position the insertion point below the Today's Date content control.

To Insert a Rich Text Content Control

The last item that users enter in the E-Mail Request Form for Weekly Specials is their favorite destinations. Because you want to allow users to format the text they enter in this content control, you use the rich text content control. The difference between a plain text and rich text content control is that the users can format text as they enter it in the rich text content control. The following step enters the label, Favorite Destinations:, and a rich text content control.

- With the insertion point on the paragraph mark below the Today's Date content control, type `Favorite Destinations:` as the label for the content control and then press the SPACEBAR.

- Click the Rich Text button on the Developer tab to insert a rich text content control at the location of the insertion point (Figure 8–48).

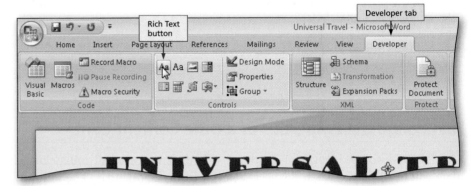

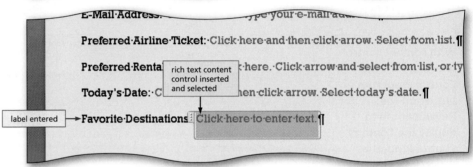

Figure 8–48

To Edit Placeholder Text

The following steps edit placeholder text for the rich text content control.

1 With the rich text content control selected, click the Design Mode button on the Developer tab to turn on design mode.

2 If necessary, scroll to page 2 to display the rich text content control.

Q&A Why did the content control move to another page (Figure 8–49)?

Because design mode displays tags, the content controls and placeholder text are not displayed in their proper positions on the screen. When you turn off design mode, the content controls will return to their original locations and the extra page should disappear.

3 If necessary, click the placeholder text to position the insertion point in it.

4 Edit the placeholder text so that it contains this instruction (Figure 8–49): Click here and type your favorite travel destinations (i.e., city, state, country).

5 Click the Design Mode button on the Developer tab to turn off design mode.

6 Scroll to display the top of the form in the document window.

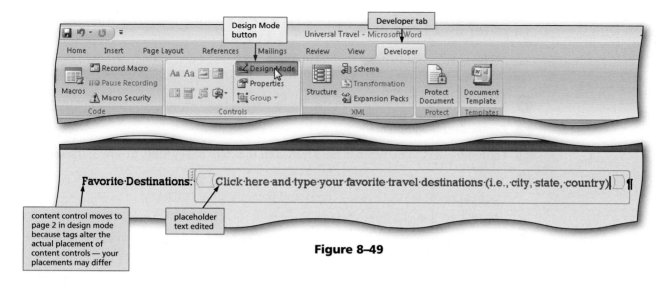

content control moves to page 2 in design mode because tags alter the actual placement of content controls — your placements may differ

placeholder text edited

Figure 8–49

To Change the Properties of a Rich Text Content Control

In the online form in this chapter, you change the same two properties for the rich text content control as for the plain text content control. That is, you enter a title and lock the content control. The following steps change the properties of the rich text content control.

1 With content control selected, click the Control Properties button on the Developer tab to display the Content Control Properties dialog box.

2 Type Favorite Destinations in the Title text box.

3 Place a check mark in the 'Content control cannot be deleted' check box (Figure 8–50).

4 Click the OK button to assign the properties to the content control.

5 Press the END key twice to position the insertion point on the paragraph mark after the Favorite Destinations content control and then press the ENTER key to position the insertion point below the Favorite Destinations content control.

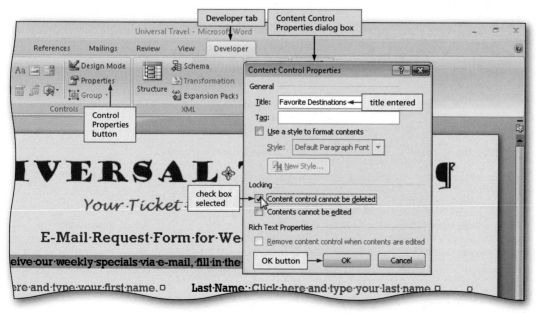

Figure 8–50

To Enter and Format Text

The next step is to enter and format the two lines of text at the bottom of the online form.

1 Be sure the insertion point is on the line below the Favorite Destinations content control.

2 Center the paragraph mark.

3 Format the text to be typed in bold font with the color of Sky Blue, Accent 3, Darker 50%.

4 Type When finished, please save the filled-in form and e-mail it to specials@universaltravel.com! and then press the ENTER key.

Q&A Why did the e-mail address change color?

In this document theme, the color for a hyperlink is a shade of rose. When you pressed the ENTER key, Word automatically formatted the hyperlink in this color.

5 Format the text to be typed in bold with the color of Black, Text 1, Lighter 50%.

6 Type Thank you for your time.

7 Position the insertion point in the line containing the hyperlink. Change the space before the paragraph to 12 point and the space after to 6 point (Figure 8–51).

8 If the text flows to a second page, reduce spacing before paragraphs in the form so that all lines fit on a single page.

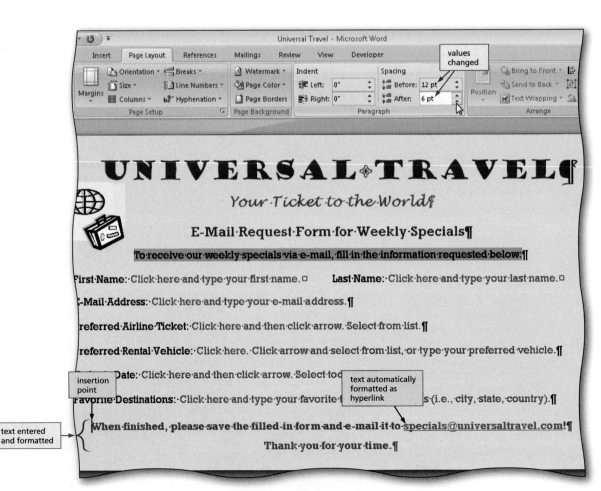

Figure 8–51

To Use the Format Painter Button

The labels for the content controls in the online form in this chapter are to be formatted to 12-point font with the color of Sky Blue, Accent 3, Darker 50%. Instead of selecting each label one at a time and then formatting it, you will format the First Name: label and then copy its format to the remaining labels on the form. The following steps copy formatting.

1

- Format the First Name: label in the form to 12-point with a color of Sky Blue, Accent 3, Darker 50%.

- Select the text that contains the formatting you wish to copy, in this case, the First Name: label.

- If necessary, display the Home tab.

- Double-click the Format Painter button on the Home tab to turn on the format painter (Figure 8–52).

Why double-click the Format Painter button?

To copy selected formats from one location to another, click the Format Painter button on the Home tab once. If you want to copy formatting to multiple locations, however, double-click the Format Painter button so that the format painter remains active until you turn it off.

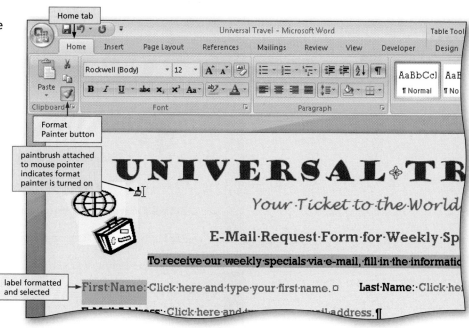

Figure 8–52

2

- Drag through the Last Name: label on the form to paste the formatting from the First Name: label to this text (Figure 8–53).

3

- Drag through these remaining labels on the form to paste formatting from the First Name: label to these labels: E-Mail Address:, Preferred Airline Ticket:, Preferred Rental Vehicle:, Today's Date:, and Favorite Destinations:.

What if the Format Painter button no longer is selected?

Repeat Step 1.

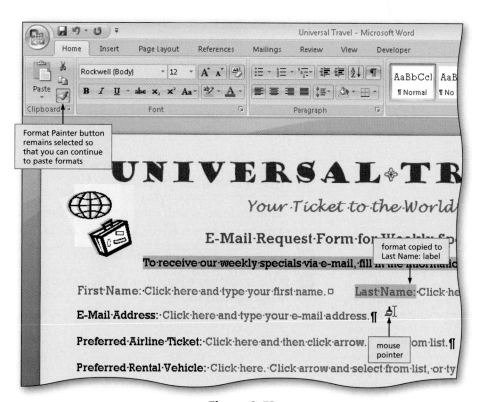

Figure 8–53

4

- Click the Format Painter button on the Home tab to turn off the format painter (Figure 8–54).

Q&A

What if my form now spills onto a second page?

Adjust the spacing above and/or below the paragraphs so that all form contents fit on a single page.

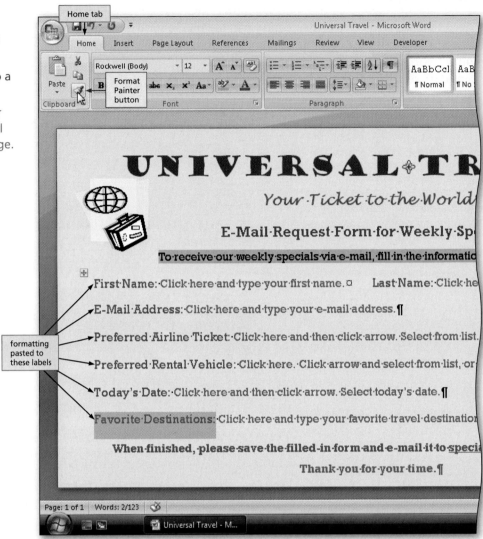

Figure 8–54

BTW

Format Painter
If you also want to copy paragraph formatting, such as alignment and line spacing, select the paragraph mark at the end of the paragraph prior to clicking the Format Painter button. If you want to copy only character formatting, such as fonts and font sizes, do not include the paragraph mark in your selected text.

To Hide Formatting Marks

You are finished with entering and formatting text on the screen. To make the form more pleasing to view, you hide formatting marks. The following steps hide formatting marks.

1 If necessary, display the Home tab.

2 If the Show/Hide ¶ button on the Home tab is selected, click it to remove formatting marks from the screen.

To Draw a Rectangle

The next step is to emphasize the data entry area of the form. The data entry area includes all the content controls in which a user enters data. To call attention to this area of the form, this online form places a rectangle around the data entry area, changes the style rectangle, and then adds a shadow to the rectangle. The first of the following steps draws the rectangle, and the subsequent steps format the rectangle.

- Position the insertion point on the line below the Favorite Destinations content control.

- Display the Insert tab.

- Click the Shapes button on the Insert tab to display the Shapes gallery (Figure 8–55).

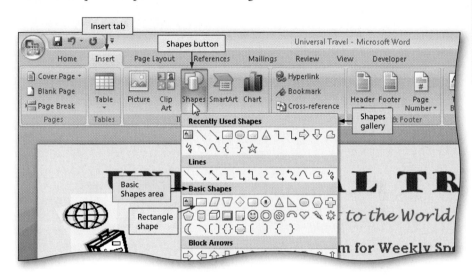

Figure 8–55

- Click Rectangle in the Basic Shapes area of the Shapes gallery, so that you can draw a rectangle on the screen.

- Position the crosshair mouse pointer as shown in Figure 8–56.

Figure 8–56

3

- Drag the mouse pointer downward and rightward to form a rectangle around the data entry area, as shown in Figure 8–57.

Figure 8–57

4

- Release the mouse button to draw the rectangle shape on top of the data entry area (Figure 8–58).

Q&A

What happened to all the text in the data entry area?

When you draw a shape in a document, Word initially places the shape in front of, or on top of, any text in the same area. You can change the stacking order of the shape so that it is displayed behind the text. Thus, the next steps place a shape behind text.

Figure 8–58

To Send a Graphic Behind Text

You want the shape graphic to be positioned behind the data entry area text, so that you can see the text in the data entry area along with the shape. The following steps send a graphic behind text.

1

- If necessary, display the Format tab.

- With the rectangle shape selected, click the Send to Back button arrow on the Format tab to display the Send to Back menu (Figure 8–59).

Q&A

My Send to Back menu did not appear. Why not?

You clicked the Send to Back button instead of the Send to Back button arrow. Repeat Step 1.

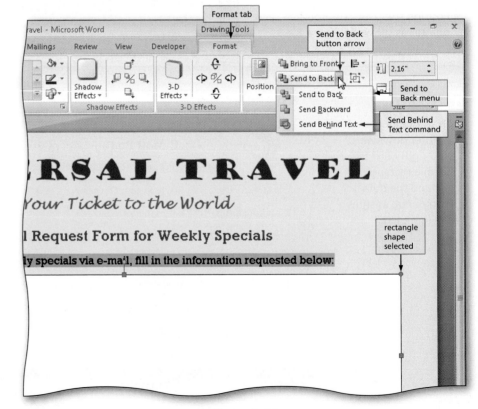

Figure 8–59

2

• Click Send Behind Text on the Send to Back menu to position the rectangle shape behind the text (Figure 8–60).

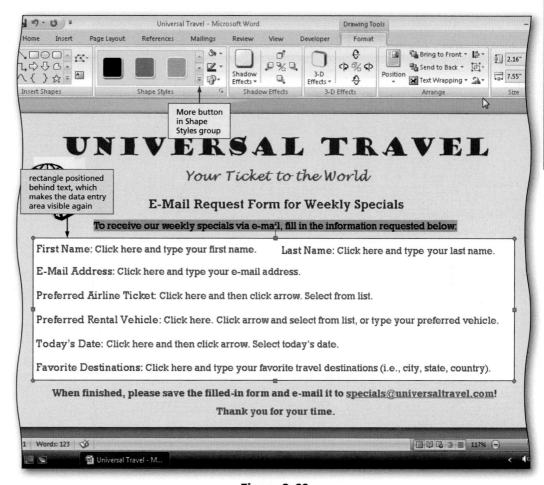

Figure 8–60

Q&A

What if I want a shape to cover text?

You would click the Bring to Front button arrow on the Format tab and then click Bring in Front of Text on the Bring to Front menu.

Other Ways

1. Right-click selected graphic, point to Order on shortcut menu, click Send Behind Text on submenu

BTW

Ordering Graphics

If you have multiple graphics displaying on the screen and would like them to overlap, you can change their stacking order by using commands on the Bring to Front and Send to Back menus. The Bring to Front command on the Bring to Front menu displays the selected object at the top of the stack, and the Send to Back command on the Send to Back menu displays the selected object at the bottom of the stack. The Bring Forward and Send Backward commands each move the graphic forward or backward one layer in the stack. These commands also are available through the shortcut menu that is displayed when you right-click a graphic.

To Apply a Shape Style

The next step is to apply a shape style to the rectangle, so that it is more colorful. Word provides a Shape Styles gallery, allowing you to change the look of the shape to a more visually appealing style. The following steps apply a style to the rectangle.

- With the shape still selected, click the More button in the Shape Styles gallery (shown in Figure 8–60 on the previous page) on the Format tab to expand the Shape Styles gallery.

- Point to Dashed Outline - Accent 4 in the Shape Styles gallery to display a live preview of that style applied to the rectangle shape in the document (Figure 8–61).

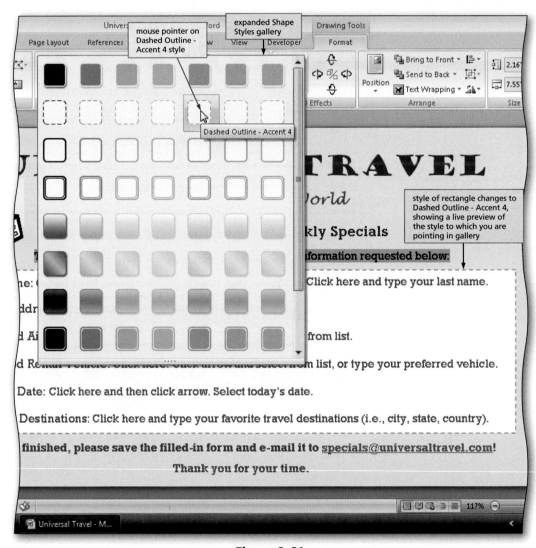

Figure 8–61

Experiment

- Point to various shape styles in the Shape Styles gallery and watch the style of the rectangle shape change.

3

- Click Dashed Outline - Accent 4 in the Shape Styles gallery to apply the selected style to the rectangle shape.

Other Ways

1. Click Advanced Tools Dialog Box Launcher in Shape Styles group, select desired colors, click OK button
2. Click Format AutoShape on shortcut menu, select desired colors, click OK button

To Add a Shadow to a Shape

To further offset the data entry area of the form, this online form has a shadow on the bottom and right edges of the rectangle shape. The following steps add a shadow to the rectangle shape.

- With the shape still selected, click the Shadow Effects button on the Format tab to display the Shadow Effects gallery.

❷
- Point to Shadow Style 4 in the Shadow Effects gallery to display a live preview of that shadow effect applied to the rectangle shape in the document (Figure 8–62).

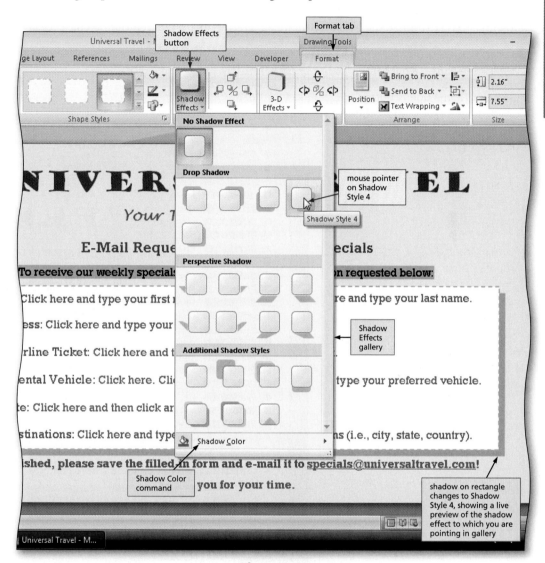

Figure 8–62

Experiment
- Point to various shadows in the Shadow Effects gallery and watch the shadow on the rectangle shape change.

❸
- Click Shadow Style 4 in the Shadow Effects gallery to apply the selected shadow to the rectangle shape.

Q&A

Can I change the color of a shadow?

Yes. Click Shadow Color in the Shadow Effects gallery and then select the desired color in the Shadow Color gallery.

To Customize a Theme Color and Save It with a New Theme Name

The final step in formatting the online form in this chapter is to change the color of the hyperlink. You would like the hyperlink to be darker, to match the company name. A document theme has twelve predefined colors for various on-screen objects including text, backgrounds, and hyperlinks. You can change any of the theme colors. The following steps customize the Foundry theme, changing its designated theme color for hyperlinks.

- Display the Page Layout tab.

- Click the Theme Colors button on the Page Layout tab to display the Theme Colors gallery (Figure 8–63).

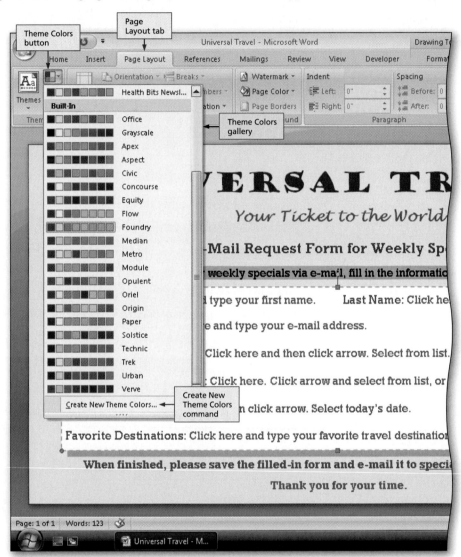

Figure 8–63

2

- Click Create New Theme Colors in the Theme Colors gallery to display the Create New Theme Colors dialog box.

- Click the Hyperlink button to display the Theme Colors gallery (Figure 8–64).

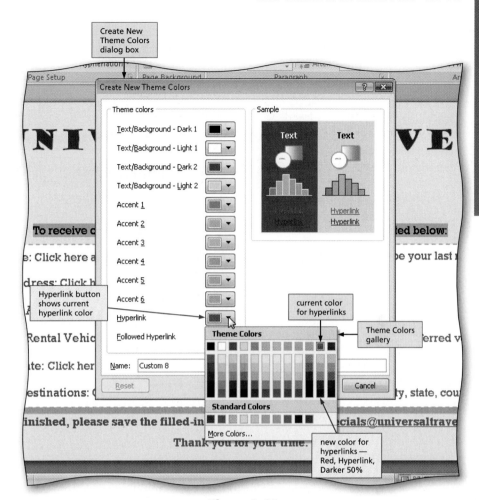

Figure 8–64

3

- Click the bottom color in the Hyperlink column (Red, Hyperlink, Darker 50%) as the new hyperlink color.

 Do I have to select colors in the specified column?

No. Word organizes suggested colors in columns. You can select any color for any item in this dialog box.

- Type Universal Travel Form in the Name text box (Figure 8–65).

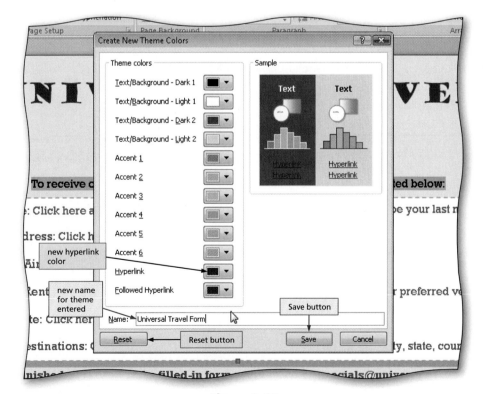

Figure 8–65

4

- Click the Save button in the Create New Theme Colors dialog box to save the modified theme with the name, Universal Travel Form, which is positioned at the top of the Theme Color gallery for future access (Figure 8–66).

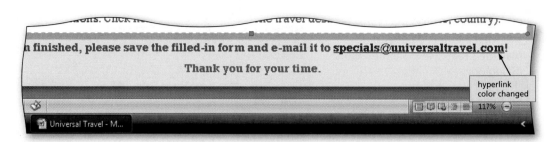

Figure 8–66

Q&A What if I do not enter a name for the modified theme?

Word assigns a name that begins with the letters, Custom, followed by a number (i.e., Custom8).

Q&A What if I wanted to reset all the original theme colors?

You would click the Reset button in the Create New Theme Colors dialog box before clicking the Save button.

Other Ways	
1. Make changes to theme colors, fonts, and/or effects; click Themes on	Page Layout tab, click Save Current Theme in Themes gallery

To Protect a Form

It is crucial that you protect a form before making it available to users. When you **protect a form**, you are allowing users to enter data only in designated areas — specifically, the content controls. The following steps protect the online form.

1

- Display the Developer tab.

- Click the Protect Document button on the Developer tab to display the Restrict Formatting and Editing task pane (Figure 8–67). (If a menu appears instead of the task pane, click Restrict Formatting and Editing on the menu to display the task pane.)

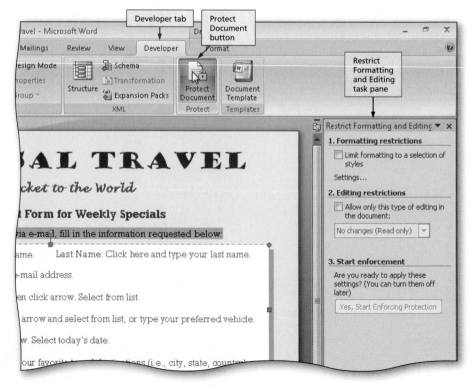
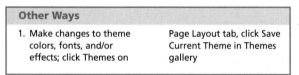

Figure 8–67

- In the Editing restrictions area, place a check mark in the 'Allow only this type of editing in the document' check box and then click its box arrow to display a list of types of allowed restrictions (Figure 8–68).

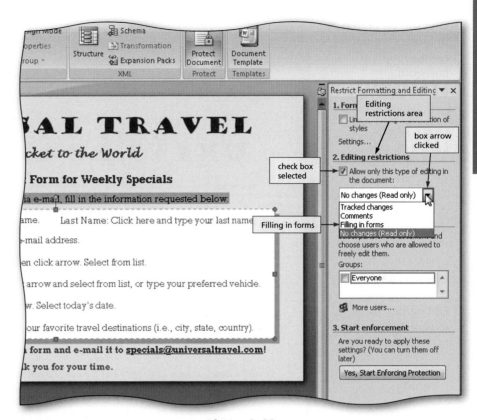

Figure 8–68

3

- Click 'Filling in forms' to instruct Word that the only editing allowed is to content controls in forms.

- In the Start enforcement area, click the Yes, Start Enforcing Protection button, which displays the Start Enforcing Protection dialog box (Figure 8–69).

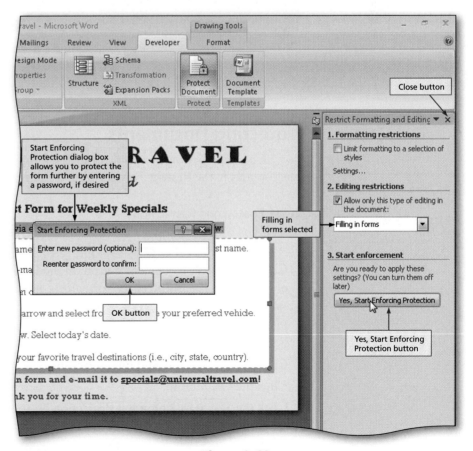

Figure 8–69

4

- Click the OK button to protect the document without a password.

What if I enter a password?

If you enter a password, only a user who knows the password will be able to unprotect the document. Chapter 9 discusses passwords in more depth.

- Close the Restrict Formatting and Editing task pane (Figure 8–70).

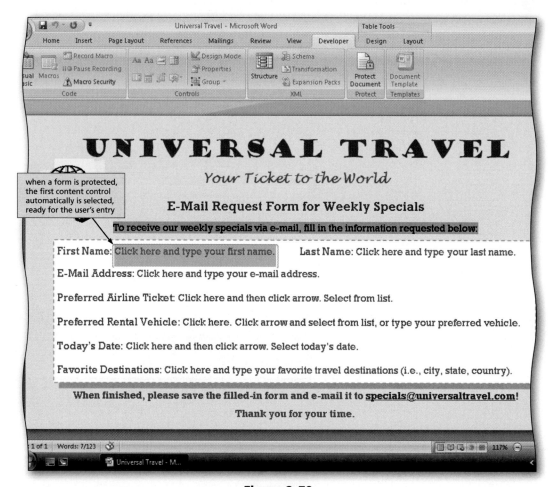

Figure 8–70

Protecting Documents

In addition to protecting a form so that it only can be filled in, Word provides several other options in the Restrict Formatting and Editing task pane.

TO SET FORMATTING RESTRICTIONS

If you wanted to restrict users from making certain types of formatting changes to a document, you would perform the following steps.

1. Click the Protect Document button on the Developer tab. (If a menu appears instead of the task pane, click Restrict Formatting and Editing on the menu to display the task pane.)

2. Place a check mark in the 'Limit formatting to a selection of styles' check box in the Formatting restrictions area.

3. Click the Settings link and then select the types of formatting you want to allow.

4. Click the OK button.

5. Click the Yes, Start Enforcing Protection button, enter a password if desired, and then click the OK button.

To Set Editing Restrictions to Tracked Changes or Comments

If you wanted to restrict users from editing a document, you would perform the following steps.

1. Click the Protect Document button on the Developer tab. (If a menu appears instead of the task pane, click Restrict Formatting and Editing on the menu to display the task pane.)

2. Place a check mark in the 'Allow only this type of editing in the document' check box in the Editing restrictions area, click the box arrow, and then click Tracked changes or Comments.

3. Click the Yes, Start Enforcing Protection button, enter a password if desired, and then click the OK button.

To Hide the Developer Tab

You are finished with the commands on the Developer tab. Thus, the following steps hide the Developer tab from the Ribbon.

1 Click the Office Button and then click the Word Options button on the Office Button menu.

2 If necessary, click Popular in the left pane.

3 If it is selected, remove the check mark in the Show Developer tab in the Ribbon check box.

4 Click the OK button to remove the Developer tab from the Ribbon.

To Save the Template Again

The online form template for this project now is complete. Thus, you should save it and quit Word.

1 Save the template with the same file name, Universal Travel.

2 Quit Word.

Working with an Online Form

When you create a template, you use the Open command on the Office Button menu to open the template so that you can modify it. After you have created a template, you then can make it available to users. Users do not open templates with the Open command in Word. Instead, a user displays a new Word document that is based on the template, which means the title bar displays the default file name, Document1 (or a similar name) rather than the template name. When Word displays a document that is based on a template, the document window contains any text and formatting associated with the template. Word provides a variety of templates such as those for memos, letters, fax cover sheets, and resumes. If a user accesses a memo template, Word displays the contents of a basic memo in a new document window.

BTW

Protected Documents
If you open an existing form that has been protected, Word will not allow you to modify the form's appearance until you unprotect it. To unprotect a document, click the Protect Document button on the Developer tab (if a menu appears instead of the task pane, click Restrict Formatting and Editing on the menu to display the task pane), click the Stop Protection button in the Restrict Formatting and Editing task pane, and then close the Restrict Formatting and Editing task pane. If the form has been protected with a password, you will be asked to enter the password when you attempt to unprotect the document.

To Use Windows Explorer to Display a New Document That Is Based on a Template

When you save the template to a USB flash drive, as instructed earlier in this chapter, a user can display a new document that is based on the template through Windows Explorer. This allows the user to work with a new document instead of risking the chance of altering the original template. The following steps display a new Word document that is based on the Universal Travel template.

- Click the Start button on the Windows Vista taskbar to display the Start menu (Figure 8–71).

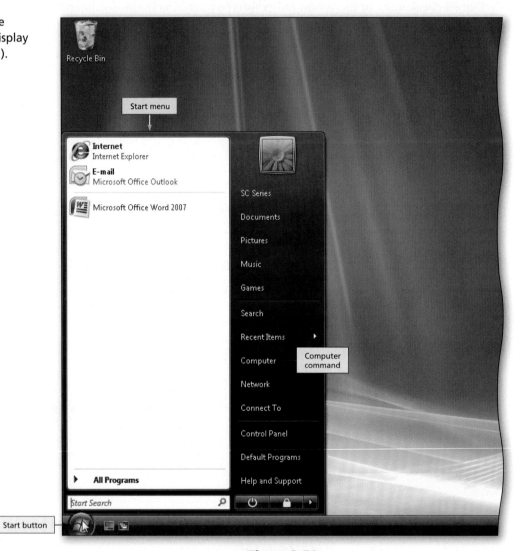

Figure 8–71

BTW

Internet Explorer vs. Windows Explorer
Internet Explorer is a Web browser included with the Windows operating system. Windows Explorer is a file manager that is included with the Windows operating system. It enables you to perform functions related to file management, such as displaying a list of files, organizing files, and copying files.

2

- Click Computer on the Start menu to display the Explorer window.

- When the Explorer window opens, if necessary, locate your USB flash drive.

- Click the Universal Travel file to select it (Figure 8–72).

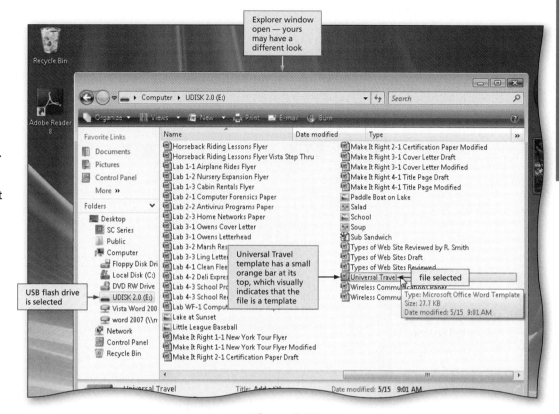

Figure 8–72

3

- Double-click the Universal Travel file in the Explorer window, which starts Word and displays a new document window that is based on the contents of the Universal Travel template (Figure 8–73).

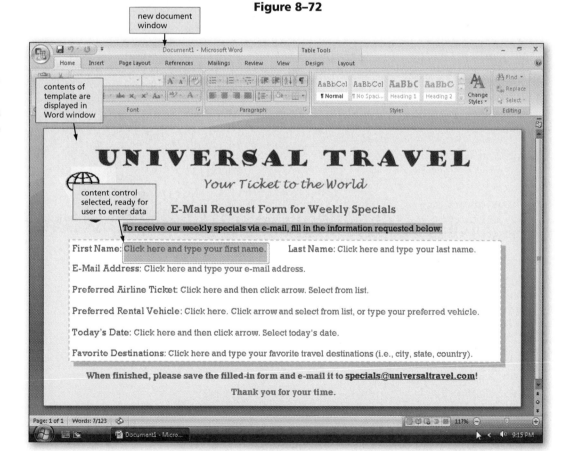

Figure 8–73

To Fill In a Form and Save It

The next step is to enter data in the form. To advance from one content control to the next, a user can click the content control or press the TAB key. To move to a previous content control, a user can click it or press SHIFT+TAB. The following steps fill in the Universal Travel form.

1

- With the First Name content control selected, type Howard and then press the TAB key.

- Type Blasdel in the Last Name content control and then press the TAB key.

- Type blasdel@worldlink .net in the E-Mail Address content control.

- Press the TAB key to select the Preferred Airline Ticket content control and then click its arrow to display the list of choices (shown in Figure 8–1b on page WD 571).

- Click Business in the list and then press the TAB key.

- Type Convertible in the Preferred Rental Vehicle content control and then press the TAB key.

- Click the Today's Date arrow to display the calendar (Figure 8–74).

2

- Click May 29, 2008 in the calendar and then press the TAB key.

- Type Orlando, Florida, and Paris, France in the Favorite Destinations content control to complete the entries in the form (Figure 8–75).

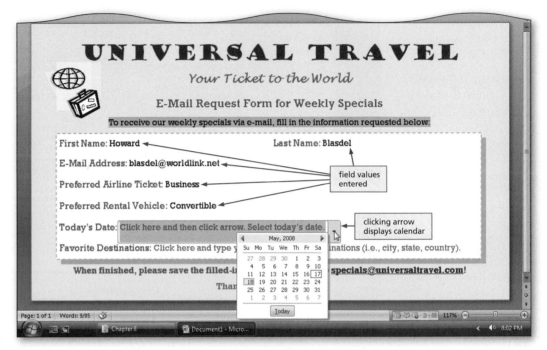

Figure 8–74

Figure 8–75

3

- Click the Save button on the Quick Access Toolbar and then save the file on your USB flash drive with the file name, Blasdel E-Mail Request Form.

Q&A Can I print the form?

You can print the document as you print any other document. Keep in mind, however, that the colors used were designed for viewing online. Thus, different color schemes would have been selected if the form had been designed for a printout.

Working with Templates

If you want to modify the template, open it by clicking the Open command on the Office Button menu, clicking the template name, and then clicking the Open button in the dialog box. Then, you must **unprotect the form** by clicking the Protect Document button on the Developer tab and then clicking the Stop Protection button in the Restrict Formatting and Editing task pane. (If a menu appears instead of the task pane when you click the Protect Document button, click Restrict Formatting and Editing on the menu to display the task pane.)

When you created the template in this chapter, you saved it on a USB flash drive. In environments other than an academic setting, you would not save the template on a USB flash drive. Instead, you would save it in the Templates folder, which is the folder Word initially displays in the Save As dialog box for a template file type (shown in Figure 8–3 on page WD 574). When you save a template in the Templates folder, you can locate the template by clicking the Office Button, clicking New, and then clicking My templates, which displays the template in the New dialog box (Figure 8–76).

BTW

Conserving Ink and Toner
You can instruct Word to print draft quality documents to conserve ink or toner by clicking the Office Button, clicking the Word Options button, clicking Advanced in the left pane of the Word Options dialog box, scrolling to the Print area, placing a check mark in the 'Use draft quality' check box, and then clicking the OK button. Click the Office Button, point to Print, and then click Quick Print.

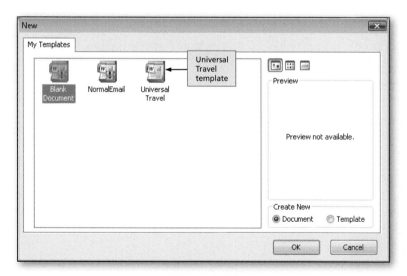

Figure 8–76

To Quit Word

The final steps are to quit Word and close Windows Explorer.

1 Quit Word.

2 If Windows Explorer is still open, close the window.

Chapter Summary

In this chapter, you have learned how to create an online form. Topics covered included saving a document as a template, changing paper size, inserting content controls, editing placeholder text, changing properties of content controls, using the Format Painter, and protecting a form. The items listed below include all the new Word skills you have learned in this chapter.

1. Save a Document as a Template (WD 574)
2. Change Paper Size (WD 577)
3. Adjust the Contrast of a Graphic (WD 584)
4. Highlight Text (WD 586)
5. Show the Developer Tab (WD 588)
6. Insert a Borderless Table in a Form (WD 589)
7. Show Gridlines (WD 592)
8. Insert a Plain Text Content Control (WD 593)
9. Edit Placeholder Text (WD 594)
10. Change the Properties of a Plain Text Content Control (WD 595)
11. Hide Gridlines (WD 599)
12. Insert a Drop-Down List Content Control (WD 601)
13. Change the Properties of a Drop-Down List Content Control (WD 602)
14. Insert a Combo Box Content Control (WD 604)
15. Change the Properties of a Combo Box Content Control (WD 605)
16. Insert a Date Content Control (WD 606)
17. Change the Properties of a Date Content Control (WD 607)
18. Insert a Rich Text Content Control (WD 608)
19. Change the Properties of a Rich Text Content Control (WD 609)
20. Use the Format Painter Button (WD 611)
21. Draw a Rectangle (WD 613)
22. Send a Graphic Behind Text (WD 614)
23. Apply a Shape Style (WD 616)
24. Add a Shadow to a Shape (WD 617)
25. Customize a Theme Color and Save It with a New Theme Name (WD 618)
26. Protect a Form (WD 620)
27. Set Formatting Restrictions (WD 622)
28. Set Editing Restrictions to Tracked Changes or Comments (WD 623)
29. Hide the Developer Tab (WD 623)
30. Use Windows Explorer to Display a New Document That Is Based on a Template (WD 624)
31. Fill In a Form and Save It (WD 626)

If you have a SAM user profile, you may have access to hands-on instruction, practice, and assessment. Log in to your SAM account (http://sam2007.course.com) to launch any assigned training activities or exams that relate to the skills covered in this chapter.

BTW

Quick Reference
For a table that lists how to complete the tasks covered in this book using the mouse, Ribbon, shortcut menu, and keyboard, see the Quick Reference Summary at the back of this book, or visit the Word 2007 Quick Reference Web page (scsite.com/wd2007/qr).

Learn It Online

Test your knowledge of chapter content and key terms.

Instructions: To complete the Learn It Online exercises, start your browser, click the Address bar, and then enter the Web address scsite.com/wd2007/learn. When the Word 2007 Learn It Online page is displayed, click the link for the exercise you want to complete and then read the instructions.

Chapter Reinforcement TF, MC, and SA
A series of true/false, multiple choice, and short answer questions that test your knowledge of the chapter content.

Flash Cards
An interactive learning environment where you identify chapter key terms associated with displayed definitions.

Practice Test
A series of multiple choice questions that test your knowledge of chapter content and key terms.

Who Wants To Be a Computer Genius?
An interactive game that challenges your knowledge of chapter content in the style of a television quiz show.

Wheel of Terms
An interactive game that challenges your knowledge of chapter key terms in the style of the television show *Wheel of Fortune*.

Crossword Puzzle Challenge
A crossword puzzle that challenges your knowledge of key terms presented in the chapter.

Apply Your Knowledge

Reinforce the skills and apply the concepts you learned in this chapter.

Filling In an Online Form
Instructions: In this assignment, you access a template through Windows Explorer. The template contains an online form. You are to fill in the form, save it, and print it. The template is located on the Data Files for Students. See the inside back cover of this book for instructions on downloading the Data Files for Students, or contact your instructor for information about accessing the required files.

Perform the following tasks:
1. Start Windows Explorer. In the Explorer window, select the USB flash drive. Double-click the Apply 8-1 That Pool Place template in Windows Explorer.
2. When Word displays a new document based on the Apply 8-1 That Pool Place template, if necessary, hide formatting marks and change the zoom to page width. Your screen should look like Figure 8–77 on the next page.
3. With the First Name content control selected, type Celaine and then press the TAB key.
4. With the Last Name content control selected, type Raam and then press the TAB key.
5. Click the Today's Date content control arrow, click May 29, 2008 in the calendar and then press the TAB key.
6. With the E-Mail Address content control selected, type cr@linkworld.net and then press the TAB key.
7. Click the Pool Size content control arrow and then review the list. Press the ESCAPE key because none of these choices meets your criteria. Type 7,000 gallons as the pool size and then press the TAB key.
8. Click the Type of Pool content control arrow and then click Liner in the list.

Continued >

Apply Your Knowledge *continued*

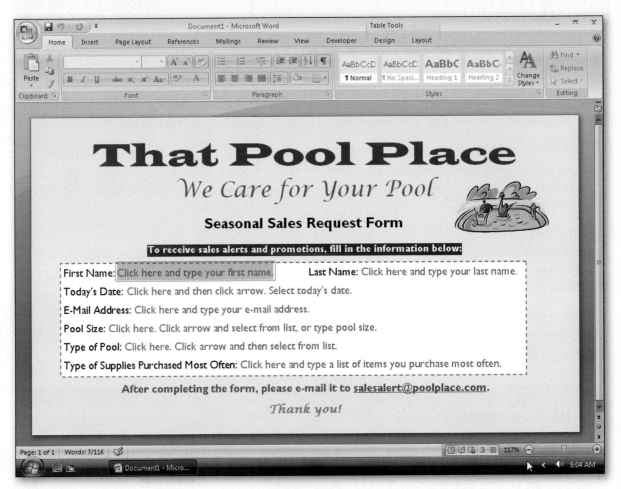

Figure 8–77

9. Click the Type of Supplies Purchased Most Often content control and then type chlorine and water test kits as the supplies.

10. Save the file with the name Apply 8-1 Raam Form. Print the form. Close the document.

11. Open the Apply 8-1 That Pool Place template from the Data Files for Students.

12. Unprotect the Apply 8-1 That Pool Place template.

13. Save the template with a new name, Apply 8-1 That Pool Place Modified.

14. Change the Today's Date content control to the format M/d/yyyy (i.e., 5/20/2008).

15. Adjust the contrast of the graphic to +30 %.

16. Protect the modified template.

17. Save the modified template.

18. Print the modified template.

Extend Your Knowledge

Extend the skills you learned in this chapter and experiment with new skills. You may need to use Help to complete the assignment.

Working with Picture Content Controls, Text Boxes, Shadows, Themes, and Passwords

Instructions: Start Word. Open the document, Extend 8-1 Pampered Pals Draft, from the Data Files for Students. See the inside back cover of this book for instructions on downloading the Data Files for Students, or contact your instructor for information about accessing the required files.

You will add a pattern fill effect to the page color, add a picture content control in a text box and format the text box, rotate graphics, change the highlight color, change the shadow color, nudge the shadow, change theme colors, reset theme colors, save a modified theme, and protect a form with a password.

Perform the following tasks:

1. Use Help to review and expand your knowledge about these topics: fill effects, picture content controls, text boxes, rotating graphics, shadows, changing theme colors, and protecting forms with passwords.

2. Add a pattern fill effect, of your choice, to the page color.

3. Add a simple text box to the empty space in the bottom-right corner of the data entry area. Resize the text box so that it fits completely in the data entry area.

4. In the text box, type the label, Pet Photo:, and then below the label, insert a picture content control. Resize the picture content control so that it fits in the text box (Figure 8–78). Remove the border from the text box.

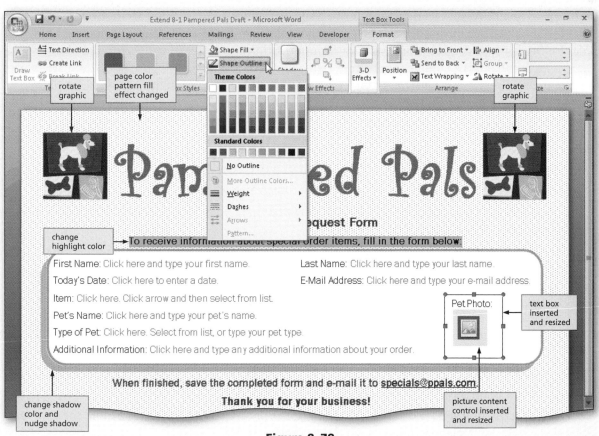

Figure 8–78

Continued >

Extend Your Knowledge *continued*

5. Rotate the graphics at the top of the form so that the dogs are angled instead of horizontal. If necessary, move the rotated graphics so that they do not cover text in the form title.

6. Change the highlight color of the third line of text to a color other than Gray-25%. If necessary, change the text color so that you can read the text in the new highlight color.

7. Change the color of the shadow on the rectangle to a color other than the default.

8. Nudge the shadow up, down, left, and/or right so that it looks different from the default shadow.

9. Change the theme colors for Text/Background - Dark 1 and Accent 3. Reset the theme colors.

10. Change the theme colors for Accent 1 and Hyperlink. Save the modified theme colors.

11. Make any necessary formatting changes to the form.

12. Protect the form with a password.

13. Change the document properties as specified by your instructor.

14. Save the revised document with a new file name.

15. Test the form. When filling in the form, use the picture called Dog on the Data Files for Students for the picture content control.

16. Submit the online form in the format specified by your instructor.

Make It Right

Analyze a document and correct all errors and/or improve the design.

Formatting an Online Form

Instructions: Start Word. Open the document, Make It Right 8-1 Party Tunes Draft, from the Data Files for Students. See the inside back cover of this book for instructions on downloading the Data Files for Students, or contact your instructor for information about accessing the required files.

The document is an online form whose elements are not formatted (Figure 8–79). You are to change the graphic's wrapping style; change the page color; change fonts, font sizes, and font colors; change the graphic's contrast; remove the table border; edit placeholder text; change content control properties; use the Format Painter; draw a rectangle and format it; and protect the form.

Perform the following tasks:

1. Change the graphic's wrapping style to In Front of Text.

2. Change the page color to a color of your choice (other than white).

3. Change the font, font size, and font color for the first three lines and last two lines of text. Center the five lines.

4. Change the graphic's contrast and move the graphic to an appropriate location on the form.

5. Remove the border from the 2 × 1 table that surrounds the First Name and Last Name content controls. Show table gridlines.

6. Edit all placeholder text so that each content control contains meaningful instructions.

7. For each content control, change the properties as follows: add a title and set the locking so that the content control cannot be deleted.

8. Change the format of the First Name: label. Use the Format Painter to copy the formatting to all other labels in the data entry area of the form.

9. Draw a rectangle around the data entry area. Format the rectangle so that it is behind the text. Add a shape style and a shadow to the rectangle.

10. Hide table gridlines. Protect the form.

11. Change the document properties as specified by your instructor.

12. Save the revised document with a new file name and then submit it in the format specified by your instructor.

13. Save the revised document with a new file name. Test the form.

14. Submit the online form in the format specified by your instructor.

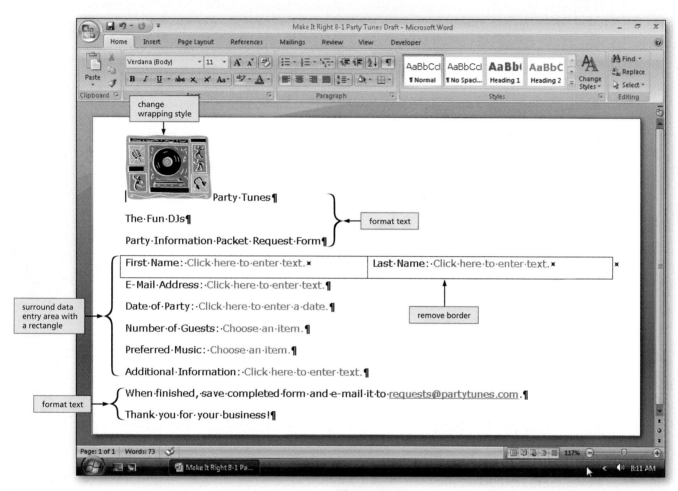

Figure 8–79

In the Lab

Design and/or create a document using the guidelines, concepts, and skills presented in this chapter. Labs are listed in order of increasing difficulty.

Lab 1: Creating an Online Form

Problem: You work as a part-time assistant at Andrew County Public Library. Your supervisor has asked you to prepare the event notification request form shown in Figure 8–80.

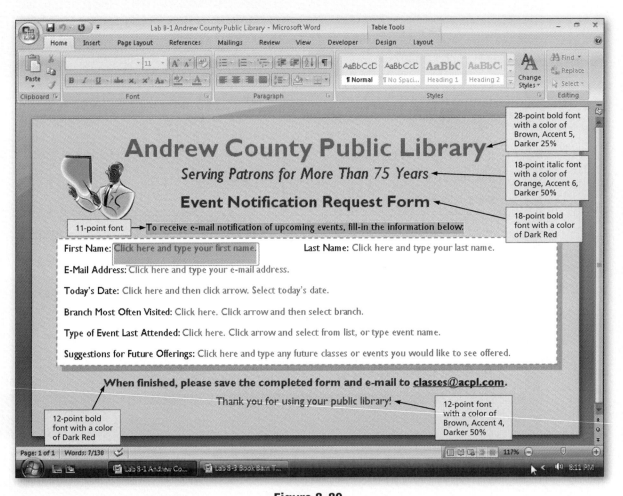

Figure 8–80

Perform the following tasks:

1. Save a blank document as a template, called Lab 8-1 Andrew County Public Library, for the online form.

2. If necessary, change the view to page width.

3. Change the paper size to a height of 8.5 inches and a width of 4.75 inches.

4. Change the margins as follows: top — 0.25", bottom — 0", left — 0.5", and right — 0.5".

5. Change the theme fonts to Origin. Change the theme colors to Trek.

6. Change the page color to Light Yellow, Background 2, Darker 10%.

7. Enter and format the company name, business tag line, and form title as shown in Figure 8–80 (or with similar fonts). Insert the clip art image (which is installed by default with Word). Change the wrapping style of the graphic to In Front of Text. If necessary, resize the graphic and move to the location shown.

8. Enter the instructions above the data entry area and highlight the line Gray-25%.

9. In the data entry area, enter the labels as shown in Figure 8–80 and the content controls as follows: First Name, Last Name, and E-Mail Address are plain text content controls. Today's Date is a date content control. Branch Most Often Visited is a drop-down list content control with these choices: River Fork, Eakins, Main, and Manning. Type of Event Last Attended is a combo box content control with these choices: Computer Class, Author Lecture, Book Discussion, Children's Program, and Craft/Hobby Class. Suggestions for Future Offerings is a rich text content control.

10. Edit the placeholder text of all content controls to match Figure 8–80. Change the properties of the content controls so that each contains a title and all have locking set so that the content control cannot be deleted.

11. Enter the two lines below the data entry area as shown in Figure 8–80.

12. Adjust spacing above and below paragraphs as necessary so that all contents fit on a single screen.

13. Draw a rectangle around the data entry area. Change the shape style of the rectangle to Dashed Outline - Accent 5. Apply Shadow Style 4 to the rectangle.

14. Protect the form.

15. Save the form again and submit it in the format specified by your instructor.

16. Access the template through Windows Explorer. Fill in the form using personal data and submit it in the format specified by your instructor.

In the Lab

Lab 2: Creating an Online Form with Clip Art from the Web

Problem: You work part-time for Entrée Express, a company that delivers meals to the customer's door. Your supervisor has asked you to prepare the online weekly menu request form shown in Figure 8–81.

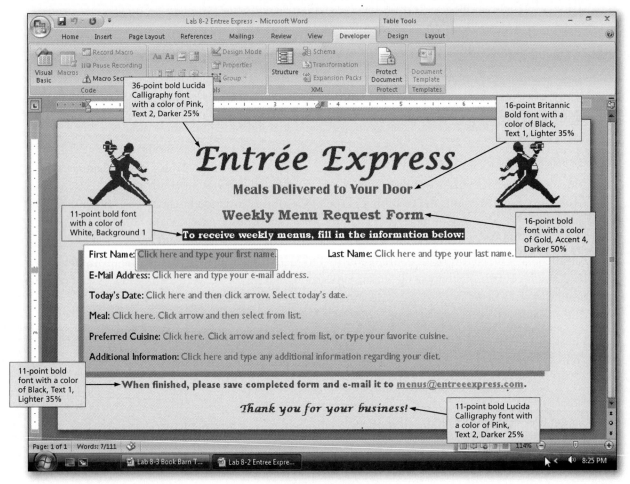

Figure 8–81

Perform the following tasks:

1. Save a blank document as a template, called Lab 8-2 Entree Express, for the online form.

2. If necessary, change the view to page width.

3. Change the paper size to a height of 8.5 inches and a width of 4.75 inches.

4. Change the margins as follows: top — 0.25", bottom — 0", left — 0.5", and right — 0.5".

5. Change the theme fonts to Origin. Change the theme colors to Opulent.

6. Change the page color to Orange, Accent 6, Lighter 80%.

7. Enter and format the company name, business tag line, and form title as shown in Figure 8–81 (or with similar fonts). Locate a clip art image on the Web similar to the one in the figure (or insert the image on the Data Files for Students) and insert it twice. Change the wrapping style of the graphics to In Front of Text. If necessary, resize the graphics. Move the graphics to the locations shown. Flip the graphic on the right.

8. Enter the instructions above the data entry area and highlight the line violet.

9. In the data entry area, enter the labels as shown in Figure 8–81 and the content controls as follows: First Name, Last Name, and E-Mail Address are plain text content controls. Today's Date is a date content control. Meal is a drop-down list content control with these choices: Breakfast, Lunch, and Dinner. Preferred Cuisine is a combo box content control with these choices: American, Asian, French, Italian, Mexican, Southwestern, and Vegetarian. Additional Information is a rich text content control.

10. Edit the placeholder text of all content controls to match Figure 8–81. Change the properties of the content controls so that each contains a title and all have locking set so that the content control cannot be deleted.

11. Enter the two lines below the data entry area as shown in Figure 8–81.

12. Adjust spacing above and below paragraphs as necessary so that all contents fit on the screen.

13. Change the theme color for the hyperlink color to Light Yellow, Hyperlink, Darker 50%.

14. Draw a rectangle around the data entry area. Change the shape style of the rectangle to Linear Up Gradient - Accent 5. Apply Shadow Style 3 to the rectangle.

15. Protect the form.

16. Save the form again and submit it in the format specified by your instructor.

17. Access the template through Windows Explorer. Fill in the form using personal data and submit it in the format specified by your instructor.

In the Lab

Lab 3: Creating an Online Form with Clip Art from the Web and a Texture Fill Effect

Problem: You work part-time for the Book Barn, a bookshop that specializes in rare and out-of-print books. Your supervisor has asked you to prepare an e-mail request form.

Perform the following tasks:

1. Save a blank document as a template, called Lab 8-3 Book Barn, for the online form.

2. If necessary, change the view to page width.

3. Change the paper size to a height of 8.5 inches and a width of 4.75 inches.

4. Change the margins as follows: top — 0.25", bottom — 0", left — 0.5", and right — 0.5".

5. Change the theme fonts to Office. Change the theme colors to Aspect.

6. Change the page color to Tan, Background 2, Darker 10%.

7. Enter and format the company name, business tag line, and form title as shown in Figure 8–82 on the next page (or with similar fonts). Locate a clip art image on the Web similar to the one in the figure. Change the wrapping style of the graphic to In Front of Text. If necessary, resize the graphic and move it to the location shown.

8. Enter the instructions above the data entry area and highlight the line dark yellow.

9. In the data entry area, enter the labels as shown in Figure 8–82 and the content controls as follows: First Name, Last Name, and E-Mail Address are plain text content controls. Today's Date is a date content control. Genre is a combo box content control with these choices: Mystery, Science Fiction, Romance, Historical, Juvenile, and Nonfiction. Second Choice If Written Book Is Unavailable is a drop-down list content control with these choices: Audio Book and DVD/VHS Movie. Particular Items Sought is a rich text content control.

10. Edit the placeholder text of all content controls to match Figure 8–82. Change the properties of the content controls so that each contains a title and all have locking specified so that the content control cannot be deleted.

Continued >

In the Lab continued

11. Enter the two lines below the data entry area as shown in Figure 8–82.

12. Change the font size and color of the E-Mail Address: label as shown in Figure 8–82. Use the Format Painter to copy the format from this label to the remaining labels in the data entry area of the form.

13. Adjust spacing above and below paragraphs as necessary so that all contents fit on the screen.

14. Draw a rectangle around the data entry area. Change the shape style of the rectangle to Compound Outline - Accent 2. Add the Parchment texture fill effect to the rectangle. Apply Shadow Style 4 to the rectangle. Color the shadow Red, Accent 2.

15. Protect the form.

16. Save the form again and submit it in the format specified by your instructor.

17. Access the template through Windows Explorer. Fill in the form using personal data and submit it in the format specified by your instructor.

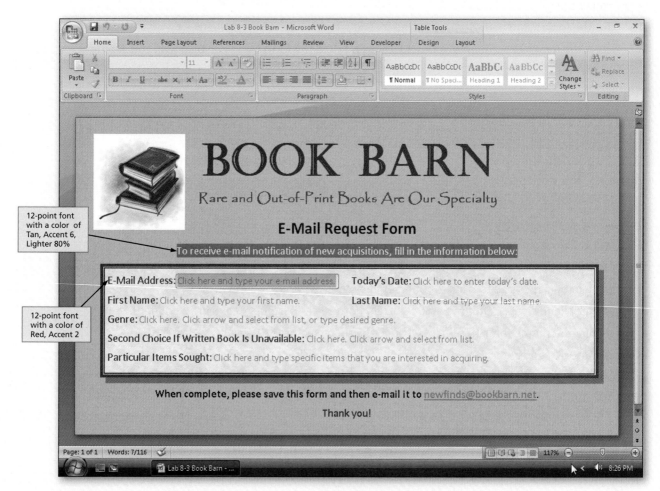

Figure 8–82

Cases and Places

Apply your creative thinking and problem solving skills to design and implement a solution.

• EASIER   •• MORE DIFFICULT

• 1: Create an Online Form for an Auto Dealership

Your boss at Cool Ride Auto Sales, a new and used car dealership, recently decided to explore online auto sales. He has asked you to create an online form that customers can complete when they have an inquiry about purchasing a car. Create a template that contains the business name (Cool Ride Auto Sales), the business tag line (Quality Cars – Guaranteed!), and appropriate clip art. The third line should have the text, Auto Search Form. The fourth line should be highlighted and should read: To receive information, fill in the information requested below:. The data entry area should contain two plain text content controls on the first line placed within a table: First Name and Last Name. The second line should contain a plain text content control with the label, E-Mail Address. The third line should contain a drop-down list content control with the label, Price Range. The choices for this drop-down list are as follows: < $5,000; $5,000 – $10,000; $10,000 – $20,000; $20,000 – $30,000; and > $30,000. The fourth line should contain a combo box content control with the label, Desired Style. The choices for this content control are Sedan, SUV, Van/Minivan, Truck, Sports Car, and Luxury. The fifth line should contain a date content control with the label, Today's Date. The sixth line in the data entry area should have a rich text content control with the label, Additional Information. Below the data entry area, add this message: Save this form and e-mail to deals@coolrides.com. On the last line, include the text: Thank you for your time. Use meaningful instructional text for all content controls. (For example, the instructional text for the First Name text box content control could be as follows: Click here and then type your first name.) Draw a rectangle around the data entry area of the form. Add a shadow to the rectangle. Protect the form and test it.

•• 2: Create an Online Form for a Real Estate Office

You work part-time for your neighbor's real estate office. She has asked you to design a template for an online information form that prospective buyers can complete to receive information about new listings that might interest them. The top of the form should have the name of the real estate office (Richards Realty), with the tag line: Great homes at great prices. The third line should be: New Listing Alert Request Form. The fourth line should read: For information about new listings, fill in the information below. Be sure to highlight this line so that it stands out. Include appropriate clip art, and add plain text content controls for buyer's first name, last name, and e-mail address. Add a drop-down list content control with the label, Type of House. The choices for this content control should include the following: Condo, Ranch, Two-Story, Split-Level. Use a combo box content control with the label, Price Range. The choices should include the following: $100,000 – $150,000; $150,000 – $200,000; $200,000 – $300,000; and > $300,000. Include a date content control so that form users can enter the current date and a rich text content control where they can provide additional information about their home search. Use meaningful instructional text for all content controls. Draw a rectangle with a shadow around the data entry area. Protect the form and test it.

•• 3: Create an Online Form for a Property Management Agency

As a part-time assistant at Sunshine Rentals, you have been assigned the project of designing an online form that clients can access via the Web in order to inquire about rental properties in Florida. Include the company name and appropriate clip art, as well as the tag line: We Cover All of Florida! The third line should read: Rental Request Form. The fourth line should be highlighted and should read: Complete the form below to receive rental information. Include plain text content controls for all pertinent information, such as first name, last name, and e-mail address. Add a drop-down list content

Continued >

Cases and Places *continued*

control for general location (North, South, East, West, Central, and Island). Use a combo box content control for type of unit (Condo, House, Hotel/Motel, and Cabin). Provide a plain text content control for number of guests and a date content control for the date. Include another combo box content control labeled, Desired Amenities, with these choices: Pool, Kitchen, Pets Allowed, Kitchen, Beachside, Beach Access, Wheelchair Access. Use meaningful instructional text for all content controls. Draw a rectangle with a shadow around the data entry area. Protect the form and test it.

•• 4: Create an Online Form for Your Future Business

Make It Personal

Most people, at some point, wish they owned their own business, or at least worked for themselves rather than someone else. Considering your major and/or your job skills and experience, what type of business would you open if you could? With this choice in mind, design an online form that would help facilitate your business. The form could gather information from customers or disperse information to them. Use the techniques and skills you learned in this chapter to design the form. Include appropriate clip art, a company name and tag line, and other appropriate elements. Add content controls to the form as necessary. Use meaningful instructional text for all content controls. When the form is complete, protect it and test it.

•• 5: Create an Online Form for Your School

Working Together

For this assignment, you will form a team to investigate a campus organization, club, or facility that could benefit from using an online form. For example, a fitness facility might benefit from an online form that alerts members to open court times or special events. The library might find it easier if it could inform patrons of new books and other publications and materials as they become available. A club or organization might use an online form to gather information about members' interests or inform members of upcoming events or meetings. Once you have made your choice, as a team, choose a title, clip art, and tag line. Decide on the overall design of the form, as well as the fonts, colors, and other visual elements. Each member then should design an area of the form. First, determine what information is required for the form to be effective and helpful. Then, decide which choices to include in the various content controls you include. Be sure to include at least one of each of the following content controls: plain text, combo box, drop-down list, rich text box, building block, and photo. Use the techniques and skills you learned in this chapter to format and design the form so that it is attractive and easy to use.

9 | Enhancing an Online Form and Working with Macros, Document Security, and XML

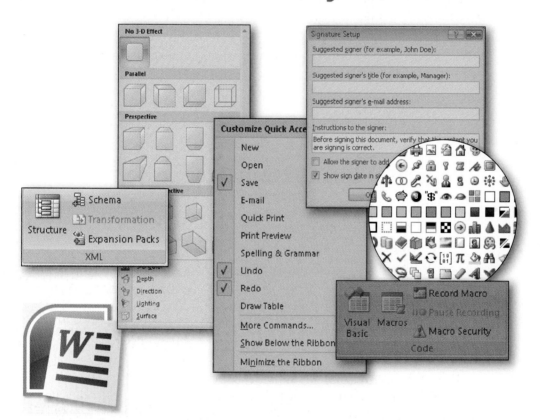

Objectives

You will have mastered the material in this chapter when you can:

- Unprotect a document
- Specify macro settings
- Use fill effects
- Convert a table to text
- Add a 3-D effect to a shape
- Rotate a graphic
- Insert and edit a field
- Record and execute a macro

- Customize the Quick Access Toolbar
- Edit a macro's VBA code
- Save a document with a password
- Use the Document Inspector
- Add a signature line or a digital signature
- Work with XML

9 | Enhancing an Online Form and Working with Macros, Document Security, and XML

Introduction

Word provides many tools that allow you to improve the appearance, functionality, and security of your documents, as well as provide formats for sharing document data with other programs. This chapter discusses tools used to perform the following tasks:

- Enhance the look of graphics and shapes with fill effects and 3-D effects.
- Automate a series of tasks with a macro.
- Secure a document with digital signatures, passwords, and other settings.
- Use XML formats if data will be shared with other programs.

Project — Online Form Revised

This chapter is divided into three separate projects:

1. The first improves the visual appearance of and adds macros to the online form created in Chapter 8.
2. The second incorporates security in a document.
3. The third uses XML so that a document's data can be shared and re-used by other programs.

The first project in this chapter uses Word to produce the online form shown in Figure 9–1a. This project begins with the Universal Travel online form created in Chapter 8. Thus, you will need the online form template created in Chapter 8 to complete this project. (If you did not create the template, see your instructor for a copy.)

This project modifies the fonts and font colors of the text in the Universal Travel online form and enhances the contents of the form to include a texture fill effect, a 3-D effect, and a picture fill effect. The graphic in the form is rotated, and the date automatically displays the computer date, instead of requiring the user to enter the date.

This form also includes macros to automate tasks. A **macro** is a set of commands and instructions grouped together to allow a user to accomplish a task automatically. One macro allows the user to hide the Developer tab by pressing a shortcut key or clicking a button on the Quick Access Toolbar. Another macro specifies how the form is displayed initially on a user's Word screen. As shown in Figure 9–1b, when a document contains macros, Word may generate security warnings that allow you to enable or disable macros. If you are sure the macros are from a trusted source and free of viruses, then enable the macros. Otherwise, disable them to protect your computer from potentially harmful viruses or other malicious software.

The second and third projects are presented when they are discussed later in the chapter.

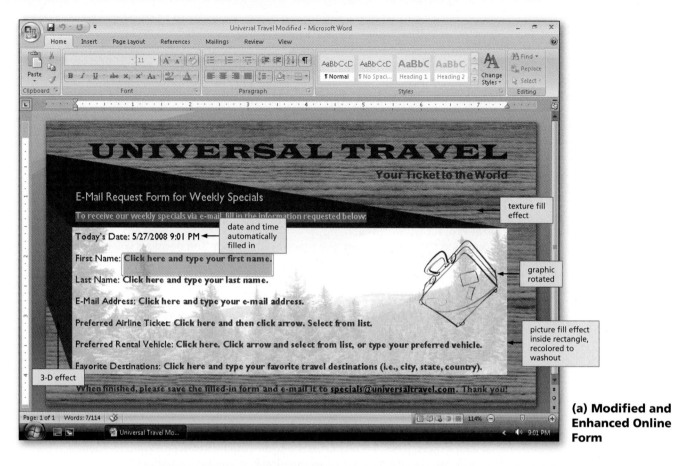

(a) Modified and Enhanced Online Form

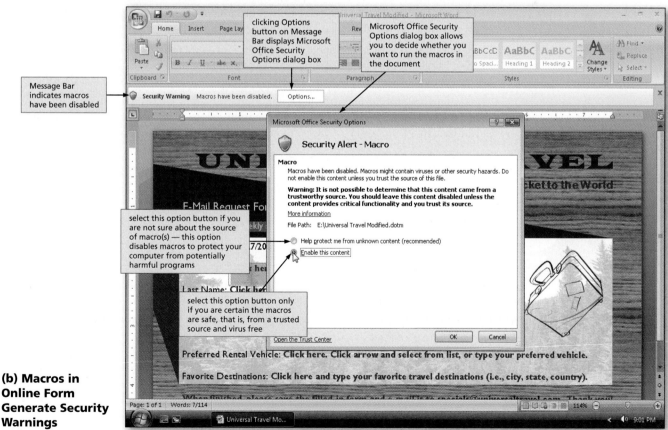

(b) Macros in Online Form Generate Security Warnings

Figure 9–1

Overview

As you read through this chapter, you will learn how to create the online form shown in Figure 9–1 on the previous page, make a document more secure, and prepare a document data for use in other programs by performing these general tasks:

- Enhance the look of an online form.
- Add macros to automate tasks.
- Incorporate security in a document.
- Use XML.

Plan Ahead

General Project Guidelines

When creating a Word document, the actions you perform and decisions you make will affect the appearance and characteristics of the finished document. As you enhance an online form, such as the project shown in Figure 9–1, add macros, incorporate security, and use XML, you should follow these general guidelines:

1. **Save the form to be modified as a macro-enabled template.** If you plan to include macros in a template for a form, be sure to save the template as a macro-enabled template. Basic Word templates cannot store macros.

2. **Enhance the visual appeal of a form.** Use colors and images that complement one another. Draw the user's attention to important sections. Arrange data entry fields in logical groups on the form and in an order that users would expect.

3. **Add macros to automate tasks.** In Word, a macro consists of VBA code. **VBA**, which stands for **Visual Basic for Applications**, is a powerful programming language included with Word that allows users to customize and extend the capabilities of Word. Word can generate the VBA code associated with a macro automatically, or you can write the VBA code yourself. To add macros, you do not need a computer programming background. To write VBA code, however, you should be familiar with computer programming.

4. **Incorporate security in a document.** Word provides several tools that allow you to secure your documents. For example, you can add a digital signature, insert a signature line, mark the document as final, save the document with a password, and customize Word settings.

5. **Determine how the form data will be analyzed.** If the data entered in the form will be analyzed by a program outside of Word, create the data entry fields so that the entries are stored in a format, such as XML, that can be shared with other programs.

When necessary, more specific details concerning the above guidelines are presented at appropriate points in the chapter. The chapter also will identify the actions performed and decisions made regarding these guidelines during the creation of the documents in this chapter.

To Start Word

If you are using a computer to step through the project in this chapter and you want your screens to match the figures in this book, you should change your computer's resolution to 1024 × 768. For information about how to change a computer's resolution, read Appendix D.

The following steps start Word and verify Word settings.

1 Start Word.

2 If the Word window is not maximized, click its Maximize button.

3 If the Print Layout button on the status bar is not selected, click it so that Word is in Print Layout view.

If the rulers are displayed, click the View Ruler button on the vertical scroll bar because you will not use the rulers to perform tasks in this project.

 If the edges of the page do not extend to the edge of the document window, click View on the Ribbon and then click Page Width on the View tab to zoom page width.

To Save a Macro-Enabled Template

The first project in this chapter contains macros. To provide added security to templates, a basic Word template does not contain macros. Word instead provides a specific type of template, called a **macro-enabled template**, in which you can store macros. Thus, the first step in this chapter is to open the Universal Travel template created in Chapter 8 and to save it as a macro-enabled template. (If you did not create the template, see your instructor for a copy.) The following steps open an existing Word template from a USB flash drive and then save it with a new name as a Word macro-enabled template.

1
- Open the template named Universal Travel from the USB flash drive.

2
- Click the Office Button and then click Save As on the Office Button menu to display the Save As dialog box.

- Type Universal Travel Modified in the File name text box to change the file name.

- Click the Save as type box arrow and then click Word Macro-Enabled Template in the list to change the file type (Figure 9–2).

3
- Click the Save button in the Save As dialog box to save the file called Universal Travel Modified as a macro-enabled template on the USB flash drive.

Q&A

How does Word differentiate between a Word template and a Word macro-enabled template?

A Word template has an extension of .dotx, whereas a Word macro-enabled template has an extension of .dotm. Also, the icon for a macro-enabled template contains an exclamation point.

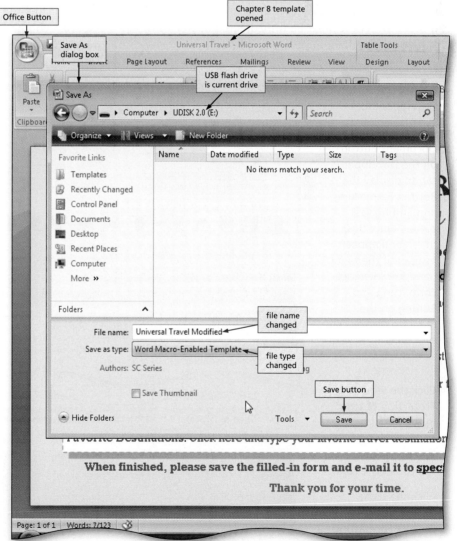

Figure 9–2

BTW

Macro-Enabled Documents

The steps on the previous page showed how to create a macro-enabled template. If you wanted to create a macro-enabled document, you would click the Office Button, click Save As, click the Save as type box arrow, click Word Macro-Enabled Document, and then click the Save button.

To Show the Developer Tab

Many of the tasks you will perform in this chapter use commands on the Developer tab. Thus, the following steps show the Developer tab on the Ribbon.

1 Click the Office Button and then click the Word Options button on the Office Button menu.

2 If necessary, click Popular in the left pane of the Word Options dialog box.

3 If it is not selected, place a check mark in the Show Developer tab in the Ribbon check box.

4 Click the OK button to show the Developer tab on the Ribbon.

To Unprotect a Document

The Universal Travel Modified template is protected. Recall that Chapter 8 showed how to protect a form so that users could enter data only in designated areas, specifically, the content controls. Before this form can be modified, it must be unprotected. Later in this project, after you have completed the modifications, you will protect the document again. The following steps unprotect a document.

- Display the Developer tab.

- Click the Protect Document button on the Developer tab to display the Restrict Formatting and Editing task pane (Figure 9–3). (If a menu appears instead of the task pane, click Restrict Formatting and Editing on the menu to display the task pane.)

- Click the Stop Protection button in the Restrict Formatting and Editing task pane to unprotect the form.

- Click the Close button in the Restrict Formatting and Editing task pane to close the task pane.

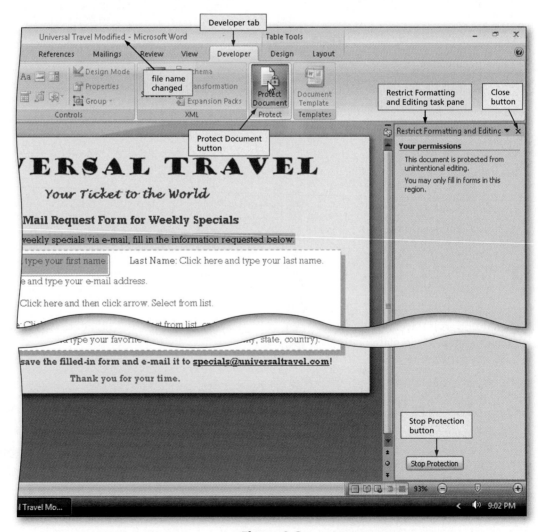

Figure 9–3

Word Macro Settings

A **computer virus** is a type of malicious software, or malware, which is a potentially damaging computer program that affects, or infects, a computer negatively by altering the way the computer works without the user's knowledge or permission. Currently, more than 180,000 known viruses and other malicious programs exist. The increased use of networks, the Internet, and e-mail has accelerated the spread of computer viruses and other malicious programs.

To combat this evil, most computer users run **antivirus programs** that search for viruses and other malware and destroy the malicious programs before they ever have a chance to infect the computer. Macros are a known carrier of viruses and other malware. For this reason, you can specify a macro setting in Word to reduce the chance your computer will be infected with a macro virus. These macro settings allow you to enable or disable macros. An **enabled macro** is a macro that Word will execute, and a **disabled macro** is a macro that is unavailable to Word.

As shown in Figure 9–1b on page WD 643, you can instruct Word to display a security warning if it opens a document that contains a macro(s). If you are confident of the source (author) of the document and macros, enable the macros. If you are uncertain about the reliability of the source of the document and macros, then disable the macros.

To Specify Macro Settings in Word

This project shows how to create macros. When you open the online form in this chapter, you want the macros enabled. At the same time, your computer should be protected from potentially harmful macros. Thus, you will specify a macro setting that allows you to enable or disable the macros each time you open this project or any document that contains a macro from an unknown source. The following steps specify macro settings.

1

- Click the Macro Security button on the Developer tab to display the Trust Center dialog box.

- If it is not selected already, click the 'Disable all macros with notification' option button, which causes Word to alert you when a document contains a macro so that you can decide whether to enable or disable the macro (Figure 9–4).

2

- Click the OK button.

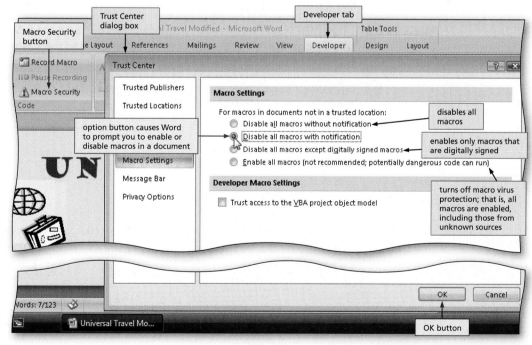

Figure 9–4

Enhancing a Form

The look of this form in this chapter is enhanced from the one in Chapter 8 by performing these steps:

1. Delete the current clip art image, and change the color scheme and font set.
2. Apply a texture fill effect for the page color.
3. Change the fonts, colors, and alignments of the first four lines of text.
4. Convert the 2 × 1 table containing the First Name and Last Name content controls to text so that each of the content controls is on a separate line.
5. Combine the last two lines of text and change their colors.
6. Add a 3-D effect to the rectangle shape.
7. Fill the rectangle with a picture.
8. Insert a new clip art image and rotate it.
9. Delete the date content control and replace it with a date field.
10. Modify the style of the placeholder text.

The following pages apply these changes to the form.

To Delete a Graphic and Change Theme Colors and Fonts

The online form in this chapter has a different clip art image and uses the Module color scheme and Solstice font set. The following steps delete the current clip art image and change the theme colors and the theme fonts.

1 Click the clip art image of the luggage to select it and then press the DELETE key to delete the clip art image.

2 Display the Home tab. Click the Change Styles button on the Home tab, point to Colors on the Change Styles menu, and then select Module in the Colors gallery to change the document theme colors to Module.

3 Click the Change Styles button on the Home tab, point to Fonts on the Change Styles menu, and then select Solstice in the Fonts gallery to change the document theme fonts to Solstice.

To Save a New Theme

In the previous steps, you modified the color scheme and font set. So that you can use this same combination of color scheme and font set again in the future, you save these new settings with a theme name. The next steps save the current theme settings with a new theme name.

1
- Display the Page Layout tab.

- Click the Themes button on the Page Layout tab to display the Themes gallery (Figure 9–5).

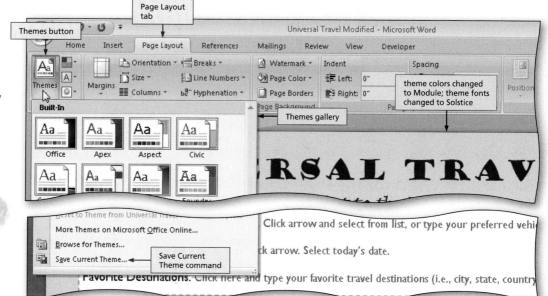

Figure 9–5

2
- Click Save Current Theme in the Themes gallery to display the Save Current Theme dialog box.

- Type Universal Travel Modified in the File name text box as the custom theme name (Figure 9–6).

3
- Click the Save button to add the theme to the Themes gallery as a custom theme.

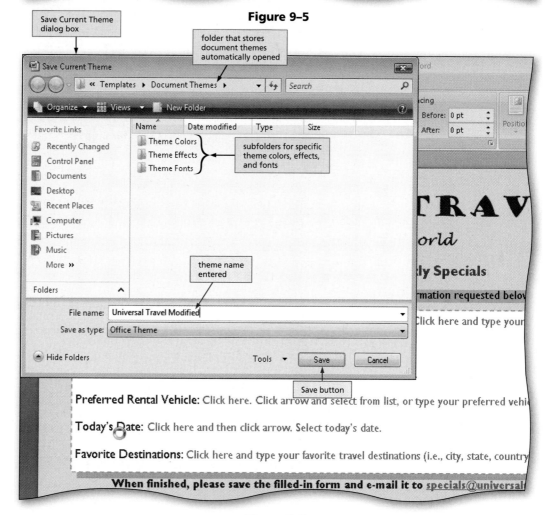

Figure 9–6

TO SET A THEME AS A DEFAULT

The current default theme is the Office theme, which means that new documents are based on this theme. If you wanted to change the default on which new documents are based, you would perform the following steps.

1. Select the theme you want to be the default theme, or select the color scheme, font set, and theme effects you would like to use as the default.

2. Click the Change Styles button on the Home tab and then click Set as Default, which uses the current settings for the new default.

To Use a Fill Effect for the Page Color

Instead of a color for the page color, this online form uses a texture for the page color. Word provides a gallery of 24 predefined textures you can apply to a page. These textures resemble various wallpaper patterns. The following steps change the page color to a texture fill effect.

1

- Click the Page Color button on the Page Layout tab to display the Page Color gallery (Figure 9–7).

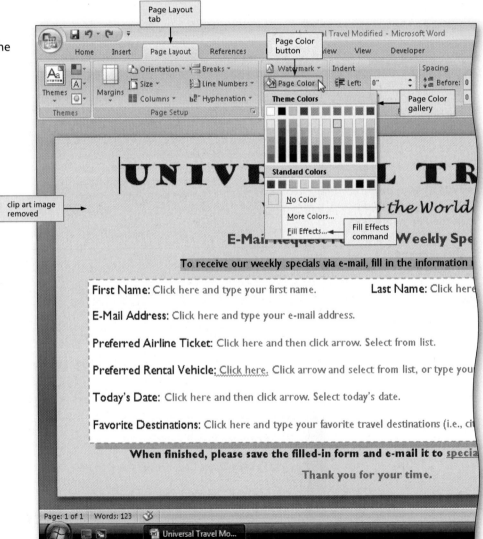

Figure 9–7

2

- Click Fill Effects in the Page Color gallery to display the Fill Effects dialog box.

- Click the Texture tab in the dialog box to display the Texture sheet.

- Scroll to the bottom of the Texture gallery and then click Oak to select the Oak texture (Figure 9–8).

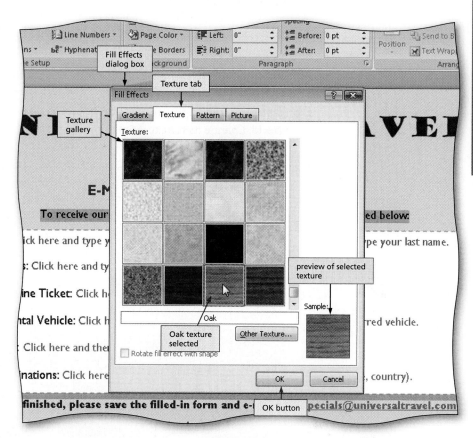

Figure 9–8

3

- Click the OK button to use the Oak texture as the page color in the document (Figure 9–9).

Q&A

How would I remove a texture page color?

You would click the Page Color button on the Page Layout tab and then click No Color in the Page Color gallery.

Figure 9–9

To Format Text

The next step in modifying the online form for this project is to change the formats of the company name, business tag line, form name, and form instructions.

1 Select the first line of text, UNIVERSAL TRAVEL, and then change its font to Wide Latin. Right-align the line of text.

2 Select the second line of text, which contains the business tag line: Your Ticket to the World. Change its font to Arial Rounded MT Bold. Change its color to Green, Accent 4, Darker 50%. Right-align the line of text.

3 Select the third line of text, which contains the form name, E-Mail Request Form for Weekly Specials. Remove the bold format from the text. Change its color to Gold, Accent 1, Lighter 40%. Left-align the line of text.

4 Select the fourth line of text, which are the user instructions that currently are highlighted gray. Change the highlight color to Dark Yellow. Change the font color to Gray-25%, Background 2. Left-align the line of text (Figure 9–10).

Figure 9–10

To Change the Properties of a Plain Text Content Control

In this online form, the First Name and Last Name content controls are on separate lines. In Chapter 8, you selected the 'Content control cannot be deleted' check box in the Content Control Properties dialog box so that users accidentally could not delete the content control while filling in the form. This selected check box, however, prevents you from moving a content control. Thus, the following steps change the locking properties of the First Name and Last Name content controls so that you can rearrange them.

1 Display the Developer tab.

2 Click the First Name content control to select it.

3 Click the Control Properties button on the Developer tab to display the Content Control Properties dialog box.

4 Remove the check mark from the 'Content control cannot be deleted' check box (Figure 9–11).

5 Click the OK button to assign the modified properties to the content control.

6 Click the Last Name content control to select it and then click the Control Properties button on the Developer tab to display the Content Control Properties dialog box.

7 Remove the check mark from the 'Content control cannot be deleted' check box, and then click the OK button to assign the modified properties to the content control.

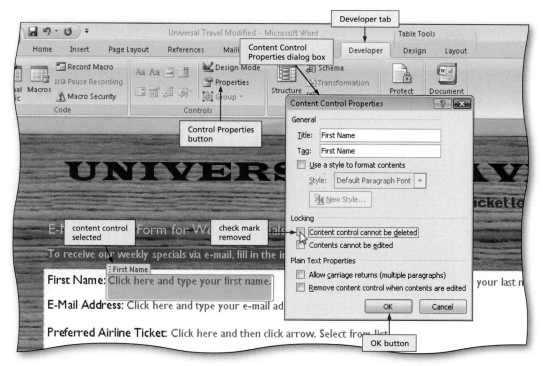

Figure 9–11

To Convert a Table to Text

The First Name and Last Name content controls currently are in a 2 × 1 table. In this project, these content controls are on separate lines, one below the other. That is, they are not in a table. The following steps convert the table to regular text, placing a paragraph break at the location of the second column.

1

- Position the insertion point somewhere in the table.

- Display the Layout tab.

- Click the Convert to Text button on the Layout tab to display the Convert Table To Text dialog box.

- In the 'Separate text with' area, click Paragraph marks, which will place a paragraph mark at the location of each new column in the table (Figure 9–12).

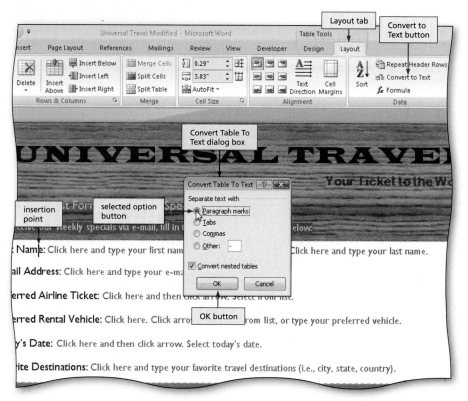

Figure 9–12

● Click the OK button to convert the table to text, separating each column with a paragraph mark (Figure 9–13).

Why did the Last Name content control move below the First Name content control?

The 'Separate text with' area controls how the table is converted to text. The Paragraph marks setting converts each column in the table to a line of text below the previous line. The Tabs setting places a tab character where each column was located, and the Commas setting places a comma where each column was located.

❸

● Click anywhere to remove the selection from the text.

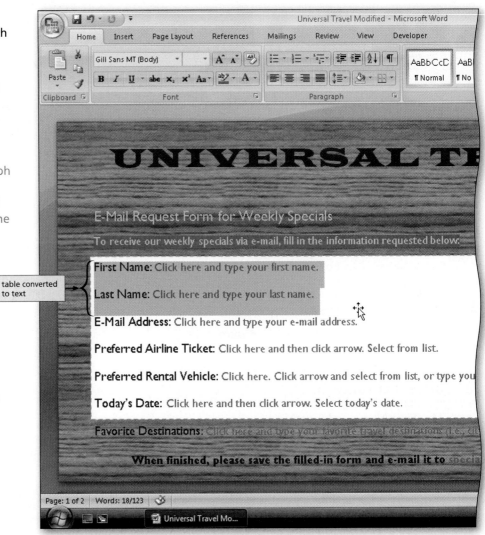

Figure 9–13

To Change the Properties of a Plain Text Content Control

You are finished moving the First Name and Last Name content controls. The following steps reset the locking properties of these content controls.

❶ Display the Developer tab.

❷ Click the First Name content control to select it and then click the Control Properties button on the Developer tab to display the Content Control Properties dialog box.

❸ Place a check mark in the 'Content control cannot be deleted' check box and then click the OK button to assign the modified properties to the content control.

❹ Repeat Steps 2 and 3 for the Last Name content control.

To Resize the Rectangle Shape

With the First Name and Last Name content controls on separate lines, the rectangle outline in the data entry area now is too short. The following steps extend the rectangle shape downward so that it surrounds the entire data entry area.

1 If necessary, click the rectangle shape to select it.

2 Position the mouse pointer on the bottom-middle sizing handle of the rectangle shape.

3 Drag the bottom-middle sizing handle downward so that the shape includes the Favorite Destinations content control (Figure 9–14).

4 Release the mouse button.

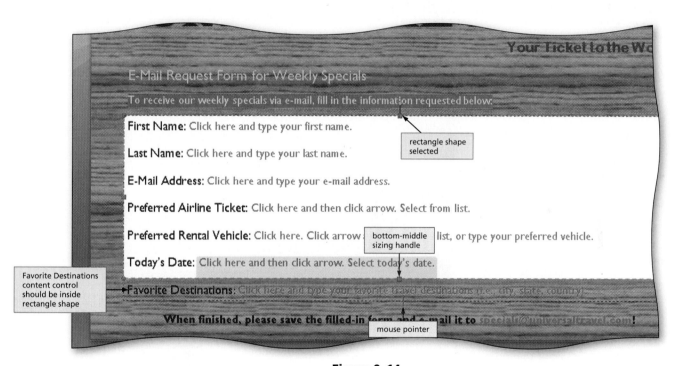

Figure 9–14

To Modify and Format Text

Because the First Name and Last Name content controls are on separate lines, the last line of the online form now spills onto a second page. So that the form fits on a single page, you delete the last line of the form and place a thank-you message at the end of the new last line. The following steps modify and format text below the data entry area of the form.

1 Scroll to display the second page of the online form and then delete the line of text on this page. If necessary, press the BACKSPACE key as many times as required to delete the page entirely. Scroll to display page one in the document window.

2 Change the exclamation point at the end of the last line to a period, press the SPACEBAR, and then type Thank You!

3 Select the line and change its font color to Green, Accent 4, Darker 50%. Click anywhere to remove the selection from the text (Figure 9–15 on the next page).

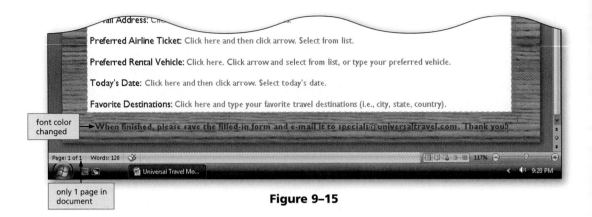

only 1 page in document

Figure 9–15

To Modify a Style Using the Styles Task Pane

When the font color of the line below the data entry area changed, the hyperlink color also changed. In this project, the hyperlink should be a dark red color (similar to the company name) so that it is noticeable. The Hyperlink style is not in the Styles gallery. To modify a style that is not in the Styles gallery, you can use the Styles task pane. The following steps modify the Hyperlink style using the Styles task pane.

1

- If necessary, scroll to display the entire form in the window.

- Select the hyperlink in the form.

- Display the Home tab.

- Click the Styles Dialog Box Launcher to display the Styles task pane.

- Click Hyperlink in the list of styles in the task pane and then click the Hyperlink box arrow to display the Hyperlink menu (Figure 9–16).

Q&A

What if the style I want to modify is not in the list?

Click the Manage Styles button at the bottom of the task pane, locate the style, and then click the Modify button in the dialog box.

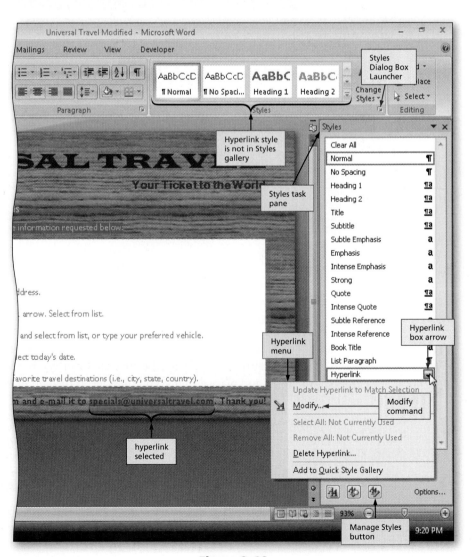

Figure 9–16

- Click Modify on the Hyperlink menu to display the Modify Style dialog box.

- Click the Bold button in the dialog box.

- Click the Font Color box arrow to display the Font Color gallery (Figure 9–17).

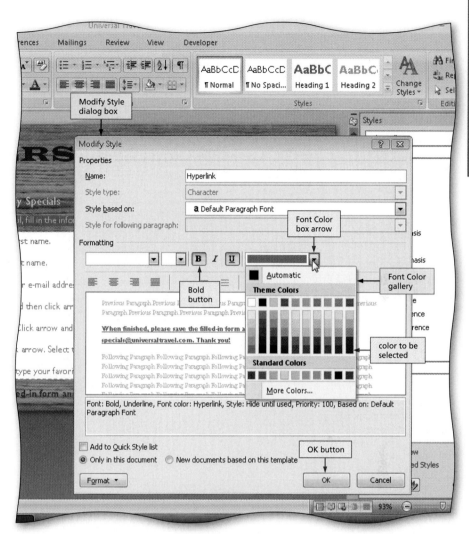

Figure 9–17

❸

- Click Red, Accent 6, Darker 50% as the new hyperlink color.

- Click the OK button. Close the Styles task pane.

- Click outside the selected text to remove the selection (Figure 9–18).

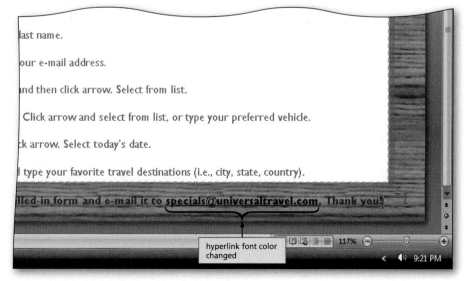

Figure 9–18

To Add a 3-D Effect to a Shape

To give the data entry area of the form more depth, this online form has a 3-D effect added to the rectangle shape. A shape can have either a 3-D effect or a shadow effect. Thus, when you add the 3-D effect, the shadow effect will disappear. The following steps add a 3-D effect to the rectangle shape.

1

- Click the rectangle shape to select it.

- Display the Format tab.

- Click the 3-D Effects button on the Format tab to display the 3-D Effects gallery.

2

- Point to 3-D Style 9 in the 3-D Effects gallery to display a live preview of that 3-D effect applied to the rectangle shape in the document (Figure 9–19).

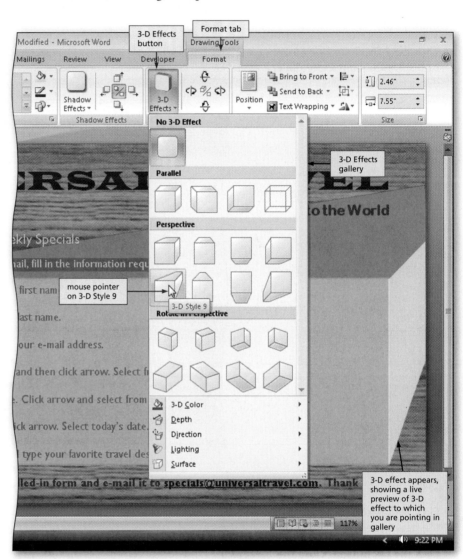

Figure 9–19

Experiment

- Point to various effects in the 3-D Effects gallery and watch the 3-D effect change on the rectangle shape.

3

- Click 3-D Style 9 in the 3-D Effects gallery to apply the selected 3-D effect to the rectangle shape.

Q&A How would I remove a 3-D effect?

Click the 3-D Effects button on the Format tab and then click No 3-D Effect.

To Change the Direction of a 3-D Effect

The 3-D effect that you just added to the rectangle angles toward the top-right of the form. In this project, the 3-D effect should angle toward the top-left. The following steps change the direction of the 3-D effect.

1

- With the rectangle shape still selected, click the 3-D Effects button on the Format tab to display the 3-D Effects gallery.

- Point to Direction in the 3-D Effects gallery to display the Direction gallery.

- Point to Top Left in the Direction gallery to display a live preview of that direction applied to the 3-D effect in the document (Figure 9–20).

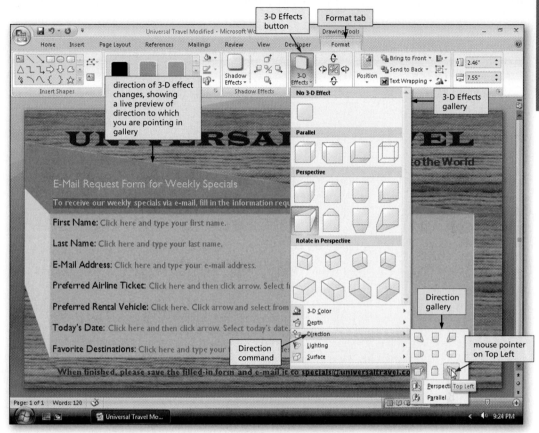

Figure 9–20

Experiment

- Point to various directions in the Direction gallery and watch the direction of the 3-D effect change.

2

- Click Top Left in the Direction gallery to apply the selected direction to the 3-D effect.

BTW

Certification
The Microsoft Certified Application Specialist (MCAS) program provides an opportunity for you to obtain a valuable industry credential — proof that you have the Word 2007 skills required by employers. For more information see Appendix G or visit the Word 2007 Certification Web page (scsite.com/wd2007/cert).

To Change the Color of a 3-D Effect

The 3-D color in this project is dark green. The following steps change the 3-D color.

- With the rectangle shape still selected, click the 3-D Effects button on the Format tab to display the 3-D Effects gallery.

- Point to 3-D Color in the 3-D Effects gallery to display the 3-D Color gallery.

- Point to Green, Accent 4, Darker 50% in the 3-D Color gallery to display a live preview of that 3-D color in the document (Figure 9–21).

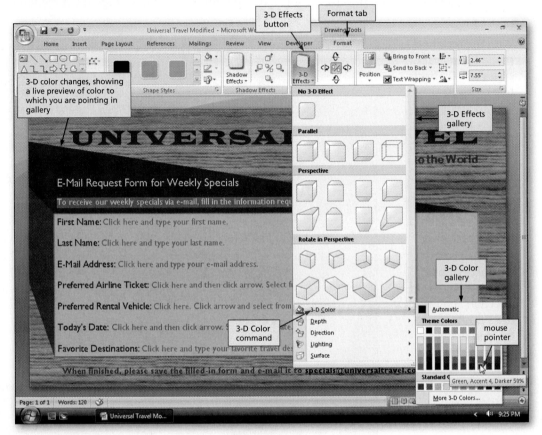

Figure 9–21

Experiment

- Point to various colors in the 3-D Color gallery and watch the 3-D color change.

2

- Click Green, Accent 4, Darker 50% in the 3-D Color gallery to apply the selected 3-D color.

To Fill a Shape with a Picture

The rectangle in this online form contains a picture of pine trees on a mountainside. The picture, called Trees, was taken with a digital camera and is located on the Data Files for Students. See the inside back cover of this book for instructions on downloading the Data Files for Students, or contact your instructor for information about accessing the required files. The next steps fill a shape with a picture.

①

• With the rectangle shape still selected, click the Shape Fill button arrow on the Format tab to display the Shape Fill gallery (Figure 9–22).

My Shape Fill gallery did not display. Why not?

You clicked the Shape Fill button instead of the Shape Fill button arrow. Repeat Step 1.

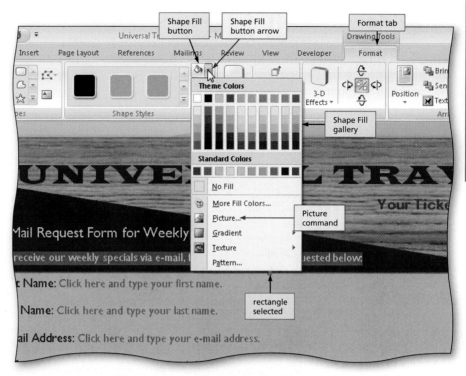

Figure 9–22

②

• Click Picture in the Shape Fill gallery to display the Select Picture dialog box.

• With your USB flash drive connected to one of the computer's USB ports, locate and then click the file called Trees on the USB flash drive to select the file.

• Click the Insert button in the dialog box to fill the rectangle shape with the picture (Figure 9–23).

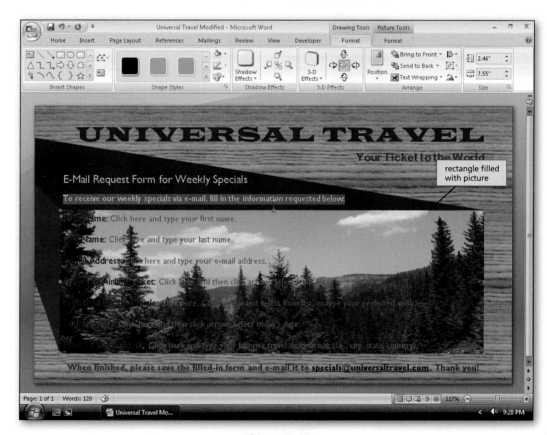

Figure 9–23

To Change the Color of a Picture

The text in the rectangle shape is difficult to read because the picture just inserted is too colorful. You can experiment with adjusting the brightness, contrast, and color of a picture so that the text is readable. In this project, the color is changed to the washout setting so that the text is easier to read. The following steps change the color of the picture to washout.

1

• Display the Picture Tools Format tab.

• With the rectangle shape still selected, click the Recolor button on the Picture Tools Format tab to display the Recolor gallery.

• Point to Washout in the Recolor gallery to display a live preview of the Washout color applied to the picture (Figure 9–24).

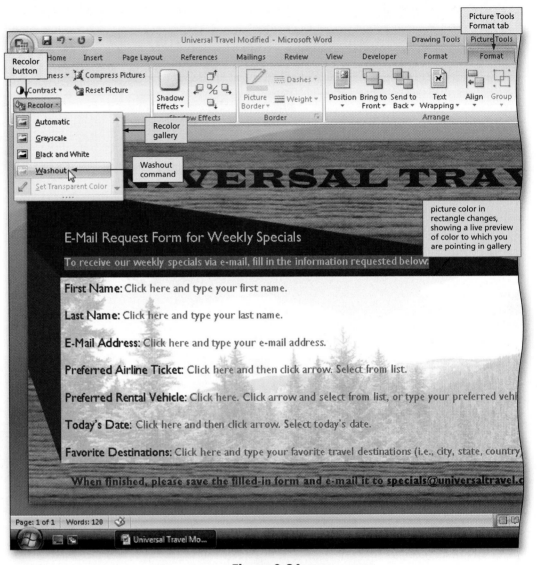

Figure 9–24

 Experiment

• Point to various colors in the Recolor gallery and watch the picture color change.

2

• Click Washout in the Recolor gallery to apply the Washout color to the picture.

To Insert Clip Art from the Web

The next step is to insert a luggage image from the Web in the form.

Note: The following steps assume your computer is connected to the Internet. If it is not, go directly to the shaded steps below that are titled To Insert a Graphic File from the Data Files for Students.

1 Display the Insert tab. Click the Clip Art button on the Insert tab to display the Clip Art task pane.

2 In the Clip Art task pane, type `luggage` in the Search for text box.

3 Click the Go button to display a list of clips that match the description, luggage.

4 Scroll to and then click the luggage clip art that matches the one in Figure 9–25 on the next page.

5 Close the Clip Art task pane.

To Insert a Graphic File from the Data Files for Students

If you do not have access to the Internet, you can insert the clip art file in the Word document from the Data Files for Students. See the inside back cover of this book for instructions on downloading the Data Files for Students, or contact your instructor for information about accessing the required files. Only perform these steps if you were not able to insert the luggage clip art from the Web in the steps at the top of this page.

1 Display the Insert tab. Click the Insert Picture from File button on the Insert tab to display the Insert Picture dialog box.

2 With your USB flash drive connected to one of the computer's USB ports, locate and then click the file called Luggage on the USB flash drive to select the file.

3 Click the Insert button in the dialog box to insert the picture at the location of the insertion point in the document.

To Scale the Graphic, Change Its Wrapping Style, and Move It

Because the graphic's original size is too large, you will scale it to 70 percent of its original size. Then, you will change its wrapping so that the picture can be positioned in front of the text. Finally, you will move the graphic to its correct location.

1 With the graphic still selected, click the Size Dialog Box Launcher on the Picture Tools Format tab to display the Size dialog box.

2 Change the values in the Height and Width text boxes in the Scale area to 70%.

3 Close the Size dialog box.

4 Click the Text Wrapping button on the Format tab to display the Text Wrapping menu.

5 Click In Front of Text on the Text Wrapping menu to change the graphic from inline to floating with In Front of Text wrapping.

6 Point inside the selected graphic, and when the mouse pointer has a four-headed arrow attached to it, drag the graphic to the location shown in Figure 9–25.

To Rotate a Graphic

The image of the luggage in this form is angled to the left more. In Word, you can rotate a floating graphic. The following steps rotate a graphic.

- Position the mouse pointer on the graphic's rotate handle (Figure 9–25).

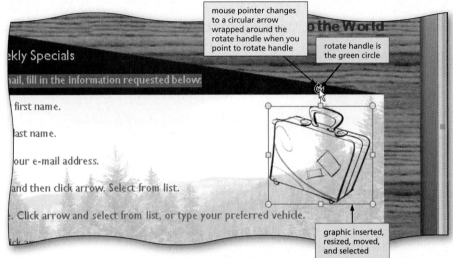

Figure 9–25

- Drag the rotate handle leftward and downward to rotate the graphic as shown in Figure 9–26.

Q&A

Can I drag the rotate handle in any direction?

You can drag the rotate handle clockwise or counter-clockwise.

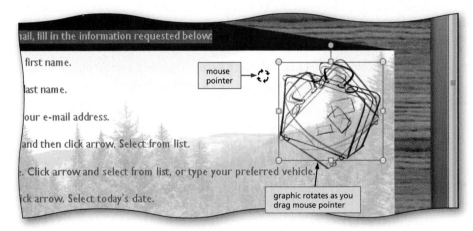

Figure 9–26

- Release the mouse button to position the graphic in the location where you dragged the rotate handle (Figure 9–27). (You may need to rotate the graphic a few times to position it in the desired location.)

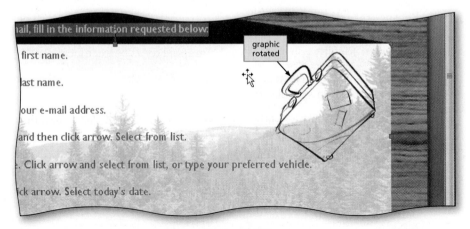

Figure 9–27

To Change the Properties of a Date Content Control

In this online form, instead of the user entering the current date, the system date will be filled in automatically by Word. Thus, the Today's Date content control is not needed and can be deleted. To delete the content control, you first will need to remove the check mark from the 'Content control cannot be deleted' check box in the Content Control Properties dialog box. The following steps change the locking properties of the Today's Date content control and then delete the content control.

1 Display the Developer tab.

2 Click the Today's Date content control to select it.

3 Click the Control Properties button on the Developer tab to display the Content Control Properties dialog box.

4 Remove the check mark from the 'Content control cannot be deleted' check box (Figure 9–28).

5 Click the OK button to assign the modified properties to the content control.

6 Click the Today's Date content control to select it again and then press the DELETE key to delete it.

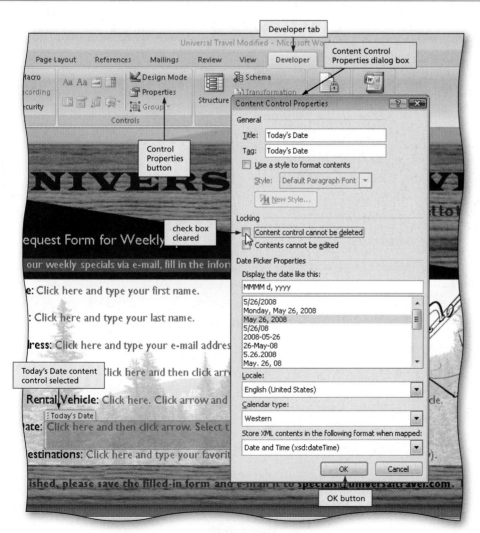

Figure 9–28

To Insert a Date Field

The next step is to instruct Word to display the current date and time at the location of the insertion point. The current date and time is a field. Recall that a field is a set of codes that instructs Word to perform a certain action. The following steps insert the date and time as a field in the form at the location of the insertion point.

 1

- Display the Insert tab.

- With the insertion point positioned as shown in Figure 9–29, click the Quick Parts button on the Insert tab to display the Quick Parts menu.

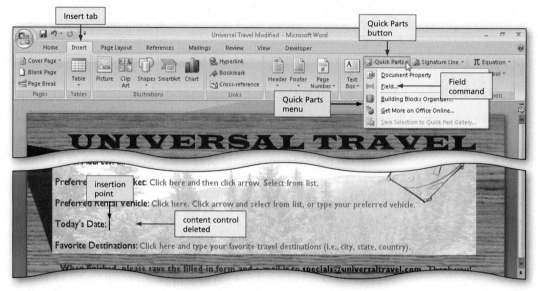

Figure 9–29

2

- Click Field on the Quick Parts menu to display the Field dialog box.

- Scroll through the Field names list and then click Date, which displays the Date formats list in the Field properties area.

- Click the format, 5/26/2008 9:35:34 PM, in the Date formats list — your date and time will differ (Figure 9–30).

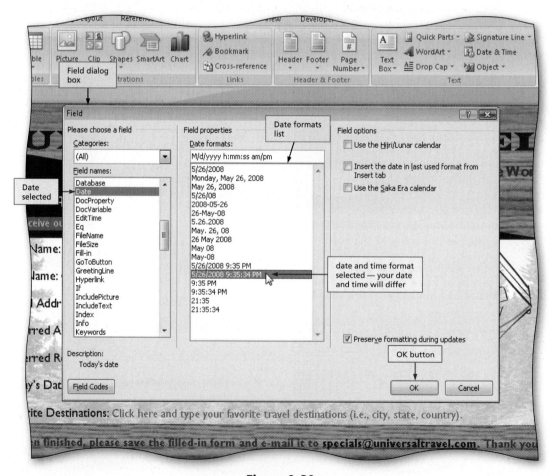

Figure 9–30

3

• Click the OK button to insert the current date and time at the location of the insertion point (Figure 9–31).

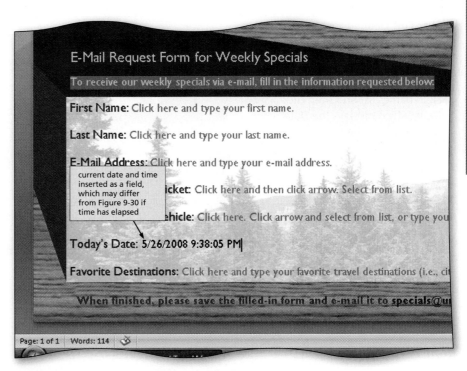

Figure 9–31

To Edit a Field

When looking at the date and time in the form, you decide not to include the seconds in the time. That is, you want just the hours and minutes. Thus, following steps edit the field.

1

• Right-click the date field to display a shortcut menu (Figure 9–32).

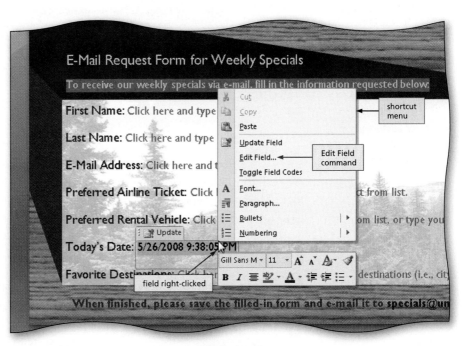

Figure 9–32

2

- Click Edit Field on the shortcut menu to display the Field dialog box.

- If necessary, scroll through the Field names list and then click Date, which displays the Date formats list in the Field properties area.

- Select the desired date format, in this case, 5/26/2008 9:38 PM (Figure 9–33).

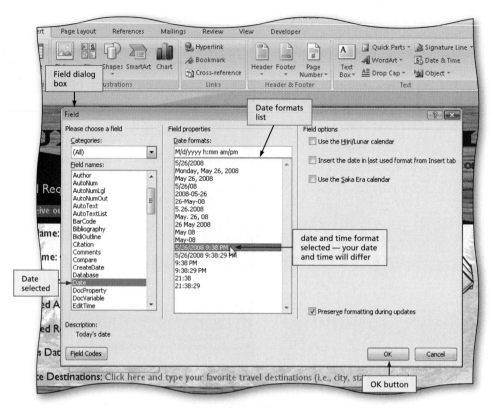

Figure 9–33

3

- Click the OK button to insert the edited current date and time at the location of the insertion point (Figure 9–34).

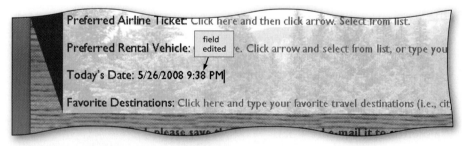

Figure 9–34

To Move Text

Because the user no longer enters data in the date field, the date field is not in a logical location. Typically, all content controls are placed together. In this online form, the current date is positioned at the top of the data entry area. The following steps move the date so that it is above the First Name content control.

1 Select the entire date line.

2 Use drag-and-drop editing to move the selection so that it is positioned just above the First Name content control.

3 If the graphic also moves when you move the text, drag the graphic to the correct location.

To Modify a Style Using the Manage Styles Button

The font color of placeholder text, such as 'Click here and type your first name.', is a little too light. In this online form, the placeholder text is dark green and bold. The Placeholder Text style is not in the Styles gallery, nor is it in the Styles task pane — because it is hidden. When you cannot locate a style you wish to update, you can display all possible styles through the Manage Styles button. The following steps modify the hidden Placeholder Text style.

- Display the Home tab.

- Click the Styles Dialog Box Launcher on the Home tab to display the Styles task pane (Figure 9–35).

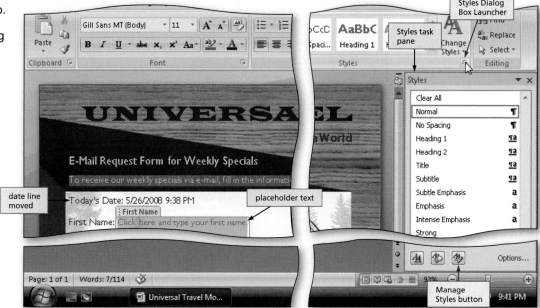

Figure 9–35

- Click the Manage Styles button in the Styles task pane to display the Manage Styles dialog box.

- Click the Sort order box arrow and then click Alphabetical so that the styles are listed in alphabetical order.

- Scroll through the list of styles and select the one you wish to modify, Placeholder Text, in this case, and then click the Modify button to display the Modify Style dialog box.

- Click the Bold button in the dialog box.

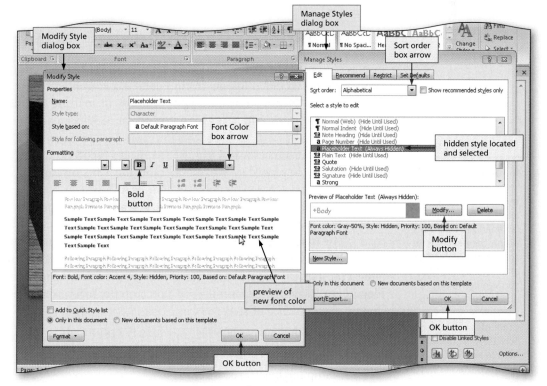

Figure 9–36

- Click the Font Color box arrow and then click Green, Accent 4, Darker 50% as the new placeholder text color (Figure 9–36).

3

- Click the OK button in each open dialog box. Close the Styles task pane.

- If necessary, click outside the selected text to remove the selection (Figure 9–37).

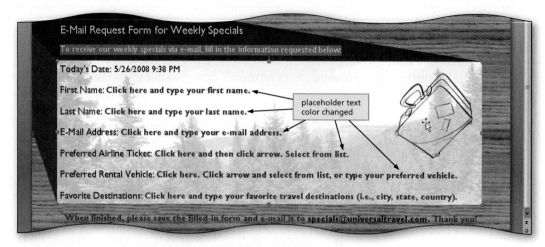

Figure 9–37

To Save a Template Again

The enhancements to the appearance of the online form are complete. You have performed many tasks since the last save and should save the template again.

1 Save the template again with the same file name, Universal Travel Modified.

Using a Macro to Automate a Task

A **macro** consists of a series of Word commands or instructions that are grouped together as a single command. This single command is a convenient way to automate a difficult or lengthy task. Macros often are used to simplify formatting or editing activities, to combine multiple commands into a single command, or to select an option in a dialog box using a shortcut key.

To create a macro, you can use the macro recorder or the Visual Basic Editor. With the macro recorder, Word generates the VBA instructions associated with the macro automatically as you perform actions in Word. If you wanted to write the VBA instructions yourself, you would use the Visual Basic Editor. This chapter uses the macro recorder to create a macro and the Visual Basic Editor to modify it.

The **macro recorder** creates a macro based on a series of actions you perform while the macro recorder is recording. The macro recorder is similar to a video camera: after you start the macro recorder, it records all actions you perform while working in a document and stops recording when you stop the macro recorder. To record a macro, you follow this sequence of steps:

1. Start the macro recorder and specify options about the macro.
2. Execute the actions you want recorded.
3. Stop the macro recorder.

After you record a macro, you can execute the macro, or play it, any time you want to perform the same set of actions.

BTW

Naming Macros
If you give a new macro the same name as an existing built-in command in Microsoft Word, the new macro actions will replace the existing actions. Thus, you should be careful not to name a macro FileSave or after any other menu commands. To view a list of built-in macros in Word, click the View Macros button on the Developer tab to display the Macros dialog box. Click the Macros in box arrow and then click Word commands.

To Record a Macro and Assign It a Shortcut Key

Before sending this online form to users, you want to hide the Developer tab because it contains commands that the users do not need. To simplify this task, the macro in this project hides the Developer tab. In Word, you can assign a shortcut key to a macro so that you can execute the macro by pressing the shortcut key instead of using a dialog box to execute it. The following steps record a macro that hides the Developer tab; the macro is assigned the shortcut key, ALT+D.

1

- Display the Developer tab.

- Click the Record Macro button on the Developer tab to display the Record Macro dialog box.

- Type HideDeveloperTab in the Macro name text box.

- Click the 'Store macro in' box arrow and then click Documents Based On Universal Travel Modified.

- In the Description text box, type this sentence (Figure 9–38): Hides the Developer tab.

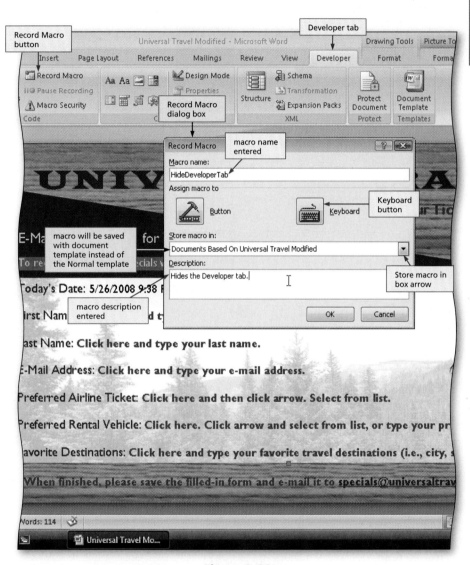

Figure 9–38

Do I have to name a macro?

If you do not enter a name for the macro, Word assigns a default name. Macro names can be up to 255 characters in length and can contain only numbers, letters, and the underscore character. A macro name cannot contain spaces or other punctuation.

What is the difference between storing a macro with the document template versus the Normal template?

Macros saved in the Normal template are available to all future documents; macros saved with the document template are available only with a document based on the template.

2

- Click the Keyboard button to display the Customize Keyboard dialog box.

- Press ALT+D to display the characters ALT+D in the 'Press new shortcut key' text box (Figure 9–39).

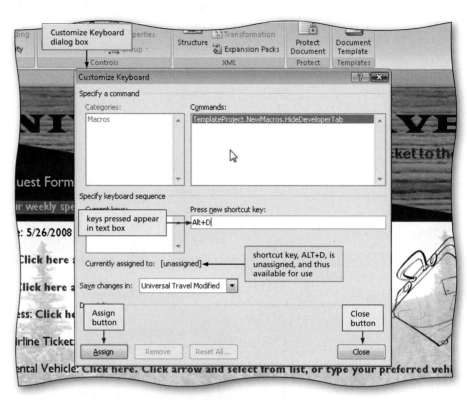

Q&A Can I type the letters in the shortcut key (ALT+D) in the text box?

Although typing the letters places them in the text box, the shortcut key is valid only if you press the shortcut key combination itself.

Figure 9–39

3

- Click the Assign button to assign the shortcut key, ALT+D, to the macro named HideDeveloperTab.

- Click the Close button, which closes the dialog box, places a Macro Recording button on the status bar, and starts the macro recorder (Figure 9–40).

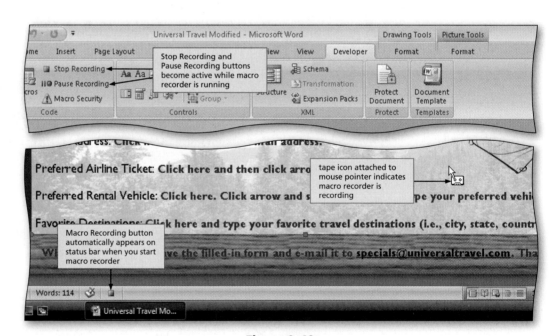

Q&A How do I record the macro?

While the macro recorder is running, any action you perform in Word will be part of the macro — until you stop or pause the macro.

Figure 9–40

Q&A What is the purpose of the Pause Recording button?

If, while recording a macro, you want to perform some actions that should not be part of the macro, click the Pause Recording button to suspend the macro recorder. The Pause Recording button changes to a Resume Recorder button that you click when you want to continue recording.

4

- Click the Office Button to display the Office Button menu (Figure 9–41).

Q&A What happened to the tape icon?

While recording a macro, the tape icon might disappear from the mouse pointer when the mouse pointer is in a menu, on the Ribbon, or in a dialog box.

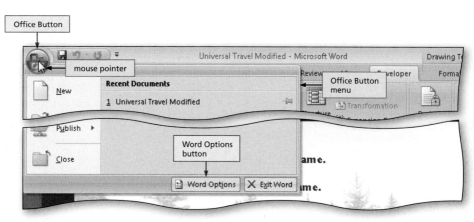

Figure 9–41

5

- Click the Word Options button on the Office Button menu to display the Word Options dialog box.

- If necessary, click Popular in the left pane.

- Remove the check mark from the Show Developer tab in the Ribbon check box (Figure 9–42).

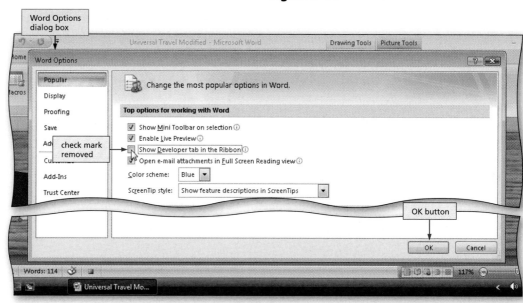

Figure 9–42

6

- Click the OK button to remove the Developer tab from the Ribbon (Figure 9–43).

7

- Click the Macro Recording button on the status bar to turn off the macro recorder, that is, to stop recording actions you perform in Word.

Q&A What if I made a mistake while recording the macro?

Delete the macro and record it again. To delete a macro, click the View Macros button on the Developer tab, select the macro name in the list, click the Delete button, and then click the Yes button.

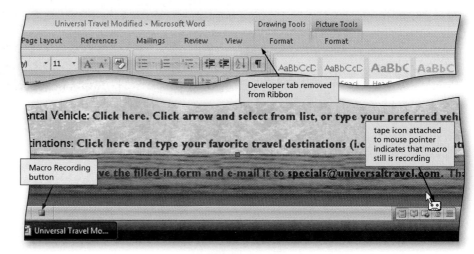

Figure 9–43

Other Ways

1. Click Macro Recording button on status bar

To Run a Macro

The next step is to execute, or run, the macro to ensure that it works. Recall that this macro hides the Developer tab, which means you must be sure the Developer tab shows on the Ribbon before running the macro. Because you created a shortcut key for the macro in this project, the following steps show the Developer tab so that you can run the HideDeveloperTab macro using the shortcut key, ALT+D.

1 Click the Office Button and then click the Word Options button on the Office Button menu. If necessary, click Popular in the left pane of the Word Options dialog box.

2 If it is not selected, place a check mark in the Show Developer tab in the Ribbon check box.

3 Click the OK button to show the Developer tab on the Ribbon.

4 With the Developer tab showing on the Ribbon, press ALT+D, which causes Word to perform the instructions stored in the HideDeveloperTab macro, that is, to hide the Developer tab on the Ribbon.

To Add a Macro as a Button to the Quick Access Toolbar

Word allows you to add buttons to and delete buttons from the Quick Access Toolbar, as shown in Appendix E on pages APP 27 through APP 32. You also can assign a command, such as a macro, to a button on the Quick Access Toolbar. This project shows how to create a button for the HideDeveloperTab macro so that instead of pressing the shortcut keys, you can click the button to hide the Developer tab. The following steps assign the HideDeveloperTab macro to a new button on the Quick Access Toolbar.

1

- Click the Customize Quick Access Toolbar button on the Quick Access Toolbar to display the Customize Quick Access Toolbar menu (Figure 9–44).

Q&A

What happens if I click the commands listed on the Customize Quick Access Toolbar menu?

If the command does not have a check mark beside it and you click it, Word places the command on the Quick Access Toolbar. If the command has a check mark beside it and you click it, Word removes the command from the Quick Access Toolbar.

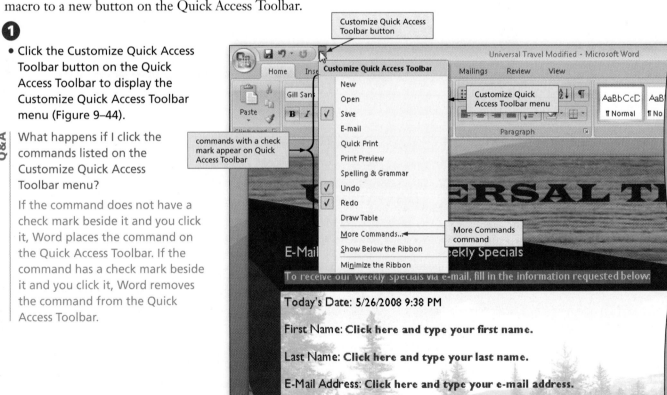

Figure 9–44

2

- Click More Commands on the Customize Quick Access Toolbar menu to display the Word Options dialog box with Customize selected in the left pane (Figure 9–45).

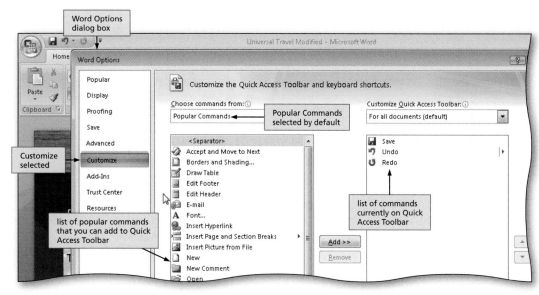

Figure 9–45

3

- Click the 'Choose commands from' box arrow to display a list of categories of commands (Figure 9–46).

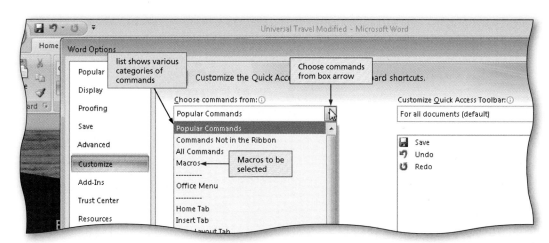

Figure 9–46

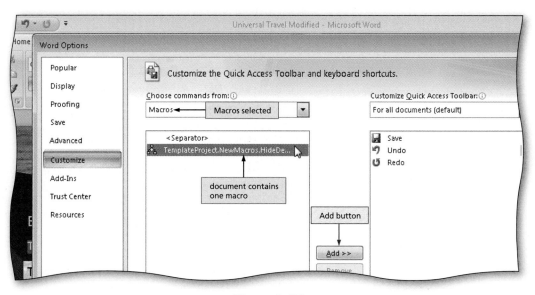

4

- Click Macros in the list to display the macro in this document (Figure 9–47).

Figure 9–47

5

- If necessary, click the macro to select it.

- Click the Add button to display the selected macro in the Customize Quick Access Toolbar list.

- Click the Modify button to display the Modify Button dialog box.

- Change the name in the Display name text box to `Hide Developer Tab`, which will be the text that appears in the ScreenTip for the button.

- Scroll through the list of symbols and click the eraser icon as the new face for the button (Figure 9–48).

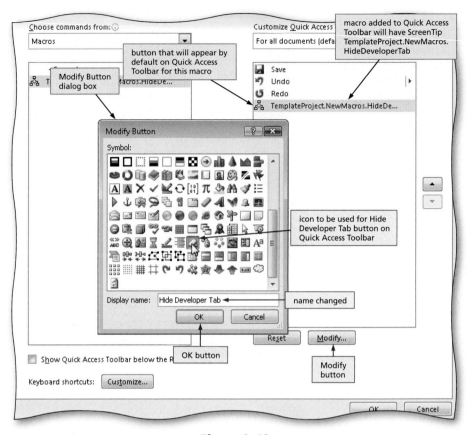

Figure 9–48

6

- Click the OK button in the Modify Button dialog box to change the button characteristics in the Customize Quick Access Toolbar list (Figure 9–49).

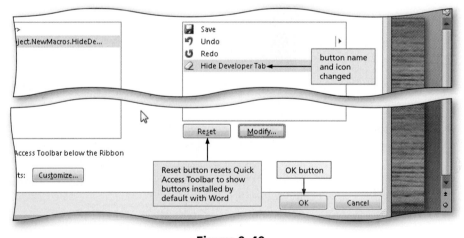

Figure 9–49

7

- Click the OK button to add the button to the Quick Access Toolbar (Figure 9–50).

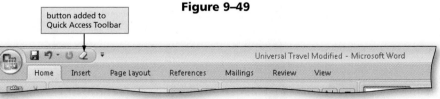

Figure 9–50

Other Ways

1. Right-click Quick Access Toolbar, click Customize Quick Access Toolbar on shortcut menu

To Run the Macro by Clicking the Button on the Quick Access Toolbar

The next step is to execute, or run, the macro again to ensure that it works — by clicking the button on the Quick Access Toolbar. Recall that this macro hides the Developer tab, which means you must be sure the Developer tab shows on the Ribbon before clicking the button. The following steps show the Developer tab so that you can test the macro by clicking the button that is assigned to the Quick Access Toolbar.

BTW

Quick Access Toolbar
You can add any object (button, box, etc.) on the Ribbon to the Quick Access Toolbar by right-clicking the object and then clicking Add to Quick Access Toolbar.

1 Click the Office Button and then click the Word Options button on the Office Button menu. If necessary, click Popular in the left pane of the Word Options dialog box.

2 If it is not selected, place a check mark in the Show Developer tab in the Ribbon check box.

3 Click the OK button to show the Developer tab on the Ribbon.

4 With the Developer tab showing on the Ribbon, point to the Hide Developer Tab button on the Quick Access Toolbar to ensure the ScreenTip displays correctly (Figure 9–51).

5 Click the Hide Developer Tab button on the Quick Access Toolbar, which causes Word to perform the instructions stored in the HideDeveloperTab macro, that is, to hide the Developer tab on the Ribbon.

Figure 9–51

To Delete a Button from a Toolbar

If you no longer plan to use a button on the Quick Access Toolbar, you can delete it. The following steps delete the Hide Developer Tab button from the Quick Access Toolbar.

1

• Right-click the button to be deleted from the Quick Access Toolbar, in this case the Hide Developer Tab button, to display a shortcut menu (Figure 9–52).

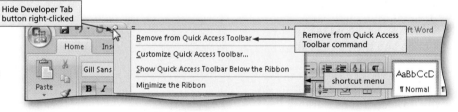

Figure 9–52

2

• Click Remove from Quick Access Toolbar on the shortcut menu to remove the button from the Quick Access Toolbar.

To Rename a Macro

If you wanted to rename a macro, you would perform the following steps.

1. Click the View Macros button on the Developer tab to display the Macros dialog box.

2. Click the Organizer button to display the Organizer dialog box.

3. Click the macro to rename and then click the Rename button.

4. Enter the new macro name in the New name text box and then click the OK button to rename the macro.

5. Close the Organizer dialog box.

To DELETE A MACRO

If you wanted to delete a macro, you would perform the following steps.

1. Click the View Macros button on the Developer tab to display the Macros dialog box.
2. Click the Delete button and then click the Yes button.
3. Close the Macros dialog box.

Automatic Macros

The previous section showed how to create a macro, assign it a unique name (HideDeveloperTab) and a shortcut key, and then on the Quick Access Toolbar, add a button that executes the macro. This section creates an **automatic macro**, which is a macro that executes automatically when a certain event occurs. Word has five prenamed automatic macros. Table 9–1 lists the name and function of these automatic macros.

Table 9–1 Automatic Macros	
Macro Name	**Event That Causes Macro to Run**
AutoClose	Closing a document that contains the macro
AutoExec	Starting Word
AutoExit	Quitting Word
AutoNew	Creating a new document based on a template that contains the macro
AutoOpen	Opening a document that contains the macro

The automatic macro you choose depends on when you want certain actions to occur. In this project, when a user creates a new Word document that is based on the Universal Travel Modified template, you want to be sure that the zoom is set to page width. Thus, the AutoNew automatic macro is used in this online form.

To Create an Automatic Macro

The online form in this chapter is displayed properly when the zoom is set to page width. Thus, you will record the steps to zoom to page width in the AutoNew macro. The following steps create an AutoNew macro, using the macro recorder.

1

- Show the Developer tab on the Ribbon and then display the Developer tab.

- Click the Record Macro button on the Developer tab to display the Record Macro dialog box.

- Type AutoNew in the Macro name text box.

- Click the 'Store macro in' box arrow and then click Documents Based On Universal Travel Modified.

- In the Description text box, type this sentence (Figure 9–53): Specifies how the form initially is displayed.

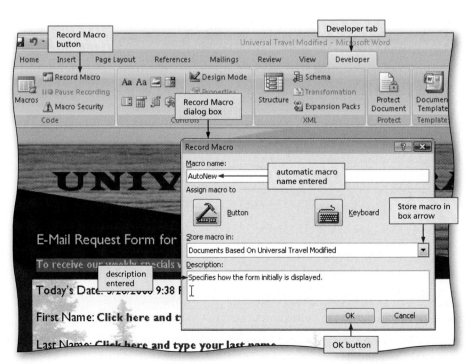

Figure 9–53

2

- Click the OK button to close the Record Macro dialog box and start the macro recorder.

- Display the View tab.

- Click the Page Width button on the View tab to zoom page width (Figure 9–54).

3

- Click the Macro Recording button on the status bar to turn off the macro recorder, that is, stop recording actions you perform in Word.

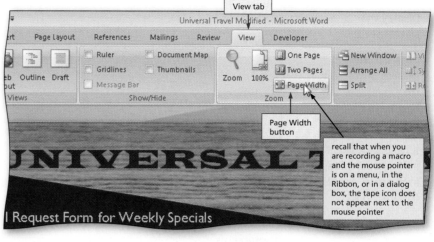

Figure 9–54

Q&A

How do I test an automatic macro?

Activate the event that causes the macro to execute. For example, the AutoNew macro runs whenever you create a new Word document that is based on the template.

To Run the AutoNew Macro

The next step is to execute, or run, the AutoNew macro to ensure that it works. To run the AutoNew macro, you need to create a new Word document that is based on the Universal Travel Modified template. This macro contains instructions to zoom page width. To verify that the macro works as intended, you will change the zoom to 100% before testing the macro.

1 Use the Zoom Out button on the status bar to change the zoom to 100%.

2 Save the template with the same name, Universal Travel Modified.

3 Click the Start button on the Windows Vista taskbar to display the Start menu. Click Computer on the Start menu to display the Explorer window.

4 Locate your USB flash drive in the Explorer window and then double-click the file named Universal Travel Modified to display a new document window that is based on the contents of the Universal Travel Modified template, which should be zoomed to page width as shown in Figure 9–1a on page WD 643.

5 Close the new document that displays the form in the Word window. Click the No button when Word asks if you want to save the changes to the new document.

6 Change the zoom back to page width.

BTW

Automatic Macros
A document can contain only one AutoClose macro, one AutoNew macro, and one AutoOpen macro. The AutoExec and AutoExit macros, however, are not stored with the document; instead, they must be stored in the Normal template. Thus, only one AutoExec macro and only one AutoExit macro can exist for all Word documents.

To Edit a Macro's VBA Code

In addition to zooming page width when the online form displays in new document window, you would like to be sure that the Developer tab is hidden and the formatting marks are hidden. As mentioned earlier, a macro consists of VBA instructions. To edit a recorded macro, you use the Visual Basic Editor.

The steps on the next page use the Visual Basic Editor to add VBA instructions to the AutoNew macro. These steps are designed to show the basic composition of a VBA procedure and illustrate the power of VBA code statements.

- Display the Developer tab.

- Click the View Macros button on the Developer tab to display the Macros dialog box.

- If necessary, select the macro to be edited, in this case, AutoNew (Figure 9–55).

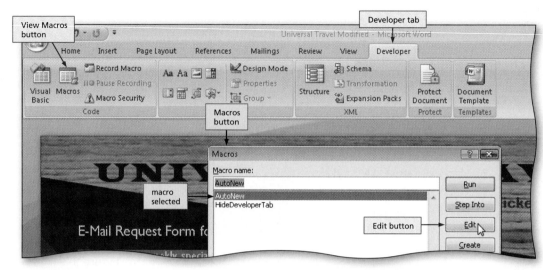

Figure 9–55

- Click the Edit button to start the Visual Basic Editor and display the VBA code for the AutoNew macro in the Code window — your screen may appear differently depending on previous Visual Basic Editor settings (Figure 9–56).

Q&A What if the Code window does not appear in the Visual Basic Editor?

In the Visual Basic Editor, click View on the menu bar and then click Code. If it still does not appear and you are in a network environment, this feature may be disabled for some users.

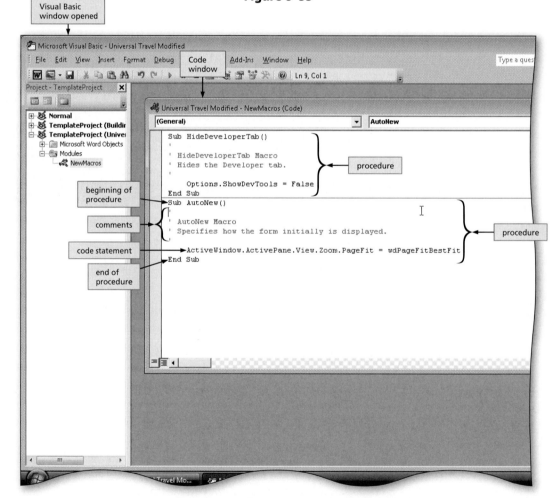

Figure 9–56

Q&A What are the lines of text (instructions) in the Code window?

The named set of instructions associated with a macro is called a **procedure**. It is this set of instructions — beginning with the words Sub and continuing sequentially to the line with the words End Sub — that executes when you run the macro. The instructions within a procedure are called **code statements**.

3

- Position the insertion point at the end of the second-to-last line in the AutoNew macro and then press the ENTER key to insert a blank line for a new code statement.

- On a single line, type `Options .ShowDevTools = False` and then press the ENTER key, which enters the VBA code statement that hides the Developer tab.

What are the lists that appear in the Visual Basic Editor as I enter code statements?

The lists present valid statement elements to assist you with entering code statements. Ignore them because they are beyond the scope of this chapter.

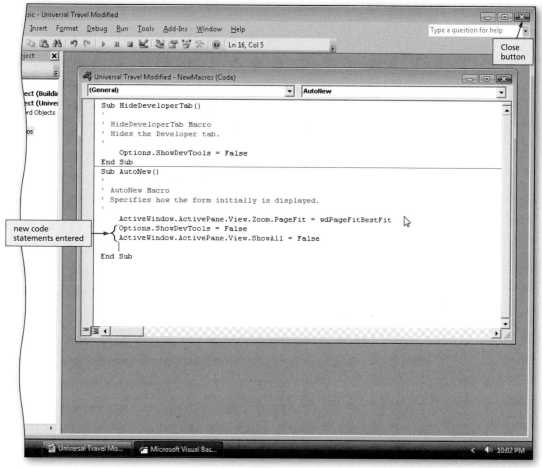

Figure 9–57

- On a single line, type `ActiveWindow.ActivePane.View.ShowAll = False` and then press the ENTER key, which enters the VBA code statement that turns off formatting marks (Figure 9–57).

4

- Click the Close button on the right edge of the Microsoft Visual Basic window title bar.

To Run the AutoNew Macro

The next step is to execute, or run, the AutoNew macro again to ensure that it works. To be sure the macro works as intended, you first will display the formatting marks and ensure the Developer tab is on the Ribbon. The AutoNew macro should hide the formatting marks and hide the Developer tab.

1 Display the Home tab. If necessary, click the Show/Hide ¶ button on the Home tab to display formatting marks.

2 Ensure the Developer tab appears on the Ribbon.

3 Save the template with the same name, Universal Travel Modified.

④ Click the Start button on the Windows Vista taskbar to display the Start menu and then click Computer on the Start menu to display the Explorer window.

⑤ Locate your USB flash drive in the Explorer window and then double-click the file named Universal Travel Modified to display a new document window that is based on the contents of the Universal Travel Modified template, which should be zoomed to page width as shown in Figure 9–1a on page WD 643.

⑥ Close the new document that displays the form in the Word window. Click the No button when Word asks if you want to save the changes to the new document.

⑦ Close the Explorer window.

⑧ In the Word window, hide formatting marks on the screen.

VBA

BTW

VBA
VBA includes many more statements than those presented in this project. You may need a background in computer programming if you plan to write VBA code instructions in macros you develop and if the VBA code instructions are beyond those instructions presented in this project.

As shown in the steps on pages WD 680 and WD 681, a VBA procedure begins with a Sub statement and ends with an End Sub statement. The Sub statement is followed by the name of the procedure, which is the macro name (AutoNew). The parentheses following the macro name in the Sub statement are required. They indicate that arguments can be passed from one procedure to another. Passing arguments is beyond the scope of this chapter, but the parentheses still are required. The End Sub statement signifies the end of the procedure and returns control to Word.

Comments often are added to a procedure to help you remember the purpose of the macro and its code statements at a later date. Comments begin with an apostrophe (') and appear in green in the Code window. The macro recorder, for example, placed four comment lines below the Sub statement. These comments display the name of the macro and its description, as entered in the Record Macro dialog box. Comments have no effect on the execution of a procedure; they simply provide information about the procedure, such as its name and description, to the developer of the macro.

For clarity, code statement lines are indented four spaces. Table 9–2 explains the function of each element of a code statement.

Table 9–2 Elements of a Code Statement

Code Statements

Element	Definition	Examples
Keyword	Recognized by Visual Basic as part of its programming language. Keywords appear in blue in the Code window.	Sub End Sub
Variable	An item whose value can be modified during program execution.	ActiveWindow.ActivePane.View.Zoom.PageFit
Constant	An item whose value remains unchanged during program execution.	False
Operator	A symbol that indicates a specific action.	=

To Protect a Form

You now are finished enhancing the online form and adding macros to it. The following steps protect the online form so that users are restricted to entering data only in content controls.

1 Show the Developer tab and then display the Developer tab.

2 Click the Protect Document button on the Developer tab to display the Restrict Formatting and Editing task pane. (If a menu appears instead of the task pane, click Restrict Formatting and Editing on the menu to display the task pane.)

3 In the Editing restrictions area, if necessary, place a check mark in the 'Allow only this type of editing in the document' check box and then click its box arrow and select 'Filling in forms' in the list.

4 In the Start enforcement area, click the Yes, Start Enforcing Protection button and then click the OK button in the dialog box to protect the document without a password.

5 Close the Restrict Formatting and Editing task pane.

To Run the Compatibility Checker

Assume you have considered saving this template in the Word 97-2003 format so that it can be opened by users with earlier versions of Microsoft Word. Before saving a document or template in an earlier format, however, you want to ensure that all of its elements (such as fields, building blocks, and content controls) are compatible (will work with) earlier versions of Word. The following steps run the compatibility checker.

• Click the Office Button and then point to Prepare to display the Prepare submenu (Figure 9–58).

Figure 9–58

- Click Run Compatibility Checker on the Prepare submenu to display the Microsoft Office Word Compatibility Checker dialog box, which shows any content that may not be supported by earlier versions of Word (Figure 9–59).

- Analyze the results of the compatibility checker: Because the compatibility checker indicated that content controls are not supported in earlier versions of Word, you will not save the template in the Word 97-2003 format.

- Click the OK button in the dialog box.

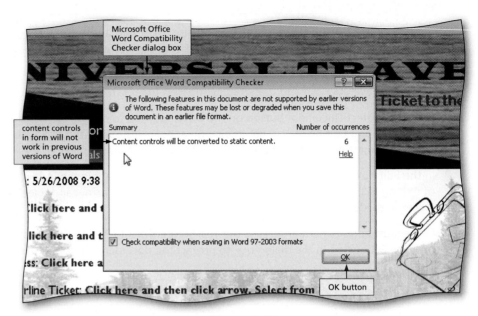

Figure 9–59

To Save the Document Again and Close the Template

You now are finished with the first project in this chapter, enhancing the online form and adding macros to it. Thus, you will save it a final time and close it. You will leave Word running for the next project in the chapter.

1 Save the template again with the same name, Universal Travel Modified.

2 Click the Office Button and then click Close on the Office Button menu to close the template and leave Word running.

Incorporating Security and Functionality in a Document

The project for this section of the chapter is a business letter that incorporates both security and functionality because you intend to share the letter with others. For example, you may want to e-mail a document to others for their review, signature, or information and ensure that the document cannot be modified. When preparing documents to be shared, you might want to consider several modifications to the document:

1. Save a document with a password.
2. Save frequently used data as building blocks.
3. Remove personal information, hidden text, and other nonessential content.
4. Add a signature line and/or digital signature.
5. Save the document as an XPS file.

The following pages apply these modifications to a letter.

> **Save a document with a password.**
> To keep unauthorized users from accessing files, save the file with a password and keep your password confidential. Choose a password that is easy to remember and that no one can guess. Do not use any part of your first or last name, your spouse's or child's name, telephone number, street address, license plate number, Social Security number, birthday, and so on. Be sure your password is at least six characters long, and if possible, use a mixture of numbers and letters.

To Save a Document with a Password

The first step in this project is to open the document, Best Business Solutions Draft, from the Data Files for Students. See the inside back cover of this book for instructions on downloading the Data Files for Students, or contact your instructor for information about accessing the required files. Then, you will save the document with a new file name and with a password. Saving the file with a password protects unauthorized users from altering the contents of a file. The following steps save a file with a password.

- Open the file called Best Business Solutions Draft from the Data Files for Students.

 **Experiment**

- Scroll through the letter to familiarize yourself with its contents.

- Click the Office Button and then click Save As to display the Save As dialog box.

- Type Best Business Solutions Modified as the new file name.

- Click the Tools button in the dialog box to display the Tools menu (Figure 9–60).

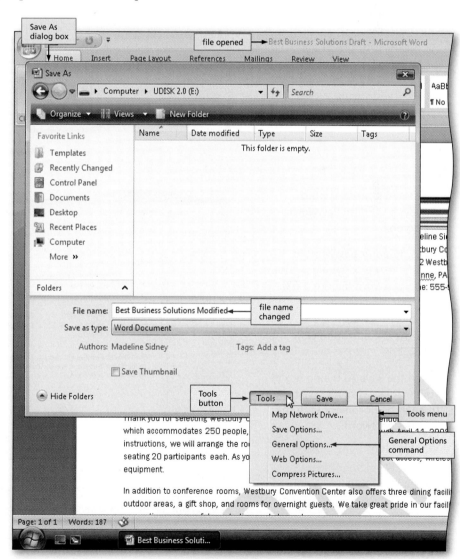

Figure 9–60

- Click General Options on the Tools menu to display the General Options dialog box.

- In the 'Password to modify' text box, type computer as the password (Figure 9–61).

Q&A Why do dots appear in the text box instead of the word, computer?

Many programs display a series of dots instead of the actual characters so that others cannot see your password as you type it.

Q&A Is the word, computer, a good password?

For purposes of this project, the password was designed to be easy to remember. In real-world settings, you should choose more secure passwords.

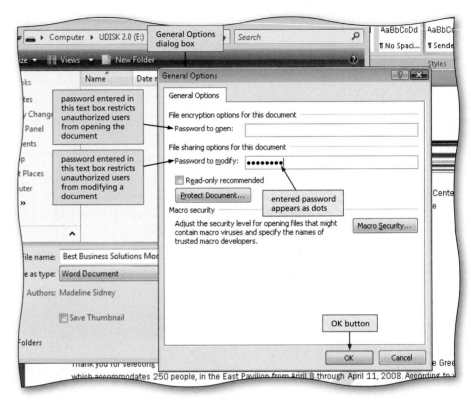

Figure 9–61

- Click the OK button, which displays a Confirm Password dialog box.

- In the 'Reenter password to modify' text box, type computer as the password (Figure 9–62).

- Click the OK button to close the dialog box.

- When the Save As dialog box is visible again, click its Save button to save the document with the entered password.

Q&A What if I forget my password?

Do not forget your password because you will not be able to modify the document without it.

Q&A When will the password be requested?

When the document is opened, a Password dialog box will appear that requests the password.

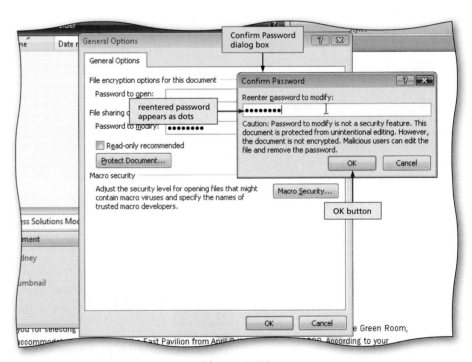

Figure 9–62

To Create a Building Block

Recall that if you use the same text or graphic frequently, you can store the text or graphic in a **building block** and then use the stored building block entry in the open document, as well as in future documents. Because the company contact information in this letter may be needed again in future documents, you create a building block for this information. The following steps create a building block.

1 Select the text to be a building block, in this case, the five lines in the inside address.

2 Display the Insert tab. Click the Quick Parts button on the Insert tab to display the Quick Parts menu.

3 Click Save Selection to Quick Part Gallery on the Quick Parts menu to display the Create New Building Block dialog box.

4 Type Best Business Solutions in the Name text box (Figure 9–63).

5 Click the OK button to store the building block entry in the Quick Parts gallery and close the dialog box. If Word displays another dialog box, click the Yes button.

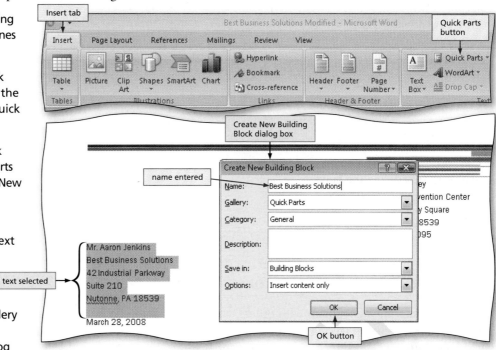

Figure 9–63

To Modify a Building Block

When you save a building block in the Quick Parts gallery, it appears when you click the Quick Parts button on the Insert tab. When you point to the building block in the Quick Parts gallery, the ScreenTip displays the building block name. If you want to display more information when the user points to the building block, you can include a description as an Enhanced ScreenTip. The following steps modify a building block to include a description.

1

• Click the Quick Parts button on the Insert tab to display the Quick Parts gallery.

Experiment

• Point to the Best Business Solutions building block in the Quick Parts gallery to display the ScreenTip.

2

• Right-click the Best Business Solutions building block to display a shortcut menu (Figure 9–64).

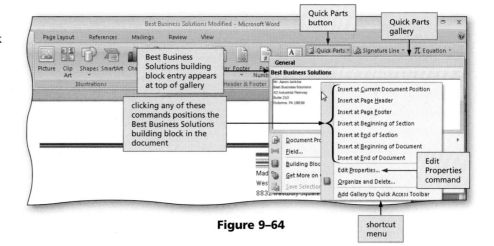

Figure 9–64

- Click Edit Properties on the shortcut menu to display the Modify Building Block dialog box, which is filled in with information related to the Best Business Solutions building block.

- Type `Conference Room Reservation` in the Description text box (Figure 9–65).

- Click the OK button to store the building block entry and close the dialog box.

- Click the Yes button when asked if you want to redefine the building block entry.

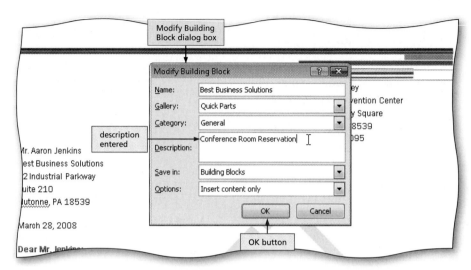

Figure 9–65

To Use the Document Inspector

Before sharing a document with others, you should proofread it to be sure it is free from spelling and grammar errors. When sending an electronic file, you also want to check the content of the information that may be stored with the document. Word includes a Document Inspector that checks a document for content you might not want to share with others such as comments, tracked changes, annotations, personal information, and data formatted as hidden text. The following steps use the Document Inspector to remove personal information and other similar content from a document.

- Click the Office Button and then point to Prepare on the Office Button menu (Figure 9–66).

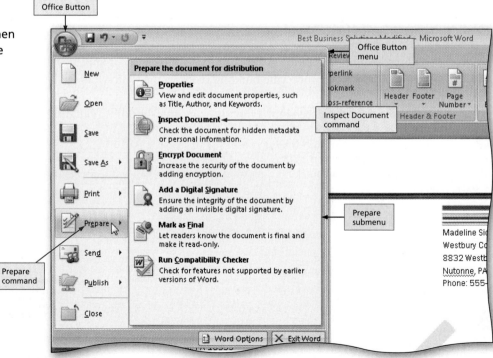

Figure 9–66

2

- Click Inspect Document on the Prepare submenu to display the Document Inspector dialog box.

- Review the list of items in the Document Inspector dialog box and, if necessary, place a check mark for content you may want to remove; in this case, select all items in the list (Figure 9–67).

Q&A

What is an annotation?

If you have a Tablet PC, you can enter ink annotations (handwriting) in a comment in the document.

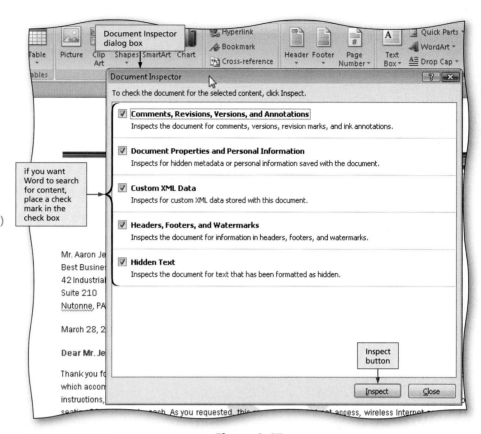

Figure 9–67

3

- Click the Inspect button so that Word searches for content that you selected and displays the search results in the dialog box (Figure 9–68).

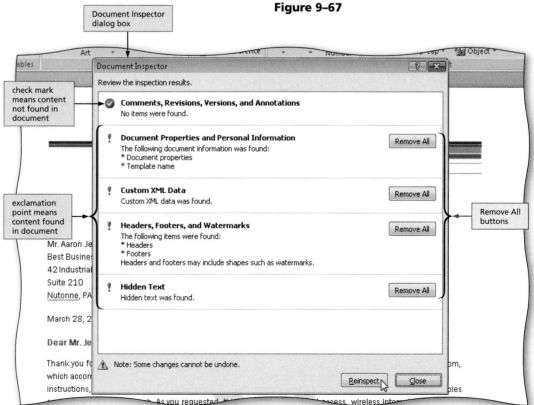

Figure 9–68

- Review the inspection results and determine which content you want to remove from the document.

- Click the first Remove All button to remove document properties and personal information.

- Click the next Remove All button to remove XML data.

- Click the next Remove All button to remove headers, footers, and watermarks.

- Click the next Remove All button to remove hidden text (Figure 9–69).

Q&A

What if the document contained an ink annotation?

The inspection would have located it, and you would have clicked the Remove All button to remove the ink annotation.

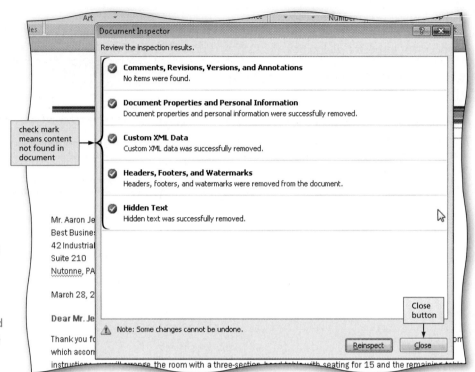

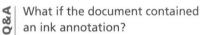

Figure 9–69

- Click the Close button to close the dialog box.

Digital Signatures

Some users attach a **digital signature** to a document to verify its authenticity. A digital signature is an electronic, encrypted, and secure stamp of authentication on a document. This signature confirms that the file originated from the signer (file creator) and that it has not been altered.

A digital signature references a digital certificate. A **digital certificate** is an attachment to a file, macro project, or e-mail message that vouches for its authenticity, provides secure encryption, or supplies a verifiable signature. Many users who receive online forms enable the macros based on whether they are digitally signed by a developer on the user's list of trusted sources.

You can obtain a digital certificate from a commercial certification authority or from your network administrator, or you can create a digital signature yourself. A digital certificate you create yourself is not issued by a formal certification authority. Documents using such a certificate are referred to as self-signed documents. Certificates you create yourself are considered unauthenticated and still will generate a warning when opened at certain security levels. Many users, however, consider self-signed documents safer to open than those with no certificates at all.

Once a digital signature is added, the document becomes a read-only document, which means that modifications cannot be made to it. Thus, you only should create a digital signature when the document is final. In Word, you can add two types of digital signatures to a document: (1) a signature line or (2) an invisible digital signature. The following sections address each of these types of digital signatures.

To Add a Signature Line to a Document

A digital signature line, which resembles a printed signature placeholder, allows a recipient of the electronic file to type a signature, include an image of his or her signature, or write a signature using the ink feature on a Tablet PC. Digital signature lines enable organizations to use paperless methods of obtaining signatures on official documents such as contracts. The following steps add a digital signature line to a document.

- Position the insertion point at the location for the digital signature, in this case, at the very bottom of the document.

- Click the Signature Line button on the Insert tab to display the Signature Setup dialog box.

- If a dialog box appears about signature services, click its OK button.

- Type the name of the person who should sign the document, Aaron Jenkins, in this case.

- If available, type the signer's e-mail address, jenkins@bbs.com, in this case.

- Place a checkmark in the 'Allow the signer to add comments in the Sign dialog' check box so that the recipient can add a message back to you (Figure 9–70).

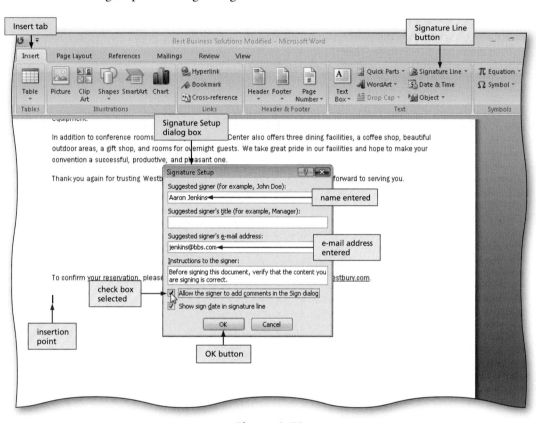

Figure 9–70

- Click the OK button to insert a signature line in the document at the location of the insertion point (Figure 9–71).

Q&A

How does a recipient insert his or her digital signature?

When the recipient opens the document, a Message Bar appears that contains a View Signatures button. The recipient can click the View Signatures button to display the Signatures task pane, click the requested signature box arrow, and then click Sign in the menu (or double-click the signature line in the document) to display a dialog box that the recipient then completes.

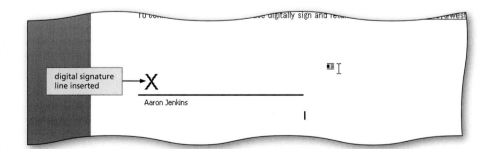

Figure 9–71

To Add an Invisible Digital Signature to a Document

An invisible digital signature does not appear as a tangible signature in the document. If the status bar displays a Signatures button, the document has an invisible digital signature. The following steps add an invisible digital signature to a document.

1
- Click the Office Button and then point to Prepare to display the Prepare submenu (Figure 9–72).

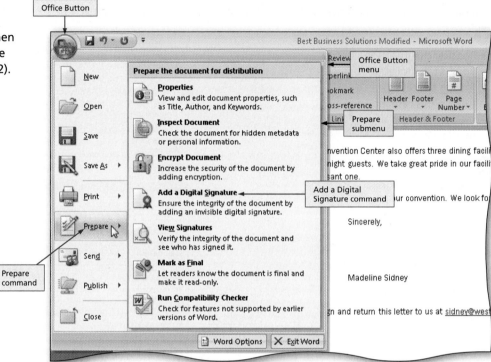

Figure 9–72

2
- Click Add a Digital Signature on the Prepare submenu to display the Sign dialog box.

- If a dialog box about signature services appears, click its OK button.

Q&A
What if a dialog box appears indicating I need a digital ID?

If necessary, select the 'Get your own digital ID' option button, click the OK button, and then follow the on-screen instructions.

- In the 'Purpose for signing this document' text box, type Verify its authenticity. (Figure 9–73).

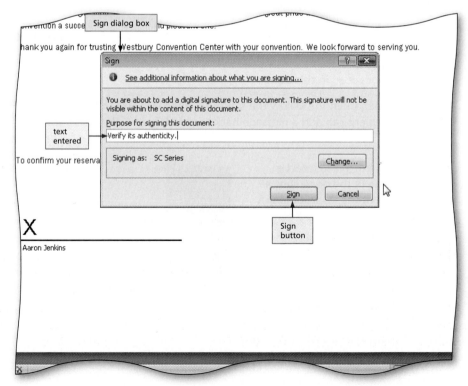

Figure 9–73

- Click the Sign button to add the digital signature, show the Signatures button on the status bar, and display the Signatures task pane, which lists all current digital signatures in the document — your list may differ (Figure 9–74).

- If a dialog box appears indicating the signature has been saved successfully, click its OK button.

- Click the Close button on the Signatures task pane.

Q&A

How can I view the digital signatures in a document?

Click the Signatures button on the status bar or click the Office Button, point to Prepare, and then click View Signatures.

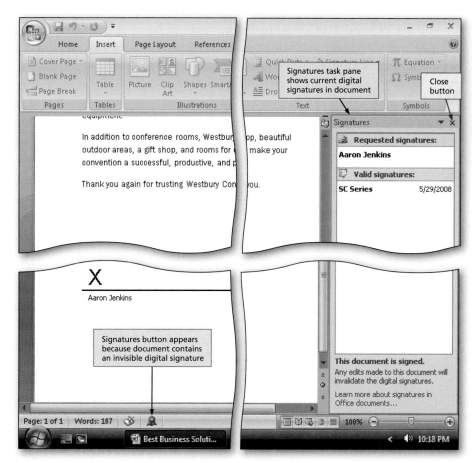

Figure 9–74

XPS

XPS, which stands for XML Paper Specification, is a file format developed by Microsoft that shows all elements of a printed document as an electronic image. Like the PDF format, users can view a XPS document without the software that created the original document. Thus, the XPS format enables users easily to share documents with others. Windows Vista has built-in capability to view, navigate, and print an XPS file; for other operating systems, users can download a viewer.

Microsoft provides a free add-in utility that enables you to convert a Word document to an XPS format. To check if the utility has been downloaded to your computer, click the Office Button menu and then point to Save As. If your Save As submenu contains the PDF or XPS command, then the add-in utility has been installed. If your Save As submenu contains the 'Find add-ins for other file formats' command, then the add-in utility has not been installed. To download the add-in utility, click 'Find add-ins for other file formats' on the Save As submenu to display the 'Enable support for other file formats, such as PDF and XPS' Help window. Scroll through the Help window and then click the Microsoft Save as PDF or XPS Add-in for 2007 Microsoft Office Programs, which displays a Web page at Microsoft's site. Follow the instructions at that Web page to download and install this add-in utility.

With the XPS add-in utility installed on your computer, you can save your documents as XPS files or e-mail the document to others as a XPS file.

To Save a Document in an XPS Format

If the XPS add-in utility is installed on your computer, you can save the document displayed in the Word window as an XPS file. The original Word document remains intact — Word creates a copy of the file in an XPS format. The following steps save an XPS version of the current document.

1

- Click the Office Button and then point to Save As on the Office Button menu to display the Save As submenu (Figure 9–75).

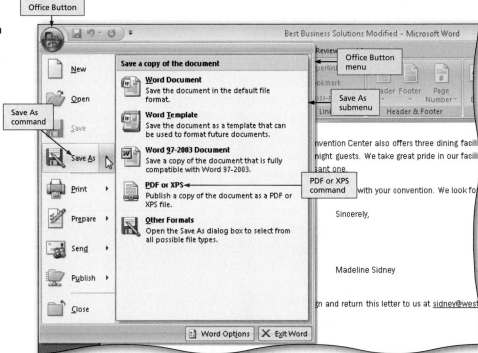

Figure 9–75

2

- Click PDF or XPS on the Save As submenu to display the Publish as PDF or XPS dialog box.

Q&A What if the PDF or XPS command is not on my Save As submenu?

The XPS add-in utility has not been installed on your computer. See the discussion on the previous page for information about installing the XPS add-in utility.

- If necessary, click the 'Save as type' box arrow and then click XPS Document.

- If necessary, place a check mark in the 'Open file after publishing' check box, so that you can see the XPS document that Word creates (Figure 9–76).

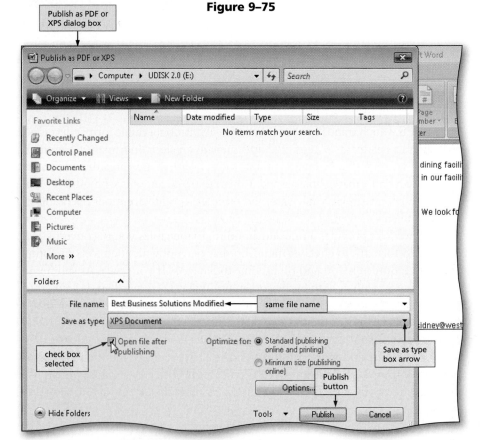

Figure 9–76

3

- Click the Publish button, which creates an XPS file of the current document, starts your default XPS viewer program, and displays the XPS file in the viewer window, which in this case is Internet Explorer (Figure 9–77).

4

- Click the Close button to close the XPS file and exit the viewer.

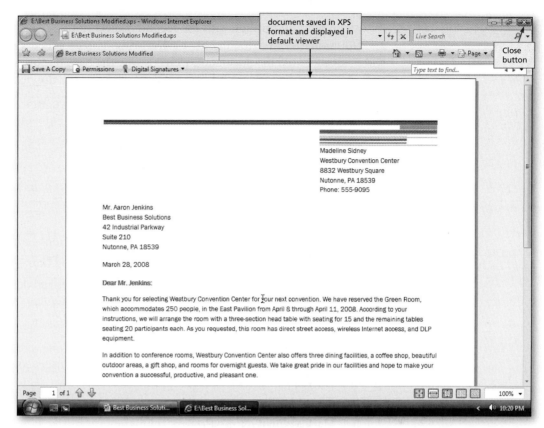

Figure 9–77

To Customize How Word Opens E-Mail Attachments

When a user e-mails you a Word document as an attachment, Word displays the document in Full Screen Reading view. This view is designed to increase the readability and legibility of an on-screen document. Full Screen Reading view, however, does not represent how the document will look when it is printed. For this reason, many users prefer working in Print Layout view to read documents. To exit Full Screen Reading view, click the Close button in the upper-right corner of the screen. As an alternative, you can instruct Word not to use Full Screen Reading view when opening e-mail attachments. The following steps customize how Word opens e-mail attachments.

1 Click the Office Button and then click the Word Options button to display the Word Options dialog box. If necessary, click Popular in the left pane.

2 Remove the check mark from the 'Open e-mail attachments in Full Screen Reading view' check box.

3 Click the OK button.

To Close the Document

You now are finished with the second project in this chapter, incorporating security and functionality in a document. Earlier when you attached a digital signature, Word automatically saved the document, which is why the Save button is dimmed. The following step closes the document and leaves Word running for the next project in the chapter.

 Click the Office Button and then click Close on the Office Button menu to close the document and leave Word running.

To Set a Default Save Location

If you wanted to change the default location that Word uses when it saves a document, you would perform the following steps.

1. Click the Office Button and then click the Word Options button.
2. Click Save in the left pane of the Word Options dialog box.
3. In the 'Default file location' text box, type the new desired default save location.
4. Click the OK button.

To Mark a Document as Final

If you wanted to mark a document as final so that users could not edit it, you would perform the following steps.

1. Click the Office Button and then point to Prepare.
2. Click Mark as Final on the Prepare submenu.
3. Click the OK button.

Working with XML

The final project in this chapter converts an online form to the XML format so that the data in the form can be shared with other programs. XML is a popular format for structuring data, which allows the data to be reused and shared. **XML**, which stands for eXtensible Markup Language, is a language used to encapsulate data and a description of the data in a single text file, the **XML file**. XML uses **tags** to describe data items. Each data item is called an **element**. Businesses often create standard XML file layouts and tags to describe commonly used types of data.

In Word, you have three options for structuring an XML document:

1. Save a file in a default XML format, in which Word parses up the document into individual components that can be used by other programs.

2. Incorporate content controls in a template, which can interact directly with programs stored on central sites such as a SharePoint Server.

3. Specifically identify sections of the document as XML elements. This feature is available only in the stand-alone version of Microsoft Office Word 2007 and in Microsoft Office Professional 2007.

This project guides you through the first and third options. Chapter 8 presented the second option. If you are stepping through this project on a computer, you must have the stand-alone version of Microsoft Office Word 2007 or Microsoft Office Professional 2007 to perform the steps related to option 3.

To Save a Document in the Default XML Format

The first step in this project is to open the document, That Pool Place - No Schema Attached, from the Data Files for Students. See the inside back cover of this book for instructions on downloading the Data Files for Students, or contact your instructor for information about accessing the required files. Then, you will save the document in the XML format. The following steps save a file in the XML format.

- Open the file called That Pool Place - No Schema Attached from the Data Files for Students.

- Click the Office Button and then click Save As to display the Save As dialog box.

- Click the 'Save as type' box arrow and then click Word XML Document in the list (Figure 9–78).

- Click the Save button to save the template as an XML document.

Q&A

How can I identify an XML document?

XML documents typically have an .xml extension.

Figure 9–78

To Close the Document

You now are finished saving a file in the default XML format. The following step closes the document and leaves Word running for the next steps in the chapter.

1 Click the Office Button and then click Close on the Office Button menu to close the document and leave Word running.

To Attach a Schema File

An **XML schema** is a special type of XML file that describes the layout of elements in other XML files. Word users typically do not create XML schema files. Computer programmers or other technical personnel create an XML schema file and provide it to Word users. XML schema files, often simply called schema files, usually have an extension of .xsd.

The schema file to be used in this project is on the Data Files for Students. See the inside back cover of this book for instructions on downloading the Data Files for Students, or contact your instructor for information about accessing the required files. The steps on the next page attach a schema to a file.

1

- Open the file called That Pool Place from the Data Files for Students.

- Use the Save As command to save the file with the new name, That Pool Place - Schema Attached.

2

- Display the Developer tab.

- Click the Schema button on the Developer tab to display the Templates and Add-ins dialog box (Figure 9–79).

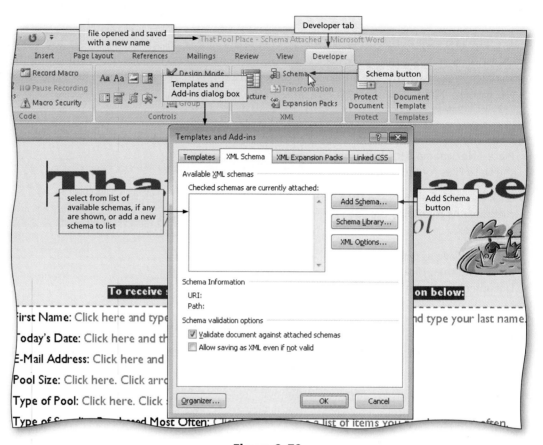

Figure 9–79

3

- Click the Add Schema button to display the Add Schema dialog box.

- Locate the file called That Pool Place.xsd on the Data Files for Students.

- Click That Pool Place.xsd in the list of schema files (Figure 9–80).

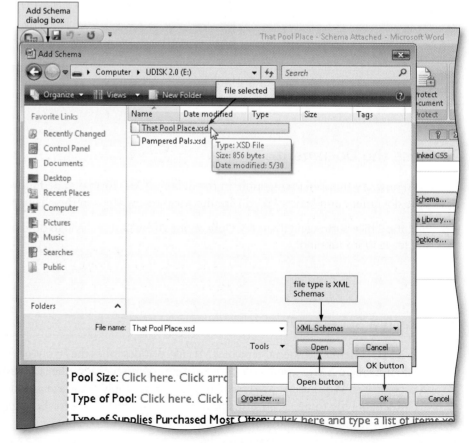

Figure 9–80

4
- Click the Open button in the Add Schema dialog box to display the Schema Settings dialog box.

- Type `urn:form-schema-1` in the URI text box, and then type `That Pool Place` in the Alias text box (Figure 9–81).

Q&A

What is a URI and an alias?

Word uses the URI, also called a **namespace**, to refer to the schema. Because these names are difficult to remember, you can define a namespace alias. In a setting outside of an academic environment, a computer administrator would provide you with the appropriate namespace entry.

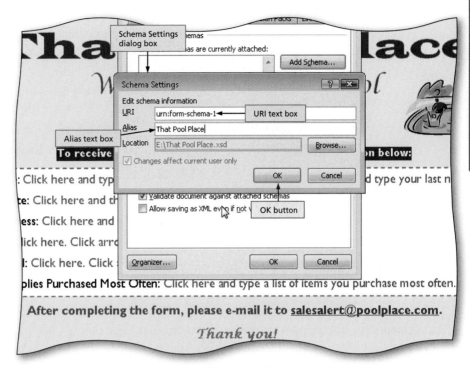

Figure 9–81

5
- Click the OK button to add the schema to the Schema Library and then add the namespace alias to the list of available schemas in the XML Schema sheet in the Templates and Add-ins dialog box.

- If necessary, place a check mark in the That Pool Place check box (Figure 9–82).

6
- Click the OK button, which causes Word to attach the selected schema to the open document and display the XML Structure task pane in the Word window.

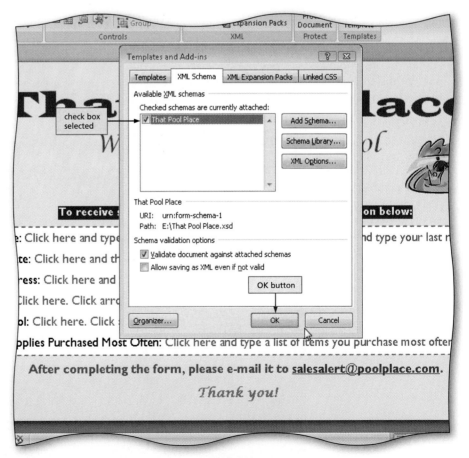

Figure 9–82

To Delete a Schema from the Schema Library

To delete a schema from a document, you would remove the check mark from the schema name in the XML Schema sheet in the Templates and Add-ins dialog box (Figure 9–82 on the previous page). If you wanted to delete a schema altogether from the Schema Library, you would do the following.

1. Click the Schema button on the Developer tab to display the Templates and Add-ins dialog box.
2. Click the Schema Library button to display the Schema Library dialog box.
3. Click the schema you want to delete in the 'Select a schema' list and then click the Delete Schema button.
4. When Word displays a dialog box asking if you are sure you wish to delete the schema, click the Yes button.
5. Click the OK button and then click the Cancel button.

To Add a Parent and Child XML Element

After a schema has been attached to a document, the next step is to add XML elements to the document. XML elements are data items whose value often changes. The online form in this project has eight XML elements: First Name, Last Name, Today's Date, E-Mail Address, Pool Size, Type of Pool, Type of Supplies Purchased Most Often, and the entire online form itself. The first step is to add the entire online form XML element, called the **parent element**, to the document and then add the elements subordinate to the parent, called the **child elements**.

The following steps add XML elements to the document, which is called tagging the text. First, you select the item to be tagged and then you add the desired XML element to apply the tag.

- Position the insertion point at the top of the document.

- In the 'Choose an element to apply to your current selection' list in the XML Structure task pane, double-click ThatPoolPlace{That Pool Place} to display the 'Apply to entire document' dialog box (Figure 9–83).

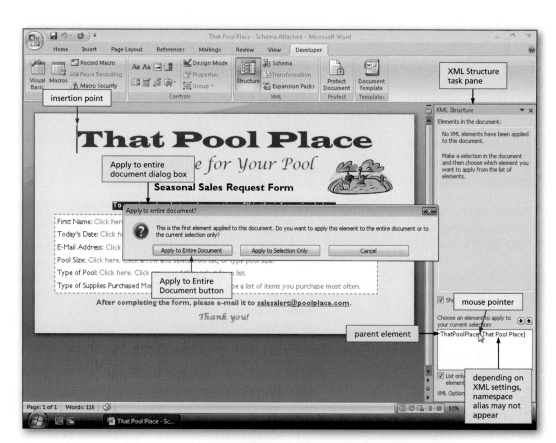

Figure 9–83

2

- Click the Apply to Entire Document button to place start and end tags on the entire document, that is, to tag the parent element.

- Be sure the 'Show XML tags in the document' check box contains a check mark (Figure 9–84).

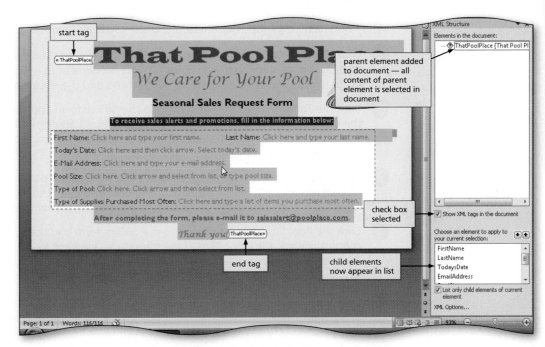

Figure 9–84

3

- Click the First Name content control in the online form and then click its label to select the content control.

Q&A

What if the item to select is not a content control?

Drag through the item you want to assign to the child element.

- Click FirstName in the 'Choose an element to apply to your current selection' list, which places start and end tags on the text selected in the document and moves the selected child element below the parent element in the 'Elements in the document' list in the task pane (Figure 9–85).

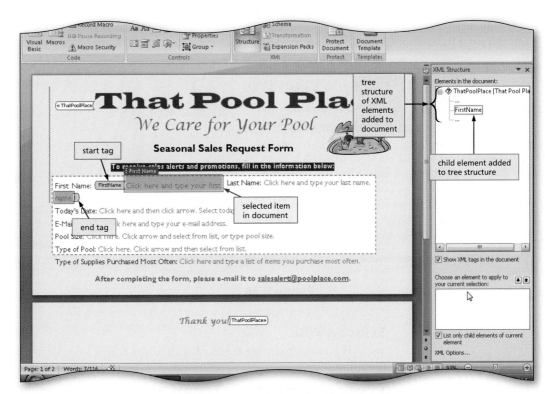

Figure 9–85

To Add XML Elements

The next steps add the remaining child XML elements to the XML tree structure.

1 Click the Last Name content control in the online form and then click its label to select the content control. Click LastName in the 'Choose an element to apply to your current selection' list to tag the text selected in the document and add the element to the XML tree structure.

2 Click the Today's Date content control in the online form and then click its label to select the content control. Click TodaysDate in the 'Choose an element to apply to your current selection' list to tag the text selected in the document and add the element to the XML tree structure.

3 Click the E-Mail Address content control in the online form and then click its label to select the content control. Click EmailAddress in the 'Choose an element to apply to your current selection' list to tag the text selected in the document and add the element to the XML tree structure.

4 Click the Pool Size content control in the online form and then click its label to select the content control. Click PoolSize in the 'Choose an element to apply to your current selection' list to tag the text selected in the document and add the element to the XML tree structure.

5 Click the Type of Pool content control in the online form and then click its label to select the content control. Click TypeOfPool in the 'Choose an element to apply to your current selection' list to tag the text selected in the document and add the element to the XML tree structure.

6 Click the Type of Supplies Purchased Most Often content control in the online form and then click its label to select the content control. Click TypeOfSupplies in the 'Choose an element to apply to your current selection' list to tag the text selected in the document and add the element to the XML tree structure.

7 Click anywhere to remove the selection from the text (Figure 9-86).

8 Remove the check mark from the 'Show XML tags in the document' check box so that the tags no longer appear in the document window.

Figure 9–86

To Remove a Tag

If you wanted to remove a tag that was added to a document, you would perform the following steps.

1. Right-click the start or end tag and then click Remove tag on the shortcut menu — which instructs Word to remove both the start and end tag.

or

2. Right-click the element name in the XML Structure task pane and then click Remove tag on the shortcut menu.

To Save a Document in the Default XML Format

The next step in this project is to save the XML document.

1 Click the Office Button and then click Save As to display the Save As dialog box.

2 Click the 'Save as type' box arrow and then click Word XML Document in the list.

3 Click the Save button to save the template as an XML document. Close the XML Structure task pane.

To Set Exceptions to Editing Restrictions

When users open an online form, you want them to be able to edit only the placeholder text. You can use the Restrict Formatting and Editing task pane to allow editing in just certain areas of the document, a procedure called adding users excepted from restrictions. The following steps set exceptions to editing restrictions.

1

- Click the Protect Document button on the Developer tab to display the Restrict Formatting and Editing task pane.

2

- If necessary, place a check mark in the 'Allow only this type of editing in the document' check box and then change the associated text box to No changes (Read only), which instructs Word to prevent any editing to the document.

- Click the First Name placeholder text. Press and hold the CTRL key while clicking the rest of the placeholder text in the online form.

- Place a check mark in the Everyone check box in the Exceptions (optional) area, which instructs Word that the selected text can be edited — the rest of the form will be read only (Figure 9–87).

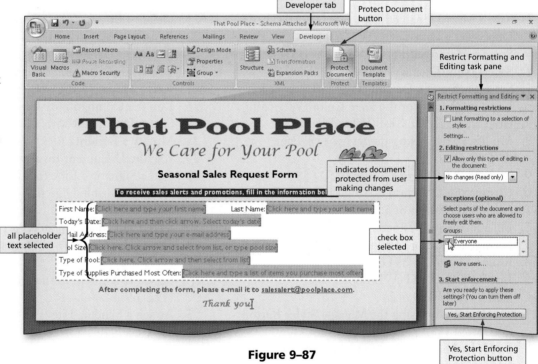

Figure 9–87

3

- Click the Yes, Start Enforcing Protection button in the Restrict Formatting and Editing task pane.

- Click the OK button in the Start Enforcing Protection dialog box.

- Close the Restrict Formatting and Editing task pane.

BTW

Quick Reference
For a table that lists how to complete the tasks covered in this book using the mouse, Ribbon, shortcut menu, and keyboard, see the Quick Reference Summary at the back of this book, or visit the Word 2007 Quick Reference Web page (scsite.com/wd2007/qr).

To Save an XML Document as a Template and Quit Word

The next step is to save the document as a template with a new name so that a user can open a new document window based on the template and then quit Word.

1 Click the Office Button and then click Save As to display the Save As dialog box.

2 Change the file name to That Pool Place Modified - Schema Attached.

3 Click the 'Save as type' box arrow and then click Word Template in the list.

4 Click the Save button to save the template so that users can create new documents based on the template.

5 Click the Close button on the Word title bar.

Chapter Summary

In this chapter, you learned how to enhance the look of graphics and shapes with fill effects and 3-D effects; automate a series of tasks with a macro; secure a document with digital signatures, passwords, and other settings; and use XML for data that will be shared with other programs. The items listed below include all the new Word skills you have learned in this chapter.

1. Save a Macro-Enabled Template (WD 645)
2. Unprotect a Document (WD 646)
3. Specify Macro Settings in Word (WD 647)
4. Save a New Theme (WD 648)
5. Set a Theme as a Default (WD 650)
6. Use a Fill Effect for the Page Color (WD 650)
7. Convert a Table to Text (WD 653)
8. Modify a Style Using the Styles Task Pane (WD 656)
9. Add a 3-D Effect to a Shape (WD 658)
10. Change the Direction of a 3-D Effect (WD 659)
11. Change the Color of a 3-D Effect (WD 660)
12. Fill a Shape with a Picture (WD 660)
13. Change the Color of a Picture (WD 662)
14. Rotate a Graphic (WD 664)
15. Insert a Date Field (WD 666)
16. Edit a Field (WD 667)
17. Modify a Style Using the Manage Styles Button (WD 669)
18. Record a Macro and Assign It a Shortcut Key (WD 671)
19. Run a Macro (WD 674)
20. Add a Macro as a Button to the Quick Access Toolbar (WD 674)

21. Delete a Button from a Toolbar (WD 677)
22. Rename a Macro (WD 677)
23. Delete a Macro (WD 678)
24. Create an Automatic Macro (WD 678)
25. Edit a Macro's VBA Code (WD 679)
26. Run the Compatibility Checker (WD 683)
27. Save a Document with a Password (WD 685)
28. Modify a Building Block (WD 687)
29. Use the Document Inspector (WD 688)
30. Add a Signature Line to a Document (WD 691)
31. Add an Invisible Digital Signature to a Document (WD 692)
32. Save a Document in an XPS Format (WD 694)
33. Customize How Word Opens E-Mail Attachments (WD 695)
34. Save a Document in the Default XML Format (WD 697)
35. Attach a Schema File (WD 697)
36. Delete a Schema from the Schema Library (WD 700)
37. Add a Parent and Child XML Element (WD 700)
38. Remove a Tag (WD 702)
39. Set Exceptions to Editing Restrictions (WD 703)

If you have a SAM user profile, you may have access to hands-on instruction, practice, and assessment. Log in to your SAM account (http://sam2007.course.com) to launch any assigned training activities or exams that relate to the skills covered in this chapter.

Learn It Online

Test your knowledge of chapter content and key terms.

Instructions: To complete the Learn It Online exercises, start your browser, click the Address bar, and then enter the Web address scsite.com/wd2007/learn. When the Word 2007 Learn It Online page is displayed, click the link for the exercise you want to complete and then read the instructions.

Chapter Reinforcement TF, MC, and SA
A series of true/false, multiple choice, and short answer questions that test your knowledge of the chapter content.

Flash Cards
An interactive learning environment where you identify chapter key terms associated with displayed definitions.

Practice Test
A series of multiple choice questions that test your knowledge of chapter content and key terms.

Who Wants To Be a Computer Genius?
An interactive game that challenges your knowledge of chapter content in the style of a television quiz show.

Wheel of Terms
An interactive game that challenges your knowledge of chapter key terms in the style of the television show *Wheel of Fortune*.

Crossword Puzzle Challenge
A crossword puzzle that challenges your knowledge of key terms presented in the chapter.

Apply Your Knowledge

Reinforce the skills and apply the concepts you learned in this chapter.

Working with XML
Instructions: Start Word. Open the document, Apply 9-1 Pampered Pals Draft, from the Data Files for Students. See the inside back cover of this book for instructions on downloading the Data Files for Students, or contact your instructor for information about accessing the required files.

In this assignment, you attach an XML schema file, add XML elements to a template (Figure 9–88), save a file as an XML file, set exceptions to editing restrictions, and save an XML document as a template.

Figure 9–88

Continued >

Apply Your Knowledge *continued*

Perform the following tasks:

1. Unprotect the template.

2. Save the template in the default XML format using the file name Apply 9-1 Pampered Pals - No Schema Attached.

3. Attach the XML schema file called Pampered Pals.xsd to the Pampered Pals template. Use urn:form-schema-2 as the URI and Pampered Pals as the alias. The schema file is on the Data Files for Students. See the inside back cover of this book for instructions on downloading the Data Files for Students, or contact your instructor for information about accessing the required files.

4. Add the parent element, PamperedPals, to the template.

5. Add all the child elements to the template — one for each data entry field.

6. Save the document as an XML document using the file name, Apply 9-1 Pampered Pals - Schema Attached.

7. Set exceptions to editing restrictions so that all users can edit only the placeholder text in the document. Protect the document without a password.

8. Save the XML document as a template using the name, Apply 9-1 Pampered Pals Modified - Schema Attached.

9. Submit the files in the format specified by your instructor.

Extend Your Knowledge

Extend the skills you learned in this chapter and experiment with new skills. You may need to use Help to complete the assignment.

Working with Document Security

Instructions: Start Word. Open the document, Extend 9-1 Innovative Products Letter Draft, from the Data Files for Students. See the inside back cover of this book for instructions on downloading the Data Files for Students, or contact your instructor for information about accessing the required files.

You will create your own digital ID, add an invisible digital signature to a document, add a digital signature line, save the document as an XPS file, and encrypt the document.

Perform the following tasks:

1. Use Help to review and expand your knowledge about these topics: creating a digital ID, invisible digital signatures, signature lines, XPS files, and document encryption.

2. Create your own digital ID.

3. Add a digital signature line to the document. Use your personal information in the signature line.

4. Add an invisible digital signature to the document.

5. Save the document as an XPS file. View and print the XPS file. Familiarize yourself with the buttons and commands in the XPS viewer (Figure 9–89). Close the XPS file.

6. Encrypt the document. Be sure to use a password you will remember.

7. Save the document with a new file name. Then, close the document and re-open it. Enter the password when prompted.

8. View the signatures in the document.

9. Sign the document; that is, enter your digital signature (type it or select an image).

10. Save the document again. Change the document properties as specified by your instructor. Submit the document in the format specified by your instructor.

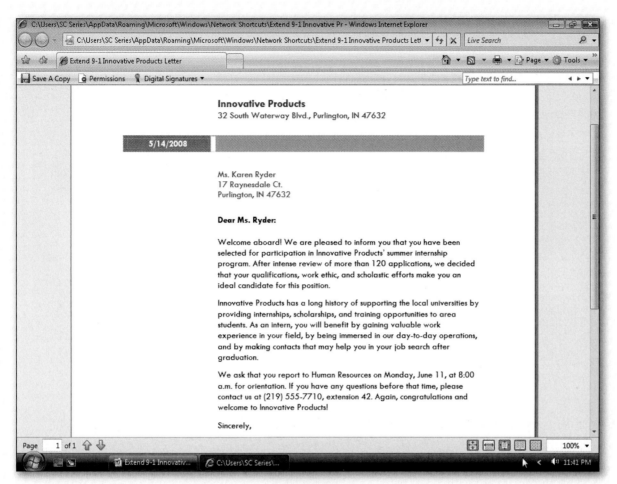

Figure 9–89

Make It Right

Analyze a document and correct all errors and/or improve the design.

Formatting an Online Form

Instructions: Start Word. Open the document, Make It Right 9-1 Parent Athletic Association Letter Draft, from the Data Files for Students. See the inside back cover of this book for instructions on downloading the Data Files for Students, or contact your instructor for information about accessing the required files.

The document is a letter that requires finishing touches before sending (Figure 9–90 on the next page). You are to add and edit a building block, change the font set and save the modified theme, run the compatibility checker, save the document with a password, use the Document Inspector, and disable Full Screen Reading view for e-mail attachments.

Perform the following tasks:
1. Add a building block for the contact information (inside address). Save it to the Quick Parts gallery. Use the name, Nicholas Blake. Do not enter a description.
2. Edit the building block for Nicholas Blake to include this description: Athlete of the Year.
3. Change the font set to one of your choice. Save the modified theme with the name PAA. If approved by your instructor, set the modified theme as the default.
4. Run the compatibility checker to determine if this document can be saved in the Word 97-2003 format. Add a comment to the document indicating the results of the compatibility checker.

Continued >

Make It Right *continued*

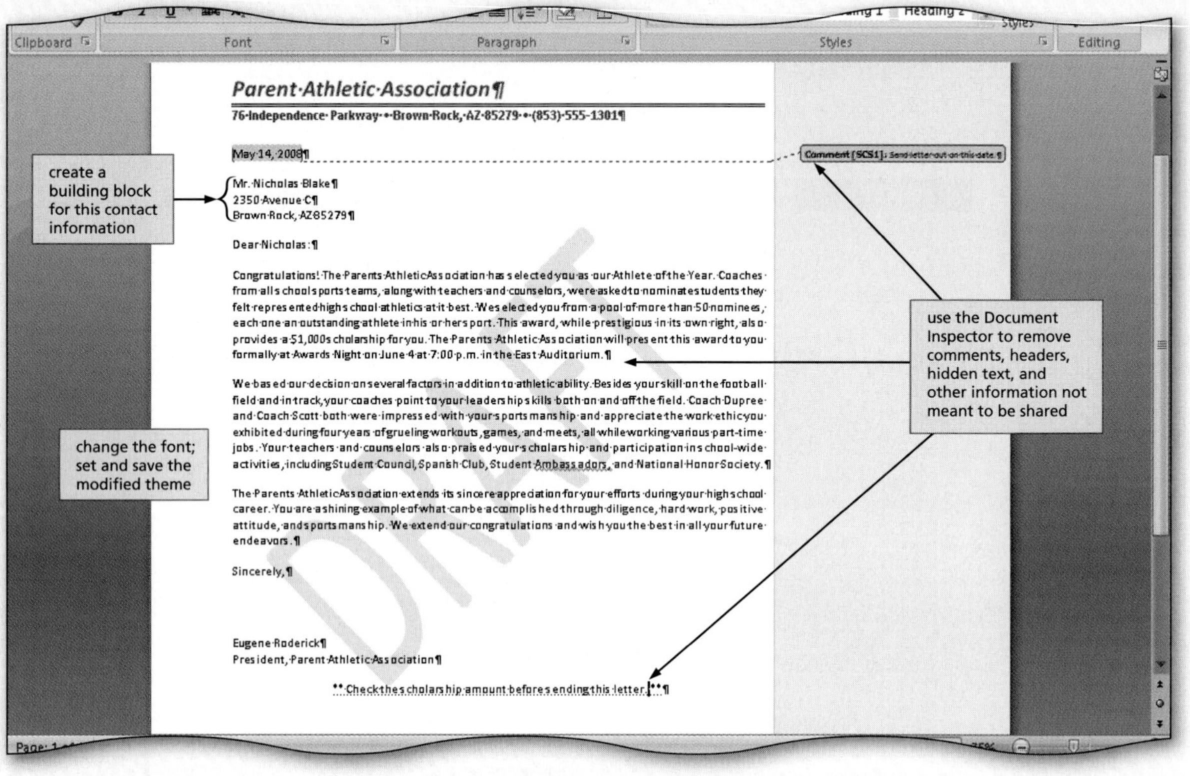

Figure 9–90

5. Save the document with a new name and a password of your choice. Be sure to select a password you will remember.

6. Use the Document Inspector to determine the types of personal information and other hidden content that is in the document. What are the results? Remove the comments, document properties, headers, footers, and hidden text.

7. Change the document properties as specified by your instructor. Save the document again.

8. E-mail a copy of the document to yourself.

9. Disable the open e-mail attachments in Full Screen Reading view setting.

10. Open the e-mail attachment.

11. Submit the document in the format specified by your instructor.

In the Lab

Design and/or create a document using the guidelines, concepts, and skills presented in this chapter. Labs are listed in order of increasing difficulty.

Lab 1: Enhancing the Graphics and Shapes of an Online Form

Problem: You created the online form shown in Figure 8-80 on page WD 634 for Andrew County Public Library. Your supervisor has asked you to change the form's appearance. You modify the form so that it looks like the one shown in Figure 9–91.

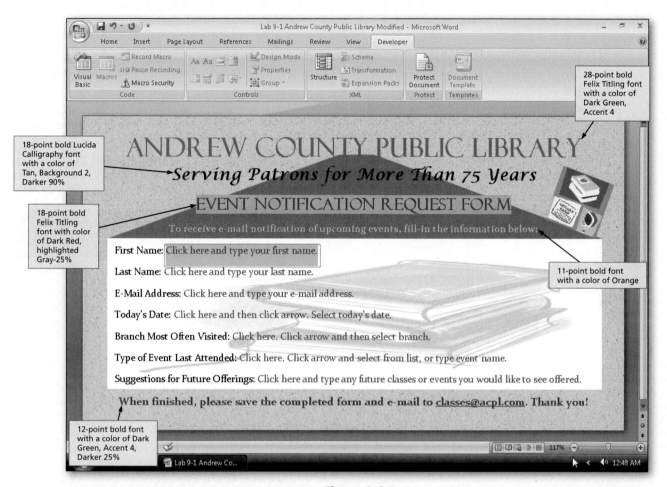

Figure 9–91

Perform the following tasks:

1. Open the template called Lab 8-1 Andrew County Public Library that you created in Lab 1 of Chapter 8. Save the template with a new file name of Lab 9-1 Andrew County Public Library Modified. If you did not complete the lab in Chapter 8, see your instructor for a copy.

2. Use the Recycled paper fill effect for the page color.

3. Change the color scheme to Aspect. Change the font set to Flow.

4. Edit the last two lines so that the text fits on a single line as shown in Figure 9–91.

5. Modify the formats of the company name, business tag line, form title, user instruction, and thank you lines as shown in Figure 9–91 (or with similar fonts).

6. Convert the table to text for the 2 × 1 table containing the First Name and Last Name content controls. Extend the rectangle to cover the entire data entry area.

7. Add the 3-D Style 10 to the rectangle shape. Change the 3-D color to Orange, Accent 1, Lighter 80%.

8. Modify the style of the placeholder text to the color Orange, Accent 1, Darker 25%.

9. Use the picture fill effect to place a picture in the rectangle shape. Use the picture called Books from the Data Files for Students. See the inside back cover of this book for instructions on downloading the Data Files for Students, or contact your instructor for information about accessing the required files.

10. Change the color of the picture in the rectangle to washout.

Continued >

In the Lab *continued*

11. Remove the current clip art and insert the one shown in the figure (or a similar image). Format the image as floating In Front of Text. Resize the clip art. Recolor it to Accent color 4 Light. Rotate the graphic as shown in the figure.

12. Protect the form.

13. Save the form again and submit it in the format specified by your instructor.

14. Access the template through Windows Explorer. Fill in the form and submit the filled-in form in the format specified by your instructor.

In the Lab

Lab 2: Adding a Field and Macros to an Online Form

Problem: You created the online form shown in Figure 8-81 on page WD 636 for Entrée Express. Your supervisor has asked you to change the form's appearance, add a field, and add some macros. You modify the form so that it looks like the one shown in Figure 9–92.

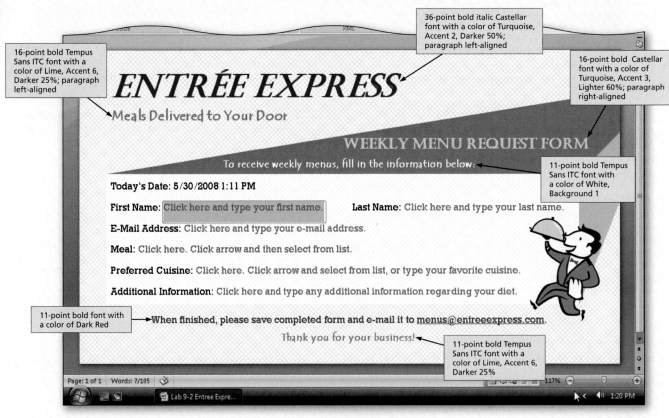

Figure 9–92

Perform the following tasks:

1. Open the template called Lab 8-2 Entree Express that you created in Lab 2 of Chapter 8. Save the template as a macro-enabled template with a new file name of Lab 9-2 Entree Express Modified. If you did not complete the lab in Chapter 8, see your instructor for a copy.

2. Change the color scheme to Flow. Change the font set to Foundry.

3. Use the page color Turquoise, Accent 3, Lighter 60%. Apply the Outlined diamond pattern fill effect to the page color.

4. Modify the formats of the company name, business tag line, form title, user instruction, and thank you lines as shown in Figure 9–92 (or with similar fonts).

5. Remove the Today's Date content control. Insert a date field from Quick Parts in the format 5/31/2008.

6. Edit the date field so that it displays the date and time in the format of 5/31/2008 1:10 PM. Move the date line to the top of the data entry form.

7. Add the 3-D Style 9 to the rectangle shape. Change the 3-D color to Dark Teal, Text 2, Lighter 80%. Change the pattern inside the rectangle to 90%.

8. Remove the current clip art and insert the one shown in the figure (or a similar image). Format the image as floating In Front of Text. Resize the clip art. Rotate the graphic as shown in the figure.

9. Record a macro that hides the Developer tab. Assign it the shortcut key, ALT+D. Run the macro to test it.

10. Create an automatic macro called AutoNew using the macro recorder. The macro should change the view to page width.

11. Protect the form.

12. Save the form again and submit it in the format specified by your instructor.

13. Access the template through Windows Explorer. Fill in the form and submit the filled-in form in the format specified by your instructor.

In the Lab

Lab 3: Enhancing the Look of an Online Form and Adding Macros to It

Problem: You created the online form shown in Figure 8-82 on page WD 638 for the Book Barn. Your supervisor has asked you to change the form's appearance, add a field, and add some macros. You modify the form so that it looks like the one shown in Figure 9–93.

Figure 9–93

Continued >

In the Lab *continued*

Perform the following tasks:

1. Open the template called Lab 8-3 Book Barn that you created in Lab 3 of Chapter 8. Save the template as a macro-enabled template with a new file name of Lab 9-3 Book Barn Modified. If you did not complete the lab in Chapter 8, see your instructor for a copy.

2. Use the Stationery paper fill effect for the page color.

3. Change the color scheme to Equity. Change the font set to Opulent.

4. Edit the last two lines so that the form fits on a single line as shown in Figure 9–93 on the previous page.

5. Modify the formats of the company name, business tag line, form title, user instruction, and thank you lines as shown in Figure 9–93 (or with similar fonts).

6. Convert the two tables in the data entry area to text. Extend the rectangle to cover the entire data entry area.

7. Remove the Today's Date content control. Insert a date field from Quick Parts in the format 5/31/2008 1:39:25 PM.

8. Add the 3-D Style 9 to the rectangle shape. Change the direction to Top Left. Change the 3-D color to Tan, Background 2, Darker 10%.

9. Modify the style of the placeholder text to the color Brown, Accent 6, Darker 50%.

10. Use the picture fill effect to place a picture in the rectangle shape. Use the picture called Barn from the Data Files for Students. See the inside back cover of this book for instructions on downloading the Data Files for Students, or contact your instructor for information about accessing the required files.

11. Change the color of the picture in the rectangle to washout.

12. Remove the current clip art and insert the one shown in the figure (or a similar image). Format the image as floating In Front of Text. Resize the clip art. Rotate the graphic as shown in the figure.

13. Record a macro that hides the Developer tab. Assign it the shortcut key, ALT+D. Run the macro to test it.

14. Add a button to the Quick Access Toolbar for the macro created in Step 13. Test the button and then delete the button.

15. Create an automatic macro called AutoNew using the macro recorder. The macro should change the view to page width.

16. Edit the macro so that it also hides the Developer tab and hides formatting marks.

17. Protect the form.

18. Save the form again and submit it in the format specified by your instructor.

19. Access the template through Windows Explorer. Fill in the form and submit the filled-in form in the format specified by your instructor.

Cases and Places

Apply your creative thinking and problem solving skills to design and implement a solution.

● Easier ●● More Difficult

● 1: Modify an Online Form for an Auto Dealership

You created the online form for Cool Ride Auto Sales that was defined in Cases and Places Assignment 1 in Chapter 8 on page WD 639. Your boss was pleased with the results and by the response from customers. You and your boss, however, believe the form can be improved by enhancing its appearance. Make the following modifications to the form: Change the company name, slogan, and title to a different font and color; change the page color to a texture or fill pattern; change the highlight; and change the font and color of the last line. Add a 3-D effect to the rectangle; if necessary, resize the rectangle to include all text. In the rectangle, add a suitable picture fill effect and recolor it using the Washout effect. If necessary, delete the last line on the form so that the entire form's contents fit on one page. Delete the existing clip art, replace it with new clip art, and then rotate it. Use the concepts and techniques presented in this chapter to modify the online form.

●● 2: Modify an Online Form for a Real Estate Office

You created the online form for Richards Realty that was defined in Cases and Places Assignment 2 in Chapter 8 on page WD 639. Your neighbor was pleased with the results, but now she wants you to make a few modifications to the form you created. Make the following modifications to the form: change the company name, slogan, and title to a different font and color; change the page color to a texture or fill pattern; and change the font and color of the last line. Add a 3-D effect to the rectangle; if necessary, resize the rectangle to include all text. Change the direction and color of the 3-D effect. In the rectangle, add a suitable picture fill effect and recolor it using the Washout effect. If necessary, delete the last line on the form so that the entire form's contents fit on one page. Delete the existing clip art, replace it with new clip art, and then rotate it. Use the concepts and techniques presented in this chapter to modify the online form. When finished, mark the document as final.

●● 3: Modify an Online Form for a Property Management Agency

You created the online form for Sunshine Rentals that was defined in Cases and Places Assignment 3 in Chapter 8 on page WD 639. Your boss has asked you to change the form's appearance by changing its clip art, fonts and font color, and page color. He has decided that the slogan should be changed to: We've Got Florida Covered. He wants you to add a picture as fill and a 3-D effect to the rectangle, and resize it so that it contains all data entry area text. In addition, delete the date content control and insert a date field in its place. Then, move the date content control to the top of the form. Specify the appropriate macro security level. Add a macro to the form and assign it to a button on the Quick Access Toolbar. Then, add an AutoNew macro that controls how the form initially is displayed on the screen. Use the concepts and techniques presented in this chapter to modify the online form.

●● 4: Create an Online Form for Your Future Business

Make It Personal

You created the online form that was defined in Cases and Places Assignment 4 in Chapter 8 on page WD 640. Now you have decided to make a few embellishments and improvements to your form. Use the concepts and techniques you learned in this chapter to modify the form. Set your USB flash drive

Continued >

Cases and Places *continued*

as the default save location. At a minimum, you should change all fonts, font colors, and clip art; use a pattern or texture fill effect for the page; move the date content control to the top of the form and change it to a date field that includes date and time; and add a 3-D effect to the data entry area. When finished, mark the document as final.

•• 5: Create an Online Form for Your School

Working Together

You created the online form that was defined in Cases and Places Assignment 5 in Chapter 8 on page WD 640. Now your team has decided to make a few embellishments and improvements to your form. Use the concepts and techniques you learned in this chapter to modify the form. At a minimum, you should change all fonts, font colors, and clip art; use a pattern or texture fill effect for the page; move the date content control to the top of the form and change it to a date field that includes date and time; and add a 3-D effect to the data entry area. Add three macros to the form and assign each to a button on the Quick Access Toolbar. Then, add an AutoNew macro that controls how the form initially is displayed on the screen. Assign each team member a section of the form to modify. Then, as a team, determine which changes look best in the new form and implement the changes.

Blogging Feature
Creating a Blog Post

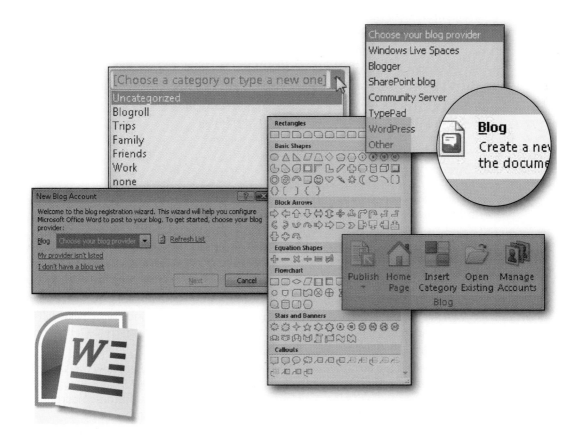

Objectives

You will have mastered the material in this feature when you can:

- Create a new blog post
- Crop a picture
- Change the shape of a picture
- Insert a blog category
- Display the Web page associated with your blog
- Publish a blog post

Blogging Feature Introduction

A **blog**, short for **Weblog**, is an informal Web site consisting of date- or time-stamped articles, or **posts**, in a diary or journal format, usually listed in reverse chronological order. Blogs reflect the interests, opinions, and personalities of the author, called the **blogger**, and sometimes of the site visitors as well.

Project — Blog Post

Blogs have become an important means of worldwide communication. Businesses create blogs to communicate with employees, customers, and vendors. Teachers create blogs to collaborate with other teachers and students, and home users create blogs to share aspects of their personal life with family, friends, and others.

The project in this feature creates a blog post and then publishes it to a registered blog account at WordPress.com, which is a blogging service on the Web. Figure 1a shows the blog Web page with just one post; Figure 1b shows a new blog post created in Word and published to a Web site; Figure 1c shows the updated blog Web page, which shows the new post published at the top of the Web page.

Overview

As you read through this feature, you will learn how to create the blog post shown in Figure 1b and then publish it by performing these general tasks:

- Create the blog post.
- Publish the blog post.

Plan
Ahead

> **General Project Guidelines**
> When creating a blog post, the actions you perform and decisions you make will affect the appearance and characteristics of the finished document. As you create a blog post, such as the project shown in Figure 1, you should follow these general guidelines:
>
> 1. **Create a blog account on the Web.** Many Web sites exist that allow users to set up a blog free or for a fee. Blogging services that work with Word 2007 include Blogger, Community Server, SharePoint blog, TypePad, and WordPress.com. For illustration purposes in this feature, a free blog account was created at WordPress.com.
>
> 2. **Register your blog account in Word.** Before you can use Word to publish a blog post, you must register your blog account in Word. This step establishes a connection between Word and your blog account. The first time you create a new blog post, Word will ask if you want to register a blog account. You can click the Register Later button if you want to learn how to create a blog post without registering a blog account.
>
> 3. **Create a blog post.** Use Word to enter the text and any graphics in your blog post. Some blogging services accept graphics directly from a Word blog post. Others require that you use a picture hosting service to store pictures you use in a blog post.
>
> 4. **Publish a blog post.** When you publish a blog post, the blog post in the Word document is copied to your account at the blogging service. Once the post is published, it appears at the top of the blog Web page. You may need to click the Refresh button in the browser window to display the new post.

(a) Blog Web Page Before New Posting

**(b) Blog Post Created in Word
and Published to Web Site**

**(c) Blog Web Site
with New Posting**

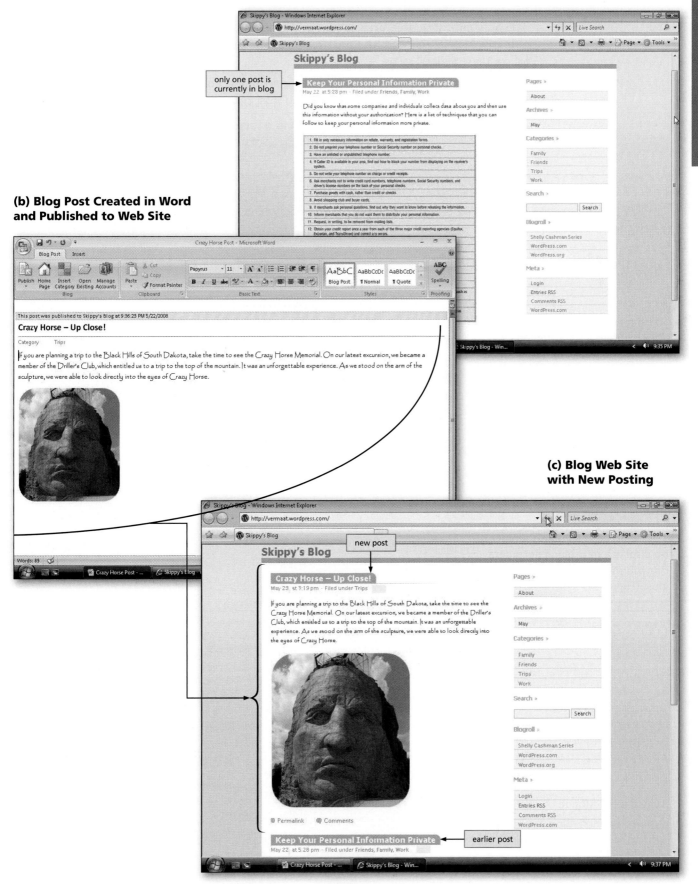

Figure 1

Creating the Blog Post

The blog post in this feature contains a title (Crazy Horse - Up Close!) above a paragraph of text, which is followed by a picture. To create the blog post in this feature, you will follow these general steps:

1. Start Word and create a new blank document for your blog post.
2. Enter the text in the blog post and then format the text.
3. Insert the picture in the blog post and then format the picture.

To Create a Blank Word Document for a Blog Post

The following steps create a blog post based on the current document. Because the current document is blank, the new blog post also will be blank. The following steps create a new blank Word document for a blog post.

- Start Word.

- With a blank document in the Word window, click the Office Button and then point to Publish on the Office Button menu to display the Publish submenu (Figure 2).

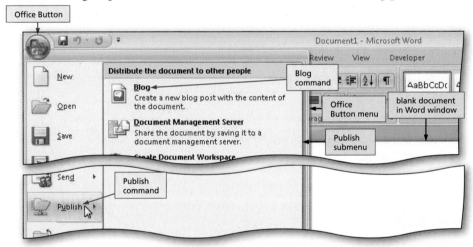

Figure 2

3

- Click Blog on the Publish submenu to display a new blank document for your blog post (Figure 3).

Q&A What if a Register a Blog Account dialog box appears?

Click the Register Later button to skip the registration process at this time. Or, if you have a blog account, you can click the Register Now button and follow the instructions to register your account.

Q&A Why did the Ribbon change?

When creating a blog post, the Ribbon in Word changes to display only the tools required to create and publish a blog post.

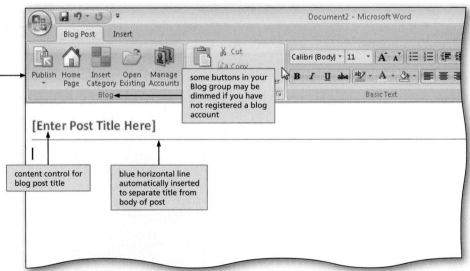

Figure 3

Other Ways

1. Click Office Button, click New, click New blog post, click Create button

To Enter Text

The next step is to enter the blog post title and paragraph of text in the blog post.

1 Click the Enter Post Title Here content control and then type `Crazy Horse - Up Close!` as the title.

2 Position the insertion point below the blue horizontal line and then type this paragraph of text

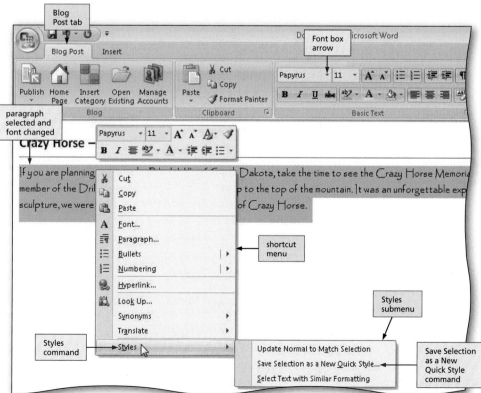

title entered

paragraph entered

Crazy Horse – Up Close!

If you are planning a trip to the Black Hills of South Dakota, take the time to see the Crazy Horse Memorial. On our latest excursion, we became a member of the Driller's Club, which entitled us to a trip to the top of the mountain. It was an unforgettable experience. As we stood on the arm of the sculpture, we were able to look directly into the eyes of Crazy Horse.

insertion point

Figure 4

(Figure 4): `If you are planning a trip to the Black Hills of South Dakota, take the time to see the Crazy Horse Memorial. On our latest excursion, we became a member of the Driller's Club, which entitled us to a trip to the top of the mountain. It was an unforgettable experience. As we stood on the arm of the sculpture, we were able to look directly into the eyes of Crazy Horse.`

To Format Text and Create a New Style Based on the Formatted Text

The paragraph of text below the title in this blog post is formatted with the Papyrus font. Thus, you will change the format of the paragraph of text. Because you want future posts to use the same font, you will create a Quick Style based on the new formats. The following steps select and format the paragraph and then create a Quick Style based on the formats in the selected paragraph.

1 Triple-click the paragraph below the title to select it. Use the Font box arrow on the Blog Post tab to change the font of the selected text to Papyrus.

2 Right-click the selected paragraph to display a shortcut menu. Point to Styles on the shortcut menu to display the Styles submenu (Figure 5).

3 Click Save Selection as a New Quick Style on the Styles submenu to display the Create New Style from Formatting dialog box.

4 Type `Blog Post` in the Name text box. Click the OK button to create the new Quick Style and add it to the Styles gallery.

Figure 5

To Insert a Picture

The next step in creating the blog post is to insert a picture of the Crazy Horse Memorial below the paragraph of text. The picture, which was taken with a digital camera, is available on the Data Files for Students. See the inside back cover of this book for instructions on downloading the Data Files for Students, or contact your instructor for information about accessing the required files. The following steps insert a picture from the USB flash drive.

1 Position the insertion point at the end of the paragraph of text and then press the ENTER key.

2 Display the Insert tab.

3 Click the Insert Picture from File button on the Insert tab to display the Insert Picture dialog box.

4 With your USB flash drive connected to one of the computer's USB ports, locate and then click the file called Crazy Horse on the USB flash drive to select the file (Figure 6).

5 Click the Insert button in the dialog box to insert the picture at the location of the insertion point in the document.

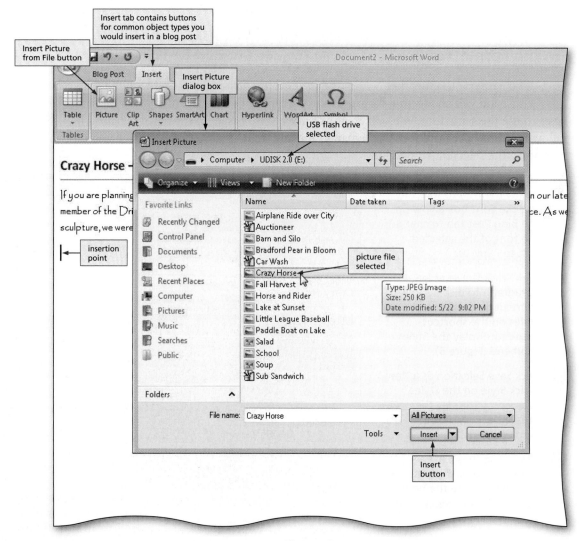

Figure 6

To Crop a Graphic

The next step is to format the picture just inserted. Currently, the image of Crazy Horse's head is not centered in the picture. To make the focal point of the picture centered, you would like to remove a section of the left edge and also the top edge from the picture. Word allows you to **crop**, or remove edges from, a graphic. The following steps crop a picture.

- Click the Crop button on the Format tab, which changes the graphic's sizing handles to cropping handles and also attaches a cropping image to the mouse pointer.

- Position the mouse pointer on the middle-left cropping handle so that it looks like a sideways letter T (Figure 7).

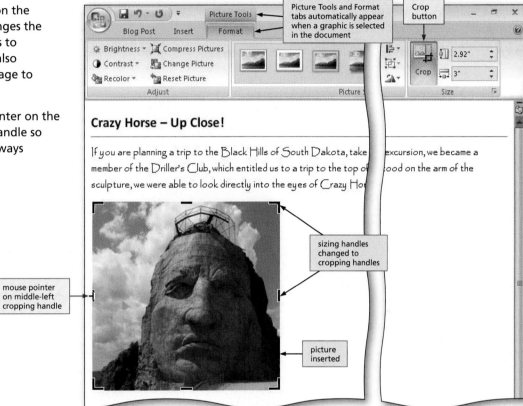

Figure 7

- Drag the middle-left cropping handle rightward to the location of the mouse pointer shown in Figure 8.

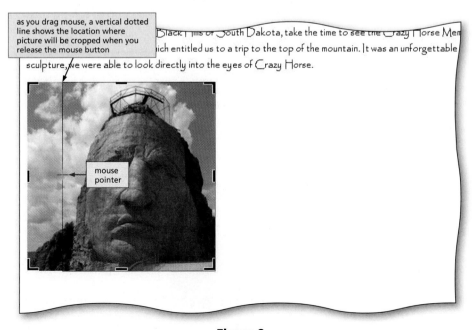

Figure 8

- Release the mouse button to crop the graphic to the location shown in Figure 8 on the previous page.

- Position the mouse pointer on the middle-top cropping handle so that it looks like an upside-down letter T and then drag the cropping handle downward to the location of the mouse pointer shown in Figure 9.

- Release the mouse button to crop the graphic to the location shown in Figure 9.

- Click the Crop button on the Format tab to deactivate the cropping tool, which changes the cropping handles on the graphic back to sizing handles.

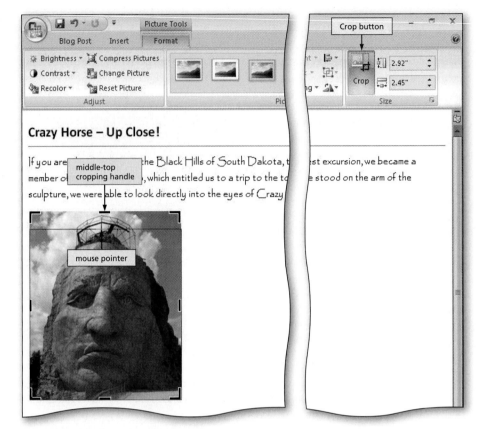

Figure 9

Other Ways
1. With graphic selected, click Size Dialog Box Launcher on Format tab, enter values   in Crop from text boxes, click Close button

To Change a Picture Shape

The picture in the blog post currently has a rectangle shape. In this feature, the picture is the shape of a rounded rectangle. Thus, the following steps change the shape of the picture.

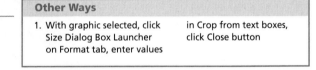

- With the picture selected, click the Picture Shape button on the Format tab to display the Picture Shape gallery (Figure 10).

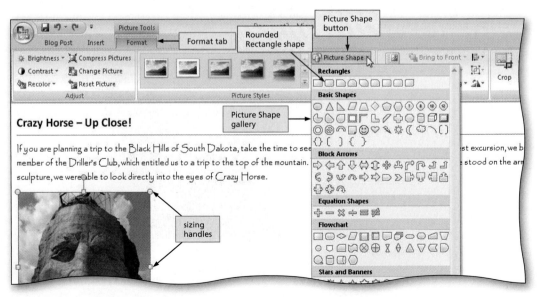

Figure 10

- Click Rounded Rectangle in the Picture Shape gallery to apply the rounded rectangle shape to the selected picture.

- Click outside of the picture to remove the selection from the picture (Figure 11).

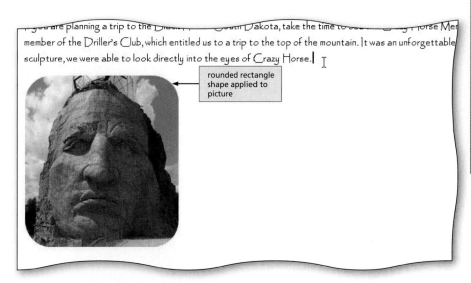

Figure 11

To Insert a Category

In this feature, the blog post is associated with the Trips category. This category already has been created in the blog account that was registered with Word. The following steps associate this blog post with the Trips category in the registered blog account.

Note: If you have not registered a blog account, you will not be able to perform the following steps.

- Display the Blog Post tab.

- Click the Insert Category button on the Blog Post tab to insert the Category drop-down list content control in the blog post (Figure 12).

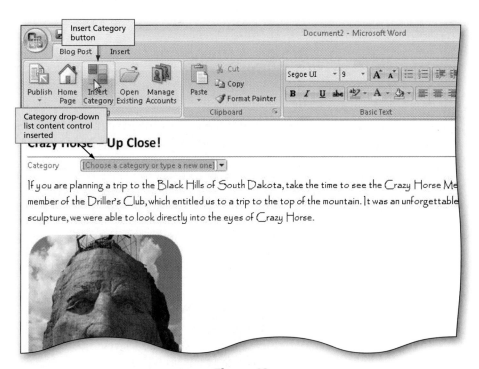

Figure 12

2

- Click the 'Choose a category or type a new one' box arrow to display a list of categories associated with the registered blog account (Figure 13).

Q&A

What if I do not have anything in the list?

Either your blog account is not registered or your account does not have any categories. In this case, skip Step 3.

3

- Click Trips in the list, so that this blog post is categorized in the Trips category when you publish the blog post.

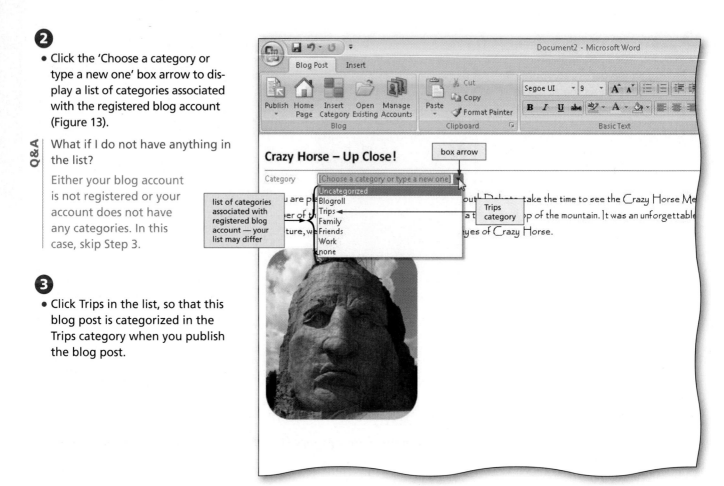

Figure 13

To Save a Document

You are finished entering and formatting the content of the blog post. The next step is to save the blog post.

1 With a USB flash drive connected to one of the computer's USB ports, click the Save button on the Quick Access Toolbar to display the Save As dialog box.

2 Type `Crazy Horse Post` in the File name text box to change the file name.

3 Select your USB flash drive as the save location.

4 Click the Save button in the Save As dialog box to save the document on the USB flash drive with the file name, Crazy Horse Post.

Publishing the Blog Post

With the blog post created and saved, the next step is to publish it. The next series of steps displays the blog Web page associated with the registered account, publishes the blog post, and then redisplays the updated blog Web page. If you do not have a registered account, you will not be able to perform these steps on a computer.

To Display a Blog Web Page in a Web Browser Window

Before publishing the blog post, you want to verify the correct blog account is associated with Word. The following steps display the current blog account's Web page in a browser window.

1

- Position the mouse pointer on the Home Page button on the Blog Post tab (Figure 14).

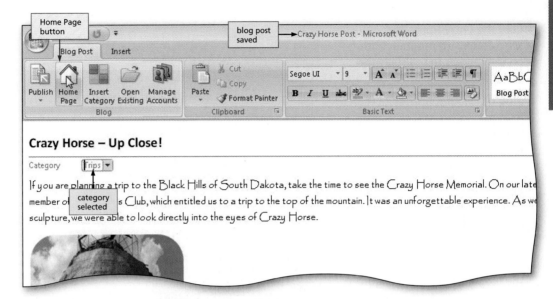

Figure 14

2

- Click the Home Page button on the Blog Post tab, which starts the default browser (Internet Explorer, in this case) and displays the Web page associated with the registered blog account in the browser window (Figure 15).

Q&A

What if the wrong Web page is displayed?

You may have multiple blog accounts registered with Word. To select a different blog account registered with Word, switch back to Word, click the Manage Accounts button on the Blog Post tab, click the desired account in the Blog Accounts dialog box, and then click the Close button. Then, repeat Steps 1 and 2.

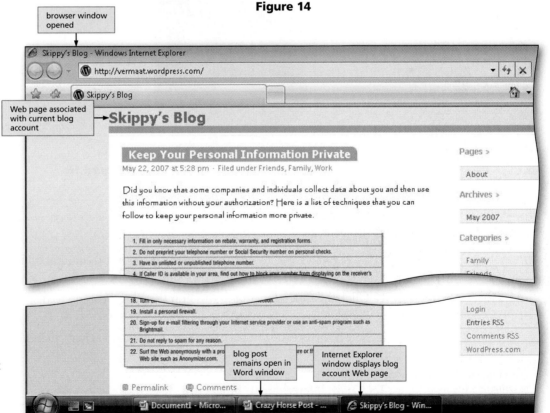

Figure 15

To Publish a Blog Post

The final step in this feature is to publish the blog post, so that it appears at the top of the Web page associated with this blog account. The following steps publish the blog post.

- Click the Crazy Horse Post - Microsoft Word program button on the taskbar to redisplay the Word window.

- Click the Publish button on the Blog Post tab, which causes Word to display a brief message that it is contacting the blog provider and then display a message on the screen that the post was published (Figure 16).

- To view the newly published post, click the Home Page button on the Blog Post tab again (Figure 1c on page WD 717). You may need to click the Refresh button in your browser window to display the most current Web page contents.

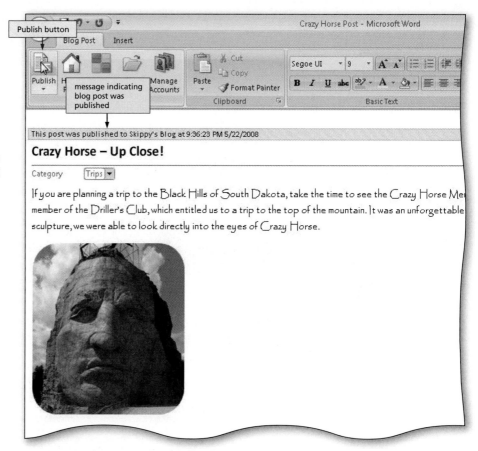

Figure 16

TO OPEN AN EXISTING BLOG POST

If you wanted to open an existing blog post to modify or view it in Word, you would perform the following steps.

1. Click the Open Existing button on the Blog Post tab to display the Open Existing Post dialog box.

2. Select the title of the post you wish to open and then click the OK button.

BTW

Quick Reference
For a table that lists how to complete the tasks covered in this book using the mouse, Ribbon, shortcut menu, and keyboard, see the Quick Reference Summary at the back of this book, or visit the Word 2007 Quick Reference Web page (scsite.com/wd2007/qr).

To Quit Word

You are finished with the project in this feature and should quit Word and close your browser window.

1. Quit Word.

2. Close your browser window.

Feature Summary

In this feature, you have learned how to create a new blog post, crop a picture, change the shape of a picture, and publish a blog post. The items listed below include all the new Word skills you have learned in this feature.

1. Create a Blank Word Document for a Blog Post (WD 718)
2. Crop a Graphic (WD 721)
3. Change a Picture Shape (WD 722)
4. Insert a Category (WD 723)
5. Display a Blog Web Page in a Web Browser Window (WD 725)
6. Publish a Blog Post (WD 726)
7. Open an Existing Blog Post (WD 726)

 If you have a SAM user profile, you may have access to hands-on instruction, practice, and assessment. Log in to your SAM account (http://sam2007.course.com) to launch any assigned training activities or exams that relate to the skills covered in this feature.

In the Lab

Design and/or create a document using the guidelines, concepts, and skills presented in this chapter. Labs are listed in order of increasing difficulty.

Lab 1: Creating a Blog Post from Supplied Data

Problem: Your assignment is to use Word to create the blog post that is shown on the Web page in Figure 1a on page WD 717.

Instructions:

1. Start Word and create a new blank document for a blog post.
2. Type `Keep Your Personal Information Private` as the blog title.
3. Type the following as the paragraph of text below the blue line in the blog post document:
   `Did you know that some companies and individuals collect data about you and then use this information without your authorization? Here is a list of techniques that you can follow to keep your personal information more private.`
4. Format the blog post paragraph entered in Step 3 to the Papyrus font. Create a new style called Blog Post that is based on the paragraph with the modified font.
5. Below the paragraph entered in Step 3, insert the graphic called Privacy Tips, which is located on the Data Files for Students. See the inside back cover of this book for instructions on downloading the Data Files for Students, or contact your instructor for information about accessing the required files.
6. Resize the graphic to 50 percent of its original size.
7. Remove the title from the top of the image by cropping the top of the image.
8. Save the blog post with the name Lab BF-1 Privacy. Submit the blog post in the format specified by your instructor.
9. If you have permission and your instructor requests it, create a blog account on the Web. Register your blog account in Word. Display the blog account's Web page in a browser window. Use Word to publish the blog post created in these steps to your Web blog account. Display the updated blog Web page in a browser window. Submit the blog Web page in a format requested by your instructor.

In the Lab

Lab 2: Creating Your Own Blog Post

Problem: In this assignment, you are to create a blog post that presents your interests, opinions, or personality.

Instructions:

1. Decide on an issue, idea, or opinion about a topic that you would like to share on a blog.

2. Start Word and create a new blank blog post document.

3. Enter an appropriate blog title for your blog. Enter at least 250 words in text below the title that presents your discussion.

4. Format the blog post paragraph entered in Step 3 by changing the font, and font size if desired, to one of your choice. Create a new style called Blog Post that is based on the paragraph with the modified font.

5. Below the paragraph entered in Step 3, insert an appropriate graphic. The graphic may be a table, picture, clip art image, SmartArt, or chart. Resize the graphic, if necessary. Crop the graphic, if necessary.

6. Save the blog post with a name that appropriately reflects its content. Submit the blog post in the format specified by your instructor.

7. If you have permission and your instructor requests it, create a blog account on the Web. Register your blog account in Word. Display the blog account's Web page in a browser window. Use Word to publish the blog post created in these steps to your Web blog account. Display the updated blog Web page in a browser window. Submit the blog Web page in a format requested by your instructor.

Appendix A
Project Planning
Guidelines

Using Project Planning Guidelines

The process of communicating specific information to others is a learned, rational skill. Computers and software, especially Microsoft Office 2007, can help you develop ideas and present detailed information to a particular audience.

Using Microsoft Office 2007, you can create projects such as Word documents, Excel spreadsheets, Access databases, and PowerPoint presentations. Computer hardware and productivity software such as Microsoft Office 2007 minimizes much of the laborious work of drafting and revising projects. Some communicators handwrite ideas in note-books, others compose directly on the computer, and others have developed unique strategies that work for their own particular thinking and writing styles.

No matter what method you use to plan a project, follow specific guidelines to arrive at a final product that presents information correctly and effectively (Figure A–1). Use some aspects of these guidelines every time you undertake a project, and others as needed in specific instances. For example, in determining content for a project, you may decide that a bar chart communicates trends more effectively than a paragraph of text. If so, you would create this graphical element and insert it in an Excel spreadsheet, a Word document, or a PowerPoint slide.

Determine the Project's Purpose

Begin by clearly defining why you are undertaking this assignment. For example, you may want to track monetary donations collected for your club's fundraising drive. Alternatively, you may be urging students to vote for a particular candidate in the next election. Once you clearly understand the purpose of your task, begin to draft ideas of how best to communicate this information.

Analyze Your Audience

Learn about the people who will read, analyze, or view your work. Where are they employed? What are their educational backgrounds? What are their expectations? What questions do they have?

PROJECT PLANNING GUIDELINES

1. DETERMINE THE PROJECT'S PURPOSE
Why are you undertaking the project?

2. ANALYZE YOUR AUDIENCE
Who are the people who will use your work?

3. GATHER POSSIBLE CONTENT
What information exists, and in what forms?

4. DETERMINE WHAT CONTENT TO PRESENT TO YOUR AUDIENCE
What information will best communicate the project's purpose to your audience?

Figure A–1

Design experts suggest drawing a mental picture of these people or finding photographs of people who fit this profile so that you can develop a project with the audience in mind.

By knowing your audience members, you can tailor a project to meet their interests and needs. You will not present them with information they already possess, and you will not omit the information they need to know.

Example: Your assignment is to raise the profile of your college's nursing program in the community. How much do they know about your college and the nursing curriculum? What are the admission requirements? How many of the applicants admitted complete the program? What percent pass the state Boards?

Gather Possible Content

Rarely are you in a position to develop all the material for a project. Typically, you would begin by gathering existing information that may reside in spreadsheets or databases. Web sites, pamphlets, magazine and newspaper articles, and books could provide insights of how others have approached your topic. Personal interviews often provide perspectives not available by any other means. Consider video and audio clips as potential sources for material that might complement or support the factual data you uncover.

Determine What Content to Present to Your Audience

Experienced designers recommend writing three or four major ideas you want an audience member to remember after reading or viewing your project. It also is helpful to envision your project's endpoint, the key fact you wish to emphasize. All project elements should lead to this ending point.

As you make content decisions, you also need to think about other factors. Presentation of the project content is an important consideration. For example, will your brochure be printed on thick, colored paper or transparencies? Will your PowerPoint presentation be viewed in a classroom with excellent lighting and a bright projector, or will it be viewed on a notebook computer monitor? Determine relevant time factors, such as the length of time to develop the project, how long readers will spend reviewing your project, or the amount of time allocated for your speaking engagement. Your project will need to accommodate all of these constraints.

Decide whether a graph, photograph, or artistic element can express or emphasize a particular concept. The right hemisphere of the brain processes images by attaching an emotion to them, so audience members are more apt to recall these graphics long term rather than just reading text.

As you select content, be mindful of the order in which you plan to present information. Readers and audience members generally remember the first and last pieces of information they see and hear, so you should put the most important information at the top or bottom of the page.

Summary

When creating a project, it is beneficial to follow some basic guidelines from the outset. By taking some time at the beginning of the process to determine the project's purpose, analyze the audience, gather possible content, and determine what content to present to the audience, you can produce a project that is informative, relevant, and effective.

Appendix B
Introduction to Microsoft Office 2007

What Is Microsoft Office 2007?

Microsoft Office 2007 is a collection of the more popular Microsoft application software. It is available in Basic, Home and Student, Standard, Small Business, Professional, Ultimate, Professional Plus, and Enterprise editions. Each edition consists of a group of programs, collectively called a suite. Table B–1 lists the suites and their components. **Microsoft Office Professional Edition 2007** includes these six programs: Microsoft Office Word 2007, Microsoft Office Excel 2007, Microsoft Office Access 2007, Microsoft Office PowerPoint 2007, Microsoft Office Publisher 2007, and Microsoft Office Outlook 2007. The programs in the Office suite allow you to work efficiently, communicate effectively, and improve the appearance of the projects you create.

Table B–1

	Microsoft Office Basic 2007	Microsoft Office Home & Student 2007	Microsoft Office Standard 2007	Microsoft Office Small Business 2007	Microsoft Office Professional 2007	Microsoft Office Ultimate 2007	Microsoft Office Professional Plus 2007	Microsoft Office Enterprise 2007
Microsoft Office Word 2007	✓	✓	✓	✓	✓	✓	✓	✓
Microsoft Office Excel 2007	✓	✓	✓	✓	✓	✓	✓	✓
Microsoft Office Access 2007					✓	✓	✓	✓
Microsoft Office PowerPoint 2007		✓	✓	✓	✓	✓	✓	✓
Microsoft Office Publisher 2007				✓	✓	✓	✓	✓
Microsoft Office Outlook 2007	✓		✓				✓	✓
Microsoft Office OneNote 2007		✓				✓		
Microsoft Office Outlook 2007 with Business Contact Manager				✓	✓	✓		
Microsoft Office InfoPath 2007						✓	✓	✓
Integrated Enterprise Content Management						✓	✓	✓
Electronic Forms						✓	✓	✓
Advanced Information Rights Management and Policy Capabilities						✓	✓	✓
Microsoft Office Communicator 2007							✓	✓
Microsoft Office Groove 2007						✓		✓

Microsoft has bundled additional programs in some versions of Office 2007, in addition to the main group of Office programs. Table B–1 on the previous page lists the components of the various Office suites.

In addition to the Office 2007 programs noted previously, Office 2007 suites can contain other programs. Microsoft Office OneNote 2007 is a digital notebook program that allows you to gather and share various types of media, such as text, graphics, video, audio, and digital handwriting. Microsoft Office InfoPath 2007 is a program that allows you to create and use electronic forms to gather information. Microsoft Office Groove 2007 provides collaborative workspaces in real time. Additional services that are oriented toward the enterprise solution also are available.

Office 2007 and the Internet, World Wide Web, and Intranets

Office 2007 allows you to take advantage of the Internet, the World Wide Web, and intranets. The Microsoft Windows operating system includes a **browser**, which is a program that allows you to locate and view a Web page. The Windows browser is called Internet Explorer.

One method of viewing a Web page is to use the browser to enter the Web address for the Web page. Another method of viewing a Web page is clicking a hyperlink. A **hyperlink** is colored or underlined text or a graphic that, when clicked, connects to another Web page. Hyperlinks placed in Office 2007 documents allow for direct access to a Web site of interest.

An **intranet** is a private network, such as a network used within a company or organization for internal communication. Like the Internet, hyperlinks are used within an intranet to access documents, pages, and other destinations on the intranet. Unlike the Internet, the materials on the network are available only for those who are part of the private network.

Online Collaboration Using Office

Organizations that, in the past, were able to make important information available only to a select few, now can make their information accessible to a wider range of individuals who use programs such as Office 2007 and Internet Explorer. Office 2007 allows colleagues to use the Internet or an intranet as a central location to view documents, manage files, and work together.

Each of the Office 2007 programs makes publishing documents on a Web server as simple as saving a file on a hard disk. Once placed on the Web server, users can view and edit the documents and conduct Web discussions and live online meetings.

Using Microsoft Office 2007

The various Microsoft Office 2007 programs each specialize in a particular task. This section describes the general functions of the more widely used Office 2007 programs, along with how they are used to access the Internet or an intranet.

Microsoft Office Word 2007

Microsoft Office Word 2007 is a full-featured word processing program that allows you to create many types of personal and business documents, including flyers, letters, resumes, business documents, and academic reports.

Word's AutoCorrect, spelling, and grammar features help you proofread documents for errors in spelling and grammar by identifying the errors and offering suggestions for corrections as you type. The live word count feature provides you with a constantly updating word count as you enter and edit text. To assist with creating specific documents, such as a business letter or resume, Word provides templates, which provide a formatted document before you type the text of the document. Quick Styles provide a live preview of styles from the Style gallery, allowing you to preview styles in the document before actually applying them.

Word automates many often-used tasks and provides you with powerful desktop publishing tools to use as you create professional looking brochures, advertisements, and newsletters. SmartArt allows you to insert interpretive graphics based on document content.

Word makes it easier for you to share documents for collaboration. The Send feature opens an e-mail window with the active document attached. The Compare Documents feature allows you easily to identify changes when comparing different document versions.

Word 2007 and the Internet   Word makes it possible to design and publish Web pages on the Internet or an intranet, insert a hyperlink to a Web page in a word processing document, as well as access and search the content of other Web pages.

Microsoft Office Excel 2007

Microsoft Office Excel 2007 is a spreadsheet program that allows you to organize data, complete calculations, graph data, develop professional looking reports, publish organized data to the Web, and access real-time data from Web sites.

In addition to its mathematical functionality, Excel 2007 provides tools for visually comparing data. For instance, when comparing a group of values in cells, you can set cell backgrounds with bars proportional to the value of the data in the cell. You can also set cell backgrounds with full-color backgrounds, or use a color scale to facilitate interpretation of data values.

Excel 2007 provides strong formatting support for tables with the new Style Preview gallery.

Excel 2007 and the Internet   Using Excel 2007, you can create hyperlinks within a worksheet to access other Office documents on the network or on the Internet. Worksheets saved as static, or unchanging Web pages can be viewed using a browser. The person viewing static Web pages cannot change them.

In addition, you can create and run queries that retrieve information from a Web page and insert the information directly into a worksheet.

Microsoft Office Access 2007

Microsoft Office Access 2007 is a comprehensive database management system (DBMS). A **database** is a collection of data organized in a manner that allows access, retrieval, and use of that data. Access 2007 allows you to create a database; add, change, and delete data in the database; sort data in the database; retrieve data from the database; and create forms and reports using the data in the database.

Access 2007 and the Internet   Access 2007 lets you generate reports, which are summaries that show only certain data from the database, based on user requirements.

Microsoft Office PowerPoint 2007

Microsoft Office PowerPoint 2007 is a complete presentation graphics program that allows you to produce professional looking presentations. With PowerPoint 2007, you can create informal presentations using overhead transparencies, electronic presentations using a projection device attached to a personal computer, formal presentations using 35mm slides or a CD, or you can run virtual presentations on the Internet.

PowerPoint 2007 and the Internet   PowerPoint 2007 allows you to publish presentations on the Internet or other networks.

Microsoft Office Publisher 2007

Microsoft Office Publisher 2007 is a desktop publishing program (DTP) that allows you to design and produce professional quality documents (newsletters, flyers, brochures, business cards, Web sites, and so on) that combine text, graphics, and photographs. Desktop publishing software provides a variety of tools, including design templates, graphic manipulation tools, color schemes or libraries, and various page wizards and templates. For large jobs, businesses use desktop publishing software to design publications that are **camera ready**, which means the files are suitable for production by outside commercial printers. Publisher 2007 also allows you to locate commercial printers, service bureaus, and copy shops willing to accept customer files created in Publisher.

Publisher 2007 allows you to design a unique image, or logo, using one of more than 45 master design sets. This, in turn, permits you to use the same design for all your printed documents (letters, business cards, brochures, and advertisements) and Web pages. Publisher includes 70 coordinated color schemes; 30 font schemes; more than 10,000 high-quality clip art images; 1,500 photographs; 1,000 Web-art graphics; 340 animated graphics; and hundreds of unique Design Gallery elements (quotations, sidebars, and so on). If you wish, you also can download additional images from the Microsoft Office Online Web page on the Microsoft Web site.

Publisher 2007 and the Internet   Publisher 2007 allows you easily to create a multipage Web site with custom color schemes, photographic images, animated images, and sounds.

Microsoft Office Outlook 2007

Microsoft Office Outlook 2007 is a powerful communications and scheduling program that helps you communicate with others, keep track of your contacts, and organize your schedule. Outlook 2007 allows you to view a To-Do bar containing tasks and appointments from your Outlook calendar. Outlook 2007 allows you to send and receive electronic mail (e-mail) and permits you to engage in real-time communication with family, friends, or coworkers using instant messaging. Outlook 2007 also provides you with the means to organize your contacts, and you can track e-mail messages, meetings, and notes with a particular contact. Outlook's Calendar, Contacts, Tasks, and Notes components aid in this organization. Contact information is available from the Outlook Calendar, Mail, Contacts, and Task components by accessing the Find a Contact feature. **Personal information management (PIM)** programs such as Outlook provide a way for individuals and workgroups to organize, find, view, and share information easily.

Microsoft Office 2007 Help

At any time while you are using one of the Office programs, you can interact with **Microsoft Office 2007 Help** for that program and display information about any topic associated with the program. Several categories of help are available. In all programs, you can access Help by pressing the F1 key on the keyboard. In Publisher 2007 and Outlook 2007, the Help window can be opened by clicking the Help menu and then selecting Microsoft Office Publisher or Outlook Help command, or by entering search text in the 'Type a question for help' text box in the upper-right corner of the program window. In the other Office programs, clicking the Microsoft Office Help button near the upper-right corner of the program window opens the program Help window.

The Help window in all programs provides several methods for accessing help about a particular topic, and has tools for navigating around Help. Appendix C contains detailed instructions for using Help.

Collaboration and SharePoint

While not part of the Microsoft Office 2007 suites, SharePoint is a Microsoft tool that allows Office 2007 users to share data using collaborative tools that are integrated into the main Office programs. SharePoint consists of Windows SharePoint Services, Office SharePoint Server 2007, and, optionally, Office SharePoint Designer 2007.

Windows SharePoint Services provides the platform for collaboration programs and services. Office SharePoint Server 2007 is built on top of Windows SharePoint Services. The result of these two products is the ability to create SharePoint sites. A SharePoint site is a Web site that provides users with a virtual place for collaborating and communicating with their colleagues while working together on projects, documents, ideas, and information. Each member of a group with access to the SharePoint site has the ability to contribute to the material stored there. The basic building blocks of SharePoint sites are lists and libraries. Lists contain collections of information, such as calendar items, discussion points, contacts, and links. Lists can be edited to add or delete information. Libraries are similar to lists, but include both files and information about files. Types of libraries include document, picture, and forms libraries.

The most basic type of SharePoint site is called a Workspace, which is used primarily for collaboration. Different types of Workspaces can be created using SharePoint to suit different needs. SharePoint provides templates, or outlines of these Workspaces, that can be filled in to create the Workspace. Each of the different types of Workspace templates contain a different collection of lists and libraries, reflecting the purpose of the Workspace. You can create a Document Workspace to facilitate collaboration on documents. A Document Workspace contains a document library for documents and supporting files, a Links list that allows you to maintain relevant resource links for the document, a Tasks list for listing and assigning To-Do items to team members, and other links as needed. Meeting Workspaces allow users to plan and organize a meeting, with components such as Attendees, Agenda, and a Document Library. Social Meeting Workspaces provide a place to plan social events, with lists and libraries such as Attendees, Directions, Image/Logo, Things To Bring, Discussions, and Picture Library. A Decision Meeting Workspace is a Meeting Workspace with a focus on review and decision-making, with lists and libraries such as Objectives, Attendees, Agenda, Document Library, Tasks, and Decisions.

Users also can create a SharePoint site called a WebParts page, which is built from modules called WebParts. WebParts are modular units of information that contain a title bar and content that reflects the type of WebPart. For instance, an image WebPart would contain a title bar and an image. WebParts allow you quickly to create and modify a SharePoint site, and allow for the creation of a unique site that can allow users to access and make changes to information stored on the site.

Large SharePoint sites that include multiple pages can be created using templates as well. Groups needing more refined and targeted sharing options than those available with SharePoint Server 2007 and Windows SharePoint Services can add SharePoint Designer 2007 to create a site that meets their specific needs.

Depending on which components have been selected for inclusion on the site, users can view a team calendar, view links, read announcements, and view and edit group documents and projects. SharePoint sites can be set up so that documents are checked in and out, much like a library, to prevent multiple users from making changes simultaneously. Once a SharePoint site is set up, Office programs are used to perform maintenance of the site. For example, changes in the team calendar are updated using Outlook 2007, and changes that users make in Outlook 2007 are reflected on the SharePoint site. Office 2007 programs include a Publish feature that allows users easily to save file updates to a SharePoint site. Team members can be notified about changes made to material on the site either by e-mail or by a news feed, meaning that users do not have to go to the site to check to see if anything has been updated since they last viewed or worked on it. The search feature in SharePoint allows users quickly to find information on a large site.

Appendix C
Microsoft Office Word 2007 Help

Using Microsoft Office Word Help

This appendix shows how to use Microsoft Office Word Help. At any time while you are using one of the Microsoft Office 2007 programs, you can use Office Help to display information about all topics associated with the program. This appendix uses Microsoft Office Word 2007 to illustrate the use of Office Help. Help in other Office 2007 programs responds in a similar fashion.

In Office 2007, Help is presented in a window that has Web browser-style navigation buttons. Each Office 2007 program has its own Help home page, which is the starting Help page that is displayed in the Help window. If your computer is connected to the Internet, the contents of the Help page reflect both the local help files installed on the computer and material from Microsoft's Web site. As shown in Figure C–1, two methods for accessing Word's Help are available:

1. Microsoft Office Word Help button near the upper-right corner of the Word window
2. Function key F1 on the keyboard

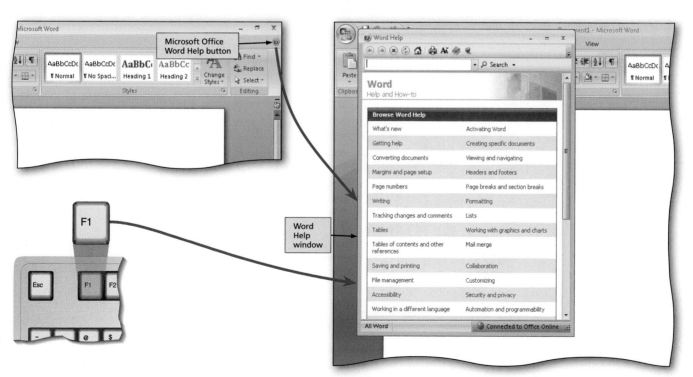

Figure C–1

To Open the Word Help Window

The following steps open the Word Help window and maximize the window.

1

• Start Microsoft Word, if necessary. Click the Microsoft Office Word Help button near the upper-right corner of the Word window to open the Word Help window (Figure C–2).

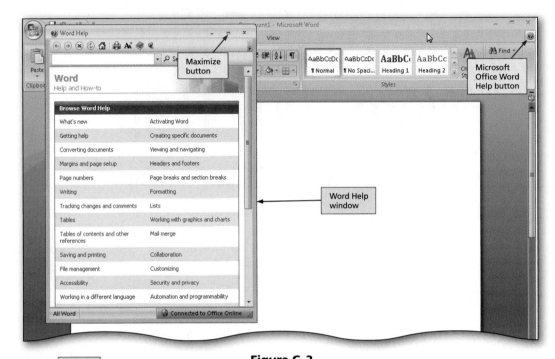

Figure C–2

2

• Click the Maximize button on the Help title bar to maximize the Help window (Figure C–3).

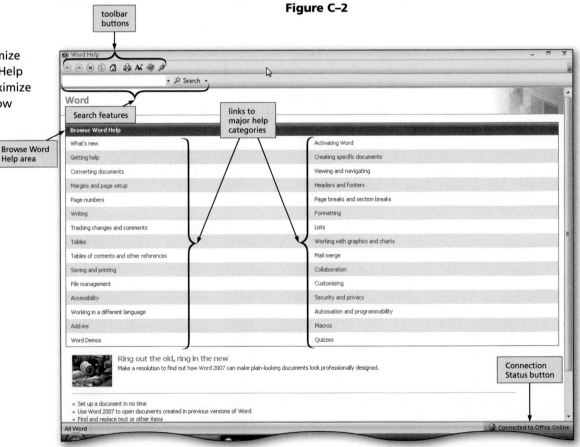

Figure C–3

The Word Help Window

The Word Help window provides several methods for accessing help about a particular topic, and also has tools for navigating around Help. Methods for accessing Help include searching the help content installed with Word, or searching the online Office content maintained by Microsoft.

Figure C–3 shows the main Word Help window. To navigate Help, the Word Help window includes search features that allow you to search on a word or phrase about which you want help; the Connection Status button, which allows you to control where Word Help searches for content; toolbar buttons; and links to major Help categories.

Search Features

You can perform Help searches on words or phrases to find information about any Word feature using the 'Type words to search for' text box and the Search button (Figure C–4a). Click the 'Type words to search for' text box and then click the Search button or press the ENTER key to initiate a search of Word Help.

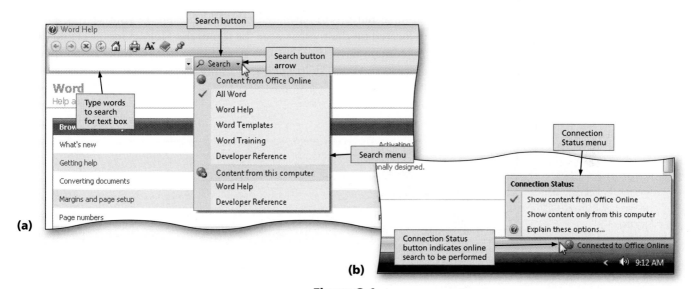

Figure C–4

Word Help offers the user the option of searching the online Help Web pages maintained by Microsoft or the offline Help files placed on your computer when you install Word. You can specify whether Word Help should search online or offline from two places: the Connection Status button on the status bar of the Word Help window, or the Search button arrow on the toolbar. The Connection Status button indicates whether Help currently is set up to work with online or offline information sources. Clicking the Connection Status button provides a menu with commands for selecting online or offline searches (Figure C–4b). The Connection Status menu allows the user to select whether Help searches will return content only from the computer (offline), or content from the computer and from Office Online (online).

Clicking the Search button arrow also provides a menu with commands for an online or offline search (Figure C–4a). These commands determine the source of information that Help searches for during the current Help session only. For example, assume that your preferred search is an offline search because you often do not have Internet access. You would set Connection Status to 'Show content only from this computer'. When you have Internet access, you can select an online search from the Search menu to search Office Online for information for your current search session only. Your search will use the Office Online resources until you quit Help. The next time you start Help, the Connection Status once again will be offline. In addition to setting the source of information that Help searches for during the current Help session, you can use the Search menu to further target the current search to one of four subcategories of online Help: Word Help, Word Templates, Word Training, and Developer Reference. The local search further can target one subcategory, Developer Reference.

In addition to searching for a word or string of text, you can use the links provided on the Browse Word Help area (Figure C–3 on page APP 10) to search for help on a topic. These links direct you to major help categories. From each major category, subcategories are available to further refine your search.

Finally, you can use the Table of Contents for Word Help to search for a topic the same way you would in a hard copy book. The Table of Contents is accessed via a toolbar button.

Toolbar Buttons

You can use toolbar buttons to navigate through the results of your search. The toolbar buttons are located on the toolbar near the top of the Help Window (Figure C–5). The toolbar buttons contain navigation buttons as well as buttons that perform other useful and common tasks in Word Help, such as printing.

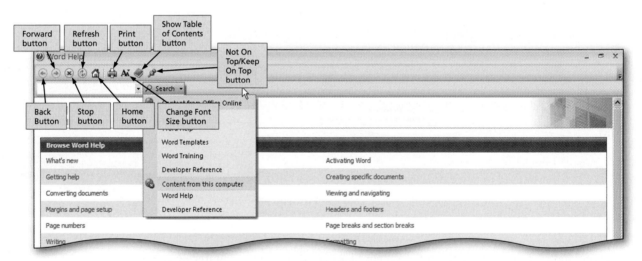

Figure C–5

The Word Help navigation buttons are the Back, Forward, Stop, Refresh, and Home buttons. These five buttons behave like the navigation buttons in a Web browser window. You can use the Back button to go back one window, the Forward button to go forward one window, the Stop button to stop loading the current page, and the Home button to redisplay the Help home page in the Help window. Use the Refresh button to reload the information requested into the Help window from its original source. When getting Help information online, this button provides the most current information from the Microsoft Help Web site.

The buttons located to the right of the navigation buttons — Print, Change Font Size, Show Table of Contents, and Not on Top — provide you with access to useful and common commands. The Print button prints the contents of the open Help window. The Change Font Size button customizes the Help window by increasing or decreasing the size of its text. The Show Table of Contents button opens a pane on the left side of the Help window that shows the Table of Contents for Word Help. You can use the Table of Contents for Word Help to navigate through the contents of Word Help much as you would use the Table of Contents in a book to search for a topic. The Not On Top button is an example of a toggle button, which is a button that can be switched back and forth between two states. It determines how the Word Help window behaves relative to other windows. When clicked, the Not On Top button changes to Keep On Top. In this state, it does not allow other windows from Word or other programs to cover the Word Help window when those windows are the active windows. When in the Not On Top state, the button allows other windows to be opened or moved on top of the Word Help window.

You can customize the size and placement of the Help window. Resize the window using the Maximize and Restore buttons, or by dragging the window to a desired size. Relocate the Help window by dragging the title bar to a new location on the screen.

Searching Word Help

Once the Word Help window is open, several methods exist for navigating Word Help. You can search for help by using any of the three following methods from the Help window:

1. Enter search text in the 'Type words to search for' text box
2. Click the links in the Help window
3. Use the Table of Contents

To Obtain Help Using the Type Words to Search for Text Box

Assume for the following example that you want to know more about watermarks. The following steps use the 'Type words to search for' text box to obtain useful information about watermarks by entering the word, watermark, as search text. The steps also navigate in the Word Help window.

- Type watermark in the 'Type words to search for' text box at the top of the Word Help window.

- Click the Search button arrow to display the Search menu.

- If it is not selected already, click All Word on the Search menu to select the command. If All Word is already selected, click the Search button arrow again to close the Search menu.

Q&A

Why select All Word on the Search menu?

Selecting All Word on the Search menu ensures that Word Help will search all possible sources for information on your search term. It will produce the most complete search results.

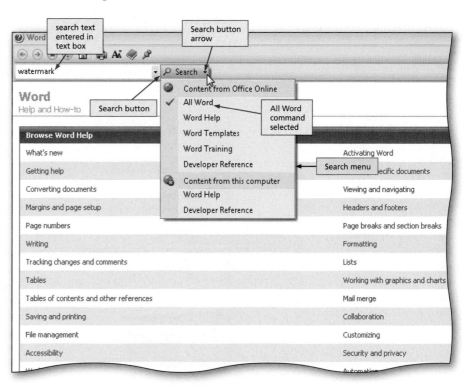

Figure C–6

2

- Click the Search button to display the search results (Figure C–7).

Q&A

Why do my results differ?

If you do not have an Internet connection, your results will reflect only the content of the Help files on your computer. When searching for help online, results also can change as material is added, deleted, and updated on the online Help Web pages maintained by Microsoft.

Q&A

Why were my search results not very helpful?

When initiating a search, keep in mind to check the spelling of the search text; and to keep your search very specific, with fewer than seven words, to return the most accurate results.

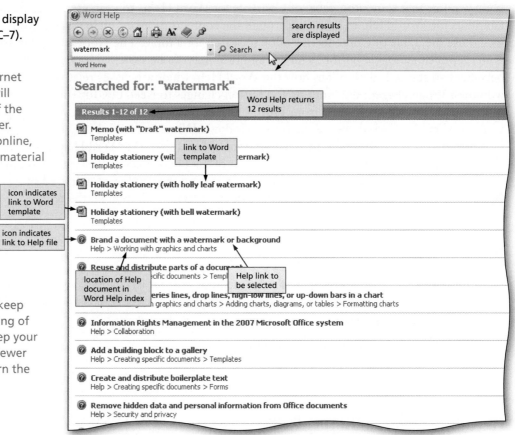

Figure C–7

3

- Click the 'Brand a document with a watermark or background' link to open the Help document associated with the link in the Help window (Figure C–8).

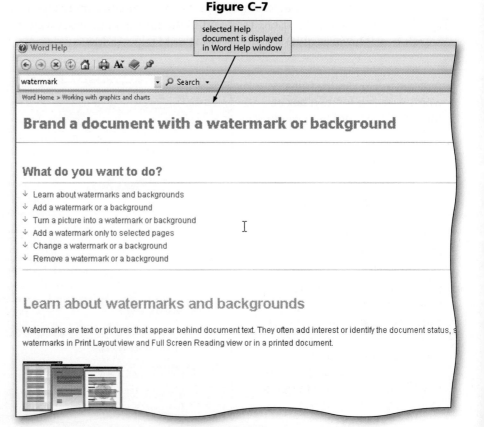

Figure C–8

4

- Click the Home button on the taskbar to clear the search results and redisplay the Word Help home page (Figure C–9).

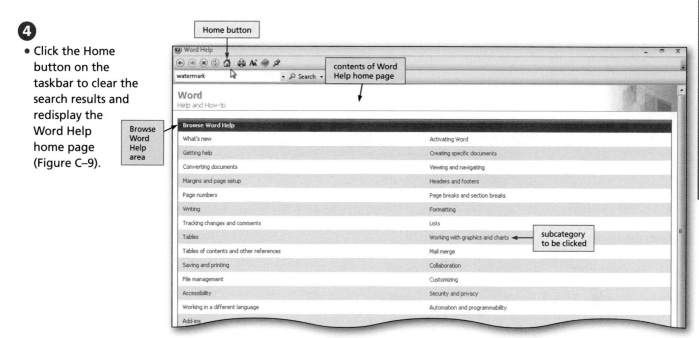

Figure C–9

To Obtain Help Using the Help Links

If your topic of interest is listed in the Browse Word Help area, you can click the link to begin browsing Word Help categories instead of entering search text. You browse Word Help just like you would browse a Web site. If you know in which category to find your Help information, you may wish to use these links. The following steps find the watermark Help information using the category links from the Word Help home page.

1

- Click the 'Working with graphics and charts' link to open the 'Working with graphics and charts' page.

- Click the 'Brand a document with a watermark or background' link to open the Help document associated with the link (Figure C–10).

 What does the Show All link do?

In many Help documents, additional information about terms and features is available by clicking a link in the document to display additional information in the Help document. Clicking the Show All link opens all the links in the Help document that expand to additional text.

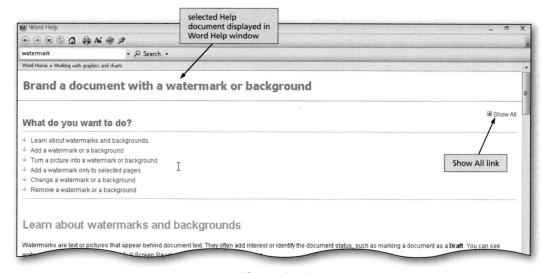

Figure C–10

To Obtain Help Using the Help Table of Contents

A third way to find Help in Word is through the Help Table of Contents. You can browse through the Table of Contents to display information about a particular topic or to familiarize yourself with Word. The following steps access the watermark Help information by browsing through the Table of Contents.

- Click the Home button on the toolbar.
- Click the Show Table of Contents button on the toolbar to open the Table of Contents pane on the left side of the Help window. If necessary, click the Maximize button on the Help title bar to maximize the window (Figure C–11).

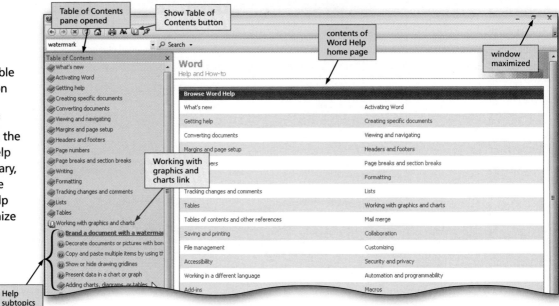

Figure C–11

- Click the 'Working with graphics and charts' link in the Table of Contents pane to view a list of Help subtopics.
- Click the 'Brand a document with a watermark or background' link in the Table of Contents pane to view the selected Help document in the right pane (Figure C–12).

Q&A

How do I remove the Table of Contents pane when I am finished with it?

The Show Table of Contents button acts as a toggle switch. When the Table of Contents pane is visible, the button changes to Hide Table of Contents. Clicking it hides the Table of Contents pane and changes the button to Show Table of Contents.

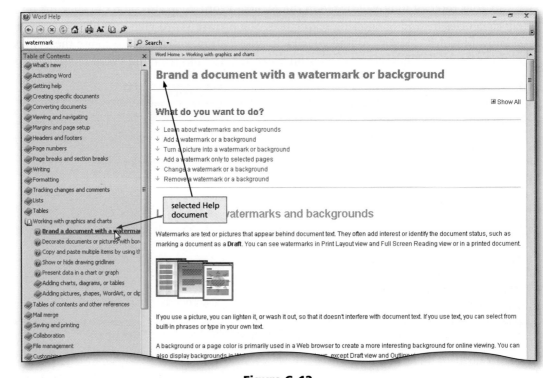

Figure C–12

Obtaining Help while Working in Word

Often you may need help while working on a document without already having the Help window open. For example, you may be unsure about how a particular command works, or you may be presented with a dialog box that you are not sure how to use. Rather than opening the Help window and initiating a search, Word Help provides you with the ability to search directly for help.

Figure C–13 shows one option for obtaining help while working in Word. If you want to learn more about a command, point to the command button and wait for the Enhanced ScreenTip to appear. If the Help icon appears in the Enhanced ScreenTip, press the F1 key while pointing to the command to open the Help window associated with that command.

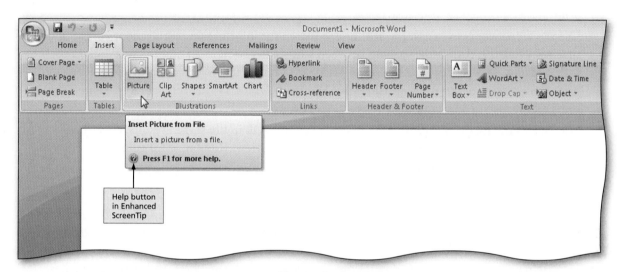

Figure C–13

Figure C–14 shows a dialog box with a Get help button in it. Pressing the F1 key while the dialog box is displayed opens a Help window. The Help window contains help about that dialog box, if available. If no help file is available for that particular dialog box, then the main Help window opens.

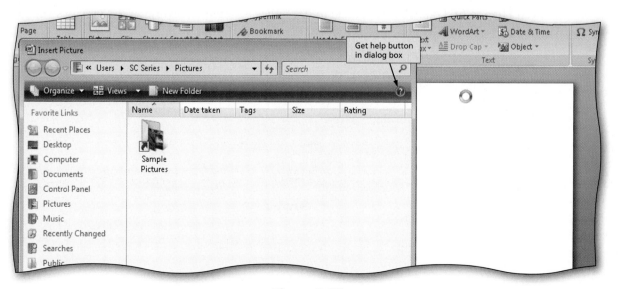

Figure C–14

Use Help

1 Obtaining Help Using Search Text

Instructions: Perform the following tasks using Word Help.

1. Use the 'Type words to search for' text box to obtain help about landscape printing. Use the Connection Status menu to search online help if you have an Internet connection.

2. Click Select page orientation in the list of links in the search results. Double-click the Microsoft Office Word Help window title bar to maximize it. Read and print the information. At the top of the printout, write down the number of links Word Help found.

3. Use the Search menu to search for help offline. Repeat the search from Step 1. At the top of the printout, write down the number of links that Word Help found searching offline. Submit the printouts as specified by your instructor.

4. Use the 'Type words to search for' text box to search for information online about adjusting line spacing. Click the 'Adjust the spacing between a list bullet or number and the text' link in the search results. If necessary, maximize the Microsoft Office 2007 Word Help window. Read and print the contents of the window. Close the Microsoft Office Word Help window. Submit the printouts as specified by your instructor.

5. For each of the following words and phrases, click one link in the search results, click the Show All link, and then print the page: page zoom; date; print preview; Ribbon; word count; and citation. Submit the printouts as specified by your instructor.

2 Expanding on Word Help Basics

Instructions: Use Word Help to better understand its features and answer the questions listed below. Answer the questions on your own paper, or submit the printed Help information as specified by your instructor.

1. Use Help to find out how to customize the Help window. Change the font size to the smallest option and then print the contents of the Microsoft Office Word Help window. Change the font size back to its original setting. Close the window.

2. Press the F1 key. Search for information about tables, restricting the search results to Word Templates. Print the first page of the Search results.

3. Search for information about tables, restricting the search results to Word Help files. Print the first page of the Search results.

4. Use Word Help to find out what happened to the Office Assistant, a feature in the previous version of Word. Print out the Help document that contains the answer.

Appendix D
Publishing Office 2007 Web Pages to a Web Server

With the Office 2007 programs, you use the Save As command on the Office Button menu to save a Web page to a Web server using one of two techniques: Web folders or File Transfer Protocol. A **Web folder** is an Office shortcut to a Web server. **File Transfer Protocol (FTP)** is an Internet standard that allows computers to exchange files with other computers on the Internet.

You should contact your network system administrator or technical support staff at your Internet access provider to determine if their Web server supports Web folders, FTP, or both, and to obtain necessary permissions to access the Web server. If you decide to publish Web pages using a Web folder, you must have the Office Server Extensions (OSE) installed on your computer.

Using Web Folders to Publish Office 2007 Web Pages

When publishing to a Web folder, someone first must create the Web folder before you can save to it. If you are granted permission to create a Web folder, you must obtain the Web address of the Web server, a user name, and possibly a password that allows you to access the Web server. You also must decide on a name for the Web folder. Table D–1 explains how to create a Web folder.

Office 2007 adds the name of the Web folder to the list of current Web folders. You can save to this folder, open files in the folder, rename the folder, or perform any operations you would to a folder on your hard disk. You can use your Office 2007 program or Windows Explorer to access this folder. Table D–2 explains how to save to a Web folder.

Table D–1 Creating a Web Folder

1. Click the Office Button and then click Save As or Open.

2. When the Save As dialog box (or Open dialog box) appears, click the Tools button arrow, and then click Map Network Drive... When the Map Network Drive dialog box is displayed, click the 'Connect to a Web site that you can use to store your documents and pictures' link.

3. When the Add Network Location Wizard dialog box is displayed, click the Next button. If necessary, click Choose a custom network location. Click the Next button. Click the View examples link, type the Internet or network address, and then click the Next button. Click 'Log on anonymously' to deselect the check box, type your user name in the User name text box, and then click the Next button. Enter the name you want to call this network place and then click the Next button. Click to deselect the 'Open this network location when I click Finish' check box, and then click the Finish button.

Table D–2 Saving to a Web Folder

1. Click the Office Button, click Save As.

2. When the Save As dialog box is displayed, type the Web page file name in the File name text box. Do not press the ENTER key.

3. Click the Save as type box arrow and then click Web Page to select the Web Page format.

4. Click Computer in the Navigation pane.

5. Double-click the Web folder name in the Network Location list.

6. If the Enter Network Password dialog box appears, type the user name and password in the respective text boxes and then click the OK button.

7. Click the Save button in the Save As dialog box.

Using FTP to Publish Office 2007 Web Pages

When publishing a Web page using FTP, you first must add the FTP location to your computer before you can save to it. An FTP location, also called an **FTP site**, is a collection of files that reside on an FTP server. In this case, the FTP server is the Web server.

To add an FTP location, you must obtain the name of the FTP site, which usually is the address (URL) of the FTP server, and a user name and a password that allows you to access the FTP server. You save and open the Web pages on the FTP server using the name of the FTP site. Table D–3 explains how to add an FTP site.

Office 2007 adds the name of the FTP site to the FTP locations list in the Save As and Open dialog boxes. You can open and save files using this list. Table D–4 explains how to save to an FTP location.

Table D–3 Adding an FTP Location
1. Click the Office Button and then click Save As or Open.
2. When the Save As dialog box (or Open dialog box) appears, click the Tools button arrow, and then click Map Network Drive... When the Map Network Drive dialog box is displayed, click the 'Connect to a Web site that you can use to store your documents and pictures' link.
3. When the Add Network Location Wizard dialog box appears, click the Next button. If necessary, click Choose a custom network location. Click the Next button. Click the View examples link, type the Internet or network address, and then click the Next button. If you have a user name for the site, click to deselect 'Log on anonymously' and type your user name in the User name text box, and then click Next. If the site allows anonymous logon, click Next. Type a name for the location, click Next, click to deselect the 'Open this network location when I click Finish' check box, and click Finish. Click the OK button.
4. Close the Save As or the Open dialog box.

Table D–4 Saving to an FTP Location
1. Click the Office Button and then click Save As.
2. When the Save As dialog box is displayed, type the Web page file name in the File name text box. Do not press the ENTER key.
3. Click the Save as type box arrow and then click Web Page to select the Web Page format.
4. Click Computer in the Navigation pane.
5. Double-click the name of the FTP site in the Network Location list.
6. When the FTP Log On dialog box appears, enter your user name and password and then click the OK button.
7. Click the Save button in the Save As dialog box.

Appendix E
Customizing Microsoft Office Word 2007

This appendix explains how to change the screen resolution in Windows Vista to the resolution used in this book. It also describes how to customize the Word window by changing the Ribbon, Quick Access Toolbar, and the color scheme.

Changing Screen Resolution

Screen resolution indicates the number of pixels (dots) that the computer uses to display the letters, numbers, graphics, and background you see on the screen. When you increase the screen resolution, Windows displays more information on the screen, but the information decreases in size. The reverse also is true: as you decrease the screen resolution, Windows displays less information on the screen, but the information increases in size.

The screen resolution usually is stated as the product of two numbers, such as 1024×768 (pronounced "ten twenty-four by seven sixty-eight"). A 1024×768 screen resolution results in a display of 1,024 distinct pixels on each of 768 lines, or about 786,432 pixels. The figures in this book were created using a screen resolution of 1024×768.

The screen resolutions most commonly used today are 800×600 and 1024×768, although some Office specialists set their computers at a much higher screen resolution, such as 2048×1536.

To Change the Screen Resolution

The following steps change the screen resolution from 1280×1024 to 1024×768. Your computer already may be set to 1024×768 or some other resolution.

1

- If necessary, minimize all programs so that the Windows Vista desktop appears.

- Right-click the Windows Vista desktop to display the Windows Vista desktop shortcut menu (Figure E–1).

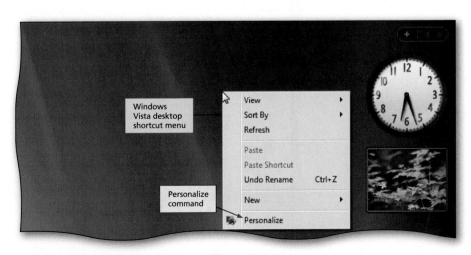

Figure E–1

- Click Personalize on the shortcut menu to open the Personalization window.

- Click Display Settings in the Personalization window to display the Display Settings dialog box (Figure E–2).

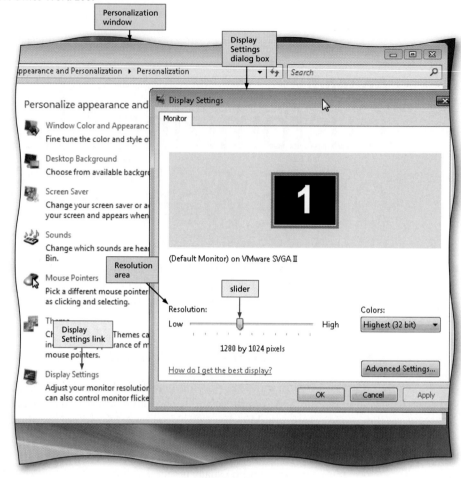

Figure E–2

- Drag the slider in the Resolution area so that the screen resolution changes to 1024 × 768 (Figure E–3).

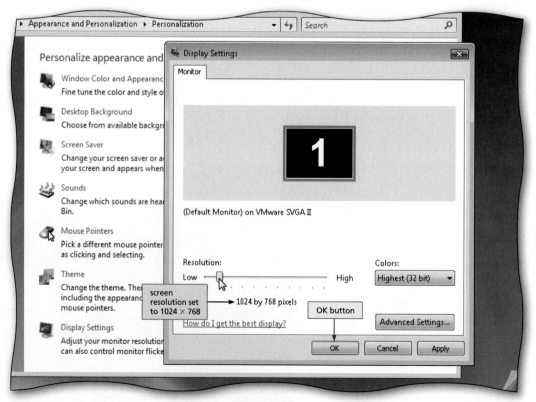

Figure E–3

4

- Click the OK button to change the screen resolution from 1280 × 1024 to 1024 × 768 (Figure E–4).

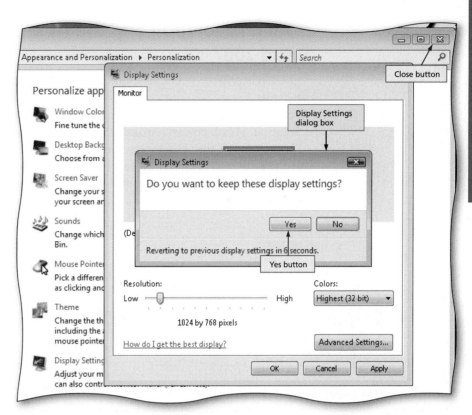

Figure E–4

5

- Click the Yes button in the Display Settings dialog box to accept the new screen resolution (Figure E–5).

Q&A

What if I do not want to change the screen resolution after seeing it applied after I click the OK button?

You either can click the No button in the inner Display Settings dialog box, or wait for the timer to run out, at which point Windows Vista will revert to the original screen resolution.

- Click the Close button to close the Personalization window.

Figure E–5

Screen Resolution and the Appearance of the Ribbon in Word 2007

Changing the screen resolution affects how the Ribbon appears in Word 2007 programs. Figure E–6 shows the Word Ribbon at the screen resolutions of 800 × 600, 1024 × 768, and 1280 × 1024. All of the same commands are available regardless of screen resolution. Word, however, makes changes to the groups and the buttons within the groups to accommodate the various screen resolutions. The result is that certain commands may need to be accessed differently depending on the resolution chosen. A command that is visible on the Ribbon and available by clicking a button at one resolution may not be visible and may need to be accessed using its group button at a different resolution.

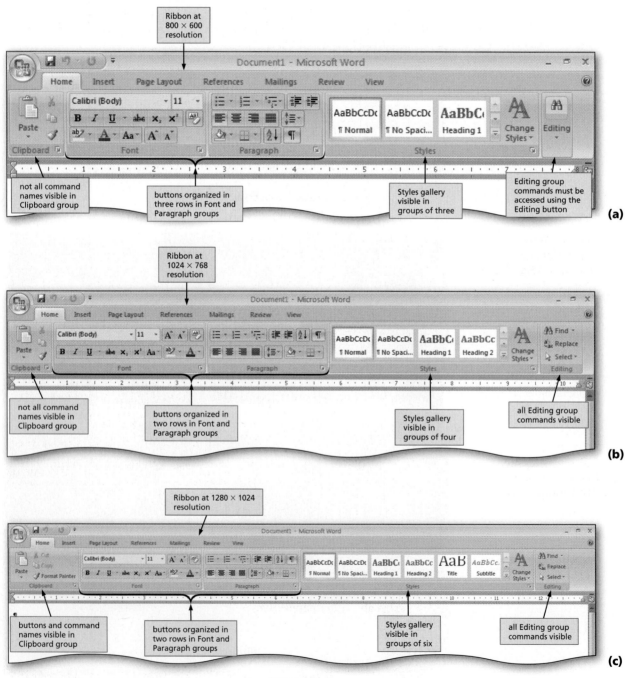

Figure E–6

Comparing the three Ribbons, notice changes in content and layout of the groups and galleries. In some cases, the content of a group is the same in each resolution, but the layout of the group differs. For example, the same buttons appear in the Font and Paragraph groups in the three resolutions, but the layouts differ. The buttons are displayed in three rows at the 800×600 resolution, and in two rows in the 1024×768 and 1280×1024 resolutions. In other cases, the content and layout are the same across the resolution, but the level of detail differs with the resolution. In the Clipboard group, when the resolution increases to 1280×1024, the names of all the buttons in the group appear in addition to the buttons themselves. At the lower resolution, only the buttons appear.

Changing resolutions also can result in fewer commands being visible in a group. Comparing the Editing groups, notice that the group at the 800×600 resolution consists of an Editing button, while at the higher resolutions, the group has three buttons visible. The commands that are available on the Ribbon at the higher resolutions must be accessed using the Editing button at the 800×600 resolution.

Changing resolutions results in different amounts of detail being available at one time in the galleries on the Ribbon. The Styles gallery in the three resolutions presented show different numbers of styles. At 800×600, you can scroll through the gallery three styles at a time, at 1024×768, you can scroll through the gallery four styles at a time, and at 1280×1024, you can scroll through the gallery six styles at a time.

Customizing the Word Window

When working in Word, you may want to make your working area as large as possible. One option is to minimize the Ribbon. You also can modify the characteristics of the Quick Access Toolbar, customizing the toolbar's commands and location to better suit your needs.

To Minimize the Ribbon in Word

The following steps minimize the Ribbon.

- Start Word.

- Maximize the Word window, if necessary.

- Click the Customize Quick Access Toolbar button on the Quick Access Toolbar to display the Customize Quick Access Toolbar menu (Figure E–7).

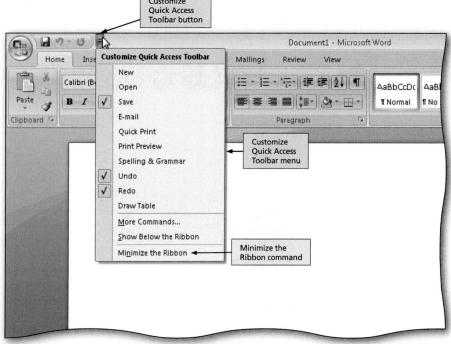

Figure E–7

- Click Minimize the Ribbon on the Quick Access Toolbar menu to reduce the Ribbon display to just the tabs (Figure E–8).

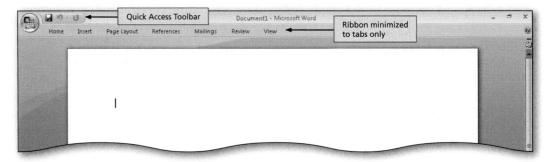

Figure E–8

Customizing and Resetting the Quick Access Toolbar

The Quick Access Toolbar, located to the right of the Microsoft Office Button by default, provides easy access to some of the more frequently used commands in Word (Figure E–7). By default, the Quick Access Toolbar contains buttons for the Save, Undo, and Redo commands. Customize the Quick Access Toolbar by changing its location in the window and by adding additional buttons to reflect which commands you would like to be able to access easily.

To Change the Location of the Quick Access Toolbar

The following steps move the Quick Access Toolbar to below the Ribbon.

- Double-click the Home tab to redisplay the Ribbon.

- Click the Customize Quick Access Toolbar button on the Quick Access Toolbar to display the Customize Quick Access Toolbar menu (Figure E–9).

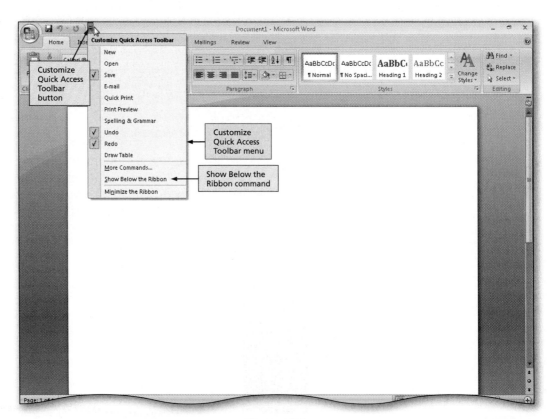

Figure E–9

- Click Show Below the Ribbon on the Quick Access Toolbar menu to move the Quick Access Toolbar below the Ribbon (Figure E–10).

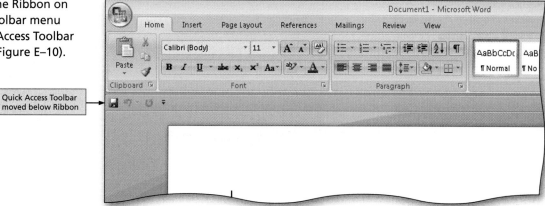

Quick Access Toolbar moved below Ribbon

Figure E–10

To Add Commands to the Quick Access Toolbar Using the Customize Quick Access Toolbar Menu

Some of the more commonly added commands are available for selection from the Customize Quick Access Toolbar menu. The following steps add the Quick Print button to the Quick Access Toolbar.

- Click the Customize Quick Access Toolbar button to display the Customize Quick Access Toolbar menu (Figure E–11).

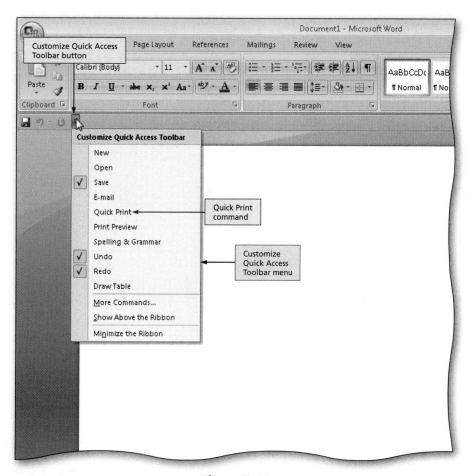

Figure E–11

• Click Quick Print on the Quick Access Toolbar menu to add the Quick Print button to the Quick Access Toolbar (Figure E–12).

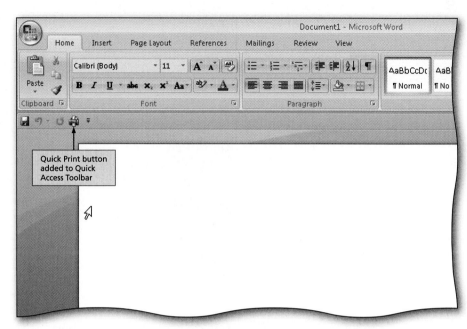

Figure E–12

To Add Commands to the Quick Access Toolbar Using the Shortcut Menu

Commands also can be added to the Quick Access Toolbar from the Ribbon. Adding an existing Ribbon command that you use often to the Quick Access Toolbar makes the command immediately available, regardless of which tab is active.

• Click the Review tab on the Ribbon to make it the active tab.

• Right-click the Spelling & Grammar button on the Review tab to display a shortcut menu (Figure E–13).

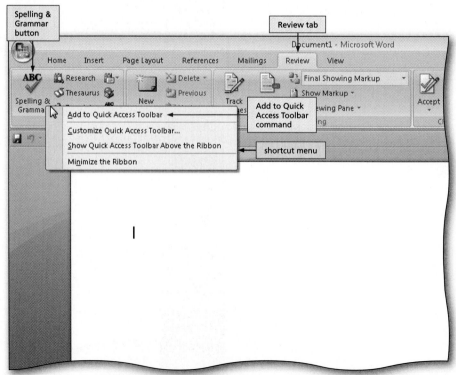

Figure E–13

2
- Click Add to Quick Access Toolbar on the shortcut menu to add the Spelling & Grammar button to the Quick Access Toolbar (Figure E–14).

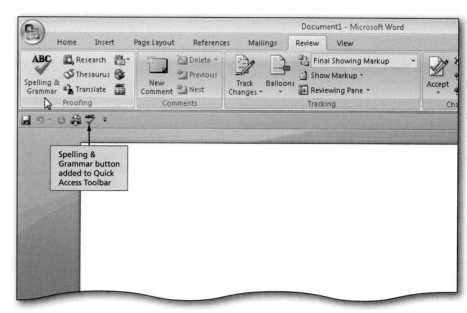

Figure E–14

To Add Commands to the Quick Access Toolbar Using Word Options

Some commands do not appear on the Ribbon. They can be added to the Quick Access Toolbar using the Word Options dialog box.

1
- Click the Office Button to display the Office Button menu (Figure E–15).

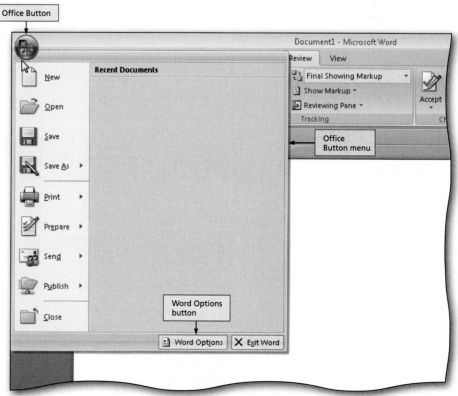

Figure E–15

- Click the Word Options button on the Office Button menu to display the Word Options dialog box (Figure E–16).

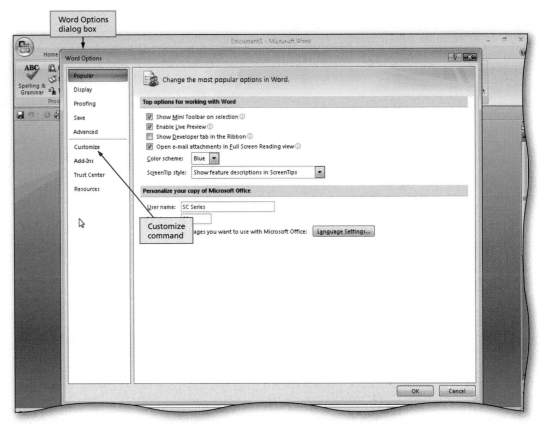

Figure E–16

- Click Customize in the left pane.

- Click the 'Choose commands from' box arrow to display the 'Choose commands from' list.

- Click Commands Not in the Ribbon in the 'Choose commands from' list.

- Scroll to display the Web Page Preview command.

- Click Web Page Preview to select it (Figure E–17).

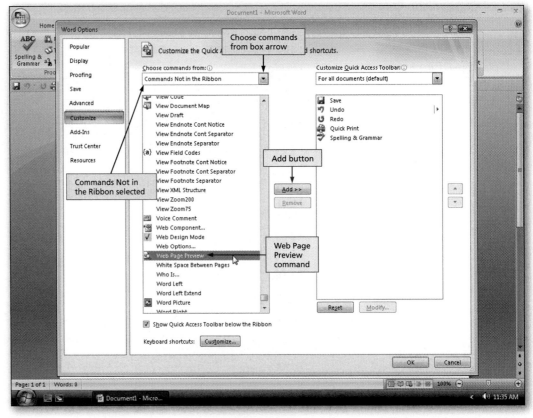

Figure E–17

4

• Click the Add button to add the Web Page Preview button to the list of buttons on the Quick Access Toolbar (Figure E–18).

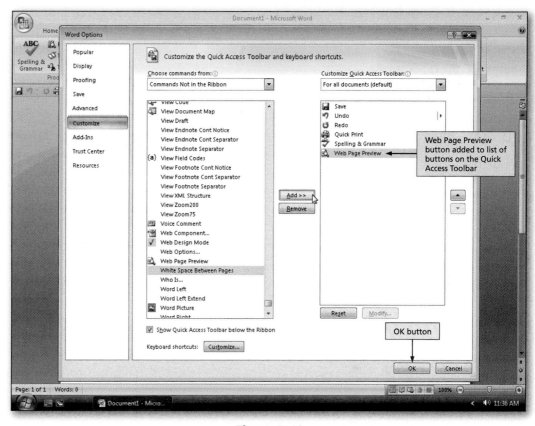

Figure E–18

5

• Click the OK button to add the Web Page Preview button to the Quick Access Toolbar (Figure E–19).

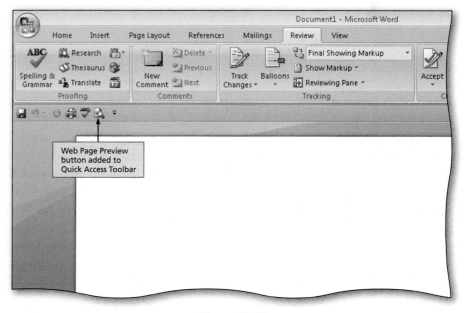

Figure E–19

Other Ways

1. Click Customize Quick Access Toolbar button, click More Commands, select commands to add, click Add button, click OK button

To Remove a Command from the Quick Access Toolbar

1

• Right-click the Web Page Preview button on the Quick Access Toolbar to display a shortcut menu (Figure E–20).

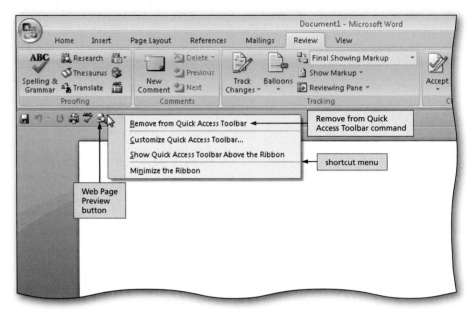

Figure E–20

2

• Click Remove from Quick Access Toolbar on the shortcut menu to remove the button from the Quick Access Toolbar (Figure E–21).

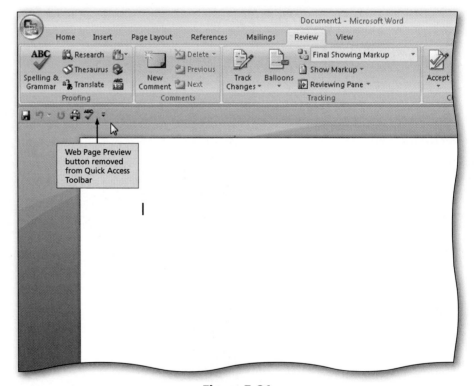

Figure E–21

Other Ways

1. Click Customize Quick Access Toolbar button, click More Commands, click the command you wish to remove in the Customize Quick Access Toolbar list, click Remove button, click OK button

2. If the command appears on the Customize Quick Access Toolbar menu, click the Customize Quick Access Toolbar button, click the command you wish to remove

To Reset the Quick Access Toolbar

1

- Click the Customize Quick Access Toolbar button on the Quick Access Toolbar.

- Click More Commands on the Quick Access Toolbar menu to display the Word Options Dialog box.

- Click the Show Quick Access Toolbar below the Ribbon check box to deselect it (Figure E–22).

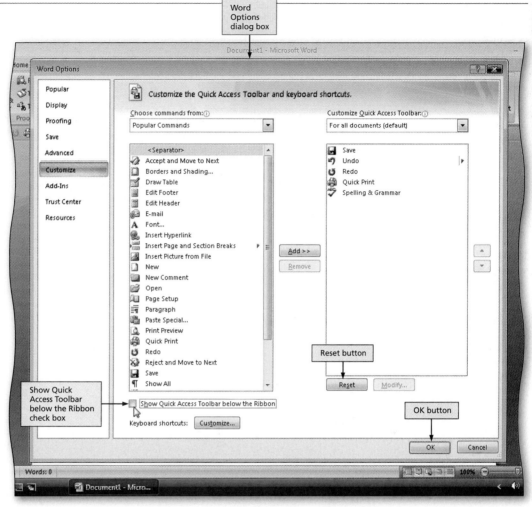

Figure E–22

- Click the Reset button, click the Yes button in the dialog box that appears, and then click the OK button in the Word Options dialog box, to reset the Quick Access Toolbar to its original position to the right of the Office Button, with the original three buttons (Figure E–23).

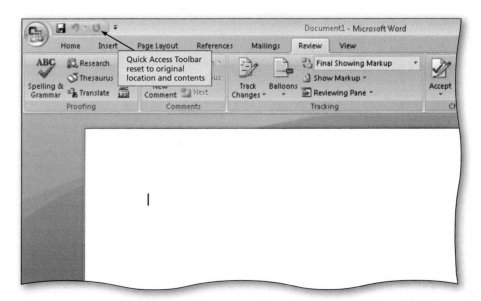

Figure E–23

Changing the Word Color Scheme

The Microsoft Word window can be customized by selecting a color scheme other than the default blue one. Three color schemes are available in Word.

To Change the Word Color Scheme

The following steps change the color scheme.

1

- Click the Office Button to display the Office Button menu.

- Click the Word Options button on the Office Button menu to display the Word Options dialog box.

- If necessary, click Popular in the left pane. Click the Color scheme box arrow to display a list of color schemes (Figure E–24).

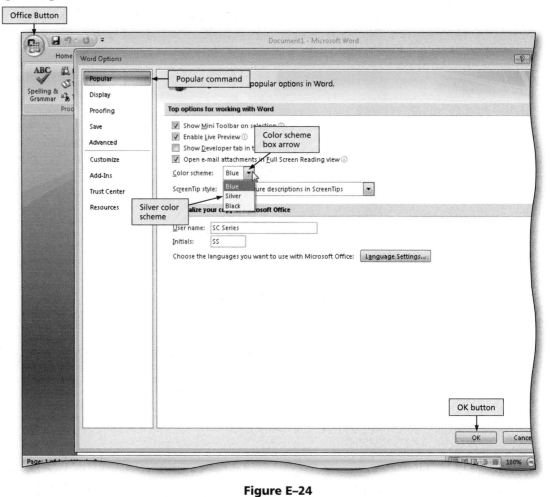

Figure E–24

2

- Click Silver in the list.

- Click the OK button to change the color scheme to silver (Figure E–25).

Q&A How do I switch back to the default color scheme?

Follow the steps for changing the Word color scheme, and select Blue from the list of color schemes.

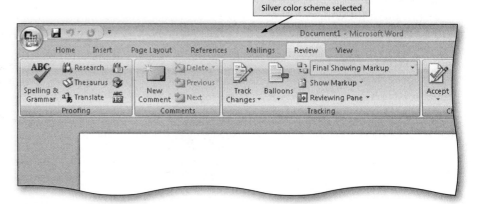

Figure E–25

Appendix F

Steps for the Windows XP User

For the XP User of this Book

For most tasks, no differences exist between using Word under the Windows Vista operating system and using Word under the Windows XP operating system. With some tasks, however, you will see some differences, or need to complete the tasks using different steps. This appendix shows how to Start Word, Save a Document, Open a Document, Insert a Picture, and Insert Text from a File while using Microsoft Office under Windows XP.

To Start Word

The following steps, which assume Windows is running, start Word based on a typical installation. You may need to ask your instructor how to start Word for your computer.

1 Click the Start button on the Windows taskbar to display the Start menu.

- Point to All Programs on the Start menu to display the All Programs submenu.

- Point to Microsoft Office on the All Programs submenu to display the Microsoft Office submenu (Figure F–1).

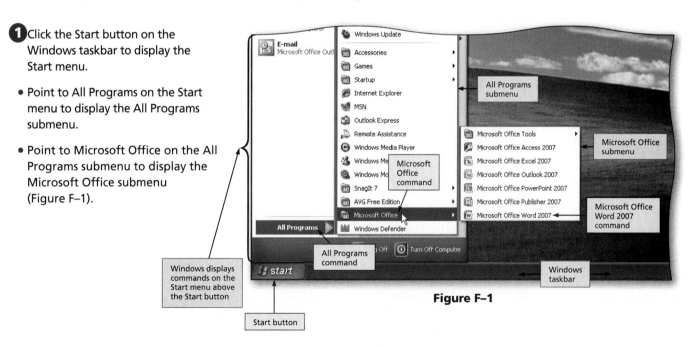

Figure F–1

- Click Microsoft Office Word 2007 to start Word and display a new blank document in the Word window (Figure F–2).

- If the Word window is not maximized, click the Maximize button next to the Close button on its title bar to maximize the window.

- If the Print Layout button is not selected, click it so that your screen layout matches Figure F–2.

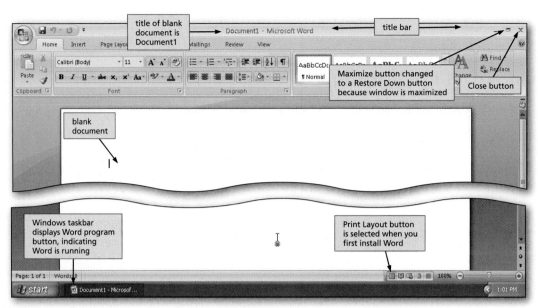

Figure F–2

Other Ways

1. Double-click Word icon on desktop, if one is present	2. Click Microsoft Office Word 2007 on Start menu

To Save a Document

After editing, you should save the document. The following steps save a document on a USB flash drive using the file name, Horseback Riding Lessons Flyer.

- With a USB flash drive connected to one of the computer's USB ports, click the Save button on the Quick Access Toolbar to display the Save As dialog box (Figure F–3).

Q&A

Do I have to save to a USB flash drive?

No. You can save to any device or folder. A **folder** is a specific location on a storage medium. You can save to the default folder or a different folder. You also can create your own folders, which is explained later in this book.

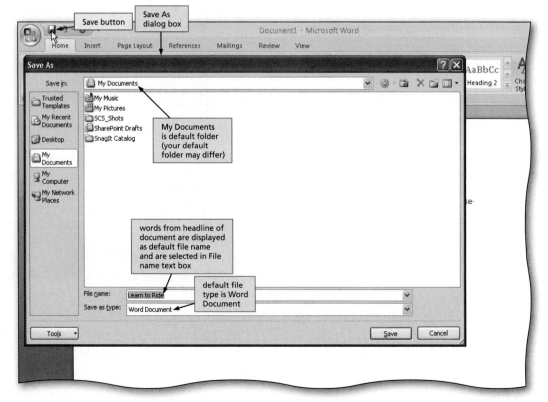

Figure F–3

2

- Type the name of your file (Horseback Riding Lessons Flyer in this example) in the File name text box to change the file name. Do not press the ENTER key after typing the file name (Figure F–4).

Q&A

What characters can I use in a file name?

A file name can have a maximum of 255 characters, including spaces. The only invalid characters are the backslash (\), slash (/), colon (:), asterisk (*), question mark (?), quotation mark ("), less than symbol (<), greater than symbol (>), and vertical bar (|).

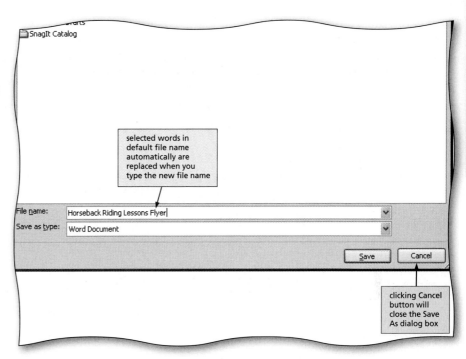

Figure F–4

3

- Click the Save in box arrow to display a list of available drives and folders (Figure F–5).

Q&A

Why is my list of files, folders, and drives arranged and named differently from those shown in the figure?

Your computer's configuration determines how the list of files and folders is displayed and how drives are named. You can change the save location by clicking shortcuts on the **My Places bar**.

Q&A

How do I save the file if I am not using a USB flash drive?

Use the same process, but be certain to select your device in the Save in list.

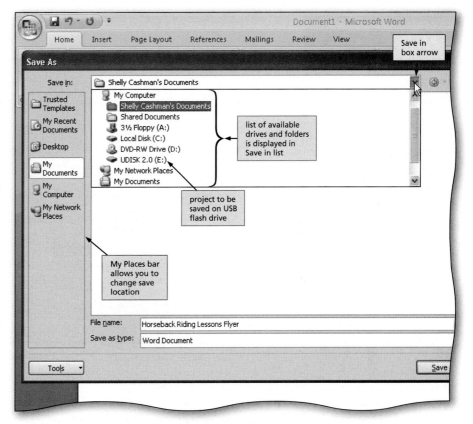

Figure F–5

- Click UDISK 2.0 (E:) in the Save in list to select the USB flash drive, Drive E in this case, as the new save location (Figure F–6).

- Click the Save button to save the document.

Q&A What if my USB flash drive has a different name or letter?

It is very likely that your USB flash drive will have a different name and drive letter and be connected to a different port. Verify the device in your Save in list is correct.

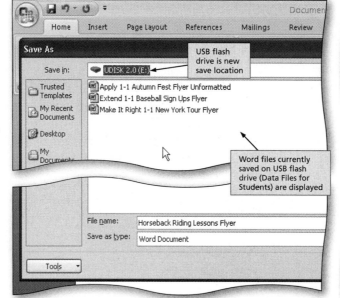

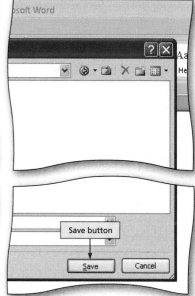

Figure F–6

Other Ways

1. Click Office Button, click Save, type file name, select drive or folder, click Save button

2. Press CTRL+S or press SHIFT+F12, type file name, select drive or folder, click Save button

To Open a Document

The following steps open the Horseback Riding Lessons Flyer file from the USB flash drive.

1

- With your USB flash drive connected to one of the computer's USB ports, click the Office Button to display the Office Button menu.

- Click Open on the Office Button menu to display the Open dialog box.

- If necessary, click the Look in box arrow and then click UDISK 2.0 (E:) to select the USB flash drive, Drive E in this case, in the Look in list as the new open location.

- Click Horseback Riding Lessons Flyer to select the file name (Figure F–7).

- Click the Open button to open the document.

Q&A How do I open the file if I am not using a USB flash drive?

Use the same process, but be certain to select your device in the Look in list.

Figure F–7

Other Ways

1. Click Office Button, double-click file name in Recent Documents list

2. Press CTRL+O, select file name, press ENTER

To Insert a Picture

The following steps insert a centered picture, which, in this example, is located on the same USB flash drive that contains the saved flyer.

1 Position the insertion point where you want the picture to be located. Click Insert on the Ribbon to display the Insert tab.

2 Click the Insert Picture from File button on the Insert tab to display the Insert Picture dialog box.

3 With your USB flash drive connected to one of the computer's USB ports, if necessary, click the Look in box arrow and then click UDISK 2.0 (E:) to select the USB flash drive, Drive E in this case, in the Look in list as the device that contains the picture. Select the file name of the picture file.

4 Click the Insert button in the dialog box to insert the picture at the location of the insertion point in the document.

To Insert Text from a File

The following steps insert text from a file located on the USB flash drive.

1 Click where you want to insert the text. Click Insert on the Ribbon to display the Insert tab.

2 Click the Object button arrow to display the Object menu. Click Text from File to display the Insert File dialog box.

3 With your USB flash drive connected to one of the computer's USB ports, if necessary, click the Look in box arrow and then click UDISK 2.0 (E:) to select the USB flash drive, Drive E in this case, in the Look in list as the device that contains the file. Select the file name of the file to be inserted.

4 Click the Insert button in the dialog box to insert the file at the location of the insertion point in the document.

Appendix G
Microsoft Business Certification Program

What Is the Microsoft Business Certification Program?

The Microsoft Business Certification Program enables candidates to show that they have something exceptional to offer – proved expertise in Microsoft Office 2007 programs. The two certification tracks allow candidates to choose how they want to exhibit their skills, either through validating skills within a specific Microsoft product or taking their knowledge to the next level and combining Microsoft programs to show that they can apply multiple skill sets to complete more complex office tasks. Recognized by businesses and schools around the world, more than 3 million certifications have been obtained in more than 100 different countries. The Microsoft Business Certification Program is the only Microsoft-approved certification program of its kind.

What Is the Microsoft Certified Application Specialist Certification?

The Microsoft Certified Application Specialist certification exams focus on validating specific skill sets within each of the Microsoft Office system programs. Candidates can choose which exam(s) they want to take according to which skills they want to validate. The available Application Specialist exams include:

- Using Microsoft® Windows Vista™
- Using Microsoft® Office Word 2007
- Using Microsoft® Office Excel® 2007
- Using Microsoft® Office PowerPoint® 2007
- Using Microsoft® Office Access 2007
- Using Microsoft® Office Outlook® 2007

> For more information and details on how Shelly Cashman Series textbooks map to Microsoft Certified Application Specialist certification, visit scsite.com/off2007/cert.

What Is the Microsoft Certified Application Professional Certification?

The Microsoft Certified Application Professional certification exams focus on a candidate's ability to use the 2007 Microsoft® Office system to accomplish industry-agnostic functions, for example Budget Analysis and Forecasting, or Content Management and Collaboration. The available Application Professional exams currently include:

- Organizational Support
- Creating and Managing Presentations
- Content Management and Collaboration
- Budget Analysis and Forecasting

Index

Quick Reference Summary

In the Microsoft Office Word 2007 program, you can accomplish a task in a number of ways. The following table provides a quick reference to each task presented in this textbook. The first column identifies the task. The second column indicates the page number on which the task is discussed in the book. The subsequent four columns list the different ways the task in column one can be carried out.

Microsoft Office Word 2007 Quick Reference Summary

Task	Page Number	Mouse	Ribbon	Shortcut Menu	Keyboard Shortcut
1.5 Line Spacing	WD 86		Line spacing button on Home tab	Paragraph | Indents and Spacing tab	CTRL+5
Address, Validate	WD 348		Edit Recipient List button on Mailings tab | Validate addresses link		
AddressBlock Merge Field, Add	WD 357		Address Block button on Mailings tab		
Arrange All Open Documents	WD 435		Arrange All button on View tab		
AutoCorrect Entry, Create	WD 93	Office Button | Word Options button | Proofing | AutoCorrect Options button			
AutoCorrect Options Menu, Display	WD 92	Point to text automatically corrected, point to small blue box, click AutoCorrect Options button			
Background Color, Add	WD 221		Page Color button on Page Layout tab		
Bibliographical List, Create	WD 113		Bibliography button on References tab | Insert Bibliography		
Bibliographical List, Modify Source and Update List	WD 117		Manage Sources button on References tab | select source | Edit button		

Microsoft Office Word 2007 Quick Reference Summary *(continued)*

Task	Page Number	Mouse	Ribbon	Shortcut Menu	Keyboard Shortcut
Bibliography Style, Change	WD 95		Bibliography Style box arrow on References tab		
Blank Page, Insert	WD 535		Blank Page button on Insert tab		
Blog Post, Create Blank Document for	WD 718	Office Button | Publish | Blog			
Blog Post, Insert Category	WD 723		Insert Category button on Blog Post tab		
Blog Post, Open Existing	WD 726		Open Existing button on Blog Post tab		
Blog Post, Publish	WD 726		Publish button on Blog Post tab		
Blog Web Page, Display in Web Browser Window	WD 725		Home Page button on Blog Post tab		
Bold	WD 34	Bold button on Mini toolbar	Bold button on Home tab	Font | Font tab | Bold in Font style list	CTRL+B
Bookmark, Add	WD 551		Bookmark button on Insert tab		
Bookmark, Go To	WD 552	In Bookmark dialog box, click name | Go To button			F5
Border, Paragraph	WD 161, WD 231, WD 396		Border button arrow on Home tab | Borders and Shading		
Building Block, Create	WD 170		Quick Parts button on Insert tab | Save Selection to Quick Part Gallery		ALT+F3
Building Block, Edit Properties	WD 518, WD 687		Quick Parts button on Insert tab | Building Blocks Organizer | select building block | Edit Properties button	Right-click building block on Quick Parts menu | Edit Properties	
Building Block, Insert	WD 172		Quick Parts button on Insert tab | building block name		F3
Building Blocks Organizer	WD 516		Quick Parts button on Insert tab | Building Blocks Organizer		
Bullets, Apply	WD 32	Bullets button on Mini toolbar	Bullets button on Home tab	Bullets	ASTERISK KEY | SPACEBAR
Bullets, Customize	WD 278		Bullets button on the Home tab | Define New Bullet		
Capital Letters	WD 86		Change Case button on Home tab | UPPERCASE	Font	CTRL+SHIFT+A
Caption, Add	WD 509		Insert Caption button on References tab		

Microsoft Office Word 2007 Quick Reference Summary *(continued)*

Task	Page Number	Mouse	Ribbon	Shortcut Menu	Keyboard Shortcut
Case of Letters, Change	WD 86		Change Case button on Home tab	Font | Font tab	SHIFT+F3
Center	WD 26	Center button on Mini toolbar	Center button on Home tab	Paragraph | Indents and Spacing tab	CTRL+E
Character Spacing, Modify	WD 240		Font Dialog Box Launcher on Home Tab | Character Spacing tab	Font | Character Spacing tab	
Character Style, Create	WD 276		More button in Styles gallery | Save Selection as New Quick Style	Styles | Save Selection	
Chart Table	WD 269		Object button arrow on Insert tab		
Chart Type, Change	WD 272			Chart Type | Standard Types tab	
Chart, Move Legend	WD 270			Format Legend | Placement tab	
Chart, Resize	WD 271	Drag sizing handle			
Citation Placeholder, Insert	WD 101		Insert Citation button on References tab | Add New Placeholder		
Citation, Insert	WD 547		Mark Citation button on References tab		ALT+SHIFT+I
Citation, Insert and Create Source	WD 96		Insert Citation button on References tab | Add New Source		
Citation, Edit	WD 98	Click citation, Citation Options box arrow | Edit Citation			
Close Document	WD 60	Office Button | Close			
Color Text	WD 152, WD 240	Font Color button arrow on Mini toolbar	Font Color button arrow on Home tab		
Column Break, Insert	WD 420		Insert Page and Section Breaks button on Page Layout tab | Column		
Column Break, Remove	WD 421		Cut button on Home tab		DELETE
Columns, Balance	WD 438		Insert Page and Section Breaks button on Page Layout tab		
Columns, Change Number	WD 410, WD 433		Columns button on Page Layout tab		
Columns, Increase Width	WD 414	Drag column boundaries	Columns button on Page Layout tab | More Columns		
Combine Revisions	WD 502		Compare button on Review tab | Combine on Compare menu		

Microsoft Office Word 2007 Quick Reference Summary *(continued)*

Task	Page Number	Mouse	Ribbon	Shortcut Menu	Keyboard Shortcut
Comment, Delete One	WD 496		Delete Comment button on Review tab	Right-click comment | Delete Comment	
Comment, Edit	WD 493	Click balloon, type new text			
Comment, Insert	WD 488		Insert Comment button on Review tab		CTRL+ALT+M
Comments, Balloons Setting, Turn On	WD 488		Balloons button on Review tab | Show Only Comments and Formatting in Balloons		
Comments, Delete All	WD 499		Delete Comment button arrow on Review tab | Delete All Comments in Document		
Compare Documents	WD 500		Compare button on Review tab | Compare on Compare menu		
Compared Documents, Display Original and Revised Documents	WD 500		Show Source Documents button on Review tab		
Compatibility Checker	WD 683	Office Button | Prepare | Run Compatibility Checker			
Compress Pictures	WD 524	Tools button in Save As dialog box | Compress Pictures on Tools menu	Compress Pictures button on Format tab		
Content Control, Change Text	WD 187, WD 534	Triple-click content control, change text			
Content Control, Combo Box, Change Properties	WD 605		Control Properties button on Developer tab		
Content Control, Combo Box, Insert	WD 604		Combo Box button on Developer tab		
Content Control, Date, Change Properties	WD 607		Control Properties button on Developer tab		
Content Control, Date, Insert	WD 606		Date Picker button on Developer tab		
Content Control, Drop-Down List, Change Properties	WD 602		Control Properties button on Developer tab		
Content Control, Drop-Down List, Insert	WD 601		Drop-Down List button on Developer tab		

Microsoft Office Word 2007 Quick Reference Summary *(continued)*

Task	Page Number	Mouse	Ribbon	Shortcut Menu	Keyboard Shortcut
Content Control, Plain Text, Change Properties	WD 595		Control Properties button on Developer tab		
Content Control, Plain Text, Insert	WD 593		Text button on Developer tab		
Content Control, Rich Text, Change Properties	WD 609		Control Properties button on Developer tab		
Content Control, Rich Text, Insert	WD 608		Rich Text button on Developer tab		
Copy	WD 189, WD 428		Copy button on Home tab	Copy	CTRL+C
Count Words	WD 107	Word Count indicator on status bar	Word Count button on Review tab		CTRL+SHIFT+G
Cover Page, Insert	WD 533		Cover Page button on Insert tab		
Cross-Reference, Create	WD 511		Cross-reference button on References tab		
Cross-Reference, Update Manually	WD 511			Right-click reference | Update Field	Select reference, F9
Cut	WD 121, WD 257		Cut button on Home tab	Cut	CTRL+X
Data Source, Associate with Main Document	WD 340		Select Recipients button on Mailings tab | Use Existing List		
Data Source, Create	WD 323		Start Mail Merge button on Mailings tab		
Date, Insert	WD 168, WD 330		Insert Date and Time button on Insert tab		
Delete	WD 59				DELETE
Developer Tab, Show	WD 588	Office Button | Word Options button | Popular | Show Developer tab in the Ribbon check box			
Dictionary, Custom, View or Modify Entries	WD 127	Office Button | Word Options button | Proofing | Custom Dictionaries button			
Dictionary, Set Custom	WD 127	Office Button | Word Options button | Proofing | Custom Dictionaries button | select desired dictionary name | Change Default button			
Digital Signature, Add to a Document	WD 692	Office Button | Prepare | Add a Digital Signature			

Microsoft Office Word 2007 Quick Reference Summary (continued)

Task	Page Number	Mouse	Ribbon	Shortcut Menu	Keyboard Shortcut
Document Inspector	WD 688	Office Button | Prepare | Inspect Document			
Document Map	WD 537		Document Map check box on View tab		
Document Properties, Set or View	WD 51	Office Button | Prepare | Properties			
Documents, Switch Between	WD 189	Program button on Windows taskbar	Switch Windows button on View tab		ALT+TAB
Double-Space Text	WD 87		Line spacing button on Home tab	Paragraph | Indents and Spacing	CTRL+2
Double-Underline	WD 35		Font Dialog Box Launcher on Home tab	Font | Font tab	CTRL+SHIFT+D
Drawing Canvas, Display Automatically	WD 314	Office Button | Word Options button | Advanced | Editing Options area			
Drawing Canvas, Format	WD 315		Drawing Tools Format tab		
Drawing Canvas, Insert	WD 314		Shapes button on Insert tab | New Drawing Canvas		
Drawing Canvas, Resize	WD 320	Drag a sizing handle	Shape Width and Shape Height text boxes on Format tab	Format Drawing Canvas | Size tab	
Drop Cap	WD 417		Drop Cap button on Insert tab		
Editing Restrictions, Set	WD 623		Protect Document button on Developer tab | set options in task pane		
E-Mail, Customize Opening	WD 695	Office Button | Word Options button | Popular			
E-Mail Document, as Attachment	WD 478	Office Button | Send | E-mail			
E-Mail Document, as PDF Attachment	WD 449	Office Button | Send | E-mail as PDF Attachment			
Envelope, Address and Print	WD 203		Envelopes button on Mailings tab | Envelopes tab | Print button		
Exceptions, Set Editing Restrictions	WD 703		Protect Document button on Developer tab		
Field Codes, Display or Remove	WD 261, WD 331, WD 341			Toggle Field Codes	ALT+F9
Field Codes, Print	WD 342	Office Button | Word Options button | Advanced			

Microsoft Office Word 2007 Quick Reference Summary *(continued)*

Task	Page Number	Mouse	Ribbon	Shortcut Menu	Keyboard Shortcut
Field, Edit	WD 667			Edit Field	
Field, Insert	WD 666		Quick Parts button on Insert tab		
Field, Lock	WD 345				CTRL+F11
Field, Unlock	WD 345				CTRL+SHIFT+F11
File, Create from Existing File	WD 165	Office Button	New	New from existing			
Fill Effect for Background, Add	WD 222, WD 650		Page Color button on Page Layout tab	Fill Effects	Pattern tab		
Find Format	WD 274	Select Browse Object button on vertical scroll bar	Find icon	Find button on Home tab		CTRL+F
Find Text	WD 124	Select Browse Object button on vertical scroll bar	Find icon	Find button on Home tab		CTRL+F
Find and Replace Text	WD 123	Select Browse Object button on vertical scroll bar	Find icon	Replace tab	Replace button on Home tab		CTRL+H
First-Line Indent Paragraphs	WD 88	Drag First Line Indent marker on ruler	Paragraph Dialog Box Launcher on Home tab	Indents and Spacing tab	Paragraph	Indents and Spacing tab	TAB
Folder, Create While Saving	WD 321	Save button on Quick Access Toolbar	Create a new, empty folder button			F12
Font, Change	WD 29	Font box arrow on Mini toolbar	Font box arrow on Home tab	Font	Font tab	CTRL+SHIFT+F
Font, Change Case	WD 243		Change Case button on Home tab		SHIFT+F3
Font Settings, Modify Default	WD 242		Font Dialog Box Launcher on Home Tab	Default button	Yes button		
Font Size, Change	WD 28	Font Size box arrow on Mini toolbar	Font Size box arrow on Home tab	Font	Font tab	CTRL+SHIFT+P
Font Size, Decrease	WD 152	Shrink Font button on Mini toolbar	Shrink Font button on Home tab	Font	Font tab	CTRL+SHIFT+<
Font Size, Decrease 1 Point	WD 86			Font	Font tab	CTRL+[
Font Size, Increase	WD 151	Grow Font button on Mini toolbar	Grow Font button on Home tab		CTRL+SHIFT+>
Font Size, Increase 1 Point	WD 86			Font	Font tab	CTRL+]
Footer, Insert Formatted	WD 261		Footer button on Design tab		
Footnote Reference Mark, Insert	WD 100		Insert Footnote button on References tab		CTRL+ALT+F

Microsoft Office Word 2007 Quick Reference Summary *(continued)*

Task	Page Number	Mouse	Ribbon	Shortcut Menu	Keyboard Shortcut
Footnote, Delete	WD 106	Delete note reference mark in document window	Cut button Home tab		BACKSPACE | BACKSPACE
Footnote, Edit	WD 106	Double-click note reference mark in document window	Show Notes button on References tab		
Footnote, Move	WD 106	Drag note reference mark in document window	Cut button on Home tab | Paste button on Home tab		
Footnote Style, Modify	WD 102		Click footnote text | Styles Dialog Box Launcher | Manage Styles button | Modify button	Style | Footnote Text | Modify button	
Format Characters	WD 240		Font Dialog Box Launcher on Home Tab		
Format Painter	WD 611		Format Painter button on Home tab		
Formatting Marks	WD 14, WD 248, WD 515		Show/Hide ¶ button on Home tab		CTRL+SHIFT+*
Formatting Restrictions, Set	WD 622		Protect Document button on Developer tab | set options in task pane		
Formatting, Clear	WD 162		Clear Formatting button on Home tab		CTRL+ SPACEBAR
Go To, Section	WD 258	Page number in document button on status bar	Find button arrow on Home tab | Go To on Find menu		CTRL+G
Graphic, Adjust Brightness	WD 404		Brightness button on Format tab	Format Picture | Picture	
Graphic, Adjust Contrast	WD 584		Contrast button on Format tab	Format Picture | Picture	
Graphic, Crop	WD 721		Crop button on Format tab		
Graphic, Flip	WD 403		Rotate button on Format tab		
Graphic, Format as Floating	WD 402		Text Wrapping button on Format tab	Text Wrapping	
Graphic, Insert	WD 153		Clip Art button on Insert tab		
Graphic, Recolor	WD 156		Recolor button on Format tab	Format Picture | Picture | Recolor button	
Graphic, Resize	WD 46	Drag sizing handle	Format tab in Picture Tools tab or Size Dialog Box Launcher on Format tab	Size | Size tab	
Graphic, Restore	WD 404		Reset Picture button on Format tab		

Microsoft Office Word 2007 Quick Reference Summary *(continued)*

Task	Page Number	Mouse	Ribbon	Shortcut Menu	Keyboard Shortcut
Graphic, Rotate	WD 664	Drag rotate handle			
Graphic, Send Behind Text	WD 614		Send to Back button on Format tab	Order | Send Behind Text	
Graphic, Set Transparent Color	WD 157		Recolor button on Format tab | Set Transparent Color		
GreetingLine Merge Field, Edit	WD 332			Right-click field | Edit Greeting Line	
Gridlines, Show/ Hide	WD 592, WD 599		View Table Gridlines button on Layout tab		
Hanging Indent, Create	WD 116	Drag Hanging Indent marker on ruler	Paragraph Dialog Box Launcher on Home tab | Indents and Spacing tab	Paragraph | Indents and Spacing tab	CTRL+T
Hanging Indent, Remove	WD 86		Paragraph Dialog Box Launcher on Home tab | Indents and Spacing tab	Paragraph | Indents and Spacing tab	CTRL+SHIFT+T
Header & Footer, Close	WD 83	Double-click dimmed document text	Close Header and Footer button on Design tab		
Header, Different for Section	WD 259		Header button on Insert Tab | Edit Header		
Header, Display	WD 80	Double-click dimmed header	Header button on Insert tab | Edit Header		
Header, Distance from Edge	WD 261		Page Setup Dialog Box Launcher on Page Layout tab | Layout tab		
Header, Insert Formatted	WD 260		Header button on Design tab		
Headers, Alternating	WD 548		Header button on Insert tab | Edit Header | Different Odd & Even Pages		
Help	WD 60		Office Word Help button		F1
Hidden Text, Format Text as	WD 366		Font Dialog Box Launcher | Font tab	Font | Font tab	
Hidden Text, Hide/ Show	WD 367		Show/Hide ¶ button on Home tab		CTRL+SHIFT+*
Highlight Text	WD 586		Text Highlight Color button on Home tab		
Hyperlink, Format Text as	WD 220		Insert Hyperlink button on Insert tab	Hyperlink	CTRL+K
Hyperlink, Insert	WD 552		Select text | Insert Hyperlink button on Insert tab		
Hyperlink, Remove	WD 163		Hyperlink button on Insert tab | Remove Link button	Remove Hyperlink	

Microsoft Office Word 2007 Quick Reference Summary *(continued)*

Task	Page Number	Mouse	Ribbon	Shortcut Menu	Keyboard Shortcut
IF Field, Insert	WD 338		Rules button on Mailings tab		
Indent Paragraph	WD 196, WD 233	Drag Left Indent marker on ruler	Increase Indent button on Home tab	Paragraph | Indents and Spacing sheet	CTRL+M
Index Entry, Delete	WD 546	Display formatting marks, delete entry			
Index Entry, Edit	WD 546	Display formatting marks, change text inside quotation marks			
Index Entry, Mark	WD 512		Select text | Mark Entry button on References tab		ALT+SHIFT+X
Index, Build	WD 544		Insert Index button on References tab		
Index, Change Format	WD 547		Insert Index button on References tab		
Index, Delete	WD 547	Select index, drag through field code, delete index entry			
Index, Update	WD 546		Update Index button on References tab		Select index, F9
Insert Document in Existing Document	WD 251		Object button arrow on Insert tab		
Insertion Point, Move to Beginning of Document	WD 24	Scroll to top of document, click			CTRL+HOME
Insertion Point, Move to End of Document	WD 25	Scroll to bottom of document, click			CTRL+END
Italicize	WD 36	Italic button on Mini toolbar	Italic button on Home tab	Font | Font tab	CTRL+I
Justify Paragraph	WD 86, WD 411		Justify button on Home tab	Paragraph | Indents and Spacing tab	CTRL+J
Left-Align	WD 86		Align Text Left button on Home tab	Paragraph | Indents and Spacing tab	CTRL+L
Line Break, Enter	WD 194				SHIFT+ENTER
Link Object	WD 469		Copy object | Paste button on Home tab | Paste Special		
Linked Object, Break Links	WD 476	Office Button | Prepare | Edit Links to Files | Break Link button		Linked Object | Links | Break Link button	CTRL+SHIFT+F9
Linked Object, Edit	WD 476	Double-click linked object			
Macro Settings, Specify	WD 647	Office Button | Word Options button | Trust Center	Macro Security button on Developer tab		
Macro, Delete	WD 678		View Macros button on Developer tab | Delete button		

Microsoft Office Word 2007 Quick Reference Summary *(continued)*

Task	Page Number	Mouse	Ribbon	Shortcut Menu	Keyboard Shortcut
Macro, Edit VBA Code	WD 679		View Macros button Developer tab | Edit button		
Macro, Pause Recording	WD 672	Pause Recording button on status bar			
Macro, Record	WD 671, WD 678	Macro Recording button on status bar	Record Macro button on Developer tab		
Macro, Rename	WD 677		View Macros button on Developer tab | Organizer button		
Macro, Run	WD 674		View Macros button on Developer tab | Run button		
Mail Merge Fields, Insert	WD 333		Insert Merge Field button arrow on Mailings tab		
Mail Merge to New Document Window	WD 363		Finish & Merge button on Mailings tab | Edit Individual Documents		
Mail Merge to Printer	WD 344		Finish & Merge button on Mailings tab | Print Documents		
Mail Merge, Directory	WD 358		Start Mail Merge button on Mailings tab		
Mail Merge, Envelopes	WD 356		Start Mail Merge button on Mailings tab		
Mail Merge, Identify Main Document	WD 309		Start Mail Merge button on Mailings tab		
Mail Merge, Mailing Labels	WD 350		Start Mail Merge button on Mailings tab		
Mail Merge, Select Records	WD 345		Edit Recipient List button on Mailings tab		
Mail Merge, Sort Data Records	WD 348		Edit Recipient List button on Mailings tab		
Mail Merged Data, View	WD 349		View Merged Data button on Mailings tab		
Main Document File, Convert	WD 368		Start Mail Merge button on Mailings tab		
Margin, Gutter	WD 550		Margins button on Page Layout tab		
Margins, Change Settings	WD 313, WD 389, WD 579	Drag margin boundary on ruler	Margins button on Page Layout tab		
Markup, Select Next	WD 496		Next Change button on Review tab		

Microsoft Office Word 2007 Quick Reference Summary *(continued)*

Task	Page Number	Mouse	Ribbon	Shortcut Menu	Keyboard Shortcut
Markups, Change How Document is Displayed	WD 496		Display for Review box arrow on Review tab		
Markups, Display in Balloons	WD 492		Balloons button on Review tab | Show Revisions in Balloons		
Markups, Display Inline	WD 492		Balloons button on Review tab | Show All Revisions Inline		
Markups, Print	WD 495	Office Button | Print | Print | Print what box arrow | Document showing markup			
Markups, Select Items to Display	WD 496		Show Markup button on Review tab		
Merge Condition, Remove	WD 348		Edit Recipient List button on Mailings tab | Filter link | Clear All button		
Move Selected Text	WD 121	Drag and drop selected text	Cut button on Home tab | Paste button on Home tab	Cut | Paste	CTRL+X, CTRL+V
Multilevel List, Change Levels	WD 336		Increase (Decrease) Indent button on Home tab	Increase Indent or Decrease Indent	TAB, SHIFT+TAB
Multilevel List, Create	WD 335		Multilevel List button on Home tab		
Nonbreaking Space, Insert	WD 171		Symbol button on Insert tab | More Symbols | Special Characters tab		CTRL+SHIFT+SPACEBAR
Numbered List, Enter	WD 519		Numbering button on Home tab		
Numbered List, Format	WD 519		Numbering button arrow on Home tab		
Open Document	WD 56	Office Button | Open			CTRL+O
Outline, Create	WD 525	Outline button on status bar	Outline View on View tab		
Page Border, Add	WD 48		Page Borders button on Page Layout tab		
Page Break, Delete	WD 256		Cut button on Home tab	Cut	CTRL+X, BACKSPACE
Page Break, Manual	WD 112		Page Break button on Insert tab		CTRL+ENTER
Page Number, Insert	WD 82		Insert Page Number button on Design tab		
Page Numbers, Start at Different Number	WD 262		Insert Page Number button on Design tab | Format Page Numbers on Insert Page Number menu		

Microsoft Office Word 2007 Quick Reference Summary *(continued)*

Task	Page Number	Mouse	Ribbon	Shortcut Menu	Keyboard Shortcut
Page Orientation	WD 362		Page Orientation button on Page Layout tab		
Paper Size, Change	WD 577		Page Size button on Page Layout tab		
Paragraph, Add Space Above	WD 79		Line spacing button on Home tab | Add Space Before (After) Paragraph	Paragraph | Indents and Spacing tab	CTRL+0 (zero)
Paragraph, Decrease Indent	WD 196	Decrease Indent button on Mini toolbar	Decrease Indent button on Home tab	Paragraph | Indents and Spacing tab	CTRL+SHIFT+M
Paragraph, Remove Space After	WD 195		Line spacing button on Home tab | Remove Space After Paragraph	Paragraph | Indents and Spacing tab	
Paragraphs, Change Spacing Above and Below	WD 50		Spacing Before box arrow on Page Layout tab	Paragraph | Indents and Spacing tab	
Password-Protect File	WD 685	Office Button | Save As | Tools button | General Options			
Paste	WD 191, WD 430, WD 436		Paste button on Home tab	Paste	CTRL+V
Picture Border, Change	WD 45		Picture Border button on Format tab		
Picture Style, Apply	WD 44		Picture Tools and Format tabs | More button in Picture Styles gallery		
Picture, Change Color	WD 662		Recolor button on Picture Tools Format tab		
Picture, Change Shape	WD 722		Picture Shape button on Format tab		
Picture, Insert	WD 41		Picture button on Insert tab		
Placeholder Text, Edit	WD 594		Design Mode button on Developer tab		
Print Document	WD 54	Office Button | Print | Print			CTRL+P
Print Document Properties	WD 130	Office Button | Print | Print | Print what box arrow			
Print Preview	WD 201	Office Button | Print | Print Preview			
Print Specific Pages	WD 253	Office Button | Print | Print			CTRL+P
Print, Draft	WD 347	Office Button | Word Options button | Advanced | Print area			

Microsoft Office Word 2007 Quick Reference Summary *(continued)*

Task	Page Number	Mouse	Ribbon	Shortcut Menu	Keyboard Shortcut
Protect Document	WD 620		Protect Document button on Developer tab		
Quick Access Toolbar, Add Macro as Button	WD 674	Customize Quick Access Toolbar button on Quick Access Toolbar			
Quick Access Toolbar, Delete Button	WD 677			Right-click button | Remove from Quick Access Toolbar	
Quick Style, Create	WD 90		More button in Styles gallery | Save Selection as a New Quick Style	Styles | Save Selection as a New Quick Style	
Quit Word	WD 55	Close button on right side of Word title bar			ALT+F4
Quote Style, Apply	WD 532		More button in Styles group on Home tab		CTRL+SHIFT+S
Rectangle, Draw	WD 613		Shapes button on Insert tab		
Remove Character Formatting (Plain Text)	WD 87		Font Dialog Box Launcher on Home tab | Font tab	Font | Font tab	CTRL+SPACEBAR
Remove Paragraph Formatting	WD 87		Font Dialog Box Launcher on Home tab	Font | Font tab	CTRL+Q
Research Task Pane, Use	WD 128	Hold down ALT key, click word to look up			
Reveal Formatting	WD 248				SHIFT+F1
Reviewer Information, Change	WD 490	Office Button | Word Options button	Track Changes button arrow on Review tab | Change User Name on Track Changes menu		
Reviewing Pane, Display Vertically	WD 493		Reviewing Pane button arrow on Review tab | Reviewing Pane Vertical		
Right-Align Paragraph	WD 81		Align Text Right button on Home tab	Paragraph | Indents and Spacing tab	CTRL+R
Rulers, Display	WD 87	View Ruler button on vertical scroll bar	View Ruler on View tab		
Save Document as Template	WD 574	Office Button | Save As | Word Template			F12
Save Document as Web Page	WD 218	Office Button | Save As | Other Formats			F12
Save Document, Previous Word Format	WD 477	Office Button | Save As | Word 97-2003 Document			F12
Save Document, Same Name	WD 53	Save button on Quick Access Toolbar			CTRL+S

Microsoft Office Word 2007 Quick Reference Summary *(continued)*

Task	Page Number	Mouse	Ribbon	Shortcut Menu	Keyboard Shortcut
Save New Document	WD 19	Save button on Quick Access Toolbar			CTRL+S
Save, as XML File	WD 697	Office Button | Save As			
Save, as XPS File	WD 694	Office Button | Save As			
Save, Macro-Enabled Template	WD 645	Office Button | Save As			
Schema, Attach File	WD 697		Schema button on Developer tab		
Schema, Delete	WD 700		Schema button on Developer tab | Schema Library button		
Search for and Highlight Text	WD 514	Click Select Browse Object button on vertical scroll bar | Find icon	Find button on Home tab | entered desired text | Reading Highlight button | Highlight All		CTRL+F
Section Break, Continuous	WD 409		Insert Page and Section Breaks button on Page Layout tab | Continuous		
Section Break, Delete	WD 251			Cut	DELETE or BACKSPACE
Section Break, Next Page	WD 250, WD 418		Breaks button on Page Layout tab		
Section Number, Display on Status Bar	WD 249			Section	
Section, Formatting	WD 259	Double-click section break notation			
Select Block of Text	WD 33	Click at beginning of text, hold down SHIFT key and click at end of text to select; or drag through text			CTRL+SHIFT+RIGHT ARROW and/or DOWN ARROW
Select Browse Object Menu, Use	WD 118	Select Browse Object button on vertical scroll bar			ALT+CTRL+HOME
Select Character(s)	WD 120	Drag through character(s)			CTRL+SHIFT+RIGHT ARROW
Select Entire Document	WD 120	Point to left of text and triple-click			CTRL+A
Select Graphic	WD 46	Click graphic			
Select Line	WD 27	Point to left of line and click			SHIFT+DOWN ARROW
Select Lines	WD 30	Point to left of first line and drag up or down			CTRL+SHIFT+DOWN ARROW
Select Nonadjacent Text	WD 277	Drag through text, press and hold CTRL key, drag through more text			

Microsoft Office Word 2007 Quick Reference Summary *(continued)*

Task	Page Number	Mouse	Ribbon	Shortcut Menu	Keyboard Shortcut
Select Paragraph	WD 90	Triple-click paragraph			SHIFT+DOWN ARROW
Select Paragraphs	WD 30	Point to left of first paragraph, double-click, and drag up or down			
Select Sentence	WD 120	Press and hold down CTRL key and click sentence			CTRL+SHIFT+RIGHT ARROW
Select Word	WD 59	Double-click word			CTRL+SHIFT+RIGHT ARROW
Select Words	WD 33	Drag through words			CTRL+SHIFT+RIGHT ARROW
Shade Paragraph	WD 232		Shading button arrow on Home tab		
Shape, 3-D Effect, Change Color	WD 660		3-D Effects button on Format tab	3-D Color		
Shape, 3-D Effect, Change Direction	WD 659		3-D Effects button on Format tab	Direction		
Shape, Add Text	WD 319		Edit Text button on Drawing Tools Format tab	Add Text	
Shape, Add 3-D Effect	WD 658		3-D Effects button on Format tab		
Shape, Add Shadow	WD 617		Shadow Effects button on Format tab		
Shape, Apply Style	WD 318, WD 616		Advanced Tools Dialog Box Launcher in Shape Styles group	Format AutoShape	
Shape, Fill with Picture	WD 660		Shape Fill button arrow on Format tab	Picture		
Shape, Insert	WD 316		Shapes button on Insert tab		
Shape, Remove 3-D Effect	WD 658		3-D Effects button on Format tab	No 3-D Effect		
Show First Line Only	WD 527		Show First Line Only check box on Outlining tab		
Signature Line, Add to a Document	WD 691		Signature Line button on Insert tab		
Single-Space Lines	WD 86		Line spacing button on the Home tab	Paragraph	Indents and Spacing tab	CTRL+1
Small Uppercase Letters	WD 86		Font Dialog Box Launcher on Home tab	Font tab	Font	Font tab	CTRL+SHIFT+K
SmartArt Graphic, Add Shape	WD 441		Add Shape button on Design tab		
SmartArt Graphic, Add Text	WD 237, WD 442	Click Text Pane control on SmartArt graphic	Text Pane button on SmartArt Tools Design tab		

Microsoft Office Word 2007 Quick Reference Summary (continued)

Task	Page Number	Mouse	Ribbon	Shortcut Menu	Keyboard Shortcut
SmartArt Graphic, Apply Style	WD 239		More button in SmartArt Styles gallery		
SmartArt Graphic, Change Colors	WD 238		Change Colors button on SmartArt Tools Design tab		
SmartArt Graphic, Change Layout	WD 440		Click selection in Layouts gallery on SmartArt Tools Design tab	Change Layout	
SmartArt Graphic, Insert	WD 235		Insert SmartArt Graphic button on Insert tab		
SmartArt Graphic, Outline	WD 446		Shape Outline button on Format tab		
SmartArt Graphic, Remove Formats	WD 240		Reset Graphic button on SmartArt Tools Design tab		
Sort Paragraphs	WD 200		Sort button on Home tab		
Source, Edit	WD 104	Click citation, Citation Options box arrow | Edit Source			
Spelling and Grammar	WD 125	Spelling and Grammar Check icon on status bar | Spelling	Spelling & Grammar button on Review tab	Right-click flagged text | Spelling	F7
Spelling and Grammar Check as You Type	WD 16	Spelling and Grammar Check icon on status bar		Correct word on shortcut menu	
Split Window	WD 434	Double-click split box	Split button on View tab		
Split Window, Remove	WD 437	Double-click split bar	Remove Split button on View tab		
Status Bar, Customize	WD 249			Right-click status bar | click desired element	
Style Set, Change	WD 37		Change Styles button on Home tab | Style Set on Change Styles menu		
Styles Task Pane, Open	WD 25		Styles Dialog Box Launcher on Home tab		ALT+CTRL+SHIFT+S
Styles, Apply	WD 24		Styles gallery on Home tab		
Styles, Modify	WD 90, WD 405, WD 424, WD 656		Styles Dialog Box Launcher on Home tab	Update [*style name*] to Match Selection	
Style, Modify Using Manage Styles Button	WD 669		Styles Dialog Box Launcher on Home tab		
Subdocument, Insert	WD 528		Insert Subdocument button on Outlining tab		

Microsoft Office Word 2007 Quick Reference Summary *(continued)*

Task	Page Number	Mouse	Ribbon	Shortcut Menu	Keyboard Shortcut
Subscript	WD 86		Font Dialog Box Launcher on Home tab	Font | Font tab	CTRL+EQUAL SIGN
Superscript	WD 86		Font Dialog Box Launcher on Home tab	Font | Font tab	CTRL+SHIFT+PLUS SIGN
Symbol, Insert	WD 398		Symbol button on Insert tab		ALT | NUM LOCK key | type ANSI code
Synonym, Find	WD 124		Thesaurus on Review tab	Synonyms | desired word	SHIFT+F7
Tab Stops, Set	WD 158, WD 167	Click tab selector, click ruler on desired location	Paragraph Dialog Box Launcher | Tabs button	Paragraph | Tabs button	
Table of Authorities, Create	WD 547		Insert Table of Authorities button on References tab		
Table of Contents, Add Text to	WD 538		Add Text button on References tab		
Table of Contents, Change Format	WD 541	Select table | Table of Contents button on table	Select table | Table of Contents button on References tab		
Table of Contents, Create	WD 536		Table of Contents button on References tab		
Table of Contents, Update	WD 540	Select table | Update Table button on table	Select table | Update Table button on References tab		Select table, F9
Table of Figures	WD 542, WD 543		Insert Table of Figures button on References tab		
Table of Figures, Update	WD 543		Select table of figures | click Update Table of Figures button on References tab		Select table, F9
Table, Add Column	WD 264		Insert Columns to the Left (or Right) button on Layout tab		
Table, Align Data in Cells	WD 268		Align [location] button on Layout tab		
Table, Apply Style	WD 176		More button in Table Styles gallery		
Table, Border	WD 267		Line Weight box arrow on Design tab | Borders button arrow		
Table, Change Row Height	WD 290	Drag border	Table Properties button on Layout tab	Table Properties	
Table, Convert Text to Table	WD 361		Table button on Insert tab | Convert Text to Table		
Table, Convert to Text	WD 653		Convert to Text button on Layout tab		
Table, Delete Column	WD 263		Delete button on Layout tab	Delete Columns	

Microsoft Office Word 2007 Quick Reference Summary *(continued)*

Task	Page Number	Mouse	Ribbon	Shortcut Menu	Keyboard Shortcut
Table, Delete Contents	WD 283				DELETE
Table, Delete Rows	WD 186, WD 264		Delete button on Layout tab | Delete Rows		
Table, Display Text Vertically in Cell	WD 284		Text Direction button on Layout tab		
Table, Distribute Rows	WD 283		Select Table button on Layout tab | Select Table		
Table, Draw	WD 280		Table button on Insert tab | Draw Table		
Table, Erase Lines	WD 282		Eraser button on Design tab		
Table, Insert	WD 173		Table button on Insert tab		
Table, Insert Borderless	WD 589		Table button on Insert tab | Borders button arrow on Design tab | No Border		
Table, Merge Cells	WD 287		Merge Cells button on Layout tab	Merge Cells	
Table, Modify Properties	WD 364		Table Properties button on Layout tab		
Table, Move	WD 267	Drag move handle			
Table, Non-Breaking Across Pages	WD 279		Table Properties button on the Table Tools Layout tab | Row tab		
Table, Resize Columns	WD 177	Double-click column boundary	AutoFit button on Layout tab	AutoFit | AutoFit to Contents	
Table, Select	WD 179	Click table move handle	Select button on Layout tab | Select Table on Select menu		
Table, Select Cell	WD 178	Click left edge of cell			
Table, Select Column	WD 178	Click border at top of column			
Table, Select Multiple Adjacent Cells, Rows, or Columns	WD 178	Drag through cells, rows, or columns			
Table, Select Multiple Nonadjacent Cells, Rows, or Columns	WD 178	Select first cell, row, or column, hold down CTRL key while selecting next cell, row, or column			
Table, Select Next Cell	WD 178	Drag through cell			TAB
Table, Select Previous Cell	WD 178	Drag through cell			SHIFT+TAB
Table, Select Row	WD 178	Click to left of row			

Microsoft Office Word 2007 Quick Reference Summary *(continued)*

Task	Page Number	Mouse	Ribbon	Shortcut Menu	Keyboard Shortcut
Table, Shade Cells (Remove Shade)	WD 288		Shading button arrow on Design tab		
Table, Sort	WD 365		Sort button on Layout tab		
Table, Split Cells	WD 287		Split Cells button on Layout tab	Split Cells	
Table, Sum Columns	WD 265		Formula button on Layout tab		
Table, Wrapping	WD 284			Table Properties | Table tab	
Tag, Remove	WD 702			Remove tag	
Text Box, Fill	WD 523		Select text box | Shape Fill button arrow on Format tab		
Text Box, Insert	WD 427		Text Box button on Insert tab		
Text Box, Position	WD 431	Drag text box			
Text Boxes, Link	WD 521		Select first text box | Create Link button on Format tab | click the second text box		
Theme Colors, Change	WD 39		Change Styles button on Home tab | Colors on Change Styles menu		
Theme Colors, Create New	WD 618		Theme Colors button on Page Layout tab | Create New Theme Colors		
Theme Fonts, Change	WD 40		Change Styles button on Home tab | Fonts on Change Styles menu		
Theme Fonts, Customize	WD 255		Change Styles button on Home tab | Fonts on Change Styles menu | Create new Theme Fonts		
Theme, Change	WD 467		Themes button on Page Layout tab		
Theme, Save New	WD 648		Themes button on Page Layout tab | Save Current Theme		
Theme, Set as Default	WD 650		Change Styles button on Home tab | Set as Default		
Thumbnails, Display	WD 538		Thumbnails check box on View tab		
Track Changes, Turn On/Off	WD 491, WD 492	Click Tracking Changes button on status bar	Track Changes button arrow on Review tab | Track Changes		CTRL+SHIFT+E

Microsoft Office Word 2007 Quick Reference Summary *(continued)*

Task	Page Number	Mouse	Ribbon	Shortcut Menu	Keyboard Shortcut
Tracked Change, Accept	WD 496		Accept and Move to Next button on Review tab	Right-click tracked change | Accept Change	
Tracked Change, Reject	WD 496		Reject and Move to Next button on Review tab	Right-click tracked change | Reject Change	
Tracked Changes, Accept All	WD 507		Accept and Move to Next button arrow on Review tab | Accept All Changes in Document		
Tracked Changes, Change Options	WD 499		Track Changes button arrow on Review tab | Change Tracking Options		
Tracked Changes, Display All Reviewers	WD 506		Show Markup button on Review tab | Reviewers | All Reviewers		
Tracked Changes, Display One Reviewer	WD 506		Show Markup button on Review tab | Reviewers | deselect non-target reviewers		
Tracked Changes, Reject All	WD 507		Reject and Move to Next button arrow on Review tab | Reject All Changes in Document		
Tracking Changes Button, Display on Status Bar	WD 490			Right-click status bar | Track Changes	
Underline	WD 35		Underline button on Home tab	Font | Font tab	CTRL+U
Underline Words, Not Spaces	WD 86				CTRL+SHIFT+W
Unprotect Document	WD 646		Protect Document button on Developer tab		
User Information, Change	WD 312	Office Button | Word Options button			
Watermark, Create	WD 245		Watermark button on Page Layout tab		
White Space, Hide	WD 486	Double-click Hide White Space button			
White Space, Show	WD 487	Double-click Show White Space button			
WordArt, Fill Color	WD 393		Shape Fill button arrow on WordArt Tools Format tab	Format WordArt | Fill Effects button	
WordArt, Insert	WD 391		WordArt button on Insert tab		

Microsoft Office Word 2007 Quick Reference Summary *(continued)*

Task	Page Number	Mouse	Ribbon	Shortcut Menu	Keyboard Shortcut
WordArt, Shape	WD 395		Change WordArt Shape button on Format tab		
XML Element, Add Parent and Child	WD 700	Open XML Structure task pane | select element			
Zoom	WD 46, WD 244	Zoom Out and Zoom In buttons on status bar	Zoom button on View tab		
Zoom Page Width	WD 576		Page Width button on View tab |		
Zoom, Two Pages	WD 447		Two Pages button on View tab		